Civil War
Medal of Honor
Recipients

ALSO BY ROBERT P. BROADWATER
AND FROM MCFARLAND

*The Battle of Fair Oaks: Turning Point
of McClellan's Peninsula Campaign* (2011)

*Gettysburg as the Generals Remembered It:
Postwar Perspectives of Ten Commanders* (2010)

*General George H. Thomas:
A Biography of the Union's "Rock of Chickamauga"* (2009)

*Did Lincoln and the Republican Party Create the Civil War?
An Argument* (2008)

*American Generals of the Revolutionary War:
A Biographical Dictionary* (2007; paperback 2012)

*The Battle of Olustee, 1864:
The Final Union Attempt to Seize Florida* (2006)

*Chickamauga, Andersonville, Fort Sumter and Guard Duty at Home:
Four Civil War Diaries by Pennsylvania Soldiers* (edited by; 2006)

*The Battle of Perryville, 1862:
Culmination of the Failed Kentucky Campaign* (2005; paperback 2011)

Civil War Medal of Honor Recipients

A Complete Illustrated Record

ROBERT P. BROADWATER

McFarland & Company, Inc., Publishers
Jefferson, North Carolina, and London

> The present work is a reprint of the library bound edition of Civil War Medal of Honor Recipients: A Complete Illustrated Record, *first published in 2007 by McFarland.*

LIBRARY OF CONGRESS CATALOGUING-IN-PUBLICATION DATA

Broadwater, Robert P., 1958–
    Civil War Medal of Honor recipients : a complete illustrated record / Robert P. Broadwater.
       p.   cm.
    Includes bibliographical references and index.

    ISBN 978-0-7864-6906-2
    softcover : 50# alkaline paper ∞

    1. United States. Army — History — Civil War, 1861–1865.
    2. United States. Navy — History — Civil War, 1861–1865.
    3. United States. Marine Corps — History — Civil War, 1861–1865.
    4. Medal of Honor.   5. United States — History — Civil War, 1861–1865 — Anecdotes.   6. Courage — United States — History — 19th century — Anecdotes.   7. Soldiers — United States — Biography.
    8. Sailors — United States — Biography.   9. Heroes — United States — Biography.   10. United States — History — Civil War, 1861–1865 — Biography.   I. Title.
    E491.B65 2012
    973.7′6 — dc22   2007023786

BRITISH LIBRARY CATALOGUING DATA ARE AVAILABLE

© 2007 Robert P. Broadwater. All rights reserved

No part of this book may be reproduced or transmitted in any form or by any means, electronic or mechanical, including photocopying or recording, or by any information storage and retrieval system, without permission in writing from the publisher.

On the cover: *top row* David Buckingham, William Carney, Henry Barnum; *bottom row* Andrew Tomlin (photographs courtesy of U.S. Army War College), Adelbert Ames, Frank Baldwin (both courtesy of Hall of Heroes); background image and ribbon © 2012 shutterstock

Manufactured in the United States of America

McFarland & Company, Inc., Publishers
  Box 611, Jefferson, North Carolina 28640
    www.mcfarlandpub.com

To my father,
Paul W. Broadwater,
the person from whom I first learned the principles
of honor, devotion to duty, and sacrifice.
He was the first hero of my childhood,
and has remained as a shining example to me
through all of my adult years.

Contents

Preface 1
A Note on Sources 3
History of the Medal of Honor in the Civil War 4

The Recipients (with Descriptions of Their Actions) 7

Names by Branch of Service
    U.S. Army 227
    U.S. Marine Corps 235
    U.S. Navy 235

Names by Regiment and by Naval Ship 239

Listing by Place of Action 259

Listing by Act of Heroism
    Advancing the Colors 277
    Capturing Artillery 278
    Capturing Enemy Prisoners 278
    Capturing an Enemy Flag 278
    Capturing an Enemy Vessel 281
    Carrying Water to Comrades 281
    Delivering Messages Under Fire 281
    Escaping from the Enemy 281
    Fighting in the Big Shanty, Georgia, Raid 281
    Killing a Confederate General 281
    Killing the Murderer of Colonel Ellsworth 281
    Pressing an Attack 281
    Procuring Ammunition 282
    Sacrificing One's Safety to Save a Comrade 282
    Saving Artillery from Capture 284
    Saving the Command 284
    Saving the Regimental Colors 284

>   Scouting the Enemy, or Behind Enemy Lines 284
>   Serving After Expiration of Enlistment 285
>   Showing Gallantry Under Fire 285
> Listing by State or Country of Birth 289
> Listing by Birth Year of Recipient 301
> Listing by Year of Issuance 309
>
> *Appendices* 321
>   A: *First Six Winners of the Medal of Honor* 321
>   B: *Winners of More Than One Medal of Honor* 322
>   C: *Posthumously Awarded Medals of Honor* 322
>   D: *Civilian Recipients* 322
>   E: *Black Soldiers* 323
> *Index* 325

Preface

The Congressional Medal of Honor was created to acknowledge acts of superior bravery and heroism committed by soldiers and sailors during the Civil War. For a nation not inclined to follow the pomp and circumstance of the European military, it was intended to recognize those who went above and beyond the call of duty, and not to reward individuals who merely did what was expected of them. From the time of its creation, the medal represented heroism, and those upon whom it was bestowed instantly became heroes.

The Congressional Medal of Honor became the most coveted award in the military, and a badge of honor and prestige to the public at large. For officers and men serving in the military forces of the United States, the Medal of Honor signified the highest degree of heroism on the battlefield, and those to whom it was awarded were to be admired, honored, and emulated.

In many instances, the act that earned a soldier or sailor a Medal of Honor occurred at a critical and defining moment in that part of the battle, and for that reason, historians and students of the period have long been drawn to accounts of these acts. Unfortunately, until now, the researcher has been forced to trudge through a mountain of material in order to glean the information he sought, as a result of the fact that previously published Civil War Medal of Honor books present only an alphabetical listing of the winners, with their citations. For the person interested in finding out if Medals of Honor were awarded for particular battles, or to members of particular units, it was necessary to pore over the alphabetical listing, name by name, in an effort to find the answers to such questions. I have gone through this drudgery myself, in my personal research, and have felt akin to a medieval scholar searching for knowledge in the stacks of an ancient monastery.

It occurred to me that the available published material on the Civil War Congressional Medal of Honor was not user-friendly, and that someone should organize the material, by categories, into one book that would be easy for the casual researcher and historian to navigate. That "someone" quickly became me, as I became excited over the prospect of being able to provide Civil War buffs with a reference book that would fill a research need. Indeed, I was amazed to discover that, with all of the thousands of books written on the Civil War, no one had ever thought to tackle this project before.

Where possible, the recipient's year of birth has been taken from his official citation. Other sources were also consulted to determine a recipient's year of birth. In cases where there was a discrepancy between sources, the date from the citation has been used.

The purpose of this work is to provide the reader with information about the Civil War Medal of Honor recipients in an easy to use format, putting the material at the researcher's finger tips by breaking it down into its various categories. In addition to the alphabetical listing of recipients, with the citations of their acts of heroism as recorded in the War Department, and the listings of recipients by various categories, there is a history of the medal in the Civil War. It is hoped that this new offering to the history of the Civil War Medal of Honor will facilitate research about these first winners of America's most distinguished military award for bravery, and that in doing so, it may help to honor and perpetuate the memory of the Army, Navy, and Marine heroes of the Civil War.

A Note on Sources

The original Medal of Honor citations, compiled from the War Department's records, have served as the foundation for the preparation of this book, and are the source of most of the material contained herein. These records are the most comprehensive collection of Medal of Honor material available to the historian or researcher. Additional historic and background information on the Medal of Honor was obtained from the following sources:

Beyer, W.F., and O.F. Keydel. *Deeds of Valor: How America's Civil War Heroes Won the Congressional Medal of Honor.* Detroit: Perrien-Keydel Co., 1903.

Epstrein, Samuel, and Beryl Epstein. *The Andrews Raid; or, The Great Locomotive Chase.* New York: Coward-McCann, Inc., 1956.

Schott, Joseph L. *Action Above and Beyond.* New York: Popular Library, 1962.

History of the Medal of Honor

The Congressional Medal of Honor was the brainchild of Lieutenant Colonel Edward Townsend, adjutant general of the United States Army. In November of 1861, following the various reverses that had befallen Union arms in the opening campaigns of the Civil War, Townsend sought to establish an award that would inspire Northern soldiers and recognize their heroic actions. Medals had never been embraced by the American military, as they were viewed as too European. The influx of foreign-born officers who had come to America in search of commissions in the Union army caused Townsend to re-evaluate the existing medal policy. Foreign officers, with all their shiny medals, were they envy of American soldiers, and the adjutant general wanted to create an American award for bravery. He began by writing a proposal to Secretary of War Edwin Stanton. The following week, Townsend had an informal meeting with Stanton, during which the subject of medals came up. Stanton was hesitant. He expressed concern over possible resistance to the idea, and specifically cited General Winfield Scott's disdain for medals. Secretary of the Navy Gideon Welles was also present at the meeting, and he was much more responsive to Townsend's suggestion. Stating that Winfield Scott had no influence over the Navy, Welles was determined to push forward immediately the creation of a Navy medal. He submitted the idea to Congress, which speedily passed a bill that was signed into law by President Lincoln on December 21, 1861. The Navy bill provided for the manufacture of two hundred medals to be awarded to enlisted personnel of the Navy and Marines. Officers were excluded; it was felt that gallantry in combat was a condition of being an officer and a gentleman. Welles set to work devising an appropriate design for the award, which was now being called the Congressional Medal of Honor. The final design was submitted by the United States Mint, in Philadelphia. What Welles adopted was a five-pointed star, tipped with trefoils, with a crown of laurel and oak in the middle of thirty-four stars. The goddess Minerva, symbolizing the United States, stands with her left hand resting on fasces, signifying authority, while her right hand holds a shield emblazoned with the U.S. coat of arms. Minerva is in the act of repelling Discord,

Men of the 114th Pennsylvania Infantry Zouaves. Colonel Charles Collis won the Medal of Honor for leading these men in a charge against the Confederate position at Fredericksburg, Virginia, in 1862 (U.S. Army War College).

represented by snakes. The medal was suspended from a red, white and blue ribbon, and attached to a clasp adorned with a Naval anchor.

The creation of a Naval award prodded the War Department into action, and legislation was introduced in Congress on February 17, 1862, to authorize a medal of honor for the Army. An amended version of the Navy bill was presented on May 13, 1862, and was finally approved and signed into law by President Lincoln on July 12, 1862. In order to economize expenditures, the Army adopted the design of the Navy medal, the only change being the adoption of an eagle to replace the anchor on the clasp. Though both services now had approval for their medals, there were no actual awards to present to recipients, as Congress did not get around to appropriating funds for the purchase of the medals until March of 1863. The Navy was approved to purchase two hundred medals, while the Army was cleared to obtain an initial order of two thousand. The initial Army legislation, like that of the Navy, excluded officers from being eligible for the award. By the time Congress appropriated money for the purchase of the medals, that act had been amended so that all members of the Army, officer or enlisted, could receive the medal.

Though the Navy had been the first to create the award, the Army would make the first presentation of the Medal of Honor. In April of 1862, a group of twenty-one volunteers, led by the mysterious spy James J. Andrews, had attempted a daring raid deep into Confederate Georgia. The mission of the raiders was to disrupt Confederate transportation and communication between Atlanta and Chattanooga. They captured a train at Big Shanty, Georgia, some two hundred miles behind enemy lines, and attempted to carry out their plan of destroying track and bridges but were severely hampered by an active pursuit from the Confederates. The raiders kept up a running fight until their fuel was expended and they were forced to abandon their train and make a run for it on foot. All were captured by Southern cavalry; Andrews and six other raiders were executed and the remaining fourteen raiders were sent to a Confederate prison, from which eight escaped in October of 1862. In March of 1863, the remaining six raiders were paroled and sent north. When they reached Washington, these raiders had an audience with Secretary Stanton. The head of the War Department had just recently received the initial shipment of the Medals of Honor, and on March 25, 1863, he presented one to each of the six men in recognition of their daring deeds. The members of Andrews' Raiders received the first of more than twenty-one hundred medals to be awarded by the Army for service in the Civil War. Some nine hundred of those would be revoked by a military review panel in 1917, leaving the Army total for the war at 1,200. The number distributed by the Navy to sailors and Marines was 327. The army also had the distinction of awarding the last Medals of Honor for service in the war. In 1917, Henry Lewis and Henry C. Peters, both from the 47th Ohio Infantry, were awarded the Medal of Honor for their services at Vicksburg, some fifty-four years earlier.

The Congressional Medal of Honor was created during the Civil War to recognize exceptional gallantry and courage of those in service to the nation. In the almost one hundred fifty years since its inception, it has come to represent the bravery and sacrifice that best exemplifies what a free people can and will do to preserve and protect that freedom.

The Recipients (with Descriptions of Their Actions)

Adams, James F. Birth: Virginia, 1844. Private in Company D, 1st West Virginia Cavalry. On November 12, 1864, at Nineveh, Va., Private Adams captured the state flag of the 14th Virginia Cavalry. Adams was awarded his medal on November 26, 1864.

Adams, John G. B. Birth: Massachusetts, 1841. Second Lieutenant, Company I, 19th Massachusetts Infantry. During the fighting at Fredericksburg, on December 16, 1862, Lieutenant Adams seized the regiment's state and national colors from the hands of their mortally wounded bearers and boldly advanced across the field to a point where the regiment rallied on their standards. Adams was awarded his medal on December 16, 1896.

Aheam, Michael. Enlisted in France. Paymaster's Steward serving aboard the U.S.S. *Kearsarge*. On June 19, 1864, Aheam exhibited coolness and marked gallantry when the *Kearsarge* sank the Confederate Raider *Alabama*, of the coast of Cherbourg, France. Aheam was awarded his medal on December 31, 1864.

John Adams (U.S. Army War College)

Alber, Frederick. Birth: Germany, 1838. Private in Company A, 17th Michigan Infantry. On May 12, 1864, during the fighting at Spotsylvania, Virginia, Alber saw that Lieutenant Charles H. Todd, of his regiment, was being captured by a small group of Confederates. He immediately charged the Confederates, shooting one and knocking another over with the butt of his musket. Alber not only rescued his officer from capture, he took both of the Confederates he had engaged prisoner. Alber was awarded his medal on July 30, 1896.

Albert, Christian. Birth: Ohio, 1833. Private in Company G, 47th Ohio Infantry. On May 22, 1863, Private Albert exhibited extreme gallantry at Vicksburg, Mississippi, while in charge of a volunteer storming party. Albert was awarded his medal on August 10, 1895.

Allen, Abner P. Birth: Illinois, 1839. Corporal in Company K, 39th Illinois Infantry. On April 2, 1865, Allen was cited for heroism in advancing his regimental flag during the assault of Fort Gregg, Va. Allen was awarded his medal on May 12, 1865.

Allen, James. Birth: Ireland, 1843. Private in Company F, 16th New York Infantry. On September 14, 1862, at South Mountain, Md., Allen, alone and slightly wounded, noticed a squad of 14 Confederate soldiers. Through imagination and bluff he was able to secure the surrender of all 14 Confederates, who happened to be carrying with them the colors of the 16th Georgia Infantry. Allen was awarded his medal on September 11, 1890.

Allen, Nathaniel M. Birth: Massachusetts, 1840. Corporal in Company B, 1st Massachusetts Infantry. On July 2, at Gettysburg, Pennsylvania, when the 1st Massachusetts was withdrawing from the field in the face of the enemy, Allen was acting as one of the color bearers, carrying the national colors. Noticing that the bearer of the regimental flag had been shot down, Allen advanced in the face of the onrushing enemy to retrieve the banner from beneath the body of its fallen bearer. Allen was awarded his medal on March 29, 1899.

Ames, Adelbert. [photograph p. 9] Birth: Maine, 1835. First Lieutenant in the 5th U.S. Artillery. On July 21, 1861, at the battle of First Manassas, Virginia, Ames commanded a section of Griffin's Battery. He refused to leave the field, continuing to service his guns, even though he had been severely wounded. He did not assent to quit the fight until he had become so weak from loss of blood that he could not even sit on the caisson. Ames was awarded his medal on June 22, 1894.

Ammerman, Robert W. Birth: Pennsylvania, 1841. Private in Company B, 148th

Nathaniel Allen (U.S. Army War College)

Pennsylvania Infantry. On May 12, 1864, while fighting at Spotsylvania, Virginia, Private Ammerman captured the battle flag of the 8th North Carolina Infantry in close combat. Ammerman was awarded his medal on January 31, 1865.

Anderson, Bruce. Birth: New York, 1845. Private in Company K, 142nd New York Infantry. On January 15, 1865, during the expedition against Fort Fisher, North Carolina, Private Anderson volunteered to go in advance of the assaulting column to cut down the palisade fence that was blocking their path, in the face of enemy fire. Anderson was awarded his medal on December 28, 1914.

Anderson, Charles W. Birth: Louisiana, 1844. Private in Company K, 1st New York Cavalry. On March 2, 1865, at Waynesboro, Va., Private Anderson captured a Confederate flag from a unit unknown to him or his commanders. Anderson was awarded his medal on March 26, 1865.

Anderson, Everett W. Birth: Louisiana, 1839. Sergeant in Company M, 15th Pennsylvania Cavalry. On January 14, 1864, Sergeant Anderson single-handedly captured Brigadier General Robert B. Vance at Crosby's Creek, Tennessee. Anderson was awarded his medal on December 3, 1894.

Anderson, Frederick C. Birth: Massachusetts, 1842. Private in Company A, 18th Massachusetts Infantry. On August 21, 1864, at Weldon Railroad, Va., Private Anderson captured the colors of the 27th South Carolina, along with its bearer. Anderson was awarded his medal on September 6, 1864.

Adelbert Ames (Hall of Heroes)

Charles Anderson (U.S. Army War College)

Anderson, Marion T. Birth: Indiana, 1839. Captain of Company D, 51st Indiana Infantry. On December 16, 1864, Anderson was leading his company in an attack on the Confederate lines at Nashville, Tennessee. He gallantly pressed home the assault, staying at the head of his company while it swept over five lines of the enemy's works before falling severely wounded. Anderson was awarded his medal on September 1, 1893.

Anderson, Peter. Birth: Wisconsin, 1847. Private in Company B, 31st Wisconsin Infantry. On March 19, 1865, at Bentonville, North Carolina, Private Anderson single-handedly dragged an abandoned piece of artillery from the field, preventing it from falling into enemy hands. Anderson was awarded his medal on June 16, 1865.

Marion Anderson (U.S. Army War College)

Anderson, Robert. Birth: Ireland, 1841. Quartermaster aboard the U.S.S. *Keokuk*. During an assault on the Confederate defenses in Charleston, South Carolina, Anderson was stationed at the wheel when a shot penetrated the wheelhouse, scattering bits of iron about the cabin. He used his own body as a shield to protect his commanding officer from the deadly shards. Anderson was awarded his medal on July 10, 1863.

Anderson, Thomas. Birth: Pennsylvania, 1841. Corporal in Company I, 1st West Virginia Cavalry. On April 8, 1865, at Appomattox Station, Virginia, Corporal Anderson was credited with capturing a Confederate flag. Anderson was awarded his medal on May 3, 1865.

Peter Anderson (U.S. Army War College)

Angling, John. Birth: Maine, 1850. Cabin Boy aboard the U.S.S. *Pontoosuc*. Angling was cited for skill and gallantry in performing his duties during the expeditions against Fort Fisher, North Carolina, in December of 1864 and January of 1865. Angling was awarded his medal on June 22, 1865.

Apple, Andrew O. Birth: Pennsylvania, 1845. Corporal in Company I, 12th West Virginia Infantry. On April 2, 1865, at Petersburg, Virginia, Corporal Apple showed marked gallantry in advancing his regimental colors in the assault on Fort Gregg. Apple was awarded his medal on May 12, 1865.

Appleton, William H. Birth: New Hampshire, 1843. First Lieutenant of Company H, 4th United States Colored Troops. On June 15, 1864, while fighting along the Petersburg, Virginia, lines, Lieutenant Appleton showed conspicuous gallantry in leading and inspiring his troops in a desperate assault at New Market Heights, being himself the first man to enter the enemy's works. Appleton was awarded his medal on February 18, 1891.

Archer, James W. Birth: Illinois. First Lieutenant and Adjutant in the 59th Indiana Infantry. On October 4, 1862, at Corinth, Mississippi, Lieutenant Archer voluntarily took command of another regiment, with the consent of one or more of his senior officers. Archer rallied the shaken command and gallantly led it forward in the attack. Archer was awarded his medal on August 2,1897.

Archer, Lester. Birth: New York, 1838. Sergeant in Company E, 96th New York Infantry. On September 29, 1864, at Fort Harrison, Virginia, Sergeant Archer displayed extreme gallantry in advancing his regiment's colors and placing them on the enemy fort. Archer was awarded his medal on April 6, 1865.

Archinal, William. Birth: Germany, 1840. Corporal in Company I, 30th Ohio Infantry. On May 22, 1863, at Vicksburg, Mississippi, Corporal Archinal showed conspicuous gallantry in the charge of the volunteer storming party, Archinal was awarded his medal on July 10, 1894.

Armstrong, Clinton L. Birth: Indiana, 1844. Private in Company D, 83rd Indiana Infantry. On May 22, 1863, at Vicksburg, Mississippi, Private Armstrong showed conspicuous gallantry in the charge of the volunteer storming party. Armstrong was awarded his medal on August 15, 1894.

Arnold, Abraham K. Birth: Pennsylvania, 1837. Captain of the 5th United States Cavalry. On May 10, 1864, at Davenport Bridge, Virginia, Captain Arnold led a gallant charge against a superior force of the enemy to extricate his command from a perilous position to which it had been ordered. Arnold was awarded his medal on September 1, 1893.

William Archinal (Hall of Heroes)

Arther, Matthew. Birth: Scotland, 1835. Signal Quartermaster aboard the U.S.S. *Carondelet*. On February 6 and 14, 1862, at Forts Henry and Donelson, Tennessee, Arther showed conspicuous valor and devotion in faithfully serving as captain of the rifled bow gun. Arther was awarded his medal on July 10, 1863.

Asten, Charles. Birth: Canada, 1834. Quarter Gunner aboard the U.S.S. *Signal*. On May 5, 1864, at Red River, the U.S.S. *Signal* was engaged by a large force of enemy batteries and sharpshooters. The ship returned fire until it was totally disabled, and Gunner Asten was conspicuous in keeping his gun in the engagement. Asten was awarded his medal on December 31, 1864.

Atkinson, Thomas E. Birth: Massachusetts, 1824. Yeoman aboard the U.S.S. *Richmond*. On August 5, 1864, at Mobile Bay, Alabama, Yeoman Atkinson was commended for coolness and energy in supplying the rifle ammunition which was under his sole charge. Atkinson was awarded his medal on December 31, 1864.

Avery, James. Birth: Scotland, 1825. Seaman aboard the U.S.S. *Metacomet*. On August 5, 1864, at Mobile Bay, Alabama, Seaman Avery braved enemy fire that his commander stated to be "one of the most galling" he had ever seen to rescue 10 men from the U.S.S. *Tecumseh*. Avery was awarded his medal on January 15, 1866.

Avery, William B. Birth: Rhode Island, 1840. Lieutenant in the 1st New York Marine Artillery. On June 5, 1862, at Tranter's Creek, North Carolina, Lieutenant Avery handled his battery with the greatest coolness amidst the hottest fire. Avery was awarded his medal on September 2, 1893.

Ayers, David. Birth: Ohio, 1841. Sergeant of Company A, 57th Ohio Infantry. On May 22, 1863, at Vicksburg, Mississippi, Sergeant Ayers showed exceptional gallantry in the charge of the volunteer storming party. Ayers was awarded his medal on April 13, 1894.

Ayers, John G. K. Birth: Michigan, 1837. Private in Company H, 8th Missouri Infantry. On May 22, 1863, at Vicksburg, Mississippi, Private Ayers showed conspicuous gallantry in the charge of the volunteer storming party. Ayers was awarded his medal on August 31, 1895.

John Ayers (U.S. Army War College)

Babcock, William J. Birth: Connecticut, 1841. Sergeant in Company E, 2nd Rhode Island Infantry. On April 2, 1865, at Petersburg, Virginia, Sergeant Babcock planted his regiment's flag on the Confederate parapets while the enemy still occupied the works, and was the first of his regiment to enter the works. Babcock was awarded his medal on March 2, 1895.

Bacon, Elijah W. Birth: Connecticut. Private in Company F, 14th Connecticut Infantry. On July 3, 1863, at Gettysburg, Pennsylvania, Private Bacon captured the flag of the 16th North Carolina Infantry. Bacon was awarded his medal on December 1, 1864.

Baird, Absalom. Birth: Pennsylvania. Brigadier General of United States Volunteers. On September 1, 1864, at Jonesboro, Georgia, General Baird voluntarily led a detached brigade in an

Absalom Baird (Hall of Heroes)

assault upon the enemy's works. Baird was awarded his medal on April 22, 1896.

Baker, Charles. Birth: District of Columbia, 1809. Quarter Gunner aboard the U.S.S. *Metacomet*. On August 5, 1864, at Mobile Bay, Alabama, Gunner Baker exhibited exceptional gallantry when he braved enemy fire his commander stated to the "one of the most galling" he had ever seen to rescue 10 members of the crew of the sunken U.S.S. *Tecumseh*. Baker was awarded his medal on January 15, 1866.

Baldwin, Charles. Birth: Delaware, 1839. Coal Heaver aboard the U.S.S. *Wyalusing*. On May 25, 1864, at Roanoke River, North Carolina, Baldwin volunteered to attempt the destruction of the Confederate Ram Albermarle by swimming the river with two torpedoes. When Baldwin neared the Confederate vessel, he was challenged by a sentry and forced to abandon the plan. He escaped the fire of the enemy, but spent two days, without food, in making his way back to his mother ship. Baldwin was awarded his medal on December 31, 1864.

Charles Baker (U.S. Army War College)

Charles Baldwin (U.S. Army War College)

Baldwin, Frank D. Birth: Michigan, 1842. Captain of Company D, 19th Michigan Infantry. On July 12, 1864, at Peach Tree Creek, Georgia, Captain Baldwin led his company in a counter charge, and singly entered the enemy line, bringing back two commissioned officers and the guidon of a Georgia regiment. Baldwin was awarded his medal on December 3, 1891.

Ballen, Frederick. Birth: Germany, 1842. Private in Company B, 47th Ohio Infantry. On May 3, 1863, at Vicksburg, Mississippi, Private Ballen was one of a party that volunteered to attempt to run the enemy's batteries with a steam tug and 2 barges loaded with sustenance stores. Ballen was awarded his medal on November 6, 1908.

Banks, George L. [photograph p. 14] Birth: Indiana, 1839. Sergeant in Company C, 15th Indiana Infantry. On November 25, 1863, at Missionary Ridge, Tennessee, Sergeant Banks, as color bearer, led his regiment forward, though he himself was wounded, being the first to plant his banner upon the parapet of the enemy. Banks was awarded his medal on September 28, 1897.

Barber, James A. [photograph p. 14] Birth: Rhode Island, 1841. Corporal in Company G, 1st

Frank Baldwin (Hall of Heroes)

George Banks (U.S. Army War College)   *James Barber (U.S. Army War College)*

Rhode Island Light Artillery. On April 2, 1865, at Petersburg, Virginia, Corporal Barber volunteered to accompany an infantry assaulting party and turned the cannon captured in the attack on the enemy. Barber was awarded his medal on June 20, 1866.

Henry Barnum (U.S. Army War College)

Barker, Nathaniel C. Birth: New Hampshire, 1836. Sergeant in Company E, 11th New Hampshire Infantry. On May 12, 1864, at Spotsylvania, Virginia, Sergeant Barker, after seeing six color bearers of his regiment be killed, picked up both of the regiment's flags and carried them through the remainder of the battle. Barker was awarded his medal on September 23, 1897.

Barnes, William H. Birth: Maryland. Private in Company C, 38th United States Colored Infantry. On September 29, 1864, at Chapin's Farm, Virginia, Private Barnes, although wounded, was among the first to enter the enemy's works. Barnes received his medal on April 6, 1865.

Barnum, Henry A. Birth: New York, 1833. Colonel of the 149th

New York Infantry. On November 23, 1863, at Chattanooga, Tennessee, Colonel Barnum conspicuously led his men forward despite the fact that he was severely wounded. Barnum was awarded his medal in July of 1889.

Barnum, James. Birth: Massachusetts, 1816. Boatswain's Mate aboard the U.S.S. *New Ironsides*. In December of 1864 and January of 1865, Barnum exhibited meritorious conduct during the expeditions against Fort Fisher, North Carolina. Barnum was awarded his medal on June 22, 1865.

Barrell, Charles L. Birth: 1842. First Lieutenant of Company C, 102nd United States Colored Infantry. In April of 1865, at Camden, South Carolina, Lieutenant Barrell performed hazardous service in marching through the enemy's country to bring relief to his command. Barrell was awarded his medal on May 14, 1891.

Barrick, Jesse T. Birth: Ohio, 1841. Corporal in Company H, 3rd Minnesota Infantry. From May 26 to June 2, 1863, at Duck River, Tennessee, Corporal Barrick captured two Confederate guerrilla officers. Barrick was awarded his medal on March 3, 1917.

Barringer, William H. Birth: 1841. Private in Company F, 4th West Virginia Infantry. On May 22, 1863, at Vicksburg, Mississippi, Private Barringer displayed exceptional gallantry in the charge of the storming party, Barringer was awarded his medal on July 12, 1894.

Charles Barrell (U.S. Army War College)

Barry, Augustus. Birth: Ireland, 1840. Sergeant Major of the 16th United States Infantry. Was issued a Medal of Honor for gallantry in various actions taking place between 1863 to 1865. Was awarded his medal on February 28, 1870.

Barter, Gurdon H. Birth: New York, 1843. Landsman aboard the U.S.S. *Minnesota*. On January 15, 1865, at Fort Fisher, North Carolina, Landsman Barter showed conspicuous gallantry fighting with the landing party from his ship. He remained at the front after more than two-thirds of his party had retreated, not withdrawing until after dark. Barter was awarded his medal on June 22, 1865.

Barton, Thomas. Birth: Ohio, 1831. Seaman aboard the U.S.S. *Hunchback*. On October 3, 1862, at Franklin, Virginia, Seaman Barton acted promptly when an ignited shell fell out of a howitzer onto the deck. Disregarding the danger to himself, Barton seized a pail of water and threw it on the shell, preventing it from exploding and doing injury to the crew. Barton was awarded his medal on April 3, 1863.

Bass, David L. [photograph p. 16] Birth: Ireland, 1843. Seaman aboard the U.S.S. *Minnesota*. On January 15, 1865, at Fort Fisher, North Carolina, Seaman Bass exhibited exceptional gallantry as part of the landing party from his ship. Bass advanced to the top of the sand hill, remaining there after two-thirds of his party had retreated, and not withdrawing until after dark. Bass was awarded his medal on June 22, 1865.

Batchelder, Richard N. [photograph p. 16] Birth: New Hampshire, 1832. Lieutenant Colonel and Chief Quartermaster of the Union 2nd Corps. From October 13 to

15, 1863, between Catlett's Station and Fairfax Station, Virginia, Colonel Batchelder moved his wagon train without the usual military escort, through a heavy attack by a superior enemy by arming his teamsters and conducting a running fight between those two points. Batchelder was awarded his medal on May 20, 1895.

Bates, Delavan. Birth: New York, 1840. Colonel of the 30th United States Colored Infantry. On July 30, 1864, at Cemetery Hill, Virginia, Colonel Bates gallantly led his regiment forward until he was shot through the face and head. Bates was awarded his medal on June 22, 1891.

David Bass (U.S. Army War College)

Bates, Norman F. Birth: Vermont, 1839. Sergeant of Company F, 4th Iowa Cavalry. On April 16, 1865, at Columbus, Georgia, Sergeant Bates captured a Confederate flag and its bearer. Bates was awarded his medal on June 17, 1865.

Baybutt, Philip. Birth: England, 1844. Private in Company A, 2nd Massachusetts Cavalry. On September 24, 1864, at Luray, Virginia, Private Baybutt captured an enemy flag. Baybutt was awarded his medal on October 19, 1864.

Bazaar, Philip. Birth: Chile. Ordinary Seaman aboard the U.S.S. *Santiago de Cuba*. On January 15, 1865, at Fort Fisher, North Carolina, Seaman Bazaar displayed conspicuous bravery as part of the landing party from his ship, being one of six members of the fleet to enter the fort. Bazaar was awarded his medal on June 22, 1865.

Richard Batchelder (U.S. Army War College)

Beatty (Beattie), Alexander M. [photograph p. 17] Birth: Vermont, 1828. Captain of Company F, 3rd Vermont Infantry. On June 5, 1864, at Cold Harbor, Virginia, Captain Beatty, under a heavy fire from the enemy, removed a wounded member of his command to a place of safety. Beatty was awarded his medal on April 25, 1894.

Beaty, Powhatan. [photograph p. 17] Birth: Virginia, 1837. First Sergeant of Company G, 5th United Stated Colored Infantry. On September 29, 1864, at Chapin's Farm, Virginia, Sergeant Beaty assumed command of his company after all of the officers had been killed or wounded and led it gallantly forward. Beaty was awarded his medal on April 6, 1865.

Delavan Bates (U.S. Army War College)

Pohatan Beaty (U.S. Army War College)

Alexander Beatty (Beattie) (U.S. Army War College)

Beaufort, Jean J. Birth: France. Corporal in Company A, 2nd Louisiana Infantry (Colored). On May 20, 1863, at Port Hudson, Louisiana, Corporal Beaufort volunteered to go within enemy lines at the head of a party of eight to destroy a signal station which greatly aided in the operations against Port Hudson that followed. Beaufort was awarded his medal on July 20, 1897.

Beaumont, Eugene B. [photograph p. 18] Birth: Pennsylvania, 1837. Major and Assistant Adjutant General, Cavalry Corps, Army of the Mississippi. On December 17, 1864, at Harpeth River, Tennessee, Major Beaumont charged an enemy position with the 4th U.S. Cavalry, dispersing the gunners from a Confederate battery and capturing the guns. On April 2, 1865, at Selma, Alabama, he led a charge that captured the last line of enemy works. Beaumont was awarded his medal on March 30, 1898.

Bebb, Edward J. [photograph p. 18] Birth: Ohio, 1839. Private in Company D, 4th Iowa Cavalry. On April 16, 1865, at Columbus, Georgia, Private Bebb captured an enemy flag. Bebb was awarded his medal on June 17, 1865.

Beckwith, Wallace A. Birth: Connecticut. Private in Company F, 21st Connecticut Infantry. On February 13, 1862, at Fredericksburg, Virginia, Private Beckwith volunteered to man a battery, serving with heroism until the termination of the engagement. Beckwith was awarded his medal on February 15, 1897.

Beddows, Richard. Birth: England, 1843. Private in the 34th New York Battery. On May 18, 1864, at Spotsylvania, Virginia, Private Beddows saved the battery guidon, under heavy fire from the enemy, after his horse had become unmanageable from the bursting of a shell. Beddows was awarded his medal on July 10, 1896.

Eugene Beaumont (U.S. Army War College)

Beebe, William S. Birth: New York, 1841. First Lieutenant, Ordnance Department, U.S. Army. On April 23, 1864, at Cane River Crossing, Louisiana, Lieutenant Beebe volunteered to lead a successful assault on a fortified enemy position. Beebe was awarded his medal on June 30, 1897.

Beech, John P. Birth: England, 1844. Sergeant of Company B, 4th New Jersey Infantry. On May 1, 1864, at Spotsylvania Courthouse, Virginia, Sergeant Beech showed exceptional courage when he volunteered to service the guns of a battery in which all of its members had been killed or wounded. Beech was awarded his medal on May 12, 1894.

Edward Bebb (U.S. Army War College)

Begley, Terrence. Birth: Ireland. Sergeant of Company D, 7th New York Heavy Artillery. On June 3, 1864, at Cold Harbor, Virginia, Sergeant Begley shot a Confederate color bearer, rushed forth and seized his colors under heavy fire from the enemy. Begley was awarded his medal on December 1, 1864.

Belcher, Thomas. Birth: Maine, 1834. Private in Company I, 9th Maine Infantry. On September 29, 1864, at Chapin's Farm, Virginia, Private Belcher took the guidon from the hands of its mortally wounded bearer and advanced them nearer to the enemy battery than any other man. Belcher was awarded his medal on April 6, 1865.

Bell, George. [photograph p. 19] Birth: England, 1839. Captain of the Afterguard aboard

William Beebe (Hall of Heroes)

the U.S.S. *Santee*. On November 7, 1861, at Galveston, Texas, Bell served as pilot of the U.S.S. *Santee* and evinced more coolness in the passing of the four forts and the Confederate steamer *General Rusk* than was ever seen before by his commanding officer, although being severely wounded at the time. Bell was awarded his medal on July 10, 1863.

Bell, James B. Birth: Ohio, 1835. Sergeant in Company H. 11th Ohio Infantry. On November 25, 1863, at Missionary Ridge, Tennessee, Sergeant Bell advanced his colors to the summit of the ridge, being the first to plant them inside the enemy's works, even though he had been wounded five times. The date that Bell's medal was awarded is unknown.

Benedict, George G. Birth: Vermont, 1826. Second Lieutenant of Company C, 12th Vermont Infantry. On July 3, 1863, at Gettysburg, Pennsylvania, Lieutenant Benedict passed through a murderous fire of grape and canister to deliver orders and re-formed the crowded lines. Benedict was awarded his medal on June 27, 1892.

Benjamin, John F. Birth: New York. Corporal in Company M, 2nd New York Cavalry. On April 6, 1865, at Sailors Creek, Virginia, Corporal Benjamin captured the battle flag of the 9th Virginia Infantry. Benjamin was awarded his medal on May 3, 1865.

Benjamin, Samuel N. [photograph p. 20] Birth: New York, 1839. First Lieutenant in the 2nd United States Artillery. From Bull Run to Spotsylvania, Va., Lieutenant Benjamin showed particularly distinguished service as an artillery officer. Benjamin was awarded his medal on June 11, 1877.

Bennett, Orren. Birth: Pennsylvania. Private in Company D, 141st Pennsylvania Infantry. On April 6, 1865, at Sailors Creek, Virginia, Private Bennett captured a Confederate flag. Bannett was awarded his medal on May 10, 1865.

Bennett, Orson W. Birth: Michigan, 1841. First Lieutenant of Company A, 102nd United States Colored Infantry. On November 30, 1864, at Honey Hill, South

George Bell (Hall of Heroes)

George Benedict (U.S. Army War College)

Samuel Benjamin (U.S. Army War College)

William Bensinger (U.S. Army War College)

Carolina, Lieutenant Bennett led a small party 100 yards in advance of the Union lines to rescue 3 pieces of abandoned artillery. Bennett brought the guns back, preventing their capture. Bennet was awarded his medal on March 9, 1887.

Bensinger, William. Birth: Ohio, 1840. Private in Company G, 21st Ohio Infantry. In April of 1862, at Big Shanty, Georgia, Private Bensinger participated in a raid 200 miles inside enemy territory, captured a train, and attempted to destroy bridges and track between Chattanooga and Atlanta. Bensinger was awarded his medal on March 25, 1863. (second to receive the Medal of Honor)

Benyaurd, William H. Birth: Pennsylvania, 1841. First Lieutenant in the Engineer Corps. On April 1, 1865, at Five Forks, Virginia, Lieutenant Benyaurd voluntarily advanced in a reconnaissance beyond the skirmishers, and in the same battle rode to the front, with the commanding general, to encourage the men to resume the advance, which they did. Benyaurd was awarded his medal on September 7, 1897.

William Benyaurd (U.S. Army War College)

Betham, Asa. Birth: New York, 1838. Coxswain aboard the U.S.S. *Pontoosuc*. From December 24, 1864 to January 22, 1865, at Fort Fisher, North Carolina, Coxswain Betham exhibited exceptional skill and courage under fire during the expeditions to capture the Confederate stronghold. Bethem was awarded his medal on June 22, 1865.

Betts, Charles M. Birth: Pennsylvania, 1838. Lieutenant Colonel of the 15th Pennsylvania Cavalry. On April 19, 1865, at Greensboro, North Carolina, Colonel Betts, with a force of 75 men, surprised and captured an entire battalion of the enemy's cavalry. Betts was awarded his medal on October 10, 1892.

Beyer, Hillary. Birth: Pennsylvania, 1837. Second Lieutenant of Company H, 90th Pennsylvania Infantry. On September 17, 1862, at Antietam, Maryland, Lieutenant Beyer remained alone on the line of battle, after his command had been forced to retreat, to care for his wounded comrades. He was able to carry one of them to safety before withdrawing himself. Beyer was awarded his medal on October 30, 1896.

Charles Betts (U.S. Army War College)

Bibber, Charles J. Birth: Maine, 1838. Gunner's Mate aboard the U.S.S. *Agawam*. On December 23, 1864, at Fort Fisher, North Carolina, Gunner's Mate Bibber volunteered to be part of a crew to tow a powder boat close to Fort Fisher to be exploded. Bibber was awarded his medal on December 31, 1864.

Bickford, Henry H. Birth: Michigan, 1838. Corporal of Company E, 8th New York Cavalry. On March 2, 1865, at Waynesboro, Virginia, Corporal Bickford was responsible

Hillary Beyer (U.S. Army War College)

Henry Bickford (U.S. Army War College)

for recapturing a flag that had been taken by the Confederates. Bickford was awarded his medal on March 26, 1865.

Bickford, John F. Birth: Maine, 1843. Captain of the Top aboard the U.S.S. *Kearsarge*. On June 19, 1864, at Cherbourg, France, Bickford exhibited marked coolness under fire during the engagement with the C.S.S. *Alabama*. Bickford was awarded his medal on December 31, 1864.

Bickford, Matthew. Birth, Illinois, 1839. Corporal of Company G, 8th Missouri Infantry. On May 22, 1863, at Vicksburg, Mississippi, Corporal Bickford exhibited extreme gallantry in the charge of the volunteer storming party. Bickford was awarded his medal on August 31, 1894.

Bieger, Charles. Birth: Germany, 1844. Private in Company D, 4th Missouri Cavalry. On February 22, 1864, at Ivy Farm, Mississippi, Private Bieger, under heavy fire, voluntarily rode beyond the line of battle to rescue his captain, whose horse had been killed in the charge, and who was surrounded by the enemy's skirmishers. Bieger was awarded his medal on July 8, 1897.

Binder, Richard. Birth: Pennsylvania, 1840. Sergeant in the United States Marine Corps. From December 24 to 25, 1864 and January 13 to 15, 1865, at Fort Fisher, North Carolina, Sergeant Binder, as captain of a gun performed his duties with skill and courage. Binder was awarded his medal in 1865.

Bingham, Henry H. Birth: Pennsylvania, 1841. Captain of Company G, 140th Pennsylvania Infantry. On May 6, 1864, at the Wilderness, Virginia, Captain Bingham rallied a portion of troops who had started to withdraw and led them in an attack against the enemy. Bingham was awarded his medal on August 31, 1893.

Richard Binder (U.S. Army War College)

Henry Bingham (U.S. Army War College)

Birdsall, Horatio L. Birth: New York, 1833. Sergeant in Company B, 3rd Iowa Cavalry. On April 16, 1865, at Columbus, Georgia, Sergeant Birdsall captured a Confederate flag. Birdsall was awarded his medal on June 17, 1865.

Bishop, Francis A. Birth: Pennsylvania, 1840. Private in Company C, 57th Pennsylvania Infantry. On May 12, 1864, at Spotsylvania, Virginia, Private Bishop captured a Confederate flag. Bishop was awarded his medal on December 1, 1864.

Black, John C. [photograph p. 23] Birth: Mississippi, 1839. Lieutenant Colonel of the 37th Illinois Cavalry. On December 7, 1862, at Prairie Grove, Arkansas, Colonel

Black gallantly pressed forward an attack after two other regiments had already been repulsed, capturing a battery, after being severely wounded. Black was awarded his medal on October 31, 1893.

Black, William P. Birth: Kentucky, 1842. Captain of Company K, 37th Illinois Infantry. On March 7, 1862, at Pea Ridge, Arkansas, Captain Black single-handedly confronted the Confederates and checked their advance within 100 yards of the Union line. Black was awarded his medal on October 2, 1893.

Blackmar, Wilmon W. Birth: Pennsylvania. Lieutenant in Company H, 1st West Virginia Cavalry. On April 1, 1865, at Five Forks, Virginia, Lieutenant Blackmar, without orders, led a successful advance upon the enemy at a critical stage of the battle. Blackmar was awarded his medal on October 23, 1897.

Blackwood, William R.D. Birth: Ireland, 1838. Surgeon of the 48th Pennsylvania Infantry. On April 2, 1865, at Petersburg, Virginia, Surgeon Blackwood exposed himself

John Black (U.S. Army War College)

William Black (Hall of Heroes)

William Blackwood (U.S. Army War College)

Wilmon Blackmar (Hall of Heroes)

beyond the call of duty to save several wounded officers and men from the battlefield. Blackwood was awarded his medal on July 21, 1897.

Blagheen, William. Birth: England, 1832. Ship's Cook aboard the U.S.S. *Brooklyn*. On August 5, 1864, at Mobile Bay, Alabama, Blagheen performed his duties in the powder division with marked coolness and gallantry. Blagheen was awarded his medal on December 31, 1864.

Blair, Robert M. Birth: Vermont, 1836. Boatswain's Mate aboard the U.S.S. *Pontoonsuc*. From December 24, 1864 till January 22, 1865, at Fort Fisher, North Carolina, Boatswain Mate Blair exhibited skill and gallantry while performing his duties under fire. Blair was awarded his medal on June 22, 1865.

Blake, Robert. Birth: Virginia. Listed as Contraband, United States Navy. On December 25, 1863, at John's Island, South Carolina, Blake, an escaped slave, served the rifled gun bravely throughout the engagement. Blake was awarded his medal on April 16, 1864.

Milton Blickensderfer (Hall of Heroes)

Blasdel, Thomas A. Birth: Indiana. Private in Company A, 83rd Indiana Infantry. On May 22, 1863, at Vicksburg, Mississippi, Private Blasdel exhibited exceptional gallantry in the charge of the volunteer storming party. Blasdel was awarded his medal on August 11, 1894.

Blickensderfer, Milton. Birth: Pennsylvania, 1835. Corporal in Company E, 126th Ohio Infantry. On April 3, 1865, at Petersburg, Virginia, Corporal Blickensderfer captured a Confederate flag. Blickensderfer was awarded his medal on May 10, 1865.

Bliss, George N. Birth: Rhode Island, 1837. Captain of Company C, 1st Rhode Island Cavalry. On September 28, 1864, at Waynesboro, Virginia, Captain Bliss was in command of the provost guard when he saw the Union lines in retreat before a Confederate attack. He quickly gathered his guard and, without orders, charged into the oncoming Confederates, receiving three saber wounds and being taken prisoner in the process. Bliss was awarded his medal on August 3, 1897.

George Bliss (U.S. Army War College)

Bliss, Zenas R. Birth: Maine, 1835. Colonel of the 7th Rhode Island Infantry. On December 13, 1862, at Fredericksburg, Virginia, Colonel Bliss displayed exceptional gallantry in encouraging his regiment, while under heavy fire from the enemy. Bliss boldly exposed himself to the Confederate fire by arising in front of the prone men of his command, advancing to within short range of the enemy, and firing several shots. Bliss was awarded his medal on December 30, 1898.

Blodgett, Welis H. Birth: Illinois, 1839. First Lieutenant of Company D, 37th Illinois Infantry. On September 30, 1862, at Newtonia, Missouri, Lieutenant Blodgett, along with an orderly, captured an armed Confederate picket of eight men. Blodgett was awarded his medal on February 15, 1894.

Zenas Bliss (U.S. Army War College)

Blucher, Charles. Birth: Germany. Corporal in Company H, 188th Pennsylvania Infantry. On September 29, 1864, at Fort Harrison, Virginia, Corporal Blucher was the first to plant the national colors on the Confederate fortifications. Blucher was awarded his medal on April 6, 1865.

Blunt, John W. Birth: New York, 1840. First Lieutenant of Company K, 6th New York Cavalry. On October 19, 1864, at Cedar Creek, Virginia, Lieutenant Blunt voluntarily led a charge across a narrow bridge of the creek against the enemy lines. In it unknown when Lieutenant Blunt was awarded his medal.

Boehm, Peter M. [photograph p. 23] Birth: New York, 1845. Second Lieutenant of Company K, 15th New York Cavalry. On March 31, 1865, at Dinwiddie Courthouse, Virginia, Lieutenant Boehm, taking a flag from the hands of its bearer, rode to the front of the line that was being driven back and rallied the men, reformed the line, and drove the Confederates back. Boehm was awarded his medal on December 15, 1898.

Wells Blodgett (U.S. Army War College)

Bois, Frank. Birth: Canada, 1841. Quartermaster, U.S. Navy aboard the U.S.S. *Cincinnati*. On May 27, 1863, at Vicksburg, Mississippi, Quartermaster Bois showed extreme gallantry in servicing the ship's guns in action against the Confederate batteries. Bois was awarded his medal on July 10, 1863.

Bond, William. Birth: Massachusetts, 1839. Boatswain's Mate aboard the U.S.S. *Kearsarge*. On June 19, 1864, at Cherbourg, France, Boatswain's Mate Bond exhibited exceptional coolness and good conduct in the fighting that resulted in the sinking of the Confederate Raider *Alabama*. Bond was awarded his medal on December 31, 1864.

Bonebrake, Henry G. Birth: Pennsylvania, 1838. Lieutenant of Company G, 17th Pennsylvania Cavalry. On April 1, 1865, at Five Forks, Virginia, Lieutenant Bonebrake fought a hand-to-hand struggle to capture a Confederate flag. Bonebrake was awarded his medal on May 3, 1865.

Bonnaffon, Sylvester, Jr. Birth: Pennsylvania, 1844. First Lieutenant of Company G, 99th Pennsylvania Infantry. On October 27, 1864, at Boydton Plank Road, Virginia, Lieutenant Bonnaffon checked the rout of his troops, rallied them to go forward, while being severely wounded himself. Bonnaffon was awarded his medal on September 29, 1893.

Peter Boehm (U.S. Army War College)

Boody, Robert. Birth: Maine, 1836. Sergeant of Company B, 40th New York Infantry. On May 2, 1863, at Chancellorsville, Virginia, Sergeant Boody risked his life to save Captain George B. Carse from the battlefield. Boody was awarded his medal on July 8, 1896.

Boon, Hugh P. Birth: Pennsylvania, 1831. Captain of Company B, 1st West Virginia Cavalry. On April 6, 1865, at Sailors Creek, Virginia, Captain Boon captured a Confederate flag. Boon was awarded his medal on May 3, 1865.

Boss, Orlando. [photograph p. 27] Birth: Massachusetts, 1844. Corporal in Company F, 25th Massachusetts Infantry. On June 3, 1864, at Cold Harbor, Virginia, Corporal Boss risked his life to rescue his lieutenant who was lying mortally wounded between the opposing lines. Boss was awarded his medal on May 10, 1888.

Bouquet, Nicholas. Birth: Germany, 1842. Private in Company D, 1st Iowa Infantry. On August 10, 1861, at Wilson's Creek, Missouri, Private Bouquet left the line of battle to capture a rider less horse and hitch it to a disabled cannon, thus saving the piece from capture. Bouquet was awarded his medal on February 16, 1897.

Bourke, John G. Birth: Pennsylvania, 1846. Private in Company E, 15th Pennsylvania Cavalry. On December 31, 1862, at Stone's River, Tennessee, Private Bourke displayed exceptional gallantry in action. Bourke was awarded his medal on November 16, 1887.

Orlando Boss (U.S. Army War College)

Bourne, Thomas. Birth: England, 1834. Seaman and Gun Captain aboard the U.S.S. *Varuna*. On April 24, 1862, at Forts Jackson and St. Philip, south of New Orleans, Seaman Bourne exhibited exceptional gallantry in combat with the enemy. Bourne was awarded his medal on April 3, 1863.

Boury, Richard. Birth: Ohio, 1830. Sergeant in Company C, 1st West Virginia Cavalry. On March 5, 1865, at Charlottesville, Virginia, Sergeant Boury captured a Confederate flag. Boury was awarded his medal on March 26, 1865.

Boutwell, John W. Birth: New Hampshire, 1845. Private in Company B, 18th New Hampshire Infantry. On April 2, 1865, at Petersburg, Virginia, Private Boutwell risked his life to rescue a fallen comrade who had been shot through both legs from a galling enemy fire. The date of Boutwell's award is unknown.

John Bourke (Hall of Heroes)

Nicholas Bouquet (U.S. Army War College)

Bowen, Chester B. Birth: New York, 1842. Corporal in Company I, 19th New York Cavalry. On September 19, 1864, at Winchester, Virginia, Corporal Bowen captured a Confederate flag. Bowen was awarded his medal on September 27, 1864.

Bowen, Emmer. Birth: New York, 1830. Private in Company C, 127th Illinois Infantry. On May 22, 1863, at Vicksburg, Mississippi, Private Bowen exhibited exceptional gallantry in the charge of the volunteer storming party. Bowen was awarded his medal on July 21, 1894.

Bowman, Edward R. Birth: Maine, 1828. Quartermaster, U.S. Navy aboard the U.S.S. *Ticonderoga*. From January 13 to 15, 1865, at Fort Fisher, North Carolina, Quartermaster Bowman displayed outstanding courage in the performance of his duties in maintaining a well-placed fire on the Confederate fortress. Bowman was awarded his medal on June 22, 1865.

Thomas Box (U.S. Army War College)

Box, Thomas J. Birth: New York, 1833. Captain of Company D, 27th Indiana Infantry. On May 14, 1864, at Resaca, Georgia, Captain Box captured the flag of the 38th Alabama Infantry. Box was awarded his medal on April 7, 1865.

Boynton, Henry V. Birth: Massachusetts, 1835. Lieutenant Colonel of the 35th Ohio Infantry. On November 25, 1863, at Missionary Ridge, Tennessee, Colonel Boynton, though wounded, led his regiment gallantly in the face of a severe fire from the enemy.

Henry Boynton (U.S. Army War College)

Bradley, Amos. Birth: New York, 1827. Landsman aboard the U.S.S. *Varuna*. On April 24, 1862, at Forts Jackson and St. Philip, south of New Orleans, Landsman Bradley exhibited exceptional gallantry in performing his duties. Bradley was awarded his medal on April 3, 1863.

Bradley, Charles. Birth: Ireland, 1838. Boatswain's Mate aboard the U.S.S. *Louisville*. While acting as captain in the thick of battle, Bradley consistently showed attention to duty, bravery and coolness in action against the enemy. Bradley was awarded his medal on April 3, 1863.

Bradley, Thomas W. [photograph p. 29] Birth: England, 1844. Sergeant of Company H, 124th New York Infantry. On May 3, 1863, at Chancellorsville, Virginia,

Thomas Bradley (U.S. Army War College)

Sergeant Bradley volunteered to go for ammunition in the face of a heavy fire of musketry and canister. Bradley was awarded his medal on June 10, 1896.

Brady, James. Birth: Massachusetts, 1842. Private in Company F, 10th New Hampshire Infantry. On September 29, 1864, at Chapin's Farm, Virginia, Private Brady captured a Confederate flag. Brady was awarded his medal on April 6, 1865.

Brandle, Joseph E. Birth: Ohio, 1839. Private in Company C, 17th Michigan Infantry. On November 16, 1863, at Lenoire, Tennessee, Private Brandle, while regimental color bearer, and having been twice wounded, without the sight in one eye, still held on to the colors until ordered to the rear by his regimental commander. Brandle was awarded his medal on July 20, 1897.

Brannigan, Felix. Birth: Ireland. Private in Company A, 74th New York Infantry. On May 2, 1863, at Chancellorsville, Virginia, Private Brannigan volunteered on a dangerous scouting service and brought in valuable information. Brannigan was awarded his medal on June 29, 1866.

Brant, William, Jr. Birth: New Jersey, 1842. Lieutenant in Company B, 1st New Jersey Veteran Battalion. On April 3, 1865, at Petersburg, Virginia, Lieutenant Brant captured the battle flag of the 46th North Carolina Infantry. Brant was awarded his medal on May 10, 1865.

Bras, Edgar A. Birth: Iowa, 1841. Sergeant in Company K, 8th Iowa Infantry. On April 8, 1865, at Spanish Fort, in Mobile, Alabama, Sergeant Bras captured a Confederate flag. Brass was awarded his medal on June 8, 1865.

Brazell, John. Birth: Pennsylvania, 1837. Quartermaster aboard the U.S.S. *Richmond*. On August 5, 1864, at Mobile Bay, Alabama, Quartermaster Brazell showed coolness and good conduct as a gun captain during that engagement. Brazell was awarded his medal on December 31, 1864.

Breen, John. Birth: New York, 1827. Boatswain's Mate aboard the U.S.S. *Commodore Perry*. On October 3, 1862, at Franklin, Virginia, Boatswain's Mate Breen exhibited exceptional heroism performing his duties while the *Commodore Perry* battled against the Confederate batteries along the banks of Blackwater River. Breen was awarded his medal on April 3, 1863.

Brennan, Christopher. Birth: Ireland, 1832. Seaman aboard the U.S.S. *Mississippi*. From April 24 to 25, 1862, at Forts Jackson and St. Philip, south of New Orleans, Seaman Brennan showed skill and courage in the entire engagement that resulted in the taking of St. Philip and Jackson and the surrender of New Orleans. Brennan was awarded his medal on July 10, 1863.

Brest, Lewis. Birth: Pennsylvania, 1842. Private in Company D, 57th Pennsylvania Infantry. On April 6, 1865, at Sailors Creek, Virginia, Private Brest captured a Confederate flag. Brest was awarded his medal on May 10, 1865.

Brewer, William J. Birth: New York, 1843. Private in Company C, 2nd New York Cavalry. On April 4, 1865, at Appomattox, Virginia, Private Brewer captured an engineer flag from the Army of Northern Virginia. Brewer was awarded his medal on May 3, 1865.

Breyer, Charles. Birth: Pennsylvania, 1844. Sergeant in Company I, 90th Pennsylvania Infantry. On August 23, 1862, at Rappahannock Station, Virginia, Sergeant Breyer disposed of an unexploded shell, saving the life of a comrade whose arm had been taken off by that same shell. Breyer was awarded his medal on July 8, 1896.

Lewis Brest (Hall of Heroes)

Briggs, Elijah A. Birth: Connecticut. Corporal in Company B, 2nd Connecticut Heavy Artillery. On April 3, 1865, at Petersburg, Virginia, Corporal Briggs captured a Confederate flag. Briggs was awarded his medal on May 10, 1865.

Bringle, Andrew. Birth: New York. Corporal of Company F, 10th New York Cavalry. On April 6, 1865, at Sailors Creek, Virginia, Corporal Bringle charged the enemy and assisted Sgt. Norton in capturing a fieldpiece and two prisoners. Bringle was awarded his medal on July 3, 1865.

Brinn, Andrew. Birth: Scotland, 1829. Seaman aboard the U.S.S. *Mississippi*. On March 14, 1863, at Port Hudson, Louisiana, Seaman Brinn remained, under a heavy fire, on board the grounded vessel until all the abandoning crew had landed. After asking to be assigned some duty, he was finally ordered to save himself. Brinn was awarded his medal on July 10, 1863.

Bronner, August F. Birth: Germany, 1835. Private in Company C, 1st New York Artillery. On June 30, 1862, at White Oak Swamp, Virginia, Private Bronner continued

John Brosnan (U.S. Army War College)

to fight after being severely wounded. The date Bronner's medal was awarded is unknown.

Bronson, James H. Birth: Pennsylvania, 1838. First Sergeant of Company D, 5th United States Colored Infantry. On September 29, 1864, at Chapin's Farm, Virginia, Sergeant Bronson took command of his company after all of the officers had been killed or wounded, gallantly leading it. Bronson was awarded his medal on April 6, 1865.

Brosnan, John. [photograph p. 30] Birth: Ireland, 1846. Sergeant of Company E, 164th New York Infantry. On June 17, 1864, at Petersburg, Virginia, Sergeant Brosnan exposed himself to a heavy enemy fire to rescue a wounded comrade, being wounded himself in the process. Brosnan was awarded his medal on January 18, 1894.

Brouse, Charles W. Birth: Indiana, 1839. Captain of Company K, 100th Indiana Infantry. On November 25, 1863, at Missionary Ridge, Tennessee, Captain Brouse encouraged his men by refusing to lie down, even though his men had been ordered to do so, walking along the top of the works until he fell severely wounded. Brouse was awarded his medal on May 16, 1899.

Brown, Charles. Birth: Pennsylvania, 1841. Sergeant of Company C, 50th Pennsylvania Infantry. On August 19, 1864, at Weldon Railroad, Virginia, Sergeant Brown captured the flag of the 47th Virginia Infantry. Brown was awarded his medal on December 1, 1864.

Brown, Edward, Jr. Birth: Ireland, 1841. Corporal in Company G, 62nd New York infantry. On May 3 and 4, 1863, at Fredericksburg, Virginia, Corporal Brown, while severely wounded, carried the colors and continued at his post until being ordered to the rear. Brown was awarded his medal on November 24, 1880.

Brown, Henri Le Ferve. Birth: New York, 1842. Sergeant in Company B, 72nd New York Infantry. On May 6, 1864, at the Wilderness, Virginia, Sergeant Brown crossed the field of battle three times with loads of ammunition in a blanket on his back enabling the regiment to hold its position until reinforced. Brown was awarded his medal on June 23, 1896.

Edward Brown (U.S. Army War College)

Brown, James. Birth: New York, 1826. Quartermaster aboard the U.S.S. *Albatross*. On May 4, 1863, at Fort DeRussy, in the Red River area, Quartermaster Brown exhibited exceptional gallantry in performing his duty while under heavy fire from the enemy. Brown was awarded his medal on April 16, 1864.

Brown, Jeremiah Z. Birth: Pennsylvania, 1839. Captain of Company K, 148th Pennsylvania Infantry. On October 27, 1864, at Petersburg, Virginia, Captain Brown, with 100 volunteers, assaulted and captured the enemy works. Brown was awarded his medal on June 22, 1896.

Brown, John (True name was **Thomas Hayes**). Birth: Scotland, 1826. Captain of the Forecastle aboard the U.S.S. *Brooklyn*. On August 5, 1864, at Mobile Bay, Alabama, Brown fought his gun with skill and courage in the fight with the Confederate ram *Tennessee* and the Rebel forts. Brown was awarded his medal on December 31, 1864.

Jeremiah Brown (U.S. Army War College)

Brown, John H. Birth: Massachusetts, 1842. First Sergeant in Company A, 47th Ohio Infantry. On May 19, 1863, at Vicksburg, Mississippi, Sergeant Brown carried a message from Col. A.C. Parry to Gen. Hugh Ewing through a terrific fire. Brown was awarded his medal on August 24, 1896.

Brown, John Harties. Birth: Canada, 1834, Captain of Company D, 12th Kentucky Infantry. On November 30, 1864, at Franklin, Tennessee, captain Brown captured a Confederate flag. Brown was awarded his medal on February 13, 1865.

Brown, Morris, Jr. Birth: New York, 1842. Captain of Company A, 126th New York Infantry. On July 3, 1863, at Gettysburg, Pennsylvania, Captain Brown captured a Confederate flag. Brown was awarded his medal on March 6, 1869.

Robert Brown (U.S. Army War College)

Brown, Robert. Birth: Norway, 1830. Captain of the Top aboard the U.S.S. *Richmond*. On August 5, 1864, at Mobile Bay, Alabama, Brown was cool and courageous at his station throughout the prolonged action. Brown was awarded his medal on December 31, 1864.

Brown, Robert B. Birth: Ohio, 1844. Private in Company A, 15th Ohio Infantry. On November 25, 1863, at Missionary Ridge, Tennessee, Private Brown captured the flag and color bearer of the 9th Mississippi Infantry. Brown was awarded his medal on March 27, 1890.

Brown, Uriah. Birth: Ohio, 1841. Private of Company G, 30th Ohio Infantry. On May 22, 1863, at Vicksburg, Mississippi, Private Brown, though wounded himself, dragged five of his wounded comrades to safety. Brown was awarded his medal on August 15, 1894.

Brown, William H. Birth: Maryland, 1836. Landsman aboard the U.S.S. *Brooklyn*. On August 5, 1864, at Mobile Bay, Alabama, Landsman Brown remained steadfast at his post and performed his duties in the powder division throughout the furious action which resulted in the surrender of the ram *Tennessee* and the damaging and destruction of batteries at Fort Morgan. Brown was awarded his medal on December 31, 1864.

William H. Brown (Hall of Heroes)

Brown, Wilson. Birth: Mississippi, 1841. Landsman aboard the U.S.S. *Hartford*. On August 5, 1864, at Mobile Bay, Alabama, Landsman Brown was knocked unconscious by an enemy shell burst which killed a man on the ladder above him. Regaining consciousness, he promptly returned to the shell whip and continued to perform his duties even though 4 of the 6 men at this station had been killed or wounded.

Brown, Wilson W. Birth, 1839: Ohio. Private in Company F, 21st Ohio Infantry. In April of 1862, at Big Shanty, Georgia, Brown was one of 22 men who penetrated nearly 200 miles into enemy territory, captured a railroad train, and attempted to destroy bridges and track between Chattanooga and Atlanta. Brown was awarded his medal in September of 1863.

Wilson Brown [Mississippi, 1841] (U.S. Army War College)

Brownell, Francis E. [photograph p. 34] Birth: New York, 1840. Private in Company A, 11th New York Infantry. On May 24, 1861, at Alexandria, Virginia, Private

The Recipients — **Brownell**

Francis Brownell (Hall of Heroes)

Louis Bruner (U.S. Army War College)

Brownell killed the murderer of Colonel Elmer Ellsworth at the Marshall House. This was the first deed done to merit the Medal of Honor. Brownell was awarded his medal on January 26, 1877.

Brownell, William P. Birth: New York, 1838. Coxswain aboard the U.S.S. *Benton*. On May 2, 1863, at Great Gulf Bay, Mississippi, Brownell served gallantly against the enemy as captain of a 9-inch gun. Brownell was awarded his medal on April 16, 1864.

Bruner, Louis J. Birth: Indiana, 1843. Private in Company H, 5th Indiana Cavalry. On December 2, 1863, at Walker's Ford, Tennessee, Private Bruner passed through enemy lines, under fire, and conveyed to a battalion, then in a perilous position and liable to be captured, information that enabled it to reach a point of safety. Bruner was awarded his medal on March 9, 1896.

Brush, George W. Birth: New York, 1842. Lieutenant in Company B, 34th United States Colored Infantry. On May 24, 1864, at Ashepoo River, South Carolina, Lieutenant Brush voluntarily commanded a boat crew that went to the rescue of a large number of Union soldiers on board the stranded steamer Boston and succeeded in conveying them to shore. Brush was awarded his medal on January 21, 1897.

George Brush (U.S. Army War College)

Bruton, Christopher C. (True name **Christopher Braton**). Birth: 1840. Captain of Company C, 22nd New York Cavalry. On March 2, 1865, at Waynesboro, Virginia, Captain Bruton captured General Jubal Early's headquarters flag. Bruton was awarded his medal on March 26, 1865.

Brutsche, Henry. Birth: Pennsylvania, 1846. Landsman aboard the U.S.S. *Tacony*. On October 31, 1864, at Plymouth, North Carolina, Landsman Brutsche, during the capture of Plymouth distinguished himself when he participated in landing and spiking a 9-inch gun while under a devastating fire from the enemy. Brutsche was awarded his medal on December 31, 1864.

Bryant, Andrew S. Birth: Massachusetts, 1841. Sergeant of Company A, 46th Massachusetts Infantry. On May 23, 1863, at New Bern, North Carolina, Sergeant Bryant, with 16 men, repulsed for half an hour a fierce attack of a strong Confederate force, thus saving the city of New Bern from capture. Bryant was awarded his medal on August 13, 1873.

Andrew Bryant (U.S. Army War College)

Buchanan, George A. Birth: New York, 1842. Private in Company G, 148th New York Infantry. On September 29, 1864, at Chapin's Farm, Virginia, Private Buchanan took position in advance of the skirmish line and drove the enemy's cannoneers from their guns. He was mortally wounded in the assault. Buchanan's medal was awarded on April 6, 1865.

Buck, Frederick Clarence. Birth: Connecticut, 1843. Corporal in Company A, 21st Connecticut Infantry. On September 29, 1864, at Chapin's Farm, Virginia. Corporal Buck, although wounded, refused to leave the field until the fight closed. Buck was awarded his medal on April 6, 1865.

Buck, James. Birth: Maryland, 1808. Quartermaster aboard the U.S.S. *Brooklyn*. From April 24 to 25, 1862, at Forts Jackson and St. Philip, south of New Orleans, Buck, though severely wounded, continued to perform his duty until positively ordered below. Buck was awarded his medal on April 3, 1863.

Buckingham, David E. [photograph p. 36] Birth: Delaware, 1840. First Lieutenant of Company E, 4th Delaware Infantry. On February 5, 1865, at Rowanty Creek, Virginia, Lieutenant Buckingham swam the partly frozen creek, under fire, to try to capture a crossing. Buckingham was awarded his medal on February 13, 1895.

Buckles, Abram J. (True name **Abraham C. Buckles.**) Birth: Indiana, 1846. Sergeant of Company E,

Abram Buckles (U.S. Army War College)

19th Indiana Infantry. On May 5, 1864, at the Wilderness, Virginia, Sergeant Buckles, though seriously wounded, carried the regimental colors until wounded again. Buckles was awarded his medal on December 4, 1893.

Buckley, Dennis. Birth: Canada, 1844. Private in Company G, 136th New York Infantry. On July 20, 1864, at Peach Tree Creek, Georgia, Private Buckley captured the flag of the 31st Mississippi Infantry. Buckley was awarded his medal on April 7, 1865.

Buckley, John C. Birth: West Virginia, 1842. Sergeant in Company G, 4th West Virginia Infantry. On May 22, 1863, at Vicksburg, Mississippi, Sergeant Buckley exhibited exceptional gallantry in the charge of the volunteer storming party. Buckley was awarded his medal on July 9, 1864.

David Buckingham (U.S. Army War College)

Bucklyn, John K. [photograph p. 37] Birth: Rhode Island, 1834. First Lieutenant in Battery E, 1st Rhode Island Light Artillery. On May 3, 1863, at Chancellorsville, Virginia, Lieutenant Bucklyn fought his battery until all of his ammunition was expended, and with many of the gunners and most of the horses killed or wounded, and the enemy within 25 yards of the guns, succeeded in disabling one piece and bringing the other safely off. Bucklyn was awarded his medal on July 13, 1899.

Buffington, John E. Birth: Maryland, 1841. Sergeant in Company C, 6th Maryland Infantry. On April 2, 1865, at Petersburg, Virginia, Sergeant Buffington was the first enlisted man of the 3rd Division to mount the parapet of the

John Buckley (Hall of Heroes)

John Bucklyn (U.S. Army War College)

Robert Buffum (Hall of Heroes)

enemy's line. The date of Buffington's award is unknown.

Buffum, Robert. Birth: Massachusetts, 1828. (3rd to receive the Medal of Honor) Private in Company H, 21st Ohio Infantry. In April of 1862, at Big Shanty, Georgia, Private Buffum was one of 22 volunteers who penetrated 200 miles into enemy territory, captured a railroad train, and attempted to destroy bridges and track between Chattanooga and Atlanta. Buffum was awarded his medal on March 25, 1863.

Buhrman, Henry G. Birth: Ohio. Private in Company H, 54th Ohio Infantry. On May 22, 1863, at Vicksburg, Mississippi, Private Buhrman exhibited exceptional gallantry in the charge of the volunteer storming party. Burhman was awarded his medal on July 12, 1894.

Bumgarner, William. Birth: 1837. Sergeant of Company A, 4th West Virginia Infantry. On May 22, 1863, at Vicksburg, Mississippi, Sergeant Bumgarner exhibited exceptional gallantry in the charge of the volunteer storming party. Bumgarner was awarded his medal on July 10, 1894.

Burbank, James H. Birth: Holland, 1838. Sergeant of Company K, 4th Rhode Island Infantry. On October 3, 1862, at Blackwater, Virginia, Sergeant Burbank showed exceptional gallantry in action while on detached service on board the gunboat Barney. Burbank was awarded his medal on July 27, 1896.

Burger, Joseph. Birth: Austria, 1848. Private in Company H, 2nd Minnesota Infantry. On February 15, 1863, at Nolensville, Tennessee, Private Burger was one of a detachment of 16 men who heroically defended a wagon train against the attack of 125 Confederate cavalry, repulsed the attack and saved the train. Burger was awarded his medal on September 11, 1897.

Burk, E. Michael. Birth: Ireland, 1847. Private in Company D, 125th New York Infantry. On May 12, 1864, at Spotsylvania, Virginia, Private Burk received a bullet wound in the chest in the act of capturing a Confederate flag. Burk was awarded his medal on December 1, 1864.

Burk, Thomas. Birth: New York, 1842. Sergeant in Company H, 97th New York Infantry. On May 6, 1864, at the Wilderness, Virginia, Sergeant Burk, at the risk of his own life, went back while the Rebels were still firing, and finding Col. Wheelock unable to move, alone and unaided carried him off the field. Burk was awarded his medal on August 24, 1896.

Burke, Daniel W. Birth: Connecticut, 1841. First Sergeant in Company B, 2nd United States Infantry. On September 20, 1862, at Shepherdstown Ford, Virginia, Sergeant Burke voluntarily attempted to spike a gun in the face of the enemy. Burke was awarded his medal on April 21, 1892.

Burke, Thomas. Birth: Ireland, 1842. Private in Company A, 5th New York Cavalry. On June 30, 1863, at Hanover Courthouse, Virginia, Private Burke captured a Confederate flag. Burke was awarded his medal on February 11, 1878.

Burns, James M. Birth: Ohio, 1845. Sergeant of Company B, 1st West Virginia Infantry. On May 15, 1864, at New Market, Virginia, Sergeant Burns rallied a few men to support the colors, which were in danger of being captured, and bore them to a place of safety. Burns was awarded his medal on November 20, 1896.

James Burns (U.S. Army War College)

Burns, John M. Birth: New York, 1835. Seaman aboard the U.S.S. *Lackawana*. On August 5, 1864, at Mobile Bay, Alabama, Seaman Burns exhibited exceptional gallantry in assisting the powder division throughout a prolonged action, even though he was severely wounded. Burns was awarded his medal on December 31, 1864.

Burritt, William W. Birth: New York. Private in Company G, 113th Illinois Infantry. On April 27, 1863, at Vicksburg, Mississippi, Private Burritt voluntarily acted as a fireman on a steam tug that ran the Confederate blockade and passed the batteries under a heavy fire. Burritt was awarded his medal on July 8, 1896.

Burton, Albert. Birth: England, 1838. Seaman aboard the U.S.S. *Wabash*. On January 15, 1865, at Fort Fisher, North Carolina, Seaman Burton, as part of the sip's landing party, succeeded in reaching the angle of the fort and was one of the few who entered the fort. Burton was awarded his medal on June 22, 1865.

Butterfield, Daniel. Birth: New York, 1831. Brigadier General, United States Volunteers. On June 27, 1862, at Gaines Mill, Virginia, General Butterfield seized the colors of the 83rd Pennsylvania at a critical moment and encouraged the men to renew the attack. Butterfield was awarded his medal on September 26, 1893.

Butterfield, Franklin G. Birth: Vermont, 1842. First Lieutenant of Company C, 6th Vermont Infantry. On May 4, 1863, at Salem Heights, Virginia, Lieutenant Butterfield took command of a skirmish line and covered the movement of his regiment out of a precarious position. Butterfield was awarded his medal on May 4, 1891.

Daniel Butterfield (Hall of Heroes)

Butts, George. Birth: New York, 1838. Gunner's Mate aboard the U.S.S. *Signal*. On May 5, 1864, at Red River, Louisiana, Butts, although on the sick list, courageously carried out his duties during the entire engagement. Butts was awarded his medal on December 31, 1864.

Byrnes, James. Birth: Ireland, 1838. Boatswain's Mate aboard the U.S.S. *Louisville*. Byrnes carried out his duties through the thick of battle and acting as captain of the 9-inch gun consistently showed attention to duty, bravery, and coolness in action against the enemy. Byrnes was awarded his medal on April 3, 1863.

Cadwallader, Abel G. Birth: Maryland, 1841. Corporal in Company H, 1st Maryland Infantry. On February 6, 1865, at Hatcher's Mill, Virginia, Corporal Cadwallader gallantly planted the colors on the enemy's works in advance of the arrival of his regiment. Cadwallader was awarded his medal on January 5, 1897.

Cadwell, Luman L. Birth: New York, 1836. Sergeant of Company B, 2nd New York Cavalry. On September 20, 1864, at Alabama Bayou, Louisiana, Sergeant Cadwell swam the bayou under fire and captured and brought back a boat with which the command crossed and routed the enemy. Cadwell was awarded his medal on August 17, 1894.

Caldwell, Daniel. Birth: Pennsylvania, 1842. Sergeant in Company H, 13th Pennsylvania

Frank Butterfield (Hall of Heroes)

Cavalry. On February 6, 1865, at Hatcher's Run, Virginia, Sergeant Caldwell captured the flag of the 33rd North Carolina Infantry. Caldwell was awarded his medal on February 25, 1865.

Calkin, Ivers S. Birth: New York, 1836. First Sergeant of Company M, 2nd New York Cavalry. On April 6, 1865, at Sailors Creek, Virginia, Sergeant Calkin captured the flag of the 18th Virginia Infantry. Calkin was awarded his medal on May 3, 1865.

Callahan, John H. Birth: Kentucky. Private in Company B, 122nd Illinois Infantry. On April 9, 1865, at Fort Blakely, Alabama, Private Callahan captured a Confederate flag. Callahan was awarded his medal on June 8, 1865.

John Callahan (Hall of Heroes)

Camp, Carlton N. Birth: New Hampshire, 1845. Private in Company B, 18th New Hampshire Infantry. On April 2, 1865, at Petersburg, Virginia, Private Camp rescued a comrade from the picket line who had been severely wounded. The date of Camp's award is unknown.

Campbell, James A. Birth: New York, 1844. Private in Company A, 2nd New York Cavalry. On January 22, 1865, at Woodstock, Virginia, Private Campbell rushed back when his command was retreating to rescue his commanding officer, who had been unhorsed and left behind. At Amelia Courthouse, Virginia, he would later capture two Confederate flags on April 5, 1865. Campbell was awarded his medal on October 30, 1897.

Campbell, William. Birth: Indiana, 1838. Boatswain's Mate aboard the

James Campbell (U.S. Army War College)

U.S.S. *Ticonderoga*. On December 24 to 25, 1864, and January 13 to 15, 1865, in actions against Fort Fisher, North Carolina, Campbell served as captain of a gun and performed his duties with skill and courage. Campbell was awarded his medal on June 22, 1865.

The Recipients — Carey 41

Charles Capehart (U.S. Army War College)

Henry Capehart (U.S. Army War College)

Campbell, William. Birth: Ireland, 1840. Private in Company I, 30th Ohio Infantry. On May 22, 1863, at Vicksburg, Mississippi, Private Campbell exhibited exceptional gallantry in the charge of the volunteer storming party. Campbell was awarded his medal on August 14, 1894.

Capehart, Charles E. Birth: Pennsylvania, 1833. Major of the 1st West Virginia Cavalry. On July 4, 1863, at Monterey Mountain, Pennsylvania, Major Capehart charged down the side of the mountain upon the Confederate's retreating wagon train destroying and capturing many wagons and capturing many prisoners. Capehart was awarded his medal on April 7, 1898.

Capehart, Henry. Birth: Pennsylvania, 1825. Colonel of 1st West Virginia Cavalry. On May 22, 1864, at Greenbrier River, West Virginia, Colonel Capehart rescued a drowning soldier, while under fire from the enemy. Capehart was awarded his medal on February 12, 1895.

Capron, Horace, Jr. Birth: Maryland, 1840. Sergeant in Company G, 8th Illinois Cavalry. In June of 1862, at Chickahominy and Ashland, Virginia, Sergeant Capron exhibited gallantry in action. Capron was awarded his medal on September 27, 1865.

Carey, Hugh. Birth: Ireland. Sergeant of Company E, 82nd New York Infantry. On July 2, 1863, at Gettysburg, Pennsylvania, Sergeant Carey captured the flag of the

William Carney (U.S. Army War College)

Eugene Carr (U.S. Army War College)

7th Virginia Infantry. Carey was awarded his medal on February 6, 1888.

Carey, James L. Birth: New York, 1839. Sergeant in Company G, 10th New York Cavalry. On April 9, 1865, at Appomattox Courthouse, Virginia, Sergeant Carey bravely urged his men forward in a charge. The date of Carey's award is unknown.

Carlisle, Casper R. Birth: Pennsylvania. Private in Company F, Independent Pennsylvania Light Artillery. On July 2, 1863, at Gettysburg, Pennsylvania, Private Carlisle saved a gun of his battery, under heavy fire, even though most of the horses and drivers had been killed or wounded. Carlisle was awarded his medal on December 21, 1892.

Carman, Warren. Birth: New York. Private in Company H, 1st New York Cavalry. On March 2, 1865, at Waynesboro, Virginia, Private Carman captured a Confederate flag and several prisoners. Carman was awarded his medal on March 26, 1865.

Carmin, Isaac H. Birth: New Jersey, 1841. Corporal in Company A, 48th Ohio Infantry. On May 22, 1863, at Vicksburg, Mississippi, Corporal Carmin saved his regimental flag from capture and also risked his life to throw a shell with a burning fuse from among his comrades. Carmin was awarded his medal on February 25, 1895.

Carney, William H. Birth: Virginia, 1840. Sergeant in Company C, 54th Massachusetts Colored Infantry. On July 18, 1863, at Fort Wagner, South Carolina, Sergeant Carney Seized the regimental flag, after its bearer had been shot down, and led the way to the parapet, where he planted the banner. When the attack was repulsed, Carney brought the flag safely off, even though he had been twice wounded. Carney was awarded his medal on May 23, 1900.

Carr, Eugene A. Birth: New York, 1830. Colonel of the 3rd Illinois Cavalry. On March 7, 1862, at Pea Ridge, Arkansas, Colonel Carr gallantly directed the deployment of his command and held his ground under a brisk fire of shot and shell in which he was wounded several times. Carr was awarded his medal on January 16, 1894.

Carr, Franklin. Birth: Ohio, 1844. Corporal in Company D, 124th Ohio Infantry. On December 16, 1864, at Nashville, Tennessee, Corporal Carr recaptured a U.S. guidon from a Confederate battery. Carr was awarded his medal on February 24, 1865.

Carr, William M. Birth: Maryland, 1829. Master-at-Arms aboard the U.S.S. *Richmond*. On August 5, 1864, at Mobile Bay, Alabama, Carr displayed exceptional skill and courage in the performance of his duties. Carr was awarded his medal on December 31, 1864.

Carson, William J. Birth: Pennsylvania, 1840. Musician in Company E, 15th United States Infantry. On September 19, 1863, at Chickamauga, Georgia, at a critical stage of the battle, Musician Carson noticed the lines of the 18th U.S. Infantry wavering, and he used his own initiative to bugle "to the colors," causing the regiment to form on him and checking the enemy advance. He later repeated the action with the 2nd Ohio Infantry. Carson was awarded his medal on January 27, 1894.

Cart, Jacob. Birth: Pennsylvania, 1843. Private in Company A, 7th Pennsylvania Reserve Infantry. On December 13, 1862, at Fredericksburg, Virginia, Private Cart captured the flag of the 19th Georgia Infantry. Cart was awarded his medal on November 25, 1864.

Carter, John J. Birth: New York, 1842. Second Lieutenant of Company B, 33rd New York Infantry. On September 17, 1862, at Antietam, Maryland, Lieutenant Carter, while commanding a detached company, saw the remainder of his regiment being thrown back by the Confederates, and, without orders made a countercharge checking the Confederate assault. Carter was awarded his medal on September 10, 1897.

Carter, Joseph F. Birth: Maryland, 1842. Captain of Company D, 3rd Maryland Infantry. On March 25, 1865, at Fort Stedman, Virginia, Captain Carter captured the flag of the 51st Virginia Infantry. he was also captured, but escaped bringing a number of prisoners with him. Carter was awarded his medal on July 9, 1891.

John Carter (U.S. Army War College)

Caruana, Orlando E. Birth: North Carolina, 1844. Private in Company K, 51st New York Infantry. On March 14, 1862, at New Bern, North Carolina, Private Caruana saved the wounded color bearer and the colors from capture. Caruana was awarded his medal on November 14, 1890.

Casey, David. Birth: Ireland, 1842. Private in Company C, 25th Massachusetts Infantry. On June 3, 1864, at Cold Harbor, Virginia, Private Casey, seeing the color bearers of the regiment being shot down, rushed forward, through a heavy enemy fire, to rescue the flag. Casey was awarded his medal on September 14, 1888.

Casey, Henry. Birth: Pennsylvania, 1837. Private in Company C, 20th Ohio Infantry. On April 22, 1863, at Vicksburg, Mississippi, Private Casey volunteered to serve as one of the crew on a transport that passed the Confederate forts, under heavy fire. Casey was awarded his medal on September 23, 1897.

Cassidy, Michael. Birth: Ireland, 1837. Landsman aboard the U.S.S. *Lackawana*. On August 5, 1864, at Mobile Bay, Alabama, Landsman Cassidy displayed great coolness and courage performing the duties of first sponger during the battle. Cassidy was awarded his medal on December 31, 1864.

Catlin, Isaac S. Birth: New York, 1835. Colonel of the 109th New York Infantry. On July 30, 1864, at Petersburg, Virginia, Colonel Catlin received a severe wound while heroically endeavoring to rally his troops. Catlin was awarded his medal on January 13, 1899.

Cayer, Ovila. Birth: Canada. Sergeant on Company A, 14th United States Infantry. On August 19, 1864, at Weldon Railroad, Virginia, Sergeant Cayer assumed command of his regiment after all of the officers had been disabled, continuing the attack. Cayer was awarded his medal on February 15, 1867.

Chamberlain, Joshua L. Birth: Maine, 1828. Colonel of the 20th Maine Infantry. On July 2, 1863, at Gettysburg, Pennsylvania, Colonel Chamberlain showed exceptional heroism and tenacity in holding his position on Little Round Top against repeated assaults, then mounted a bayonet charge that swept the Confederates from his front. Chamberlain was awarded his medal on August 11, 1893.

Isaac Catlin (U.S. Army War College)

Joshua Chamberlain (U.S. Army War College)

Joseph Chambers (Hall of Heroes)

Stephen Chandler (U.S. Army War College)

Henry Chandler (U.S. Army War College)

Chamberlain, Orville T. Birth: Indiana, 1841. Second Lieutenant in Company G, 74th Indiana Infantry. On September 20, 1863, at Chickamauga, Georgia, Lieutenant Chamberlain exposed himself to a galling fire to gather ammunition for his men from another regiment. Chamberlain was awarded his medal on March 11, 1896.

Chambers, Joseph B. Birth: Pennsylvania. Private in Company F, 100th Pennsylvania Infantry. On March 25, 1865, at Petersburg, Virginia, Private Chambers captured the flag of the 1st Virginia Infantry. Chambers was awarded his medal on July 27, 1871.

Chandler, Henry F. Birth: Massachusetts, 1835. Sergeant in Company E, 59th Massachusetts Infantry. On June 17, 1864, at Petersburg, Virginia, Sergeant Chandler refused to go to the rear, even though he was seriously wounded, and participated in the attack of his regiment that carried the enemy breastworks. Chandler was awarded his medal on March 30, 1898.

Chandler, James B. Birth: Massachusetts, 1838. Coxswain aboard the U.S.S. *Richmond*. On August 5, 1864, at Mobile Bay, Alabama, Coxswain Chandler rendered gallant service throughout the prolonged battle, even though he had just come off of the sick list. Chandler was awarded his medal on December 31, 1864.

Chandler, Stephen E. Birth: Michigan, 1841. Quartermaster Sergeant in Company A, 24th New York Cavalry. On April 5, 1865, at Amelia Springs, Virginia, Sergeant Chandler went between the lines to saved a wounded comrade from capture or death. Chandler was awarded his medal on April 4, 1898.

Chapin, Alaric B. Birth: New York. Private in Company G, 142nd New York Infantry. On January 15, 1865, at Fort Fisher, North Carolina, Private Chapin voluntarily advanced with the head of the column and cut down the palisade fence. Chapin was awarded his medal on December 28, 1914.

Chapman, John. Birth: Canada. Private in company B, 1st Maine Heavy Artillery. On April 6, 1865, at Sailors Creek, Virginia, Private Chapman captured a Confederate flag. Chapman was awarded his medal on May 10, 1865.

Chaput, Louis G. Birth: Canada, 1845. Landsman aboard the U.S.S. *Lackawana*. On August 5, 1864, at Mobile Bay, Alabama, Landsman Chaput, though severely wounded, displayed exceptional gallantry in serving his gun. Chaput was awarded his medal on December 31, 1864.

Chase, John F. Birth: Maine. Private in the 5th Maine Light Artillery. On May 3, 1863, at Chancellorsville, Virginia, Private Chase, with a comrade, continued to fire his gun, even after the others had ceased, then dragged it off the field after the horses had been shot, preventing its capture by the enemy. Chase was awarded his medal on February 7, 1888.

Child, Benjamin H. Birth: Rhode Island, 1843. Corporal in Battery A, 1st Rhode Island Light Artillery. On September 17, 1862, at Antietam, Maryland, Corporal Child was wounded and taken to the rear insensible. When he recovered, he insisted on returning to the battery, remaining in the fight until the close of the battle. Child was awarded his medal on July 20, 1897.

Chisman, William W. Birth: Indiana, 1843. Private in Company I, 83rd Indiana Infantry. On May 22, 1863, at Vicksburg, Mississippi, Private Chisman displayed exceptional gallantry in the charge of the volunteer storming party. Chisman was awarded his medal on August 15, 1894.

Benjamin Child (U.S. Army War College)

Christiancy, James I. Birth: Michigan. First Lieutenant of Company D, 9th Michigan Cavalry. On May 28, 1864, at Haws Shops, Virginia, Lieutenant Christiancy, acting as a volunteer aide, voluntarily led a part of the line in the attack, being twice wounded in the process. Christiancy was awarded his medal on October 10, 1892.

Churchill, Samuel J. Birth: Vermont. Corporal in Company G, 2nd Illinois Light Artillery. On December 15, 1864, at Nashville, Tennessee, Corporal Churchill, after the other men of the battery had been forced to seek shelter from enemy fire, stood alone in the field, manning his gun and keeping it in the battle. Churchill was awarded his medal on January 20, 1897.

Cilley, Clinton, A. Birth: New Hampshire, 1837. Captain of Company C, 2nd Minnesota Infantry. On September 20, 1863, at Chickamauga, Georgia, Captain Cilley seized the colors of a retreating regiment and led it into the thick of the attack. Cilley was awarded his medal on June 15, 1895.

Clancy, James T. Birth: New York. Sergeant in Company C, 1st New Jersey Cavalry. On October 1, 1864, at Vaughn Road, Virginia, Sergeant Clancy shot Confederate

General Dunovant during the Confederate charge, thus confusing the enemy and aiding in their repulse. Clancy was awarded his medal on July 3, 1865.

Clapp, Albert A. Birth: New York, 1841. First Sergeant on Company G, 2nd Ohio Cavalry. On April 6, 1865, at Sailors Creek, Virginia, Sergeant Clapp captured the flag of the 8th Florida Infantry. Clapp was awarded his medal on April 24, 1865.

Clark, Charles A. Birth: Maine, 1841. Lieutenant and Adjutant of the 6th Maine Infantry. On May 4, 1863, at Brooks Ford, Virginia, Lieutenant Clark, at personal risk, and with remarkable presence of mind, led the command down a precipitous embankment and saved the command from capture or destruction. Clark was awarded his medal on May 13, 1896.

Clark, Harrison. Birth: New York, 1842. Corporal of Company E, 125th New York Infantry. On July 2, 1863, at Gettysburg, Pennsylvania, Corporal Clark seized the colors and advanced with them after the color bearer had been shot down. Clark was awarded his medal on June 11, 1895.

Clark, James G. Birth: Pennsylvania. Private in Company F, 88th Pennsylvania Infantry. On June 18, 1864, at Petersburg, Virginia, Private Clark displayed distinguished bravery in action despite being severely wounded. Clark was awarded his medal on April 30, 1892.

Clark, John W. Birth: Vermont, 1830. First Lieutenant and Regimental Quartermaster for the 6th Vermont Infantry. On July 28, 1863, at Warrenton, Virginia, Lieutenant Clark defended the division train against a vastly superior force, being severely wounded in the process. Clark was awarded his medal on August 17, 1891.

Clark, William A. Birth: Pennsylvania, 1828. Corporal in Company H,

Charles Clark (U.S. Army War College)

Harrison Clark (U.S. Army War College)

2nd Minnesota Infantry. On February 15, 1863, at Nolensville, Tennessee, Corporal Clark, and a detachment of 16 men, heroically defended a wagon train against the attack of 125 enemy cavalry. Clark was awarded his medal on September 11, 1897.

Clarke, Dayton P. Birth: New York, 1840. Captain of Company F, 2nd Vermont Infantry. On May 12, 1864, at Spotsylvania, Virginia, Captain Clarke exhibited distinguished conduct in a desperate hand-to-hand fight while commanding his regiment. Clarke was awarded his medal on June 30, 1892.

Clausen, Charles H. Birth: Pennsylvania, 1842. First Lieutenant of Company H, 61st Pennsylvania Infantry. On May 12, 1864, at Spotsylvania, Virginia, Lieutenant Clausen, though severely wounded, led his regiment against the Confederates, saving a battery from capture. Clause was awarded his medal on June 25, 1864.

Clay, Cecil. Birth: Pennsylvania, 1842. Captain of Company K, 58th Pennsylvania Infantry. On September 29, 1864, at Fort Harrison, Virginia, Captain Clay led his regiment in a charge, carrying the colors of another regiment until he was wounded in the right arm. He then shifted the colors to the left hand and continued forward, even though he was subsequently wounded in the left hand. Clay was awarded his medal on April 19, 1892.

Cecil Clay (Hall of Heroes)

Cleveland, Charles F. Birth: New York. Private in Company C, 26th New York Infantry. On September 17, 1862, at Antietam, Maryland, Private Cleveland took up the colors after the color bearer had been shot and advanced them into action. Cleveland was awarded his medal on June 12, 1895.

Clifford, Robert T. Birth: Pennsylvania, 1835. Master-at-Arms aboard the U.S.S. *Shokokon*. On August 22, 1864, at New Topsail inlet, off Wilmington, North Carolina, Clifford participated in an attempt to destroy an enemy schooner. He led a charge, against three to one odds, that resulted in the retreat of the enemy and the capture of the schooner. Clifford was awarded his medal on December 31, 1864.

Clopp, John E. Birth: Pennsylvania. Private in company F, 71st Pennsylvania Infantry. On July 3, 1863, at Gettysburg, Pennsylvania, Private Clopp captured the flag of the 9th Virginia Infantry. Clopp was awarded his medal on February 2, 1865.

Clute, George W. Birth: Michigan. Corporal in Company I, 14th Michigan Infantry. On March 19, 1865, at Bentonville, North Carolina, Corporal Clute captured the flag of the 40th North Carolina Infantry. Clute was awarded his medal on August 26, 1898.

Coates, Jefferson. [photograph p. 23] Birth: Wisconsin, 1843. Sergeant in Company H, 7th Wisconsin Infantry. On July 1, 1863, at Gettysburg, Pennsylvania,

Jefferson Coates (U.S. Army War College)   *Robert Coffey (U.S. Army War College)*

Sergeant Coates exhibited unsurpassed courage in battle, where he had both eyes shot out. Coates was awarded his medal on June 29, 1866.

Cockley, David L. Birth: Ohio, 1843. First Lieutenant of Company L, 10th Ohio Cavalry. On December 4, 1864, at Waynesboro, Georgia, Lieutenant Cockley bravely led an attack of his men. Cockley was awarded his medal on August 2, 1897.

Coey, James. Birth: New York, 1841. Major of the 147th New York Infantry. On February 6, 1865, at Hatchers Run, Virginia, Major Coey advanced the regimental colors, causing the entire brigade to follow, after being severely wounded himself. Coey was awarded his medal on May 12, 1892.

Coffey, Robert J. Birth: Canada, 1842. Sergeant of Company K, 4th Vermont Infantry. On May 4, 1863, at Banks Ford, Virginia, Sergeant Coffey single-handedly captured 2 officers and 5 privates of the 8th Louisiana Infantry. Coffey was awarded his medal on May 13, 1892.

Cohn, Abraham. Birth: Prussia. Sergeant Major of the 6th New Hampshire Infantry. On May 6, 1864, at the Wilderness, Virginia, Sergeant Cohn

Abraham Cohn (Hall of Heroes)

rallied and formed his men, under heavy fire from the enemy. On July 30, 1864, at Petersburg, Virginia, he bravely carried orders to the advanced line under a severe fire. Cohn was awarded his medal on August 24, 1865.

Colbert, Patrick. Birth: Ireland, 1840. Coxswain aboard the U.S.S. *Commodore Hull.* On October 31, 1864, at Plymouth, North Carolina, Coxswain Colbert, though seriously wounded, remained at his post until the end of the action that resulted in the capture of Plymouth. Colbert was awarded his medal on December 31, 1864.

Colby, Carlos W. Birth: New Hampshire. Sergeant in Company G, 97th Illinois Infantry. On May 22, 1863, at Vicksburg, Mississippi, Sergeant Colby exhibited exceptional gallantry in the charge of the volunteer storming party. Colby was awarded his medal on January 31, 1896.

Cole, Gabriel. Birth: New York, 1831. Corporal in Company I, 5th Michigan Cavalry. On September 19, 1864, at Winchester, Virginia, Corporal Cole captured a Confederate flag. Cole was awarded his medal on September 27, 1864.

Collins, Harrison. Birth: Tennessee, 1834. Corporal of Company A, 1st Tennessee Cavalry. On December 24, 1864, at Richland Creek, Tennessee, Corporal Collins captured the flag of General Chalmer's Division. Collins was awarded his medal on February 24, 1865.

Collins, Thomas, D. Birth: New York, 1847. Sergeant of Company H. 143rd New York Infantry. On May 15, 1864, at Resaca, Georgia, Sergeant Collins captured a Confederate flag. Collins was awarded his medal on August 14, 1896.

Charles Collis (U.S. Army War College)

Collis, Charles H.T. Birth: Ireland, 1838. Colonel of the 114th Pennsylvania Infantry. On December 13, 1862, at Fredericksburg, Virginia. Colonel Collis gallantly led his regiment in battle at a critical moment. Collis was awarded his medal on March 10, 1893.

Colwell, Oliver. Birth: Ohio. First Lieutenant of Company G, 95th Ohio Infantry. On December 16, 1864, at Nashville, Tennessee, Lieutenant Colwell captured a Confederate flag. Colwell was awarded his medal on February 24, 1865.

Compson, Hartwell B. Birth: New York, 1840. Major of 8th New York Cavalry. On March 2, 1865, at Waynesboro, Virginia, Major Compson captured the headquarters flag of General Jubal Early. Compson was awarded his medal on March 26, 1865.

Conaway, John W. Birth: Indiana, 1843. Private in Company C, 83rd Indiana Infantry. On May 22, 1863, at Vicksburg, Mississippi, Private Conaway displayed exceptional gallantry in the charge of the volunteer storming party. Conaway was awarded his medal on August 11, 1894.

Conboy, Martin. [photograph p. 51] Birth: 1833. Sergeant in Company B, 37th New York Infantry. On May 5, 1862,

John Conaway (U.S. Army War College)

Martin Conboy (U.S. Army War College)

at Williamsburg, Virginia, Conboy took command of the company, while in action, after the captain and the other officers had been wounded, and handled it with skill and bravery. Conboy was awarded his medal on October 11, 1892.

Conlan, Dennis. Birth: New York, 1838. Seaman aboard the U.S.S *Agawam*. On December 23, 1864, at Fort Fisher, North Carolina, Seaman Conlan gallantly served as one of the crew in the powder boat mission designed to blow up Fort Fisher. Conlan was awarded his medal on December 31, 1864.

Connell, Trustrim. Birth: Pennsylvania. Corporal in Company I, 138th Pennsylvania Infantry. On April 6, 1865, at Sailors Creek, Virginia, Corporal Trustrim captured a Confederate flag. Connell was awarded his medal on May 10, 1865.

Conner, Richard. Birth: Pennsylvania. Private in Company F, 6th New Jersey Infantry. On August 30, 1862, at Bull Run, Virginia, Private Conner voluntarily returned to the battlefield to bring off the regimental flag that had been left behind. Conner was awarded his medal on September 17, 1897.

Connor, Thomas. Birth: Ireland, 1842. Ordinary Seaman aboard the U.S.S. *Minnesota*. On January 15, 1865, at Fort Fisher, North Carolina, Seaman Connor risked his life to remain with a wounded officer among the landing party, and waited till after dark, when he carried the wounded man from the field. Connor was awarded his medal on June 22, 1865.

Connor, William C. Birth: Pennsylvania, 1832. Boatswain's Mate aboard the U.S.S. *Howquah*. On September 25, 1864, at Wilmington, North Carolina, Connor performed his duties courageously, standing his post in the midst of a crossfire from Confederate shore batteries and Union vessels, during the destruction of the blockade runner *Lynx*. Connor was awarded his medal on December 31, 1864.

Connors, James. Birth: Ireland. Private in Company E, 43rd New York Infantry. On September 22, 1864, at Fisher's Hill, Virginia, Private Connors captured a Confederate flag. Connors was awarded his medal on October 6, 1864.

Cook, John. [photograph p. 52] Birth: Ohio, 1847. Bugler in Battery B, 4th United States Artillery. On September 17, 1862, at Antietam, Maryland, Bugler Cook, only fifteen years old, volunteered to act as a cannoneer, bravely serving the gun under a severe enemy fire. Cook was awarded his medal on June 30, 1894.

Cook, John H. Birth: England. Sergeant in Company A, 119th Illinois Infantry. On April 9, 1864, at Pleasant Hill, Louisiana, Sergeant Cook voluntarily left the brigade

John Cook (U.S. Army War College)

quartermaster, where he had been detailed as a clerk, and rejoined his regiment as an acting first lieutenant, leading the line toward the enemy. Cook was awarded his medal on September 19, 1890.

Cooke, Walter H. Birth: Pennsylvania. Captain in Company K, 4th Pennsylvania Infantry Militia. On July 21, 1861, at Bull Run, Virginia, Captain Cooke gallantly served on the staff of Colonel David Hunter, participating in the entire battle, even though his term of service had expired the previous day. Cooke was awarded his medal on May 19, 1887.

Cooper, John. Birth: Ireland, 1832. Coxswain aboard the U.S.S. *Brooklyn*. On August 5, 1864, at Mobile Bay, Alabama, Coxswain Cooper fought his gun with skill and courage throughout the battle that resulted in the surrender of the ram *Tennessee* and the damage and destruction of Fort Morgan. Cooper was awarded his medal on December 31, 1864. Cooper was the recipient of a second Medal of Honor. On April 26, 1865, at Mobile Bay, Alabama, during a terrific fire, Cooper advanced through exploding shells to rescue a wounded man and bring him to safety. He was awarded his second medal on June 29, 1865.

Copp, Charles D. Birth: New Hampshire, 1840. Second Lieutenant in Company C, 9th New Hampshire Infantry. On December 13, 1862, at Fredericksburg, Virginia, Lieutenant Copp seized the regimental colors, after the bearer had been shot down, rallying the regiment under a heavy fire. Copp was awarded his medal on June 28, 1890.

Corcoran, John. Birth: Rhode Island, 1842. Private in Company G, 1st Rhode Island Light Artillery. On April 2, 1865, at Petersburg, Virginia, Private Corcoran was one of a detachment of 20 men who accompanied an infantry assaulting party, and turned captured enemy guns against the Confederates. Corcoran was awarded his medal on November 2, 1887.

Charles Copp (U.S. Army War College)

Corcoran, Thomas E. Birth: New York, 1838. Landsman aboard the U.S.S. *Cincinnati*. In 1863, at Vicksburg, Mississippi, Landsman Corcoran fought bravely amid incessant enemy fire of shot and shell, never ceasing to do his duty until the ship went down. Corcoran was awarded his medal on July 10, 1863.

Corliss, George W. Captain of Company C, 5th Connecticut Infantry. On August 9, 1862, at Cedar Mountain, Virginia, Captain Corliss, though severely wounded and permanently disabled, planted the colors in the earth and kept the flag flying. Corliss was awarded his medal on September 10, 1897.

Corliss, Stephen P. Birth: New York, 1832. First Lieutenant in Company F, 4th New York Heavy Artillery. On April 2, 1865, at South Side Railroad, Virginia, Lieutenant Corliss raised the fallen colors and rushed them forward, in advance of the troops, placing them on the enemy works. Corliss was awarded his medal on January 17, 1895.

Thomas Corcoran (Hall of Heroes)

Corson, Joseph K. [photograph p. 54] Birth: Pennsylvania, 1836. Assistant Surgeon in the 6th Pennsylvania Infantry Reserves. On October 14, 1863, at Bristoe Station, Virginia, Surgeon Corson, with one companion, rescued a wounded soldier who had been left behind when the regiment fell back, despite a galling enemy artillery fire. Corson was awarded his medal on May 13, 1899.

Cosgriff, Richard H. Birth: New York, 1844. Private in Company L, 4th Iowa Cavalry. On April 16, 1865, at Columbus, Georgia, Private Cosgriff captured a Confederate flag in a personal encounter with its bearer. Cosgriff was awarded his medal on June 17, 1865.

Cosgrove, Thomas. Birth: Ireland. Private in Company F, 40th Massachusetts Infantry. On May 15, 1864, at Drury's

Stephen Corliss (U.S. Army War College)

Joseph Corson (U.S. Army War College)

John Coughlin (Hall of Heroes)

Bluff, Virginia, Private Cosgrove personally received the surrender of 7 armed Confederates concealed in a cellar. Cosgrove was awarded his medal on November 7, 1896.

Cotton, Peter. Birth: New York, 1839. Ordinary Seaman aboard the U.S.S. *Baron De Kalb*. From December 23 to 27, 1862, Cotton distinguished himself in the expedition made up the Yazoo River capturing two enemy transports. Cotton was awarded his medal on April 3, 1863.

Coughlin, John. Birth: Vermont. Lieutenant Colonel of the 10th New Hampshire Infantry. On May 9, 1864, at Swifts Creek, Virginia, Colonel Coughlin led his regiment forward to interpose it between the attacking Confederates and Hunt's Battery, repulsing the attack and saving the guns. Coughlin was awarded his medal on August 31, 1893.

Cox, Robert M. Birth: Ohio. Corporal in Company K, 55th Illinois Infantry. On May 22, 1863, at Vicksburg, Mississippi, Corporal Cox bravely defended the colors planted on the outward parapet of Fort Hill. Cox was awarded his medal on December 31, 1892.

Coyne, John N. Birth: New York, 1839. Sergeant in Company B, 70th New York Infantry. On May 5, 1862, at Williamsburg, Virginia, Sergeant Coyne captured a Confederate flag after a severe hand-to-hand struggle. Coyne was awarded his medal on April 18, 1888.

Cranston, William W. Birth: Ohio. Private in Company A, 66th Ohio Infantry. On May 2, 1863, at Chancellorsville, Virginia, Private Cranston was on of four men who volunteered to bring a wounded Confederate officer from within the enemy's lines in the face of constant fire. Cranston was awarded his medal on December 15, 1892.

Crawford, Alexander. Birth: Pennsylvania, 1842. Fireman aboard the U.S.S. *Wyalusing*. On May 25, 1864, at Roanoke River, North Carolina, Fireman Crawford volunteered to take part in a mission to destroy the Confederate ram *Albemarle*. He displayed unfailing devotion to duty, even though the mission had to be aborted. Crawford was awarded his medal on December 31, 1864.

Creed, John. Birth: Ireland. Private in Company D, 23rd Illinois Infantry. On September 22, 1864, at Fisher's Hill, Virginia, Private Creed captured a Confederate flag. Creed was awarded his medal on October 6, 1864.

Cripps, Thomas. Birth: Pennsylvania, 1837, Quartermaster aboard the U.S.S. *Richmond*. On August 5, 1864, at Mobile Bay, Alabama, Cripps fought his gun with skill and courage, despite damage to the ship and the loss of several men. Cripps was awarded his medal on December 31, 1864.

Crocker, Henry H. Birth: Connecticut, 1840. Captain of Company F, 2nd Massachusetts Cavalry. On October 19, 1864, at Cedar Creek, Virginia, Captain Crocker led a charge that resulted in the capture of 14 enemy prisoners, though he himself was wounded. Crocker was awarded his medal on January 10, 1896.

Crocker, Ulric L. Birth: Ohio. Private in Company M, 6th Michigan Cavalry. On October 26, 1864, at Cedar Creek, Virginia, Private Crocker captured the flag of the 18th Georgia Infantry. Crocker was awarded his medal on October 26, 1864.

Henry Crocker (Hall of Heroes)

Croft, James E. Birth: England. Private in the 12th Wisconsin Light Artillery. On October 5, 1864, at Allatoona, Georgia, Croft took the place of a gunner who had been shot down and inspired his comrades by his bravery. Croft was awarded his medal on March 20, 1897.

Cronin, Cornelius. Birth: Michigan, 1836. Chief Quartermaster aboard the U.S.S. *Richmond*. On August 5, 1864, at Mobile Bay, Alabama, Quartermaster Cronin remained cool and vigilant at his station throughout the prolonged action. Cronin was awarded his medal on December 31, 1864.

Crosier, William H.H. Birth: New York, 1843. Sergeant of Company G, 149th New York Infantry. On July 20, 1864, at Peach Tree Creek, Georgia, Sergeant Crosier, though severely wounded, stripped the regimental colors from their staff and brought them back into the line. Crosier was awarded his medal on January 12, 1892.

Cornelius Cronin (U.S. Army War College)

Cross, James E. [photograph p. 56] Birth: New York, 1840. Corporal in Company K, 12th New York Infantry. On July 18, 1861, at Blackburn's Ford, Virginia,

Corporal Cross refused to retreat when a part of the regiment was driven back in disorder, remaining upon the skirmish line for some time thereafter and firing at the enemy. Cross was awarded his medal on April 5, 1898.

Crowley, Michael. Birth: New York, 1829. Private in Company A, 22nd New York Cavalry. On March 2, 1865, at Waynesboro, Virginia, Private Crowley captured a Confederate flag. Crowley was awarded his medal on December 1, 1864.

Cullen, Thomas. Birth: Ireland, 1839. Corporal in Company I, 82nd New York Infantry. On October 14, 1863, at Bristoe Station, Virginia, Corporal Cullen captured the flag of a North Carolina regiment. Cullen was awarded his medal on December 1, 1864.

James Cross (U.S. Army War College)

Cummings, Amos J. Birth: New York, 1841. Sergeant Major in the 26th New Jersey Infantry. On May 4, 1863, at Salem Heights, Virginia, Sergeant Cummings rendered great assistance in the heat of action in rescuing a part of the field batteries from a dangerous and exposed position. Cummings was awarded his medal on March 28, 1894.

Cumpston, James M. Birth: Ohio. Private in Company D, 91st Ohio Infantry. From August to November of 1864, in the Shenandoah Valley, Virginia, Private Cumpston captured a Confederate flag. The date of Cumpston's award is unknown.

Cunningham, Francis M. Birth: Pennsylvania, 1837. First Sergeant in Company H, 1st West Virginia Cavalry. On April 6, 1865, at Sailors Creek, Virginia, Sergeant Cunningham captured the flag of the 12th Virginia Infantry. Cunningham was awarded his medal on May 3, 1865.

Francis Cunningham (Hall of Heroes)

Cunningham, James S. Birth: Pennsylvania, 1840. Private in Company D, 8th Missouri Infantry. On May 22, 1863, at Vicksburg, Mississippi, Private Cunningham displayed exceptional gallantry in the charge of the volunteer storming party. Cunningham was awarded his medal on July 30, 1894.

Curran, Richard. Birth: Ireland, 1838. Assistant Surgeon of the 33rd New York

Richard Curran (U.S. Army War College)

Infantry. On September 17, 1862, at Antietam, Maryland, Surgeon Curran exposed himself to great danger in succoring the wounded and conducting them to safety. Curran was awarded his medal on March 30, 1898.

Curtis, John C. Birth: Connecticut. Sergeant Major of the 9th Connecticut Infantry. On August 5, 1862, at Baton Rouge, Louisiana, Curtis captured 2 enemy prisoners. Curtis was awarded his medal on December 2, 1896.

Curtis, Josiah M. Birth: Ohio, 1844. Second Lieutenant of Company I, 12th West Virginia Infantry. On April 2, 1865, at Petersburg, Virginia, Lieutenant Curtis seized the colors of his regiment after two color bearers had fallen and advanced them inside the enemy works. Curtis was awarded his medal on May 12, 1865.

Josiah Curtis (U.S. Army War College)

Curtis, Newton Martin. Birth: New York, 1835. Brigadier General of U.S. Volunteers. On January 15, 1865, at Fort Fisher, North Carolina, General Curtis was the first man to pass through the stockade, personally leading each assault on the traverses, and was wounded four times. Curtis was awarded his medal on November 28, 1891.

Custer, Thomas W. Birth: Ohio, 1845. Second Lieutenant on Company B, 6th Michigan Cavalry. On May 10, 1863, at Namozine Church, Virginia, Lieutenant Custer captured a Confederate flag. Custer was awarded his medal on May 3, 1865. ***Custer won a second Medal of Honor on April 6, 1865, at Sailors Creek, Virginia, when he captured two stands of Confederate colors. His medal was awarded on May 26, 1865.

Newton Martin Curtis (U.S. Army War College)

Cutcheon, Byron M. Birth: New Hampshire, 1836. Major of the 20th Michigan Infantry. On May 10, 1863, at Horseshoe Bend, Kentucky, Major Cutcheon led his regiment in a charge against a house occupied by the enemy with distinguished gallantry. Cutcheon was awarded his medal on June 29, 1891.

Cutts, James M. [photograph p. 56] Birth: District of Columbia, 1838. Captain in the 11th United States Infantry. At the Wilderness, Spot-

Byron Cutcheon (Hall of Heroes)

The Recipients — Darrough

James Cutts (U.S. Army War College)

Andrew Davidson (Hall of Heroes)

George Davis (U.S. Army War College)

sylvania, and Petersburg, Virginia, Captain Cutts displayed constant gallantry in action. Cutts was awarded his medal on May 2, 1891.

Darrough, John S. Birth: Kentucky. Sergeant of Company F, 113th Illinois Infantry. On October 10, 1864, at Eastport, Mississippi, Sergeant Darrough saved the life of a captain. Darrough was awarded his medal on February 5, 1895.

Davidsizer, John A. Birth: Pennsylvania. Sergeant in Company A, 1st Pennsylvania Cavalry. On April 5, 1865, at Paine's Crossroads, Virginia, Sergeant Davidsizer captured a Confederate flag. Davidsizer was awarded his medal on May 3, 1865.

Davidson, Andrew. Birth: Vermont, 1819. Assistant Surgeon in the 47th Ohio Infantry. On May 3, 1863, at Vicksburg, Mississippi, Surgeon Davidson voluntarily attempted to run the enemy's batteries. Davidson was awarded his medal on October 17, 1892.

Davidson, Andrew. Birth: Scotland, 1840. First Lieutenant in Company H, 30th United States Infantry Colored. On July 30, 1864, at Petersburg, Virginia, Lieutenant Davidson gallantly assisted in rallying and saving the command after the commander had fallen. Davidson was awarded his medal on October 17, 1892.

Davis, Charles C. Birth: Pennsylvania, 1830. Major of the 7th Pennsylvania Cavalry. On June 27, 1863, at Shelbyville, Tennessee, Major Davis led one of the most desperate and successful charges of the war. Davis was awarded his medal on June 14, 1894.

Davis, Freeman. Birth: Ohio. Sergeant in Company B, 80th Ohio Infantry. On November 25, 1863, at Missionary Ridge, Tennessee, Sergeant Davis seeing two color bearers shot down, recovered both flags and saved them from capture. Davis was awarded his medal March 30, 1894.

Davis, George E. Birth: Massachusetts, 1839. First Lieutenant of Company D, 10th Vermont Infantry. On July 9, 1864, at Monocacy, Mary-

John Davis (Hall of Heroes)

David Day (U.S. Army War College)

land, Lieutenant Davis held the approaches to two bridges against repeated assaults of superior numbers. Davis was awarded his medal on May 27, 1892.

Davis, Harry. Birth: Ohio, 1841. Private in Company G, 46th Ohio Infantry. On July 28, 1864, at Atlanta, Georgia, Private Davis captured the flag of the 30th Louisiana Infantry. Davis was awarded his medal on December 2, 1864.

Davis, John. Birth: New Jersey. Quarter gunner aboard the U.S.S. *Valley City*. On February 10, 1862, at Elizabeth City, North Carolina, Gunner Davis covered a barrel of gun powder with his own body to protect it from a fire that was burning on deck. Davis was awarded his medal on April 3, 1863.

Davis, John. Birth: Kentucky. Private in Company F, 17th Indiana Mounted Infantry. In April of 1865, at Culloden, Georgia, Private Davis captured the flag of the Worrill Grays. Davis was awarded his medal on June 17, 1865.

Davis, Joseph. Birth: Wales. Corporal of Company C, 104th Ohio Infantry. On November 30, 1864, at Franklin, Tennessee, Corporal Davis captured a Confederate flag. Davis was awarded his medal on February 4, 1865.

Davis, Martin, K. Birth: Illinois, 1843. Sergeant in Company H, 116th Illinois Infantry. On may 22, 1863, at Vicksburg, Mississippi, Sergeant Davis exhibited exceptional gallantry in the charge of the volunteer storming party. Davis was awarded his medal on July 26, 1894.

Davis, Samuel W. Birth: Maine, 1845. Ordinary Seaman aboard the U.S.S. *Brooklyn*. On August 5, 1864, at Mobile Bay, Alabama, Seaman Davis exhibited exceptional gallantry throughout the battle that resulted in the surrender of the ram *Tennessee* and the damage and destruction of Fort Morgan. Davis was awarded his medal on December 31, 1864.

Davis, Thomas. Birth: Wales. Private in Company C, 2nd New York Heavy Artillery. On April 6, 1865, at Sailors Creek, Virginia, Private Davis captured a Confederate flag. Davis was awarded his medal on May 3, 1865.

Day, Charles. Birth: New York, 1844. Private in Company K, 210th Pennsylvania Infantry. On February 6, 1865, at Hatchers Run, Virginia, Private Day seized the colors of another regiment that had been thrown into confusion and bore them throughout the engagement. Day was awarded his medal on July 20, 1897.

Day, David F. Birth: Ohio, 1847. Private in Company D, 57th Ohio Infantry. On May 22, 1863, at Vicksburg, Mississippi, Private Day exhibited exceptional gallantry in the charge of the volunteer storming party. Day was awarded his medal on January 2, 1895.

Deakin, Charles. Birth: New York, 1837. Boatswain's Mate aboard the U.S.S. *Richmond*. On August 5, 1864, at Mobile Bay, Alabama, Deakin exhibited skill and courage throughout the prolonged battle that resulted in the surrender of the ram *Tennessee* and the damage and destruction of Fort Morgan. Deakin was awarded his medal on December 31, 1864.

Patrick De Lacey (U.S. Army War College)

Deane, John M. Birth: Massachusetts, 1840. Major of 29th Massachusetts Infantry. On March 25, 1865, at Fort Stedman, Virginia, Major Deane, observing an abandoned gun at Fort Haskill, and calling for volunteers, worked the piece until the enemy's advancing line was routed. Deane was awarded his medal on March 8, 1895.

De Castro, Joseph H. Birth: Massachusetts. Corporal in Company I, 19th Massachusetts Infantry. On July 3, 1863, at Gettysburg, Pennsylvania, Corporal De Castro captured the flag of the 19th Virginia Infantry. De Castro was awarded his medal on December 1, 1864.

De Lacey, Patrick. Birth: Pennsylvania, 1834. First Sergeant in Company A, 143rd Pennsylvania Infantry. On May 6, 1864, at the Wilderness, Virginia, Sergeant De Lacey, running ahead of the line, shot a Confederate color bearer, contributing to the success of the attack. De Lacey was awarded his medal on April 24, 1894.

Deland, Frederick N. Birth: Massachusetts, 1843. Private in Company B, 40th Massachusetts Infantry. On May 27, 1863, at Port Hudson, Louisiana, Private Deland volunteered to fill a ditch in the enemy line with fascines under a heavy fire from the enemy. Deland was awarded his medal on June 22, 1896.

Delaney, John C. Birth: Ireland, 1848. Sergeant in Company I, 107th Pennsylvania Infantry. On February 6, 1864, at Dabny's Mills, Virginia, Sergeant Delaney sprang between the lines to save a wounded comrade about to be burned in the brush. Delaney was awarded his medal on August 29, 1894.

Frederick Deland (Hall of Heroes)

DeLavie, Hiram H. Birth: Ohio. Sergeant in Company I, 11th Pennsylvania Infantry. On April 1, 1865, at Five Forks, Virginia, Sergeant De Lavie captured a Confederate flag. De Lavie was awarded his medal on May 10, 1865.

Dempster, John. Birth: Scotland, 1839. Coxswain aboard the U.S.S. *New Ironsides*. On December 24 to 25, 1864 and January 13 to 15, 1865, at Fort Fisher, North Carolina, Dempster exhibited exceptional gallantry in performing his duties during the two expeditions against the Confederate stronghold. Dempster was awarded his medal on June 22, 1865.

Denig, J. Henry:. Birth: Pennsylvania, 1839. Sergeant, U.S. Marine Corps, serving aboard the U.S.S. *Brooklyn*. On August 5, 1864, at Mobile Bay, Alabama, Sergeant Denig fought his gun with skill and courage throughout the engagement resulting in the surrender of the ram *Tennessee* and the damage and destruction of Fort Morgan. Denig was awarded his medal on December 31, 1864.

Denning, Lorenzo. Birth: Lorenzo, 1843. Landsman aboard the U.S.S. *Picket Boat*. On October 27, 1864, at Roanoke River, North Carolina, Landsman Denning was part of the crew that attacked the ram *Albermarle* with a spar torpedo, succeeding in jumping a log boom which encircled the ram and exploding the torpedo under the port bow of the boat. Denning was awarded his medal on December 31, 1864.

Dennis, Richard. Birth: Massachusetts, 1826. Boatswain's Mate aboard the U.S.S. *Brooklyn*. On August 5, 1864, at Mobile Bay, Alabama, Dennis exhibited exceptional gallantry and displayed skill and courage in operating the torpedo catcher during the engagement. Dennis was awarded his medal on December 31, 1864.

Densmore, William. Birth: New York, 1834. Chief Boatswain's Mate aboard the U.S.S. *Richmond*. On August 5, 1864, at Mobile Bay, Alabama, Chief Densmore fought his gun with exceptional courage throughout the engagement that resulted in the surrender of the ram *Tennessee* and the damage and destruction of Fort Morgan. Densmore was awarded his medal on December 31, 1864.

De Puy, Charles H. Birth: Michigan. First Sergeant of Company H, 1st Michigan Sharpshooters. On July 30, 1864, at Petersburg, Virginia, Sergeant De Puy aided General Bartlett in working the guns of the dismantled fort. De Puy was awarded his medal on July 30, 1896.

De Witt, Richard W. Birth: Ohio, 1838. Corporal in Company D, 47th Ohio Infantry. On May 22, 1863, at Vicksburg, Mississippi, Corporal De Witt exhibited exceptional gallantry in the charge of the volunteer storming party. De Witt was awarded his medal on August 10, 1894.

Di Cesnola, Louis P. Birth: Italy, 1832. Colonel of the 4th New York Cavalry. On June 17, 1863, at Aldie, Virginia, Colonel Di Cesnola was under arrest when he witnessed his regiment falling back from the enemy. He immediately rode to rally his men, leading them in a second charge, and pressing the attack until he was severely wounded. The date of Di Cesnola's award is unknown.

Dickey, William D. Birth: New York, 1835. Captain of Battery M, 15th New York Heavy Artillery.

William Dickey (Hall of Heroes)

On June 17, 1864, at Petersburg, Virginia, Captain Dickey remained in command of his battery after being severely wounded, and led his command in an assault on the enemy's works the following day. Dickey was awarded his medal on June 10, 1896.

Dickie, David. Birth: Scotland, 1841. Sergeant in Company A, 97th Illinois Infantry. On May 22, 1863, at Vicksburg, Mississippi, Sergeant Dickie exhibited exceptional gallantry in the charge of the volunteer storming party. Dickie was awarded his medal on January 29, 1896.

Diggins, Bartholomew. Birth: Maryland, 1832. Ordinary Seaman aboard the U.S.S. *Hartford*. On August 5, 1864, at Mobile Bay, Alabama, Seaman Diggins exhibited exceptional gallantry as a gun loader during the prolonged engagement that resulted in the surrender of the ram *Tennessee* and the damage and destruction of Fort Morgan. Diggins was awarded his medal on November 12, 1891.

Bartholomew Diggins (Hall of Heroes)

Dilger, Hubert. Birth: Germany, 1836. Captain of Battery I, 1st Ohio Light Artillery. On May 2, 1863, at Chancellorsville, Virginia, Captain Dilger fought his guns until the enemy was upon his line, then dragged one gun into the road by hand and formed a rear guard keeping the enemy at bay by the rapidity of his fire and was the last man to retreat. Dilger was awarded his medal on August 17, 1893.

Dillon, Michael A. Birth: Massachusetts, 1839. Private in Company G, 2nd New Hampshire Infantry. On May 5, 1862, at Williamsburg, Virginia, Private Dillon exhibited extreme bravery in repulsing the enemy charge on a battery. On June 25, 1862, at Oak Grove, Virginia, he crawled outside the lines and brought in important information. Dillon was awarded his medal on October 10, 1889.

Hubert Dilger (Hall of Heroes)

Ditzenback, John. Birth: New York, 1828. Quartermaster aboard the U.S.S. *Neosho*. On December 6, 1864, at Bells Mills, Tennessee, on the Cumberland River, near Nashville, Ditzenback left the pilot house after the flag and signal staffs of that vessel had been shot away and attached the flag to the stump of the

Michael Dillon (U.S. Army War College)

highest mast under a heavy fire from the enemy. Ditzenback was awarded his medal on June 22, 1865.

Dockum, Warren C. Birth: New York. Private in Company H, 121st New York Infantry. On April 6, 1865, at Sailors Creek, Virginia, Private Dockum captured the flag of the Savannah Guards after tow other men had been killed in the effort. Dockum was awarded his medal on May 10, 1865.

Dodd, Robert F. Birth: Canada, 1844. Private in Company E, 27th Michigan Infantry. On July 30, 1864, at Petersburg, Virginia, Private Dodd voluntarily assisted in carrying wounded men from the ground in front of the crater while exposed to enemy fire. Doss was awarded his medal on July 27, 1896.

Dodds, Edward E. Birth: Canada. Sergeant in Company C, 21st New York Cavalry. On July 19, 1864, at Ashby's Gap, Virginia, Sergeant Dodds rescued his wounded captain and carried him from the field to a place of safety. Dodds was awarded his medal on June 11, 1896.

Dolloff, Charles W. Birth: New York. Corporal in Company K, 1st Vermont Infantry. On April 2, 1865, at Petersburg, Virginia, Corporal Dolloff captured a Confederate flag. Dolloff was awarded his medal on April 24, 1865.

Donaldson, John. Birth: Pennsylvania, 1842. Sergeant in Company L, 4th Pennsylvania Cavalry. On April 9, 1865, at Appomattox, Virginia, Sergeant Donaldson captured the flag of the 4th Virginia Cavalry. Donaldson was awarded his medal on May 3, 1865.

Donnelly, John. Birth: England, 1839. Ordinary Seaman aboard the U.S.S. *Metacomet*. On August 5, 1864, at Mobile Bay, Alabama, Seaman Donnelly helped to rescue 10 men from the sunken Monitor *Tecumseh* during heavy fire from the enemy. Donnelly was awarded his medal on January 15, 1866.

Charles Dolloff (Hall of Heroes)

Donoghue, Timothy. Birth: Ireland, 1825. Private in Company B, 69th New York Infantry. On December 13, 1862, at Fredericksburg, Virginia, Private Donoghue voluntarily carried a wounded officer from the field who had been trapped between the lines, and was himself wounded in the process. Donoghue was awarded his medal on January 17, 1894.

Doody, Patrick. Birth: Ireland. Corporal in Company E, 164th New York Infantry. On June 7, 1864, at Cold Harbor, Virginia, Corporal Doody, after making a personal reconnaissance of the enemy, led the skirmishers in a successful night attack which enabled the pioneers to put up works. Doody was awarded his medal on December 13, 1893.

Doolen, William. Birth: Ireland, 1841. Coal Heaver aboard the U.S.S. *Richmond*. On August 5, 1864, at Mobile Bay, Alabama, Doolen was wounded in the head but refused to leave his post, rendering gallant service throughout the prolonged battle that resulted in the surrender of the ram *Tennessee* and the damage and destruction of Fort Morgan. Doolen was awarded his medal on December 31, 1864.

Dore, George H. Birth: England, 1845. Sergeant in Company D, 126th New York Infantry. On July 3, 1863, at Gettysburg, Pennsylvania, Sergeant Dore noticed that the regimental colors had been struck down by a shell and rushed out, amid an enemy charge, to rescue them. Dore was awarded his medal on December 1, 1864.

Dorley, August. Birth: Germany. Private in Company B, 1st Louisiana Cavalry. On April 11, 1865, at Mount Pleasant, Alabama, Private Dorley captured a Confederate flag. The date of Dorley's award is unknown.

Dorman, John. Birth: Ohio, 1843. Seaman aboard the U.S.S. *Carondelet*. In the various actions of the Carondelet Dorman carried out his duties courageously, although wounded several times and consistently presented an example of devotion to the flag. Dorman was awarded his medal on April 18, 1864.

Daniel Dorsey (Hall of Heroes)

Dorsey, Daniel A. Birth: Virginia. Corporal in Company H, 33rd Ohio Infantry. In April of 1862, Dorsey was a member of Andrew's raiding party that captured a railroad train at Big Shanty, Georgia in an attempt to destroy bridges and track between Chattanooga and Atlanta. Dorsey was awarded his medal on September 17, 1863.

Dorsey, Decatur. Birth: Maryland, 1836. Sergeant in Company B, 39th United States Colored Infantry. On July 30, 1864, at Petersburg, Virginia. Sergeant Dorsey planted his colors on the Confederate works in advance of his regiment, and when the regiment was driven back he carried the colors there and bravely rallied the men. Dorsey was awarded his medal on November 5, 1865.

Dougall, Allan H. Birth: Scotland. First Lieutenant and Adjutant of the 88th Indiana Infantry. On March 19, 1865, at Bentonville, North Carolina, Lieutenant Dougall, in the face of a galling enemy fire, returned to where the color bearer had fallen to save the regimental flag from capture. Dougall was awarded his medal on February 16, 1897.

Dougherty, Michael. Birth: Ireland, 1844. Private in Company B, 13th Pennsylvania Cavalry. On October 12, 1863, at Jefferson, Virginia, Private Dougherty led a detachment from his company across an open field,

Allan Dougall (Hall of Heroes)

exposed to a deadly fire, to dislodge the enemy from an unoccupied house, which he and his comrades then defended for several hours against repeated attacks, preventing the enemy from flanking the Union position. Dougherty was awarded his medal on January 23, 1897.

Dougherty, Patrick. Birth: Ireland, 1844. Landsman aboard the U.S.S. *Lackawana*. On August 5, 1864, at Mobile Bay, Alabama, Dougherty acted gallantly, and without orders, when the powder box at his gun was disabled under heavy enemy fire, and maintained a supply of powder throughout the prolonged engagement. Dougherty was awarded his medal on December 31, 1864.

Dow, George P. Birth: New Hampshire. Sergeant in Company C, 7th New Hampshire Infantry. In October, 1864, near Richmond, Virginia, Sergeant Dow exhibited gallantry while in command of his company during a reconnaissance toward the Confederate capital. Dow was awarded his medal on May 10, 1884.

Dow, Henry. Birth: Scotland, 1840. Boatswain's Mate aboard the U.S.S. *Cincinnati*. On May 27, 1863, at Vicksburg, Mississippi, Dow served courageously throughout the engagement and carried out his duties to the end of this proud ship that went down with "her colors nailed to the mast." Dow was awarded his medal on July 10, 1863.

Downey, William. Birth: Ireland. Private in Company B, 4th Massachusetts Cavalry. On May 24, 1864, at Ashepoo River, South Carolina, Private Downey volunteered as a member of a boatcrew that went to the rescue of a large number of Union soldiers on board the stranded steamer Boston, conveying them to shore while exposed to a heavy fire from the enemy. Downey was awarded his medal on January 21, 1897.

Downs, Henry W. Birth: Vermont. Sergeant in Company I, 8th Vermont Infantry. On September 19, 1864, at Winchester, Virginia, Sergeant Downs crossed an open field, under heavy fire, to procure ammunition for his regiment. He then repeated the act. Downs was awarded his medal on December 13, 1893.

Drake, James M. [photograph p. 66] Birth: New Jersey, 1837. Second Lieutenant of Company D, 9th New Jersey Infantry. On May 6, 1864, at Bermuda Hundred, Virginia, Lieutenant Drake commanded the skirmish line in the advance and held his position all day and during the night. Drake was awarded his medal on March 3, 1873.

Drury, James. Birth: Ireland. Sergeant of Company C, 4th Vermont Infantry. On June 23, 1864, at Weldon Railroad, Virginia, Sergeant Drury saved the regimental colors when it was surrounded by a much larger force and after the greater part of the regiment had been killed or captured. Drury was awarded his medal on January 18, 1893.

Henry Downs (U.S. Army War College)

James Drake (U.S. Army War College)

James Duncan (Hall of Heroes)

James Dunlavy (Hall of Heroes)

Duffey, John. Birth: Massachusetts. Private in Company B, 4th Massachusetts Cavalry. On May 24, 1864, at Ashepoo River, South Carolina, Private Duffey volunteered as a member of a boat crew to rescue a large number of Union soldiers on board the stranded steamer Boston, and gallantly assisted in conveying them to shore, while being exposed to a heavy enemy fire. Duffey was awarded his medal on January 21, 1897.

Duncan, Adam. Birth: Maine, 1833. Boatswain's Mate aboard the U.S.S. *Richmond*. On August 5, 1864, at Mobile Bay, Alabama, Duncan fought his gun with skill and courage throughout the prolonged engagement that resulted in the surrender of the ram *Tennessee* and the successful attacks carried out on Fort Morgan. Duncan was awarded his medal on December 31, 1864.

Duncan, James K.L. Birth: Pennsylvania, 1845. Ordinary Seaman aboard the U.S.S. *Fort Hindman*. On March 2, 1864, near Harrisonburg, Louisiana, Seaman Duncan saw a shell burst at one of the guns start a fire in the cartridge tie and immediately seized the burning cartridge, took it from the gun, and threw it overboard, despite the immediate danger to himself. Duncan was awarded his medal on April 16, 1864.

Dunlavy, James. Birth: Indiana. Private in Company D, 3rd Iowa Cavalry. On October 25, 1864, at Osage, Kansas, Private Dunlavy captured Confederate General Marmaduke. Dunlavy was awarded his medal on April 4, 1865.

Dunn, William. Birth: Maine, 1834. Quartermaster aboard the U.S.S. *Monadnock*. From December 24 to 25, 1864 and January 13 to 15, 1865, at Fort Fisher, North Carolina, Dunn inspired his shipmates and contributed to the success of is vessel in reducing the enemy guns to silence. Dunn was awarded his medal on June 22, 1865.

Dunne, James. Birth: Michigan, 1840. Corporal of the Chicago Mercantile Battery, Illinois Light Artillery. On May 22, 1863, at Vicksburg, Mississippi, Corporal Dunne, with others, carried by hand a cannon up to and fired it through an embrasure of the enemy's works. Dunne was awarded his medal on January 15, 1895.

Dunphy, Richard D. Birth: Ireland, 1840. Coal Heaver aboard the U.S.S. *Hartford*. On August 5, 1864, at Mobile Bay, Alabama, Dunphy performed his duties with skill and courage throughout the fierce engagement that resulted in the capture of the Confederate ram *Tennessee*. Dunphy was awarded his medal on December 31, 1864.

Du Pont, Henry A. Birth: Delaware. Captain of the 5th United States Artillery. On October 19, 1864, at Cedar Creek, Virginia, Captain Du Pont gallantly exposed himself to the enemy's fire at a critical moment, when the Union line had been broken, encouraging his men to stand to their guns, and checking the advance of the enemy. Du Pont was awarded his medal on April 2, 1898.

Richard Dunphy (Hall of Heroes)

Durham, James R. Birth: West Virginia, 1833. Second Lieutenant in Company E, 12th West Virginia Infantry. On June 14, 1863, at Winchester, Virginia, Lieutenant Durham led his command over a stone wall where he was wounded. Durham was awarded his medal on March 6, 1890.

Durham, John S. Birth: New York, 1843. Sergeant in Company F, 1st Wisconsin Infantry. On October 8, 1862, at Perryville, Kentucky, Sergeant Durham seized the regimental flag, after the bearer had fallen, and advanced with it midway between the lines, amid a heavy fire from the enemy, until stopped by his commanding officer. Durham was awarded his medal on November 20, 1896.

Henry Du Pont (Hall of Heroes)

Eckes, John N. Birth: West Virginia. Private in Company E, 47th Ohio Infantry. On May 22, 1863, at Vicksburg, Mississippi, Private Eckes exhibited exceptional gallantry in the charge of the volunteer storming party. Eckes was awarded his medal on July 21, 1894.

Eddy, Samuel E. Birth: Vermont, 1822. Private in Company D, 37th Massachusetts Infantry. On April 6, 1865, at Sailors Creek, Virginia, Private Eddy saved the life of his regimental adjutant by going beyond the lines to kill one of the enemy who was in the act of firing upon the wounded officer. Eddy was assailed by several Confederates, and run through the body with a bayonet. He succeeded in killing his assailant. Eddy was awarded his medal on September 10, 1897.

Edgerton, Nathan H. Lieutenant and Adjutant in the 6th United States Colored Infantry. On September 29, 1864, at Chapin's Farm, Virginia, Lieutenant Edgerton took up the flag after three color bearers had been shot down and advanced it forward, even though he himself was wounded. Edgerton was awarded his medal on March 30, 1898.

Edwards, David. Birth: England. Private in Company H, 146th New York Infantry. On April 1, 1865, at Five Forks, Virginia, Private Edwards captured a Confederate flag. Edwards was awarded his medal on May 10, 1865.

Edwards, John. Birth: Rhode Island, 1831. Captain of the Top aboard the U.S.S. *Lackawana*. On August 5, 1864, at Mobile Bay, Alabama, Edwards, though wounded, refused to leave his post and continued to perform his duties during the prolonged engagement that resulted in the surrender of the ram *Tennessee* and the damaging and destruction of Fort Morgan. Edwards was awarded his medal on December 31, 1864.

Elliott, Alexander. Birth: Pennsylvania. Sergeant in Company A, 1st Pennsylvania Cavalry. On April 5, 1865, at Paine's Crossroads, Virginia, Sergeant Elliott captured a Confederate flag. Elliott was awarded his medal on May 3, 1865.

Elliott, Russell C. Birth: New Hampshire. Sergeant in Company B, 3rd Massachusetts Cavalry. On April 19, 1864, at Natchitoches, Louisiana, Sergeant Elliott, seeing a Confederate officer in advance of his command charged on his alone and unaided and captured him. Elliott was awarded his medal on November 20, 1896.

Ellis, Horace. Birth: Pennsylvania. Private in Company A, 7th Wisconsin Infantry. On August 21, 1864, at Weldon Railroad, Virginia, Private Ellis captured the flag of the 16th Mississippi Infantry. Ellis was awarded his medal in December of 1864.

Elise, William. Birth: England. First Sergeant in Company K, 3rd Wisconsin Cavalry. On January 14, 1865, Sergeant Elise remained at his post after receiving three wounds and only retired by the orders of his commanding officer, after being wounded the fourth time. Elise was awarded his medal on March 8, 1865.

Ellsworth, Thomas F. Birth: Massachusetts. Captain of Company B, 5th Massachusetts Infantry. On November 30, 1864, at Honey Hill, South Carolina, Captain Ellsworth, under a heavy fire, carried his wounded commanding officer from the field. Ellsworth was awarded his medal on November 18, 1895.

Elison, James M. Birth: Ohio. Sergeant in Company C, 9th Iowa Infantry. On May 22, 1863, at

James Elison (Hall of Heroes)

Vicksburg, Mississippi, Sergeant Elison carried the colors in advance of his regiment and was shot down attempting to plant them on the enemy's works. Elison was awarded his medal on September 12, 1891.

Embler, Andrew H. Birth: New York, 1834. Captain of Company D, 59th New York Infantry. On October 27, 1864, at Boydton Plank Road, Virginia, Captain Embler charged at the head of two regiments which drove the enemy's main body, gained the crest of the hill near the Burgess house and forced a barricade on the Boydton Road. Embler was awarded his medal on October 19, 1893.

Enderlin, Richard. Birth: Germany, 1843. Musician in Company C, 73rd Ohio Infantry. From July 1 to 3, 1863, at Gettysburg, Pennsylvania, Enderlin voluntarily took up a musket and served in the ranks. He voluntarily went into the enemy's lines at night, under a sharp fire, to rescue a wounded comrade. Enderlin was awarded his medal on September 11, 1897.

Engle, James E. Birth: Pennsylvania. Sergeant of Company I, 97th Pennsylvania Infantry. On May 18, 1864, at Bermuda Hundred, Virginia, Sergeant Engle volunteered to carry ammunition to the regiment, on the picket line, under a heavy fire. Engle was awarded his medal on December 17, 1896.

Andrew Embler (U.S. Army War College)

Richard Enderlin (U.S. Army War College)

The Recipients—English

English, Edmund. Birth: Ireland, 1841. First Sergeant in Company C, 2nd New Jersey Infantry. On May 6, 1864, at the Wilderness, Virginia, Sergeant English, while under orders to retreat, seized the colors, rallied the men, and drove the enemy back. English was awarded his medal on February 13, 1891.

English, Thomas. Birth: New York, 1819. Signal Quartermaster aboard the U.S.S. *New Ironsides*. From December 24 to 25, 1864 and January 13 to 15, 1865, English displayed skill and courage in the performance of hi duties in the two expeditions against Fort Fisher. English was awarded his medal on June 22, 1865.

Ennis, Charles D. Birth: Connecticut, 1843. Private in Company G, 1st Rhode Island Light Artillery. On April 2, 1865, at Petersburg, Virginia, Private Ennis was part of a detachment of 20 picked artillerymen who voluntarily accompanied an infantry assaulting party and who turned upon the enemy the guns captured in the attack. Ennis was awarded his medal on June 28, 1892.

Erickson, John P. Birth: England. Captain of the Forecastle aboard the U.S.S. *Pontoosuc*. From December 24, 1864 to February 22, 1865, Erickson faithfully carried out his duties, being severely wounded in the assault upon Fort Fisher. Erickson was awarded his medal on June 22, 1865.

Estes, Lewellyn G. Birth: Maine, 1843. Captain and Assistant Adjutant General, U.S. Volunteers. On August 30, 1864, at Flint River, Georgia, Captain Estes voluntarily led troops in a charge over a burning bridge. Estes was awarded his medal on August 29, 1894.

Evans, Coron D. Birth: Indiana. Private in Company A, 3rd Indiana Cavalry. On April 6, 1865, at Sailors Creek, Virginia, Private Evans captured the flag of the 26th Virginia Infantry. Evans was awarded his medal on May 3, 1865.

Evans, Ira H. Birth: New Hampshire, 1844. Captain of Company B, 116th United States Colored Infantry. On April 2, 1865, at Hatchers Run, Virginia, Captain Evans voluntarily passed between the lines under a heavy fire and obtained important information. Evans was awarded his medal on March 24, 1892.

Llewellyn Estes (U.S. Army War College)

Evans, James R. Birth: New York. Private in Company H, 62nd New York Infantry. On May 5, 1864, at the Wilderness, Virginia, Private Evans, in the face of an advancing enemy, went out in front of the line to rescue the regimental flag after the color bearer had fallen. Evans was awarded his medal on February 25, 1895.

Evans, Thomas. Birth: Pennsylvania. Private in Company D, 54th Pennsylvania Infantry. On June 5, 1864, at Piedmont, Virginia, Private Evans captured the flag of the 45th Virginia Infantry. Evans was awarded his medal on November 26, 1864.

Ira Evans (Hall of Heroes)

Everson, Adelbert. Birth: New York. Private in Company D, 185th New York Infantry. On April 1, 1865, at Five Forks, Virginia, Private Everson captured a Confederate flag. Everson was awarded his medal on May 10, 1865.

Ewing, John C. Birth: Pennsylvania. Private in Company E, 211th Pennsylvania Infantry. On April 2, 1865, at Petersburg, Virginia, Private Ewing captured a Confederate flag. Ewing was awarded his medal on May 20, 1865.

Falconer, John A. Birth: Michigan, 1844. Corporal in Company A, 17th Michigan Infantry. On November 20, 1863, at Knoxville, Tennessee, Corporal Falconer participated in the attack on Fort Sanders, where he conducted the "burning party" that burned a house which had sheltered enemy sharpshooters, thus insuring success to a hazardous enterprise. Falconer was awarded his medal on July 27, 1896.

Fall, Charles S. Birth: Indiana, 1842. Sergeant in Company E, 26th Michigan Infantry. On May 12, 1864, at Spotsylvania, Virginia, Sergeant Fall was the first to mount the Confederate works, where he bayoneted two of the enemy and captured a Confederate flag, but threw it away to continue the pursuit. Fall was awarded his medal on May 13, 1899.

Fallon, Thomas T. Birth: Ireland. Private in Company K, 37th New York Infantry. On May 5, 1862, at Williamsburg, Virginia, on May 30 to 31, 1862, at Fair Oaks, Virginia, and on June 14 to 15, 1864, at Big Shanty, Georgia, Private Fallon displayed conspicuous gallantry in the performance of his duties. Fallon was awarded his medal on February 13, 1891.

Falls, Benjamin. Birth: New Hampshire. Color Sergeant in Company A, 19th Massachusetts Infantry. On July 3, 1863, at Gettysburg, Pennsylvania, Sergeant Falls captured a Confederate flag. Falls was awarded his medal in December of 1864.

Fanning, Nicholas. Birth: Indiana. Private in Company B, 4th Iowa Cavalry. On April 2, 1865, at Selma, Alabama, Private Fanning captured a Confederate flag and two staff officers. Fanning was awarded his medal on June 17, 1865.

Benjamin Falls (Hall of Heroes)

Farley, William. Birth: Maine, 1835. Boatswain's Mate aboard the U.S.S. *Marblehead*. On December 25, 1863, at Legerville, Stono River, South Carolina. Farley kept up a rapid and effective fire on the enemy throughout the engagement which resulted in the enemy abandoning his position. Farley was awarded his medal on April 16, 1864.

Farnsworth, Herbert E. [photograph p. 72] Birth: New York, 1834. Sergeant Major of the 10th New York Cavalry. On June 11, 1864, at Trevilian Station, Virginia, Sergeant Farnsworth voluntarily carried a message that stopped the firing of a Union battery into his regiment, in which service he crossed a ridge in plain view and swept the fire of both armies. Farnsworth was awarded his medal on April 1, 1898.

Herbert Farnsworth (U.S. Army War College)

Charles Fasnacht (Hall of Heroes)

John Ferrell (Hall of Heroes)

Farquhar, John M. Birth: Scotland. Sergeant Major of the 89th Illinois Infantry. On December 31, 1862, at Stones River, Tennessee, Sergeant Farquhar rallied fugitives from other commands and deployed his own regiment, thereby checking the Confederate charge until a new line was established. Farquhar was awarded his medal on August 6, 1902.

Farrell, Edward. Birth: New York, 1833. Quartermaster aboard the U.S.S. *Owasco*. On April 24, 1862, at Forts Jackson and St. Philip, south of New Orleans, Farrell displayed intelligence and coolness while reporting the effect of fire from the masthead. Farrell was awarded his medal on April 3, 1863.

Fasnacht, Charles H. Birth: Pennsylvania. Sergeant in Company A, 99th Pennsylvania Infantry. On May 12, 1864, at Spotsylvania, Virginia, Sergeant Fasnacht captured the flag of the 2nd Louisiana Tigers. Fasnacht was awarded his medal on April 2, 1878.

Fassett, John B. [photograph p. 73] Birth: Pennsylvania. Captain in Company F, 23rd Pennsylvania Infantry. On July 2, 1863, at Gettysburg, Pennsylvania, Captain Fassett, while acting as a personal aide, voluntarily led a regiment to the relief of a battery and recaptured its guns from the enemy. Fassett was awarded his medal on December 29, 1894.

Fernald, Albert E. Birth: Maine, 1838. First Lieutenant of Company F, 20th Maine Infantry. On April 1, 1865, at Five Forks, Virginia, Lieutenant Fernald captured the flag of the 9th Virginia Infantry. Fernald was awarded his medal on May 10, 1865.

Ferrell, John H. Birth: Tennessee, 1823. Pilot aboard the U.S.S. *Neosho*. On December 6, 1864, at Bells Mills, Cumberland River, Tennessee, Pilot Ferrell carried out his duties courageously during the engagement. After the flag and signal staffs had been shot away, he left the pilothouse to attach the flag to the highest mast remaining. Ferrell was awarded his medal on June 22, 1865.

The Recipients — Flanagan

John Fassett (Hall of Heroes)

Eugene Ferris (U.S. Army War College)

Ferrier, Daniel T. Birth: 1841. Sergeant in Company K, 2nd Indiana Cavalry. On May 9, 1864, at Varnell's Station, Georgia, Sergeant Farrier voluntarily gave his horse to his brigade commander, during a retreat, as a result of which he was captured and confined in Confederate prisons. Ferrier was awarded his medal on March 30, 1898.

Ferris, Eugene W. Birth: Vermont, 1841. First Lieutenant and Adjutant of the 30th Massachusetts Infantry. On April 1, 1865, at Berryville, Virginia, Lieutenant Ferris displayed exceptional gallantry in resisting an attack of 5 of Mosby's cavalry. Ferris was awarded his medal on October 16, 1897.

Fesq, Frank. Birth: Germany, 1840. Private in Company A, 40th New Jersey Infantry. On April 2, 1865, at Petersburg, Virginia, Private Fesq captured the flag of the 18th North Carolina Infantry. Fesq was awarded his medal on May 10, 1865.

Finkenbiner, Henry S. Birth: Ohio, 1842. Private in Company D, 107th Ohio Infantry. On April 9, 1865, at Dingles Mill, South Carolina, Private Finkenbiner crossed the mill race on a burning bridge and ascertained the enemy's position. Finkenbiner was awarded his medal on March 30, 1898.

Fisher, John H. Birth: Pennsylvania. First Lieutenant of Company B, 55th Illinois Infantry. On May 22, 1863, at Vicksburg, Mississippi, Lieutenant Fisher exhibited exceptional gallantry in the charge of the volunteer storming party. Fisher was awarded his medal on January 16, 1894.

Fisher, Joseph. Birth: Pennsylvania, 1843. Corporal of Company C, 61st Pennsylvania Infantry. On April 2, 1865, at Petersburg, Virginia, Corporal Fisher, though painfully wounded, crawled into the enemy's works to plant his flag thereon. Fisher was awarded his medal on January 16, 1894.

Fitzpatrick, Thomas. Birth: Canada, 1837. Coxswain aboard the U.S.S. *Hartford*. On August 5, 1864, at Mobile Bay, Alabama, Coxswain Fitzpatrick's gun was disabled by a shell burst. Within a few minutes, Fitzpatrick had the gun repaired, and on new track, had sent the wounded below, and was fighting the gun again. Fitzpatrick was awarded his medal on December 31, 1864.

Flanagan, Augustin. Birth: Pennsylvania. Sergeant in Company A, 55th Pennsylvania Infantry. On September 29, 1864, Sergeant Flanagan displayed gallantry in the charge on the enemy works, rushing forward the colors and calling on the men to follow him. Flanagan was awarded his medal on April 6, 1865.

Flannigan, James. Birth: New York. Private in Company H, 2nd Minnesota Infantry. On February 15, 1863, at Nolensville, Tennessee, Private Flannigan was one of a detachment of 16 men who successfully defended a wagon train from the attack of 125 Confederate cavalry. Flannigan was awarded his medal on September 11, 1897.

Fleetwood, Christian A. Birth: Maryland. Sergeant Major of the 4th United States Colored Infantry. On September 29, 1864, at Chapin's Farm, Virginia, Sergeant Fleetwood seized the colors after two color bearers had been shot down and bore them forward through the fight. Fleetwood was awarded his medal on April 6, 1865.

Christian Fleetwood (Hall of Heroes)

Flood, Thomas. Birth: Ireland, 1840. Boy aboard the U.S.S. *Pensacola*. On April 24 to 25, 1862, at Forts Jackson and St. Philip, south of New Orleans, Flood performed his duties with coolness and fidelity like a veteran seaman. Flood was awarded his medal on April 3, 1863.

Flynn, Christopher. Birth: Ireland. Corporal in Company K, 14th Connecticut Infantry. On July 3, 1863, at Gettysburg, Pennsylvania, Corporal Flynn captured the flag of the 52nd North Carolina Infantry. Flynn was awarded his medal on December 1, 1864.

Flynn, James E. Birth: Illinois. Sergeant in Company G, 6th Missouri Infantry. On May 22, 1863, at Vicksburg, Mississippi, Sergeant Flynn exhibited exceptional gallantry in the charge of the volunteer storming party. Flynn was awarded his medal on June 19, 1894.

Follett, Joseph. Birth: New Jersey, 1843. Sergeant in Company C, 1st Missouri Light Artillery. On December 31, 1862, at Stones River, Tennessee, Sergeant Follett went to procure ammunition from the supply train when he was captured. He made good his escape and in less than an hour from the time of his capture had re-supplied the battery. Follett was awarded his medal on September 19, 1890.

Force, Manning F. Birth: District of Columbia, 1824. Brigadier General of United States Volunteers. On July 22, 1864, at Atlanta, Georgia, General Force charged upon the enemy works, and after their capture defended his position against assaults of the enemy until he was severely wounded. Force was awarded his medal on March 31, 1892.

Manning Force (Hall of Heroes)

Ford, George W. Birth: Ireland, 1844. First Lieutenant of Company E, 88th New York Infantry. On April 6, 1865, at Sailors Creek, Virginia, Lieutenant Ford captured a Confederate flag. Ford was awarded his medal on May 10, 1865.

Forman, Alexander, A. Birth: Michigan, 1843. Corporal of Company E, 7th Michigan Infantry. On May 31, 1862, at Fair Oaks, Virginia, Corporal Forman continued fighting, after he had been wounded, until he fainted from loss of blood and had to be carried from the field. Forman was awarded his medal on August 17, 1895.

Frederick Fout (Hall of Heroes)

Fout, Frederick W. Birth: Germany. Second Lieutenant in the 15th Indiana Light Artillery. On September 15, 1862, at Harpers Ferry, West Virginia, Lieutenant Fout gathered the men of the battery together and re-manned the guns, after they had been ordered to be abandoned, keeping up a steady fire until after the surrender. Fout was awarded his medal on November 2, 1896.

Fox, Henry. Birth: Germany, 1833. Sergeant in Company H, 106th Illinois Infantry. On December 23, 1862, near Jackson, Tennessee, Sergeant Fox volunteered to cross an open railway trestle, under a concentrated fire from the enemy, to secure reinforcements for the relief of his command. Fox was awarded his medal on May 16, 1899.

Fox, Henry M. Birth: Ohio, 1844. Sergeant in Company M, 5th Michigan Cavalry. On September 19, 1864, at Winchester, Virginia, Sergeant Fox captured a Confederate flag. Fox was awarded his medal on September 27, 1864.

Fox, Nicholas. Private in Company H, 28th Connecticut Infantry. On June 14, 1863, at Port Hudson, Louisiana, Private Fox made two trips across an open space in the face of severe enemy fire and secured water for the wounded. Fox was awarded his medal on April 1, 1898.

Fox, William R. Birth: Pennsylvania. Private in Company A, 95th Pennsylvania Infantry. On April 2, 1865, at Petersburg, Virginia, Private Fox bravely assisted in the capture of an enemy cannon. Fox was awarded his medal on March 28, 1879.

Foy, Charles H. Birth: New Hampshire. Signal Quartermaster aboard the U.S.S. *Rhode Island*. On January 13 to 15, 1865, at Fort Fisher, North Carolina, Foy continued to be outstanding by his good conduct and faithful services throughout the engagement. Foy was awarded his medal on June 22, 1865.

Franks, William J. Birth: North Carolina, 1830. Seaman aboard the U.S.S. *Marmora*. On March 5, 1864, at Yazoo City, Mississippi, Seaman Franks displayed exceptional gallantry in standing to his gun during the engagement. Franks was awarded his medal on April 6, 1864.

Frantz, Joseph. Birth: France, 1837. Private in Company E, 83rd Indiana Infantry. On May 22, 1863, at Vicksburg, Mississippi, Private Frantz exhibited exceptional gallantry in the charge of the volunteer storming party. Frantz was awarded his medal on August 13, 1894.

Fraser, William W. Birth: Scotland. Private in Company I, 97th Illinois Infantry. On May 22, 1863, at Vicksburg, Mississippi, Private Fraser exhibited exceptional gallantry in the charge of the volunteer storming party. Fraser was awarded his medal on October 24, 1895.

Freeman, Archibald. Birth: New York. Private in Company E, 124th New York Infantry. On May 12, 1864, at Spotsylvania, Virginia, Private Freeman captured the flag of the 17th Louisiana Infantry. Freeman was awarded his medal on December 1, 1864.

Freeman, Henry B. Birth: Ohio, 1837. First Lieutenant in the 18th United States Infantry. On December 31, 1862, at Stones River, Tennessee, Lieutenant Freeman, under a heavy fire, went to the front to rescue a field officer who had been wounded and was about to fall into enemy hands. Freeman was awarded his medal on February 17, 1894.

Henry Freeman (U.S. Army War College)

Freeman, Martin. Birth: Germany, 1814. Pilot aboard the U.S.S. *Hartford*. On August 5, 1864, at Mobile Bay, Alabama, Pilot Freeman calmly remained at his station, piloting the ships into the bay, where he rendered gallant service throughout the prolonged battle. Freeman was awarded his medal on December 31, 1864.

Freeman, William. Birth: New York, 1844. Private in Company B, 169th New York Infantry. On January 15, 1865, at Fort Fisher, North Carolina, Private Freeman carried the brigade flag forward after the bearer was wounded. Freeman was awarded his medal on May 27, 1905.

French, Samuel S. Birth: New York, 1841. Private in Company E, 7th Michigan Infantry. On May 31, 1862, at Fair Oaks, Virginia, Private French continued fighting after he had been seriously wounded until he fainted from loss of blood. French was awarded his medal on October 24, 1895.

Frey, Franz. Birth: Switzerland, 1837. Corporal in Company H, 37th Ohio Infantry. On May 22, 1863, at Vicksburg, Mississippi, Corporal Frey exhibited exceptional gallantry in the charge of the volunteer storming party. Frey was awarded his medal on August 14, 1894.

Frick, Jacob G. Birth: Pennsylvania, 1838. Colonel of the 129th Pennsylvania Infantry. On December 13, 1862, at Fredericksburg, Virginia, Colonel Frick seized the colors and led the command through a terrible fire of artillery and musketry. On May 3, 1863, at Chancellorsville, Virginia, he recaptured the colors of the regiment. Frick was awarded his medal on June 7, 1892.

Frisbee, John B. Birth: Maine, 1822. Gunner's Mate aboard the U.S.S. *Pinola*. On April 24, 1862, at Forts Jackson and St. Philip, south of New Orleans, Gunner's Mate Frisbee, under great risk to himself, closed the powder magazine after it had been set afire by enemy shelling. Frisbee was awarded his medal on April 3, 1863.

Frizell, Henry F. Birth: Missouri. Private in Company B, 6th Missouri Infantry. On May 22, 1863, at Vicksburg, Mississippi, Private Frizzell exhibited exceptional gallantry in the charge of the volunteer storming party. Frizzell was awarded his medal on July 30, 1894.

Fry, Isaac N. Birth: Pennsylvania. Orderly Sergeant, United States Marine Corps, serving aboard the U.S.S. *Ticonderoga*. On January 13 to 15, 1865, at Fort Fisher, North Carolina, Sergeant Fry performed his duties with skill and courage in maintaining a well placed fire on the enemy's batteries. Fry was awarded his medal on June 22, 1865.

Frederick Fuger (Hall of Heroes)

Fuger, Frederick. Birth: Germany. Sergeant in Battery A, 4th United States Artillery. On July 3, 1863, at Gettysburg, Pennsylvania, Sergeant Fuger, during Pickett's Charge, fought his gun after all of the other cannon in the battery had been disabled. Fuger was awarded his medal on August 24, 1897.

Funk, West. Birth: Massachusetts. Major of the 121st Pennsylvania Infantry. On April 9, 1865, at Appomattox, Virginia, Major Funk captured the flag of the 46th Virginia Infantry. Funk was awarded his medal on October 15, 1872.

Chester Furman (U.S. Army War College)

Furman, Chester S. Birth: Pennsylvania, 1842. Corporal in Company A, 6th Pennsylvania Infantry Reserves. On July 2, 1863, at Gettysburg, Pennsylvania, Corporal Furman, along with five other volunteers charged upon a log house near Devil's Den where a squad of Confederate sharpshooters were sheltered, compelling them to surrender. Furman was awarded his medal on August 3, 1897.

Furness, Frank. Captain of Company F. 6th Pennsylvania Cavalry. On June 12, 1864, at

Frank Furness (Hall of Heroes)

Trevilian Station, Virginia, Captain Furness volunteered to carry a box of ammunition across an open space, swept by enemy fire, to the relief of an outpost whose ammunition had run out. Furness was awarded his medal on October 20, 1899.

Gage, Richard J. Birth: New Hampshire. Private Company D, 104th Illinois Infantry. On July 2, 1863, at Elk River, Tennessee, Private Gage voluntarily joined a small party that, under heavy fire, captured a stockade and saved the bridge. Gage was awarded his medal on October 30, 1897.

Galloway, George N. Birth: Pennsylvania. Private in Company G, 95th Pennsylvania Infantry. On May 8, 1864, at Alsop's Farm, Virginia, Private Galloway voluntarily held an important position under heavy fire. Galloway was awarded his medal on October 24, 1895.

James Gardiner/Gardner (U.S. Army War College)

Galloway, John. Birth: Pennsylvania. Commissary Sergeant in the 8th Pennsylvania Cavalry. On April 7, 1865, at Farmville, Virginia, Sergeant Galloway rushed forward when his regiment was surprised and nearly overwhelmed to rally to men and prevent the disaster that was imminent. Galloway was awarded his medal on October 30, 1897.

Gardiner (Gardner), James. Birth: Virginia, 1839. Private in Company I, 36th United States Colored Infantry. On September 29, 1864, at Chapin's Farm, Virginia, Private Gardiner rushed in advance of his brigade, shot a Confederate officer who was on the parapet rallying his men, and then ran him through with his bayonet. Gardiner was awarded his medal on April 6, 1865.

Gardner, Charles N. Birth: Massachusetts, 1845. Private in Company E, 32nd Massachusetts Infantry. On April 1, 1865, at Five Forks, Virginia, Private Gardner captured a Confederate flag. Gardner was awarded his medal on May 10, 1865.

Gardner, Robert J. Birth: New York. Sergeant in Company K, 34th Massachusetts Infantry. On April 2, 1865, at Petersburg, Virginia, Sergeant Gardner was among the first to enter Fort Gregg, clearing the way by using his musket as a club. Gardner was awarded his medal on May 12, 1865.

Gardner, William. Birth: Ireland, 1832. Seaman aboard the U.S.S. *Calena*. On August 5, 1864, at Mobile Bay, Alabama, Seaman Gardner served gallantly during the severe battle that resulted in the surrender of the ram *Tennessee* and the damaging and destruction of Fort Morgan. Gardner was awarded his medal on December 31, 1864.

Garrett, William. Birth: England. Sergeant in Company G, 41st Ohio Infantry. On December 16, 1864, at Nashville, Tennessee, Sergeant Garrett, with several companions, rushed into the enemy's works taking possession of 4 pieces of artillery and capturing the flag of the 13th Mississippi Infantry. Garrett was awarded his medal on February 24, 1865.

Garrison, James R. Birth: New York, 1840. Coal Heaver aboard the U.S.S. *Hartford*. On August 5, 1864, at Mobile Bay, Alabama, Garrison remained at his station, even though a shell had struck his foot and severed one of his toes. Garrison was awarded his medal on December 31, 1864.

Garvin, William. Birth: Virginia, 1835. Captain of the Forecastle aboard the U.S.S. *Agawam*. On December 23, 1864, at Fort Fisher, North Carolina, Garvin served as a volunteer on the powder boat intended to blow up the fort. Garvin was awarded his medal on December 31, 1864.

Gasson, Richard. Birth: Ireland, 1842. Sergeant in Company K, 47th New York Infantry. On September 29, 1864, at Chapin's Farm, Virginia, Sergeant Gasson fell dead after advancing the colors and planting them on the enemy's works. Gasson was awarded his medal on April 6, 1865.

Gaunt, John C. Birth: Ohio. Private in Company G, 104th Ohio Infantry. On November 30, 1864, at Franklin, Tennessee, Private Gaunt captured a Confederate flag. Gaunt was awarded his medal on February 13, 1865.

Gause, Isaac. Birth: Ohio. Corporal in Company E, 2nd Ohio Cavalry. On September 13, 1864, at Berryville, Virginia, Corporal Gause captured the flag of the 8th South Carolina. Gause was awarded his medal on September 19, 1864.

Gaylord, Levi B. Birth: Massachusetts, 1840. Sergeant in Company A, 29th Massachusetts Infantry. On March 25, 1865, at Fort Stedman, Virginia, Sergeant Gaylord voluntarily assisted in working an abandoned gun while exposed to heavy fire, until the enemy's advancing line was routed by a charge. Gaylord was awarded his medal on June 22, 1896.

George, Daniel G. Birth: New Hampshire, 1840. Ordinary Seaman aboard U.S.S. *Picket Boat*. On October 27, 1864, on the Roanoke River, North Carolina, Seaman George exhibited exceptional gallantry in performing his duties during an attack against the ram *Albemarle*. George was awarded his medal on December 31, 1864.

Gere, Thomas P. Birth: New York. First Lieutenant and Adjutant of the 5th Minnesota Infantry.

Thomas Gere (Hall of Heroes)

On December 16, 1864, at Nashville, Tennessee, Lieutenant Gere captured the flag of the 4th Mississippi Infantry. Gere was awarded his medal on February 24, 1865.

Geschwind, Nicholas. Birth: France. Captain of Company F, 116th Illinois Infantry. On May 22, 1863, at Vicksburg, Mississippi, Captain Geschwind exhibited exceptional gallantry in the charge of the volunteer storming party. Geschwind was awarded his medal on August 24, 1894.

Gibbs, Wesley. Birth: Connecticut. Sergeant in Company B, 2nd Connecticut Heavy Artillery. On April 2, 1865, at Petersburg, Virginia, Sergeant Gibbs captured a Confederate flag. Gibbs was awarded his medal on May 10, 1865.

Gifford, Benjamin. Birth: New York. Private in Company H, 121st New York Infantry. On April 6, 1865, at Sailors Creek, Virginia, Private Gifford captured a Confederate flag. Gifford was awarded his medal on May 10, 1865.

Gifford, David L. Birth: Massachusetts. Private in Company B, 4th Massachusetts Cavalry. On May 24, 1864, at Ashepoo River, South Carolina, Private Gifford volunteered to be part of a boat crew that went to the rescue of a large number of soldiers on board the stranded steamer Boston and with great gallantry assisted in conveying them to shore, being exposed the entire time to a heavy fire from the Confederates. Gifford was awarded his medal on April 16, 1864.

George Gillespie (Hall of Heroes)

Gile, Frank S. Birth: Massachusetts, 1845. Landsman aboard the U.S.S. *Lehigh*. On November 16, 1863, at Charleston, South Carolina, during the hazardous task of freeing the *Lehigh*, which had been grounded, and was under heavy enemy fire from Fort Moultrie. After several previous attempts had been made, Gile succeeded in passing in a small boat from the *Lehigh* to the *Nahant* with a line bent on a hawser. This courageous action while under severe enemy fire enabled the *Lehigh* to be freed from her helpless position. Gile was awarded his medal on April 16, 1864.

Gillespie, George L. Birth: Tennessee. First Lieutenant, Corps of Engineers, U.S. Army. On May 31, 1864, at Bethesda Church, Virginia, Lieutenant Gillespie exposed himself to great danger when he volunteered to make his way through enemy lines to communicate with General Sheridan. While rendering this service, he was captured, but escaped. He was accosted by the Confederates a second time, but made good his escape, under fire. Gillespie was awarded his medal on October 27, 1897.

Gilligan, Edward L. Birth: Pennsylvania. First Sergeant of Company E, 88th Pennsylvania Infantry. On July 3, 1863, at Gettysburg, Pennsylvania, Sergeant Gilligan assisted in

Edward Gilligan (Hall of Heroes)

the capture of a Confederate flag by knocking down the color sergeant. Gilligan was awarded his medal on April 30, 1892.

Gilmore, John C. Birth: Canada. Major of the 16th New York Infantry. On May 3, 1863, at Salem Heights, Virginia, Major Gilmore seized the colors of his regiment and gallantly rallied his men under a severe fire. Gilmore was awarded his medal on October 10, 1892.

Ginley, Patrick. Birth: Ireland, 1822. Private in Company G, 1st New York Light Artillery. On August 25, 1864, at Reams Station, Virginia, Private Ginley having been left alone between the two lines, crept back into the works, put 3 charges of canister in one of the guns and fired the piece directly into a body of the enemy about to seize the works. He then rejoined his command, took the colors, and ran toward the enemy, followed by the command, which recaptured the works and guns. Ginley was awarded his medal on October 31, 1890.

Gion, Joseph. Private in Company A, 74th New York Infantry. On May 2, 1863, at Chancellorsville, Virginia, Private Gion volunteered to scout the enemy lines, and secured valuable information, Gion was awarded his medal on November 26, 1884.

Godley, Leonidus M. Birth: West Virginia. First Sergeant in Company E, 22nd Iowa Infantry. On May 22, 1863, at Vicksburg, Mississippi, Sergeant Godley led his company in the assault on the enemy's works and gained the parapet, there receiving three severe wounds. He lay all day in the sun, was taken prisoner and had his leg amputated without anesthetics. Godley was awarded his medal on August 3, 1897.

Goettel, Philip. Birth: New York. Private in Company B, 149th New York Infantry. On November 27, 1863, at Ringgold, Georgia, Private Goettel captured a Confederate flag and battery guidon. Goettel was awarded his medal on June 28, 1865.

Philip Goettel (Hall of Heroes)

Goheen, Charles A. Birth: New York. First Sergeant of Company G, 8th New York Cavalry. On March 2, 1865, at Waynesboro, Virginia, Sergeant Goheen captured a Confederate flag. Goheen was awarded his medal on March 26, 1865.

Goldsbery, Andrew E. Birth: Illinois. Private in Company E, 127th Illinois Infantry. On May 22, 1863, at Vicksburg, Mississippi, Private Goldsbery exhibited exceptional gallantry in the charge of the volunteer storming party. Goldsbery was awarded his medal on August 9, 1894.

Andrew Goldsbery (Hall of Heroes)

Goodall, Francis H. Birth: New Hampshire. First Sergeant in Company G, 11th New Hampshire Infantry. On December 13, 1862, at Fredericksburg, Virginia, Sergeant Goodall, with another soldier brought a wounded comrade into the lines under a heavy fire. Goodall was awarded his medal on December 14, 1894.

Goodman, William E. Birth: Pennsylvania, 1838. First Lieutenant of Company D, 147th Pennsylvania Infantry. On May 3, 1863, at Chancellorsville, Virginia, Lieutenant Goodman rescued the colors of the 107th Ohio Infantry from the enemy. Goodman was awarded his medal on January 11, 1894.

Goodrich, Edwin. Birth: New York 1843. First Lieutenant of Company D, 9th New York Cavalry. In November, 1864, near Cedar Creek, Virginia, Lieutenant Goodrich, while the command was falling back, returned in the face of the enemy to rescue a sergeant from under a fallen horse. Goodrich was awarded his medal on May 14, 1894.

William Goodman (U.S. Army War College)

Gould, Charles G. [photograph p. 83] Birth: Vermont, 1845. Captain in Company H, 5th Vermont Infantry. On April 2, 1865, at Petersburg, Virginia, Captain Gould was among the first to mount the enemy's works in the assault, where he received a serious bayonet wound in the face. Gould was awarded his medal on July 30, 1890.

Gould, Newton T. Birth: Illinois. Private in Company G, 113th Illinois Infantry. On May 22, 1863, at Vicksburg, Mississippi, Private Gould exhibited exceptional gallantry in the charge of the volunteer storming party. Gould was awarded his medal on September 6, 1894.

Edwin Goodrich (U.S. Army War College)

Gouraud, George E. [photograph p. 83] Birth: New York 1840. Captain and aide-de-camp, U.S. Volunteers. On November 30, 1864, at Honey Hill, South Carolina, Captain Gouraud rendered valuable assistance in rallying the men under a heavy fire. Gouraud was awarded his medal on August 21, 1893.

Grace, Peter. Birth: Massachusetts, 1845. Sergeant in Company G, 83rd Pennsylvania Infantry. On May 5, 1864, at the Wilderness, Virginia, Sergeant Grace single-handedly rescued a comrade from two Confederate guards, knocking down one and capturing the other. Grace was awarded his medal on December 27, 1894.

Charles Gould (U.S. Army War College)

Graham, Robert. Birth: England, 1841. Landsman aboard the U.S.S. *Tacony*. On October 31, 1864, at Plymouth, North Carolina, Landsman Graham, during the capture of Plymouth, distinguished himself when he participated in landing and spiking a 9-inch gun while under a devastating fire from enemy musketry. Graham was awarded his medal on December 31, 1864.

Graham, Thomas N. Second Lieutenant in Company G, 15th Indiana Infantry. On November 25, 1863, at Missionary Ridge, Tennessee, Lieutenant Graham seized the colors from a fallen bearer and, exposed to a terrible fire, carried them forward, planting them on the enemy's breastworks. Graham was awarded his medal on February 15, 1897.

George Gouraud (U.S. Army War College)

Gabriel Grant (Hall of Heroes)

Grant, Gabriel. Birth: New Jersey. Surgeon, U.S. Volunteers. On June 1, 1862, at Fair Oaks, Virginia, Surgeon Grant removed severely wounded officers and men from the field under a heavy fire. Grant was awarded his medal on July 21, 1897.

Grant, Lewis A. [photograph p. 84] Birth: Vermont, 1828. Colonel of the 5th Vermont Infantry. On May 3, 1864, at Salem Heights, Virginia, Colonel Grant displayed personal gallantry and intrepidity in the management of his brigade and in leading

The Recipients—**Graul**

Lewis Grant (U.S. Army War College)

William Graul (U.S. Army War College)

it in the assault in which he was wounded. Grant was awarded his medal on May 11, 1893.

Graul, William. Birth: Pennsylvania, 1846. Corporal of Company I, 188th Pennsylvania Infantry. On Sept 29, 1864, at Fort Harrison, Virginia, Corporal Graul was the first to advance and plant the colors of his state on the enemy fortifications. Graul was awarded his medal on April 6, 1865.

Gray, John. Birth: Scotland. Private in Company B, 5th Ohio Infantry. On June 9, 1862, at Port Republic, Virginia, Private Gray mounted an artillery horse of the enemy and captured a brass 6-pound cannon in the face of the enemy. Gray was awarded his medal on March 14, 1864.

Gray, Robert A. Birth: Pennsylvania. Sergeant in Company C, 21st Connecticut Infantry. On May 16, 1864, at Drury's Bluff, Virginia, Sergeant Gray returned in the face of enemy fire to rescue a wounded officer of his company who could not walk. Gray was awarded his medal on July 13, 1897.

Robert Gray (Hall of Heroes)

Grebe, M.R. William. Birth: Germany, 1838. Captain of Company F, 4th Missouri Cavalry. On August 31. 1864, at Jonesboro, Georgia, Captain Grebe acted as a volunteer aide carrying orders across a most dangerous part of the battlefield, was hindered by a Confederate advance and seized a rifle to take a place in the ranks and was conspicuous in repulsing the enemy. Grebe was awarded his medal on February 24, 1899.

Green, George. Birth: England, 1840. Corporal in Company H, 11th Ohio Infantry. On November 25, 1863, at Missionary Ridge, Tennessee, Corporal Green captured the flag of the 18th Alabama Infantry. Green was awarded his medal on January 12, 1892.

Greenawalt, Abraham. Birth: Pennsylvania. Private in Company G, 104th Ohio Infantry. On November 30, 1864, at Franklin, Tennessee, Private Greenawalt captured a Confederate headquarters flag. Greenawalt was awarded his medal on February 13, 1865.

Greene, John. Captain of the Forecastle aboard the U.S.S. *Varuna*. On April 24, 1862, at Forts Jackson and St. Philip, south of New Orleans, Greene remained steadfast at his gun throughout the thickest of the fight. Greene was awarded his medal on April 3, 1863.

Greene, Oliver D. Birth: New York, 1833. Major and Assistant Adjutant General U.S. Army. On September 17, 1862, at Antietam, Maryland, Major Greene formed the columns under heavy fire and put them into position. Greene was awarded his medal on December 13, 1893.

Oliver Greene (U.S. Army War College)

Gregg, Joseph O. Birth: Ohio, 1841. Private in Company F, 133rd Ohio Infantry. On June 16, 1864, near Richmond, Virginia, Private Gregg voluntarily returned to the breastworks his regiment had abandoned to notify three missing companies that the regiment was falling back. He found the enemy already in the works and refused a demand for surrender, returning to his command amid a hail of fire. Gregg was awarded his medal on May 13, 1899.

Greig, Theodore W. Birth: New York, 1843. Second Lieutenant of Company C, 61st New York Infantry. On September 17, 1862, at Antietam, Maryland, Lieutenant Greig captured the flag of the 4th Alabama Infantry, and while shot through the neck, returned it within Union lines. Greig was awarded his medal on February 10, 1887.

Joseph Gregg (U.S. Army War College)

Gresser, Ignatz. Birth: Germany, 1832. Corporal in Company D, 128th Pennsylvania Infantry. On September 17, 1862, at Antietam, Maryland. Corporal Gresser exposed himself to enemy fire to carry a wounded comrade from the field. Gresser was awarded his medal on December 12, 1895.

Gribben, James H. Birth: Ireland. Lieutenant in Company C, 2nd New York Cavalry. On April 6, 1865, at Sailors Creek, Virginia, Lieutenant Gribben captured the flag of the 12th Virginia Infantry. Gribben was awarded his medal on May 3, 1865.

Griffiths, John. Birth: Wales, 1835. Captain of the Forecastle aboard the U.S.S. *Santiago de Cuba*. On January 15, 1865, at Fort Fisher, North Carolina, Griffiths was detailed to one of the generals on shore. Griffiths bravely entered the fort in the assault and accompanied his party in carrying dispatches at the height of the battle. Griffiths was awarded his medal on June 22, 1865.

Ignatz Gresser (U.S. Army War College)

Grimshaw, Samuel. Birth: Ohio. Private in Company B, 52nd Ohio Infantry. On August 6, 1864, at Atlanta, Georgia, Private Grimshaw risked his life by picking up a lighted shell that had fallen in the midst of the company and throwing it away. Grimshaw was awarded his medal on April 5, 1894.

Grindlay, James G. Colonel of the 146th New York Infantry. On April 1, 1865, at Five Forks, Virginia, Colonel Grindlay was the first to enter the Confederate works, where he captured two Confederate flags. Grindlay was awarded his medal on August 14, 1891.

Griswold, Luke M. Birth: Massachusetts, 1837. Ordinary Seaman aboard the U.S.S. *Rhode Island*. On December 30, 1862, off Cape Hatteras, North Carolina, Seaman Griswold participated in the rescue effort for the crew of the U.S.S. *Monitor*. Griswold was awarded his medal on June 22, 1865.

James Grindlay (Hall of Heroes)

Grueb, George. Birth: Germany. Private in Company E, 158th New York Infantry. On September 29, 1864, at Chapin's Farm, Virginia, Private Grueb exhibited gallantry in advancing to the ditch of the enemy's works. Grueb was awarded his medal on April 6, 1865.

Guerin, Fritz W. Birth: New York. Private in Battery A, 1st Missouri Light Artillery. On April 28 to 29, 1863, at Grand Gulf, Mississippi, Private Guerin voluntarily took position on the steamer Cheeseman, in charge of the guns. Guerin was awarded his medal on March 10, 1896.

Guinn, Thomas. Birth: Ohio, 1836. Private in Company D, 47th Ohio Infantry. On May 22, 1863, at Vicksburg, Mississippi, Private Guin exhibited exceptional gallantry in the charge of the volunteer storming party. Guin was awarded his medal on August 21, 1894.

Gwynne, Nathaniel. Birth: Ohio. Private in Company H. 13th Ohio Cavalry. On July 30, 1864, at Petersburg, Virginia, Private Gwynne participated in a charge of the regiment even tough he was only 15 years old, and had been cautioned not to go. Gwynne suffered his left arm being crushed by a shell, and the limb had to be amputated. Gwynne was awarded his medal on January 27, 1865.

Hack, John. Birth: Germany, 1843. Private in Company B, 47th Ohio Infantry. On May 3, 1863, at Vicksburg, Mississippi, Private Hack was one of a party that volunteered and attempted to run the enemy's batteries with a steam tug and two barges loaded with subsistence stores. Hack Was awarded his medal on January 3, 1907.

Hack, Lester G. Birth: New York, 1841. Sergeant in Company F, 5th Vermont Infantry. On April 2, 1865, at Petersburg, Virginia, Sergeant Hack captured the flag of the 23rd Tennessee Infantry with several of the enemy. Hack was awarded his medal on May 10, 1865.

Hadley, Cornelius M. Birth: New York, 1838. Sergeant in Company F, 9th Michigan Cavalry. On November 20, 1863, at Knoxville, Tennessee, Sergeant Hadley voluntarily carried important dispatches through the enemy lines from General Grant to General Burnside, then besieged within Knoxville and brought back supplies. Hadley was awarded his medal on April 5, 1898.

Hadley, Osgood T. Birth: New Hampshire. Corporal in Company E, 5th New Hampshire Infantry. On September 30, 1864, at Pegram House, Virginia, Corporal Hadley, the color bearer of his regiment, defended his colors with great personal gallantry and brought them safely out of the action. Hadley was awarded his medal on July 27, 1896.

Haffee, Edmund. Birth: Pennsylvania, 1832. Quarter Gunner aboard the U.S.S. *New Ironsides*. On December 24 to 25, 1864, and January 13 to 15, 1865, at Fort Fisher, North Carolina, Haffee displayed skill and devotion in the performance of his duties. Haffee was awarded his medal on June 22, 1865.

Hagerty, Asel. Birth: Canada, 1837. Private in Company A, 61st New York Infantry. On April 6, 1865, at Sailors Creek, Virginia, Private Hagerty captured a Confederate flag. Hagerty was awarded his medal on May 10, 1865.

Haight, John H. Birth: New York, 1841. Sergeant in Company G, 72nd New York Infantry. At Williamsburg, Virginia, on May 5, 1862, Sergeant Haight carried a severely wounded comrade off the field in

John Haight (U.S. Army War College)

the face of a large force of the enemy. At Bristoe Station, Virginia, on August 27, 1862, he volunteered to search the woods for wounded, even though he was wounded himself. Haight was awarded his medal on June 8, 1888.

Haight, Sidney. Birth: Michigan, 1846. Corporal in Company E, 1st Michigan Sharpshooters. On July 30, 1864, at Petersburg, Virginia, Corporal Haight, instead of retreating, remained in the captured works, regardless of his personal safety and exposed to the firing, which he boldly and deliberately returned until the enemy was close upon him. Haight was awarded his medal on July 31, 1896.

Haley, James. Birth: Ireland, 1824. Captain of the Forecastle aboard the U.S.S. *Kearsarge*. On June 19, 1864, at Cherbourg, France, Haley was acting captain of a gun during the engagement that destroyed the C.S.S. *Alabama* and exhibited marked coolness and good conduct under fire. Haley was awarded his medal on December 31, 1864.

Hall, Francis B. Chaplain in the 16th New York Infantry. On May 3, 1863, at Salem Heights, Virginia, Chaplain Hall voluntarily exposed himself to a heavy fire during the thickest of the fight and carried wounded men to the rear for treatment and attendance. Hall was awarded his medal on February 16, 1897.

Hall, Henry Seymour. Birth: New York, 1835. Second Lieutenant in Company G, 27th New York Infantry. On June 27, 1862, at Gaines Mill, Virginia, Lieutenant Hall remained on duty and participated in the battle with his company, even though he had been wounded. Hall was awarded his medal on August 17, 1891.

Hall, Newton H. Birth: Ohio. Corporal in Company I, 104th Ohio Infantry. On November 30, 1864, at Franklin, Tennessee, Corporal Hall Captured a flag believed to belong to Stewart's Corps. Hall was awarded his medal on February 13, 1865.

Henry Hall (U.S. Army War College)

Hallock, Nathan M. Birth: New York. Private in Company K, 124th New York Infantry. On June 15, 1863, at Bristoe Station, Virginia, Private Hallock risked his life to save from death or capture a disabled officer from his company by carrying him, under a hot musketry fire, to a place of safety. Hallock was awarded his medal on September 10, 1897.

Halstead, William. Birth: New York, 1837. Coxswain aboard the U.S.S. *Brooklyn*. On August 5, 1864, at Mobile Bay, Alabama, Halstead fought his gun with skill and courage throughout the furious battle that resulted in the surrender of the ram *Tennessee* and in the damaging and destruction of batteries at Fort Morgan, Halstead was awarded his medal on December 31, 1864.

Ham, Mark G. Birth: New Hampshire, 1820. Carpenter's Mate aboard the U.S.S. *Kearsarge*. On June 19, 1864, at Cherbourg, France, Ham distinguished himself in the face of the bitter enemy fire and was highly commended by his divisional officer. Ham was awarded his medal on December 31, 1864.

Hamilton, Hugh. Birth: New York, 1830. Coxswain aboard the U.S.S. *Richmond*. On August 5, 1864, at Mobile Bay, Alabama, Hamilton performed his duties with skill and courage throughout the prolonged battle which resulted in the surrender of the ram *Tennessee* and in the successful attacks carried out on Fort Morgan. Hamilton was awarded his medal on December 31, 1864.

Hamilton, Richard. Birth: Pennsylvania, 1836. Coal Heaver aboard the U.S.S. *Picket Boat 1*. On October 27, 1864, at Roanoke River, North Carolina, Hamilton was part of the crew that made a spar torpedo attack on the Confederate ram *Albemarle*. Hamilton was awarded his medal on December 31, 1864.

Hamilton, Thomas W. Birth: Scotland, 1833. Quartermaster aboard the U.S.S. *Picket Boat 1*. On May 27, 1863, at Vicksburg, Mississippi, Hamilton was conspicuously gallant during this action, returning to his post after being severely wounded and had to be sent below. Hamilton was awarded his medal on July 10, 1863.

Hammel, Henry A. Birth: Germany. Sergeant in Battery A, 1st Missouri Light Artillery. From April 28 to 29, 1863, at Grand Gulf, Mississippi, Sergeant Hammel voluntarily took position on board the steamer Cheeseman in charge of all the guns and ammunition of the battery, and remained in charge of the same for considerable time while the steamer was unmanageable and subjected to a heavy fire from the enemy. Hammel was awarded his medal on March 10, 1896.

Hand, Allexander. Birth: Delaware, 1836. Quartermaster aboard the U.S.S. *Ceres*. On July 9, 1862, on the Roanoke River, Near Hamilton, North Carolina, Hand courageously returned the raking enemy fire and was spoken of for good conduct and cool bravery under enemy fire by the commanding officer. Hand was awarded his medal on April 3, 1863.

Haney, Milton L. Birth: Ohio. Chaplain in the 55th Illinois Infantry. On July 22, 1864, at Atlanta, Georgia, Chaplain Haney voluntarily carried a musket in the ranks of his regiment and rendered heroic service in retaking the Federal works that had been captured by the enemy. Haney was awarded his medal on November 3, 1896.

Hanford, Edward R. Birth: New York. Private in Company H, 2nd United States Cavalry. On October 9, 1864, at Woodstock, Virginia, Private Hanford captured the flag of the 32nd Battalion Virginia Cavalry. Hanford was awarded his medal on October 14, 1864.

Hanks, Joseph. Birth: Ohio. Private in Company E, 37th Ohio Infantry. On May 22, 1863, at Vicksburg, Mississippi, Private Hanks went to the rescue of a wounded comrade lying between the lines, gave him water, and brought him off the field. Hanks was awarded his medal on November 19, 1897.

Hanna, Marcus A. Birth: Maine, 1842. Sergeant in Company B, 50th Massachusetts Infantry. On July 4, 1863, at Port Hudson, Louisiana, Sergeant Hanna voluntarily exposed himself to a heavy fire to get water for comrades in the rifle pits. Hanna was awarded his medal on November 2, 1895.

Hanna, Milton. [photograph p. 90] Birth: Ohio. Corporal in Company H, 2nd Minnesota Infantry. On February 15, 1863, at Nolensville, Tennessee, Corporal Hanna was one of a detachment of 16 men who heroically defended a wagon train against

Milton Hanna (U.S. Army War College)

John Harbourne (U.S. Army War College)

Douglas Hapeman (U.S. Army War College)

the attack of 125 cavalry, repulsed the attack and saved the train. Hanna was awarded his medal on September 11, 1897.

Hanscom, Moses C. Birth: Maine. Corporal in Company F, 19th Maine Infantry. On October 14, 1863, at Bristoe Station, Virginia, Corporal Hanscom captured the flag of the 26th North Carolina. Hanscom was awarded his medal on December 1, 1864.

Hapeman, Douglas. Birth: New York, 1839. Lieutenant Colonel of the 104th Illinois Infantry. On July 20, 1864, at Peachtree Creek, Georgia, Colonel Hapeman bravely rallied his men under a severe attack, re-formed the broken ranks, and repulsed the attack. Hapeman was awarded his medal on April 5, 1898.

Harbourne, John H. Birth: England, 1840. Private in Company K, 29th Massachusetts Infantry. On June 17, 1864, at Petersburg, Virginia, Private Harbourne captured a Confederate flag. Harbourne was awarded his medal on February 24, 1897.

Harcourt, Thomas. Birth: Massachusetts, 1841. Ordinary Seaman aboard the U.S.S. *Minnesota*. On January 15, 1865, at Fort Fisher, North Carolina, Seaman Harcourt volunteered to be part of the ship's landing party. When more than two-thirds of the landing party was seized with panic from the enemy fire that killed and wounded many officers and men, Harcourt stayed with the party that remained until dark, bringing away its wounded, its arms and its colors. Harcourt was awarded his medal on June 22, 1865.

Hardenbergh, Henry M. Birth: Indiana. Private in Company G, 39th Illinois Infantry. On August 16, 1864, at Deep Bottom, Virginia, Private Hardenbergh captured a Confederate flag, though he was wounded in the shoulder. He was killed in action at Petersburg on August 28, 1864. Hardenbergh was awarded his medal on April 6, 1865.

Harding, Thomas. Birth: Connecticut, 1837. Captain of the Forecastle aboard the U.S.S. *Decotah*. On June 9, 1864, near Beaufort, North Carolina, Harding learned that one of the officers on the boat could not swim, when it was in danger of swamping. Harding told him "If we are swamped, sir, I shall carry you to the beach or I will never go there myself." Harding did not succeed in carrying out his promise, but he made repeated desperate attempts to do so, risking his own life in an effort to save his officer. Harding was awarded his medal on December 31, 1864.

Haring, Abram P. Birth: New York. First Lieutenant in Company G, 132nd New York Infantry. On February 1, 1864, at Bachelors Creek, North Carolina, Lieutenant Haring, with a command of 11 men, on picket, resisted the attack of an overwhelming force of the enemy. Haring was awarded his medal on June 28, 1890.

Harley, Bernard. Birth: New York, 1842. Ordinary Seaman aboard the U.S.S. *Picket Boat 1*. On October 27, 1864, at Roanoke River, North Carolina, Seaman Harley performed his duties with skill and courage during a spar torpedo attack on the ram *Albemarle*. Harley was awarded his medal on December 31, 1864.

Harmon, Amzi D. Birth: Pennsylvania. Corporal in Company K, 211th Pennsylvania Infantry. On April 2, 1865, at Petersburg, Virginia, Corporal Harmon captured a Confederate flag. Harmon was awarded his medal on May 20, 1865.

Harrington, Daniel. Birth: Ireland, 1849. Landsman aboard the U.S.S. *Pocahontas*. Harrington participated in a shore mission to procure meat for the ship's crew. While returning to the beach, the party was fired on from ambush and several men were hilled or wounded. Harrington was cool and courageous throughout the action, rendering gallant service against the enemy and in administering to the casualties. Harrington was awarded his medal on April 3, 1863.

Harrington, Ephraim W. Birth: Maine, 1833. Sergeant in Company G, 2nd Vermont Infantry. On May 3, 1863, at Fredericksburg, Virginia, Sergeant Harrington advanced the colors to the top of the heights and almost to the muzzle of the enemy's guns. Harrington was awarded his medal on December 13, 1893.

Harris, George W. Birth: Pennsylvania, 1835. Private in Company B, 148th Pennsylvania Infantry. On May 12, 1864, at Spotsylvania, Virginia, Private Harris captured a Confederate flag. Harris was awarded his medal on December 1, 1864.

Ephraim Harrington (Hall of Heroes)

Harris, James H. Birth: Maryland. Sergeant in Company B, 38th United States Colored Infantry. On September 29, 1864, at New Market Heights, Virginia, Sergeant Harris displayed gallantry in the assault. Harris was awarded his medal on February 18, 1874.

Harris, John. Birth: Scotland, 1839. Captain of the Forecastle aboard the U.S.S. *Metacomet*. On August 5, 1864, at Mobile Bay, Alabama, Harris braved enemy fire to aide in the rescue of ten crewmembers of the sunken U.S.S. *Tecumseh*, thereby eliciting the admiration of both friend and foe. Harris was awarded his medal on January 15, 1866.

Harris, Moses. Birth: New Hampshire. First Lieutenant in the 1st United States Cavalry. On August 28, 1864, at Smithfield, Virginia. Lieutenant Harris led an attack upon the enemy in which he exhibited personal gallantry that was so conspicuous as to inspire the men to extraordinary efforts, resulting in the complete rout of the enemy. Harris was awarded his medal on January 23, 1896.

James Harris (Hall of Heroes)

Harris, Sampson. Birth: Ohio. Private in Company K, 30th Ohio Infantry. On May 22, 1863, at Vicksburg, Mississippi, Private Harris exhibited exceptional gallantry in the charge of the volunteer storming party. Harris was awarded his medal on July 10, 1894.

Harrison, George H. Birth: Massachusetts, 1842. Seaman aboard the U.S.S. *Kearsarge*. On June 19, 1864, at Cherbourg, France, Seaman Harrison exhibited marked coolness and good conduct and was highly recommended for his gallantry under fire for the performance of his duties during the engagement with the C.S.S. *Alabama*. Harrison was awarded his medal on December 31, 1864.

Hart, John W. Birth: Germany. Sergeant in Company D, 6th Pennsylvania Infantry. On July 2, 1863, at Gettysburg, Pennsylvania, Sergeant Hart was one of six volunteers who charged a log house near Devil's Den where they captured a squad of Confederate sharpshooters. Hart was awarded his medal on August 3, 1897.

Hart, William E. Birth: New York. Private in Company B, 8th New York Cavalry. In 1864 and 1865, in the Shenandoah Valley, Virginia, Private Hart showed good conduct and services as a scout in connection with the capture of the guerrilla Harry Gilmore, and other daring acts. Hart was awarded his medal on July 3, 1872.

Hartranft, John F. [photograph p. 54] Birth: Pennsylvania, 1830. Colonel of the 4th Pennsylvania Militia. On July 21, 1861, at Bull Run, Virginia, Colonel Hartranft voluntarily served as an aide after the expiration of his term of enlistment and distinguished himself in rally-

John Hart (Hall of Heroes)

ing several regiments that had been thrown into confusion. Hartranft was awarded his medal on August 26, 1886.

Harvey, Harry. Birth: England, 1846. Corporal in Company A, 22nd New York Cavalry. On March 2, 1865, at Waynesboro, Virginia, Corporal Harvey captured a Confederate flag, along with its bearer and two other prisoners. Harvey was awarded his medal on March 26, 1865.

Haskell, Frank W. Birth: Maine, 1843. Sergeant Major of the 3rd Maine Infantry. On June 1, 1862, at Fair Oaks, Virginia, Sergeant Haskell assumed command of a portion of the left wing of his regiment after all of the officers had been killed or wounded, and led it gallantly across a stream and contributed most effectively to the success of the action. Haskell was awarded his medal on December 8, 1898.

John Hartranft (Hall of Heroes)

Haskell, Marcus M. Birth: Massachusetts. Sergeant in Company C, 35th Massachusetts Infantry. On September 17, 1862, at Antietam, Maryland, Sergeant Haskell, although wounded himself, risked his life, under a heavy fire, to rescue a badly wounded comrade and succeeded in conveying him to a place of safety. Haskell was awarded his medal on November 18, 1896.

Hastings, Smith H. Birth: Michigan, 1843. Captain of Company M, 5th Michigan Cavalry. On July 24, 1863, at Newby's Crossroads, Virginia, Captain Hastings, while in command of a squadron assigned as a rear guard of the cavalry division, was given orders to abandon a section of artillery that was in imminent danger of being captured, disregarded those orders and aided in repelling the attack and saving the guns. Hastings was awarded his medal on August 2, 1897.

Smith Hastings (U.S. Army War College)

Hatch, John P. [photograph p. 94] Birth: New York, 1822. Brigadier General, United States Volunteers. On September 14, 1862, at South Mountain, Maryland, General Hatch was severely wounded while leading one of his brigades in the attack under a heavy fire from the enemy. Hatch was awarded his medal on October 28, 1893.

John Hatch (U.S. Army War College)

Hathaway, Edward W. Birth: Massachusetts, 1838. Seaman aboard the U.S.S. *Sciota*. On June 28, 1862, at Vicksburg, Mississippi, Seaman Hathaway was struck by a bullet that severed his left arm above the elbow while displaying exceptional courage in performing his duties. The date of Hathaway's award is unknown.

Havron, John H. Birth: Ireland, 1843. Sergeant in Company G, 1st Rhode Island Light Artillery. On April 2, 1865, at Petersburg, Virginia, Sergeant Havron was one of a detachment of 20 artillerymen who voluntarily accompanied an infantry assaulting party and who turned upon the enemy the guns captured in the assault. Havron was awarded his medal on June 16, 1866.

Hawkins, Charles. Birth: Scotland, 1834. Seaman aboard the U.S.S. *Agawam*. On December 23, 1864, at Fort Fisher, North Carolina, Seaman Hawkins volunteered to be a member of the powder boat crew that attempted to blow up Fort Fisher. Hawkins was awarded his medal on December 31, 1864.

Hawkins, Gardner C. Birth: Vermont. First Lieutenant in Company E, 3rd Vermont Infantry. On April 2, 1865, at Petersburg, Virginia, Lieutenant Hawkins acted as adjutant of the regiment when the lines were wavering from well directed enemy fire. He sprang forward, and with encouraging words cheered the men, and although dangerously wounded, refused to leave the field until the enemy's works were taken. Hawkins was awarded his medal on September 30, 1893.

Martin Hawkins (Hall of Heroes)

Hawkins, Martin J. Birth: Pennsylvania. Corporal in Company A, 33rd Ohio Infantry. In April of 1862, at Big Shanty, Georgia, Corporal Hawkins was one of 22 men who captured a train at Big Shanty, Georgia, and attempted to destroy bridges and track between Chattanooga and Atlanta. Hawkins was awarded his medal in September of 1863.

Hawkins, Thomas R. Birth: Ohio. Sergeant Major of the 6th United States Colored Infantry. On September 29, 1864, at Chapin's Farm, Virginia, Sergeant Hawkins rescued the regimental colors from capture. Hawkins was awarded his medal on February 8, 1870.

Hawthorne, Harris S. Birth: New York, 1832. Corporal of Company F, 121st New York Infantry. On April 6, 1865, at Sailors Creek, Virginia, Corporal Hawthorne captured General G.W. Custis Lee. Hawthorne was awarded his medal on December 29, 1894.

Hayden, Joseph B. Birth: Maryland, 1834. Quartermaster aboard the U.S.S. *Ticonderoga*. From January 13 to 15, 1865, at Fort Fisher, North Carolina, Hayden displayed skill and courage in performing his duties during the expedition against Fort Fisher. Hayden was awarded his medal on June 22, 1865.

Hayes, John. Birth: Pennsylvania, 1831. Coxswain aboard the U.S.S. *Kearsarge*. On June 19, 1864, off Cherbourg, France, Hayes, acting as second captain of the Number 2 gun during this bitter engagement, exhibited marked coolness and good conduct and was highly recommended for his gallantry under fire by the divisional officer. Hayes was awarded his medal on December 31, 1864.

Hayes, Thomas. Birth: Rhode Island, 1840. Coxswain aboard the U.S.S. *Richmond*. On August 5, 1864, at Mobile Bay, Alabama, Hayes performed his duties in a cool and courageous manner throughout the prolonged action. Hayes was awarded his medal on December 31, 1864.

Haynes, Asbury F. Birth: Maine. Corporal in Company F, 17th Maine Infantry. On April 6, 1865, at Sailors Creek, Virginia, Corporal Haynes captured a Confederate flag. Haynes was awarded his medal on May 10, 1865.

Hays, John H. Birth: Ohio, 1844. Private in Company F, 4th Iowa Cavalry. On April 16, 1865, at Columbus, Georgia, Private Hays captured the flag and bearer of Austin's Battery. Hays was awarded his medal on May 10, 1865.

Healey, George W. Birth: Iowa. Private in Company E, 5th Iowa

George Healey (Hall of Heroes)

John Hays (U.S. Army War College)

Cavalry. On July 29, 1864, at Newnan, Georgia, Private Healey was nearly surrounded by the enemy when he captured a Confederate soldier. Later, after being joined by a comrade, he captured four more prisoners. Healey was awarded his medal on January 13, 1899.

Hedges, Joseph. Birth: Ohio, 1836. First Lieutenant in the 4th United States Cavalry. On December 17, 1864, at Harpeth River, Tennessee, Lieutenant Hedges, at the head of his regiment, charged a field battery with strong infantry supports, broke the enemy's line and with other mounted troops, captured 3 guns and many prisoners. Hedges was awarded his medal on April 5, 1898.

Heermance, William L. Birth: New York, 1837. Captain of Company C, 6th New York Cavalry. On April 30, 1863, at Chancellorsville, Virginia, Captain Heermance took command of the regiment as its senior officer when it was surrounded by J.E. B. Stuart's cavalry. The regiment cut its way through the enemy's line and escaped capture, but Heermance was desperately wounded and left for dead. He was later taken prisoner. Heermance was awarded his medal on March 30, 1898.

William Heermance (U.S. Army War College)

Heller, Henry. Birth: 1841 Sergeant in Company A, 66th Ohio Infantry. On May 2, 1863, at Chancellorsville, Virginia, Sergeant Heller was one of a party of four who voluntarily brought into the Union lines a wounded Confederate officer from whom valuable information was obtained. Heller was awarded his medal on July 29, 1892.

Helms, David H. Birth: Indiana. Private in Company B, 83rd Indiana Infantry. On May 22, 1863, at Vicksburg, Mississippi, Private Helms exhibited exceptional gallantry in the charge of the volunteer storming party. Helms was awarded his medal on July 26, 1894.

Henry, Guy V. Birth: Oklahoma. Colonel of the 40th Massachusetts Infantry. On June 1, 1864, at Cold Harbor, Virginia, Colonel Henry led the assaults of his brigade upon the enemy's works, where he had 2 horses shot under him. Henry was awarded his medal on December 5, 1893.

Henry, James. Birth: Ohio. Sergeant in Company B, 113th Illinois Infantry. On May 22, 1863, at Vicksburg, Mississippi, Sergeant Henry exhibited exceptional gallantry in the charge of the volunteer storming party. Henry was awarded his medal on July 9, 1894.

Guy Henry (Hall of Heroes)

Henry, William W. [photograph p. 97] Birth: Vermont, 1831. Colonel of the 19th Vermont Infantry. On October 19, 1864, at Cedar Creek, Virginia, Colonel Henry,

William Henry (U.S. Army War College)

though severely wounded, led his regiment in a charge that recaptured the guns of an abandoned battery. Henry was awarded his medal on December 21, 1892.

Herington, Pitt B. Birth: Michigan, 1840. Private in Company E, 11th Iowa Infantry. On June 15, 1864, at Kennesaw Mountain, Georgia, Private Herington, with a comrade, rescued a wounded comrade from between the lines, under a tremendous fire from the enemy. Herington was awarded his medal on November 27, 1899.

Herron, Francis J. Birth: Pennsylvania, 1837. Lieutenant Colonel of the 9th Iowa Infantry. On May 7, 1862, at Pea Ridge, Arkansas, Colonel Herron was foremost in leading his men, rallying them to repeated acts of daring, until himself disabled and taken prisoner. Herron was awarded his medal on September 26, 1893.

Hesseltine, Francis S. Birth: Maine, 1833. Colonel of the 13th Maine Infantry. From December 29 to 30, 1863, at Matagorda Bay, Texas, Colonel Hesseltine, in command of a detachment of 100 men, conducted a reconnaissance for two days, baffling and beating

Francis Hesseltine (U.S. Army War College)

Francis Herron (U.S. Army War College)

back an attacking force of more than a thousand Confederate cavalry. Hesseltine was awarded his medal on March 2, 1895.

Hibson, Joseph C. Birth: England, 1843. Private in Company C, 48th New York Infantry. On July 14, 1863, at Fort Wagner, South Carolina, Private Hibson responded to a call for a volunteer to reconnoiter the enemy's position, and went within the enemy's lines under fire and was exposed to great danger. Hibson was awarded his medal on October 23, 1897.

Hickey, Dennis W. Birth: New York. Sergeant in Company E, 2nd New York Cavalry. On June 29, 1864, at Stony Creek Bridge, Virginia, Sergeant Hickey, with a detachment of three men, tore up the bridge at Stony Creek being the last man on the bridge and covering the retreat until he was shot down. Hickey was awarded his medal on April 18, 1891.

Hickman, John. Birth: Virginia, 1837. Second Class Fireman aboard the U.S.S. *Richmond*. On March 14, 1863, at Port Hudson, Louisiana, Hickman showed exceptional courage in the performance of his duties. The Richmond had been hit by a Confederate shot, rupturing the steam valves in the fire room, and filling the room with steam. Hickman continued to keep the fires stoked and the ship under power until the gravity of the situation had been lessened. He was awarded his medal on July 10, 1863.

Hickok, Nathan E. Birth: Connecticut. Corporal in Company A, 8th Connecticut Infantry. On September 29, 1864, at Chapin's Farm, Virginia, Corporal Hickok captured a Confederate flag. Hickok was awarded his medal on April 6, 1865.

Higby, Charles. Birth: Pennsylvania. Private in Company F, 1st Pennsylvania Cavalry. From March 29 to April 9, 1865, in the Appomattox Campaign, Private Higby captured a Confederate flag. Higby was awarded his medal on May 3, 1865.

Higgins, Thomas J. Birth: Canada. Sergeant in Company D, 99th Illinois Infantry. On May 22, 1863, at Vicksburg, Mississippi, Sergeant Higgins continued to advance the colors, even after his regiment fell back, planting them on the parapet of the enemy, where he was captured. Higgins was awarded his medal on April 1, 1898.

Edward Hill (U.S. Army War College)

Highland, Patrick. Birth: Ireland. Corporal in Company D, 23rd Illinois Infantry. On April 2, 1865, at Petersburg, Virginia, Corporal Highland exhibited conspicuous gallantry as color bearer in the assault on Fort Gregg. Highland was awarded his medal on May 12, 1865.

Hill, Edward. Birth: New York, 1835. Captain of Company K, 6th Michigan Infantry. On June 1, 1864, at Cold Harbor, Virginia, Hill led the brigade skirmish line in a desperate charge on the enemy's masked batteries to the muzzles of the guns, where he was severely wounded. Hill was awarded his medal on December 4, 1893.

Hill, Henry. Birth: Pennsylvania. Corporal in Company C, 50th Pennsylvania Infantry. On May 6, 1864, at the Wilderness, Virginia, Corporal Hill and a companion refused to fall back when the rest of the regiment retired, but advanced instead and continued firing upon the enemy until the regiment re-formed and regained its position. Hiss was awarded his medal on September 23, 1897.

Hill, James. Birth: England, 1845. First Lieutenant in Company I, 21st Iowa Infantry. On May 16, 1863, at Champion Hill, Mississippi, Lieutenant Hill captured three of the enemy's pickets. Hill was awarded his medal on March 15, 1893.

James Hill [New York] (Hall of Heroes)

Hill, James. Birth: New York. Sergeant in Company C, 14th New York Heavy Artillery. On July 30, 1864, at Petersburg, Virginia, Sergeant Hill captured a Confederate flag after shooting down the officer holding them who was trying to rally his men. Hill was awarded his medal on December 1, 1864.

Hilliker, Benjamin F. Birth: New York, 1843. Musician in Company A, 8th Wisconsin Infantry. On June 4, 1863, at Mechanicsburg, Mississippi, Hilliker volunteered to oppose a superior Confederate force. He put aside his drum and picked up a musket, proceeding to the front of the skirmish line. While bravely opposing the enemy, Hilliker was shot in the head with a minie ball and thought to be mortally wounded, but he fully recovered. Hilliker was awarded his medal on December 17, 1897.

Hills, William G. Birth: New York, 1841. Private in Company E, 9th New York Cavalry. On September 26, 1864, at North Fork, Virginia, Private Hills volunteered to carry a severely wounded comrade out of a heavy fire of the enemy. Hills was awarded his medal on September 26, 1893.

Hilton, Alfred B. Birth: Maryland. Sergeant in Company H, 4th United States Colored Infantry. On September 29, 1864, at Chapin's Farm, Virginia, Sergeant Hilton seized the colors after the bearer had been shot down, advancing them forward until disabled at the enemy's inner line. Hilton was awarded his medal on April 6, 1865.

Hincks, William B. Birth: Maine. Sergeant Major in the 14th Connecticut Infantry. On July 3, 1863, at Gettysburg, Pennsylvania, Sergeant Hincks captured the flag of the 14th Tennessee Infantry during Pickets charge. Hincks was awarded his medal on December 1, 1864.

William Hincks (Hall of Heroes)

Hinnecan, William. Birth: Ireland, 1841. Second Class Fireman aboard the U.S.S. *Agawam*. On December 31, 1864, at Fort Fisher, North Carolina, Fireman Hinnecan volunteered to be part of the crew of the powder boat intended to blow up Fort Fisher. Hinnecan was awarded his medal on December 31, 1864.

Hodges, Addison J. Birth: Michigan, 1841. Private in Company B, 47th Ohio Infantry. On May 3, 1863, at Vicksburg, Mississippi, Private Hodges was one of the party that volunteered and attempted to run the enemy's batteries with a steam tug and two barges loaded with subsistence stores. Hodges was awarded his medal on December 13, 1907.

Hoffman, Henry. Birth: Germany. Corporal in Company M, 2nd Ohio Cavalry. On April 6, 1865, at Sailors Creek, Virginia, Corporal Hoffman captured a Confederate flag. Hoffman was awarded his medal on May 3, 1865.

Hoffman, Thomas W. Birth: Pennsylvania. Captain in Company A, 208th Pennsylvania Infantry. On April 2, 1865, at Petersburg, Virginia, Captain Hoffman prevented a retreat of his regiment during the battle. Hoffman was awarded his medal on July 19, 1895.

Hogan, Franklin. Birth: Pennsylvania. Corporal in Company A, 45th Pennsylvania Infantry. On July 30, 1864, at Petersburg, Virginia, Corporal Hogan captured the flag of the 6th Virginia Infantry. Hogan was awarded his medal on October 1, 1864.

William Hogarty (Hall of Heroes)

Hogarty, William P. Birth: New York. Private in Company D, 23rd New York Infantry. On September 17, 1862, at Antietam, Maryland, Private Hogarty exhibited distinguished gallantry in action with the battery. Hogarty was awarded his medal on June 22, 1891.

Holcomb, Daniel I. Birth: Ohio. Private in Company A, 41st Ohio Infantry. On December 16, 1864, at Brentwood Hills, Tennessee, Private Holcomb captured a Confederate guidon. Holcomb was awarded his medal on February 22, 1865.

Holehouse, James. Birth: England, 1839. Private in Company B, 7th Massachusetts Infantry. On May 3, 1863, at Marye's Heights, Fredericksburg, Virginia, Private Holehouse voluntarily and with conspicuous daring advanced beyond his regiment, which had been broken in the assault, and halted beneath the crest, Following the example, the colors were brought to the summit, and the regiment was advanced and held the position. Holehouse was awarded his medal on September 10, 1897.

Holland, Lemuel F. Birth: Ohio, 1840. Corporal in Company D, 104th Illinois Infantry. On July 2, 1863, at Elk River, Tennessee, Corporal Holland was part of a party that, under heavy fire, captured a stockade and saved the bridge. Holland was awarded his medal on October 30, 1897.

Milton Holland (Hall of Heroes)

William Holmes (Hall of Heroes)

Charles Holton (U.S. Army War College)

Holland, Milton M. Birth: Texas, 1844. Sergeant Major of the 5th United States Colored Infantry. On September 29, 1864, at Chapin's Farm, Virginia, Sergeant Holland took command of Company C, after all of the officers had been killed or wounded, and gallantly led it forward. Holland was awarded his medal on April 6, 1865.

Hollat, George. Third Class Boy aboard the U.S.S. *Varuna*. On April 24, 1862, at Forts Jackson and St. Philip, south of New Orleans, Hollat rendered gallant service through the perilous action and remained steadfast and courageous at his battle station despite extremely heavy fire. Hollat was awarded his medal on April 3, 1863.

Holmes, Lovilo N. Birth: New York, 1830. First Sergeant in Company H, 2nd Minnesota Infantry. On February 15, 1863, at Nolensville, Tennessee, Sergeant Holmes was one of a detachment of 16 men who heroically defended a wagon train against the attack of 125 Confederate cavalry, repulsed the attack and saved the train. Holmes was awarded his medal on September 11, 1897.

Holmes, William T. Birth: Illinois. Private in Company A, 3rd Indiana Cavalry. On April 6, 1865, at Sailors Creek, Virginia, Private Holmes captured the flag of the 27th Virginia Infantry. Holmes was awarded his medal on May 3, 1865.

Holton, Charles M. Birth: New York, 1838. First Sergeant in Company A, 7th Michigan Cavalry. On July 14, 1863, at Falling Waters, Virginia, Sergeant Holton captured the flag of the 55th Virginia Infantry. Holton was awarded his medal on March 21, 1899.

Lovilo Holmes (U.S. Army War College)

Holton, Edward A. Birth: Vermont. First Sergeant of Company I, 6th Vermont Infantry. On April 16, 1862, at Lees Mills, Virginia, Sergeant Holton rescued the regimental colors under a heavy fire. Holton was awarded his medal on July 9, 1892.

Homan, Conrad. Birth: Massachusetts. Color Sergeant of Company A, 29th Massachusetts Infantry. On July 30, 1864, at Petersburg, Virginia, Sergeant Homan fought his way through the enemy lines with the regimental colors after the rest of the color guard had been killed or captured. Homan was awarded his medal on June 3, 1869.

Hooker, George W. Birth: New York. First Lieutenant of Company E, 4th Vermont Infantry. On September 14, 1862, at South Mountain, Maryland, Lieutenant Hooker rode alone, in advance of his regiment, into the enemy's lines and before his own men came up received the surrender of the major of the Confederate regiment, together with the colors and 116 men, Hooker was awarded his medal on September 17, 1891.

Charles Hopkins (Hall of Heroes)

Hooper, William B. Birth: Connecticut. Corporal of Company L, 1st New Jersey Cavalry. On March 31, 1865, at Chamberlains Creek, Virginia, Corporal Hooper, with the assistance of a comrade, headed off the advance of the enemy, shooting two of his color bearers and posted himself between the enemy and the lead horses of his own command, thus saving the herd from capture. Hooper was awarded his medal on July 3, 1865.

Hopkins, Charles F. Birth: New Jersey. Corporal in Company I, 1st New Jersey Infantry. On June 27, 1862, at Gaines Mill, Virginia, Corporal Hopkins voluntarily carried a wounded comrade to safety under a heavy fire from the enemy. Hopkins was awarded his medal on July 9, 1892.

Horan, Thomas. Sergeant in Company E, 72nd New York Infantry. On July 2, 1863, at Gettysburg, Pennsylvania, Sergeant Horan captured the flag of the 8th Florida Infantry. Horan was awarded his medal on April 5, 1898.

Horne, Samuel B. Birth: Ireland, 1843. Captain of Company H, 11th Connecticut Infantry. On September 29, 1864, at Fort Harrison, Virginia, Captain Horne, while acting as an aide and carrying important messages, was severely wounded and his horse killed, but delivered the order and rejoined his general. Horne was awarded his medal on November 19, 1897.

Horsfall, William H. Birth, Kentucky, 1847. Drummer in Company G, 1st Kentucky Infantry. On May 21, 1862, at Corinth, Mississippi, Horsfall saved the life of a wounded officer lying between the lines. Horsfall was awarded his medal on August 17, 1895.

Horton, James. Birth: Massachusetts, 1838. Seaman aboard the U.S.S. *Montauk*. On September 21, 1864, when fire was discovered in the magazine light room, Seaman Horton rushed into the cabin, obtained the magazine keys, sprang into the light room and began passing put combustibles, including the box of signals in which the fire originated. Horton was awarded his medal on June 22, 1865.

Horton, Lewis A. Birth: Massachusetts, 1839. Seaman aboard the U.S.S. *Rhode Island*. On December 30, 1862, Seaman Horton participated in the hazardous task of rescuing the crew of the sinking U.S.S. *Monitor*. Horton was awarded his medal on June 22, 1865.

Hottenstine, Solomon J. Birth: Pennsylvania. Private in Company C, 107th Pennsylvania Infantry. On August 19, 1864, at Petersburg, Virginia, along the Petersburg and Norfolk Railroad, Hottenstine captured a flag belonging to a North Carolina regiment. Hottenstine was awarded his medal on February 2, 1865.

Ira Hough (U.S. Army War College)

Hough, Ira. Birth: Indiana, 1843. Private in Company E, 8th Indiana Infantry. On October 19, 1864, at Cedar Creek, Virginia, Private Hough captured a Confederate flag. Hough was awarded his medal on October 26, 1864.

Houghton, Charles H. Birth: New York, 1842. Captain in Company L, 14th New York Heavy Artillery. On July 30, 1864, at Petersburg, Virginia, Captain Houghton participated in the assault at the Crater. On March 25, 1865, at Petersburg, Virginia, he was conspicuous in the fighting at Fort Haskell, exposing himself to great danger, and being three times wounded, and suffering the loss of a leg. Houghton was awarded his medal on April 5, 1898.

Houghton, Edward J. Birth: Alabama, 1843. Ordinary Seaman aboard the U.S.S. *Picket Boat 1*. On October 27, 1864, at the Roanoke River, North Carolina, Seaman Houghton participated in the spar torpedo attack on the ram *Albemarle*, and displayed coolness and skill in the performance of his duties. Houghton was awarded his medal on December 31, 1864.

Houghton, George L. Birth: Canada. Alabama. Private in Company D, 104th Illinois Infantry. On July 2, 1863, at Elk River, Tennessee, Private Houghton voluntarily joined a party that, under a heavy fire, captured a stockade and saved the bridge. Houghton was awarded his medal on March 27, 1900.

Charles Houghton (U.S Army War College)

Houlton, William. Birth: New York. Commissary Sergeant of the 1st West Virginia Cavalry. On April 6, 1865, at Sailors

Creek, Virginia, Sergeant Houlton captured a Confederate flag. Houlton was awarded his medal on May 3, 1865.

Howard, Henderson C. Birth: 1839 Corporal in Company B, 11th Pennsylvania Infantry Reserves. On June 30, 1862, at Glendale, Virginia, Corporal Howard pursued an enemy sharpshooter when he encountered two more, whom he bayoneted in hand-to-hand combat, receiving three wounds in the process. Howard was awarded his medal on March 30, 1898.

Howard, Hiram R. Birth: Ohio, 1843. Private in Company H, 11th Ohio Infantry. On November 25, 1863, at Missionary Ridge, Tennessee, Private Howard scaled the enemy's works and in a hand-to-hand fight helped capture the flag of the 18th Alabama Infantry. Howard was awarded his medal on July 29, 1892.

Hiram Howard (U.S. Army War College)

Howard, James. Birth: New Jersey. Sergeant in Company K, 158th New York Infantry. On April 2, 1865, at Battery Wagner, near Petersburg, Sergeant Howard carried the colors in advance of the line of battle, the flagstaff being shot off while he was planting the flag on the parapet of the fort. Howard was awarded his medal on May 12, 1865.

Howard, Martin. Birth: Ireland, 1843. Landsman aboard the U.S.S. *Tacony*. On October 31, 1864, Landsman Howard carried out his duties faithfully during the capture of Plymouth, and distinguished himself by a display of coolness when he participated in landing and spiking a 9-inch gun while under a devastating fire from the enemy. Howard was awarded his medal on December 31, 1864.

Howard, Oliver O. [photograph p. 105] Birth: Maine, 1830. Brigadier General, U.S. Volunteers. On June 1, 1862, at Fair Oaks, Virginia, General Howard led the 61st New York Infantry in a charge in which he was twice severely wounded in the right arm, necessitating amputation. Howard was awarded his medal on March 29, 1893.

James Howard (Hall of Heroes)

Howard, Peter. Birth: France, 1829. Boatswain's Mate aboard the U.S.S. *Tacony*. On March 14, 1863, at Port Hudson, Louisiana, Howard served courageously throughout the battle, in which a steady fire was kept up against the enemy until the ship was enveloped in flames and abandoned. Howard was awarded his medal on July 10, 1863.

The Recipients — Hudson

Oliver O. Howard (U.S. Army War College)

Orion Howe (U.S Army War College)

Howard, Squire E. Birth: Vermont. First Sergeant in Company H, 8th Vermont Infantry. On January 14, 1863, at Bayou Teche, Louisiana, Sergeant Howard volunteered to carry an important message through the heavy fire of the enemy to bring aid and save the gunboat Calhoun. Howard was awarded his medal on January 29, 1894.

Howe, Orion P. Birth: Ohio, 1848. Musician in Company C, 5th Illinois Infantry. On May 19, 1863, at Vicksburg, Mississippi, Howe, a fourteen year old drummer boy, was severely wounded but remained on the field of battle until he had reported to General Sherman the necessity of supplying cartridges to the troops under the command of Colonel Malmborg. Howe was awarded his medal on April 23, 1896.

Howe, William H. Birth: Massachusetts. Sergeant in Company K, 29th Massachusetts Infantry. On March 25, 1865, at Fort Stedman, Virginia, Sergeant Howe served an abandoned gun under heavy fire. Howe was awarded his medal on March 25, 1865.

Hubbell, William S. Birth: Connecticut, 1837. Captain of Company A, 21st Connecticut Infantry. On September 30, 1864, at Fort Harrison, Virginia, Captain Hubbell led out a small flanking party and by a clash and at great risk captured a large number of prisoners. Hubbell was awarded his medal on June 13, 1894.

Hudson, Aaron R. Birth: Kentucky. Private in Company C, 17th Indiana Mounted Infantry. In April of 1865, at Culloden, Georgia, Private Hudson captured the flag of the Confederate Worrill Grays. Hudson was awarded his medal on June 17, 1865.

Hudson, Michael. Birth: Ireland, 1834. Sergeant in the U.S. Marine Corps serving aboard the U.S.S. *Brooklyn*. On August 5, 1864, at Mobile Bay, Alabama, Sergeant Hudson fought his gun with skill and courage throughout the furious two hour battle that resulted in the surrender of the ram *Tennessee*. Hudson was awarded his medal on December 31, 1864.

Hughes, Oliver. Birth: Tennessee, 1841. Corporal in Company C, 12th Kentucky Infantry. On June 24, 1864, at Weldon Railroad, Virginia, Corporal Hughes captured the flag of the 11th South Carolina Infantry. Hughes was awarded his medal on August 1, 1865.

Hughey, John. Birth: Ohio. Corporal in Company L, 2nd Ohio Cavalry. On April 6, 1865, at Sailors Creek, Virginia, Corporal Hughey Captured the flag of the 38th Virginia. Hughey was awarded his medal on May 3, 1865.

Huidekoper, Henry S. Birth: Pennsylvania, 1839. Lieutenant Colonel of the 150th Pennsylvania Infantry. On July 1, 1863, at Gettysburg, Pennsylvania, Colonel Huidekoper, while engaged in repelling an attack of the enemy, received a severe wound to his right arm, but instead of retiring, remained at the front in command of the regiment. Huidekoper was awarded his medal on May 27, 1905.

Hunt, Louis T. Birth: Indiana. Private in Company H, 6th Missouri Infantry. On May 22, 1863, at Vicksburg, Mississippi, Private Hunt exhibited exceptional gallantry in the charge of the volunteer storming party. Hunt was awarded his medal on July 12, 1894.

Hunter, Charles A. Birth: Massachusetts, 1843. Sergeant in Company E, 34th Massachusetts Infantry. On April 2, 1865, at Petersburg, Virginia, Sergeant Hunter carried the regimental flag in the assault on Fort Gregg and was among the foremost to enter the works. Hunter was awarded his medal on May 12, 1865.

Henry Huidekoper (Hall of Heroes)

Hunterson, John C. Birth: Pennsylvania. Private in Company B, 3rd Pennsylvania Cavalry. On June 5, 1862, on the Virginia Peninsula, Private Hunterson, while under fire between the two armies, voluntarily gave up his horse to an engineer officer whom he was accompanying on a reconnaissance and whose horse had been killed, thus enabling the officer to escape with valuable papers in his possession. Hunterson was awarded his medal on August 2, 1897.

John Hunterson (Hall of Heroes)

Huskey, Michael. Birth: New York, 1841. Fireman aboard the U.S.S. *Carondelet*. In March of 1863, at Deer Creek, Mississippi, Huskey volunteered to aid in the rescue of the tug *Ivy*, under the fire of the enemy, and set fort meritorious conduct during this hazardous mission. Huskey was awarded his medal on April 16, 1864.

Hyatt, Theodore. Birth: Pennsylvania, 1830. First Sergeant in Company D, 127th Illinois Infantry. On May 22, 1863, at Vicksburg, Mississippi, Sergeant Hyatt exhibited exceptional gallantry in the charge of the volunteer storming party. Hyatt was awarded his medal on July 9, 1894.

Hyde, Thomas W. Birth: Italy. Major of the 7th Maine. On September 17, 1862, at Antietam, Maryland, Major Hyde led his regiment in an assault on a strong body of the enemy's infantry and kept up the fight until the greater part of his men had been killed or wounded, bringing the remainder safely out of the fight. Hyde was awarded his medal on April 8, 1891.

Samuel Hymer (Hall of Heroes)

Hyland, John. Birth: Ireland, 1819. Seaman aboard the U.S.S. *Signal*. On May 5, 1864, at Red River, Louisiana, Seaman Hyland, although wounded, courageously went in full view of several hundred sharpshooters and let go the anchor, to slip the cable, when he was again wounded by the raking enemy fire. Hyland was awarded his medal on December 31, 1864.

Hymer, Samuel. Birth: Indiana, 1829. Captain of Company D, 115th Illinois Infantry. On October 13, 1864, at Buzzard's Roost Gap, Georgia, Captain Hymer, with only 41 men under his command, defended a blockhouse against the attack of Hood's Division for nearly 10 hours, thus checking the advance of the enemy and insuring the safety of the balance of the regiment, as well as that of the 8th Kentucky Infantry, then stationed at Ringgold, Georgia. Hymer was awarded his medal on March 28, 1896.

Ilgenfritz, Charles H. Birth: Pennsylvania, 1837. Sergeant of Company E,

Charles Ilgenfritz (U.S. Army War College)

207th Pennsylvania Infantry. On April 2, 1865, at Fort Sedgwick, Virginia, Sergeant Ilgenfritz, the color bearer, while pierced by seven balls, sprang forward and grasped the colors, planting them on the enemy's fort amid a murderous fire of grape, canister, and musketry. The date of Ilgenfritz's award is unknown.

Immell, Lorenzo D. Birth: Ohio. Corporal in Company F, 2nd United States Artillery. On August 10, 1861, at Wilson's Creek, Missouri, Corporal Immell displayed exceptional bravery in action. Immell was awarded his medal on July 19, 1890.

Lorenzo Immell (Hall of Heroes)

Ingalls, Lewis J. Birth: Massachusetts. Private in Company K, 8th Vermont Infantry. On September 4, 1862, at Boutte Station, Louisiana, Private Ingalls was one of 60 guards on a train that was sidetracked by a misplaced switch into an ambuscade. Ingalls, under a severe fire in which he was wounded, ran to another switch and opening it enabled the train and the surviving guards to escape. Ingalls was awarded his medal on October 20, 1899.

Inscho, Leonidus H. Birth: Ohio, 1840. Corporal in Company E, 12th Ohio Infantry. On September 14, 1862, at South Mountain, Maryland, Corporal Inscho, alone and unaided, and with his left hand disabled, captured a Confederate captain and four men. Inscho was awarded his medal on January 31, 1894.

Irlam, Joseph. Birth: England, 1840. Seaman aboard the U.S.S. *Brooklyn*. On August 5, 1864, at Mobile Bay, Alabama, Seaman Irlam carried on his duties at the wheel with only one other person after releasing all others with him to serve as replacements for men struck down at their guns. Irlam was awarded his medal on December 31, 1864.

Irsch, Francis. Birth: 1840. Captain of Company D, 45th New York Infantry. On July 1, 1863, at Gettysburg, Pennsylvania, Captain Irsch flanked the enemy and captured a number of prisoners and held a part of the town while the army was rallying on Cemetery Hill. Irsch was awarded his medal on May 27, 1892.

Irving, John. Birth: New York, 1839. Coxswain aboard the U.S.S. *Brooklyn*. On August 5, 1864, at Mobile Bay, Alabama, Irving exhibited exceptional gallantry in the performance of his duties during the battle that resulted in the surrender of the ram *Tennessee*. Irving was awarded his medal on December 31, 1864.

Irving, Thomas. Birth: England, 1842. Coxswain aboard the U.S.S. *Lehigh*. On November 16, 1863, at Charleston Harbor, South Carolina, Coxswain Irving assisted in the attempt to free the grounded Lehigh by rowing a small boat to transfer hawsers for the purpose of pulling the ship off the bar. Irving twice succeeded in making the trip, under heavy fire. Irving was awarded his medal on April 16, 1864.

Irwin, Nicholas. Birth: Denmark, 1833. Seaman aboard the U.S.S. *Brooklyn*. On August 5, 1864, at Mobile Bay, Alabama, Seaman Irwin displayed exceptional gallantry in the performance of his duties during the prolonged battle that resulted in the surrender of the ram *Tennessee*. Irwin was awarded his medal on December 31, 1864.

Irwin, Patrick. Birth: Ireland, 1839. First Sergeant in Company H, 14th Michigan Infantry. On September 1, 1864, at Jonesboro, Georgia, Sergeant Irwin participated in a charge of the regiment and was the first man over the line of enemy works, demanding and receiving the surrender of General Daniel Govan and his command. Irwin was awarded his medal on April 28, 1896.

Jackson, Frederick R. Birth: Connecticut, 1844. First Sergeant in Company F, 7th Connecticut Infantry. On June 16, 1862, at James Island, South Carolina, Sergeant Jackson had his left arm shot away during a charge on the enemy. Jackson continued on, taking part in the second and third assaults on the position, until he fell exhausted from loss of blood. Jackson was awarded his medal in 1863.

Jacobson, Eugene P. Sergeant Major of the 74th New York Infantry. On May 2, 1863, at Chancellorsville, Virginia, Sergeant Jacobson exhibited bravery in conducting a scouting party in front of the enemy. Jacobson was awarded his medal on March 29, 1865.

James, Isaac. Birth: Ohio. Private in Company H, 110th Ohio Infantry. On April 2, 1865, at Petersburg, Virginia, Private James captured a Confederate flag. James was awarded his medal on May 10, 1865.

James, John H. Birth: Massachusetts, 1835. Captain of the Top aboard the U.S.S. *Richmond*. On August 5, 1864, at Mobile Bay, Alabama, James exhibited exceptional gallantry in the performance of his duties throughout the furious two hour battle that resulted in the surrender of the ram *Tennessee*. James was awarded his medal on December 31, 1864.

James, Miles. Birth: Virginia, 1829. Corporal in Company B, 36th United States Colored Infantry. On September 30, 1864, at Chapin's Farm, Virginia, Corporal James had his arm mutilated by enemy fire. He made an immediate amputation of the limb and continued loading and discharging his musket with one arm, while urging his men forward, within 30 yards of the enemy works. James was awarded his medal on April 6, 1865.

Jamieson, Walter. Birth: France, 1842. First Sergeant in Company B, 139th New York Infantry. On July 30, 1864, at Petersburg, Virginia, Sergeant

Walter Jamieson (U.S. Army War College)

James Jardine (U.S. Army War College)

Benjamin Jellison (Hall of Heroes)

Erastus Jewett (U.S. Army War College)

Jamieson seized the regimental color after the color bearer had been shot down, and advanced it forward, planting it upon the fort in full view of the entire brigade. Jamieson was awarded his medal on April 5, 1898.

Jardine, James. Birth: Scotland, 1837. Sergeant in Company F, 54th Ohio Infantry. On May 22, 1863, at Vicksburg, Mississippi, Sergeant Jardine exhibited exceptional gallantry in the charge of the volunteer storming party. Jardine was awarded his medal on April 5, 1894.

Jellison, Benjamin H. Birth: Massachusetts. Sergeant in Company C, 19th Massachusetts Infantry. On July 3, 1863, at Gettysburg, Pennsylvania, Sergeant Jellison captured the flag of the 75th Virginia Infantry. Jellison was awarded his medal on December 1, 1864.

Jenkins, Thomas. Seaman aboard the U.S.S. *Cincinnati*. On May 27, 1863, at Vicksburg, Mississippi, Seaman Jenkins was conspicuously cool during this action, under the fire of the enemy, never ceasing to fight until the proud ship went down. Jenkins was awarded his medal on July 10, 1863.

Jennings, James T. Birth: England, 1818. Private in Company K, 56th Pennsylvania Infantry. On August 20, 1864, at Weldon Railroad, Virginia, Private Jennings captured the flag of the 55th North Carolina Infantry. Jennings was awarded his medal on December 1, 1864.

Jewett, Erastus W. Birth: Vermont, 1839. First Lieutenant in Company A, 9th Vermont Infantry. On February 2, 1864, at Newport Barracks, North Carolina, Lieutenant Jewett kept a superior force of the enemy at bay by long and persistent resistance by burning bridges, and thus covered the retreat of the garrison. Jewett was awarded his medal on September 8, 1891.

John, William. Birth: Germany. Private in Company E, 37th Ohio Infantry. On May 22, 1863, at Vicksburg, Mississippi, Private John exhibited exceptional gallantry in the charge of the volunteer storming party. John was awarded his medal on July 14, 1894.

Johndro, Franklin. Birth: Vermont. Private in Company A, 118th New York Infantry. On September 30,

1864, at Chapin's Farm, Virginia, Private Johndro captured 40 Confederate prisoners. Johndro was awarded his medal on April 6, 1865.

Johns, Elisha. Birth: Ohio, 1837. Corporal in Company B, 113th Illinois Infantry. On May 22, 1863, at Vicksburg, Mississippi, Corporal Johns exhibited exceptional gallantry in the charge of the volunteer storming party. Johns was awarded his medal on August 9, 1894. (In some listings, the last name is spelled Jones.)

Johns, Henry T. Private in Company C, 49th Massachusetts Infantry. On May 27, 1863, at Port Hudson, Louisiana, Private Johns volunteered in response to a call and took part in the movement that was made upon the enemy's works under a heavy fire there from. Johns was awarded his medal on November 25, 1893.

Johnson, Andrew. Birth: Ohio. Private in Company G, 116th Illinois Infantry. On May 22, 1863, at Vicksburg, Mississippi, Private Johnson exhibited exceptional gallantry in the charge of the volunteer storming party. Johnson was awarded his medal on August 9, 1894.

Johnson, Follett. Birth: New York, 1843. Corporal in Company H, 60th New York Infantry. On May 27, 1864, at New Hope Church, Georgia, Corporal Johnson voluntarily exposed himself to the fire of a sharpshooter enabling a comrade to shoot the sharpshooter. Johnson was awarded his medal on April 6, 1892.

Johnson, Henry. Birth: Norway, 1824. Seaman aboard the U.S.S. *Metacomet*. On August 5, 1864, at Mobile Bay, Alabama, Seaman Johnson braved enemy fire to aide in rescuing ten crew member of the *Tecumseh* after that vessel had been struck by a torpedo. Johnson was awarded his medal on February 23, 1867.

Johnson, John. Birth: Norway, 1842. Private in Company D, 2nd Wisconsin Infantry. On December 13, 1862, at Fredericksburg, Virginia, Private Johnson exhibited conspicuous gallantry in battle in which he was severely wounded while serving as connoneer manning the positions of fallen gunners. Johnson was awarded his medal on August 28, 1893.

Joseph Johnson (U.S. Army War College)

Johnson, Joseph E. Birth: Pennsylvania, 1843. First Lieutenant in Company A, 58th Pennsylvania Infantry. On September 29, 1864, at Fort Harrison, Virginia, Lieutenant Johnson, though twice severely wounded, disregarded his injuries and was among the first to enter the fort, where he was wounded a third time. Johnson was awarded his medal on April 1, 1898.

Johnson, Ruel M. Major in the 100th Indiana Infantry. On November 25, 1863, at Chattanooga, Tennessee, Major Johnson, while in command of the regiment, bravely exposed himself to the fire of the enemy, encouraging and cheering the men. Johnson was awarded his medal on August 24, 1896.

Johnson, Samuel. Birth: Pennsylvania, 1845. Private in Company G, 9th Pennsylvania Infantry Reserves. On September 17, 1862, at Antietam,

Maryland, Private Johnson captured the flag of the 1st Texas Rangers. Johnson was awarded his medal on May 30, 1863.

Johnson, Wallace W. Birth: New York. Sergeant in Company G, 6th Pennsylvania Infantry Reserves. On July 2, 1863, at Gettysburg, Pennsylvania, Sergeant Johnson, with five other volunteers, gallantly charged on a number of the enemy's sharpshooters concealed in a log house, captured them, and brought them to Union lines. Johnson was awarded his medal on August 8, 1900.

Johnston, David. Birth: Pennsylvania. Private in Company K, 8th Missouri Infantry. On may 22, 1863, at Vicksburg, Mississippi, Private Johnston exhibited exceptional gallantry in the charge of the volunteer storming party. Johnston was awarded his medal on August 16, 1884.

Wallace Johnson (Hall of Heroes)

Johnston, William P. Birth: Illinois. Landsman aboard the U.S.S. *Fort Hindman*. On March 2, 1864, at Harrisonburg, Louisiana, Landsman Johnston, despite being severely wounded in the hand, took the place of another men to sponge and lead one of the guns throughout the entire action. Johnston was awarded his medal on April 16, 1864.

Johnston, Willie. Birth: New York. Musician in Company D, 3rd Vermont Infantry. The date, place, and act associated with Johnston's medal are not on record at the War Department. Johnston was awarded his medal on September 16, 1863.

Jones, Andrew. Birth: Ireland, 1835. Chief Boatswain's Mate aboard the U.S.S. *Chickasaw*. On August 5, 1864, at Mobile Bay, Alabama, Jones,

William Johnston (Hall of Heroes)

although his enlistment was expired, volunteered for the battle of Mobile Bay, serving gallantly throughout the engagement. Jones was awarded his medal on December 31, 1864.

Jones, David. Birth: Ohio, 1841. Private in Company I, 54th Ohio Infantry. On May 22, 1863, at Vicksburg, Mississippi, Private Jones exhibited exceptional gallantry in the charge of the volunteer storming party. Jones was awarded his medal on June 13, 1894.

Jones, John. Birth: Connecticut, 1837. Landsman aboard the U.S.S. *Rhode Island*. On December 30, 1862, Jones participated in the rescue attempts for the members of the U.S.S. *Monitor*. Jones was awarded his medal on June 22, 1865.

Jones, John E. [photograph p. 113] Birth: New York, 1834. Quartermaster aboard the U.S.S. *Oneida*. On August 5, 1864, at Mobile Bay, Alabama, Jones, though wounded, carried out his duties gallantly. Jones was awarded his medal on December 31, 1864.

The Recipients — Judge

John E. Jones (U.S. Army War College)

Jones, Thomas. Birth: Maryland, 1820. Coxswain aboard the U.S.S. *Ticonderoga*. From December 24 to 25, 1864, and January 13 to 15, 1865, Jones performed his duties with skill and courage in the expeditions against Fort Fisher, North Carolina. Jones was awarded his medal on June 22, 1865.

Jones, William. Birth: Pennsylvania, 1831. Captain of the Top aboard the U.S.S. *Richmond*. On August 5, 1864, at Mobile Bay, Alabama, Jones fought his gun with skill and courage throughout the prolonged engagement that resulted in the surrender of the ram *Tennessee* and the damaging and destruction of batteries at Fort Morgan. Jones was awarded his medal on December 31, 1864.

Jones, William. Birth: Ireland, 1835. First Sergeant in Company A, 73rd New York Infantry. On May 12, 1864, at Spotsylvania, Virginia, Sergeant Jones captured the flag of the 65th Virginia Infantry. Jones was awarded his medal on December 1, 1864.

Jordan, Absalom. Birth: Ohio. Corporal in Company A, 3rd Indiana Cavalry. On April 6, 1865, at Sailors Creek, Virginia, Jordan captured a Confederate flag. Jordan was awarded his medal on May 3, 1865.

Jordan, Robert. Birth: New York, 1826. Coxswain aboard the U.S.S. *Minnesota*, temporarily attached to the U.S.S. *Mount Washington*. On April 14, 1863, at Nansemond River, Virginia, Coxswain Jordan boarded the *Mount Washington* after it had sustained several hits from the enemy and drifted against a bank. He calmly manned a 12-pound gun throughout the six hour battle that ensued, as the Confederates attempted to capture the vessel. Jordan was awarded his medal on July 10 1853.

Jordan, Thomas. Birth: Virginia, 1840. Quartermaster aboard the U.S.S. *Calena*. On August 5, 1864, at Mobile Bay, Alabama, Jordan performed his duties with skill and courage throughout the action. Jordan was awarded his medal on June 22, 1865.

Josselyn, Simeon T. Birth: New York, 1842. First Lieutenant in Company C, 13th Illinois Infantry. On November 25, 1863, at Missionary Ridge, Tennessee, Lieutenant Josselyn led his company, deployed as skirmishers, when they came upon a large body of the enemy. His command took a number of the enemy prisoners, and Josselyn shot down the color bearer and seized the colors. Josselyn was awarded his medal on April 4, 1898.

Judge, Francis W. Birth: England, 1838. First Sergeant in Company K, 79th New York Infantry. On November 29, 1863, at Fort Sanders, Knoxville, Tennessee, Sergeant Francis saw the color bearer of the 51st Georgia Infantry plant his colors on the side of the works. He sprang forward and in the face of concentrated fire seized the flag and returned to his own lines with it.

Judge was awarded his medal on November 2, 1870.

Kaiser, John. Birth: Germany. Sergeant in Company E, 2nd United States Artillery. On June 27, 1862, at Richmond, Virginia, Sergeant Kaiser displayed gallant and meritorious service during the Seven Days' battles before Richmond. Kaiser was awarded his medal on April 2, 1878.

Kaltenbach, Luther. Birth: Germany. Corporal in Company F, 12th Iowa Infantry. On December 16, 1864, at Nashville, Tennessee, Corporal Kaltenbach captured the flag of the 44th Mississippi Infantry. Kaltenbach was awarded his medal on May 12, 1865.

Kane, John. Birth: Ireland. Corporal in Company K, 100th New York Infantry. On April 2, 1865, at Petersburg, Virginia, Corporal Kane displayed exceptional gallantry as color bearer in the assault on Fort Gregg. Kane was awarded his medal on May 12, 1865.

Kane, Thomas. Birth: New Jersey, 1841. Captain of the Hold. On January 15, 1865, at Fort Fisher, North Carolina, Kane displayed outstanding skill and courage as his ship maintained its well directed fire against the fortifications on shore despite the enemy's return fire. Kane was awarded his medal on October 3, 1867.

Kappesser, Peter. Birth: Germany, 1839. Private in Company B, 149th New York Infantry. On November 24, 1863, at Lookout Mountain, Tennessee, Private Kappesser, captured a Confederate flag. Kappesser was awarded his medal on June 28, 1865.

Peter Kappesser (U.S. Army War College)

Leopold Karpeles (Hall of Heroes)

Karpeles, Leopold. Birth: Hungary. Sergeant in Company E, 57th Massachusetts Infantry. On May 6, 1864, at the Wilderness, Virginia, Sergeant Karpeles served as color bearer and rallied the retreating troops and induced them to check the enemy advance. Karpeles was awarded his medal on April 30, 1870.

Kauss (Kautz), August. Birth: Germany. Corporal in Company H, 15th New York Heavy Artillery. On April 1, 1865, at Five Forks, Virginia, Corporal Kauss captured a Confederate flag. Kauss was awarded his medal on May 10, 1865.

Keele, Joseph. Birth: Ireland. Sergeant Major in the 182nd New York Infantry. On May 23, 1864, at North Anna River, Virginia, Sergeant Keele risked his life to carry ordered to the brigade commander, which resulted in saving the works his regiment was defending. Keele was awarded his medal on October 25, 1867.

Keen, Joseph S. Birth: England, 1843. Sergeant in Company D, 13th Michigan Infantry. On October 1, 1864, near the Chattahoochie River, Georgia, Sergeant Keen, while an escaped prisoner of war within the enemy lines, observed an important movement of the enemy and at great personal risk made his way through to Union lines to bring the information to Sherman's army. Keen was awarded his medal on August 4, 1899.

Keene, Joseph. Birth: England. Private in Company B, 26th New York Infantry. On December 13, 1862, at Fredericksburg, Virginia, Private Keene seized the colors after several color bearers had been shot down and led the regiment in a charge. Keene was awarded his medal on December 2, 1892.

Kelley, Andrew J. Birth: Indiana, 1845. Private in Company E, 17th Michigan Infantry. On November 20, 1863, at Knoxville, Tennessee, Private Kelley volunteered to accompany a party charged with the mission of destroying buildings being used by enemy sharpshooters. He disregarded orders to retire, and remained to complete the firings, thus insuring the total destruction of the structures, at the imminent risk of life from the firing of the advanced enemy. Kelley was awarded his medal on April 17, 1900.

Kelley, George V. Birth: Ohio, 1845. Captain of Company A, 104th Ohio Infantry. On November 30, 1864, at Franklin, Tennessee, Captain Kelley captured a Confederate flag. Kelley was awarded his medal on February 13, 1865.

Kelley, John. Birth: Ireland. Second Class Fireman aboard the U.S.S. *Ceres*. On July 9, 1862, at Hamilton, North Carolina, on the Roanoke River, Kelley courageously carried out his duties through the engagement and was spoken of for good conduct and cool bravery under enemy fire. Kelley was awarded his medal on April 3, 1863.

Kelley, Leverett M. Birth: New York, 1841. Sergeant in Company A, 36th Illinois Infantry. On November 25, 1863, at Missionary Ridge, Tennessee, Sergeant Kelley sprang over the works just captured from the enemy, and calling on his comrades to follow, rushed forward in the face of a deadly fire and was among the first over the works on the summit, where he captured a Confederate officer. Kelley was awarded his medal on April 4, 1900.

Leverett Kelley (U.S. Army War College)

Kelly, Alexander. Birth: Pennsylvania. First Sergeant in Company F, 6th United States Colored Infantry. On September 29, 1864, at Chapin's Farm, Virginia, Sergeant Kelly gallantly seized the colors, which had fallen near the enemy's lines of abatis, raised them and rallied the men at a time of confusion and in a place of the greatest danger. Kelly was awarded his medal on April 6, 1865.

Kelly, Daniel. Birth: New York. Sergeant in Company G, 8th New York Cavalry. On March 2, 1865, at Waynesboro, Virginia, Sergeant Kelly captured a Confederate flag. Kelly was awarded his medal on March 26, 1865.

Kelly, Thomas. Birth: Ireland. Private in Company A, 6th New York Cavalry. On August 16, 1864, at Front Royal, Virginia, Private Kelly captured a Confederate flag. Kelly was awarded his medal on August 26, 1864.

Alexander Kelly (Hall of Heroes)

Kemp, Joseph. Birth: Ohio, 1844. First Sergeant in Company D, 5th Michigan Infantry. On May 6, 1864, at the Wilderness, Virginia, Sergeant Kemp captured the flag of the 31st North Carolina Infantry. Kemp was awarded his medal on December 1, 1864.

Kendall, William W. Birth: Indiana, 1839. First Sergeant in Company A, 49th Indiana Infantry. On May 17, 1863, at Black River Bridge, Mississippi, Sergeant Kendall voluntarily led the company in a charge and was the first to enter the enemy's works, taking a number of prisoners. Kendall was awarded his medal on February 12, 1894.

Kendrick, Thomas. Birth: Maine, 1839. Coxswain aboard the U.S.S. *Oneida*. On August 5, 1864, at Mobile Bay, Alabama, Kendrick exhibited courageous devotion to duty, and excellent conduct throughout the battle that resulted in the surrender of the ram *Tennessee*. Kendrick was awarded his medal on December 31, 1864.

Kenna, Barnett. Birth: England, 1827. Quartermaster aboard the U.S.S. *Brooklyn*. On August 5, 1864, at Mobile Bay, Alabama, Kenna fought his gun with skill and courage throughout the furious action that resulted in the surrender of the ram *Tennessee*. Kenna was awarded his medal on December 31, 1864.

William Kendall (U.S. Army War College)

Kennedy, John. Birth: Ireland, 1834. Private in Company M, 2nd United States Artillery. On June 11, 1864, at Trevilian Station, Virginia, Private Kennedy remained at his gun, resisting with his implements, the advancing cavalry, and thus secured the retreat of his detachment. Kennedy was awarded his medal on August 19, 1892.

Kenyon, Charles. Birth: New York, 1840. Fireman aboard the U.S.S. *Calena*. On May 15, 1862, at Drewry's Bluff, Virginia, Kenyon was severely burned while extricating a priming wire that had become bent and fixed in the bow gun while the ship underwent terrific shelling from the enemy. Kenyon hastily dressed his hands with cotton waste and oil and courageously returned to his gun while enemy sharpshooters in rifle pits along the banks continued to direct their fire at the men at the guns. Kenyon was awarded his medal on April 3, 1863.

Kenyon, John S. Birth: New York, 1843. Sergeant in Company D, 3rd New York Cavalry. On May 15, 1862, at Trenton, North Carolina, Sergeant Kenyon voluntarily left a retiring column, returned in the face of the enemy's fire, helped a wounded man upon a horse, and so enabled him to escape capture or death. Kenyon was awarded his medal on September 28, 1897.

Kenyon, Samuel P. Birth: New York. Private in Company B, 24th New York Cavalry. On April 6, 1865, at Sailors Creek, Virginia, Private Kenyon captured a Confederate flag. Kenyon was awarded his medal on May 3, 1865.

Keough, John. Birth: Ireland. Corporal in Company E, 67th Pennsylvania Infantry. On April 6, 1865, at Sailors Creek, Virginia, Corporal Keough captured the flag of the 50th Georgia Infantry. Keough was awarded his medal on May 3, 1865.

Kephart, James. Birth: Pennsylvania. Private in Company C, 13th United States Infantry. On May 19, 1863, at Vicksburg, Mississippi, Private Kephart voluntarily risked his life, under a severe enemy fire, and aided to the rear an officer who had been severely wounded and left on the field. Kephart was awarded his medal on May 13, 1899.

Kerr, Thomas R. Birth: Ireland, 1843. Captain of Company C, 14th Pennsylvania Cavalry. On August 7, 1864, at Moorefield, West Virginia, Captain Kerr captured the flag of the 8th Virginia Cavalry despite being seriously wounded. Kerr was awarded his medal on June 13, 1894.

Kiggins, John. Birth: New York. Sergeant in Company D, 149th New York Infantry. On November 24, 1863, at Lookout Mountain, Tennessee, Sergeant Kiggins waved the colors to save the lives of the men who were being fired upon by their own batteries, and thereby drew upon himself a concentrated fire from the enemy. Kiggins was awarded his medal on January 12, 1892.

James Kephart (Hall of Heroes)

Kimball, Joseph. Birth: New Hampshire. Private in Company B, 2nd West Virginia Cavalry. On April 6, 1865, at Sailors Creek, Virginia, Private Kimball captured the flag of the 6th North Carolina Infantry. Kimball was awarded his medal on May 3, 1865.

Kindig, John M. Birth: Pennsylvania. Corporal in Company A, 63rd Pennsylvania Infantry. On May 12, 1864, at Spotsylvania, Virginia, Corporal Kindig captured the flag of the 28th North Carolina Infantry. Kindig was awarded his medal on December 1, 1864.

The Recipients — King

Horatio King (Hall of Heroes)

Robert King (U.S. Army War College)

Dennis Kirby (U.S. Army War College)

King, Horatio C. Birth: Maine, 1837. Major and Quartermaster, United States Volunteers. On March 31, 1865, at Dinwiddie Courthouse, Virginia, Major King, while serving as a volunteer aide, carried orders to the reserve brigade and participated with it in the charge that repulsed the enemy. King was awarded his medal on September 23, 1897.

King, Robert H. Birth: New York, 1845. Landsman aboard the U.S.S. *Picket Boat 1*. On October 27, 1864, at Roanoke River, North Carolina, Landsman King exhibited exceptional courage during the spar torpedo attack on the ram *Albemarle*. King was awarded his medal on December 31, 1864.

King, Rufus, Jr. Birth: New York, 1838. First Lieutenant in the 4th United States Artillery. On June 30, 1862, at White Oak Swamp Bridge, Virginia, Lieutenant King succeeded to command of two batteries when his captain was wounded, and engaged a superior force of the enemy, fighting his guns most gallantly until compelled to retire. King was awarded his medal on April 2, 1898.

Kinnaird, Samuel W. Birth: New York, 1843. Landsman aboard the U.S.S. *Lackawanna*. On August 5, 1864, at Mobile Bay, Alabama, landsman Kinnaird showed presence of mind and cheerfulness that had much to do with maintaining the crew's morale. Kinnaird was awarded his medal on December 31, 1864.

Kinsey, John. Birth: Pennsylvania, 1844. Corporal in Company B, 45th Pennsylvania Infantry. On May 18, 1864, at Spotsylvania, Virginia, Corporal Kinsey seized the colors after the bearer had been shot, and with great gallantry succeeded in saving them from capture. Kinsey was awarded his medal on March 2, 1897.

Kirby, Dennis T. Birth: New York, 1838. Major of the 8th Missouri Infantry. On May 22, 1863, at Vicksburg, Mississippi, Major Kirby seized the colors after the bearer had been killed and bore them himself in the assault. Kirby was awarded his medal on January 31, 1894.

Kirk, Jonathan C. Birth: Ohio. Captain of Company F, 20th Indiana Infantry. On May 3, 1864, at

North Anna River, Virginia, Captain Kirk volunteered for dangerous service and single-handedly captured 13 armed Confederate soldiers. Kirk was awarded his medal on June 13, 1894.

Kline, Harry. Birth: Germany. Private in Company E, 40th New York Infantry. On April 6, 1865, at Sailors Creek, Virginia, Private Kline captured a Confederate flag. Kline was awarded his medal on May 10, 1865.

Kloth, Charles H. Birth: Europe. Private in the Chicago Mercantile Battery, Illinois Light Artillery. On May 22, 1863, at Vicksburg, Mississippi, Private Kloth helped carry by hand a cannon up to and fired it through an embrasure of the enemy's works. Kloth was awarded his medal on January 15, 1895.

Knight, Charles H. Birth: New Hampshire. Corporal in Company I, 9th New Hampshire Infantry. On July 30, 1864, at Petersburg, Virginia, Corporal Knight was the first to enter the exploded mine, where he was wounded, but still took several prisoners to the Union lines. Knight was awarded his medal on July 27, 1896.

Knight, William J. Birth: Ohio, 1837. Private in Company E, 21st Ohio Infantry. In April of 1862, at Big Shanty, Georgia, Private Knight was one of 22 participants who penetrated nearly 200 miles behind enemy lines, captured a train at Big Shanty and attempted to destroy bridges and track between Chattanooga and Atlanta. Knight was awarded his medal In September 1863.

William Knight (Hall of Heroes)

Knowles, Abiather J. Birth: Maine, 1830. Private in Company D, 2nd Maine Infantry. On July 21, 1861, at Bull Run, Virginia, Private Knowles gallantly removed dead and wounded from the field under heavy fire. Knowles was awarded his medal on December 27, 1894.

Knox, Edward M. Birth: New York. Second Lieutenant in the 15th New York Battery. On July 2, at Gettysburg, Pennsylvania, Lieutenant Knox held his ground with the battery after the other batteries had fallen back until compelled to draw his piece off by hand, during which time he was severely wounded. Knox was awarded his medal on October 18, 1892.

Koogle, Jacob. Birth: Maryland. First Lieutenant in Company G, 7th Maryland Infantry. On April 1, 1865, at Five Forks, Virginia, Lieutenant Koogle captured a Confederate flag. Koogle was awarded his medal on May 10, 1865.

Edward Knox (Hall of Heroes)

Kountz, John S. Birth: Ohio, 1845. Musician in Company G, 37th Ohio Infantry. On November 25, 1863, at Missionary Ridge, Tennessee, Kountz picked up a musket and joined in the charge in which he was severely wounded. Kountz was awarded his medal on August 13, 1895.

Kramer, Theodore L. Birth: Pennsylvania. Private in Company G, 188th Pennsylvania Infantry. On September 29, 1864, at Chapin's Farm, Virginia, Private Kramer took one of the first prisoners, a captain. Kramer was awarded his medal on April 6, 1865.

Kretsinger, George. Birth: New York. Private in the Chicago Mercantile Battery, Illinois Light Artillery. On May 22, 1863, at Vicksburg, Mississippi, Private Kretsinger, with others, carried by hand a cannon and fired it through an embrasure of the enemy's works. Kretsinger was awarded his medal on July 20, 1897.

John Kountz (U.S. Army War College)

Kuder, Andrew. Birth: New York. Second Lieutenant in Company G, 8th New York Cavalry. On March 2, 1865, at Waynesboro, Virginia, Lieutenant Kuder captured a Confederate flag. Kuder was awarded his medal on March 26, 1865.

Kuder, Jeremiah. Birth: Ohio. Lieutenant in Company A, 74th Indiana Infantry. On September 1, 1864, at Jonesboro, Georgia, Lieutenant Kuder captured the flags of the 8th and 19th Arkansas Infantry. Kuder was awarded his medal on April 7, 1865.

Labill, Joseph S. Birth: France. Private in Company C, 6th Missouri Infantry. On May 22, 1863, at Vicksburg, Mississippi, Private Labill exhibited exceptional gallantry in the charge of the volunteer storming party. Labill was awarded his medal on August 14, 1894.

Andrew Kuder (Hall of Heroes)

Ladd, George. Birth: New York. Private in Company H, 22nd New York Cavalry. On March 2, 1865, at Waynesboro, Virginia, Private Ladd captured a standard bearer, his flag, horse and equipment. Ladd was awarded his medal on March 26, 1865.

Lafferty, John. Birth: New York, 1842. Fireman aboard the U.S.S. *Wyalusing*. On May 25, 1864, at Roanoke River, North Carolina, Lafferty participated in the hazardous torpedo attack on the Confederate ram *Albemarle*. Lafferty was awarded his medal on December 31, 1864.

Laffey, Bartlett. Birth: Ireland, 1841. Seaman aboard the U.S.S. *Marmora*. On March 5, 1864, at Yazoo City, Mississippi, Seaman Laffey laded with a 12-pound howitzer and crew in the midst of battle, and bravely standing by his gun despite enemy rifle fire which cut the gun carriage and rammer, contributed to the turning back of the enemy. Laffey was awarded his medal on April 16, 1864.

Laing, William. Birth: New York. Sergeant in Company F, 158th New York Infantry. On September 29, 1864, at Chapin's Farm, Virginia, Sergeant Laing was among the first to scale the parapet. Laing was awarded his medal on April 6, 1865.

Lakin, Daniel. Birth: Maryland, 1834. Seaman aboard the U.S.S. *Commodore Perry*. On October 3, 1862, at Franklin, Virginia, Seaman Lakin remained at his post and performed his duties with skill and courage as the *Commodore Perry* fought a gallant battle to silence many Confederate batteries as she steamed down the Blackwater River. Lakin was awarded his medal on April 3, 1863.

Landis, James P. Birth: Pennsylvania, 1843. Chief Bugler in the 1st Pennsylvania Cavalry. On April 5, 1865, at Paine's Crossroads, Virginia, Bugler Landis captured a Confederate flag. Landis was awarded his medal on May 3, 1865.

Lane, Morgan D. Birth: New York. Private in the Signal Corps, U.S. Army. On April 6, 1865, at Jetersville, Virginia, Private Lane captured the flag of the Confederate gunboat *Nansemond*. Lane was awarded his medal on March 16, 1866.

Lanfare, Aaron S. Birth: Connecticut. First Lieutenant in Company B, 1st Connecticut Cavalry. On April 6, 1865, at Sailors Creek, Virginia, Lieutenant Lanfare captured the flag of the 11th Florida Infantry. Lanfare was awarded his medal on May 3, 1865.

Julius Langbein (Hall of Heroes)

Langbein, J.S. Julius. Birth: Germany, 1846. Musician in Company B, 9th New York Infantry. On April 19, 1862, at Camden, North Carolina, Drummer Langbein, a boy of fifteen, voluntarily and under heavy fire went to the aid of a wounded officer, procured medical assistance for him, and aided in carrying him to a place of safety. Langbein was awarded his medal on January 7, 1895.

Lann, John S. Birth: New York, 1842. Landsman aboard the U.S.S. *Magnolia*. From March 5, to 6, 1865, at St. Marks, Florida, Landsman Lann showed coolness and determination in standing by his gun while under heavy fire from the enemy and was a credit to the service he belonged to. Lann was awarded his medal on June 22, 1865.

Larimer, Smith. Birth: Ohio, 1829. Corporal in Company G, 2nd Ohio Cavalry. On April 6, 1865, at Sailors Creek, Virginia, Corporal Larimer captured the flag of General Kershaw's headquarters. Larimer was awarded his medal on May 3, 1865.

Larrabee, James W. Birth: New York. Corporal in Company I, 55th Illinois Infantry. On May 22, 1863, at Vicksburg, Mississippi, Corporal Larrabee exhibited exceptional gallantry in the charge of the volunteer storming party. Larrabee was awarded his medal on September 2, 1893.

Lawson, Gaines. Birth: Tennessee, 1841. First Sergeant in Company D, 4th Tennessee Infantry. On October 3, 1863, at Minville, Tennessee, Sergeant Lawson went to the aid of a wounded comrade between the lines and carried him to a place of safety. Lawson was awarded his medal on June 11, 1895.

Lawson, John. Birth: Pennsylvania, 1837. Landsman aboard the U.S.S. *Hartford*. On August 5, 1864, at Mobile Bay, Alabama, Landsman Lawson, though wounded in the leg by enemy fire, refused to leave his post and steadfastly continued his duties throughout the engagement. Lawson was awarded his medal on December 31, 1864.

John Lawson (U.S. Army War College)

Lawton, Henry W. Birth: Ohio, 1843. Captain in Company A, 30th Indiana Infantry. On August 3, 1864, at Atlanta, Georgia, Captain Lawton led a charge of skirmishers against the enemy's rifle pits and stubbornly and successfully resisted two determined attacks of the enemy to retake them. Lawton was awarded his medal on May 22, 1893.

Lear, Nicholas. Birth: Rhode Island, 1826. Quartermaster aboard the U.S.S. *New Ironsides*. From December 24 to 25, 1864, and January 13 to 15, 1865, at Fort Fisher, North Carolina, Lear exhibited exceptional gallantry in the performance of his duties during the expeditions against the fort. Lear was awarded his medal on June 22, 1865.

Lee, James H. Birth: New York, 1840. Seaman aboard the U.S.S. *Kearsarge*. On June 19, 1864, at Cherbourg, France, Lee exhibited marked coolness and good conduct in the bitter engagement that resulted in the destruction of the C.S.S. *Alabama*. Lee was awarded his medal on December 31, 1864.

Henry Lawton (U.S. Army War College)

Leland, George W. Birth: Georgia, 1834. Gunner's Mate aboard the U.S.S. *Lehigh*. On November 16, 1863, at Charleston, South Carolina, Leland rowed a small boat, under heavy enemy fire, to transfer hawsers from the U.S.S. *Nahant* in an attempt to free the *Lehigh*, which had grounded. He succeeded in making the trip twice, only to find that the hawsers had been cut by enemy fire. Leland was awarded his medal on April 16, 1864.

Leon, Pierre. Birth: Louisiana, 1837. Captain of the Forecastle aboard the U.S.S. *Baron De Kalb*. From December 23, to 27, 1862, during the Yazoo River, Mississippi expedition, Leon distinguished himself during the various actions as Captain of the *Forecastle*. Leon was awarded his medal on April 3, 1863.

Leonard, Edwin. Birth: Massachusetts. Sergeant in Company I, 37th Massachusetts Infantry. On June 18, 1864, at Petersburg, Virginia, Sergeant Leonard voluntarily exposed himself to the fire of a Union brigade to stop their firing on a Union skirmish line. Leonard was awarded his medal on August 16, 1894.

Leonard, William E. Birth: Pennsylvania. Private in Company F, 85th Pennsylvania Infantry. On April 16, 1864, at Deep Bottom, Virginia, Private Leonard captured a Confederate flag. Leonard was awarded his medal on April 6, 1865.

Leslie, Frank. Birth: England. Private in Company B, 4th New York Cavalry. On August 15, 1864, at Front Royal, Virginia, Private Leslie captured the flag of the 3rd Virginia Infantry. Leslie was awarded his medal on August 26, 1864.

Benjamin Levy (U.S. Army War College)

Levy, Benjamin. Birth: New York, 1845. Private in Company B, 1st New York Infantry. On June 30, 1862, at Glendale, Virginia, Private Levy, then a drummer boy, took up the musket of a sick comrade and went into the fight. When the color bearer was shot down, Levy picked up the colors and saved them from capture. Levy was awarded his medal on March 1, 1865.

Lewis, Dewitt Clinton. Birth: Pennsylvania. Captain of Company F, 97th Pennsylvania Infantry. On June 16, 1862, at Secessionville, South Carolina, Captain Lewis faced heavy enemy fire to rescue an exhausted private of his company who but for his timely action would have lost his life by drowning in the morass through which the troops were retiring. Lewis was awarded his medal on April 23, 1896.

Lewis, Henry. Birth: Michigan, 1842. Corporal in Company B, 47th Ohio Infantry. On May 3, 1863, at Vicksburg, Mississippi, Corporal Lewis was one of a party that volunteered and attempted to run the enemy's batteries with a steam tug and two barges loaded with sustenance stores. Lewis was awarded his medal on April 17, 1917.

Lewis, Samuel E. Birth: Rhode Island. Corporal in Company G, 1st Rhode Island Light Artillery. On April 2, 1865, at Petersburg, Virginia, Corporal Lewis was one of a detachment of twenty picked artillerymen who voluntarily accompanied an infantry assaulting party and who turned upon the enemy the guns captured in the assault. Lewis was awarded his medal on June 16, 1866.

Dewitt Lewis (Hall of Heroes)

Libaire, Adolphe. Captain of Company E, 9th New York Infantry. On September 17, 1862, at Antietam, Maryland, Captain Libaire seized the regimental flag after the entire color guard had been shot down and with conspicuous gallantry carried it to the extreme front, urging the line forward. Libaire was awarded his medal on April 2, 1898.

Lilley, John. Birth: Pennsylvania. Private in Company F, 205th Pennsylvania Infantry. On April 2, 1865, at Petersburg, Virginia, Private Lilley, after his regiment began to waiver, rushed forward alone to capture a Confederate flag and color bearer, Lilley was awarded his medal on May 20, 1865.

Little, Henry F.W. Birth: New Hampshire, 1842. Sergeant of Company D, 7th New Hampshire Infantry. In September of 1864, near Richmond, Virginia, Sergeant Little displayed gallantry on the skirmish line. Little was awarded his medal on January 14, 1870.

Henry Little (U.S. Army War College)

Littlefield, George H. Birth: Maine. Corporal in Company G, 1st Maine Infantry. On March 25, 1865, at Fort Fisher, Virginia, Corporal Littlefield picked up the flag, after the color sergeant had been wounded, and bore it to the front, to the great encouragement of the charging column. Littlefield was awarded his medal on June 22, 1885.

Livingston, Josiah O. Birth: Vermont. First Lieutenant and Adjutant of the 9th Vermont Infantry. On February 2, 1864, at Newport Barracks, North Carolina, Lieutenant Livingston fired the railroad bridge over which his detachment was retreating, and, although wounded himself, assisted a wounded officer over the burning structure. Livingston was awarded his medal on September 8, 1891.

Lloyd, Benjamin. Birth: England, 1839. Coal Heaver aboard the U.S.S. *Wyalusing*. On May 25, 1864, on the Roanoke River, North Carolina, Lloyd volunteered in a torpedo attack against the ram *Albemarle* and displayed exceptional gallantry. Lloyd was awarded his medal on December 31, 1864.

Lloyd, John W. Birth: New York, 1831. Coxswain aboard the U.S.S. *Wyalusing*. On May 25, 1864, at Roanoke River, North Carolina, Lloyd volunteered in a torpedo attack against the ram *Albemarle* and displayed exceptional gallantry. Lloyd was awarded his medal on December 31, 1864.

Locke, Lewis. Birth: New York. Private in Company A, 1st New Jersey Cavalry. On April 5, 1865, at Paine's Crossroads, Virginia, Private Locke captured a Confederate flag. Locke was awarded his medal on May 3, 1865.

Logan, Hugh. Birth: Ireland, 1834. Captain of the Afterguard aboard the U.S.S. *Rhode Island*. On December 30, 1862, at Mobile Bay, Alabama, Logan courageously risked his life to attempt to save the lives of the crew after the *Monitor* had been stricken. He made every effort to save others, and ultimately lost his own life in the process. Logan was awarded his medal on June 22, 1865.

Lonergan, John. Birth: Ireland, 1839. Captain of Company A, 13th Vermont Infantry. On July 2, 1863, at Gettysburg, Pennsylvania, Captain Lonergan gallantly aided in the recapture of four guns and the capture of two additional guns from the enemy, along with a number of prisoners. Lonergan was awarded his medal on October 28, 1893.

Longshore, William H. Birth: Ohio. Private in Company D, 30th Ohio Infantry. On May 22, 1863, at Vicksburg, Mississippi, Private Longshore exhibited exceptional gallantry in the charge of the volunteer storming party. Longshore was awarded his medal on August 10, 1894.

Lonsway, Joseph. Birth: New York. Private in Company D, 20th New York Cavalry. On October 16, 1864, at Murfrees Station, Virginia, Private Lonsway volunteered to swim Blackwater River to get a large flat used as a ferry on the other side. He succeeded in getting the boat across, making it possible for a detachment to cross the river and take possession of the enemy's breastworks. The date of Lonsway's award is unknown.

Lord, William. Birth: England. Musician in Company C, 40th Massachusetts Infantry. On May 16, 1864, at Drury's Bluff, Virginia, Lord went to the assistance of a wounded officer lying helpless between the lines and under fire from both sides removed him to a place of safety. Lord was awarded his medal on April 4, 1898.

Lorish, Andrew J. Birth: New York, 1832. Commissary Sergeant in the 19th New York Cavalry. On September 19, 1864, at Winchester, Virginia, Sergeant Lorish captured a Confederate flag. Lorish was awarded his medal on September 27, 1864.

Love, George M. Birth: New York. Colonel of the 116th New York Infantry. On October 19, 1864, at Cedar Creek, Virginia, Colonel Love captured the flag of the 2nd South Carolina Infantry. Love was awarded his medal on March 6, 1865.

Lovering, George M. Birth: New Hampshire, 1832. First Sergeant in Company I, 4th Massachusetts

John Lonergan (U.S. Army War College)

Joseph Lonsway (Hall of Heroes)

George Lovering (U.S. Army War College)

Infantry. On June 14, 1863, at Port Hudson, Louisiana, Sergeant Lovering, during a momentary confusion in the ranks caused by other troops rushing upon the regiment, displayed coolness and determination and rendered efficient aid in preventing a panic among the troops. Lovering was awarded his medal on November 19, 1891.

Lower, Cyrus B. Birth: Pennsylvania, 1843. Private in Company K, 13th Pennsylvania Infantry Reserves. On May 7, 1864, at the Wilderness, Virginia, Private Lower performed gallant services and displayed soldierly qualities in voluntarily rejoining his command after having been wounded. Lower was awarded his medal on July 20, 1887.

Lower, Robert A. Birth: Illinois, 1844. Private in Company K, 55th Illinois Infantry. On May 22, 1863, at Vicksburg, Mississippi, Private Lower exhibited exceptional gallantry in the charge of the volunteer storming party. Lower was awarded his medal on September 2, 1893.

Loyd, George. Birth: Ohio, 1844. Private in Company A, 122nd Ohio Infantry. On April 2, 1865, at Petersburg, Virginia, Private Loyd captured the division flag of General Heth. Loyd was awarded his medal on April 16, 1891.

Lucas, George W. Birth: Illinois, 1845. Private in Company C, 3rd Missouri Cavalry. On July 25, 1864, at Benton, Arkansas, Private Lucas pursued and killed General George M. Holt of the Arkansas Militia and captured his arms and horse. Lucas was awarded his medal in December of 1864.

Luce, Moses A. Birth: Illinois, 1842. Sergeant in Company E, 4th Michigan Infantry. On May 10, 1864, at Laurel Hill, Virginia, Sergeant Luce voluntarily returned in the face of the advancing enemy to the assistance of a wounded and helpless comrade, and carried him, at imminent peril to a place of safety. Luce was awarded his medal on February 7, 1895.

William Ludgate (U.S. Army War College)

Ludgate, William. Birth: England, 1836. Captain of Company G, 59th New York Infantry. On April 7, 1865, at Farmville, Virginia, Captain Ludgate exhibited gallantry in rallying his men and advancing with a small detachment to save a bridge about to be fired by the enemy. Ludgate was awarded his medal on August 10, 1889.

Ludwig, Carl. Birth: France. Private in the 34th New York Battery. On June 18, 1864, at Petersburg, Virginia, Private Ludwig, as gunner of his piece, inflicted singly a great loss upon the enemy and distinguished himself in the removal of the piece while under a heavy fire. Ludwig was awarded his medal on July 30, 1896.

Lunt, Alphonso M. Birth: Maine. Sergeant in Company F, 38th Massachusetts Infantry. On September 19, 1864, at Opequan Creek, Virginia, Sergeant Lunt carried his flag to the most advanced position where, left almost alone close to the enemy's lines, he refused their demand to surrender, and withdrew at great personal peril to save the flag. Lunt was awarded his flag on May 10, 1894.

Lutes, Franklin W. Birth: New York. Corporal in Company D, 111th New York Infantry. On March 31, 1865, at Petersburg, Virginia, Corporal Lutes captured the flag of the 41st Alabama Infantry, along with the color bearer and one of the color guard. Lutes was awarded his medal on April 3, 1865.

Luther, James H. Birth: Massachusetts. Private in Company D, 7th Massachusetts Infantry. On May 3, 1863, at Fredericksburg, Virginia, Private Luther was among the first to jump into the enemy's rifle pits where he captured three prisoners. Luther was awarded his medal on June 28, 1890.

Gotlieb Luty (Hall of Heroes)

Arthur MacArthur (U.S. Army War College)

Luty, Gotlieb. Birth: Pennsylvania. Corporal in Company A, 74th New York Infantry. On May 3, 1863, at Chancellorsville, Virginia, Corporal Gotlieb bravely advanced to the enemy's line under heavy fire and brought back valuable information. Luty was awarded his medal on October 5, 1876.

Lyman, Joel H. Birth: New York. Quartermaster Sergeant of Company B, 9th New York Cavalry. On September 19, 1864, at Winchester, Virginia, Sergeant Lyman attempted to capture a Confederate flag. He failed to do so, instead capturing one of the enemy's officers. Lyman was awarded his medal on August 20, 1894.

Lyon, Frederick A. Birth: Massachusetts, 1843. Corporal in Company A, 1st Vermont Cavalry. On October 19, 1864, at Cedar Creek, Virginia, Corporal Lyon, with one companion, captured a Confederate flag, three officers, and an ambulance with its mules and driver. Lyon was awarded his medal on November 26, 1864.

Lyons, Thomas. Birth: Massachusetts, 1838. Seaman aboard the U.S.S. *Pensacola*. On April 24, 1862, at forts Jackson and St. Philip, south of New Orleans, Seaman Lyons was lashed outside of the ship, on the port-sheet chain, with the lead in hand to lead the ship past the forts, and never flinched, although under a heavy fire from the forts and Rebel gunboats. Lyons was awarded his medal on February 8, 1872.

MacArthur, Arthur, Jr. Birth: Massachusetts, 1845. First Lieutenant and Adjutant of the 24th Wisconsin Infantry. On November 25, 1863, at Missionary Ridge, Tennessee, Lieutenant MacArthur seized the colors of his regiment at a critical moment and planted them on the captured works on the crest of Missionary Ridge. MacArthur was awarded his medal on June 30, 1890.

Machon, James. Birth: England, 1848. Boy aboard the U.S.S. *Brooklyn*. On August 5, 1864, at Mobile Bay, Alabama, Machon performed his duties in the powder division throughout the furious action with steadfast devotion. Machon was awarded his medal on December 31, 1864.

Mack, Alexander. Birth: Holland, 1836. Captain of the Top aboard the U.S.S. *Brooklyn*. On August 5, 1864, at Mobile Bay, Alabama, Mack, although wounded, immediately returned to his post and took charge of his gun and, as heavy enemy fire continued to fall, performed his duties with skill and courage until he was wounded again and totally disabled. Mack was awarded his medal on December 31, 1864.

Mack, John. Birth: Maine, 1843. Seaman aboard the U.S.S. *Hendrick Hudson*. From March 5 to 6, 1865, at St. Marks, Florida, Seaman Mack served with the Army in charge of Navy howitzers during the attack on St. Marks. Throughout this fierce engagement, he made remarkable efforts in assisting transport of the gun and his coolness and determination in standing by his gun while under the fire of the enemy were a credit to the service to which he belonged. Mack was awarded his medal on June 22, 1865.

Mackie, John F. Birth: New York, 1836. Corporal in the United States Marine Corps serving aboard the U.S.S. *Galena*. On May 15, 1862, at Drury's Bluff, Virginia, Corporal took part in the assault of Fort Darling, where he fearlessly maintained his musket fire against the rifle pits along the shore and when ordered to fill vacancies at guns caused by wounded men, manned the weapon with skill and courage. Mackie was awarded his medal on July 10, 1863.

Madden, Michael. Birth: Ireland, 1841. Private in Company K, 42nd New York Infantry. On September 3, 1861, at Mason's Island, Maryland, Private Madden assisted a wounded comrade to the riverbank and, under a heavy fire from the enemy, swam with him across a branch of the Potomac to Union lines. Madden was awarded his medal on March 22, 1898.

John Mackie (Hall of Heroes)

Madden, William. Birth: England, 1843. Coal Heaver aboard the U.S.S. *Brooklyn*. On August 5, 1864, at Mobile Bay, Alabama, Madden remained steadfast at his post and performed his duties on the powder division throughout the furious engagement which resulted in the surrender of the Confederate ram *Tennessee* and in the damaging and destruction of batteries at Fort Morgan. Madden was awarded his medal on December 31, 1864.

Madison, James. Birth: New York, 1842. Sergeant in Company E, 8th New York Cavalry. On March 2, 1865, at Waynesboro, Virginia, Sergeant Madison recaptured General Crook's headquarters flag after it had been taken by the Confederates. Madison was awarded his medal on March 26, 1865.

Magee, William. Birth: New Jersey. Drummer Boy in Company C, 33rd New Jersey Infantry. On December 5, 1864, at Murfreesboro, Tennessee, Magee took part in a charge and was among the first to reach a batty of the enemy, with one or two others, where he mounted the artillery horses and took the two guns into Union lines. Magee was awarded his medal on February 7, 1866.

Mahoney, Jeremiah. Sergeant in Company A, 29th Massachusetts Infantry. On November 29, 1863, at Knoxville, Tennessee, Sergeant Mahoney captured the flag of the 17th Mississippi during the attack on Fort Sanders. Mahoney was awarded his medal on December 1, 1864.

Mandy, Harry J. Birth: England. First Sergeant in Company B, 4th New York Cavalry. On August 15, 1864, at Front Royal, Virginia, Sergeant Mandy captured the flag of the 3rd Virginia Infantry. Mandy was awarded his medal on August 26, 1864.

Mangam, Richard C. Birth: Ireland. Private in Company H, 148th New York Infantry. On April 2, 1865, at Hatchers Run, Virginia, Private Mangam captured the flag of the 8th Mississippi Infantry. Mangam was awarded his medal on September 21, 1888.

Manning, Joseph S. Birth: Massachusetts, 1845. Private in Company K, 29th Massachusetts Infantry. On November 29, 1863, at Knoxville, Tennessee, Private Manning captured the flag of the 16th Georgia Infantry during the assault on Fort Sanders. Manning was awarded his medal on December 1, 1864.

Marland, William. Birth: Massachusetts, 1839. First Lieutenant in the 2nd Independent Battery, Massachusetts Light Artillery. On November 3, 1863, at Grand Coteau, Louisiana, Lieutenant Marland, after being surrounded by the enemy's cavalry, his support having surrendered, ordered a charge and saved the section of the battery that was under his command. Marland was awarded his medal on February 16, 1897.

William Marland (U.S. Army War College)

Marquette, Charles. Birth: Pennsylvania. Sergeant in Company F, 93rd Pennsylvania Infantry. On April 2, 1865, at Petersburg, Virginia, Sergeant Marquette, although wounded, was one of the first to plant colors on the enemy's breastworks. Marquette was awarded his medal on May 10, 1865.

Marsh, Albert. Birth: New York. Sergeant in Company B, 64th New York Infantry. On May 12, 1864, at Spotsylvania, Virginia, Sergeant Marsh captured a Confederate flag. Marsh was awarded his medal on December 1, 1864.

Charles Marquette (Hall of Heroes)

Marsh, Charles H. Birth: Connecticut. Private in Company D, 1st Connecticut Cavalry. On July 31, 1864, at Back Creek Valley, Virginia, Private Marsh captured a Confederate flag and its bearer. Marsh was awarded his medal on January 23, 1865.

Marsh, George. Birth: Illinois. Sergeant in Company D, 104th Illinois Infantry. On July 2, 1863, at Elk River, Tennessee, Sergeant Marsh voluntarily led a small party, under a heavy fire from the enemy, that captured a stockade and saved the bridge. Marsh was awarded his medal on September 17, 1897.

Martin, Edward S. Birth: Ireland, 1840. Quartermaster aboard the U.S.S. *Calena*. On August 5, 1864, at Mobile Bay, Alabama, Martin displayed exceptional gallantry and performed his duties with skill and courage. Martin was awarded his medal on June 22, 1865.

Martin, George. Service listed under Schwenk, Martin.

Martin, James. Birth: Ireland, 1826. Sergeant, United States Marine Corp serving aboard the U.S.S. *Richmond*. On August 5, 1864, at Mobile Bay, Alabama, Sergeant Martin fought his gun with skill and courage throughout the furious two hour engagement that resulted in the surrender of the ram *Tennessee* and in the damaging and destruction of batteries at Fort Morgan. Martin was awarded his medal on December 31, 1864.

Martin, Sylvester H. Birth: Pennsylvania. Lieutenant in Company K, 88th Pennsylvania Infantry. On August 19, 1864, at Weldon Railroad, Virginia, Lieutenant Martin gallantly made a most dangerous reconnaissance, discovering the position of the enemy and enabling the division to repulse an attack made in strong force. Martin was awarded his medal on April 5, 1894.

Martin, William. Birth: Prussia, 1842. Boatswain's Mate aboard the U.S.S. *Benton*. On December 27, 1862, on the Yazoo River, at Haines Bluff, Mississippi, Martin served courageously throughout the battle until the *Benton* was ordered to withdraw. Martin was awarded his medal on April 3, 1863.

Martin, William. Birth: Ireland, 1839. Seaman aboard the U.S.S. *Varuna*. On April 24, 1862, at Forts Jackson and St. Philip, south of New Orleans, Seaman Martin exhibited exceptional gallantry by steadfastly remaining at his station through the thickest of the fight, inflicting damage on the enemy and remaining cool and courageous although the *Varuna* was so badly damaged it was forced to beach. Martin was awarded his medal on April 3, 1863.

Mason, Elihu H. Birth: Indiana, 1831. Sergeant in Company K, 21st Ohio Infantry. In April of 1862, at Big Shanty, Georgia, Sergeant Mason, along with 21 others, captured a railroad train in an attempt to destroy bridges and track between Chattanooga and Atlanta. Mason was awarded his medal on March 25, 1863, the fourth person to receive the award.

Elihu Mason (U.S. Army War College)

Mathews, William H. Birth: England. First Sergeant in Company E, 2nd Maryland Infantry. On July 30, 1864, at Petersburg, Virginia, Sergeant Matthews captured a Confederate sergeant and two enlisted men belonging to the 17th South Carolina Infantry. Matthews was awarded his medal on July 10, 1892. (Enlisted under the name of Henry Sivel, and the original medal was issued in that name. In 1900, a replacement medal was awarded under his true name.)

Matthews, John C. Birth: Pennsylvania. Corporal in Company A, 61st Pennsylvania Infantry. On April 2, 1865, at Petersburg, Virginia, Corporal Matthews took the colors, after the color bearer had been disabled, and although severely wounded himself, carried them until the enemy's works were taken. Matthews was awarded his medal on February 13, 1891.

Matthews, Milton. Birth: Pennsylvania. Private in Company C, 61st Pennsylvania Infantry. On April 2, 1865, at Petersburg, Virginia, Private Matthews captured the flag of the 7th Tennessee Infantry. Matthews was awarded his medal on May 10, 1865.

Mattingly, Henry B. Birth: Kentucky. Private in Company B, 10th Kentucky Infantry. On September 1, 1864, at Jonesboro, Georgia, Private Mattingly captured the flags of the 6th and 7th Arkansas Infantry regiments. Mattingly was awarded his medal on April 7, 1865.

Charles Mattocks (Hall of Heroes)

Mattocks, Charles P. Birth: Vermont, 1840. Major of the 17th Maine Infantry. On April 6, 1865, at Sailors Creek, Virginia, Major Mattocks displayed extraordinary gallantry in leading a charge of his regiment that resulted in the capture of a large number of prisoners and a stand of colors. Mattocks was awarded his medal on March 29, 1899.

Maxham, Lowell M. Birth: Massachusetts. Corporal in Company F, 7th Massachusetts Infantry. On May 3, 1863, at Fredericksburg, Virginia, Corporal Maxham, though severely wounded, and in the face of a deadly fire from the enemy at short range, rushed bravely forward and was among the first to enter the enemy's works on the crest of Marye's Heights, where he helped to plant the regimental colors. Maxham was awarded his medal on August 24, 1896.

May, William. Birth: Pennsylvania, 1826. Private in Company H, 32nd Iowa Infantry. On December 16, 1864, at Nashville, Tennessee, Private May ran ahead of his regiment over the enemy's works and captured the flag and bearer of Bonanchad's Confederate Battery. May was awarded his medal on February 24, 1865.

Mayberry, John B. [photograph p. 132] Birth: Delaware. Private in Company F, 1st Delaware Infantry. On July 3, 1863, at Gettysburg, Pennsylvania, Private Mayberry captured a Confederate flag. Mayberry was awarded his medal on December 1, 1864.

John Mayberry (Hall of Heroes)

George Maynard (U.S. Army War College)

Mayes, William B. Birth: Ohio, 1837. Private in Company K, 11th Iowa Infantry. On June 15, 1864, at Kennesaw Mountain, Georgia, Private Mayes, with one companion, and under a fierce fire from the enemy at short range, went to the rescue of a wounded comrade who had fallen between the lines and carried him to a place of safety. Mayes was awarded his medal on November 27, 1899.

Maynard, George H. Birth: Massachusetts, 1836. Private in Company D, 13th Massachusetts Infantry. On December 13, 1862, at Fredericksburg, Virginia, Private Maynard voluntarily returned to the front, under a heavy fire, and carried a wounded man to a place of safety. Maynard was awarded his medal in 1888.

McAdams, Peter. Birth: Ireland, 1834. Corporal in Company A, 98th Pennsylvania Infantry. On May 3, 1863, at Salem Heights, Virginia, Corporal McAdams went 250 yards in front of his regiment toward the position of the enemy and under fire brought within the lines a wounded and unconscious comrade. McAdams was awarded his medal on April 1, 1898.

McAlwee, Benjamin F. Birth: District of Columbia, 1838. Sergeant in Company D, 3rd Maryland Infantry. On July 30, 1864, at Petersburg, Virginia, Sergeant McAlwee picked up a shell with a burning fuse and threw it over the parapet into the ditch, where it exploded. By this act he probably saved the lives of comrades at great peril to himself. McAlwee was awarded his medal on April 4, 1898.

McAnally, Charles. Birth: Ireland. Lieutenant in Company D, 69th Pennsylvania Infantry. On May 12, 1864, at Spotsylvania, Virginia, Lieutenant McAnally captured a Confederate flag in hand-to-hand combat with the bearer. McAnally was awarded his medal on August 2, 1897.

McCammon, William W. Birth: Ohio, 1836. First Lieutenant in Company E, 24th Missouri Infantry. On October 3, 1862, at Corinth, Mississippi, Lieutenant McCammon voluntarily assumed command of his company, then under fire, and so continued in command until the repulse and retreat of the enemy on the following day, the loss to his company during the battle being very great. McCammon was awarded his medal on July 9, 1896.

McCarren, Bernard. Birth: Ireland. Private in Company C, 1st Delaware Infantry. On July 3, 1863, at Gettysburg, Pennsylvania, Private McCarren captured a Confederate flag. McCarren was awarded his medal on December 1, 1864.

McCauslin, Joseph. Birth: West Virginia. Private in Company D, 12th West Virginia Infantry. On April 2, 1865, at Petersburg, Virginia, Private McCauslin exhibited conspicuous gallantry as color bearer in the assault on Fort Gregg. McCauslin was awarded his medal on May 12, 1865.

McCleary, Charles H. Birth: Ohio. First Lieutenant in Company C, 72nd Ohio Infantry. On December 16, 1864, at Nashville, Tennessee, Lieutenant McCleary captured the flag of the 4th Florida Infantry. McCleary was awarded his medal on February 24, 1865.

McClelland, James M. Birth: Ohio, 1831. Private in Company B, 30th Ohio Infantry. On May 22, 1863, at Vicksburg, Mississippi, Private McClalland exhibited exceptional gallantry in the charge of the volunteer storming party. McClelland was awarded his medal on August 13, 1894.

McClelland, Matthew. Birth: New York, 1833. First Class Fireman aboard the U.S.S. *Richmond*. On March 14, 1863, at Port Hudson, Louisiana, McClelland exhibited conspicuous gallantry after the ship's starboard and port safety valves had been damaged by enemy fire by continuing to penetrate the steam filled room to haul the fires. McClelland was awarded his medal on July 10, 1863.

McConnell, Samuel. Birth: Ohio. Captain of Company H, 199th Illinois Infantry. On April 9, 1865, at Fort Blakely, Alabama, Captain McConnell led his company in an assault, braving intense fire that mowed down his unit. Upon reaching the breastworks, he found that he had only one member of his company with him. McConnell entered the gun pit, causing the gun crew to flee, and seeing a Confederate flag bearer 30 paces away, he captured the flag and guard with the last shot in his pistol. McConnel was awarded his medal on June 8, 1865.

McCormick, Michael. Birth: Ireland, 1833. Boatswain's Mate aboard the U.S.S. *Signal*. On May 5, 1864, at Red River, Louisiana, McCormick served as gun captain, and though severely wounded early in the battle, bravely stood by his gun in the face of the enemy fire until ordered to withdraw. McCormick was awarded his medal on December 31, 1864.

McCornack, Andrew. Birth: Illinois, 1844. Private in Company I, 127th Illinois Infantry. On May 22, 1863, at Vicksburg, Mississippi,

Andrew McCornack (U.S. Army War College)

Private McCornack exhibited exceptional gallantry in the charge of the volunteer storming party. McCornack was awarded his medal on January 10, 1895.

McCullock, Adam. Birth: Maine, 1830. Seaman aboard the U.S.S. *Lackawana*. On August 5, 1864, at Mobile Bay, Alabama, Seaman McCullock was wounded when an enemy shell struck the ship. He refused to leave his station and continued to perform his duties throughout the prolonged action that resulted in the surrender of the ram *Tennessee* and in the damaging and destruction of Fort Morgan. McCullock was awarded his medal on December 31, 1864.

McDonald, George E. Birth: Rhode Island. Private in Company I, 1st Connecticut Heavy Artillery. On March 25, 1865, at Fort Stedman, Virginia, Private McDonald captured a Confederate flag. McDonald was awarded his medal on July 21, 1865.

McDonald, John. Birth: Scotland, 1817. Boatswain's Mate aboard the U.S.S. *Baron De Kalb*. From December 23 to 27, 1862, during the Yazoo River Expedition, McDonald distinguished himself in the various actions of his ship. McDonald was awarded his medal on April 3, 1863.

McDonald, John Wade. Birth: Ohio. Private in Company E, 20th Illinois Infantry. On April 6, 1862, at Shiloh, Tennessee, Private McDonald, though severely wounded himself, risked his life to carry a wounded and helpless comrade to a place of safety. McDonald was awarded his medal on August 27, 1900.

McElhinny, Samuel O. Birth: Ohio. Private in Company A, 2nd West Virginia Cavalry. On April 6, 1865, at Sailors Creek, Virginia, Private McElhinny captured a Confederate flag. McElhinny was awarded his medal on May 3, 1865.

McEnroe, Patrick H. Birth: Ireland. Sergeant in Company D, 6th New York Cavalry. On September 19, 1864, at Winchester, Virginia, Sergeant McEnroe captured the flag of the 36th Virginia Infantry. McEnroe was awarded his medal on September 27, 1864.

McFall, Daniel. Birth: New York, 1836, Sergeant in Company E, 17th Michigan Infantry. On May 12, 1864, at Spotsylvania, Virginia, Sergeant McFall captured Colonel Barker, the commander of the Confederate brigade that charged the Union batteries, That same day, he rescued Lt. George W. Harmon, of his regiment, from the enemy. McFall was awarded his medal on July 27, 1896.

McFarland, John. Birth: Massachusetts, 1840. Captain of the Forecastle aboard the U.S.S. *Hartford*. On August 5, 1864, at Mobile Bay, Alabama, McFarland performed his duties with skill and courage when the *Lackawana* ran into his ship and every man at the wheel was in danger of being crushed. He remained steadfast at his station and continued to steer the ship. McFarland was awarded his medal on December 31, 1864.

McGinn, Edward. Birth: New York. Private in Company F, 54th Ohio Infantry. On May 22, 1863, at Vicksburg, Mississippi, Private McGinn exhibited exceptional gallantry in the charge of the volunteer storming party. McGinn was awarded his medal on June 28, 1894.

McGonagle, Wilson. Birth: Ohio. Private in Company B, 30th Ohio Infantry. On May 22, 1863, at Vicksburg, Mississippi, Private McGonagle exhibited exceptional gallantry in the charge of the volunteer storming party. McGonagle was awarded his medal on August 15, 1894.

McGonnigle, Andrew J. Birth: New York, 1829. Captain and Assistant Quartermaster, United States Volunteers. On October 19, 1864, at Cedar Creek, Virginia, Captain McGonnigle was severely wounded while voluntarily leading a brigade of infantry and was commended for the greatest gallantry by General Sheridan. McGonnigle was awarded his medal on July 27, 1897.

McGough, Owen. Birth: Ireland. Corporal in Battery D, 5th United States Artillery. On July 21, 1861, at Bull Run, Virginia, Corporal McGough, through his personal exertions, under a heavy fire, brought one of the guns of his battery off the field; all the rest being captured. McGough was awarded his medal on August 28, 1897.

McGowan, John. Birth: Ireland, 1831. Quartermaster aboard the U.S.S. *Varuna*. On April 24, 1862, at forts Jackson and St. Philip, south of New Orleans, McGowan remained steadfast at the wheel throughout the thickest of the fight, continuing at his station rendering service with the greatest courage and skill until his ship, repeatedly holed and twice rammed by the enemy, was beached and sunk. McGowan was awarded his medal on April 3, 1863.

McGraw, Thomas. Birth: Ireland. Sergeant in Company B, 23rd Illinois Infantry. On April 2, 1865, at Petersburg, Virginia, Sergeant McGraw was one of the three soldiers most conspicuous for gallantry in the final assault. McGraw was awarded his medal on May 12, 1865.

McGuire, Patrick. Birth: Ireland. Private in the Chicago Mercantile Battery, Illinois Light Artillery. On may 22, 1863, at Vicksburg, Mississippi, Private McGuire, with others, carried by hand a cannon up to and fired it through an embrasure of the enemy's works. McGuire was awarded his medal on January 15, 1895.

McHale, Alexander U. Birth: Ireland, 1842. Corporal in Company H, 26th Michigan Infantry. On May 12, 1864, at Spotsylvania, Virginia, Corporal McHale captured a Confederate flag in a charge, threw the flag over in front of the works, and continued in the charge upon the enemy. McHale was awarded his medal on January 11, 1900.

McHugh, Martin. Birth: Ohio, 1837. Seaman aboard the U.S.S. *Cincinnati*. On May 27, 1863, at Vicksburg, Mississippi, Seaman McHugh was conspicuously cool under the fire of the enemy, never ceasing to fire until this proud ship went down. McHugh was awarded his medal on July 10, 1863.

McIntosh, James. Birth: Canada, 1833. Captain of the Top aboard the U.S.S. *Richmond*. On August 5, 1864, at Mobile Bay, Alabama, McIntosh performed his duties with skill and courage throughout the prolonged battle that resulted in the surrender of the ram *Tennessee* and the successful attacks carried out on Fort Morgan. McIntosh was awarded his medal on December 31, 1864.

McKay, Charles W. [photograph p. 136] Birth: New York, 1847. Sergeant in Company C, 154th New York Infantry. On May 8, 1864, at Dug Gap, Georgia, Sergeant McKay voluntarily risked his life in rescuing a wounded comrade who was lying between the lines. McKay was awarded his medal on April 13, 1894.

Charles McKay (U.S. Army War College)

Michael McKeever (U.S. Army War College)

Martin McMahon (U.S. Army War College)

McKee, George. Birth: Ireland. Color Sergeant in Company D, 89th New York Infantry. On April 2, 1865, at Petersburg, Virginia, Sergeant McKee displayed gallantry as color bearer in the assault on Fort Gregg. McKee was awarded his medal on May 12, 1865.

McKeen, Nineveh S. Birth: Illinois. First Lieutenant in Company H, 21st Illinois Infantry. On December 30, 1862, at Stone's River, Tennessee, Lieutenant McKeen, though wounded three times, captured the colors of the 8th Arkansas Infantry. McKeen was awarded his medal on June 23, 1890.

McKeever, Michael. Birth: Ireland, 1842. Private in Company K, 5th Pennsylvania Cavalry. On January 19, 1863, at Burnt Ordinary, Virginia, Private McKeever was one of a small scouting party that charged and routed a mounted force of the enemy six times their number. He led the charge in a most gallant and distinguished manner, going far beyond the call of duty. McKeever was awarded his medal on August 2, 1897.

McKnight, William. Birth: New York, 1840. Coxswain aboard the U.S.S. *Varuna*. On April 24, 1862, at forts Jackson and St. Philip, south of New Orleans, McKnight remained steadfast at his gun throughout the thickest of the fight and was instrumental in inflicting damage on the enemy until the *Varuna*, so badly damaged that she was forced to beach, was finally sunk. McKnight was awarded his medal on April 3, 1863.

McKown, Nathaniel A. Birth: Pennsylvania, 1838. Sergeant in Company B, 58th Pennsylvania Infantry. On September 29, 1864, at Chapin's Farm, Virginia, Sergeant McKown captured a Confederate flag. McKown was awarded his medal on April 6, 1865.

McLeod, James. Birth: Scotland. Captain of the Foretop aboard the U.S.S. *Pensacola*. On April 24 and 25, 1862, at forts Jackson and St. Philip, south of New Orleans, McLeod acted as gun captain of the rifled howitzer aft which was much exposed. He served this piece with great ability and activity, although no officer superintended it. McLeod was awarded his medal on April 3, 1863.

McMahon, Martin T. Birth: Canada, 1838. Captain and aide-de-camp United States Volunteers. On June 30, 1862, at White Oak Swamp, Virginia, Captain McMahon, under fire, successfully destroyed a valuable train that had been abandoned and prevented it from falling into the hands of the enemy. McMahon was awarded his medal on March 10, 1891.

McMillen, Francis M. Birth: Kentucky, 1832. Sergeant in Company C, 110th Ohio Infantry. On April 2, 1865, at Petersburg, Virginia, Sergeant McMillen captured a Confederate flag. McMillen was awarded his medal on May 10, 1865.

McVeane, John P. Birth: Canada. Corporal in Company D, 49th New York Infantry. On May 4, 1863, at Fredericksburg Heights, Virginia, Corporal McVeane shot a Confederate color bearer and seized the flag. He also approached, alone, a barn between the lines and demanded and received the surrender of a number of the enemy therein. McVeane was awarded his medal on September 21, 1870.

McWhorter, Walter F. Birth: West Virginia. Commissary Sergeant in Company E, 3rd West Virginia Cavalry. On April 6, 1865, at Sailors Creek, Virginia, Sergeant McWhorter captured the flag of the 6th Tennessee Infantry. McWhorter was awarded his medal on May 3, 1865.

McWilliams, George W. Birth: Pennsylvania, 1844. Landsman aboard the U.S.S. *Pontoosuc*. From December 24, 1864, to February 22, 1865, at Fort Fisher, North Carolina, McWilliams carried out his duties faithfully. He was severely wounded in the landing party assault on Fort Fisher, and was recommended for his gallantry, skill, and coolness in action while under the fire of the enemy. McWilliams was awarded his medal on June 22, 1865.

Meach, George E. Birth: New York. Farrier in Company I, 6th New York Cavalry. On September 19, 1864, at Winchester, Virginia, Meach captured a Confederate flag. Meach was awarded his medal on September 27, 1864.

Meagher, Thomas. Birth: Scotland. First Sergeant in Company G, 158th New York Infantry. On September 29, 1864, at Chapin's Farm, Virginia, Sergeant Meagher led a section of his men on the enemy's works, receiving a wound while scaling the parapet. Meagher was awarded his medal on April 6, 1865.

Mears, George W. Birth: Pennsylvania. Sergeant in Company A, 6th Pennsylvania Infantry Reserves. On July 2, 1863, at Gettysburg, Pennsylvania, Sergeant Mears, with five other volunteers, gallantly charged on a number of the enemy's sharpshooters concealed in a log house, captured them, and brought them in to Union lines. Mears was awarded his medal on February 16, 1897.

Melville, Charles. Birth: New Hampshire, 1828. Ordinary Seaman aboard the U.S.S. *Hartford*. On August 5, 1864, at Mobile Bay, Alabama, Seaman Melville was wounded when a shell burst between the two forward 9-inch guns, and was taken below for treatment. He promptly returned to his gun on the deck and, although scarcely able to stand, refused to go below and continued to man his post throughout the remainder of the action resulting in the capture of the ram *Tennessee*. Melville was awarded his medal on December 31, 1864.

George Mears (Hall of Heroes)

Menter, John W. Birth: New York, 1840. Sergeant in Company D, 5th Michigan Infantry. On April 6, 1865, at Sailors Creek, Virginia, Sergeant Menter captured a Confederate flag. Menter was awarded his medal on May 10, 1865.

Merriam, Henry C. Birth: Maine. Lieutenant Colonel of the 73rd United States Colored Infantry. On April 9, 1865, at Fort Blakely, Alabama, Colonel Merriam volunteered to attack the enemy's works in advance of orders and, upon permission being given, made a most gallant assault. Merriam was awarded his medal on June 28, 1894.

Merrifield, James K. Birth: Pennsylvania. Corporal in Company C, 88th Illinois Infantry. On November 30, 1864, at Franklin, Tennessee, Corporal Merrifield captured two Confederate flags and returned with them to his own lines. Merrifield was awarded his medal on March 28, 1896.

Henry Merriam (Hall of Heroes)

Merrill, Augustus. Birth: Maine. Captain in Company B, 1st Maine Infantry. On April 2, 1865, at Petersburg, Virginia, Captain Merrill, with six men, captured 69 Confederate prisoners and recaptured several soldiers who had fallen into the enemy's hands. Merrill was awarded his medal on October 23, 1891.

Merrill, George. Birth: New York. Private in Company I, 142nd New York Infantry. On January 15, 1865, at Fort Fisher, North Carolina, Private Merrill Voluntarily advanced with the head of the column and cut down the palisading. Merrill was awarded his medal on December 28, 1914.

Merritt, John G. Birth: New York. Sergeant in Company K, 1st Minnesota Infantry. On July 21, 1861, at Bull Run, Virginia, Sergeant Merritt was wounded while capturing a Confederate flag in advance of his regiment. Merritt was awarded his medal on April 1, 1880.

John Merritt (Hall of Heroes)

Meyer, Henry C. Birth: New York. Captain of Company D, 24th New York Cavalry. On June 17, 1864, at Petersburg, Virginia, Captain Meyer rendered heroic assistance to a wounded and helpless officer, in the face of heavy fire, and rescued the man, while receiving a severe wound himself in the process. Meyer was awarded his medal on March 29, 1899.

Mifflin, James. Birth: Virginia, 1839. Engineer's Cook aboard the U.S.S. *Brooklyn*. On August 5, 1864, at Mobile Bay, Alabama, Mifflin remained steadfast at his post and performed his duties in the powder division throughout the furious action that resulted in the surrender of the ram *Tennessee* and in the damaging and destruction of the batteries at Fort Morgan. Mifflin was awarded his medal on December 31, 1864.

Nelson Miles (Hall of Heroes)

Miles, Nelson A. Birth: Massachusetts. Colonel of the 61st New York Infantry. On May 2 to 3, 1863, at Chancellorsville, Virginia, Colonel Miles displayed distinguished gallantry while holding with his command an advanced position against repeated assaults by a strong force of the enemy, and was severely wounded in the process. Miles was awarded his medal on July 23, 1892.

Miller, Andrew. Birth: Germany, 1836. Sergeant in the United States Marine Corps serving aboard the U.S.S. *Richmond*. On August 5, 1864, at Mobile Bay, Alabama, Sergeant Miller fought his gun with skill and courage throughout the furious two hour battle that resulted in the surrender of the ram *Tennessee* and in the damaging and destruction of batteries at Fort Morgan. Miller was awarded his medal on December 31, 1864.

Miller, Frank. Birth: New York. Private in Company M, 2nd New York Cavalry. On April 6, 1865, at Sailors Creek, Virginia, Private Miller captured the flag of the 25th Battalion Virginia Infantry. Miller was awarded his medal on April 24, 1865.

Miller, Henry A. Birth: Germany, 1839. Captain in Company B, 8th Illinois Infantry. On April 9, 1865, at Fort Blakely, Alabama, Captain Miller captured a Confederate flag. Miller was awarded his medal on June 8, 1865.

Miller, Jacob C. Birth: Ohio. Private in Company G, 113th Illinois Infantry. On May 22, 1863, at Vicksburg, Mississippi, Private Miller exhibited exceptional gallantry in the charge of the volunteer storming party. Miller was awarded his medal on August 20, 1894.

Miller, James. Birth: Denmark, 1835. Quartermaster on the U.S.S. *Marblehead*. On December 25, 1863, during an engagement with the enemy on John's Island, Miller acted courageously under fierce hostile fire, and behaved gallantly throughout the engagement which resulted in the enemy's withdrawal and abandonment of its arms. Miller was awarded his medal on April 16, 1864.

Miller, James P. Birth: Ohio. Private in Company D, 4th Iowa Cavalry. On April 2, 1865, at Selma, Alabama, Private Miller captured the flag of the 12th Mississippi Cavalry. Miller was awarded his medal on June 17, 1865.

James Miller [Denmark, 1835] (U.S. Army War College)

Miller, John. Birth: Germany. Corporal in Company G, 8th Ohio Infantry. On July 3, 1863, at Gettysburg, Penn-

William Miller (Hall of Heroes)

George Mindil (Hall of Heroes)

sylvania, Corporal Miller captured two Confederate flags. Miller was awarded his medal on December 1, 1864.

Miller, John. Birth: Germany. Private in Company H, 8th New York Cavalry. On March 2, 1865, at Waynesboro, Virginia, Private Miller captured a Confederate flag. Miller was awarded his medal on March 26, 1865.

Miller, William E. Birth: Pennsylvania, 1836. Captain in Company H, 3rd Pennsylvania Cavalry. On July 3, 1863, at Gettysburg, Pennsylvania, Captain Miller, without orders, led a charge of his squadron upon the flank of the enemy, checked his attack, and cut off and dispersed the rear of his column. Miller was awarded his medal on July 21, 1897.

Milliken, Daniel. Birth: Maine, 1838. Quarter Gunner aboard the U.S.S. *New Ironsides*. From December 24 to 25, 1864 and January 13 to 15, 1865, Milliken and displayed coolness and skill in the assaults on the fort. Milliken was awarded his medal on June 22, 1865.

Mills, Charles. Birth: New York, 1843. Seaman aboard the U.S.S. *Minnesota*. On January 15, 1865, at Fort Fisher, North Carolina, Seaman Mills was a volunteer for the landing party from his ship. Mills charged up to the palisades and, when more than two-thirds of the men became seized with panic and retreated, he risked his life to remain with a wounded officer. Mills waited till after dark and then assisted the wounded man from the field. Mills was awarded his medal on June 22, 1865.

Mills, Frank W. Birth: New York. Sergeant in Company C, 1st New York Mounted Rifles. On September 4, 1862, at Sandy Cross Roads, North Carolina, Sergeant Mills was scouting with an advance of 3 or 4 men when he came upon an enemy column and charged them without orders, capturing the entire force of 120 men. Mills was awarded his medal on April 2, 1898.

Mindil, George W. Birth: Germany. Captain in Company I, 61st Pennsylvania Infantry. On May 5, 1862, at Williamsburg, Virginia, Captain Mindil led a charge with a part of the regiment that pierced the enemy's center, silenced some of his artillery, and, getting in his rear, caused him to abandon his position. Mindil was awarded his medal on October 25, 1893.

Mitchell, Alexander H. Birth: Pennsylvania. First Lieutenant in Company A, 105th Pennsylvania Infantry. On May 12, 1864, at Spotsylvania, Virginia, Lieutenant

Mitchell captured the flag of the 18th North Carolina Infantry. Mitchell was awarded his medal on March 27, 1890.

Mitchell, Theodore. Birth: Pennsylvania, 1835. Private in Company C, 61st Pennsylvania Infantry. On April 2, 1865, at Petersburg, Virginia, Private Mitchell captured the flag of a Tennessee Brigade. Mitchell was awarded his medal on May 10, 1865.

Moffitt, John H. Birth: New York, 1843. Corporal in Company C, 16th New York Infantry. On June 27, 1862, at Gaines Mill, Virginia, Corporal Moffitt voluntarily took up the regimental colors after several color bearers had been shot down and carried them until he was wounded himself. Moffitt was awarded his medal on March 3, 1891.

John Moffitt (U.S. Army War College)

Molbone, Archibald. Birth: Rhode Island, 1840. Sergeant in Company G, 1st Rhode Island Light Artillery. On April 2, 1865, at Petersburg, Virginia, Sergeant Molbone was one of a detachment of 20 picked artillerymen who voluntarily accompanied an infantry assaulting party and who turned upon the enemy the guns captured in the assault. Molbone was awarded his medal on June 20, 1866.

Molloy, Hugh. Birth: Illinois, 1832. Ordinary Seaman aboard the U.S.S. *Fort Hindman*. On March 2, 1864, at Harrisonburg, Louisiana, Seaman Molloy saw the first sponger mortally wounded and jumped out of the port to the forecastle, recovered the sponge and sponged the loaded gun for the remainder of the action from his exposed position, despite the extreme danger to his person from the raking fire of enemy musketry. Molloy was awarded his medal on April 16, 1864.

Hugh Molloy (U.S. Army War College)

Monaghan, Patrick. Birth: Ireland, 1843. Corporal in Company F, 48th Pennsylvania Infantry. On June 17, 1864, at Petersburg, Virginia, Corporal Monaghan recaptured the colors of the 7th New York Heavy Artillery after they had been taken by the Confederates. Monaghan was awarded his medal on December 1, 1864.

Montgomery, Robert. Birth: Ireland, 1838. Captain of the Afterguard aboard the U.S.S. *Agawam*. On December 23, 1864, at Fort Fisher, North Carolina, Montgomery was part of the volunteer crew that attempted to blow up the fort with a powder boat. Montgomery was awarded his medal on December 31, 1864.

Moore, Charles. Birth: Ireland, 1839. Landsman aboard the U.S.S. *Marblehead*. On December 25, 1863, at Legareville, South Carolina, Landsman Moore was wounded in the fierce battle, but remained at his quarters until so exhausted by the loss of blood that he had to be taken below. Moore was awarded his medal on April 16, 1864.

Moore, Charles. Seaman aboard the U.S.S. *Kearsarge*. On June 19, 1864, at Cherbourg, France, Seaman Moore acted as sponger and loader of the 11 inch pivot gun of the second division during this bitter engagement. Moore exhibited marked coolness and good conduct and was highly recommended for his gallantry under fire by the divisional officer. Moore was awarded his medal on December 31, 1864.

Moore, Daniel B. Birth: Wisconsin, 1838. Corporal on Company E, 11th Wisconsin Infantry. On April 9, 1865, at Fort Blakely, Alabama, Corporal Moore risked his own life to save an officer who had been shot down and overpowered by superior numbers. Moore was awarded his medal on August 8, 1900.

Moore, George. Birth: Pennsylvania, 1838. Seaman aboard the U.S.S. *Rhode Island*. On December 30, 1862, off Cape Hatteras, North Carolina, Seaman Moore participated in the hazardous task of rescuing the officers and crew of the sinking *Monitor*. Moore was awarded his medal on June 22, 1865.

Moore, George G. Birth: West Virginia. Private in Company D, 11th West Virginia Infantry. On September 22, 1864, at Fishers Hill, Virginia, Private Moore captured a Confederate flag. Moore was awarded his medal on October 6, 1864.

Moore, Wilbur F. Birth: Illinois. Private in Company C, 117th Illinois Infantry. On December 16, 1864, at Nashville, Tennessee, Private Moore captured the flag of a Confederate battery. Moore was awarded his medal on February 22, 1865.

Moore, William. Birth: Massachusetts, 1834. Boatswain's Mate aboard the U.S.S. *Benton*. On December 27, 1862, on the Yazoo River, at Haines Bluff, Moore served courageously in carrying lines to the shore until the *Benton* was ordered to withdraw, even though he had been wounded during the engagement. Moore was awarded his medal on April 16, 1864.

Morey, Delano. Birth: Ohio. Private in Company B, 82nd Ohio Infantry. On May 8, 1862, at McDowell, Virginia, Private Morey rushed forward after the charge of the command had been repulsed to single-handedly capture two of the enemy's sharpshooters with an empty gun. Morey was awarded his medal on August 14, 1893.

Morford, Jerome. Birth: Pennsylvania. Private in Company K, 55th Illinois Infantry. On may 22, 1863, at Vicksburg, Mississippi, Private Morford exhibited exceptional gallantry in the charge of the volunteer storming party. Morford was awarded his medal on September 2, 1893.

Morgan, James H. Birth: New York, 1840. Captain of the Top aboard the U.S.S. *Richmond*. On August 5, 1864, at Mobile Bay, Alabama, Morgan fought his gun with skill and courage throughout the furious 2 hour battle that resulted in the surrender of the ram *Tennessee* and in the damaging and destruction of batteries at Fort Morgan. Morgan was awarded his medal on December 31, 1864.

Morgan, Lewis. Birth: Ohio. Private in Company I, 4th Ohio Infantry. On May 12, 1864, at Spotsylvania, Virginia, Private Morgan captured a Confederate flag. Morgan was awarded his medal on December 1, 1864.

Morgan, Richard H. [photograph p. 143] Birth: Indiana. Corporal in Company A, 4th Iowa Cavalry. On April 16, 1865, at Columbus, Georgia, Corporal Morgan captured a Confederate flag. Morgan was awarded his medal on June 17, 1865.

Richard Morgan (Hall of Heroes)

Morrill, Walter G. Birth: Maine. Captain in Company B, 20th Maine Infantry. On November 7, 1863, at Rappahannock Station, Virginia, Captain Morrill learned that an assault was to be made on the enemy's works by other troops and voluntarily joined the storming party with about 50 men of his regiment, and by his dash and gallantry rendered effective service in the assault. Morrill was awarded his medal on April 5, 1898.

Morris, William. Birth: Pennsylvania. Sergeant in Company C, 1st New York Cavalry. On April 6, 1865, at Sailors Creek, Virginia, Sergeant Morris captured the flag of the 40th Virginia Infantry. Morris was awarded his medal on May 3, 1865.

Morrison, Francis. Birth: Pennsylvania, 1845. Private in Company H, 85th Pennsylvania Infantry. On June 17, 1864, at Bermuda Hundred, Virginia, Private Morrison voluntarily exposed himself to a heavy fire to bring off a wounded comrade. Morrison was awarded his medal on August 2, 1897.

Morrison, John G. Birth: Ireland, 1842. Coxswain aboard the U.S.S. *Carondelet*. On July 15, 1862, on the Yazoo River, Mississippi, Morrison was commended for meritorious conduct in general and especially for his heroic conduct and his inspiring example to the crew in the engagement with the Rebel ram *Arkansas*. Morrison was awarded his medal on June 22, 1865.

Morse, Benjamin. Birth: New York, 1844. Private in Company C, 3rd Michigan Infantry. On May 12, 1864, at Spotsylvania, Virginia, Private Morse captured the flag of the 4th Georgia Battery. Morse was awarded his medal on February 24, 1891.

Morse, Charles E. Birth: France. Sergeant in Company I, 62nd New York Infantry. On May 5, 1864, at the Wilderness, Virginia, Sergeant Morse took the colors from the color sergeant, who had been mortally wounded, and carried them through the fight. Morse was awarded his medal on January 14, 1890.

John Morrison (U.S. Army War College)

Morton, Charles W. Birth: Ireland, 1836. Boatswain's Mate aboard the U.S.S. *Benton*. From December 23 to 27, 1862, on the Yazoo River, at Drumgould's Bluff, Morton served courageously throughout the battle against the hostile forces. Morton was awarded his medal on April 3, 1863.

Mostroller, John W. Birth: Pennsylvania. Private in Company B, 54th Pennsylvania Infantry. On June 18, 1864, at Lynchburg, Virginia, Private Mostroller voluntarily led a charge on a Confederate battery after all of the officers in the company had become disabled, compelling the battery to be removed. Mostollar was awarded his medal on December 27, 1894.

Mulholland, St. Clair A. Birth: Ireland, 1839. Major of the 116th Pennsylvania Infantry. On May 4 to 5, 1863, at Chancellorsville, Virginia, Major Mulholland, in command, of the picket line, held the enemy in check all night to cover the retreat of the army. Mulholland was awarded his medal on March 26, 1895.

Mullen, Patrick. Birth: Maryland, 1844. Boatswain's Mate aboard the U.S.S. *Wyandank*. On March 17, 1865, on Maddox Creek, Mullen rendered gallant service to his commanding officer, loading the howitzer and tiring it so carefully so as to kill and wound many Rebels, causing their retreat. Mullen was awarded a second Medal of Honor for his actions on May 1, 1865, when he engaged in picking up the crew of a swamped ship. Mullen dived into the water to save an officer who had gone under, rescuing him from drowning. His second medal was awarded on June 29, 1865.

Mundell, Walter L. Birth: Michigan, 1839. Corporal in Company E, 5th Michigan Infantry. On April 6, 1865, at Sailors Creek, Virginia, Corporal Mundell captured a Confederate flag. Mundell was awarded his medal on May 10, 1865.

Munsell, Harvey M. Birth: New York, 1843. Sergeant in Company A, 99th Pennsylvania Infantry. On July 1 to 3, 1863, at Gettysburg, Pennsylvania, Sergeant Munsell displayed gallant and courageous conduct as color bearer. Munsell was awarded his medal on February 5, 1866.

Murphy, Charles J. Birth: England, 1832. First Lieutenant and Quartermaster of the 38th New York Infantry. On July 21, 1861, at Bull Run, Virginia, Lieutenant Murphy voluntarily remained on the field after his regiment was forced back, to care for the wounded, and was taken prisoner. Murphy was awarded his medal on April 5, 1898.

Murphy, Daniel J. Birth: Pennsylvania. Sergeant in Company F, 19th Massachusetts Infantry. On October 27, 1864, at Hatchers Run, Virginia, Sergeant Murphy captured the

Walter Mundell (Hall of Heroes)

Harvey Munsell (U.S. Army War College)

Charles Murphy (U.S. Army War College)

flag of the 47th North Carolina Infantry. Murphy was awarded his medal on December 1, 1864.

Murphy, Dennis, J.F. Birth: Ireland. Sergeant in Company F, 14th Wisconsin Infantry. On October 3, 1862, at Corinth, Mississippi. Sergeant Murphy, though wounded three times, carried the colors throughout the conflict. Murphy was awarded his medal on January 22, 1892.

Murphy, James T. Birth: Canada. Private in Company L, 1st Connecticut Heavy Artillery. On March 25, 1865, at Petersburg, Virginia, Private Murphy voluntarily assisted in working a piece of artillery that had been silenced by the enemy, conducting himself throughout the engagement in a gallant and fearless manner. Murphy was awarded his medal on October 29, 1886.

Murphy, John P. Birth: Ireland, 1844. Private in Company K, 5th Ohio Infantry. On September 17, 1862, at Antietam, Maryland, Private Murphy captured the flag of the 13th Alabama Infantry. Murphy was awarded his medal on September 11, 1866.

Murphy, Michael C. Birth: Ireland. Lieutenant Colonel of the 170th New York Infantry. On May 24, 1864, at North Anna River, Virginia, Colonel Murphy kept his regiment on the field, exposed to the fire of the enemy, for three hours without being able to fire one shot in return, because their ammunition had been exhausted. Murphy was awarded his medal on January 15, 1897.

Murphy, Patrick. Birth: Ireland, 1823. Boatswain's Mate aboard the U.S.S. *Metacomet*. On August 5, 1864, at Mobile Bay, Alabama, Murphy performed his duties with skill and courage throughout the furious two hour battle that resulted in the surrender of the ram *Tennessee* and in the damaging and destruction of batteries at Fort Morgan. Murphy was awarded his medal on December 31, 1864.

Murphy, Robinson B. Birth: Illinois. Musician in Company A, 127th Illinois Infantry. On July 28, 1864, at Atlanta, Georgia, Murphy, while acting as an orderly to the brigade commander, voluntarily led two regiments as reinforcements into line of battle, there he had his horse shot under him. Murphy was awarded his medal on July 22, 1890.

Murphy, Thomas. Birth: New York. Corporal in Company K, 158th New York Infantry. On September 30, 1864, at Chapin's Farm, Virginia, Corporal Murphy captured a Confederate flag. Murphy was awarded his medal on October 15, 1864.

Murphy, Thomas C. Birth: Ireland, 1842. Corporal of Company I, 31st Illinois Infantry. On May 22, 1863, at Vicksburg, Mississippi, Corporal Murphy voluntarily crossed the line of heavy fire of Union and Confederate forces, carrying a message to stop the firing of one Union regiment on another. Murphy was awarded his medal on August 14, 1893.

Murphy, Thomas J. Birth: Ireland. First Sergeant in Company G, 146th New York Infantry. On April 1, 1865, at Five Forks, Virginia, Sergeant Murphy captured a Confederate flag. Murphy was awarded his medal on May 10, 1865.

Myers, George S. Birth: Ohio. Private in Company F, 101st Ohio Infantry. On September 19, 1863, at Chickamauga, Georgia, Private Myers saved the regimental colors by the greatest personal devotion and bravery. Myers was awarded his medal on April 9, 1894.

Myers, William H. Birth: Pennsylvania. Private in Company A, 1st Maryland Cavalry. On April 9, 1865, at Appomattox, Virginia, Private Myers displayed extreme gallantry in action, being wounded five times. Myers was awarded his medal on June 14, 1871.

Nash, Henry H. Birth: Michigan, 1842. Corporal in Company B, 47th Ohio Infantry. On May 3, 1863, at Vicksburg, Mississippi, Corporal Nash was one of a party that volunteered and attempted to run the enemy's batteries with a steam tug and two barges loaded with subsistence stores. Nash was awarded his medal on February 15, 1909.

Naylor, David. Birth: New York, 1843. Landsman aboard the U.S.S. *Oneida*. On August 5, 1864, at Mobile Bay, Alabama, Naylor was acting as a powder boy at the 30-pounder Parrott rifle when he had his passing box shot from his hands and knocked overboard where it fell in one of the *Calena*'s boats which was under the bow. Naylor jumped overboard, recovered his box, and returned to his station, where he continued to carry out his courageous actions throughout the engagement. Naylor was awarded his medal on December 31, 1864.

Neahr, Zachariah C. Birth: New York, 1830. Private in Company K, 142nd New York Infantry. On January 15, 1865, at Fort Fisher, North Carolina, Private Neahr voluntarily advanced with the head of the column and cut down the palisading. Neahr was awarded his medal on September 11, 1890.

Neil, John. Birth: Canada, 1837. Quarter Gunner aboard the U.S.S. *Agawam*. On December 23, 1864, at Fort Fisher, North Carolina, Neil volunteered to be part of the crew of the powder boat that attempted to blow up the fort. Neil was awarded his medal on December 31, 1864.

Neville, Edwin M. Captain of Company C, 1st Connecticut Cavalry. On April 6, 1865, at Sailors Creek, Virginia, Captain Neville captured a Confederate flag. Neville was awarded his medal on May 3, 1865.

Newland, William. Birth: Massachusetts, 1841. Ordinary Seaman aboard the U.S.S. *Oneida*. On August 5, 1864, at Mobile Bay, Alabama, Seaman Newland carried out his duties as loader of the after 11-inch gun and distinguished himself by his good conduct and faithful discharge of his station, behaving splendidly under the fire of the enemy and throughout the battle that resulted in the surrender of the ram *Tennessee* and the damaging and destruction of batteries at Fort Morgan. Newland was awarded his medal on December 31, 1864.

William Newland (Hall of Heroes)

Newman, Marcellus J. Birth: Illinois, 1836. Private in Company B, 11th Illinois Infantry. On May 14, 1864, at Resaca, Georgia, Private Newman voluntarily returned, in the face of a severe fire from the enemy, and rescued a wounded comrade who had been left behind as the regiment fell back. Newman was awarded his medal on May 13, 1899.

Newman, William H. Birth: New York, 1838. Lieutenant in Company B, 86th New York Infantry. On April 6, 1865, at Amelia Springs, Virginia, Lieutenant Newman captured a Confederate flag. Newman was awarded his medal on May 10, 1865.

Nibbe, John H. Birth: Germany, 1842. Quartermaster aboard the U.S.S. *Peterel*. On April 22, 1864, on the Yazoo River, an enemy shot exploded the boilers. When all others had deserted the flag, Nibbe assisted in getting the wounded off the guard and proceeded to get ready to fire the ship despite the escaping steam at which time he was surrounded on all sides by the Confederates and forced to surrender. Nibbe was awarded his medal on June 22, 1865.

Nichols, Henry C. Birth: Vermont, 1832. Captain in Company C, 73rd United States Colored Infantry. On April 9, 1865, at Fort Blakely, Alabama, Captain Nichols voluntarily made a reconnaissance in advance of the line held by his regiment and, under a heavy fire, obtained information of great value. Nichols was awarded his medal on August 3, 1897.

Nichols, William. Birth: New York, 1837. Quartermaster aboard the U.S.S. *Brooklyn*. On August 5, 1865, at Mobile Bay, Alabama, Nichols fought his gun with skill and courage throughout the furious battle that resulted in the surrender of the ram *Tennessee* and the damaging and destruction of batteries at Fort Morgan. Nichols was awarded his medal on December 31, 1864.

Niven, Robert. Birth: New York, 1833. Second Lieutenant in Company H, 8th New York Cavalry. On March 2, 1865, at Waynesboro, Virginia, Lieutenant Niven captured two Confederate flags. Niven was awarded his medal on March 26, 1865.

Noble, Daniel. Birth: Kentucky, 1840. Landsman aboard the U.S.S. *Metacomet*. On August 5, 1864, at Mobile Bay, Alabama, Landsman Noble aided in the rescue of the crew of the sunken *Tecumseh*, thereby eliciting the admiration of both friend and foe. Noble was awarded his medal on January 15, 1866.

Nolan, John J. Birth: Ireland, 1844. Sergeant in Company K, 8th New Hampshire Infantry. On October 27, 1862, at Georgia Landing, Louisiana, Sergeant Nolan, although prostrated by a cannon shot, refused to give up the flag he was carrying as color bearer of his regiment and continued to carry it at the head of the regiment throughout the engagement. Nolan was awarded his medal on August 3, 1897.

John Nolan (U.S. Army War College)

Noll, Conrad. Birth: Germany, 1836. Sergeant in Company D, 20th Michigan Infantry. On May 12, 1864, at Spotsylvania, Virginia, Sergeant Noll seized the colors after the bearer had been shot down, and gallantly fought his way out with them, though the enemy were on the left flank and rear. Noll was awarded his medal on July 28, 1896.

North, Jasper N. Private in Company D, 4th West Virginia Infantry. On May 22, 1863, at Vicksburg, Mississippi, Private North exhibited exceptional gallantry in the charge of the volunteer storming party. North was awarded his medal on July 27, 1894.

Norton, Elliott M. Birth: Connecticut. Second Lieutenant in Company H, 6th Michigan Cavalry. On April 6, 1865, at Sailors Creek, Virginia, Lieutenant Norton captured the flag of the 44th Tennessee Infantry. Norton was awarded his medal on May 3, 1865.

Norton, John R. Birth: New York. Lieutenant in Company M, 1st New York Cavalry. On April 6, 1865, at Sailors Creek, Virginia, Lieutenant Norton captured a Confederate flag. Norton was awarded his medal on May 3, 1865.

Norton, Llewellyn P. Birth: New York, 1837. Sergeant in Company L, 10th New York Cavalry. On April 6, 1865, at Sailors Creek, Virginia, Sergeant Norton, with the assistance of Corporal Bringle, captured an enemy field piece with two prisoners. Norton was awarded his medal on July 3, 1865.

Elliott Norton (Hall of Heroes)

Noyes, William W. Birth: Vermont, 1846. Private in Company F, 2nd Vermont Infantry. On May 12, 1864, at Spotsylvania, Virginia, Private Noyes, standing upon the top of the breastworks, deliberately took aim and fired no less than fifteen shots into the enemy's lines, but a few yards away. Noyes was awarded his medal on March 22, 1892.

Nugent, Christopher. Birth: Ireland, 1840. Orderly Sergeant in the United States Marine Corps serving aboard the U.S.S. *Fort Henry*. On June 15, 1863, at Crystal River, Florida, Sergeant Nugent ordered an assault upon the Rebel breastworks. In this assault, the sergeant and his comrades drove a guard of eleven Rebels into the swamp, capturing their arms and destroying their camp equipage while gallantly withholding fire to prevent harm to a woman among the fugitives. Nugent was awarded his medal on April 16, 1864.

William Noyes (U.S. Army War College)

Nutting, Lee. Birth: New York. Captain of Company C, 61st New York Infantry. On May 8, 1864, at Todd's Tavern, Virginia, Captain Nutting led the regiment in a charge at a critical moment under a murderous fire until he fell desperately wounded. Nutting was awarded his medal on August 21, 1893.

O'Beirne, James R. [photograph p. 149] Birth: Ireland, 1844. Captain in Company C, 37th New York Infantry. From May 31 to June 1, 1864, at Fair Oaks, Virginia, Captain O'Beirne gallantly maintained the line of battle until ordered to fall back. O'Beirne was awarded his medal on January 20, 1891.

James O'Beirne (U.S. Army War College)

Henry O'Brien (Hall of Heroes)

Albert O'Connor (U.S. Army War College)

O'Brien, Henry D. Birth: Maine. Corporal in Company E, 1st Minnesota Infantry. On July 3, 1863, at Gettysburg, Pennsylvania, Corporal O'Brien took up the colors where they had fallen and rushed ahead of his regiment, close to the muzzle's of the enemy's guns, and engaged in the desperate struggle in which the enemy was defeated, and though severely wounded, held the colors until wounded a second time. O'Brien was awarded his medal on April 9, 1890.

O'Brien, Oliver. Birth: Massachusetts, 1839. Coxswain aboard the U.S.S. *John Adams*. On November 28, 1864, at Sullivan's Island, South Carolina, O'Brien was in charge of one of the boarding launches that captured the blockade runner *Beatrice* while under heavy fire from Fort Moultrie and carried out his duties with prompt and energetic conduct. O'Brien was awarded his medal on December 31, 1864.

O'Brien, Peter. Birth: Ireland. Private in Company A, 1st New York Cavalry. On March 2, 1865, at Waynesboro, Virginia, Private O'Brien captured a Confederate flag. O'Brien was awarded his medal on March 26, 1865.

O'Connell, Thomas. Birth: Ireland, 1842. Coal Heaver aboard the U.S.S. *Hartford*. On August 5, 1864, at Mobile Bay, Alabama, O'Connell, although a patient in sick bay, voluntarily reported at his station at the shell whip and continued to perform his duties with zeal and courage until his right hand was severed by an enemy shell burst. O'Connell was awarded his medal on December 31, 1864.

O'Connor, Albert. Birth: Canada, 1843. Sergeant in Company A, 7th Wisconsin Infantry. On March 31, 1865, at Gravelly Run, Virginia, Sergeant O'Connor, with a comrade, recaptured a Union officer from a detachment of nine Confederates, capturing three of the detachment. The date of O'Connor's award is unknown.

O'Connor, Timothy. Birth: Ireland, 1840. Private in Company E, 1st United States Cavalry. The date, place, and act of O'Connor's heroism are not on record at the War Department.

O'Dea, John. Birth: Ireland. Private in Company D, 8th Missouri Infantry. On

May 22, 1863, at Vicksburg, Mississippi, Private O'Dea exhibited exceptional gallantry in the charge of the volunteer storming party. O'Dea was awarded his medal on July 12, 1894.

O'Donnell, Menomen. Birth: Ireland, 1830. First Lieutenant in Company A, 11th Missouri Infantry. On May 22, 1863, at Vicksburg, Mississippi, Lieutenant O'Donnell voluntarily joined the color guard in the assault on the enemy works and when he saw indications of wavering caused the colors of his regiment to be planted in the parapet. O'Donnell was awarded his medal on September 11, 1897.

O'Donoghue, Timothy. Birth: New York, 1841. Seaman aboard the U.S.S. *Signal*. On May 5, 1864, on the Red River, Seaman O'Donoghue served as gun captain, and though wounded early in the battle, bravely stood by his gun in the face of enemy fire until ordered to withdraw. O'Donoghue was awarded his medal on December 31, 1864.

Paul Oliver (Hall of Heroes)

Oliver, Charles. Birth: Pennsylvania. Sergeant in Company M, 100th Pennsylvania Infantry. On March 25, 1865, at Petersburg, Virginia, Sergeant Oliver captured the flag of the 31st Georgia infantry. Oliver was awarded his medal on July 3, 1865.

Oliver, Paul A. Birth: at sea aboard an American flagship in the English Channel, 1831. Captain of Company D, 12th New York Infantry. On May 15, 1864, at Resaca, Georgia, Captain Oliver prevented a disaster caused by Union troops firing into each other. Oliver was awarded his medal on October 12, 1892.

David Orbansky (Hall of Heroes)

O'Neill, Stephen. Birth: Canada. Corporal in Company E, 7th United States Infantry. On May 1, 1863, at Chancellorsville, Virginia, Corporal O'Neill took up the colors, after the color bearer had been shot down, and bore them throughout the remainder of the battle. O'Neill was awarded his medal on September 28, 1891.

Opel, John N. Private in Company G, 7th Indiana Infantry. On May 5, 1864, at the Wilderness, Virginia, Private Opel captured the flag of the 50th Virginia Infantry. Opel was awarded his medal on December 1, 1864.

Orbansky, David. Birth: Prussia. Private in Company B, 58th Ohio Infantry. At Shiloh, Tennessee, and Vicksburg, Mississippi, in 1862 and 1863, Private Orbansky displayed gallantry in action. Orbansky was awarded his medal on August 2, 1879.

Charles Orr (Hall of Heroes)

Robert Orr (U.S. Army War College)

Jacob Orth (Hall of Heroes)

William Osborne (Hall of Heroes)

Orr, Charles A. Birth: New York. Private in Company G, 187th New York Infantry. On October 27, 1864, at Hatchers Run, Virginia, Private Orr and two others voluntarily, and under fire, rescued several wounded and helpless soldiers. Orr was awarded his medal on April 1, 1898.

Orr, Robert L. Birth: Pennsylvania, 1836. Major in the 61st Pennsylvania Infantry. On April 2, 1865, at Petersburg, Virginia, Major Orr carried the colors at the head of the column in the assault after two color bearers had been shot down. Orr was awarded his medal on November 28, 1892.

Ortega, John. Birth: Spain, 1840. Seaman aboard the U.S.S. *Saratoga*. Ortega served as seaman during actions of that vessel on two occasions, carrying out his duties courageously. Ortega was awarded his medal on December 31, 1864.

Orth, Jacob G. Birth: Pennsylvania. Corporal in Company D, 28th Pennsylvania Infantry. On September 17, 1862, at Antietam, Maryland, Corporal Orth captured the flag of the 7th South Carolina Infantry. Orth was awarded his medal on January 15, 1867.

Osborne, William H. Birth: Massachusetts. Private in Company C, 29th Massachusetts Infantry. On July 1, 1862, at Malvern Hill, Virginia, Private Osborne, although wounded and carried to the rear, secured another rifle and voluntarily returned to the front, where, failing to find his own regiment, he joined another and fought with it until again severely wounded and taken prisoner. Osborne was awarded his medal on April 1, 1898.

Oss, Albert. Birth: Belgium. Private in Company B, 11th New Jersey Infantry. On May 3, 1863, at Chancellorsville, Virginia, Private Oss remained in the rifle pits after the others had retreated, firing constantly, and contesting the ground step by step. Oss was awarded his medal on May 6, 1892.

Overturf, Jacob H. Birth: Indiana. Private in Company K, 83rd Indiana Infantry. On May 22, 1863, at Vicksburg, Mississippi, Private Overturf exhibited exceptional gallantry in the charge of the volunteer storming party. Overturf was awarded his medal on August 13, 1894.

Oviatt, Miles M. Birth: New York, 1841. Corporal in the United States Marine Corps serving aboard the U.S.S. *Brooklyn*. On August 5, 1864, at Mobile, Alabama, Corporal Oviatt fought his gun with skill and courage throughout the furious two hour battle that resulted in the surrender of the ram *Tennessee*. Oviatt was awarded his medal on December 31, 1864.

Packard, Loron F. Birth: New York. Private in Company E, 5th New York Cavalry. On November 27, 1863, at Raccoon Ford, Virginia, Private Packard voluntarily returned after his command hid retreated to rescue a comrade from the hands of three armed Confederates, Packard was awarded his medal on August 20, 1894.

Palmer, George H. Birth: New York, 1840. Musician in the 1st Illinois Cavalry. On September 20, 1861, at Lexington, Missouri, Palmer volunteered to fight in the trenches and led a charge that resulted in the recapture of a Union hospital, together with Confederate sharpshooters then occupying it. Palmer was awarded his medal on March 10, 1896.

Palmer, John G. Birth: Connecticut. Corporal in Company F, 21st Connecticut Infantry. On December 13, 1862, at Fredericksburg, Virginia, Corporal Palmer volunteered to assist in operating a battery upon which the enemy was concentrating its fire, and fought with the battery until the close of the engagement. Palmer was awarded his medal on October 30, 1896.

Palmer, William J. Birth: Delaware, 1836. Colonel of the 15th Pennsylvania Cavalry. On January 14, 1865, at Red Hill, Alabama, Colonel Palmer, with less than 200 men, attacked and defeated a superior force of the enemy, capturing their fieldpiece and about 100 prisoners, without losing a man. Palmer was awarded his medal on February 24, 1894.

Parker, Thomas. Birth: England. Corporal in Company B, 2nd Rhode Island Infantry. On April 2, 1865, at Petersburg, Virginia, Corporal Parker planted the first color on the enemy's works. On April 6, 1865, at Sailors Creek, Virginia, he carried the regimental colors over the creek after the regiment had broken and been repulsed. Parker was awarded his medal on May 29, 1867.

William Palmer (Hall of Heroes)

Parker, William. Birth: Massachusetts. Captain of the Afterguard aboard the U.S.S. *Cayuga*. On April 24 to 25, 1862, at Forts Jackson and St. Philip, and at New Orleans, Louisiana, Parker conscientiously performed his duties throughout the action in which attempts by three Rebel steamers to butt and board were thwarted and the ships driven off. Parker was awarded his medal on April 3, 1863.

Parks, George. Birth: New York, 1823. Captain of the Forecastle aboard the U.S.S. *Richmond*. On August 5, 1864, at Mobile Bay, Alabama, Parks performed his duties with skill and courage throughout the furious two hour battle that resulted in the surrender of the ram *Tennessee* and in the damaging and destruction of batteries at Fort Morgan. Parks was awarded his medal on December 31, 1864.

Parks, Henry Jeremiah. Birth: New York, 1848. Private in Company A, 9th New York Cavalry. On October 19, 1864, at Cedar Creek, Virginia, Private Parks, while alone and in advance of his unit, captured a color bearer, and, leaving him in the rear, returned to the front and captured three wagons and drivers. Parks was awarded his medal on October 26, 1864.

Parks, James W. Birth: Ohio. Corporal in Company F, 11th Missouri Infantry. On December 16, 1864, at Nashville, Tennessee, Corporal Parks captured a Confederate flag. Parks was awarded his medal on February 24, 1865.

Henry Parks (U.S. Army War College)

Parrott, Jacob. Birth: Ohio, 1843. Private in Company K, 33rd Ohio Infantry. In April of 1862, at Big Shanty, Georgia, Private Parrott was one of a party of 22 men who penetrated 200 miles into enemy territory and captured a railroad train in an attempt to destroy the bridges and tracks between Chattanooga and Atlanta. Parrot was awarded his medal on March 25, 1863, and was the first person to be awarded the Medal of Honor.

Parsons, Joel. Private in Company B, 4th West Virginia Infantry. On May 22, 1863, at Vicksburg, Mississippi, Private Parsons exhibited exceptional gallantry in the charge of the volunteer storming party. Parsons was awarded his medal on August 16, 1894.

Jacob Parrott (U.S. Army War College)

Patterson, John H. Birth: New York. First Lieutenant in the 11th United States Infantry. On May 5, 1864, at the Wilderness, Virginia, Lieutenant Patterson, under the heavy fire of the advancing enemy, picked up and carried several hundred yards to a place of safety a wounded officer of his regiment who was helpless and would otherwise have been burned in the forest. Patterson was awarded his medal on July 23, 1897.

Patterson, John T. Birth: Ohio. Musician in the 122nd Ohio Infantry. On June 14, 1863, at Winchester, Virginia, Patterson, with one companion, went in front of the Union line, under heavy fire, and carried back a helpless and wounded comrade, thus saving him from death or capture. Patterson was awarded his medal on May 13, 1899.

Paul, William H. Birth: Pennsylvania, 1844. Private in Company E, 90th Pennsylvania Infantry. On September 17, 1862, at Antietam, Maryland, Private Paul picked up the colors when the bearer and two of the color guard had been killed, and bore them throughout the entire battle. Paul was awarded his medal on November 3, 1896.

Pay, Byron E. Birth: New York, 1844. Private in Company H, 2nd Minnesota Infantry. On February 15, 1863, at Nolensville, Tennessee, Private Pay was one of a detachment of sixteen men who heroically defended a wagon train against the attack of 125 cavalry, repulsed the attack and saved the train. Pay was awarded his medal on September 11, 1897.

Payne, Irvin C. Birth: Pennsylvania. Corporal in Company M, 2nd New York Cavalry. On April 6, 1865, at Sailors Creek, Virginia, Corporal Payne captured a Confederate flag. Payne was awarded his medal on May 3, 1865.

Payne, Thomas H.L. Birth: Massachusetts, 1840. First Lieutenant in Company E, 37th Illinois Infantry. On April 9, 1865, at Fort Blakely, Alabama, Lieutenant Payne learned of an expected assault and requested assignment to a company that had no commissioned officers, was so assigned, and was one of the first to lead his men into the enemy's works. Payne was awarded his medal on April 1, 1898.

Pearsall, Platt. Birth: Ohio. Corporal on Company C, 30th Ohio Infantry. On May 22, 1863, at Vicksburg, Mississippi, Corporal Pearsall exhibited exceptional gallantry in the charge of the volunteer storming party. Pearsall was awarded his medal on August 14, 1894.

Pearson, Alfred L. Birth: Pennsylvania, 1838. Colonel of the 155th Pennsylvania Infantry. On March 29, 1865, at Lewis' Farm, Virginia, Colonel Pearson seized the regimental color after seeing the brigade being forced back, and called on the men to follow him. The whole brigade took up the advance and regained the lost ground. Pearson was awarded his medal on September 17, 1897.

Pease, Joachim. Birth: New York. Seaman aboard the U.S.S. *Kearsagre*. On June 19, 1864, at Cherbourg, France, Seaman Pease exhibited marked coolness and good conduct and was highly recom-

Alfred Pearson (Hall of Heroes)

mended by the divisional officer for gallantry under fire. Pease was awarded his medal on December 31, 1864.

Peck, Cassius. Birth: Vermont, 1842. Private in Company F, 1st United States Sharpshooters. On September 19, 1862, at Blackburn's Ford, Virginia, Private Peck took command of such soldiers as he could get and attacked and captured a Confederate battery of four guns. Peck was awarded his medal on October 12, 1892.

Peck, Oscar E. Birth: Connecticut, 1848. Second Class Boy aboard the U.S.S. *Varuna*. On April 24, 1862, at Forts Jackson and St. Philip, south of New Orleans, Peck served gallantly, as a powder boy, while the *Varuna* was repeatedly attacked and rammed and finally sunk. Peck was awarded his medal on April 3, 1863.

Peck, Theodore S. Birth: Vermont, 1843. First Lieutenant in Company H, 9th Vermont Infantry. On February 2, 1864, at Newport Barracks, North Carolina, Lieutenant Peck, by long and persistent resistance, and the burning of bridges, kept a superior force of the enemy at bay and covered the retreat of the garrison. Peck was awarded his medal on September 8, 1891.

Peirsol, James K. Birth: Pennsylvania. Sergeant in Company F, 13th Ohio Cavalry. On April 5, 1865, at Paine's Crossroads, Virginia, Sergeant Peirsol captured a Confederate flag. Peirsol was awarded his medal on May 3, 1865.

Pelham, William. Birth: Canada. Landsman aboard the U.S.S. *Hartford*. On August 5, 1864, at Mobile Bay, Alabama, Landsman Pelham continued to fight his gun throughout the furious two hour engagement that resulted in the surrender of the ram *Tennessee* and the damaging and destruction of batteries at Fort Morgan. Pelham was awarded his medal on December 31, 1864.

Pennypacker, Galusha. Birth: Pennsylvania, 1844. Colonel of the 97th Pennsylvania Infantry. On January 15, 1865, at Fort Fisher, North Carolina, Colonel Pennypacker gallantly led the charge over a traverse

Theodore Peck (U.S. Army War College)

William Pelham (Hall of Heroes)

Galusha Pennypacker (Hall of Heroes)

and planted the colors of one of his regiments thereon, whereupon he was severely wounded. Pennypacker was awarded his medal on August 17, 1891.

Pentzer, Patrick H. Birth: Missouri. Captain of Company C, 97th Illinois Infantry. On April 9, 1865, at Fort Blakely, Alabama, Captain Pentzer was among the first to enter the enemy's entrenchments, where he captured a Confederate general officer. Pentzer was awarded his medal on October 9, 1879.

Perry, Thomas. Birth: New York, 1836. Boatswain's mate aboard the U.S.S. *Kearsarge*. On June 19, 1864, at Cherbourg, France, Perry exhibited marked coolness and good conduct under the enemy fire and was recommended for gallantry by his divisional commander in the engagement with the raider *Alabama*. Perry was awarded his medal on December 31, 1864.

Pesch, Joseph. Birth: Prussia. Private in Battery A, 1st Missouri Light Artillery. On April 28 to 29, 1863, at Grand Gulf, Mississippi, Private Pesch voluntarily took position on board the steamer Cheeseman, in charge of all the guns and ammunition of the battery, and remained in charge of the same, although the steamer became unmanageable and was exposed for some time to a heavy fire from the enemy. Pesch was awarded his medal on March 10, 1896.

Peters, Henry C. Birth: Michigan, 1840. Private in Company B, 47th Ohio Infantry. On May 3, 1863, at Vicksburg, Mississippi, Private Peters was one of a party that volunteered and attempted to run the enemy's batteries with a steam tug and two barges loaded with subsistence stores. Peters was awarded his medal on April 5, 1917.

Peterson, Alfred. Birth: Sweden, 1838. Seaman aboard the U.S.S. *Commodore Perry*. On October 3, 1862, at Franklin, Virginia, Seaman Peterson remained at his post and performed his duties with skill and courage as the *Commodore Perry* fought a gallant battle to silence many Rebel batteries as she steamed down the Blackwater River. Peterson was awarded his medal on April 3, 1863.

Petty, Philip. Birth: England, 1840. Sergeant in Company A, 136th Pennsylvania Infantry. On December 13, 1862, at Fredericksburg, Virginia, Sergeant Petty took up the colors as they fell out of the hands of the wounded color bearer and carried them forward in the charge. Petty was awarded his medal on August 21, 1893.

Charles Phelps (Hall of Heroes)

Phelps, Charles E. Birth: Vermont, 1833. Colonel in the 7th Maryland Infantry. On May 8, 1864, at Laurel Hill, Virginia, Colonel Phelps rode to the head of the assaulting column, then much broken by severe losses and faltering under the close fire of artillery, placed himself conspicuously in front of the troops, and gallantly rallied and led them to within a few feet of the enemy's works, where he was severely wounded and captured. Phelps was awarded his medal on March 30, 1898.

Phillips, Josiah. Birth: New York. Private in Company E, 148th Pennsylvania Infantry. On April 2, 1865, at Sutherland Station, Virginia, Private Phillips captured a Confederate flag. Phillips was awarded his medal on May 10, 1865.

Phinney, William. Birth: Norway, 1824. Boatswain's Mate aboard the U.S.S. *Lackawana*. On August 5, 1864, at Mobile Bay, Alabama, Phinney showed much presence of mind in managing the gun, and gave much needed encouragement to the crew during the engagement that resulted in the capture of the prize Rebel ram *Tennessee* and in the damaging and destruction of Fort Morgan. Phinney was awarded his medal on December 31, 1864.

Phisterer, Frederick. Birth: Germany. First Lieutenant in the 19th United States Infantry. On December 31, 1862, at Stone's River, Tennessee, Lieutenant Phisterer voluntarily conveyed, under a heavy fire, information to the commander of a battalion of regular troops by which the battalion was saved from capture or annihilation. Phisterer was awarded his medal on December 12, 1894.

Frederick Phisterer (Hall of Heroes)

Pickle, Alonzo H. Birth: Canada, 1843. Sergeant in Company B, 1st Minnesota Infantry Battalion. On August 14, 1864, at Deep Bottom, Virginia, Sergeant Pickle, at the risk of his life, voluntarily went to the assistance of a wounded officer lying close to the enemy's lines and, under fire, carried him to a place of safety. Pickle was awarded his medal on June 12, 1895.

Pike, Edward M. Birth: Maine, 1838. First Sergeant in Company A, 33rd Illinois Infantry. On July 7, 1862, at Cache River, Arkansas, Sergeant Pike and a companion saved a cannon from capture, while under a severe fire at close range. Pike was awarded his medal on March 29, 1899.

Alonzo Pickle (U.S. Army War College)

Pingree, Samuel E. Birth: New Hampshire, 1832. Captain in Company F, 3rd Vermont Infantry. On April 16, 1862, at Lees Mills, Virginia, Captain Pingree gallantly led his company across a wide, deep creek, drove the enemy from the rifles pits, which were within two yards of the further

Edward Pike (U.S. Army War College)

Samuel Pingree (Hall of Heroes)

bank, and remained at the head of his men until a second time severely wounded. Pingree was awarded his medal on August 17, 1891.

Pinkham, Charles H. Birth: Massachusetts. Sergeant Major in the 57th Massachusetts Infantry. On March 25, 1865, at Fort Stedman, Virginia, Sergeant Pinkham captured the flag of the 57th North Carolina Infantry. Pinkham was awarded his medal on April 15, 1895.

Pinn, Robert. Birth: Ohio, 1843. First Sergeant in Company I, 5th United States Colored Infantry. On September 29, 1864, at Chapin's Farm, Virginia, Sergeant Pinn took command of his company after all the officers had been killed or wounded and gallantly led it in battle. Pinn was awarded his medal on April 6, 1865.

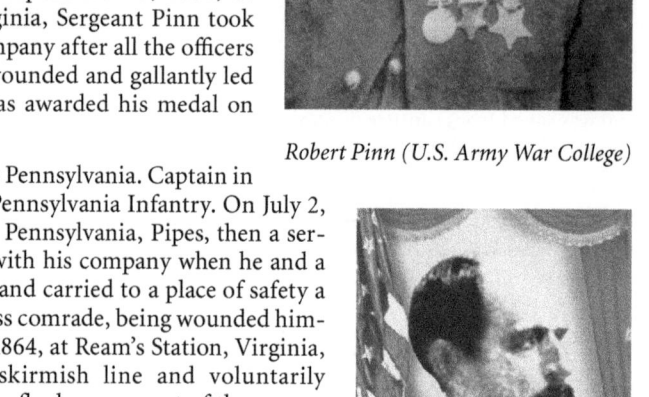

Robert Pinn (U.S. Army War College)

Pipes, James. Birth: Pennsylvania. Captain in Company A, 140th Pennsylvania Infantry. On July 2, 1863, at Gettysburg, Pennsylvania, Pipes, then a sergeant, was retiring with his company when he and a companion stopped and carried to a place of safety a wounded and helpless comrade, being wounded himself. On August 25, 1864, at Ream's Station, Virginia, he commanded a skirmish line and voluntarily assisted in checking a flank movement of the enemy, and while doing so was severely wounded. Pipes was awarded his medal on April 5, 1898.

Pitman, George J. Birth: New Jersey. Sergeant in Company C, 1st New York Cavalry. On April 6, 1865, at Sailors Creek, Virginia, Sergeant Pitman captured the flag of the Sumter Heavy Artillery. Pitman was awarded his medal on May 3, 1865.

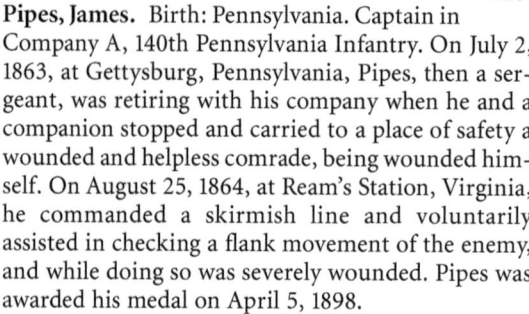

James Pipes (Hall of Heroes)

Pittinger, William. Birth: Ohio, 1840. Sergeant in Company G, 2nd Ohio Infantry. In April of 1862, at Big Shanty, Georgia, Sergeant Pittinger was on of a party of 22 men who penetrated nearly 200 miles into enemy territory and captured a railroad train in an attempt to destroy the bridges and track between Chattanooga and Atlanta. Pittinger was awarded his medal on March 23, 1863, the fifth person to be awarded the Medal of Honor.

Plant, Henry E. Birth: New York. Corporal in Company F, 14th Michigan Infantry. On March 19, 1865, at

William Pittinger (U.S. Army War College)

Bentonville, North Carolina, Corporal Plant rushed into the midst of the enemy and rescued the colors, the color bearer having fallen mortally wounded. Plant was awarded his medal on April 27, 1896.

Platt, George C. Birth: Ireland, 1842. Private in Troop H, 6th United States Cavalry. On July 3, 1863, at Fairfield, Pennsylvania, Private Platt seized the regimental flag upon the death of the standard bearer in a hand-to-hand fight and prevented it from falling into the hands of the enemy. Platt was awarded his medal on July 12, 1895.

George Platt (U.S. Army War College)

Plimley, William. Birth: New York. First Lieutenant in Company F, 120th New York Infantry. On April 2, 1865, at Hatcher's Run, Virginia, Lieutenant Plimley voluntarily accompanied a regiment in an assault on the enemy's works and acted as leader of the movement which resulted in the rout of the enemy and the capture of a large number of prisoners. Plimley was awarded his medal on April 4, 1898.

Plowman, George H. Birth: England. Sergeant Major of the 3rd Maryland Infantry. On June 17, 1864, at Petersburg, Virginia, Sergeant Plowman recaptured the colors of the 2nd Pennsylvania Provisional Artillery. Plowman was awarded his medal on December 1, 1864.

Plunkett, Thomas. Birth: Ireland. Sergeant in Company E, 21st Massachusetts Infantry. On December 11, 1862, at Fredericksburg, Virginia, Sergeant Plunkett seized the colors of the regiment, after the color bearer had been shot down, bearing them to the front where both his arms were carried away by a shell. Plunkett was awarded his medal on March 30, 1866.

Thomas Plunkett (Hall of Heroes)

Pond, George F. Birth: Illinois. Private in Company C, 3rd Wisconsin Cavalry. On May 15, 1864, at Drywood, Kansas, Private Pond, with two companions, attacked a greatly superior force of Guerrillas, routed them, and rescued several prisoners. Pond was awarded his medal on May 16, 1899.

Pond, James B. Birth: New York. First Lieutenant in Company C, 3rd Wisconsin Cavalry. On October 6, 1863, at Baxter Springs, Kansas, Lieutenant Pond, while in command of two compa-

James Pond (Hall of Heroes)

nies of cavalry, was surprised and attacked by several times his own number of guerrillas, but gallantly rallied his men, and after a severe struggle, drove the enemy outside the fortifications. He then went outside the works and, alone and unaided, fired a howitzer three times, throwing the enemy into confusion and causing him to retire. Pond was awarded his medal on March 30, 1898.

Poole, William B. Birth: Maine, 1833. Quartermaster aboard the U.S.S. *Kearsarge*. On June 19, 1864, at Cherbourg, France, Poole steered the ship during the engagement in a most cool and creditable manner and was highly commended by his divisional officer for his gallantry under fire in the engagement with the C.S.S. *Alabama*. Poole was awarded his medal on December 31, 1864.

Horace Porter (Hall of Heroes)

Porter, Ambrose. Birth: Maryland, 1839. Commissary Sergeant in Company D, 12th Missouri Cavalry. On August 7, 1864, at Tallahatchie River, Mississippi, Sergeant Porter was one of four volunteers who swam the river, under a brisk fire of the enemy's sharpshooters, and brought over a ferry boat by means of which the troops crossed and dislodged the enemy from a strong position. Porter was awarded his medal on August 24, 1905.

Porter, Horace. Birth: Pennsylvania, 1837. Captain in the Ordnance Department, United Stated Army. On September 20, 1863, at Chickamauga, Georgia, Captain Porter, acting as a volunteer aide, at a critical moment when the lines were broken, rallied enough men to hold the ground under heavy fire long enough to effect the escape of wagon trains and batteries. Porter was awarded his medal on July 8, 1902.

John Porter (Hall of Heroes)

Porter, John R. Birth: Ohio, 1838. Private in Company G, 1st Ohio Infantry. In April of 1862, at Big Shanty, Georgia, Private Porter was one of a party of 22 men who penetrated nearly 200 miles south into enemy territory and captured a railroad train in an attempt to destroy the bridges and track between Chattanooga and Atlanta. Porter was awarded his medal in September of 1863.

Porter, William. Birth: New York. Sergeant in Company H, 1st New Jersey Cavalry. On April 6, 1865, at Sailors Creek, Virginia, Sergeant Porter was among the first to check the enemy's counterchange. Porter was awarded his medal on July 3, 1865.

Post, Philip Sidney. [photograph p. 161] Birth: New York, 1833. Colonel of the 59th Illinois Infantry. On December 15 and 16, 1864, at Nashville, Tennessee, Colonel

Post led his brigade in an attack upon a strong position under terrific fire of grape, canister, and musketry, and was struck down by a grapeshot after he had reached the enemy's works. Post was awarded his medal on March 18, 1893.

Postles, James Parke. Birth: Delaware, 1840. Captain in Company A, 1st Delaware Infantry. On July 2, 1863, at Gettysburg, Pennsylvania, Captain Parke voluntarily delivered an order in the face of heavy fire of the enemy. Postles was awarded his medal on July 22, 1892.

Potter, George W. Birth: Rhode Island. Private in Company G, 1st Rhode Island Light Artillery. On April 2, 1865, at Petersburg, Virginia, Private Potter was one of a detachment of 20 picked artillerymen who accompanied an infantry assaulting party, and who turned upon the enemy the guns captured in the assault. Potter was awarded his medal on March 4, 1886.

Potter, Norman F. Birth: New York, 1826. First Sergeant in Company E, 149th New York Infantry. On November 24, 1863, at Lookout Mountain, Tennessee, Sergeant Potter captured a Confederate flag. Potter was awarded his medal on June 24, 1865.

Powell, William H. Birth: England. Major in the 2nd West Virginia Cavalry. On November 26, 1862, at Sinking Creek Valley, Virginia, Major Powell distinguished himself in a raid, where with twenty men, he charged and captured the enemy's' camp, 500 strong, without the loss of a man of gun. Powell was awarded his medal on July 22, 1890.

Power, Albert. Birth: Ohio. Private in Company A, 3rd Iowa Cavalry. On March 7, 1862, at Pea Ridge, Arkansas, Private Power, under a heavy fire and at great personal risk, went to the aid of a dismounted comrade who was surrounded by the enemy, took him up on his horse, and carried him to a place of safety. Power was awarded his medal on March 6, 1899.

Powers, Wesley J. Birth: Canada, 1845. Corporal in Company F, 147th Illinois Infantry. On April 3, 1865, at Oostanaula, Georgia, Corporal Powers voluntarily swan the river under heavy fire and secured a ferryboat, by means of which the command crossed. Powers was awarded his medal on October 24, 1895.

Prance, George. Birth: France, 1827. Captain of the Main Top aboard the U.S.S. *Ticonderoga*. December

Philip Post (Hall of Heroes)

James Postles (Hall of Heroes)

William Powell (Hall of Heroes)

24 to 25, 1864, and January 13 to 15, 1865, at Fort Fisher, North Carolina, Prance, as captain of a gun, performed his duties with skill and courage during the expeditions to capture the fort. Prance was awarded his medal on June 22, 1865.

Prentice, Joseph R. Birth: Ohio, 1838. Private in Company E, 19th United States Infantry. On December 31, 1862, at Stone's River, Tennessee, Private Prentice voluntarily rescued the body of his commanding officer, who had fallen mortally wounded. He brought off the field his mortally wounded leader under direct and constant rifle fire. Prentice was awarded his medal on February 3, 1894.

Preston, John. Birth: Ireland, 1841. Landsman aboard the U.S.S. *Oneida*. On August 5, 1864, at Mobile Bay, Alabama, Landsman Preston, though severely wounded in both eyes, attempted to return to his battle station. Preston was awarded his medal on December 31, 1864.

Preston, Noble D. First Lieutenant and Commissary in the 10th New York Cavalry. On June 11, 1864, at Trevilian Station, Virginia, Lieutenant Preston voluntarily led a charge in which he was severely wounded. Preston was awarded his medal on November 22, 1889.

Price, Edward. Birth: New York, 1840. Coxswain aboard the U.S.S. *Brooklyn*. On August 5, 1864, at Mobile Bay, Alabama, Price exhibited coolness and skill in keeping his gun in the action until the close of the action that resulted in the surrender of the ram *Tennessee* and the damage and destruction of Fort Morgan. Price was awarded his medal on December 31, 1864.

Province, George. Birth: New York, 1842. Ordinary Seaman aboard the U.S.S. *Santiago de Cuba*. On January 15, 1865, at Fort Fisher, North Carolina, Seaman Province was detailed to one of the generals on shore where he was one of six men who entered the fort from the fleet, and carried dispatches at the height of the battle. Province was awarded his medal on June 22, 1865.

Purcell, Hiram W. Birth: Pennsylvania. Sergeant in Company C, 104th Pennsylvania Infantry. On May 31, 1862, at Fair Oaks, Virginia, Sergeant Purcell was carrying the regimental color during the retreat and returned to face the enemy, flag in hand, and saved the other color, which would otherwise have been captured. Purcell was awarded his medal on May 12, 1894.

Purman, James J. Lieutenant in Company A, 140th Pennsylvania Infantry. On July 2, 1863, at Gettysburg, Pennsylvania, Lieutenant Purman voluntarily assisted a wounded comrade to a place of apparent safety while the enemy was in close proximity. He received the fire of the enemy and a wound that resulted in the amputation of his left leg. Purman was awarded his medal on October 30, 1896.

Putnam, Edgar P. [photograph p. 163] Birth: New York. Sergeant in Company D, 9th New York Cavalry. On May 27, 1864, at Crump's Creek, Virginia, Sergeant Putnam, with a small force, drove off a

James Purman (Hall of Heroes)

strong body of the enemy, charged into another force of the enemy's cavalry and stampeded them, taking 27 prisoners. Putnam was awarded his medal on May 13, 1892.

Putnam, Winthrop D. Birth: Massachusetts. Corporal in Company A, 77th Illinois Infantry. On May 22, 1863, at Vicksburg, Mississippi, Corporal Putnam, with others, carried a cannon up to and fired it through an embrasure of the enemy's works. Putnam was awarded his medal on April 4, 1898.

Pyne, George. Birth: England, 1841. Seaman aboard the U.S.S. *Magnolia*. On March 5 and 6, 1865, at St. Marks, Florida, Seaman Pyne served with the Army in charge of Navy howitzers during the attack on St. Marks. Though wounded, Pyne made remarkable efforts in the transport of the gun, and his coolness and determination in courageously standing by his gun while under the fire of the enemy was a credit to the service to which he belonged. Pyne was awarded his medal on June 22, 1865.

Quay, Matthew S. Birth: Pennsylvania, 1833. Colonel of the 134th Pennsylvania Infantry. On December 13, 1862, at Fredericksburg, Virginia, Colonel Quay voluntarily resumed duty on the eve of battle and took a conspicuous part in the charge on the heights, even though his enlistment had expired. Quay was awarded his medal on July 9, 1888.

Quinlan, James. Birth: Ireland, 1833. Major in the 88th New York Infantry. On June 19, 1862, at Savage Station, Virginia, Major Quinlan led his regiment on the enemy's battery, silenced the guns, held the position against overwhelming numbers, and covered the retreat of the 2nd Army Corps. Quinlan was awarded his medal on February 18, 1891.

Rafferty, Peter. Birth: Ireland. Private in Company B, 69th New York Infantry. On July 1, 1862, at Malvern Hill, Virginia, Private Rafferty, having been wounded, was directed to the rear, but he declined to do so, continuing in the action, until wounded again and captured by the enemy. Rafferty was awarded his medal on August 2, 1897.

Ramsbottom, Alfred. Birth: Ohio. First Sergeant in Company K, 97th Ohio Infantry. On November 30,

Edgar Putnam (U.S. Army War College)

Matthew Quay (Hall of Heroes)

Peter Rafferty (Hall of Heroes)

Charles Rand (Hall of Heroes)

George Ranney (Hall of Heroes)

Jacob Raub (U.S. Army War College)

1864, at Franklin, Tennessee, Sergeant Ramsbottom captured the flag of the 2nd Mississippi Infantry. Ramsbottom was awarded his medal on February 24, 1865.

Rand, Charles F. Birth: New York. Private in Company K, 12th New York Infantry. On July 18, 1861, at Blackburn's Ford, Virginia, Private Rand remained in action when part of his regiment broke in disorder, joined another company, and fought with it through the remainder of the engagement. Rand was awarded his medal on October 23, 1897.

Rannahan, John. Birth: Ireland, 1836. Corporal in the United States Marine Corps serving aboard the U.S.S. *Minnesota*. On January 15, 1865, at Fort Fisher, North Carolina, Corporal Rannahan exhibited exceptional gallantry as a part of the Naval landing party in the attack against the fort. Rannahan was awarded his medal on June 22, 1865.

Ranney, George E. Birth: New York, 1839. Assistant Surgeon in the 2nd Michigan Cavalry. On May 14, 1864, at Resaca, Georgia, Ranney went to the aid of a wounded soldier, lying under heavy fire between the lines, and with the aid of an orderly carried him to a place of safety. Ranney was awarded his medal on April 24, 1901.

Ranney, Myron H. Birth: New York. Private in Company G, 13th New York Infantry. On August 30, 1862, at Bull Run, Virginia, Private Ranney picked up the colors and carried them off the field after the color bearer had been shot down, and was wounded himself in the process. Ranney was awarded his medal on March 23, 1895.

Ratcliff, Edward. Birth: Virginia, 1835. First Sergeant in Company C, 38th United States Colored Infantry. On September 29, 1864, at Chapin's Farm, Virginia, Sergeant Ratcliff gallantly led his company after the commanding officer had been killed, and was the first enlisted man to enter the enemy's works. Ratcliff was awarded his medal on April 6, 1865.

Raub, Jacob F. Birth: Pennsylvania, 1840. Assistant Surgeon in the 210th Pennsylvania Infantry. On February 5, 1865, at Hatchers Run, Virginia Raub discovered a flank movement of the enemy, and, at great peril, advised the commanding general about it. Though a noncombatant, he voluntarily participated with the troops in repelling this attack. Raub was awarded his medal on April 20, 1896.

William Raymond (U.S. Army War College)

Raymond, William H. Birth: New York, 1844. Corporal in Company A, 108th New York Infantry. On July 3, 1863, at Gettysburg, Pennsylvania, Corporal Raymond voluntarily, and under a severe fire, brought a box of ammunition to his comrades on the skirmish line. Raymond was awarded his medal on March 10, 1896.

Read, Charles. Birth: New York, 1840. Ordinary Seaman aboard the U.S.S. *Magnolia*. From March 5 to 6, 1865, at St. Marks, Florida, Seaman Read made remarkable efforts in assisting transport of the gun, while serving with the Army, in charge of Navy howitzers. He displayed coolness and determination in courageously standing by his gun while under fire of the enemy and was a credit to the service to which he belonged. Read was awarded his medal on June 22, 1865.

Read, Charles A. Birth: Sweden, 1837. Coxswain aboard the U.S.S. *Kearsarge*. On June 19, 1864, at Cherbourg, France, Read exhibited marked coolness and good conduct and was highly recommended for his gallantry under fire by his divisional officer in the engagement that resulted in the destruction of the C.S.S. *Alabama*. Read was awarded his medal on December 31, 1864.

Read, George E. Birth: Rhode Island, 1838. Seaman aboard the U.S.S. *Kearsarge*. On June 19, 1864, at Cherbourg, France, Seaman Read, acting as the first loader of the No. 2 gun, exhibited marked coolness and good conduct and was highly recommended for his gallantry under fire by his divisional officer in the engagement with the C.S.S. *Alabama*. Read was awarded his medal on December 31, 1864.

Read, Morton A. Birth: New York, 1843. Lieutenant in Company D, 8th New York Cavalry. On April 8, 1865, at Appomattox Station, Virginia, Lieutenant Read captured the flag of the 1st Texas Infantry. Read was awarded his medal on May 3, 1865.

Rebmann, George F. Birth: Illinois. Sergeant in Company B, 119th Illinois Infantry. On April 9, 1865, at Fort Blakely, Alabama, Sergeant Rebmann captured a Confederate flag. Rebmann was awarded his medal on June 8, 1865.

William Reddick (U.S. Army War College)

Reddick, William H. Birth: Alabama. Corporal in Company B. 33rd Ohio Infantry. In April of 1862, Reddick, with 21 other men, penetrated 200 miles south into enemy territory and captured a railroad train at Big Shanty, Georgia, in an attempt to destroy the bridges and track between Chattanooga and Atlanta. Reddick was awarded his medal on March 25, 1863, and was the sixth man to be awarded the Medal of Honor.

Reed, Axel H. Birth: Maine. Sergeant in Company K, 2nd Minnesota Infantry. On September 19, 1863, at Chickamauga, Georgia, Sergeant Reed, while under arrest, left his place in the rear and voluntarily went to the line of battle, secured a rifle and fought gallantly during the two day battle, being released from arrest in recognition of his bravery. On November 25, 1863, at Missionary Ridge, Tennessee, he commanded his company, being among the first to enter the enemy works, where he was severely wounded, losing an arm, but declined a discharge and remained in active service to the end of the war. Reed was awarded his medal on April 2, 1898.

Reed, Charles W. Birth: Massachusetts. Bugler in the 9th Independent Battery, Massachusetts Light Artillery. On July 2, 1863, at Gettysburg, Pennsylvania, Reed rescued his wounded captain from between the lines. Reed was awarded his medal on August 16, 1895.

Charles Reed (Hall of Heroes)

Reed, George W. Birth: Pennsylvania. Private in Company E, 11th Pennsylvania Infantry. On August 21, 1864, at Weldon Railroad, Virginia, Private Reed captured the flag of the 24th North Carolina Infantry. Reed was awarded his medal on September 6, 1864.

Reed, William. Birth: Pennsylvania. Private in Company H, 8th Missouri Infantry. On May 22, 1863, at Vicksburg, Mississippi, Private Reed exhibited exceptional gallantry in the charge of the volunteer storming party. Reed was awarded his medal on December 12, 1895.

Charles Reeder (U.S. Army War College)

Reeder, Charles A. Birth: West Virginia, 1843. Private in Company G, 12th West Virginia Infantry. On April 2, 1865, at Petersburg, Virginia, Private Reeder captured a Confederate flag in the assault on Fort Gregg. Reeder was awarded his medal on April 2, 1867.

Regan, Jeremiah. Birth: Massachusetts, 1832. Quartermaster aboard the U.S.S. *Galena*. On May 15, 1862, at Drewry's Bluff, Virginia, Regan continued to man his gun throughout the engagement despite the concentration of fire directed against men at their guns by enemy sharpshooters in rifle pits along the banks. Regan was awarded his medal on April 3, 1863.

Reid, Robert. Birth: Scotland, 1842. Private in Company G, 48th Pennsylvania Infantry. On June 17, 1864, at Petersburg, Virginia, Private Reid captured the flag

Robert Reid (U.S. Army War College)

of the 44th Tennessee Infantry. Reid was awarded his medal on December 1, 1864.

Reigle, Daniel P. Birth: Pennsylvania, 1841. Corporal in Company F, 87th Pennsylvania Infantry. On October 19, 1864, at Cedar Creek, Virginia, Corporal Reigle rushed forward to capture a Confederate flag at the stone fence where the enemy's last stand was made. Reigle was awarded his medal on October 26, 1864.

Reisinger, J. Monroe. Birth: Pennsylvania. Corporal in Company H, 150th Pennsylvania Infantry. On July 1, 1863, at Gettysburg, Pennsylvania, Corporal Reisinger was specially brave and showed meritorious conduct in the face of the enemy. Reisinger was awarded his medal on January 25, 1907.

Daniel Reigle (U.S. Army War College)

Renninger, Louis. Birth: Ohio. Corporal in Company H, 37th Ohio Infantry. On May 22, 1863, at Vicksburg, Mississippi, Corporal Renninger exhibited exceptional gallantry in the charge of the volunteer storming party. Renninger was awarded his medal on August 15, 1894.

Reynolds, George. Birth: Ireland. Private in Company M, 9th New York Cavalry. On September 19, 1864, at Winchester, Virginia, Private Reynolds captured a Confederate flag. Reynolds was awarded his medal on September 27, 1864.

Rhodes, Julius D. Birth: Michigan. Private in Company F, 5th New York Cavalry. On August 28, 1862, at Thoroughfare Gap, Virginia, Private Rhodes had his horse shot from under him, at which point he voluntarily joined the 105th New York Infantry and was conspicuous in the advance on the enemy lines. On

Edmund Rice (Hall of Heroes)

August 30, 1862, at Bull Run, Virginia, he displayed gallantry on the skirmish line, where he was wounded. Rhodes was awarded his medal on March 9, 1887.

Rhodes, Sylvester D. Birth: Pennsylvania, 1842. Sergeant in Company D, 61st Pennsylvania Infantry. On September 22, 1864, at Fishers Hill, Virginia, Sergeant Rhodes was the first man to enter the enemy breastworks, where he captured one of the guns, and turned it upon the enemy. Rhodes was awarded his medal on February 16, 1897.

Rice, Charles. Birth: Russia, 1840. Coal Heaver aboard the U.S.S. *Agawam*. On December 23, 1864, at Fort Fisher, North Carolina, Rice volunteered to be part of the crew for the powder boat, and made the attempt to blow up the fort. Rice was awarded his medal on December 31, 1864.

Rice, Edmund. Birth: Massachusetts. Major of the 19th Massachusetts Infantry. On July 3, 1863, at Gettysburg, Pennsylvania, Major Rice showed conspicuous bravery in the countercharge against Pickett's division, where he fell severely wounded within the enemy's lines. Rice was awarded his medal on October 6, 1891.

Rich, Carlos H. Birth: Canada. First Sergeant in Company K, 4th Vermont Infantry. On May 5, 1864, at the Wilderness, Virginia, Sergeant Rich saved the life of an officer. Rich was awarded his medal on January 4, 1895.

Richards, Louis. Birth: New York, 1835. Quartermaster aboard the U.S.S. *Pensacola*. On April 24 and 15, 1862, at Forts Jackson and St. Philip, Louisiana, south of New Orleans, Richards steered the ship through the narrow opening, and his attention to orders contributed to the successful passage of the ship without once fouling the shore or the obstacles of the barricade. Richards, was awarded his medal on April 3, 1863.

Richardson, William R. Birth: Ohio. Private in Company A, 2nd Ohio Cavalry. On April 6, 1865, at Sailors Creek, Virginia, Private Richardson, having been captured and taken to the rear, made good his escape and rejoined the Union lines, where he furnished information of great importance as to the enemy's position and the approaches there to. Richardson was awarded his medal on April 7, 1866.

Richey, William E. Birth: Ohio, 1841. Corporal in Company A, 15th Ohio Infantry. On September 19, 1863, at Chickamauga, Georgia, Corporal Richey was in the extreme front, between the lines of the combatants, where he single handedly captured a Confederate major who was armed and mounted. Richey was awarded his medal on November 9, 1893.

Richmond, James. Birth: Maine. Private in Company F, 8th Ohio Infantry. On July 3, 1863, at Gettysburg, Pennsylvania, Private Richmond captured a Confederate flag. Richmond was awarded his medal on December 1, 1864.

Ricksecker, John H. Birth: Ohio. Private in Company D, 104th Ohio Infantry. On November 30, 1864, at Franklin, Tennessee, Private Ricksecker captured the flag of the 16th Alabama Artillery. Ricksecker was awarded his medal on February 3, 1865.

Riddell, Rudolph. Birth: New York. Lieutenant in Company I, 61st New York Infantry. On April 6, 1865, at Sailors Creek, Virginia, Lieutenant Riddell captured the flag of the 6th Alabama Cavalry. Riddell was awarded his medal on May 10, 1865.

Rudolph Riddell (Hall of Heroes)

Riley, Thomas. Birth: Ireland. Private in Company D, 1st Louisiana Cavalry. On April 4, 1865, at Fort Blakely, Alabama, Private Riley captured a Confederate flag. Riley was awarded his medal on June 8, 1865.

Ringold, Edward. Birth: Maryland, 1827. Coxswain aboard the U.S.S. *Wabash*. On October 22, 1862, at Pocataligo, South Carolina, Ringold accompanied the howitzer corps, performing his duty with such gallantry and presence of mind as to attract the attention of all around him. Ringold, knowing there was a scarcity of ammunition went through the whole line of fire with his shirt slung over his shoulder filled with fixed ammunition that he had brought from two miles to the rear of the lines. Ringold was awarded his medal on July 10, 1863.

Ripley, William Y.W. Birth: 1832. Lieutenant Colonel of the 1st United States Sharpshooters. On July 1, 1862, at Malvern Hill, Virginia, Colonel Ripley, at a critical moment, brought up two regiments, which he led against the enemy himself, being severely wounded. Ripley was awarded his medal on March 11, 1893.

Roantree, James S. Birth: Ireland, 1835. Sergeant in the United States Marine Corps, serving aboard the U.S.S. *Oneida*. On August 5, 1864, at Mobile Bay, Alabama, Sergeant Roantree performed his duties with skill and courage throughout the furious battle that resulted in the surrender of the ram *Tennessee* and in the damaging and destruction of batteries at Fort Morgan. Roantree was awarded his medal on December 31, 1864.

William Ripley (U.S. Army War College)

Robbins, Augustus I. Birth: Vermont. Second Lieutenant in Company B, 2nd Vermont Infantry. On May 12, 1864, at Spotsylvania, Virginia, Lieutenant Robbins, while voluntarily serving as a staff officer, successfully withdrew a regiment across and around a severely exposed position to the rest of the command, while being severely wounded. Robbins was awarded his medal on March 24, 1892.

Roberts, James. Birth: England, 1837. Seaman aboard the U.S.S. *Agawam*. On December 23, 1864, at Fort Fisher, North Carolina, Seaman Roberts volunteered to be part of the crew for the powder boat, and attempted to blow up the fort. Roberts was awarded his medal on December 31, 1864.

Samuel Robertson (U.S. Army War College)

Roberts, Otis O. Birth: Maine, 1842. Sergeant in Company H, 6th Maine Infantry. On November 7, 1863, at Rappahannock Station, Virginia, Sergeant Roberts captured the flag of the 8th Louisiana Infantry in hand-to-hand combat. Roberts was awarded his medal on December 28, 1863.

Robertson, Robert S. Birth: New York. First Lieutenant in Company K, 93rd New York Infantry. On May 8, 1864, at Corbin's Bridge, Virginia, Lieutenant Robertson saw a regiment breaking to the rear, seized its colors and rode with them to the front, in the face of the advancing enemy, and rallied the retreating regiment. Robertson was awarded his medal on August 2, 1897.

Robertson, Samuel. Birth: Ohio, 1843. Private in Company G, 33rd Ohio Infantry. In April of 1863, Private Robertson, along with 21 others, penetrated nearly 200 miles south into enemy territory and captured a railroad train and Big Shanty, Georgia, in an attempt to destroy the bridges and track between Chattanooga and Atlanta. Robertson was awarded his medal in September of 1863.

Robie, George F. Birth: New Hampshire. Sergeant in Company D, 7th New Hampshire Infantry. In September of 1864, at Richmond, Virginia, Sergeant Robie exhibited exceptional gallantry on the skirmish line. Robie was awarded his medal on June 12, 1883.

Robinson, Alexander. Birth: England, 1831. Boatswain's Mate aboard the U.S.S. *Howquah*. On September 25, 1864, at Wilmington, North Carolina, Robinson performed his duty faithfully under the most trying circumstances on the occasion of the destruction of the blockade runner *Lynx*. He stood firmly at his post in the midst of a crossfire from the Rebel shore batteries and his own vessels. Robinson was awarded his medal on December 31, 1864.

Robinson, Charles. Birth: Scotland, 1832. Boatswain's Mate aboard the U.S.S. *Baron de Kalb*. From December 23 to 27, 1862, on the Yazoo River Expedition, Robinson served bravely and distinguished himself in the various actions. Robinson was awarded his medal on April 3, 1863.

Robinson, Elbridge. Birth: Ohio. Private in Company C, 122nd Ohio Infantry. On June 14, 1863, at Winchester, Virginia, Private Robinson went in front of the Union line, under a heavy fire, and carried back a helpless, wounded comrade, thus saving him from death or capture. Robinson was awarded his medal on April 5, 1898.

Robinson, James H. Birth: Michigan. Private in Company B, 3rd Michigan Cavalry. On January 27, 1865, at Brownsville, Arkansas, Private Robinson successfully defended himself, single-handedly, against seven Confederate guerrillas, killing the leader, Captain W.C. Stephenson, and driving off the remainder of the party. Robinson was awarded his medal on April 4, 1865.

Robinson, John C. Birth: New York. Brigadier General, United States Volunteers. On May 8, 1864, at Laurel Hill, Virginia, General Robinson placed himself at the head of the leading brigade in a charge upon the enemy's breastworks, and was severely wounded. Robinson was awarded his medal on March 28, 1894.

Robinson, John H. Birth: Ireland. Private in Company I, 19th Massachusetts Infantry. On July 3, 1863, at Gettysburg, Pennsylvania, Private Robinson captured the flag of the 57th Virginia Infantry. Robinson was awarded his medal on December 1, 1864.

Robinson, Thomas. Birth: Ireland. Private in Company H, 81st Pennsylvania Infantry. On May 12, 1864, at Spotsylvania, Virginia, Private Robinson captured a Confederate flag in hand-to-hand combat. Robinson was awarded his medal on December 1, 1864.

John C. Robinson (Hall of Heroes)

Rock, Frederick. Birth: Germany. Private in Company A, 37th Ohio Infantry. On May 22, 1863, at Vicksburg, Mississippi, Private Rock exhibited exceptional gallantry in the charge of the volunteer storming party. Rock was awarded his medal on August 10, 1894.

Rockefeller, Charles M. Birth: New York. Lieutenant in Company A, 178th New York Infantry. On April 9, 1865, at Fort Blakely, Alabama, Lieutenant Rockefeller obtained valuable information about the enemy, that a reconnoitering party of 25 men had previously attempted and failed to obtain. The information he provided made possible the ensuing assault, during which, Rockefeller, with a few followers, captured 300 of the enemy. Rockefeller was awarded his medal on August 2, 1897.

Rodenbough, Theophilus F. Birth: Pennsylvania, 1838. Captain in the 2nd United States Cavalry. On June 11, 1864, at Trevilian Station, Virginia, Captain Rodenbough handled the regiment with great skill and valor and was severely wounded. Rodenbough was awarded his medal on September 21, 1893.

Rohm, Ferdinand F. Birth: Pennsylvania, 1843. Chief Bugler in the 16th Pennsylvania Cavalry. On August 25, 1864, at Reams Station, Virginia, Rohm, while his regiment was retiring under fire voluntarily remained behind to succor a wounded officer who was in great danger, secured assistance and removed the officer to a place of safety. Rohm was awarded his medal on October 16, 1897.

Theophilus Rodenbough (Hall of Heroes)

Rood, Oliver P. Birth: Kentucky. Private in Company B, 20th Indiana Infantry. On July 3, 1863, at Gettysburg, Pennsylvania, Private Rood captured the flag of the 21st North Carolina Infantry. Rood was awarded his medal on December 1, 1864.

Roosevelt, George W. Birth: Pennsylvania, 1844. First Sergeant in Company K, 26th Pennsylvania Infantry. On August 30, 1862, at Bull Run, Virginia, Sergeant Roosevelt recaptured the colors that had been taken by the enemy. On July 2, 1863, at Gettysburg, Pennsylvania, he captured a Confederate flag and its bearer, being severely wounded in the process. Roosevelt was awarded his medal on July 2, 1887.

Ross, Marion A. Birth: Ohio, 1832. Sergeant Major of the 2nd Ohio Infantry. In April of 1862, Sergeant Ross was on of a party of 22 men who penetrated nearly 200 miles south into the enemy's territory and captured a railroad train at Big Shanty, Georgia, in an attempt to destroy the bridges and track between Chattanooga and Atlanta. Ross was awarded his medal in September of 1863.

George Roosevelt (U.S. Army War College)

Rossbach, Valentine. Birth: Germany. Sergeant in the 34th New York Battery. On May 12, 1864, at Spotsylvania, Virginia, Sergeant Rossbach encouraged his cannoneers to hold a very dangerous position, and when all depended on several good shots it was from his piece that the most effective were delivered, causing the enemy's fire to cease and thereby relieving the critical position of the Federal troops. Rossbach was awarded his medal on July 10, 1896.

J. Levi Roush (Hall of Heroes)

Rought, Stephen. Birth: Pennsylvania, 1840. Sergeant in Company A, 141st Pennsylvania Infantry. On May 6, 1864, at the Wilderness, Virginia, Sergeant Rought captured the flag of the 13th North Carolina Infantry. Rought was awarded his medal on December 1, 1864.

Rounds, Lewis A. Birth: New York. Private in Company D, 8th Ohio Infantry. On May 12, 1864, at Spotsylvania, Virginia, Private Rounds captured a Confederate flag. Rounds was awarded his medal on December 1, 1864.

Rountry, John. Birth: Massachusetts, 1840. Fireman aboard the U.S.S. *Montauk*. On September 21, 1864, when fire was discovered in the magazine light room of the vessel, causing a panic and demoralizing the crew, Rountry, notwithstanding the cry of fire in the magazine, forced his way with hose in hand, through the frightened crowd to the light room and put out the flames. Rountry was awarded his medal on June 22, 1865.

Roush, J. Levi Birth: Pennsylvania. Corporal in Company D, 6th Pennsylvania Infantry Reserves. On July 2, 1863, at Gettysburg, Pennsylvania, Corporal Roush was one of six volunteers who charged upon a log house near Devil's Den where a squad of the enemy's sharpshooters were sheltered, and compelled their surrender. Roush was awarded his medal on August 3, 1897.

Rowand, Archibald, Jr. Birth: Pennsylvania, 1845. Private in Company K, 1st West Virginia Cavalry. During the winter of 1864–65, Private Rowand was one of two men who succeeded in getting through the enemy's lines with dispatches for General Grant. Rowand was awarded his medal on March 3, 1873.

Rowe, Henry W. Birth: New Hampshire, 1840. Private in Company I, 11th New Hampshire Infantry. On June 17, 1864, at Petersburg, Virginia, Private Rowe, with two companions, rushed and disarmed 27 enemy pickets and captured a stand of flags. Rowe was awarded his medal on December 1, 1864.

Rundle, Charles W. Birth: Ohio, 1842. Private in Company A, 116th Illinois Infantry. On May 22,

Archibald Rowand (U.S. Army War College)

1863, at Vicksburg, Mississippi, Private Rundle exhibited extreme gallantry in the charge of the volunteer storming party. Rundle was awarded his medal on July 26, 1894.

Rush, John. Birth: District of Columbia, 1835. First Class Fireman aboard the U.S.S. *Richmond*. On March 14, 1863, at Port Hudson, Louisiana, when a solid rifle shot shattered the starboard safety valve chamber and also damaged the port safety valve, the fire room of the *Richmond* immediately became filled with steam to place it in an extremely critical condition. Rush persisted in penetrating the steam filled room in order to haul the hot fires of the furnaces, and continued this action until the gravity of the situation had been lessened. Rush was awarded his medal on July 10, 1863.

Russell, Charles L. Birth: New York. Corporal in Company H, 93rd New York Infantry. On May 12, 1864, at Spotsylvania, Virginia, Corporal Russell captured the flag of the 42nd Virginia Infantry. Russell was awarded his medal on December 1, 1864.

Russell, Milton. Birth: Indiana. Captain of Company A, 51st Indiana Infantry. On December 29, 1862, at Stone's River, Tennessee, Captain Russell was the first man to cross Stone's River and, in the face of a galling fire from the concealed skirmishers of the enemy, led his men up the hillside, driving the opposing skirmishers before them. Russell was awarded his medal on September 28, 1897.

Rutherford, John T. First Lieutenant in Company L, 9th New York Cavalry. On May 11, 1864, at Yellow Tavern, Virginia, Lieutenant Rutherford led a successful charge that captured 90 prisoners. On May 27, 1864, at Hanovertown, Virginia, he led another charge upon a superior force of the enemy. Rutherford was awarded his medal on March 22, 1892.

James Rutter (U.S. Army War College)

Rutter, James M. Birth: Pennsylvania, 1841. Sergeant in Company C, 143rd Pennsylvania Infantry. On July 1, 1863, at Gettysburg, Pennsylvania, Sergeant Rutter risked his life to go to the assistance of a wounded comrade and, while under a heavy fire, removed him to a place of safety. Rutter was awarded his medal on October 30, 1896.

Ryan, Peter J. Birth: Ireland. Private in Company D, 11th Indiana Infantry. On September 19, 1864, at Winchester, Virginia, Private Ryan, with one companion, captured 14 Confederates in the severest part of the battle. Ryan was awarded his medal on April 4, 1865.

Sacriste, Louis J. Birth: Delaware, 1843. First Lieutenant in Company D, 116th Pennsylva-

Louis Sacriste (U.S. Army War College)

nia Infantry. On May 3, 1863, at Chancellorsville, Virginia, Lieutenant Sacriste saved from capture a gun of the 5th Maine Battery. On October 14, 1863, at Auburn, Virginia, he voluntarily carried orders that resulted in saving from destruction of capture the picket line of the 1st Division, 2nd Army Corps. Sacriste was awarded his medal on January 31, 1889.

Sagelhurst, John C. Birth: New York. Sergeant in Company B, 1st New Jersey Cavalry. On February 6, 1865, at Hatchers Run, Virginia, Sergeant Sagelhurst carried a severely wounded officer off the field under a heavy fire from the enemy. He also led a charge on the enemy's rifle pits. Sagelhurst was awarded his medal on January 3, 1906.

Sancrainte, Charles F. Birth: Michigan, 1840. Private in Company B, 15th Michigan Infantry. On July 22, 1864, at Atlanta, Georgia, Private Sancrainte captured the flag of the 5th Texas Regiment. Sancrainte was awarded his medal on July 25, 1892.

Sanderson, Aaron. Birth: North Carolina. Landsman aboard the U.S.S. *Wyandank*. On March 17, 1865, at Mattox Creek, Sanderson participated with a boat crew in clearing Confederates from the creek. Sanderson carried out his duties courageously in the face of a devastating fire which cut away half the oars, pierced the launch in many places and cut the barrel off a musket being fired at the enemy. Sanderson was awarded his medal on June 22, 1865.

Sands, William. Birth: Pennsylvania. First Sergeant in Company G, 88th Pennsylvania Infantry. On February 7, 1865, at Dabny's Mills, Virginia, Sergeant Sands captured a Confederate flag. Sands was awarded his medal on November 9, 1893.

Sanford, Jacob. Birth: Illinois. Private in the 55th Illinois Infantry. On May 22, 1863, at Vicksburg, Mississippi, Private Sanford exhibited exceptional gallantry in the charge of the volunteer storming party. Sanford was awarded his medal on September 2, 1893.

Sargent, Jackson. Birth: Vermont, 1842. Sergeant in Company D, 5th Vermont Infantry. On April 2, 1865, at Petersburg, Virginia, Sergeant Sargent was the first to scale the enemy works and plant the colors thereon. Sargent was awarded his medal on October 28, 1891.

Sartwell, Henry. Birth: New York, 1837. Sergeant in Company D, 123rd New York Infantry. On May 3, 1863, at Chancellorsville, Virginia, Sergeant Sartwell was severely wounded in his left arm by

Jackson Sargent (U.S. Army War College)

a gunshot. He went half a mile to the rear, but insisted on returning to his company, and continued to fight bravely until he became exhausted from loss of blood and was compelled to retire from the field. Sartwell was awarded his medal on November 17, 1896.

Saunders, James. Birth: Massachusetts, 1809. Quartermaster aboard the U.S.S. *Kearsarge*. On June 19, 1864, at Cherbourg, France, carried out his duties courageously throughout the bitter engagement with the C.S.S. *Alabama*. Saunders was awarded his medal on June 22, 1865.

Savacool, Edwin F. Birth: Michigan, 1835. Captain of Company K, 1st New York Cavalry. On April 6, 1865, at Sailors Creek, Virginia, Captain Savacool captured a Confederate flag and was mortally wounded in the process. Savacool was awarded his medal on April 24, 1865.

Savage, Auzella. Birth: Maine, 1846. Ordinary Seaman aboard the U.S.S. *Santiago de Cuba*. On January 15, 1865, at Fort Fisher, North Carolina, Seaman Savage was part of the Naval shore party that assaulted the fort. When more than two-thirds of the force fell back in panic, Savage remained steadfast, though enemy fire had shot away his flagstaff above his hands. He bravely seized the remainder of the staff and carried the colors safely off. Savage was awarded his medal on June 22, 1865.

Saxton, Rufus. Birth: Massachusetts, 1824. Brigadier General, United States Volunteers. From May 26 to 30, 1862, General Saxton displayed distinguished gallantry and good conduct in the defense of Harpers Ferry, West Virginia. Saxton was awarded his medal on April 25, 1893.

Scanlan, Patrick. Birth: Ireland. Private in Company A, 4th Massachusetts Cavalry. On May 24, 1864, at Ashepoo River, South Carolina, Private Scanlan volunteered to be part of a boat crew that went to the rescue of a large number of Union soldiers stranded aboard the steamer Boston, and with great gallantry assisted in conveying them to shore, being exposed the entire time to a heavy fire from the enemy. Scanlan was awarded his medal on January 21, 1897.

Scheibner, Martin E. Birth: Russia, 1840. Private in Company G, 90th Pennsylvania Infantry. On November 27, 1863, at Mine Run, Virginia, Private Scheibner

Rufus Saxton (U.S. Army War College)

voluntarily extinguished the burning fuse of a shell that had been thrown into the lines of the regiment by the enemy. Scheibner was awarded his medal on June 23, 1896.

Schenck, Benjamin W. Birth: Ohio, 1837. Private in Company D, 116th Illinois Infantry. On May 22, 1863, at Vicksburg, Mississippi, Private Schenck exhibited exceptional gallantry in the charge of the volunteer storming party. Schenck was awarded his medal on August 14, 1894.

Schiller, John. Birth: Germany. Private in Company E, 158th New York Infantry. On September 29, 1864, at Chapin's Farm, Virginia, Private Schiller gallantly advanced to the ditch of the enemy's works. Schiller was awarded his medal on April 6, 1865.

Schlachter, Philipp. Birth: Germany, 1841. Private in Company F, 73rd New York Infantry. On May 12, 1864, at Spotsylvania, Virginia, Private Schlachter captured the flag of the 15th Louisiana Infantry. Schlachter was awarded his medal on December 1, 1864.

Schmal, George W. Birth: Germany. Blacksmith in Company M, 24th New York Cavalry. On April 5, 1865, at Paine's Crossroads, Virginia, Schmal captured a Confederate flag. Schmal was awarded his medal on May 3, 1865.

Schmauch, Andrew. Birth: Germany. Private in Company A, 30th Ohio Infantry. On May 22, 1863, at Vicksburg, Mississippi, Private Schmauch exhibited exceptional gallantry in the charge of the volunteer storming party. Schmauch was awarded his medal on July 9, 1894.

Schmidt, Conrad. Birth: Germany. First Sergeant in Company K, 2nd United States Cavalry. On September 19, 1864, at Winchester, Virginia, Sergeant Schmidt went to the assistance of his regimental commander, whose horse had been killed under him in a charge, mounted the officer behind him, under heavy fire from the enemy, and returned him to his command. Schmidt was awarded his medal on March 16, 1896.

Schmidt, William. Birth: Ohio, 1846. Private in Company G, 37th Ohio Infantry. On November 25, 1863, at Missionary Ridge, Tennessee, Private Schmidt rescued a wounded comrade under a terrific fire. Schmidt was awarded his medal on November 9, 1895.

Schneider, George. Birth: Maryland, 1844. Sergeant in Company A, 3rd Maryland Infantry. On July 30, 1864, at Petersburg, Virginia, Sergeant Schneider seizes the colors, after the color bearer had been shot down, and planted them on the enemy's works during the charge. Schneider was awarded his medal on July 27, 1896.

Schnell, Christian. Birth: Virginia, 1838. Corporal in Company C, 37th Ohio Infantry. On May 22, 1863, at Vicksburg, Mississippi, Corporal Schnell exhibited exceptional gallantry in the charge of the volunteer storming party. Schnell was awarded his medal on July 10, 1894.

Schofield, David H. Birth: New York, 1840. Sergeant in Company K, 5th New York Cavalry. On October 19, 1864, at Cedar Creek, Virginia, Sergeant Schofield captured the flag of the 13th Virginia. Schofield was awarded his medal on October 26, 1864.

Schofield, John M. Birth: New York, 1831. Major in the 1st Missouri Infantry. On August 10, 1861, at Wilson's Creek, Missouri, Major Schofield was conspicuously gallant in leading a regiment in a successful charge against the enemy. Schofield was awarded his medal on July 2, 1892.

John Schofield (Hall of Heroes)

Schoonmaker, James M. Birth: Pennsylvania, 1842. Colonel of the 14th Pennsylvania Cavalry. On September 19, 1864, at Winchester, Virginia, Colonel Schoonmaker gallantly led a cavalry charge against the left of the enemy's line of battle, drove the enemy out of his works, and captured many prisoners. Schoonmaker was awarded his medal on May 19, 1899.

Schorn, Charles. Birth: Germany, 1842. Chief Bugler in Company M, 1st West Virginia Cavalry. On April 8, 1865, at Appomattox, Virginia, Schorn captured the flag of the Sumter Flying Artillery. Schorn was awarded his medal on May 3, 1865.

Schubert, Martin. Birth: Germany. Private in Company E, 26th New York Infantry. On December 13, 1862, at Fredericksburg, Virginia, Private Schubert relinquished a furlough for wounds, entered the battle, where he picked up the colors after several color bearers had been killed or wounded, and carried them until himself again wounded. Schubert was awarded his medal on September 1, 1893.

Schutt, George. Birth: Ireland, 1833. Coxswain aboard the U.S.S.

James Schoonmaker (U.S. Army War College)

Charles Schorn (Hall of Heroes)

Hendrick Hudson. From March 5 to 6, 1865, at St. Marks, Florida, Schutt served with the army in charge of Navy howitzers during the attack on St. Marks. Schutt made remarkable efforts in assisting transport of the gun and his coolness and determination in courageously remaining by his gun while under the heavy fire of the enemy was a credit to the service to which he belonged. Schutt was awarded his medal on June 22, 1865.

Schwan, Theodore. Birth: Germany, 1841. First Lieutenant in the 10th United States Infantry. On October 1, 1864, at Peeble's Farm, Virginia, Lieutenant Schwan risked his own life to rescue a wounded officer, while the regiment was falling back, thus saving him from death or capture. Schwan was awarded his medal on December 12, 1898.

Theodore Schwan (U.S. Army War College)

Schwenk, Martin. Birth: Germany. Sergeant in Company B, 6th United States Cavalry. In July of 1863, at Millerstown, Pennsylvania, Sergeant Schwenk exhibited bravery in attempting to carry a communication through the enemy's lines. He also rescued an officer from the hands of the enemy. Schwenk was awarded his medal on April 23, 1889.

Scott, Alexander. Birth: Canada. Corporal in Company D, 10th Vermont Infantry. On July 9, 1864, at Monocacy, Maryland, Corporal Scott, under a heavy fire from the enemy, saved the regimental colors from capture. Scott was awarded his medal on September 28, 1897.

Alexander Scott (Hall of Heroes)

Scott, John M. Birth: Ohio, 1839. Sergeant in Company F, 21st Ohio Infantry. In April of 1862, with 21 other men, Scott penetrated nearly 200 miles south into enemy territory and captured a railroad train at Big Shanty, Georgia, and attempted to destroy the bridges and track between Chattanooga and Atlanta. Scott was awarded his medal on August 4, 1866.

Scott, John Wallace. Birth: Pennsylvania, 1838. Captain in Company D, 157th Pennsylvania Infantry. On April 1, 1865, at Five Forks, Virginia, Captain Scott captured the flag of the 16th South Carolina Infantry in hand-to-hand combat. Scott was awarded his medal on April 27, 1865.

John M. Scott (U.S. Army War College)

Scott, Julian A. Birth: Vermont. Drummer in Company E, 3rd Vermont Infantry. On April 16, 1864, at Lee's Mills, Virginia, Scott crossed the creek under a terrific fire of musketry several times to assist in bringing off the wounded. Scott was awarded his medal in February of 1865.

Seaman, Elisha B. Birth: Ohio, 1838. Private in Company A, 66th Ohio Infantry. On May 2, 1863, at Chancellorsville, Virginia, Private Seaman, with three others, voluntarily brought into the Union lines a wounded Confederate officer from whom was obtained valuable information concerning the enemy. Seaman was awarded his medal on June 24, 1892.

Julian Scott (Hall of Heroes)

Seanor, James. Birth: Massachusetts, 1833. Master-at-Arms aboard the U.S.S. *Chickasaw*. On August 5, 1864, at Mobile Bay, Alabama, Seanor carried out his duties gallantly throughout the engagement that resulted in the surrender of the ram *Tennessee*. Seanor was awarded his medal on December 31, 1864.

Sears, Cyrus. Birth: New York, 1832. First Lieutenant in the 11th Ohio Light Artillery. On September 19, 1862, at Iuka, Mississippi, Lieutenant Sears, although severely wounded, fought his battery until the cannoneers and horses were nearly all killed or wounded. Sears was awarded his medal on December 31, 1892.

Seaver, Thomas O. Birth: Vermont, 1833. Colonel of the 3rd Vermont Infantry. On May 10, 1864, at Spotsylvania, Virginia, Colonel Seaver led three regiments under a most galling fire, and attacked and occupied the enemy's works. Seaver was awarded his medal on April 8, 1892.

Cyrus Sears (U.S. Army War College.)

Seitzinger, James M. Birth: Germany. Private in Company G, 116th Pennsylvania Infantry. On June 3, 1864, at Cold Harbor, Virginia, Private Seitzinger seized the colors when the color bearer went down, and bore them gallantly in a charge against the enemy. Seitzinger was awarded his medal on March 1, 1906.

Sellers, Alfred J. [photograph p. 180] Birth: Pennsylvania, 1836. Major of the 90th Pennsylvania Infantry. On July 1, 1863, at Gettysburg, Pennsylvania, Major Sellers voluntarily led the regiment under a withering

Thomas Seaver (U.S. Army War College)

fire to a position from which the enemy was repulsed. Seppers was awarded his medal on July 21, 1894.

Seston, Charles H. Birth: Indiana. Sergeant in Company I, 11th Indiana Infantry. On September 19, 1864, at Winchester, Virginia, Sergeant Seston gave gallant and meritorious service in carrying the regimental colors. Seston was awarded his medal on April 6, 1865.

Seward, Griffin. Birth: Delaware. Wagoner in Company G, 8th United States Cavalry. On October 20, 1863, at Chiricahva, Arizona, Seward displayed exceptional gallantry in action. Seward was awarded his medal on February 14, 1870.

Seward, Richard E. Birth: Maine, 1840. Paymaster's Steward United States Navy. On November 23, 1863, at Ship Island Sound, Louisiana, Seward volunteered to go on the field amidst a heavy fire to recover the bodies of two soldiers which he brought off with the aid of others. Seward was awarded his medal on April 16, 1864.

Sewell, William J. Birth: Ireland, 1835. Colonel of the 5th New Jersey Infantry. On May 3, 1863, at Chancellorsville, Virginia, Colonel Sewell assumed tie command of a brigade and rallied around his colors a mass of men from other regiments, fighting these troops with great brilliancy through several hours of desperate conflict. He remained in command though wounded, inspiring them by his presence and the gallantry of his personal example. Sewell was awarded his medal on March 25, 1896.

Shafter, William R. Birth: Michigan. First Lieutenant in Company I, 7th Michigan Infantry. On May 31, 1862, at Fair Oaks, Virginia, Lieutenant Shafter led his men in a charge against the enemy, at the close of which he was severely wounded. He remained on the field that day, and stayed to fight the following day, only by concealing his wounds. In order not to be sent home with the wounded, he concealed his wounds for another three days, until the other wounded had left the area. Shafter was awarded his medal on June 12, 1895.

Shaler, Alexander. [photograph p. 181] Birth: Connecticut, 1827. Colonel of the 65th New York

Alfred Sellers (Hall of Heroes)

William Sewell (U.S. Army War College)

William Shafter (Hall of Heroes)

Infantry. On May 3, 1863, at Fredericksburg, Virginia, Colonel Shaler pushed forward with a supporting column and pierced the enemy's works at a critical moment when the assault was about to waiver on Marye's Heights. Shaler was awarded his medal on November 25, 1893.

Shambaugh, Charles. Birth: Prussia. Corporal in Company D, 11th Pennsylvania Infantry Reserves. On June 30, 1863, at Charles City Crossroads, Virginia, Corporal Shambough captured a Confederate flag. Shambough was awarded his medal on July 17, 1866.

Shanan, Emisire. Birth: West Virginia, 1843. Corporal in Company A, 1st West Virginia, Cavalry. On April 6, 1865, at Sailors Creek, Virginia, Corporal Shanan captured the flag of the 76th Georgia Infantry. Shanan was awarded his medal on May 3, 1865.

Alexander Shaler (Hall of Heroes)

Shanes, John. Birth: West Virginia. Private in Company K, 14th West Virginia infantry. On July 20, 1864, at Carter's Farm, Virginia, Private Shanes charged upon a Confederate fieldpiece in advance of his comrades and by his individual exertions silenced the piece. Shanes was awarded his medal on January 31, 1896.

Shapland, John. Birth: England, 1832. Private in Company D, 104th Illinois Infantry. On July 2, 1863, at Elk River, Tennessee, Private Shapland voluntarily joined a small party that, under a heavy fire, captured a stockade and saved the bridge. Shapland was awarded his medal on October 30, 1897.

Sharp, Hendrick. Birth: Spain 1815. Seaman aboard the U.S.S. *Richmond*. On August 5, 1864, at Mobile Bay, Alabama, Seaman Sharp fought his gun with skill and courage throughout the furious two hour battle that resulted in the surrender of the ram *Tennessee* and in the damaging and destruction of the batteries at Fort Morgan. Sharp was awarded his medal on December 31, 1864.

Shea, Joseph H. Birth: Maryland. Private in Company K, 92nd New York Infantry. On September 29, 1864, at Chapin's Farm, Virginia, Private Shea exhibited exceptional gallantry in bringing in wounded from the field under heavy fire. Shea was awarded his medal in March of 1866.

Shellenberger, John S. Corporal in Company B, 85th Pennsylvania Infantry. On August 16, 1864, at Deep Run, Virginia, Corporal Shellenberger captured a Confederate flag. Shellenberger was awarded his medal on April 6, 1865.

Irwin Shepard (U.S. Army War College)

Shepard, Irwin. Birth: New York, 1843. Corporal in Company E, 17th Michigan Infantry. On November 20, 1863, at Knoxville, Tennessee, Corporal Shepard accompanied a small party detailed to destroy buildings within the enemy lines from which sharpshooters had been firing. He disregarded an order to retire, remaining and completing the mission of firing the buildings, thus insuring their total destruction, at the imminent risk of his life from the fire of the advancing enemy. Shepard was awarded his medal on August 3, 1897.

Shepard, Louis C. Birth: Ohio, 1843. Ordinary Seaman aboard the U.S.S. *Wabash*. On January 15, 1865, at Fort Fisher, North Carolina, Seaman Shepard served as part of the Naval landing party that assaulted the fort. He succeeded in reaching the angle of the fort, and in going on, to be one of the few that entered the fort, from that service. Shepard was awarded his medal on June 22. 1865.

Louis Shepard (Hall of Heroes)

Shepard, William. Birth: Indiana. Private in Company A, 3rd Indiana Cavalry. On April 6, 1865, at Sailors Creek, Virginia, Private Shepard captured a Confederate flag. Shepard was awarded his medal on May 3, 1865.

Sheridan, James. Birth: New Jersey, 1831. Quartermaster aboard the U.S.S. *Oneida*. On August 5, 1864, at Mobile Bay, Alabama, Sheridan was recommended for his gallantry and intelligence, serving courageously throughout this battle that resulted in the surrender of the ram *Tennessee* and the damaging of Fort Morgan. Sheridan was awarded his medal on December 31, 1864.

Marshall Sherman (Hall of Heroes)

Sherman, Marshall. Birth: Vermont. Private in Company C, 1st Minnesota Infantry. On July 3, 1863, at Gettysburg, Pennsylvania, Corporal Sherman captured the flag of the 28th Virginia Infantry. Sherman was awarded his medal on December 1, 1864.

Shiel, John. Corporal in Company E, 90th Pennsylvania Infantry. On December 13, 1862, at Fredericksburg, Virginia, Corporal Shiel carried a dangerously wounded comrade into the Union lines thereby preventing his capture by the enemy. Shiel was awarded his medal on January 21, 1897. (Name is also listed as Shields.)

Shields, Bernard. Birth: Ireland. Private in Company E, 2nd West Virginia Cavalry. On April 8, 1865, at Appomattox, Virginia, Private Shields captured the flag of the Washington Artillery. Shields was awarded his medal on May 3, 1865.

Shilling, John. [photograph p. 183] Birth: England, 1832. First Sergeant in Company H, 3rd Delaware Infantry. On August 21, 1864, at Weldon Railroad, Virginia,

Sergeant Shilling captured a Confederate flag. Shilling was awarded his medal on September 6, 1864.

Shipley, Robert F. Birth: New York. Sergeant in Company A, 140th New York Infantry. On April 1, 1865, at Five Forks, Virginia, Sergeant Shipley captured the flag of the 9th Virginia Infantry in hand-to-hand combat. Shipley was awarded his medal on May 10, 1865.

John Shilling (Hall of Heroes)

Robert Shipley (Hall of Heroes)

Shipman, William. Birth: New York, 1831. Coxswain aboard the U.S.S. *Minnesota*. On January 15, 1865, at Fort Fisher, North Carolina, Shipman exhibited exceptional gallantry as a member of the Naval landing party that assaulted the fort. Shipman was awarded his medal on June 22, 1865.

Shivers, John. Birth: Canada, 1830. Private in the United States Marine Corps serving aboard the U.S.S. *Minnesota*. On January 15, 1865, at Fort Fisher, North Carolina, Private Shivers exhibited exceptional gallantry as a participant in the Naval landing party that assaulted the fort. Shivers was awarded his medal on June 22, 1865.

Shoemaker, Levi. Birth: West Virginia, 1840. Sergeant in Company A, 1st West Virginia Cavalry. On November 12, 1864, at Nineveh, Virginia, Sergeant Shoemaker captured the flag of the 22nd Virginia Cavalry. Shoemaker was awarded his medal on November 26, 1864.

Shopp, George J. Birth: Pennsylvania, 1834. Private in Company E, 191st Pennsylvania Infantry. On April 1, 1865, at Five Forks, Virginia, Private Shopp captured a Confederate flag. Shopp was awarded his medal on April 27, 1865.

Shubert, Frank. Birth: Germany. Sergeant in Company E, 43rd New York Infantry. On April 2, 1865, at Petersburg, Virginia, Sergeant Shubert captured two markers. Shubert was awarded his medal on May 10, 1865.

Shutes, Henry. Birth: Maryland, 1804. Captain of the Forecastle aboard the U.S.S. *Wissahickon*. From April 24 to 25, 1862, at Forts Jackson and St. Philip, south of New Orleans, Shutes performed his duties with skill and courage. On February 27, 1863, at Fort McAllister, his seamanlike qualities as a gunner's mate were outstanding.

The Recipients — Sickles

Daniel Sickles (U.S. Army War College)

William Sickles (Hall of Heroes)

Shutes was awarded his medal on January 15, 1866.

Sickles, Daniel E. Birth: New York, 1825. Major General United States Volunteers. On July 2, 1863, at Gettysburg, Pennsylvania, General Sickles displayed conspicuous gallantry on the field vigorously contesting the advance of the enemy and continuing to encourage his troops after being himself severely wounded. Sickles was awarded his medal on October 30, 1897.

Sickles, William H. Birth: New York. Sergeant in Company B, 7th Wisconsin Infantry. On March 31, 1865, at Gravelly Run, Virginia, Sergeant Sickles, with a comrade, attempted to capture an enemy stand of colors and detachment of nine Confederates, but succeeded in capturing three prisoners and dispersing the rest. The date of Sickles award is not recorded at the War Department.

Sidman, George E. Birth: New York, 1844. Private in Company C, 16th Michigan Infantry. On June 27, 1862, at Gaines Mill, Virginia, Private Sidman rallied his comrades to charge vastly superior forces until wounded in the hip, even though he was but a sixteen-year-old drummer boy. Sidman was awarded his medal on April 6, 1892.

Simkins, Lebbeus. Birth: New York, 1836. Coxswain aboard the U.S.S. *Richmond*. On August 5, 1864, at Mobile Bay, Alabama, Simkins performed his duties with skill and courage throughout the furious two hour battle that resulted in the surrender of the ram *Tennessee* and in the damaging and destruction of batteries at Fort Morgan. Simkins was awarded his medal on December 31, 1864.

Simmons, John. Birth: New York. Private in Company D, 2nd New York Heavy Artillery. On April 6, 1865, at Sailors Creek, Virginia, Private Simmons captured a Confederate flag. Simmons was awarded his medal on April 24, 1865.

Simmons, William T. Birth: Illinois, 1843. Lieutenant in Company C, 11th Missouri Infantry. On December 16, 1864, at Nashville, Tennessee, Lieutenant Simmons captured the flag of the 34th Alabama Infantry after being the first to enter the enemy works. Simmons was awarded his medal on February 24, 1865.

Simonds, William Edgar. Sergeant Major of the 25th Connecticut Infantry. On April 14, 1863, at Irish Bend, Louisiana, Sergeant Simmons displayed great gallantry, under a heavy fire from the enemy, in calling in the skirmishers and assisting in forming the line of battle. Simmons was awarded his medal on February 25, 1899.

Simons, Charles J. Birth: India, 1843. Sergeant in Company A, 9th New Hampshire Infantry. On July 30, 1864, at Petersburg, Virginia, Sergeant Simons was one of the first in the exploded mine, captured a number of prisoners, and was himself captured, but escaped. Simons was awarded his medal on July 27, 1896.

Sivel, Henry. See William H. Matthews.

Charles Simons (U.S. Army War College)

Skellie, Ebenezer. Birth: New York. Corporal in Company D, 112th New York infantry. On September 29, 1864, at Chapin's Farm, Virginia, Corporal Skellie took up the colors of his regiment, the color bearer having fallen, and carried them through the first charge, also, in the second charge, after all the color bearers had been killed or wounded he carried the colors up to the enemy's works, where he fell wounded. Skellie was awarded his medal on April 6, 1865.

Sladen, Joseph A. Birth: England. Private in Company A, 33rd Massachusetts Infantry. On May 14, 1864, at Resaca, Georgia, Private Sladen was detailed as a headquarters clerk, but voluntarily engaged in action at a critical moment and by personal example inspired the troops to repel the enemy. Sladen was awarded his medal on July 19, 1895.

Ebenezer Skellie (Hall of Heroes)

Slagle, Oscar. Birth: Ohio. Private in Company D, 104th Illinois Infantry. On July 2, 1863, at Elk River, Tennessee, Private Slagle voluntarily joined a small party that, under a heavy fire, captured a stockade and saved the bridge. Slagle was awarded his medal on October 30, 1897.

Slavens, Samuel. Birth: Ohio, 1831. Private in Company E, 33rd Ohio Infantry. In April of 1862, Slavens, along with 21 other companions, penetrated nearly 200 miles south into enemy territory and captured a railroad train at Big Shanty, Georgia in an attempt to destroy the bridges and track between Chattanooga and Atlanta. Slavens was awarded his medal on July 28, 1883.

Samuel Slavens (U.S. Army War College)

Sloan, Andrew J. Birth: Pennsylvania. Private in Company H, 12th Iowa Infantry. On December 16, 1864, at Nashville, Tennessee, Private Sloan captured the flag of the 1st Louisiana Battery. Sloan was awarded his medal on February 24, 1865.

Slusher, Henry C. Birth: Pennsylvania. Private in Company F, 22nd Pennsylvania Cavalry. On September 11, 1863, at Moorefield, West Virginia, Private Slusher voluntarily crossed a branch of the Potomac River under fire to rescue a wounded comrade held prisoner by the enemy and was wounded and taken prisoner in the attempt. Slusher was awarded his medal on April 4, 1898.

Smalley, Reuben. Birth: New York, 1839. Private in Company F, 83rd Indiana Infantry. On May 22, 1863, at Vicksburg, Mississippi, Private Smalley exhibited exceptional gallantry in the charge of the volunteer storming party. Smalley was awarded his medal on July 9, 1894.

Henry Slusher (Hall of Heroes)

Smalley, Reuben S. Birth: Pennsylvania, 1837. Private in Company D, 104th Illinois Infantry. On July 2, 1863, at Elk River, Tennessee, Private Smalley voluntarily joined a small party that, under a heavy fire, captured a stockade and saved the bridge. Smalley was awarded his medal on October 30, 1897.

Smith, Alonzo. Birth: New York, 1842. Sergeant in Company C, 7th Michigan Infantry. On October 27, 1864, at Hatchers Runs, Virginia, Sergeant Smith captured the flag of the 26th Virginia Infantry while outside his lines far from his comrades. Smith was awarded his medal on December 1, 1864.

Smith, Andrew Jackson. [photograph p. 187] Birth: 1843. Corporal in the 55th Massachusetts Infantry. On November 30, 1864, at Honey Hill, South Carolina, Corporal Smith saved his regimental colors after the color bearer had been killed. Smith was awarded his medal on March 3, 1865.

Smith, Charles H. Birth: Maine. Colonel of the 1st Maine Cavalry. On June 24, 1864, at St. Mary's Church, Virginia, Colonel Smith remained in the fight to the close, although severely wounded. Smith was awarded his medal on April 11, 1895.

Col. Charles H. Smith (Hall of Heroes)

Smith, Charles H. Birth: Maine, 1826. Coxswain aboard the U.S.S. *Rhode Island*. On December 30, 1862, at Mobile Bay, Alabama, Smith risked his life in a gallant attempt to rescue members of a sunken sister ship. Although he too lost his life during the hazardous operation, he made every effort possible to save the lives of his fellow men. Smith was awarded his medal on June 22, 1865.

Andrew Smith (U.S. Army War College)

Smith, David L. Sergeant in Battery E, 1st New York Light Artillery. On April 6, 1862, at Warwick Courthouse, Virginia, Sergeant Smith procured water and extinguished a fire when a shell struck an ammunition chest, exploding a number of cartridges, thus preventing the explosion of the remaining ammunition. Smith was awarded his medal on August 6, 1906.

Smith, Edwin. Birth: New York, 1841. Ordinary Seaman serving aboard the U.S.S. *Whitehead*. On October 3, 1862, at Franklin, Virginia, Seaman Smith swam to shore with a line, under heavy fire, when the ship became grounded. His fearless action enabled the ship to maintain a steady fire and keep the enemy in check during the battle. Smith was awarded his medal on April 3, 1863.

Smith, Francis M. Birth: Maryland, 1842. First Lieutenant and Adjutant of the 1st Maryland Infantry. On February 6, 1865, at Dabney's Mills, Virginia, Lieutenant Smith voluntarily remained with the body of his regimental commander under a heavy fire after the brigade had retired and brought the body off the field. Smith was awarded his medal on August 13, 1895.

Francis Smith (U.S. Army War College)

Smith, Henry I. Birth: England, 1840. First Lieutenant in Company B, 7th Iowa Infantry. On March 15, 1865, at Black River, North Carolina, Lieutenant Smith voluntarily and under fire rescued a comrade from death by drowning. Smith was awarded his medal on September 7, 1894.

Smith, James (Ovid). [photograph p. 189] Birth: Virginia, 1845. Private in Company I, 2nd Ohio Infantry. In April of 1862 Smith was one of 22 men who penetrated nearly 200 miles into enemy territory and captured a railroad train at Big Shanty, Georgia, in an attempt to destroy bridges and track between Chattanooga and Atlanta. Smith was awarded his medal on July 6, 1864.

Smith, James. Birth: New York, 1826. Captain of the Forecastle aboard the U.S.S. *Richmond*. On August 5, 1864, at Mobile Bay, Alabama, Smith fought his gun with skill and courage throughout the prolonged battle that resulted in the surrender of the ram *Tennessee* and in the successful attacks carried out on Fort Morgan. Smith was awarded his medal on December 31, 1864.

Smith, John. Birth: Massachusetts, 1831. Captain of the Forecastle aboard the U.S.S. *Lackawana*. On August 5, 1864, at Mobile Bay, Alabama, Smith served his gun but found that he could not depress it enough to bring it to bear when alongside the Confederate ram *Tennessee*. Smith threw a hand holystone into one of the ports at a Rebel using abusive language against the crew of the ship. He continued his daring action throughout the engagement that resulted in the surrender of the *Tennessee* and in the damaging and destruction of Fort Morgan. Smith was awarded his medal on December 31, 1864.

Smith, John. Birth: New York, 1826. Second Captain of the Top aboard the U.S.S. *Richmond*. On August 5, 1864, at Mobile Bay, Alabama, Smith fought his gun with

skill and courage throughout the furious two hour battle that resulted in the surrender of the ram *Tennessee* and in the damaging and destruction of batteries at Fort Morgan. Smith was awarded his medal on December 31, 1864.

Smith, Joseph S. Birth: Maine, 1836. Lieutenant Colonel and Commissary of Subsistence, 2nd Army Corps. On October 27, 1864, at Bull Run, Virginia, Colonel Smith led a part of the brigade, saved two pieces of artillery, captured a flag and secured a number of prisoners. Smith was awarded his medal on May 25, 1892.

James (Ovid) Smith (U.S. Army War College)

Joseph Smith (U.S. Army War College)

Smith, Oloff. Birth: Sweden, 1833. Coxswain aboard the U.S.S. *Richmond*. On August 5, 1864, at Mobile Bay, Alabama, Smith performed his duties with skill and courage throughout the furious two hour battle that resulted in the surrender of the ram *Tennessee* and in the damaging and destruction of batteries at Fort Morgan. Smith was awarded his medal on December 31, 1864.

Smith, Otis W. Birth: Ohio. Private in Company G, 95th Ohio Infantry. On December 16, 1864, at Nashville, Tennessee, Private Smith captured the flag of the 6th Florida Infantry. Smith was awarded his medal on February 24, 1865.

Smith, Richard. Birth: New York. Private in Company B, 95th New York Infantry. On August 21, 1864, at Weldon Railroad, Virginia, Private Smith captured two Confederate officers and twenty enlisted men of Hagood's Brigade while they were attempting to make their way back through the woods. Smith was awarded his medal on March 13, 1865.

Smith, S. Rodmond. [photograph p. 190] Birth: Delaware. Captain of Company C, 4th Delaware Infantry. On February 5, 1865, at Rowanty Creek, Virginia, Captain Smith swam the partly frozen creek, under fire, to establish a crossing. Smith was awarded his medal on April 8, 1895.

S. Rodmond Smith (Hall of Heroes)

Smith, Thaddeus S. Birth: Pennsylvania, 1847. Corporal in Company E, 6th Pennsylvania Infantry Reserves. On July 2, 1863, at Gettysburg, Pennsylvania, Corporal Smith was one of six volunteers who charged upon a log house near Devil's Den, where a squad of the enemy's sharpshooters were sheltered, and compelled their surrender. Smith was awarded his medal on May 5, 1900.

Smith, Thomas. Birth: England, 1838. Seaman aboard the U.S.S. *Magnolia*. From March 5 to 6, 1865, at St. Marks, Florida, Seaman Smith served with the Army in charge of Navy howitzers during the attack on the town, and throughout this fierce engagement made remarkable efforts in assisting transport of the gun, and his coolness and determination in courageously standing by his gun while under fire of the enemy was a credit to the service to which he belonged. Smith was awarded his medal on June 22, 1865.

Smith, Walter B. Birth: New York, 1827. Ordinary Seaman aboard the U.S.S. *Richmond*. On August 5, 1864, at Mobile Bay, Alabama, Seaman Smith was cool and courageous at his station throughout the prolonged action rendering outstanding service at the 100-pounder rifle on the topgallant forecastle, and while firing his musket into the gun ports of the C.S.S. *Tennessee*. Smith was awarded his medal on December 31, 1864.

Smith, Willard M. Birth: New York, 1840. Corporal in the United States Marines serving aboard the U.S.S. *Brooklyn*. On August 5, 1864, at Mobile Bay, Alabama, Corporal Smith fought his gun with skill and courage throughout the furious two hour battle that resulted in the surrender of the ram *Tennessee*. Smith was awarded his medal on December 31, 1864.

Smith, William. Birth: Ireland, 1838. Quartermaster aboard the U.S.S. *Kearsarge*. On June 19, 1864, at Cherbourg, France, Smith carried out his duties as acting captain of the 11-inch pivot gun courageously and deserved special notice for the deliberate and cool manner in which he acted throughout the bitter engagement. It is stated by Rebel officers that this gun was more destructive and did more damage than any other gun of the Kearsarge in the action against the C.S.S. *Alabama*. Smith was awarded his medal on December 31, 1864.

Smith, Wilson. Birth: New York. Corporal in Cattery H, 3rd New York Light Artillery. On September 6, 1862, at Washington, North Carolina, Corporal Smith took command of a gun after the lieutenant in charge had disappeared, and fired the same so rapidly and effectively that the enemy was repulsed, although for a time a hand-to-hand conflict was had over the gun. Smith was awarded his medal on April 24, 1896.

Snedden, James. Birth: Scotland. Musician in Company E, 54th Pennsylvania Infantry. On June 5, 1864, at Piedmont, Virginia, Snedden left his place in the rear, too the rifle of a disabled soldier, and fought through the remainder of the action. Snedden was awarded his medal on September 11, 1897.

Southard, David. Birth: New Jersey. Sergeant in Company C, 1st New Jersey Cavalry. On April 6, 1865, at Sailors Creek, Virginia, Sergeant Southard was the first man over the works in the charge, capturing a Confederate flag. Southard was awarded his medal on July 3, 1865.

Sova, Joseph E. Birth: New York. Saddler in Company H, 8th New York Cavalry. From March 29 to April 9, 1865, during the Appomattox Campaign, Sova captured a Confederate flag. Sova was awarded his medal on May 3, 1865.

Sowers, Michael. Birth: Pennsylvania, 1844. Private in Company L, 4th Pennsylvania Cavalry. On December 1, 1864, at Stony Creek Station, Virginia, Private Sowers had his horse shot out from under him and voluntarily and on foot participated in the cavalry charge made upon one of the forts, conducting himself throughout with great personal bravery. Sowers was awarded his medal on February 16, 1897.

Spalding, Edward B. Birth: Illinois, 1840. Sergeant in Company E, 52nd Illinois Infantry. On April 6, 1862, at Shiloh, Tennessee, Sergeant Spalding, although twice wounded, and thereby crippled for life, remained fighting in open ground to the close of the battle. Spalding was awarded his medal on January 15, 1894.

Sperry, William J. Birth: Vermont. Major in the 6th Vermont Infantry. On April 2, 1865, at Petersburg, Virginia, Major Sperry, with the assistance of a few men, captured two pieces of artillery and turned them upon the enemy. Sperry was awarded his medal on August 12, 1892.

Spillane, Timothy. Birth: Ireland. Private in Company C, 16th Pennsylvania Cavalry. On February 7, 1865, at Hatchers Run, Virginia, Private Spillane exhibited gallantry and good conduct in action, bravery in a charge and reluctance to leave the field after being twice wounded. Spillane was awarded his medal on September 16, 1880.

Sprague, Benona. Birth: New York. Corporal in Company F, 116th Illinois Infantry. On May 22, 1863, at Vicksburg, Mississippi, Corporal Sprague exhibited exceptional gallantry in the charge of the volunteer storming party. Sprague was awarded his medal on July 10, 1894.

Sprague, John W. Birth: New York, 1817. Colonel of the 63rd Ohio Infantry. On July 22, 1862, at Decatur, Georgia, Colonel Sprague, with a small command, defeated an overwhelming force of the enemy and saved the trains of the corps. Sprague was awarded his medal on January 18, 1894.

John Sprague (Hall of Heroes)

Sprowle, David. Birth: New York, 1811. Orderly Sergeant in the United States Marine Corps serving aboard the U.S.S. *Richmond*. On August 5, 1864, at Mobile Bay, Alabama, Sergeant Sprowle inspired the men of the Marine guard and directed a division of great guns throughout the furious battle that resulted in the surrender of the ram *Tennessee* and in the damaging and destruction of batteries at Fort Morgan. Sprowle was awarded his medal on December 31, 1864.

The Recipients — Spurling

Andrew Spurling (Hall of Heroes)

Charles Stacey (Hall of Heroes)

Julius Stahel (U.S. Army War College)

David Stanley (U.S. Army War College)

Spurling, Andrew B. Birth: Maine. Lieutenant Colonel in the 2nd Maine Cavalry. On march 23, 1865, at Evergreen, Alabama, Colonel Spurling advanced alone in the darkness beyond the picket line, came upon three of the enemy, fired upon them, wounded two, and captured the whole party. Spurling was awarded his medal on September 10, 1897.

Stacey, Charles. Birth: England. Private in Company D, 55th Ohio Infantry. On July 2, 1863, at Gettysburg, Pennsylvania, Private Stacey voluntarily took an advanced position on the skirmish line for the purpose of ascertaining the location of the Confederate sharpshooters, and under heavy fire held the position thus taken until the company of which he was a member went back to the main line. Stacey was awarded his medal on June 23, 1896.

Stahel, Julius. Birth: Hungary, 1825. Major General, United States Volunteers. On June 5, 1864, at Piedmont, Virginia, General Stahel led his division into action until he was severely wounded. Stahel was awarded his medal on November 4, 1893.

Stanley, David S. Birth: Ohio, 1828. Major General, United States Volunteers. On November 30, 1864, at Franklin, Tennessee, General Stanley, at a critical moment, rode to the front of one of his brigades, reestablished its lines, and gallantly led it in a successful assault. Stanley was awarded his medal on March 29, 1893.

Stanley, William A. Birth: Massachusetts, 1831. Shell Man aboard the U.S.S. *Hartford*. On August 5, 1864, at Mobile Bay, Alabama, Stanley, though severely wounded, continued to pass shell until forced by the loss of blood to go below. Stanley was awarded his medal on December 31, 1864.

Starkins, John H. Birth: New York. Sergeant in the 34th New York Battery. On November 16, 1863, at Campbell Station, Tennessee, Sergeant Starkins brought off his piece without losing a man. Starkins was awarded his medal on July 30, 1896.

Steele, John W. Birth: Vermont, 1835. Major and Aide-de-Camp, United States Volunteers. On November 29, 1864, at Spring Hill, Tennessee, during a night attack of the enemy upon the wagon and ammunition train of this officer's corps, major Steele gathered up a force of stragglers and others, assumed command of it, though himself a staff officer, and attacked and dispersed the enemy's forces, thus saving the train. Steele was awarded his medal on September 28, 1897.

Steinmetz, William. Birth: Kentucky. Private in Company G, 83rd Indiana Infantry. On May 22, 1863, at Vicksburg, Mississippi, Private Steinmetz exhibited exceptional gallantry in the charge of the volunteer storming party. Steinmetz was awarded his medal on July 12, 1894.

Stephens, William G. Birth: New York. Private in the Chicago Mercantile Battery, Illinois Light Artillery. On May 22, 1863, at Vicksburg, Mississippi, Private Stephens carried by hand, with others, a cannon up to and fired it through an embrasure of the enemy's works. Stephens was awarded his medal on December 21, 1894.

Sterling, James E. Birth: Maine, 1838. Coal Heaver aboard the U.S.S. *Brooklyn*. On August 5, 1864, at Mobile Bay, Alabama, Sterling, though wounded, courageously remained at his post and continued passing shell until struck down a second time and completely disabled. Sterling was awarded his medal on December 31, 1864.

Sterling, John T. Birth: Illinois. Private in Company D, 11th Indiana Infantry. On September 19, 1864, at Winchester, Virginia, Private Sterling, with one companion, captured fourteen of the enemy in the severest part of the battle. Sterling was awarded his medal on April 4, 1865.

Stevens, Daniel D. Birth: Tennessee, 1840. Quartermaster aboard the U.S.S. *Canonicus*. On January 13, 1865, at Fort Fisher, North Carolina, Stevens gallantly replaced the flag when it was shot away on two separate occasions. Stevens was awarded his medal on July 15, 1870.

Daniel Stevens (Hall of Heroes)

Stevens, Hazard. Birth: Rhode Island, 1842. Captain and Assistant Adjutant General, United States Volunteers. On April 19, 1863, at Fort Huger, Virginia, Captain Stevens gallantly led a party that assaulted and captured the fort. Stevens was awarded his medal on June 13, 1894.

Stewart, George W. Birth: New Jersey. First Sergeant in Company E, 1st New Jersey Cavalry. On April 5, 1865, at Paine's Crossroads, Virginia, Sergeant Stewart captured a Confederate flag. Stewart was awarded his medal on May 3, 1865.

Hazard Stevens (U.S. Army War College)

Stewart, Joseph. Birth: Ireland. Private in Company G, 1st Maryland Infantry. On April 1, 1865, at Five Forks, Virginia,

Private Stewart captured a Confederate flag. Stewart was awarded his medal on April 27, 1865.

Stickels, Joseph. Birth: Ohio. Sergeant in Company A, 83rd Ohio Infantry. On April 9, 1865, at Fort Blakely, Alabama, Sergeant Stickels captured a Confederate flag. Stickels was awarded his medal on June 8, 1865.

Stockman, George H. Birth: Germany, 1833. First Lieutenant in Company C, 6th Missouri Infantry. On May 22, 1863, at Vicksburg, Mississippi, Lieutenant Stockman exhibited exceptional gallantry in the charge of the volunteer storming party. Stockman was awarded his medal on July 9, 1894.

Stoddard, James. Birth: North Carolina, 1838. Seaman aboard the U.S.S. *Marmora*. On March 5, 1864, at Yazoo City, Mississippi, Seaman Stoddard landed with the gun crew in the midst of heated battle and bravely standing by his gun despite enemy rifle fire which cut the gun carriage and rammer, contributed to the turning back of the enemy during the fierce engagement. Stoddard was awarded his medal on April 16, 1864.

Stokes, George. Birth: England, 1838. Private in Company C, 122nd Illinois Infantry. On December 16, 1864, at Nashville, Tennessee, Private Stokes captured a Confederate flag. Stokes was awarded his medal on February 24, 1865.

Stolz, Frank. Birth: Indiana, 1844. Private in Company G, 83rd Indiana Infantry. On May 22, 1863, at Vicksburg, Mississippi, Private Stolz exhibited exceptional gallantry in the charge of the volunteer storming party. Stolz was awarded his medal on July 9, 1894.

Storey, John H.R. Birth: Pennsylvania. Sergeant in Company F, 109th Pennsylvania Infantry. On May 28, 1864, at Dallas, Georgia, Sergeant Storey, while bringing in a wounded comrade, under a destructive fire, was himself wounded in the right leg, which was amputated on the same day. Storey was awarded his medal on August 29, 1896.

Stout, Richard. Birth: New York, 1836. Landsman aboard the U.S.S. *Isaac Smith*. On January 30, 1863, at Stono River, South Carolina, Landsman Stout carried out his duties bravely throughout the action when the ship was trapped in a Confederate ambush and forced to strike its colors. Stout was awarded his medal on April 16, 1864.

Strahan, Robert. Birth: New Jersey. Captain of the Top aboard the U.S.S. *Kearsarge*. On June 19, 1864, at Cherbourg, France, Strahan carried out his duties in the face of heavy enemy fire and exhibited marked coolness and good conduct throughout the engagement with the C.S.S. *Alabama*. Strahan was awarded his medal on December 31, 1864.

Strausbaugh, Bernard A. Birth: Pennsylvania. First Sergeant in Company A, 3rd Maryland Infantry. On June 17, 1864, at Petersburg, Virginia, Sergeant Strausbaugh recaptured the colors of the 2nd Pennsylvania Provisional Artillery. Strausbaugh was awarded his medal on December 1, 1864.

Richard Stout (Hall of Heroes)

Streile, Christian. Birth: Germany. Private in Company I, 1st New Jersey Cavalry. On April 5, 1865, at Paine's Crossroads, Virginia, Private Streile captured a Confederate flag. Streile was awarded his medal on May 3, 1865.

Strong, James N. Birth: 1818. Sergeant in Company C, 49th Massachusetts Infantry. On May 27, 1863, at Port Hudson, Louisiana, Sergeant Strong volunteered in response to a call and took part in the movement that was made upon the enemy's works under a heavy fire there from in advance of the general assault. Strong was awarded his medal on November 25, 1893.

James Sturgeon (Hall of Heroes)

Sturgeon, James K. Birth: Ohio. Private in Company F, 46th Ohio Infantry. On June 15, 1864, at Kennesaw Mountain, Georgia, Private Sturgeon advanced beyond the lines, and in an encounter with three Confederates shot two and took the other prisoner. Sturgeon was awarded his medal on January 2, 1895.

Sullivan, James. Birth: New York, 1833. Ordinary Seaman aboard the U.S.S. *Agawam*. On December 23, 1864, at Fort Fisher, North Carolina, Seaman Sullivan volunteered to be part of the crew of the powder boat intended to blow up the fort. Sullivan was awarded his medal on December 31, 1864.

Sullivan, John. Birth: New York, 1839. Seaman aboard the U.S.S. *Monticello*. From June 23 to 25, 1864, at Wilmington, North Carolina, Seaman Sullivan took part in a reconnaissance of enemy defenses of Wilmington that covered a period of two days and one night. He courageously carried out his duties during this action, which resulted in the capture of a mail carrier and mail, the cutting of a telegraph wire, and the capture of a large group of prisoners. Sullivan was awarded his medal on April 3, 1864.

Sullivan, Timothy. Birth: Ireland, 1835. Coxswain aboard the U.S.S. *Louisville*. Sullivan served during the various actions of the Louisville as first captain of a 9-inch gun and throughout his period of service, was especially commanded for his attention to duty, bravery, and coolness in action. Sullivan was awarded his medal on April 3, 1863.

Summers, James C. Birth: West Virginia, 1838. Private in Company H, 4th West Virginia Infantry. On May 22, 1863, at Vicksburg, Mississippi, Private Summers exhibited exceptional gallantry in the charge of the volunteer storming party. Summers was awarded his medal on February 25, 1895.

Summers, Robert. Birth: Prussia, 1838. Chief Quartermaster aboard the U.S.S. *Ticonderoga*. From January 13 to 15, 1865, at Fort Fisher, North Carolina, Summers exhibited gallantry in performing his duties during the three days of fighting at the fort. Summers was awarded his medal on June 22, 1865.

Surles, William H. Birth: Ohio, 1845. Private in Company G, 2nd Ohio Infantry. On October 8, 1862, at Perryville, Kentucky, Private Surles, in the hottest part of the fire, stepped in front of his colonel to shield him from the enemy's fire. Surles was awarded his medal on August 19, 1891.

Swan, Charles A. Birth: Pennsylvania, 1838. Private in Company K, 4th Iowa Cavalry. On April 2, 1865, at Selma, Alabama, Private Swan captured a Confederate flag supposed to belong to the 11th Mississippi Infantry. Swan was awarded his medal on June 17, 1865.

Swanson, John. Birth: Sweden, 1842. Seaman aboard the U.S.S. *Santiago de Cuba*. On January 15, 1865, at Fort Fisher, North Carolina, Seaman Swanson was one of the boat crew detailed to a general on shore, where he bravely carried dispatches at the height of the battle. He was also one of six men who entered the fort in the assault from the fleet. Swanson was awarded his medal on June 22, 1865.

Swap, Jacob E. Birth: New York. Private in Company H, 83rd Pennsylvania Infantry. On May 5, 1864, at the Wilderness, Virginia, Private Swap, although assigned to other duty, voluntarily joined his regiment in a charge and fought with it until severely wounded. Swap was awarded his medal on November 19, 1897.

Swatton, Edward. Birth: New York, 1836. Seaman aboard the U.S.S. *Santiago de Cuba*. On January 15, 1865, at Fort Fisher, North Carolina, Seaman Swatton was one of the boat crew detailed to one of the generals on shore. He bravely entered the fort in the assault and accompanied his party in carrying dispatches at the height of the battle. He was one of six men who entered the fort in the assault from the fleet. Swatton was awarded his medal on June 22, 1865.

Wager Swayne (U.S. Army War College)

Swayne, Wager. Birth: Ohio, 1834. Lieutenant Colonel of the 43rd Ohio Infantry. On October 4, 1862, at Corinth, Mississippi, Colonel Swayne displayed conspicuous gallantry in restoring order at a critical moment and leading his regiment in a charge. Swayne was awarded his medal on August 19, 1893.

Swearer, Benjamin. Birth: Maryland, 1825. Seaman aboard the U.S.S. *Pawnee*. On August 29, 1861, at Fort Clark, North Carolina, Seaman Swearer took part in a mission to land troops and to remain inshore and provide protection. He rendered gallant service throughout the action and had the honor of being the first man to raise the flag on the captured fort. Swearer was awarded his medal on April 3, 1863.

Benjamin Swearer (Hall of Heroes)

Sweatt, Joseph G. [photograph p. 197] Birth: New Hampshire, 1843. Private in Company C, 6th Massachusetts Infantry. On May 15, 1863, at Carrsville, Virginia,

Private Sweatt was ordered to retreat, but instead turned and rushed back to the front, in the face of heavy fire from the enemy, in an endeavor to rescue his wounded comrades, remaining by them until overpowered and taken prisoner. Sweatt was awarded his medal on March 22, 1892.

Sweeney, James. Birth: England. Private in Company A, 1st Vermont Cavalry. On October 19, 1864, at Cedar Creek, Virginia, Private Sweeney, with one companion, captured a North Carolina flag, three officers, and an ambulance with its mules and driver. Sweeney was awarded his medal on October 26, 1864.

Swegheimer, Jacob. Birth: Germany, 1843. Private in Company I, 54th Ohio Infantry. On May 22, 1863, at Vicksburg, Mississippi, Private Swegheimer exhibited exceptional gallantry in the charge of the volunteer storming party. Swegheimer was awarded his medal on July 14, 1894.

Joseph Sweatt (U.S. Army War College)

Swift, Frederic W. Birth: Connecticut, 1831. Lieutenant Colonel of the 17th Michigan Infantry. On November 16, 1863, at Lenoire Station, Tennessee, Colonel Swift seized the colors and rallied the regiment after three color bearers had been shot down and the regiment had become demoralized and was in imminent danger of capture. Swift was awarded his medal on February 15, 1897.

Swift, Harlan J. Birth: New York, 1843. Second Lieutenant in Company H, 2nd New York Infantry Militia. On July 30, 1864, at Petersburg, Virginia, Lieutenant Swift advanced with his regiment and captured the enemy's line. He then saw four of the enemy retiring toward their second line, advanced upon them alone, compelled their surrender, and regained his regiment with the four prisoners. Swift was awarded his medal on July 20, 1897.

Sype, Peter. Birth: Michigan, 1841. Private in Company B, 47th Ohio Infantry. On May 3, 1863, at Vicksburg, Mississippi, Private Sype was one of a party that volunteered and Attempted to run the enemy's batteries with a steam tug and two barges loaded with subsistence stores. Sype was awarded his medal on September 13, 1911.

Frederic Swift (Hall of Heroes)

Tabor, William S. Birth: Massachusetts, 1844. Private in Company K, 15th New Hampshire Infantry. In July of 1863, at Port Hudson, Louisiana, Private Tabor exposed himself to the enemy only a few feet away to render valuable services for the protection of his comrades. Tabor was awarded his medal on March 10, 1896.

Taggart, Charles A. Birth: Massachusetts, 1843. Private in Company B, 37th Massachusetts Infantry. On April 6, 1865, at Sailors Creek, Virginia, Private Taggert captured a Confederate flag. Taggert was awarded his medal on May 10, 1865.

Talbott, William. Birth: Maine, 1812. Captain of the Forecastle aboard the U.S.S. *Louisville*. On January 10 to 11, 1863, at Arkansas Post, Arkansas, Talbott carried out his duties as captain of the 9-inch gun and was conspicuous for ability and bravery throughout the engagement with the enemy. Talbott was awarded his medal on April 16, 1865.

Tallentine, James. Birth: England, 1840. Quarter Gunner aboard the U.S.S. *Tacony*. On October 31, 1864, at Plymouth, North Carolina, Tallentine distinguished himself by a display of coolness when he participated in landing and spiking a 9-inch gun while under devastating fire from the enemy. He later gave his life while courageously engaged in storming Fort Fisher, North Carolina. Tallentine was awarded his medal on December 31, 1864.

Charles Taggart (U.S. Army War College)

Tanner, Charles B. Birth: Pennsylvania, 1842. Second Lieutenant in Company H, 1st Delaware Infantry. On September 17, 1862, at Antietam, Maryland, Lieutenant Tanner carried of the colors, which had fallen within 20 yards of the enemy's lines, the color guard of Nine men having all been killed or wounded. He himself was wounded three times. Tanner was awarded his medal on December 13, 1889.

Charles Tanner (Hall of Heroes)

Taylor, Anthony. Birth: New Jersey, 1837. First Lieutenant in Company A, 15th Pennsylvania Cavalry. On September 20, 1863, at Chickamauga, Georgia, Lieutenant Taylor held out to the last with a small force against the advance of superior numbers of the enemy. Taylor was awarded his medal on November 2, 1896.

Taylor, George. Birth: New York, 1830. Armorer aboard the U.S.S. *Lackawana*. On August 5, 1864, at Mobile Bay, Alabama, Taylor, although wounded, went into the shell room, where an enemy shell had exploded and started a fire, and with his hand extinguished the fire from explosion. Taylor was awarded his medal on December 31, 1864.

Taylor, Henry H. Birth: Illinois. Sergeant in Company C, 45th Illinois Infantry. On June 25, 1863, at Vicksburg, Mississippi, Sergeant Taylor was the first to plant the Union colors on the enemy's works. Taylor was awarded his medal on September 1, 1893.

Taylor, John. Seaman at the Navy Yard, New York. On September 9, 1865, at Brooklyn, New York, Seaman Taylor acted with promptness, coolness, and good judgment in rescuing from drowning Commander S.D. Trenchard who fell overboard in attempting to get on a ferry boat, which had collided with an English steamer, and needed immediate assistance. Taylor was awarded his medal on January 15, 1866.

Taylor, Joseph. Birth: England. Private in Company E, 7th Rhode Island Infantry. On August 18, 1864, at Weldon Railroad, Virginia, Private Taylor, while acting as an orderly to a general officer on the field and alone, encountered a picket of three of the enemy and compelled their surrender. Taylor was awarded his medal on July 20, 1897.

Taylor, Richard. Birth: Alabama. Private in Company E, 18th Indiana Infantry. On October 19, 1864, at Cedar Creek, Virginia, Private Taylor captured a Confederate flag. Taylor was awarded his medal on November 21, 1864.

Taylor, Thomas. Birth: Maine, 1834. Coxswain aboard the U.S.S. *Metacomet*. On August 5, 1864, at Mobile Bay, Alabama, Taylor encouraged the men of the forward pivot gun when the officer in command displayed cowardice, doing honor to the occasion. Taylor was awarded his medal on June 22, 1865.

Taylor, William. Birth: District of Columbia. Sergeant in Company H and Second Lieutenant in Company M, 1st Maryland Infantry. On May 23, 1862, at Front Royal, Virginia, Sergeant Taylor, though painfully wounded, obeyed an order to burn a bridge, persevered in the attempt, and burned the bridge, preventing its use by the enemy. On August 19, 1864, at Weldon Railroad, Virginia, he took the place of a disabled officer on a hazardous reconnaissance beyond the lines of the army, and was taken prisoner in the attempt. Taylor was awarded his medal on August 2, 1897.

Taylor, William G. Birth: Pennsylvania, 1831. Captain of the Forecastle aboard the U.S.S. *Ticonderoga*. On December 24 to 25, 1864, at Fort Fisher, North Carolina, Taylor acted as a gun captain and performed his duties with coolness and skill as his ship took position in the line of battle and delivered its fire on the batteries on shore. Taylor was awarded his medal on June 22, 1865.

Terry, John D. Birth: Maine. Sergeant in Company E, 23rd Massachusetts Infantry. On March 14, 1862, at New Bern, North Carolina, Sergeant Terry lost his leg by a shot in the thickest part of the fight, and still encouraged the men until carried off the field. Terry was awarded his medal on October 12, 1867.

Thackrah, Benjamin. Birth: Scotland. Private in Company H, 115th New York Infantry. On April 1, 1864, at Fort Gates, Florida, Private Thackrah was a volunteer in the surprise and capture of the enemy's picket. Thackrah was awarded his medal on May 2, 1890.

Thatcher, Charles M. Birth: Michigan, 1844. Private in Company B, 1st Michigan Sharpshooters. On July 31, 1864, at Petersburg, Virginia, Private Thatcher, instead of retreating or surrendering when the works were captured, regardless of his personal safety, continued to return the enemy's fire until he was captured. Thatcher was awarded his medal on July 31, 1896.

Thaxter, Sidney W. Birth: Maine, 1839. Major of the 1st Maine Cavalry. On October, 27, 1864, at Hatchers Run, Virginia, Major Thaxter voluntarily remained and participated in the battle with conspicuous gallantry even though his term of enlistment had expired. Thaxter was awarded his medal on September 10, 1897.

Thielberg, Henry. Birth: Germany, 1833. Seaman aboard the U.S.S. *Mount Washington*. On April 14, 1863, at Nansemond River, North Carolina, Seaman Thielberg assisted in hauling up and raising the flagstaff, and then volunteered to go up to the pilot house and observe the movements of the enemy, although three shells struck within a few inches of his head, and remained at his post until ordered to descend. Thielberg was awarded his medal on July 10, 1863.

Sidney Thaxter (U.S. Army War College)

Thomas, Hampton S. Birth: Pennsylvania, 1837. Major of the 1st Pennsylvania Cavalry. On April 5, 1865, at Amelia Springs, Virginia, Major Thomas displayed conspicuous gallantry in the capture of a field battery and a number of battle flags and in the destruction of the enemy's wagon train. Thomas was awarded his medal on January 15, 1894.

Thomas, Stephen. Birth: Vermont. Colonel of the 8th Vermont Infantry. On October 19, 1864, at Cedar Creek, Virginia, Colonel Thomas displayed distinguished conduct in a desperate hand-to-hand encounter, in which the advance of the enemy was checked. Thomas was awarded his medal on July 25, 1892.

Thompkins, George W. Birth: New York. Corporal in Company F, 124th New York Infantry. On March 25, 1865, at Petersburg, Virginia, Corporal Thompkins captured the flag of the 49th Alabama Infantry. Thompkins was awarded his medal on April 6, 1865.

Stephen Thomas (Hall of Heroes)

Thompson, Allen. Birth: New York, 1847. Private in Company I, 4th New York Heavy Artillery. On April 1, 1865, at White Oak Road, Virginia, Private Thompson made a hazardous reconnaissance through timber and slashings preceding the Union line of battle, signaling the troops and leading them through the obstruction. Thompson was awarded his medal on April 22, 1896.

Thompson, Charles A. Birth: Ohio, 1843. Sergeant in Company D, 17th Michigan

Charles Thompson (U.S. Army War College)

Infantry. On May, 12, 1864, at Spotsylvania, Virginia, Sergeant Thompson, after the regiment was surrounded and all resistance seemed useless, fought single-handed for the colors and defused to give them up until he had appealed to his superior officers. Thompson was awarded his medal on July 27, 1896.

Thompson, Freeman C. Birth: Ohio, 1845. Corporal in Company F, 116th Ohio Infantry. On April 2, 1865, at Petersburg, Virginia, Corporal Thompson was twice knocked from the parapet of Fort Gregg by blows from enemy muskets but at the third attempt fought his way into the works. Thompson was awarded his medal on May 12, 1865.

Thompson, Henry A. Birth: England, 1841. Private in the United States Marine Corps serving aboard the U.S.S. *Minnesota*. On January 15, 1865, at Fort Fisher, North Carolina, Private Thompson was a volunteer for the Naval landing party and advanced through the palisade and nearer to the fort than any man from his ship. Thompson was awarded his medal on June 22, 1865.

J. (James) Harry Thompson (Hall of Heroes)

Thompson, James. Birth: New York. Private in Company K, 4th New York Heavy Artillery. On April 1, 1865, at White Oak Road, Virginia, Private Thompson made a hazardous reconnaissance through timber and slashings, preceding the Union line of battle, signaling the troops and leading them through the obstructions. Thompson was awarded his medal on April 22, 1896.

Thompson, James B. Birth: Pennsylvania. Sergeant in Company G, 1st Pennsylvania Rifles. On July 1, 1863, at Gettysburg, Pennsylvania, Sergeant Thompson captured the flag of the 15th Georgia Infantry. Thompson was awarded his medal on December 1, 1864.

Thompson, J. (James) Harry. Birth: England. Surgeon in the United States Volunteers. On March 14, 1862, at New Bern, North Carolina, Surgeon Thompson voluntarily reconnoitered the enemy's position and carried orders under the hottest fire. Thompson was awarded his medal on November 11, 1870.

Thompson, John. Birth: Denmark, 1838. Corporal in Company C, 1st Maryland Infantry. On February 6, 1865, at Hatchers Run, Virginia, Corporal Thompson, as color bearer, with the most conspicuous gallantry, preceded his regiment in the assault and planted his flag upon the enemy's works. Thompson was awarded his medal on September 10, 1897.

Thompson, Thomas. Birth: Ohio, 1839. Sergeant in Company A, 66th Ohio Infantry. On May 2, 1863, at Chancellorsville, Virginia, Sergeant Thompson was one of a party of four who voluntarily brought into the Union lines, under fire, a wounded Confederate officer from whom was obtained valuable information concerning the enemy. Thompson was awarded his medal on July 16, 1892.

Thompson, William. Birth: New Jersey. Signal Quartermaster aboard the U.S.S. *Mohican*. On November 7, 1861, at Hilton Head, South Carolina, Thompson displayed gallantry in the actions against Forts Beauregard and Walker, steadfastly steering the ship with a steady and bold heart under the batteries, was wounded by a piece of shell, but remained at his station until he fell from loss of blood. Legs were afterward amputated. Thompson was awarded his medal on July 10, 1863.

Thompson, William P. Birth: New York. Sergeant in Company G, 20th Indiana Infantry. On May 6, 1864, at the Wilderness, Virginia, Sergeant Thompson captured the flag of the 55th Virginia, Infantry. Thompson was awarded his medal on December 1, 1864.

Thomson, Clifford. First Lieutenant of Company A, 1st New York Cavalry. On May 2, 1863, at the Wilderness, Virginia, Lieutenant Thomson volunteered to ascertain the character of approaching enemy troops, rode up so closely as to distinguish the features of the enemy, and as he wheeled to return they opened fire with musketry, the Union troops returning same. Under a terrific fire from both sides, he rode back unhurt to the Federal lines, averting a disaster to the Army by his heroic act. Thomson was awarded his medal on November 27, 1896.

Clifford Thomson (U.S. Army War College)

Thorn, Walter. Birth: New York. Second Lieutenant in Company G, 116th United States Colored Infantry. On January 1, 1865, at Dutch Gap Canal, Virginia, Lieutenant Thorn learned that the picket guard had not yet been withdrawn after the fuse to the mined bulkhead had been lit. He mounted the bulkhead, at great personal danger and warned the guard of its danger. Thorn was awarded his medal on December 8, 1898.

Tibbets, Andrew W. Birth: Indiana. Private in Company I. 3rd Iowa Cavalry. On April 15, 1865, at Columbus, Georgia, Private Tibbetts captured the flag of Austin's Battery. Tibbetts was awarded his medal on June 17, 1865.

Andrew Tibbets (Hall of Heroes)

Tilton, William. Birth: Vermont. Sergeant in Company C, 7th New Hampshire Infantry. In 1864, during the Richmond Campaign, Sergeant Tilton exhibited gallantry in his conduct in the field. Tilton was awarded his medal on February 20, 1884.

Tinkham, Eugene M. Birth: Connecticut. Corporal in Company H, 148th New York Infantry. On June 3, 1864, at Cold Harbor, Virginia, Corporal Tinkham, though wounded himself, voluntarily left the rifle pits, crept out between the lines and, exposed to the severe fire of the enemy's guns at close range, brought within the lines two wounded and helpless comrades. Tinkham was awarded his medal on April 5, 1898.

Titus, Charles. Birth: New Jersey, 1838. Sergeant in Company H, 1st New Jersey Cavalry. On April 6, 1865, at Sailors Creek, Virginia, Sergeant Titus was among the first to check the enemy's counstercharge. Titus was awarded his medal on July 3, 1865.

Toban, James W. Birth: Michigan, 1844. Sergeant in Company C, 9th Michigan Cavalry. On February 11, 1865, at Aiken, South Carolina, Sergeant Toban voluntarily and at great personal risk, returned in the face on the advance of the enemy, and rescued from impending death or capture, Major William C. Stevens, 9th Michigan Cavalry, who had been thrown from his horse. Toban was awarded his medal on July 9, 1896.

Tobie, Edward P. Birth: Maine. Sergeant Major in the 1st Maine Cavalry. From March 29 to April 9, 1865, during the Appomattox Campaign, Sergeant Tobie, though severely wounded at Sailors Creek and Farmville, refused to go to the hospital, remaining with the regiment, performed the full duties of Adjutant upon the wounding of that officer, and was present for duty at Appomattox. Tobie was awarded his medal on April 1, 1898.

Tobin, John M. Birth: Ireland. First Lieutenant and Adjutant in the 9th Massachusetts Infantry. On July 1, 1862, at Malvern Hill, Virginia, Lieutenant Tobin voluntarily took command of the 9th Massachusetts, while adjutant, bravely fighting from 3 p.m. until dusk, rallying and reforming the regiment under fire, twice picked up the regimental flag, the color bearer having been shot down, and placed it in worthy hands. Tobin was awarded his medal on March 11, 1896.

Todd, Samuel. Birth: New Hampshire, 1815. Quartermaster aboard the U.S.S. *Brooklyn*. On August 5, 1864, at Mobile Bay, Alabama, Todd performed his duty with outstanding skill and courage throughout the furious battle that resulted in the surrender of the ram *Tennessee* and in the damaging and destruction of batteries at Fort Morgan. Todd was awarded his medal on December 31, 1864.

Toffey, John J. Birth: New York, 1844. First Lieutenant in Company G, 33rd New Jersey Infantry. On November

John Toffey (U.S. Army War College)

23, 1863, at Chattanooga, Tennessee, Lieutenant Toffey although excused from duty on account of sickness, went to the front in command of a storming party and with conspicuous gallantry participated in the assault of Missionary Ridge, was here wounded and permanently disabled. Toffey was awarded his medal on September 10, 1897.

Tomlin, Andrew J. Birth: New Jersey, 1844. Corporal in the United States Marine Corps serving aboard the U.S.S. *Wabash*. On January 15, 1865, at Fort Fisher, North Carolina, Corporal Tomlin was one of 200 Marines assembled to hold a line of entrenchments in the rear of the fort which the enemy threatened to attack in force. When one of his comrades was struck down by enemy fire, he unhesitatingly advanced under a withering fire of musketry into an open plain close to the fort and assisted the wounded man to a place of safety. Tomlin was awarded his medal on June 22, 1865.

Andrew Tomlin (U.S. Army War College)

Tompkins, Aaron B. Birth: New Jersey. Sergeant in Company G, 1st New Jersey Cavalry. On April 5, 1965, at Sailors Creek, Virginia, Sergeant Tompkins charged into the enemy's works and captured a Confederate flag. Tompkins was awarded his medal on July 3, 1865.

Tompkins, Charles H. Birth: Virginia. First Lieutenant in the 2nd United States Cavalry. On June 1, 1861, at Fairfax, Virginia, Lieutenant Tompkins twice charged through the enemy's lines and, taking a carbine from an enlisted man, shot the enemy's captain. Tompkins was awarded his medal on November 13, 1893.

Toohey, Thomas. Birth: New York, 1835. Sergeant in Company F, 24th Wisconsin Infantry. On November 30, 1864, at Franklin, Tennessee, Sergeant Toohey voluntarily assisted in working the guns of a battery near right of the regiment after nearly every man had left them, the fire of the enemy being hotter at this than at any other point on the line. The date of Toohey's award is not recorded at the War Department.

Toomer, William. Birth: Ireland. Sergeant in Company G, 127th Illinois Infantry. On may 22, 1863, at Vicksburg, Mississippi, Sergeant Toomer exhibited exceptional gallantry in the charge of the volunteer storming party. Toomer was awarded his medal on July 9, 1864.

Torgler, Ernst (Ernert). Birth: Germany, 1840. Sergeant in Company G, 37th Ohio Infantry. On July 28, 1864, at Ezra Chapel, Georgia, Sergeant Torgler risked his life to save his commanding officer, then badly wounded, from capture. Torgler was awarded his medal on May 10, 1894.

Tozier, Andrew J. Birth: Maine. Sergeant in Company I, 20th Maine Infantry. On July 2, 1863, at Gettysburg, Pennsylvania, Sergeant Tozier, a color bearer, at the crisis of the engagement, stood alone in an advanced position, the regiment having been borne back, and defended his colors with musket and ammunition picked up at his feet. Tozier was awarded his medal on August 13, 1898.

Tracy, Amasa A. Birth: Maine, 1829. Lieutenant Colonel of the 2nd Vermont Infantry. On October 19, 1864, at Cedar Creek, Virginia, Colonel Tracy took command of and led the brigade in the assault of the enemy's works. Tracy was awarded his medal on June 24, 1892.

Tracy, Benjamin F. Birth: New York, 1830. Colonel of the 109th New York Infantry. On May 6, 1864, at the Wilderness, Virginia, Colonel Tracy seized the colors and led the regiment when other regiments had retired and then reformed his line and held it. Tracy was awarded his medal on June 21, 1895.

Tracy, Charles H. Birth: Connecticut. Sergeant in Company A, 37th Massachusetts Infantry. On May 12, 1864, at Spotsylvania, Virginia, Sergeant Tracy, at the risk of his own life, assisted in carrying to a place of safety a wounded and helpless officer. On April 2, 1865, he advanced with the pioneers, under heavy fire, assisted in removing two lines of chevaux de frise; was twice wounded but advanced to the third line, where he was again severely wounded, losing a leg. Tracy was awarded his medal on November 19, 1897.

Tracy, William G. Birth: New York. Second Lieutenant in Company I, 122nd New York Infantry. On May 2, 1863, at Chancellorsville, Virginia, Lieutenant Tracy was sent outside the lines to obtain information of great importance and having succeeded in his mission, was surprised upon his return by a large force of the enemy, regaining the Union lines only after greatly imperiling his life. Tracy was awarded his medal on May 2, 1895.

Traynor, Andrew. Birth: New Jersey. Corporal in Company D, 1st Michigan Cavalry. On March 16, 1864, at Mason's Hill, Virginia, Corporal Traynor, after having been surprised and captured by a detachment of guerrillas, participated with other prisoners in seizing arms of the enemy, killing two of the guerrillas, and enabling all of the prisoners to escape. Traynor was awarded his medal on September 28, 1897.

Treat, Howell B. Birth: Ohio, 1833. Sergeant in Company I, 52nd Ohio Infantry. On May 11, 1864, at Buzzard's Roost, Georgia, Sergeant Treat risked his life to save a wounded comrade. Treat was awarded his medal on August 14, 1894.

Amasa Tracy (Hall of Heroes)

Benjamin Tracy (U.S. Army War College)

Charles Tracy (Hall of Heroes)

Tremain, Henry E. Birth: New York. Major and Aide-de-Camp, United States Volunteers. On May 15, 1864, at Resaca, Georgia, Major Tremain voluntarily rode between the lines while two brigades of Union troops were firing into each other and stopped the firing. Tremain was awarded his medal on June 30, 1892.

Tribe, John. Birth: New York, 1841. Private in Company G, 5th New York Cavalry. On August 25, 1862, at Waterloo Bridge, Virginia, Private Tribe voluntarily assisted in the burning and destruction of the bridge under heavy fire of the enemy. Tribe was awarded his medal on June 11, 1895.

Tripp, Othniel. Birth: Maine, 1826. Chief Boatswain's Mate aboard the U.S.S. *Seneca*. On January 15, 1865, at Fort Fisher, North Carolina, Tripp boldly charged through the gap in the stockade although the center of the line, being totally unprotected, fell back along the open beach and left too few in the ranks to attempt an offensive operation. Tripp was awarded his medal on June 22, 1865.

Henry Tremain (Hall of Heroes)

Trogden, Howell G. Birth: North Carolina, 1840. Private in Company B, 8th Missouri Infantry. On May 22, 1863, at Vicksburg, Mississippi, Private Trogden exhibited exceptional gallantry in the charge of the volunteer storming party. He carried his regiment's flag and tried to borrow a gun to defend it. Trogden was awarded his medal on August 3, 1894.

Truell, Edwin M. Birth: Massachusetts. Private in Company E, 12th Wisconsin Infantry. On July 21, 1864, at Atlanta, Georgia, Private Truell, although severely wounded in a charge, remained with the regiment until again severely wounded, losing his leg. Truell was awarded his medal on March 11, 1870.

Truett, Alexander, H. Birth: Maryland, 1834. Coxswain aboard the U.S.S. *Richmond*. On August 5, 1864, at Mobile Bay, Alabama, Truett performed his duties with skill and courage throughout the furious two hour battle that resulted in the surrender of the ram *Tennessee* and in the damaging and destruction of batteries at Fort Morgan. Truett was awarded his medal on December 31, 1864.

Tucker, Allen. Birth: Connecticut. Sergeant in Company F, 10th Connecticut Infantry. On April 2, 1865, at Petersburg, Virginia, Sergeant Tucker displayed gallantry as color bearer in the assault on Fort Gregg. Tucker was awarded his medal on May 12, 1865.

Tucker, Jacob R. Birth: Pennsylvania, 1845. Corporal in Company G, 4th Maryland Infantry. On April 1, 1865, at Petersburg, Virginia, Corporal Tucker was one of three soldiers most conspicuous in the final assault. Tucker was awarded his medal on April 22, 1871.

Tweedale, John. [photograph p. 207] Birth: Pennsylvania, 1841. Private in Company B, 15th Pennsylvania Cavalry. On December 31, 1862, at Stone's River, Ten-

nessee, Private Tweedale exhibited exceptional gallantry in action. Tweedale was awarded his medal on November 18, 1887.

Twombly, Voltaire P. Birth: Iowa, 1842. Corporal in Company F, 2nd Iowa Infantry. On February 15, 1862, at Fort Donelson, Tennessee, Corporal Twombly took the colors after three color bearers had fallen, and although most instantly knocked down by a spent ball, immediately arose and bore the colors to the end of the engagement. Twombly was awarded his medal on March 12, 1897.

John Tweedale (Hall of Heroes)

Voltaire Twombly (U.S. Army War College)

Tyrrell, George William. Birth: Ireland. Corporal in Company H, 5th Ohio Infantry. On May 14, 1864, at Resaca, Georgia, Corporal Tyrrell captured a Confederate flag. Tyrrell was awarded his medal on April 7, 1865.

Uhrl, George. Birth: Germany. Sergeant in Battery F, 5th United States Light Artillery. On June 30, 1862, at White Oak Swamp Bridge, Virginia, Sergeant Uhrl was one of a party of three who, under heavy fire from the advancing enemy, voluntarily secured and saved from capture a field gun belonging to another battery, and which had been deserted by its officers and men. Uhrl was awarded his medal on April 4, 1898.

Urell, M. Emmet. Birth: Ireland. Private in Company E, 82nd New York Infantry. On October 14, 1863, at Bristoe Station, Virginia, Private Urell displayed gallantry in action while detailed as color bearer, being severely wounded. Urell was awarded his medal on June 6, 1870.

Wilson Vance (U.S. Army War College)

Vale, John. Birth: England. Private in Company H, 2nd Minnesota Infantry. On February 15, 1863, at Nolensville, Tennessee, Private Vale was one of a detachment of sixteen men who heroically defended a wagon train against the attack of 125 cavalry, repulsed the attack and saved the train. Vale was awarded his medal on September 11, 1897.

Vance, Wilson. Birth: Ohio, 1845. Private in Company B, 21st Ohio Infantry. On December 31, 1862, at Stone's River, Tennessee, Private Vance voluntarily, and under a heavy fire, while his command was falling back, rescued a wounded and helpless comrade from death or capture. Vance was awarded his medal on September 17, 1897.

Vanderslice, John M. Birth: Pennsylvania, 1846. Private in Company D, 8th Pennsylvania Cavalry. On February 6, 1865, at Hatchers Run, Virginia, Private Vanderslice was the first man to reach the enemy's rifle pits, which were taken in the charge. Vanderslice was awarded his medal on September 1, 1893.

Van Matre, Joseph. Birth: West Virginia. Private in Company G, 116th Ohio Infantry. On April 2, 1865, at Petersburg, Virginia, Private Van Matre climbed upon the parapet of Fort Gregg and fired down into the fort as fast as the loaded guns could be passed up to him by comrades. Van Matre was awarded his medal on May 12, 1865.

Vantine, Joseph E. Birth: Pennsylvania, 1835. First Class Fireman aboard the U.S.S. *Richmond*. On March 14, 1863, at Port Hudson, Louisiana, Vantine penetrated the steam filled fire room, after the port and starboard safety valves had been damaged by enemy fire, and courageously hauled the hot fires of the furnaces, continuing this action until the gravity of the situation had been lessened. Vantine was awarded his medal on July 10, 1863.

John Vanderslice (U.S. Army War College)

Van Winkle, Edward (Edwin). Birth: New York. Corporal in Company C, 148th New York Infantry. On September 29, 1864, at Chapin's Farm, Virginia, Corporal Van Winkle took position in advance of the skirmish line and drove the enemy's cannoneers from their guns. Van Winkle was awarded his medal on April 6, 1865.

Vaughn, Pinkerton R. Birth: Pennsylvania, 1839. Sergeant in the United States Marine Corps serving aboard the U.S.S. *Mississippi*. On March 14, 1863, at Port Hudson, Louisiana, Sergeant Vaughn rendered invaluable assistance to his commanding officer, remaining with the ship until the crew had landed and the ship had been fired to prevent its falling into enemy hands. Persistent until the last, and conspicuously cool under the heavy shellfire, Sergeant Vaughn was finally ordered to save himself as he saw fit. Vaughn was awarded his medal on July 10, 1863.

Joseph Vantine (Hall of Heroes)

Veal, Charles. Birth: Virginia, 1838. Private in Company D, 4th United States Colored Infantry. On September 29, 1864, at Chapin's Farm, Virginia, Private Veal seized the national colors after two color bearers had been shot down close to the enemy's works, and bore them through the remainder of the battle. Veal was awarded his medal on April 6, 1865.

Veale, Moses. Birth: Pennsylvania, 1832. Captain in Company F, 109th Pennsylvania Infantry. On October 28, 1863, at Wauhatchie, Tennessee, Captain Veale exhibited exceptional gallantry in action manifesting throughout the engagement coolness, zeal, judgment and courage. Veale was awarded his medal on January 17, 1894.

Veazey, Wheelock G. Birth: New Hampshire, 1835. Colonel of the 16th Vermont Infantry. On July 3, 1863, at Gettysburg, Pennsylvania, Colonel Veazey rapidly assembled his regiment and charged the enemy's flank, under heavy fire, and destroyed a Confederate brigade, all this with new troops in their first battle. Veazey was awarded his medal on September 8, 1891.

Vernay, James D. Birth: Illinois, 1834. Second Lieutenant in Company B, 11th Illinois Infantry. On April 22, 1863, at Vicksburg, Mississippi, Lieutenant Vernay served gallantly as a volunteer with the crew of the steamer Horizon that, under a heavy fire, passed the Confederate batteries. Vernay was awarded his medal on April 1, 1898.

Wheelock Veazey (U.S. Army War College)

Verney, James W. Birth: Maine, 1834. Chief Quartermaster aboard the U.S.S. *Pontoosuc*. During the Fort Fisher Expeditions of December and January of 1864 and 1865, Verney carried out his duties throughout this period and was recommended for gallantry and skill and for his cool courage while under fire of the enemy throughout the various actions. Verney was awarded his medal on June 22, 1865.

Vifquain, Victor. Birth: Belgium. Lieutenant Colonel in the 97th Illinois Infantry. On April 9, 1865, at Fort Blakely, Alabama, Colonel Vifquain captured a Confederate flag. Vifquain was awarded his medal on June 8, 1865.

Victor Vifquain (Hall of Heroes)

Von Vegesack, Ernest. Birth: Sweden. Major and Aide-de-Camp, United States Volunteers. On June 27, 1862, at Gaines Mill, Virginia, Major Von Vegesack successfully and advantageously charged the position of troops under fire. Von Vegesack was awarded his medal on August 23, 1893.

Wageman, John H. Birth: Ohio. Private in Company I, 60th Ohio Infantry. On June 17, 1864, at Petersburg, Virginia, Private Wageman

Ernest Von Vegesack (Hall of Heroes)

remained with the command after being severely wounded, until he had fired all the cartridges in his possession, when he had to be carried from the field. Wageman was awarded his medal on July 27, 1896.

Wagg, Maurice. Birth: England, 1837. Coxswain aboard the U.S.S. *Rhode Island.* On December 31, 1862, at Cape Hatteras, North Carolina, Wagg participated in the hazardous task of rescuing the officers and crew of the sinking Monitor, distinguishing himself by meritorious conduct during this operation. Wagg, was awarded his medal on December 31, 1864.

Wagner, John W. Birth: Maryland, 1844. Corporal in Company F, 8th Missouri Infantry. On May 22, 1863, at Vicksburg, Mississippi, Corporal Wagner exhibited exceptional gallantry in the charge of the volunteer storming party. Wagner was awarded his medal on December 14, 1894.

John Wainwright (U.S. Army War College)

Wainwright, John. Birth: New York, 1839. First Lieutenant in Company F, 97th Pennsylvania Infantry. On January 15, 1865, at Fort Fisher, North Carolina, Lieutenant Wainwright exhibited gallant and meritorious conduct, where, as first lieutenant, he commanded the regiment. Wainwright was awarded his medal on June 24, 1890.

Walker, James C. Birth: Ohio, 1843. Private in Company K, 31st Ohio Infantry. On November 25, 1863, at Missionary Ridge, Tennessee, Private Walker seized the flag and carried it forward after two bearers had fallen, assisted in capturing a battery, and captured the flag of the 41st Alabama Infantry. Walker was awarded his medal on November 25, 1895.

Walker, Dr. Mary E. [photograph p. 211] Birth: New York, 1832. Contract Acting Assistant Surgeon (civilian), United States Army. At Bull Run, Virginia; Patent Office Hospital, Washington, D.C.; Chattanooga, Tennessee; Richmond, Virginia; and Atlanta, Georgia, Dr. Walker rendered valuable service through

James Walker (U.S. Army War College)

Mary Walker (U.S. Army War College)

her untiring efforts to care for the sick and wounded. She was also a prisoner of war, while acting as a contract surgeon. Walker was awarded her medal on November 11, 1865, by a special presentation made by President Johnson. In 1917, her medal was stricken from the rolls on the grounds that she was not enrolled in the military, and thus not eligible for the distinction. In 1977, President Carter restored the Medal of Honor to her, reinstating walker as the only woman and one of only two civilians to be awarded the honor for the Civil War.

Wall, Jerry. Birth: New York, 1841. Private in Company B, 126th New York Infantry. On July 3, 1863, at Gettysburg, Pennsylvania, Private Wall captured a Confederate flag. Wall was awarded his medal on December 1, 1864.

Waller, Francis A. Birth: Ohio, 1840. Corporal in Company I, 6th Wisconsin Infantry. On July 1, 1863, at Gettysburg, Pennsylvania, Corporal Waller captured the flag of the 2nd Mississippi Infantry. Waller was awarded his medal on December 1, 1864.

Walling, William H. Birth: New York, 1830. Captain in Company C, 142nd New York Infantry. On December 25, 1864, at Fort Fisher, North Carolina, Captain Walling captured the flag of the fort after it had been shot down by the fire of the fleet. Walling was awarded his medal on March 28, 1892.

Walsh, John. Birth: Ireland, 1841. Corporal in Company D, 5th New York Cavalry. On October 19, 1864, at Cedar Creek, Virginia, Corporal Walsh recaptured the flag of the 15th New Jersey Infantry. Walsh was awarded his medal on October 26, 1864.

Walton, George W. Birth: Pennsylvania. Private in Company C, 97th Pennsylvania Infantry. On August 29, 1864, at Petersburg, Virginia, Private Walton went outside the trenches, under heavy fire, and rescued a comrade who had been wounded and thrown out of the trench by an exploding shell. Walton was awarded his medal on August 6, 1902.

Wambsgan, Martin. Birth: Germany. Private in Company D, 90th New York Infantry. On October 19, 1864, at Cedar Creek, Virginia, Private Wambsgan sprang forward and bore off the regimental colors after the color bearer had fallen on the field of battle. Wambsgan was awarded his medal on November 3, 1895.

Ward, James. Birth: New York, 1833. Quarter Gunner aboard the U.S.S. *Lackawanna*. On August 5, 1864, at Mobile Bay, Alabama, Ward, though wounded, refused to go below, rendering aid at one of the guns and serving bravely throughout the action that resulted in the surrender of the ram *Tennessee* and the damaging and

Thomas Ward (Hall of Heroes)

William Ward (U.S. Army War College)

Francis Warren (Hall of Heroes)

destruction of the batteries at Fort Morgan. Ward was awarded his medal on December 31, 1864.

Ward, Nelson W. Birth: Ohio. Private in Company M, 11th Pennsylvania Cavalry. On June 25, 1864, at Staunton River Bridge, Virginia, Private Ward went alone in front of his regiment, under a heavy fire, to secure the body of his captain, who had been killed in the action. Ward was awarded his medal on September 10, 1897.

Ward, Thomas J. Birth: West Virginia. Private in Company C, 116th Illinois Infantry. On May 22, 1863, at Vicksburg, Mississippi, Private Ward exhibited exceptional gallantry in the charge of the volunteer storming party. Ward was awarded his medal on July 27, 1894.

Ward, William H. Birth: Michigan, 1840. Captain of Company B, 47th Ohio Infantry. On May 3, 1863, at Vicksburg, Mississippi, Captain Ward voluntarily commanded the expedition which, under cover of darkness, attempted to run the enemy's batteries. Ward was awarded his medal on January 2, 1895.

Warden, John. Birth: Illinois, 1841. Corporal in Company E, 55th Illinois Infantry. On May 22, 1863, at Vicksburg, Mississippi, Corporal Warden exhibited exceptional gallantry in the charge of the volunteer storming party. Warded was awarded his medal on September 2, 1893.

Warfel, Henry C. Birth: Pennsylvania. Private in Company A, 1st Pennsylvania Cavalry. On April 5, 1865, at Paine's Crossroads, Virginia, Private Warfel captured Virginia State colors. Warfel was awarded his medal on May 3, 1865.

Warren, David. Birth: Scotland, 1836. Coxswain aboard the U.S.S. *Monticello*. From June 23 to 25, 1864, at Wilmington, North Carolina, Warren courageously carried out his duties which resulted in the capture of a mail carrier and mail, cutting a telegraph wire, and the capture of a large number of prisoners. Warren was awarded his medal on December 31, 1864.

Warren, Francis E. Birth: Massachusetts. Corporal in Company C, 49th Massachusetts Infantry. On May 27, 1863, at Port Hudson, Louisiana, Corporal Warren volunteered to take part in the movement that was made upon the enemy's works under a heavy fire in advance of the general assault. Warren was awarded his medal on September 30, 1893.

Alexander Webb (Hall of Heroes)

James Webb (U.S. Army War College)

John Weeks (Hall of Heroes)

Webb, Alexander S. Birth: New York, 1835. Brigadier General, United States Volunteers. On July 3, 1863, at Gettysburg, Pennsylvania, General Webb displayed distinguished personal gallantry in leading his men forward at a critical period in the contest. Webb was awarded his medal on September 28, 1891.

Webb, James. Birth: New York, 1841. Private in Company F, 5th New York Infantry. On August 30, 1862, at Bull Run, Virginia, Private Webb, though severely wounded, voluntarily carried information to a battery commander that enabled him to save his guns from capture. Webb was awarded his medal on September 17, 1897.

Webber, Alason P. Birth: New York, 1828. Musician in the 86th Illinois Infantry. On June 27, 1864, at Kennesaw Mountain, Georgia, Webber voluntarily joined a charge against the enemy, which was repulsed. By his rapid firing in the face of the enemy, he enabled many of the wounded to return to Federal lines, while he, with others, held the advance of the enemy while temporary works were being constructed. Webber was awarded his medal on June 22, 1896.

Webster, Henry S. Birth: New York, 1835. Landsman aboard the U.S.S. *Susquehanna*. On January 15, 1865, at Fort Fisher, North Carolina, Landsman Webster displayed exceptional gallantry as a volunteer of the Naval landing party in its attack on the fort. Webster was awarded his medal on June 22, 1865.

Weeks, Charles H. Birth: New Jersey, 1837. Captain of the Foretop aboard the U.S.S. *Montauk*. On September 21, 1864, Weeks displayed great presence of mind and rendered valuable service in extinguishing the fire that was discovered in the magazine of the ship which were imperiling the ship and the men on board. Weeks was awarded his medal on October 3, 1867.

Weeks, John H. Birth: Connecticut, 1845. Private in Company H. 152nd New York Infantry. On May 12, 1864, at Spotsylvania, Virginia, Private Weeks captured a Confederate flag and bearer. Weeks was awarded his medal on December 1, 1864.

Weir, Henry C. Birth: New York. Captain and Assistant Adjutant General, United States Volunteers. On June 24, 1864, at St. Mary's Church, Virginia, Captain Weir, as the division was being pressed back, dismounted and gave his horse to a wounded officer, thus enabling him to escape. Afterwards, he rallied and took command of some stragglers and helped to repel the last charge of the enemy. Weir was awarded his medal on May 18, 1899.

Welch, George W. Birth: Iowa. Private in Company A, 11th Missouri Infantry. On December 16, 1864, at Nashville, Tennessee, Private Welch captured the flag of the 13th Alabama Infantry. Welch was awarded his medal on February 24, 1865.

Welch, Richard. Birth: Ireland. Corporal in Company E, 37th Massachusetts Infantry. On April 2, 1865, at Petersburg, Virginia, Corporal Welch captured a Confederate flag. Welch was awarded his medal on May 10, 1865.

Welch, Stephen. Birth: New York. Sergeant in Company C, 154th New York Infantry. On May 8, 1864, at Dug Gap, Georgia, Sergeant Welch risked his life in rescuing a wounded comrade under fore of the enemy. Welch was awarded his medal on April 13, 1894.

Wells, Henry S. Private in Company C, 148th New York Infantry. On September 29, 1864, at Chapin's Farm, Virginia, Private Wells, with two comrades, took position in advance of the skirmish line, within a short distance of the enemy's gunners, and drove them from their guns. Wells was awarded his medal on April 6, 1865.

Wells, Thomas M. Birth: Ireland. Chief Bugler in the 6th New York Cavalry. On October 19, 1864, at Cedar Creek, Virginia, Wells captured the flag of the 44th Georgia Infantry. Wells was awarded his medal on October 26, 1864.

William Wells (Hall of Heroes)

Wells, William. Birth: Vermont, 1837. Major in the 1st Vermont Cavalry. On July 3, 1863, at Gettysburg, Pennsylvania, Major Wells led the second battalion of his regiment in a daring charge. Wells was awarded his medal on September 8, 1891.

Wells, William. Birth: Germany, 1832. Quartermaster aboard the U.S.S. *Richmond*. On August 5, 1864, at Mobile Bay, Alabama, Wells performed his duties with skill and courage throughout the furious two hour battle that resulted in the surrender of the ram *Tennessee* and in the damaging and destruction of the batteries at Fort Morgan. Wells was awarded his medal on December 31, 1864.

Welsh, Edward. [photograph p. 215] Birth: Ireland. Private in Company D, 54th Ohio Infantry.

Edward Welsh (Hall of Heroes)

On May 22, 1863, at Vicksburg, Mississippi, Private Welsh exhibited exceptional gallantry in the charge of the volunteer storming party. Welsh was awarded his medal on May 11, 1894.

Welsh, James. Birth: Ireland. Private in Company E, 4th Rhode Island Infantry. On July 30, 1864, at Petersburg, Virginia, Private Welsh bore the regimental colors after the color sergeant had been wounded and the color corporal bearing the colors killed, thus saving the colors from capture. Welsh was awarded his medal on June 3, 1905.

Westerhold, William. Birth: Prussia. Sergeant in Company G, 52nd New York Infantry. On May 12, 1864, at Spotsylvania, Virginia, Sergeant Westerhold captured the flag of the 23rd Virginia, Infantry. Westerhold was awarded his medal on December 1, 1864.

Weston, John. Birth: Kentucky. Major in the 4th Kentucky Cavalry. On April 13, 1865, at Wetumpka, Alabama, Major Weston captured two canoes and ferried his men across an unfordable river. He defeated the enemy, and found the Confederate steamers anchored midstream., By a ruse, he obtained possession of a boat, with which he reached the steamers and demanded and received their surrender. Weston was awarded his medal on April 9, 1898.

Wheaton, Lloyd. Birth: Michigan, 1838. Lieutenant Colonel of the 8th Illinois Infantry. On April 9, 1865, at Fort Blakely, Alabama, Colonel Wheaton led the right wing of his regiment, and, springing through an embrasure, was the first to enter the enemy's works, against a strong fire of artillery and infantry. Wheaton was awarded his medal on January 16, 1894.

Wheeler, Daniel D. Birth: Vermont, 1841. First Lieutenant in Company G, 4th Vermont Infantry. On May 3, 1863, at Salem Heights, Virginia, Lieutenant Wheeler displayed distinguished bravery in action where he was wounded and had a horse shot from under him. Wheeler was awarded his medal on March 28, 1892.

Wheeler, Henry W. Birth: Arkansas, 1842. Private in Company A, 2nd Maine Infantry. On July 21, 1861, at Bull Run, Virginia, Private Wheeler assisted his commanding officer in removing the dead and wounded from the field under a heavy fire of artillery and infantry. Wheeler was awarded his medal on April 5, 1898.

Wherry, William M. [photograph p. 216] Birth: Missouri, 1836. First Lieutenant in Company D, 3rd Missouri Infantry Reserves. On August 10, 1861, at Wilson's Creek, Missouri, Lieutenant Wherry displayed conspicuous coolness and heroism in rallying troops that were recoiling under heavy fire. Wherry was awarded his medal on October 30, 1895.

Daniel Wheeler (U.S. Army War College)

William Wherry (Hall of Heroes)

Edward Whitaker (Hall of Heroes)

Whitaker, Edward W. Birth: Connecticut, 1841. Captain of Company E, 1st Connecticut Cavalry. On June 29, 1864, at Reams Station, Virginia, Captain Whitaker voluntarily carried dispatches from the commanding general to General George G. Meade, forcing his way with a single troop of cavalry through an infantry division of the enemy in the most distinguished manner, though he lost half his escort. Whitaker was awarded his medal on April 2, 1898.

White, Adam. Birth: Switzerland. Corporal in Company G, 11th West Virginia Infantry. On April 2, 1865, at Hatchers Run, Virginia, Corporal White captured a Confederate flag. White was awarded his medal on June 13, 1865.

White, J. Henry. Birth: Pennsylvania. Private in Company A, 90th Pennsylvania Infantry. On August 23, 1862, at Rappahannock Station, Virginia, Private White, at imminent risk of his life, crawled to a nearby spring within the enemy's range, and exposed to constant fire filled a large number of canteens, and returned to the relief of his comrades who were suffering from want of water. White was awarded his medal on May 5, 1900.

White, Joseph. Birth: District of Columbia, 1840. Captain of the Gun aboard the U.S.S. *New Ironsides*. From December 23 to 25, 1864, and January 13 to 15, 1865, at Fort Fisher, North Carolina, White performed his duties with skill and courage during the two expeditions against Fort Fisher. White was awarded his medal on June 22, 1865.

White, Patrick H. Birth: Ireland, 1833. Captain of the Chicago Mercantile Battery, Illinois Light Artillery. On May 22, 1863, at Vicksburg, Mississippi, Captain White, with others, carried by hand a cannon up to and fired it through an embrasure of the enemy's works. White was awarded his medal on April 4, 1898.

Whitehead, John M. Birth: Indiana, 1823. Chaplain in the 15th Indiana Infantry. On December 31, 1862, at Stones River, Tennessee, Whitehead went to the front during a desperate contest and unaided carried to the rear several wounded and helpless soldiers. Whitehead was awarded his medal on April 4, 1898.

Whitfield, Daniel. Birth: New Jersey, 1821. Quartermaster aboard the U.S.S. *Lackawanna*. On August 5, 1864, at Mobile Bay, Alabama, Whitfield courageously carried out his duties during the prolonged action that resulted in the capture of the ram *Tennessee* and in the damaging and destruction of Fort Morgan. Whitfield was awarded his medal on December 31, 1864.

Whitman, Frank M. Birth: Maine, 1838. Private in Company G, 35th Massachusetts Infantry. On September 17, 1862, at Antietam, Maryland, Private Whitman was instrumental in saving the lives of several of his comrades at the imminent risk of his own life. On May 18, 1864, at Spotsylvania, Virginia, he was foremost in the line in the assault, receiving a wound that cost him a leg. Whitman was awarded his medal on February 21, 1874.

Whitmore, John. Birth: Illinois, 1844. Private in Company F, 119th Illinois Infantry. On April 9, 1865, at Fort Blakely, Alabama, Private Whitmore captured a Confederate flag. Whitmore was awarded his medal on June 8, 1865.

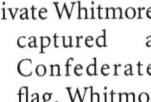

Frank Whitman (U.S. Army War College)

Whitney, William G. Birth: Michigan, 1840. Sergeant in Company B, 11th Michigan Infantry. On September 20, 1863, at Chickamauga, Georgia, Sergeant Whitney went outside the Union lines, as the enemy was preparing to charge, and at great exposure to himself, removed cartridge boxes from the dead and wounded, bringing the same within the Union lines, the ammunition being used with good effect in again repulsing the attack. Whitney was awarded his medal on October 21, 1895.

John Whitmore (U.S. Army War College)

Whittier, Edward N. [photograph p. 218] Birth: Maine, 1840. First Lieutenant in 5th Battery, Maine Light Artillery. On September 22, 1864, at Fishers Hill, Virginia, Lieutenant Whittier went over the enemy's works with the assaulting column, to gain quicker possession of the guns and to turn them upon the enemy. Whittier was awarded his medal on January 13, 1892.

Widick, Andrew J. Birth: Illinois. Private in Company B, 116th Illinois Infantry. On May 22, 1863, at Vicksburg, Mississippi, Private Widick exhibited exceptional gallantry in the charge of the volunteer storming party. Widick was awarded his medal on August 11, 1894.

Wilcox, Franklin L. Birth: New York, 1831. Ordinary Seaman aboard the U.S.S. *Minnesota*. On January 15, 1865, at Fort Fisher, North Carolina, Seaman Wilcox displayed exceptional gallantry as a member of the Naval landing party assaulting the fort. Wilcox was awarded his medal on June 22, 1865.

Wilcox, William H. Birth: New Hampshire. Sergeant in Company G, 9th New Hampshire Infantry. On May 12, 1864, at Spotsylvania, Virginia, Sergeant Wilcox

Edward Whittier (U.S. Army War College)

Perry Wilkes (Hall of Heroes)

took command of his company after the officers had been wounded, conducting himself gallantly. Wilcox was awarded his medal on July 28, 1896.

Wiley, James. Birth: Ohio. Sergeant in Company B, 59th New York Infantry. On July 3, 1863, at Gettysburg, Pennsylvania, Sergeant Wiley captured the flag of a Georgia regiment. Wiley was awarded his medal on December 1, 1864.

Wilhelm, George. Birth: Ohio, 1830. Captain in Company F, 56th Ohio Infantry. On May 16, 1863, at Champion Hill, Mississippi, Captain Wilhelm having been badly wounded in the chest and captured. made a prisoner of his captor and brought him into camp. Wilhelm was awarded his medal on November 17, 1887.

Wilkes, Henry. Birth: New York, 1845. Landsman aboard the U.S.S. *Picket Boat*. On October 27, 1864, at the Roanoke River, North Carolina, Landsman Wilkes was part of the crew that participated in a spar torpedo attack on the Confederate ram *Albemarle*. Wilkes was awarded his medal on December 31, 1864.

Wilkes, Perry. Birth: Indiana, 1830. Pilot serving aboard the U.S.S. *Signal*. On May 5, 1864, at Red River, Louisiana, Wilkes, acting as pilot throughout the battle, stood by his wheel until it was disabled in his hands by a bursting enemy shell. Wilkes was awarded his medal on December 31, 1864.

Wilkins, Leander A. Birth: New Hampshire. Sergeant in Company H, 9th New Hampshire Infantry. On July 30, 1864, at Petersburg, Virginia, Sergeant Wilkins recaptured the colors of the 21st Massachusetts Infantry in a hand-to-hand encounter. Wilkins was awarded his medal on December 1, 1864.

Willcox, Orlando B. [photograph p. 219] Birth: Michigan. Colonel of the 1st Michigan Infantry. On July 21, 1861, at Bull Run, Virginia, Colonel Willcox led repeated

Orlando Willcox (Hall of Heroes)

charges until wounded and taken prisoner. Willcox was awarded his medal on March 2, 1895.

Williams, Anthony. Birth: Massachusetts, 1832. Sailmaker's Mate aboard the U.S.S. *Pontoosuc*. From December 23 to 25, 1864 and January 13 to 15, 1865, at Fort Fisher, North Carolina, Williams carried out his duties faithfully throughout the engagements against the fort and was recommended for gallantry and skill and for his cool courage while under the fire of the enemy. Williams was awarded his medal on June 22, 1865.

Williams, Augustus. Birth: Norway, 1842. Seaman aboard the U.S.S. *Santiago de Cuba*. On January 15, 1865, at Fort Fisher, North Carolina, Seaman Williams exhibited exceptional gallantry as a volunteer with the Naval landing party that assaulted the fort. Williams was awarded his medal on June 22, 1865.

Williams, Elwood N. Birth: Pennsylvania, 1842. Private in Company A, 28th Illinois Infantry. On April 6, 1862, at Shiloh, Tennessee, Private Williams, with one companion, under a heavy fire from both sides, retrieved a box of ammunition that had been abandoned between the lines and delivered it within the line of his regiment. His companion was mortally wounded in the attempt. Williams was awarded his medal on September 28, 1897.

Williams, George C. Birth: England. Quartermaster Sergeant in the 1st Battalion, 14th United States Infantry. On June 17, 1862, at Gaines Mill, Virginia, Sergeant Williams voluntarily left his place of safety in the rear, joined a company, and fought with distinguished gallantry through the action. Williams was awarded his medal on August 28, 1897.

Elwood Williams (Hall of Heroes)

Williams, John. Birth: New Jersey. Boatswain's Mate Aboard the U.S.S. *Mohican*. On November 1, 1861, at Hilton Head, South Carolina, Williams was cool and courageous at his battle station, maintaining a steady fire against the enemy in the engagement with forts Beauregard and Walker. Williams was awarded his medal on July 10, 1863.

Williams, John. Birth: Louisiana, 1828. Captain of the Maintop aboard the U.S.S. *Pawnee*. On June 26, 1861, at Mathias Point, Virginia, Williams, although wounded by a musket ball in the thigh, retained the charge of his boat, and, when the staff was shot away, held the stump in his hand, with the flag, until alongside the *Freeborn*. Williams was awarded his medal on April 3, 1863.

Williams, John. Birth: Pennsylvania, 1832. Seaman aboard the U.S.S. *Commodore Perry*. On October, 3, 1862, at Franklin, Virginia, Seaman Williams remained at his post and did his duties with skill and courage as the *Commodore Perry* fought a gallant battle to silence many Rebel batteries as she steamed down the Blackwater River. Williams was awarded his medal on April 3, 1863.

Williams, Le Roy. Birth: New York, 1845. Sergeant in Company G, 8th New York Heavy Artillery. On June 3, 1864, at Cold Harbor, Virginia, Sergeant Williams voluntarily exposed himself to the fire of enemy sharpshooters to locate the body of his colonel who had been killed near the enemy lines. He recovered the body and returned it to Union lines, having approached within a few feet of Confederate pickets. Williams was awarded his medal on April 1, 1898.

Williams, Peter. Birth: Norway, 1831. Seaman aboard the U.S.S. *Monitor*. On March 9, 1862, at Hampton Roads, Virginia, Seaman Williams gallantly served throughout the engagement with the C.S.S. *Merrimack*, piloting the *Monitor* throughout the battle. Williams was awarded his medal on April 3, 1863.

Williams, Robert. Birth: New York, 1837. Signal Quartermaster aboard the U.S.S. *Benton*. From December 23 to 27, 1862, at Yazoo River, Mississippi, Williams served courageously throughout the battle against hostile forces in which the enemy had the dead range of the vessel and were punishing her with heavy fire. Williams was awarded his medal on April 3, 1863.

Williams, William. Birth: Ireland, 1840. Landsman aboard the U.S.S. *Lehigh*. On November 16, 1863, at Charleston, South Carolina, Landsman Williams undertook the hazardous task of freeing the Lehigh, which had been grounded and was under heavy fire from Fort Moultrie. Williams succeeded in passing a hawser from the *Nahant* in a small boat to the *Lehigh*, enabling it to be freed from its helpless position. Williams was awarded his medal on April 16, 1864.

Williams, William H. Birth: Ohio. Private in Company C, 82nd Ohio Infantry. On July 20, 1864, at Peach Tree Creek, Georgia, Private Williams voluntarily went beyond the lines to observe the enemy. He also aided a wounded comrade. Williams was awarded his medal on June 19, 1894.

James Williamson (U.S. Army War College)

Williamson, James A. Birth: Kentucky, 1829. Colonel in the 4th Iowa Infantry. On December 29, 1862, at Chickasaw Bayou, Mississippi, Colonel Williamson led his regiment against a superior force, strongly entrenched, and held his ground when all support had been withdrawn. Williamson was awarded his medal on January 17, 1895.

Willis, Richard. Birth: England, 1826. Coxswain aboard the U.S.S. *New Ironsides*. From December 23 to 25, 1864 and January 13 to 15, 1865, at Fort Fisher, North Carolina, Willis displayed exceptional gallantry in performing his duties during the expeditions against Fort Fisher. Willis was awarded his medal on June 22, 1865.

Williston, Edward B. Birth: Vermont. First Lieutenant in the 2nd United States Artillery. On June 12, 1864, at Trevilian Station, Virginia, Lieutenant Williston displayed distinguished gallantry in action. Williston was awarded his medal on April 6, 1892.

Wilson, Charles E. Birth: Pennsylvania. Sergeant in Company A, 1st New Jersey Cavalry. On April 6, 1865, at Sailors Creek, Virginia, Sergeant Wilson charged the enemy works, colors in hand, and had two horses shot from under him. Wilson was awarded his medal on July 3, 1865.

Wilson, Christopher W. Birth: Ireland. Private in Company E, 73rd New York Infantry. On May 12, 1864, at Spotsylvania, Virginia, Private Wilson took the flag from the wounded color bearer and carried it in the charge, in which he also captured the flag of the 56th Virginia Infantry. Wilson was awarded his medal on December 30, 1898.

Wilson, Francis A. Birth: Pennsylvania. Corporal in Company B, 95th Pennsylvania Infantry. On April 2, 1865, at Petersburg, Virginia, Corporal Wilson was among the first to penetrate the enemy's lines where he captured a cannon. Wilson was awarded his medal on June 25, 1880.

Wilson, John. Birth: England. Sergeant in Company L, 1st New Jersey Cavalry. On March 31, 1865, at Chamberlains Creek, Virginia, Sergeant Wilson, with one comrade, headed off the advance of the enemy, shooting two of his color bearers, also posted himself between the enemy and the lead horses of his own command, thus saving the heard from capture. Wilson was awarded his medal on July 3, 1865.

John Wilson [England] (U.S. Army War College)

Wilson, John A. Birth: Ohio, 1832. Private in Company C, 21st Ohio Infantry. In April of 1862, at Big Shanty, Georgia, Private Wilson was one of 22 men who penetrated nearly 200 miles south into enemy territory and captured a railroad train, and attempted to destroy the bridges and track between Chattanooga and Atlanta. Wilson was awarded his medal in September of 1863.

Wilson, John M. Birth: Washington Territory. First Lieutenant, United States Engineers. On August 6, 1862, at Malvern Hill, Virginia, Lieutenant Wilson remained on duty, while suffering from an acute illness and very weak, and participated in the action of that date. Wilson was awarded his medal on July 3, 1897.

Winegar, William W. Birth: New York. Lieutenant in Company B, 19th New York Cavalry. On April 1, 1865, at Five Forks, Virginia, Lieutenant Winegar captured a Confederate flag and its guard. Winegar was awarded his medal on May 3, 1865.

John M. Wilson (Hall of Heroes)

William Withington (U.S. Army War College)

John Wollam (Hall of Heroes)

Wisner, Lewis S. Birth: New York. First Lieutenant in Company K, 124th New York Infantry. On May 12, 1864, at Spotsylvania, Virginia, Lieutenant Wisner, while serving as an engineer officer, voluntarily exposed himself to the enemy's fire. Wisner was awarded his medal on January 2, 1895.

Withington, William H. Birth: Massachusetts, 1835. Captain of Company B, 1st Michigan Infantry. On July 21, 1861, at Bull Run, Virginia, Captain Withington remained on the field under heavy fire to succor his superior officer. Withington was awarded his medal on January 7, 1895.

Wollam, John. Birth: Ohio. Private in Company C, 33rd Ohio Infantry. In April of 1862, at Big Shanty, Georgia, Private Wollam was one of 22 men who penetrated nearly 200 miles south into enemy territory and captured a railroad train and attempted to destroy the bridges and track between Chattanooga and Atlanta. Wollam was awarded his medal on July 20, 1864.

Wood, H. Clay. Birth: Maine, 1832. First Lieutenant in the 11th United States Infantry. On August 10, 1861, at Wilson's Creek, Missouri, Lieutenant Wood displayed distinguished gallantry in the battle. Wood was awarded his medal on October 28, 1893.

Wood, Mark. [photograph p. 223] Birth: England. Private in Company C, 21st Ohio Infantry. In April of 1862, at Big Shanty, Georgia, Private Wood was one of 22 men who penetrated nearly 200 miles south into enemy territory and captured a railroad train and

Mark Wood (Hall of Heroes); at left: *H. Clay Wood (U.S. Army War College);*

attempted to destroy the bridges and track between Chattanooga and Atlanta. Wood was awarded his medal in September of 1863.

Wood, Richard H. Birth: New Jersey. Captain in Company A, 97th Illinois Infantry. On May 22, 1863, at Vicksburg, Mississippi, Captain Wood exhibited exceptional gallantry in the charge of the volunteer storming party. Wood was awarded his medal on December 12, 1895.

Wood, Robert B. Birth: Ohio, 1836. Coxswain aboard the U.S.S. *Mount Washington*. On April 14, 1863, at Nansemond River, North Carolina, Wood continued to fight as his gun for six hours, despite a strike on the head by a spent ball. Wood was awarded his medal on July 10, 1863.

Woodall, William H. Civilian scout, United States Army, serving in General Philip Sheridan's Headquarters. From March 29 to April 9, 1865, during the campaigning around Richmond, Petersburg, and the Confederate retreat to Appomattox, Woodall captured the flag of Brigadier General Rufus Barringer's headquarters flag. Woodall was awarded his medal on April 25, 1865. In 1916, Woodall's medal was rescinded by order of the review committee because of the fact that he was a civilian, and therefore not eligible to receive it. In 1989, the U.S. Army Board of Correction of Records restored the medal to him.

Woodbury, Eri D. Birth: New Hampshire. Sergeant in Company E, 1st Vermont Cavalry. On October 19, 1864, at Cedar Creek, Virginia, Sergeant Woodbury encountered four Confederate infantrymen retreating, drew his saber, and compelled them to surrender, along with their muskets and the flag of the 12th North Carolina Infantry.

Woodruff, Alonzo. Birth: Michigan, 1839. Sergeant in the 1st United States Sharpshooters. On October 27, 1864, at Hatchers Run, Virginia, Sergeant Woodruff went to the assistance of a wounded and overpowered comrade, and in hand-to-hand combat effected his rescue. Woodruff was awarded his medal on January 29, 1896.

Woodruff, Carle A. Birth: New York, 1841. First Lieutenant in the 2nd United States Artillery. On July 24, 1863, at Newby's Crossroads, Virginia, Lieutenant Woodruff, while in command of a section of the battery, was attacked by the enemy and ordered to abandon his guns. Woodruff disregarded his orders and aided in repelling the attack and saving the guns. Woodruff was awarded his medal on September 1, 1893.

Woods, Daniel A. Birth: West Virginia, 1847. Private in Company K, 1st West Virginia Cavalry. On April 6, 1865, at Sailors Creek, Virginia, Private Woods captured the flag of the 18th Florida Infantry. Woods was awarded his medal on May 3, 1865.

Woods, Samuel. Birth: California, 1835. Seaman aboard the U.S.S. *Mount Washington*. On April 14, 1863, at Nansemond River, Virginia, Seaman Woods fearlessly jumped into the river to rescue a comrade who had been struck by a bullet and

Carle Woodruff (U.S. Army War College)

fallen overboard. The man sank below the surface before Woods could reach him. Woods was awarded his medal on July 10, 1863.

Woodward, Evan M. Birth: Pennsylvania, 1838. First Lieutenant and Adjutant in the 2nd Pennsylvania Infantry Reserves. On December 13, 1862, at Fredericksburg, Virginia, Lieutenant Woodward advanced between the lines and captured the flag of the 19th Georgia Infantry. Woodward was awarded his medal on December 14, 1894.

Woon, John. Birth: England, 1823. Boatswain's Mate aboard the U.S.S. *Pittsburgh*. On April 29, 1863, at Grand Gulf, Mississippi, Woon showed courage and devotion to duty throughout the bitter engagement. Woon was awarded his medal on July 10, 1863.

Woram, Charles B. Birth: New York, 1845. Seaman aboard the U.S.S. *Oneida*. On August 5, 1864, at Mobile Bay, Alabama, Seaman Worman acted as aid to the executive officer carrying orders intelligently and correctly, distinguishing himself by his cool courage throughout the battle that resulted in the surrender of the ram *Tennessee* and the damaging of Fort Morgan. Woram was awarded his medal on December 31, 1864.

Wortick (Wertick), Joseph. Birth: Pennsylvania. Private in Company A, 8th Missouri Infantry. On May 22, 1863, at Vicksburg, Mississippi, Private Wortick exhibited exceptional gallantry in the charge of the volunteer storming party. Wortick was awarded his medal on July 14, 1894.

William Wray (U.S. Army War College)

Wray, William J. Birth: Pennsylvania, 1846. Sergeant in Company K, 1st United States Veteran Reserve Corps. On July 12, 1864, at Fort Stevens, Washington, D.C., Sergeant Wray rallied the company at a critical moment during a change of position under fire. Wray was awarded his medal on December 15, 1892.

Wright, Albert D. Birth: Pennsylvania, 1844. Captain in Company G, 43rd United States Colored Infantry. On July 30, 1864, at Petersburg, Virginia, Captain Wright advanced beyond the enemy's lines, capturing a stand of colors and its color guard, being wounded in the process. Wright was awarded his medal on May 1, 1893.

Wright, Edward. Birth: New York, 1829. Quartermaster aboard the U.S.S. *Cayuga*. From April 24 to 25, 1862, at forts Jackson and St. Philip, south of New Orleans, Wright con-

Albert Wright (U.S. Army War College)

scientiously performed his duties throughout the action in which attempts by three rebel steamers to butt and board were repelled, and the ships driven off or forced to surrender. Wright was awarded his medal on April 3, 1863.

Wright, Robert. Birth: Ireland. Private in Company G, 14th United States Infantry. On October 1, 1864, at Chapel House Farm, Virginia, Private Wright was commended for gallantry in action. Wright was awarded his medal on November 25, 1869.

Wright, Samuel. Birth: Indiana. Corporal in Company H, 2nd Minnesota Infantry. On February 15, 1863, at Nolensville, Tennessee, Corporal Wright was one of a detachment of sixteen men who heroically defended a wagon train against the attack of 125 cavalry and saved the train. Wright was awarded his medal on September 11, 1897.

Samuel Wright (Hall of Heroes)

Wright, Samuel C. Birth: Massachusetts. Private in Company E, 29th Massachusetts Infantry. On September 17, 1862, at Antietam, Maryland, Private Wright voluntarily advanced under a destructive fire and removed a fence that would have impeded a contemplated charge. Wright was awarded his medal on January 29, 1896.

Wright, William. Birth: England, 1835. Yeoman aboard the U.S.S. *Monticello*. From June 23 to 25, 1864, at Wilmington, North Carolina, Yeoman Wright took part in a reconnaissance of the enemy defenses and courageously carried out his cutting of a telegraph wire and the capture of a large group of prisoners. Wright was awarded his medal on December 31, 1864.

Yeager, Jacob F. Birth: Pennsylvania, 1841. Private in Company H, 101st Ohio Infantry. On May 11, 1864, at Buzzard's Roost, Georgia, Private Yeager seized a shell with fuse burning that had fallen in the ranks of his company and threw it into a stream, thereby probably saving his comrades from injury. Yeager was awarded his medal on August 3, 1897.

Young, Andrew J. Birth: Pennsylvania. Sergeant in Company F, 1st Pennsylvania Cavalry. On April 5, 1865, at Paine's Crossroads, Virginia, Sergeant Young captured a Confederate flag. Young was awarded his medal on May 3, 1865.

Young, Benjamin F. Birth: Canada, 1844. Corporal in Company I, 1st Michigan Sharpshooters. On June 17, 1864, at Petersburg, Virginia, Corporal Young captured the flag of the 35th North Carolina Infantry. Young was awarded his medal in December of 1864.

Young, Cavalry M. Birth: Ohio. Sergeant in Company I, 3rd Iowa Cavalry. On October 25, 1864, at Osage, Kansas, Sergeant Young displayed gallantry in capturing Confederate General Cabell. Young was awarded his medal on April 4, 1865.

Young, Edward B. Birth: New Jersey, 1835. Coxswain aboard the U.S.S. *Calena*. On August 5, 1864, at Mobile Bay, Alabama, Young performed his duties with skill and courage throughout the action that resulted in the surrender of the ram *Tennessee* and in the damaging and destruction of the batteries at Fort Morgan. Young was awarded his medal on June 22, 1865.

Young, Horatio N. Birth: Maine, 1845. Seaman aboard the U.S.S. *Lehigh*. On November 16, 1863, at Charleston, South Carolina, Seaman Young, during the hazardous task of freeing the *Lehigh*, which had become grounded under enemy fire, successfully passed a hawser from the *Nahant*, in a small boat, enabling his ship to be freed from its helpless position. Young was awarded his medal on April 16, 1864.

Horatio Young (Hall of Heroes)

Young, James M. Birth: New York. Private in Company B, 72nd New York Infantry. On May 6, 1864, at the Wilderness, Virginia, Private Young, with two companions, voluntarily went in the forest to reconnoiter the enemy's position, was fired upon and one of his companions disabled. Young took the wounded man upon his back and, under fire, carried him within Union lines. Young was awarded his medal on April 2, 1898.

Young, William. Birth: New York, 1835. Boatswain's Mate aboard the U.S.S. *Cayuga*. From April 24 to 25, 1862, at forts Jackson and St. Philip, south of New Orleans, Young calmly manned a Parrot gun throughout the action in which attempts by three Rebel steamers to butt and board were thwarted and the ships driven off and captured. Young was awarded his medal on April 3, 1863.

John Younker (U.S. Army War College)

Younker, John L. Birth: Germany, 1836. Private in Company A, 12th United States Infantry. On August 9, 1862, at Cedar Mountain, Virginia, Private Younker voluntarily carried an order, at great risk of life in the face of a fire of grape and canister, in doing so he was wounded. Younker was awarded his medal on November 1, 1893.

Names by Branch of Service

U.S. Army
Adams, James F.
Adams, John G.B.
Alber, Frederick
Albert, Christian
Allen, Abner P.
Allen, James
Allen, Nathaniel
Ames, Adelbert
Ammerman, Robert W.
Anderson, Bruce
Anderson, Charles W.
Anderson, Everett W.
Anderson, Frederick C.
Anderson, Marion T.
Anderson, Peter
Anderson, Thomas
Apple, Andrew O.
Appleton, William H.
Archer, James W.
Archer, Lester
Archinal, William
Armstrong, Clinton L.
Arnold, Abraham K.
Ayers, David
Ayers, John G.K.
Babcock, William J.
Bacon, Elijah W.
Baird, Absalom
Baldwin, Frank D.
Ballen, Frederick
Banks, George L.
Barber, James A.
Barker, Nathaniel C.
Barnes, William H.
Barnum, Henry A.

The Battle of First Manasass, Virginia. Though the battle took place before Congress had authorized the Medal of Honor, Adelbert Ames was recognized for his gallantry on that field, when he refused to leave his section of the 5th United States Artillery. Ames was the only participant of the battle to be awarded the Medal of Honor (U.S. Army War College).

Barrell, Charles L.
Barrick, Jesse T.
Barringer, William H.
Barry, Augustus
Batchelder, Richard N.
Bates, Delaven
Bates, Norman
Baybutt, Philip
Beaty, Powhatan
Beaufort, Jean J.
Beaumont, Eugene B.
Bebb, Edward J.
Beckwith, Wallace A.
Beebe, William S.
Beech, John P.
Begley, Terrence
Belcher, Thomas
Bell James B.
Benedict, George G.
Benjamin, John F.
Benjamin, Samuel N.
Bennett, Orren
Bennett, Orson W.
Bensinger, William
Benyaurd, William H.
Betts, Charles M.
Beyer, Hillary
Bickford, Henry H.
Bickford, Matthew
Bieger, Charles
Bingham, Henry H.
Birdsall, Horatio L.
Bishop, Francis A.
Black, John C.
Black, William P.
Blackmar, Wilmon W.
Blackwood, William R.D.
Blair, Robert M.
Blasdel, Thomas A.
Blickensderfer, Milton
Bliss, George N.
Bliss, Zenas R.
Blodgett, Welis H.
Blucher, Charles
Blunt, John W.
Boehm, Peter M.
Bonebrake, Henry G.
Bonnaffon, Sylvester, Jr.
Boody, Robert
Boon, Hugh P.
Boquet, Nicholas

Boss, Orlando
Bourke, John G.
Boury, Richard
Boutwell, John W.
Bowen Chester B.
Bowen, Emmer
Box, Thomas J.
Boynton, Henry V.
Bradley, Thomas W.
Brady, James
Brandle, Joseph E.
Brannigan, Felix
Brant, William
Bras, Edgar A.
Brest, Lewis F.
Brewer, William J.
Breyer, Charles
Briggs, Elijah A.
Bringle, Andrew
Bronner, August F.
Bronson, James H.
Brosnan, John
Brouse, Charles W.
Brown, Charles
Brown, Edward, Jr.
Brown, Henri Le Ferve
Brown, Jeremiah Z.
Brown, John H.
Brown, John Harties
Brown, Morris, Jr.
Brown, Robert B.
Brown, Uriah
Brown, Wilson W.
Brownell, Francis E.
Bruner, Louis J.
Brush, George W.
Bruton, Christopher C.
Bryant, Andrew S.
Buchanan, George A.
Buck, F. Clarence
Buckingham, David E.
Buckles, Abram J.
Buckley, Denis
Buckley, John C.
Bucklyn, John K.
Buffington, John E.
Buffum, Robert
Buhrman, Henry G.
Bumgarner, William
Burbank, James H.
Burger, Joseph

Burk, E. Michael
Burk, Thomas
Burke, Daniel W.
Burke, Thomas
Burns, James M.
Burritt, William W.
Butterfield, Daniel
Butterfield, Frank G.
Cadwallader, Abel G.
Cadwell, Luman L.
Caldwell, Daniel
Calkin, Ivers S.
Callahan, John H.
Camp, Carlton N.
Campbell, James A.
Campbell, William
Capehart, Charles E.
Capehart, Henry
Capron, Horace, Jr.
Carey, Hugh
Carey, James L.
Carlisle, Casper R.
Carman, Warren
Carmin, Isaac H.
Carney, William H.
Carr, Eugene A.
Carr, Franklin
Carson, William J.
Cart, Jacob
Carter, John J.
Carter, Joseph F.
Caruana, Orlando E.
Casey, David
Casey, Henry
Catlin, Isaac S.
Cayer, Ovila
Chamberlain, Joshua L.
Chamberlain, Orville T.
Chambers, Joseph B.
Chandler, Henry F.
Chandler, James B.
Chandler, Stephen E.
Chapin, Alaric B.
Chapman, John
Chase, John F.
Child, Benjamin H.
Chisman, William W.
Christiancy, James I.
Churchill, Samuel J.
Cilley, Clinton A.
Clancy, James T.

Clapp, Albert A.
Clark, Charles A.
Clark, Harrison
Clark, James G.
Clark, John W.
Clark, William A.
Clarke, Dayton P.
Clausen, Charles H.
Clay, Cecil
Cleveland, Charles F.
Clopp, John E.
Clute, George W.
Coates, Jefferson
Cockley, David L.
Coey, James
Coffey, Robert J.
Cohn, Abraham
Colby, Carlos W.
Cole, Gabriel
Collins, Harrison
Collins, Thomas D.
Collis, Charles H.T.
Colwell, Oliver
Compson, Hartwell B.
Conaway, John W.
Conboy, Martin
Connell, Trustrim
Conner, Richard
Connors, James
Cook, John
Cook, John H.
Cooke, Walter H.
Copp, Charles D.
Corcoran, John
Corliss, George W.
Corliss, Stephen P.
Corson, Joseph K.
Cosgriff, Richard H.
Cosgrove, Thomas
Coughlin, John
Cox, Robert M.
Coyne, John N.
Cranston, William W.
Creed, John
Crocker, Henry H.
Crocker, Ulric L.
Croft, James E.
Crosier, William H.H.
Cross, James E.
Crowley, Michael
Cullen, Thomas

Cummings, Amos J.
Cumpston, James M.
Cunningham, Francis M.
Cunningham James, S.
Curran, Richard
Curtis, John C.
Curtis, Josiah M.
Curtis, Newton Martin
Custer, Thomas W.
Cutcheon, Byron M.
Cutts, James M.
Darrough, John S.
Davidsizer, John A.
Davidson, Andrew
Davidson, Andrew
Davis, Charles C.
Davis, Freeman
Davis, George, E.
Davis, Harry
Davis, John
Davis, Joseph
Davis, Martin K.
Davis, Thomas
Day, Charles
Day, David F.
Deane, John M
De Castro, Joseph H.
De Lacey, Patrick
Deland, Frederick N.
Delaney, John C.
De Lavie, Hiram H.
De Puy, Charles H.
De Will, Richard W.
Di Cesnola, Louis P.
Dickey, William D.
Dickie, David
Dilger, Hubert
Dillon, Michael A.
Dockum, Warren C.
Dodd, Robert F.
Dodds, Edward E.
Dulloff, Charles W.
Donaldson, John
Donoghue, Timothy
Doody, Patrick
Dore, George E.
Dorley, August
Dorsey, Daniel A.
Dorsey, Decatur
Dougall, Allan H.
Dougherty, Michael

Dow, George P.
Downey, William
Downs, Henry W.
Drake, James M.
Drury, James
Duffey, John
Dunlavy, James
Dunne, James
Du Pont, Henry A.
Durham, James R.
Durham John S.
Eckes, John N.
Eddy, Samuel E.
Edgerton, Nathan H.
Edwards, David
Elliott, Alexander
Elliott, Russell C.
Ellis, Horace
Elise, William
Ellsworth, Thomas
Elison, James M.
Embler, Andrew H.
Enderlin, Richard
Engle, James E.
English, Edmund
Ennis, Charles D.
Estes, Lewellyn G.
Evans, Coron, D.
Evans, Ira H.
Evans, James R.
Evans, Thomas
Everson, Adelbert
Ewing, John C.
Falconer, John A.
Fall, Charles S.
Fallon, Thomas T.
Falls, Benjamin F.
Fanning, Nicholas
Farnsworth, Herbert E.
Farquhar, John M.
Fasnacht, Charles H.
Fernald, Albert E.
Ferrier, Daniel T.
Ferris, Eugene W.
Fesq, Frank
Finkenbiner, Henry S.
Fisher, John H.
Fisher, Joseph
Flanagan, Augustin
Flannigan, James
Fleetwood, Christian A.

Branch of Service (U.S. Army)

Follett, Joseph L.
Force, Manning F.
Ford, George W.
Forman, Alexander A.
Fout, Frederick W.
Fox, Henry
Fox, Henry M.
Fox, Nicholas
Fox, William R.
Frantz, Joseph
Fraser, Willaim W.
Freeman, Archibald
Freeman, Henry B.
Freeman, William H.
French, Samuel S.
Frey, Franz
Frick, Jacob G.
Frizzell, Henry F.
Fuger, Frederick
Funk, West
Furman, Chester S.
Furness, Frank
Gage, Richard J.
Galloway, George N.
Galloway, John
Gardiner, James
Gardner, Charles N.
Gardner, Robert J.
Garrett, William
Gasson, Richard
Gaunt, John C.
Gauese, Isaac
Gaylord, Levi B.
Gere, Thomas P.
Geschwind, Nicholas
Gibbs, Wesley
Gifford, Benjamin
Gifford, David L.
Gillespie, George E.
Gilligan, Edward L.
Gilmore, John C.
Ginley, Patrick
Gion, Joseph
Godley, Leonidus M.
Goettel, Philip
Goheen, Charles A.
Goldsbery, Andrew E.
Goodall, Francis H.
Goodman, William E.
Goodrich, Edwin
Gould, Charles G.

Gould, Newton, T.
Gouraud, George E.
Grace, Peter
Graham, Thomas N.
Grant, Gabriel
Grant, Lewis A.
Graul, William
Gray, John
Gray, Robert A.
Grebe, M.R. William
Green, George
Greenawalt, Abraham
Greene, Oliver D.
Gregg, Joseph O.
Greig, Theodore W.
Gresser, Ignatz
Gribben, James H.
Grimshaw, Samuel
Grindlay, James G.
Grueb, George
Guerin, Fritz W.
Guinn, Thomas
Gwynne, Nathaniel
Hack, John
Hack, Lester G.
Hadley, Cornelius M.
Hadley, Osgood T.
Hagerty, Asel
Haight, John H.
Haight, Sidney
Hall, Francis B.
Hall, Henry Seymour
Hall, Newton H.
Hallock, Nathan M.
Hammel, Henry A.
Haney, Milton L.
Hanford, Edward R.
Hanks, Joseph
Hanna, Marcus A.
Hanna, Milton
Hanscom, Moses C.
Hapeman, Douglas
Harbourne, John H.
Hardenbergh, Henry, M.
Haring, Abram P.
Harmon Amzi D.
Harrington, Ephraim W.
Harris, George W.
Harris, James H.
Harris, Moses
Harris, Sampson

Hart, John W.
Hart, William E.
Hartranft, John F.
Harvey, Harry
Haskell, Frank W.
Haskell, Marcus M.
Hastings, Smith H.
Hatch, John P.
Havron, John H.
Hawkins, Gardner C.
Hawkins, Martin J.
Hawkins, Thomas R.
Hawthorne, Harris S.
Haynes, Asbury F.
Hays, John H.
Healey, George W.
Hedges, Joseph
Heermance, William L.
Heller, Henry
Helms, David H.
Henry, Guy V.
Henry, James
Henry, William W.
Herington, Pitt B.
Herron, Francis J.
Hesseltine, Francis, S.
Hibson, Joseph C.
Hickey, Dennis W.
Hickok, Nathan E.
Higby, Charles
Higgins, Thomas J.
Highland, Patrick
Hill, Edward
Hill, Henry
Hill, James
Hill, James
Hilliker, Benjamin F.
Hills, William G.
Hilton, Alfred B.
Hincks, William B.
Hodges, Addison J.
Hoffman, Henry
Hoffman, Thomas W.
Hogan, Franklin
Hogarty, William P.
Holcomb, Daniel I.
Holehouse, James
Holland, Lenuel F.
Holland, Milton M.
Holmes, Lovilo N.
Holmes, William T.

Holton, Charles M.
Holton, Edward A.
Homan, Conrad
Hooker, George W.
Hooper, William B.
Hopkins, Charles F.
Horan, Thomas
Horne, Samuel B.
Horsfall, William H.
Hottenstine, Solomon J.
Hough, Ira
Houghton, Charles H.
Houghton, George L.
Houlton, William
Howard, Henderson C.
Howard, Hiram R.
Howard, James
Howard, Oliver O.
Howard, Squire E.
Howe, Orion P.
Howe, William H.
Hubbell, William S.
Hudson, Aaron R.
Hughes, Oliver
Hughey, John
Huidekoper, Henry S.
Hunt, Louis T.
Hunter, Charles A.
Hunterson, John C.
Hyatt, Theodore
Hyde, Thomas W.
Hymer, Samuel
Ilgenfritz, Charles H.
Immell, Lorenzo D.
Ingalls, Lewis J.
Inscho, Leonidus H.
Irsch, Francis
Irwin, Patrick
Jackson, Frederick R.
Jacobson, Eugene P.
James, Isaac
James, Miles
Jamieson, Walter
Jardine, James
Jellison, Benjamin H.
Jennings, James T.
Jewett, Erastus W.
John, William
Johndro, Franklin
Johns, Elisha
Johns, Henry T.

Johnson, Andrew
Johnson, Follett
Johnson, John
Johnson, Joseph E.
Johnson, Ruel M.
Johnson, Samuel
Johnson, Wallace W.
Johnston, David
Johnston, Willie
Jones, David
Jones, William
Jordan, Absalom
Josselyn, Simeon T.
Judge, Francis W.
Kaiser, John
Kaltenbach, Luther
Kane, John
Kappesser, Peter
Karpeles, Leopold
Kauss, August
Keele, Joseph
Keen, Joseph S.
Keene, Joseph
Kelley, Andrew J.
Kelley, George V.
Kelley, John
Kelley, Leverett M.
Kelly, Alexander
Kelly, Daniel
Kelly, Thomas
Kemp, Joseph
Kendall, William W.
Kennedy, John
Kenyon, John S.
Kenyon, Samuel P.
Keough, John
Kephart, James
Kerr, Thomas R.
Kiggins, John
Kimball, Joseph
Kindig, John M.
King, Horation C.
King, Robert H.
King, Rufus, Jr.
Kinsey, John
Kirby, Dennis T.
Kirk, Jonathan C.
Kline, Harry
Kloth, Charles H.
Knight, Charles H.
Knight, William J.

Knowles, Abiather J.
Knox, Edward M.
Koogle, Jacob
Kountz, John S.
Kramer, Theodore L.
Kretsinger, George
Kuder, Andrew
Kuder, Jeremiah
Labill, Joseph S.
Ladd, George
Laing, William
Landis, James P.
Lane, Morgan D.
Lanfare, Aaron S.
Langbein, J.C. Julius
Larimer, Smith
Larrabee, James W.
Lawson, Gaines
Lawton, Henry W.
Leonard, Edwin
Leonard, William E.
Leslie, Frank
Levy, Benjamin
Lewis Dewitt Clinton
Lewis, Henry
Lewis, Samuel E.
Libaire, Adolphe
Lilley, John
Little, Henry F.W.
Littlefield, George H.
Livingston, Josiah O.
Locke, Lewis
Lonergan, John
Longshore, William H.
Lonsway, Joseph
Lord, William
Lorish, Andrew J.
Love, George M.
Lovering, George M.
Lower, Cyrus B.
Lower, Robert A.
Loyd, George
Lucas, George W.
Luce, Moses A.
Ludgate, William
Ludwig, Carl
Lunt, Alphonso M.
Lutes, Franklin W.
Luther, James H.
Luty, Gotlieb
Lyman, Joel H.

Lyon, Frederick A.
MacArthur, Arthur, Jr.
Madden, Michael
Madison, James
Magee, William
Mahoney, Jeremiah
Mandy, Harry J.
Mangam, Richard C.
Manning, Joseph S.
Marland, William
Marquette, Charles
Marsh, Albert
Marsh, Charles H.
Marsh, George
Martin, Sylvester H.
Mason, Elihu H.
Mathews, William H.
Matthews, John C.
Matthews, Milton
Mattingly, Henry B.
Mattocks, Charles P.
Maxham, Lowell M.
May, William
Mayberry, John B.
Mayes, William B.
Maynard, George H.
McAdams, Peter
McAlwee, Benjamin F.
McAnally, Charles
McCammon, William W.
McCarren, Bernard
McCauslin, Joseph
McCleary, Charles H.
McClelland, James M.
McConnell, Samuel
McCornack, Andrew
McDonald, George E.
McDonald, John Wade
McElhinny, Samuel O.
McEnroe, Patrick H.
McFall, Daniel
McGinn, Edward
McGonagle, Wilson
McGonnigle, Andrew J.
McGough, Owen
McGraw, Thomas
McGuire, Patrick
McHale, Alexander U.
McKay, Charles W.
McKee, George
McKeen, Nineveh S.

McKeever, Michael
McKown, Nathaniel A.
McMahon, Martin T.
McMillen, Francis M.
McVeane, John P.
McWhorter, Walter F.
Meach, George E.
Meagher, Thoomas
Mears, George W.
Menter, John W.
Merriam, Henry C.
Merrifield, James K.
Merrill, Augustus
Merril, George
Merritt, John G.
Meyer, Henry C.
Miles, Nelson A.
Miller, Frank
Miller, Henry A.
Miller, Jacob C.
Miller, James P.
Miller, John
Miller, John
Miller, William E.
Mills, Frank W.
Mindil, George W.
Mitchell, Alexander H.
Mitchell, Theodore
Moffitt, John H.
Molbone, Archibald
Monaghan, Patrick
Moore, Daniel B.
Moore, George G.
Moore, Wilbur F.
Morey, Delano
Morford, Jerome
Morgan, Lewis
Morgan, Richard H.
Morrill, Walter G.
Morris, William
Morrison, Francis
Morse, Benjamin
Morse, Charles E.
Mostoller, John W.
Mulholland, St. Clair A.
Mundell, Walter L.
Munsell, Harvey M.
Murphy, Charles J.
Murphy, Daniel J.
Murphy, Dennis J.F.
Murphy, James T.

Murphy, John P.
Murphy, Michael C.
Murphy, Robinson B.
Murphy, Thomas
Murphy, Thomas C.
Murphy, Thomas J.
Myers, George S.
Myers, William H.
Nash, Henry H.
Neahr, Zachariah C.
Neville, Edwin M.
Newman, Marcellus J.
Newman, William H.
Nichols, Henry C.
Niven, Robert
Noll, Conrad
North, Jasper N.
Norton, Elliott M.
Norton, John R.
Norton, Llewellyn P.
Noyes, William W.
Nutting, Lee
O'Beirne, James R.
O'Brien, Henry D.
O'Brien, Peter
O'Connor, Albert
O'Connor, Timothy
O'Dea, John
O'Donnell, Memomen
Oliver, Charles
Oliver, Paul A.
O'Neill, Stephen
Opel, John N.
Orbansky, David
Orr, Charles A.
Orr, Robert L.
Orth, Jacob G.
Osborne, William H.
Oss, Albert
Overturf, Jacob H.
Packard, Loron F.
Palmer, George H.
Palmer, John G.
Palmer, William J.
Parker, Thomas
Parks, Henry Jeremiah
Parks, James W.
Parrott, Jacob
Parsons, Joel
Patterson, John H.
Patterson, John T.

Paul, William H.
Pay, Byron E.
Payne, Irvin C.
Payne, Thomas H.L.
Pearsall, Platt
Pearson, Alfred L.
Peck, Cassius
Peck, Theodore S.
Peirsol, James K.
Pennypacker, Galusha
Pentzer, Patrick H.
Pesch, Joseph
Peters, Henry C.
Petty, Philip
Phelps, Charles E.
Phillips, Josiah
Phisterer, Frederick
Pckle, Alonzo H.
Pike, Edward M.
Pingree, Samuel E.
Pinkham, Charles H.
Pinn, Robert
Pipes, James
Pitman, George J.
Pittinger, William
Plant, Henry E.
Platt, George C.
Plimley, William
Plowman, George H.
Plunkett, Thomas
Pond, George F.
Pond, James B.
Porter, Ambrose
Porter, Horace
Porter, John R.
Porter, William
Post, Philip Sidney
Postles, James Parke
Potter, George W.
Potter, Norman F.
Powell, William H.
Power, Albert
Powers, Wesley J.
Prentice, Joseph R.
Preston, Noble D.
Purcel, Hiram W.
Purman, James J.
Putnam, Edgar P.
Putnam, Winthrop D.
Quay, Matthew S.
Quinlan, James

Rafferty, Peter
Ramsbottom, Alfred
Rand, Charles F.
Ranney, George E.
Ranney, Myron H.
Ratcliff, Edward
Raub, Jacob F.
Raymond, William H.
Read, Morton A.
Rebmann, George F.
Reddick, William H.
Reed, Axel H.
Reed, Charles W.
Reed, George W.
Reed, William
Reeder, Charles A.
Reid, Robert
Reigle, Daniel P.
Reinsinger, J. Monroe
Renninger, Louis
Reynolds, George
Rhodes, Julius D.
Rhodes, Sylvester D.
Rice, Edmund
Rich, Carlos H.
Richardson, William R.
Richey, William E.
Richmond, James
Ricksecker, John H.
Riddell, Rudolph
Riley, Thomas
Ripley, William Y.W.
Robbins, Augustus I.
Roberts, Otis O.
Robertson, Robert S.
Robertson, Samuel
Robie, George F.
Robinson, Elbridge
Robinson, James H.
Robinson, John C.
Robinson, John H.
Robinson, Thomas
Rock, Frederick
Rockefeller, Charles M.
Rodenbough, Theophilus F.
Rohm, Ferdinand F.
Rood, Oliver P.
Roosevelt, George W.
Ross, Marion A.
Rossbach, Valentine
Rounds, Lewis A.

Roush, Levi J.
Rowland, Archibald H., Jr.
Rowe, Henry W.
Rundle, Charles W.
Russell, Charles L.
Russell, Milton
Rutherford, John T.
Rutter, James M.
Ryan, Peter J.
Sacriste, Louis J.
Sagelhurst, John C.
Sancrainte, Charles F.
Sands, William
Sanford, Jacob
Sargent, Jackson
Sartwell, Henry
Savacool, Edwin F.
Saxton, Rufus
Scanlan, Patrick
Scheibner, Martin E.
Schenck, Benjamin W.
Shiller, John
Schlachter, Philipp
Schmal, George W.
Schmauch, Andrew
Schmidt, Conrad
Schmidt, William
Schneider, George
Schnell, Christian
Schofield, John M.
Schoonmaker, James M.
Schorn, Charles
Schubert, Martin
Schwan, Theodore
Schwenk, Martin
Scofield, David H.
Scott, Alexander
Scott, John M.
Scott, John Wallace
Scott, Julian A.
Seaman, Elisha B.
Seanor, James
Sears, Cyrus
Seaver, Thomas O.
Seitzinger, James M.
Sellers, Alfred J.
Seston, Charles H.
Seward, Griffin
Sewell, William J.
Shafter, William R.
Shanan, Emisire

Shaler, Alexander
Shambaugh, Charles
Shanes, John
Shapland, John
Shea, Joseph H.
Shellenberger, John S.
Shepard, Irwin
Shepard, William
Sherman, Marshall
Shiel, John
Shields, Bernard
Shilling, John
Shipley, Robert F.
Shipman, William
Shoemaker, Levi
Shopp, George J.
Shubert, Frank
Sickles, Daniel E.
Sickles William H.
Sidman, George E.
Simmons, John
Simmons, William T.
Simonds, William Edgar
Simons, Charles J.
Skellie, Ebenezer
Sladen, Joseph A.
Slagle, Oscar
Slavens, Samuel
Sloan, Andrew J.
Slusher, Henry C.
Smalley, Reuben
Smalley, Reuben S.
Smith, Alonzo
Smith, Andrew Jackson
Smith, Charles H.
Smith, David L.
Smith, Francis M.
Smith, Henry I.
Smith, James (Ovid)
Smith, Joseph S.
Smith, Otis W.
Smith, Richard
Smith, S. Rodmond
Smith, Thaddeus S.
Smith, Wilson
Snedden, James
Southard, David
Sova, Joseph E.
Sowers, Michael
Spalding, Edward B.
Sperry, William J.

Spillane, Timothy
Sprague, Benona
Sprague, John W.
Spurling, Andrew B.
Stacey, Charles
Stahel, Julius
Stanley, David S.
Starkins, John H.
Steele, John W.
Steinmetz, William
Stephens, William G.
Sterling, John T.
Stevens, Hazard
Stewart, George W.
Stewart, Joseph
Stickels, Joseph
Stockman, George H.
Stokes, George
Stolz, Frank
Storey, John H.R.
Strausbaugh, Bernard A.
Streile, Christian
Strong, James N.
Sturgeon, James K.
Summers, James C.
Surles, William H.
Swan, Charles A.
Swap, Jacob E.
Swayne, Wager
Sweatt, Joseph G.
Sweeney, James
Swegheimer, Jacob
Swift, Frederic W.
Swift, Harlan J.
Sype, Peter
Tabor, William S.
Taggert, Charles A.
Tanner, Charles R.
Taylor, Anthony
Taylor, George
Taylor, Henry H.
Taylor, Joseph
Taylor, Richard
Taylor, William
Terry, John D.
Thackrah, Benjamin
Thatcher, Charles M.
Thaxter, Sidney W.
Thomas, Hampton S.
Thomas, Stephen
Thompkins, George W.

Thompson, Allen
Thompson, Charles A.
Thompson, Freeman C.
Thompson, James
Thompson, James B.
Thompson, J. (James) Harry
Thompson, John
Thompson, Thomas
Thompson, William P.
Thomson, Clifford
Thorn, Walter
Tibbetts, Andrew W.
Tilton, William
Tinkham, Eugene M.
Titus, Charles
Toban, James W.
Tobie, Edward P.
Tobin, John M.
Toffey, John J.
Tompkins, Aaron B.
Tompkins, Charles H.
Toohey, Thomas
Toomer, William
Torgler, Ernst
Tozier, Andrew J.
Tracy, Amasa A.
Tracy, Benjamin F.
Tracy, Charles H.
Tracy, William G.
Traynor, Andrew
Treat, Howell B.
Tremain, Henry E.
Tribe, John
Trogden, Howell G.
Truell, Edwin M.
Tucker, Allen
Tucker, Jacob R.
Tweedale, John
Twombly, Voltaire P.
Tyrrell, George William
Uhrl, George
Urell, M. Emmet
Vale, John
Vance, Wilson
Vanderslice, John M.
Van Matre, Joseph
Van Winkle, Edward
  (Edwin)
Veal, Charles
Veale, Moses
Veazey, Wheelock G.

Branch of Service (U.S. Marine Corps; U.S. Navy)

Vernay, James D.
Vifquain, Victor
Von Vegesack, Ernest
Wageman, John H.
Wagner, John W.
Wainwright, John
Walker, James C.
Walker, Dr. Mary E.
Wall, Jerry
Waller, Francis A.
Walling, William H.
Walsh, John
Walton, George W.
Wambsgan, Martin
Ward, Nelson W.
Ward, Thomas J.
Ward, William H.
Warden, John
Warfel, Henry C.
Warren, Francis E.
Webb, Alexander S.
Webb, James
Webber, Alason P.
Weeks, John H.
Weir, Henry C.
Welch, George W.
Welch, Richard
Welch, Stephen
Wells, Henry S.
Wells, Thomas M.
Wells, William
Welsh, Edward
Welsh, James
Westerhold, William
Weston, John F.
Wheaton, Lloyd
Wheeler, Daniel D.
Wheeler, Henry W.
Wheery, William M.
Whitaker, Edward W.
White, Adam
White, J. Henry
White, Patrick H.
Whitehead, John M.
Whitman, Frank M.
Whitmore, John
Whitney, William G.
Whittier, Edward N.
Widick, Andrew J.
Wilcox, William H.
Wiley, James

Wilhelm, George
Wilkins, Leander A.
Willcox, Orlando B.
Williams, Elwood N.
Williams, George C.
Williams, Le Roy
Williams, William H.
Williamson, James A.
Williston, Edward B.
Wilson, Charles E.
Wilson, Christopher W.
Wilson, Francis A.
Wilson, John
Wilson, John A.
Wilson, John M.
Winegar, William W.
Wisner, Lewis S.
Withington, William H.
Wollam, John
Wood, H. Clay
Wood, Mark
Wood, Richard H.
Woodall, William H.
Woodbury, Eri D.
Woodruff, Alonzo
Woodruff, Carle A.
Woods, Daniel A.
Woodward, Evan M.
Wortick, (Wertick) Joseph
Wray, William J.
Wright, Albert D.
Wright, Robert
Wright, Samuel
Wright, Samuel C.
Yeager, Jacob F.
Young, Andrew J.
Young, Benjamin F.
Young, Cavalry M.
Young, James M.
Younker, John L.

U.S. Marine Corps

Avery, William B.
Binder, Richard
Denig, J. Henry
Flynn, Christopher
Flynn, James E.
Fry, Isaac N.
Hudson, Michael
Mackie, John F.
Martin, James

Miller, Andrew
Nugent, Christopher
Oviatt, Miles M.
Rannahan, John
Roantree, James S.
Rought, Stephen
Shivers, John
Smith, Willard M.
Sprowle, David
Thompson, Henry A.
Tomlin, Andrew J.
Vaughn, Pinkerton R.

U.S. Navy

Aheam, Michael
Anderson, Robert
Angling, John
Arther, Matthew
Asten, Charles
Atkinson, Thomas E.
Avery, James
Baker, Charles
Baldwin, Charles
Barnum, James
Barter, Gurdon H.
Barton, Thomas
Bass, David L.
Bazaar, Philip
Beatty, Alexander M.
Beddows, Richard
Bell, George
Betham, Asa
Bibber, Charles J.
Bickford, John F.
Blagheen, William
Blake, Robert
Bois, Frank
Bond, William
Bourne, Thomas
Bowman, Edward R.
Bradley, Amos
Bradley, Charles
Brazell, John
Breen, John
Brennan, Christopher
Brinn, Andrew
Brown, James
Brown, John
Brown, Robert
Brown, William H.
Brown, Wilson

235

Branch of Service (U.S. Navy)

Brownell, William P.
Brutsche, Henry
Buck, James
Burns, John M.
Burton, Albert
Butts, George
Byrnes, James
Campbell, William
Carr, William
Cassidy, Michael
Chaput, Louis G.
Clifford, Robert T.
Colbert, Patrick
Conlan, Dennis
Connor, Thomas
Connor, William C.
Cooper, John
Corcoran, Thomas E.
Cotton, Peter
Crawford, Alexander
Cripps, Thomas
Cronin, Cornelius
Davis, John
Davis, Samuel W.
Deakin, Charles
Dempster, John
Denning, Lorenzo
Dennis, Richard
Densmore, William
Diggins, Bartholomew
Ditzenback, John
Donnelly, John
Doolen, William
Dorman, John
Dougherty, Patrick
Dow, Henry
Duncan, Adam
Duncan, James K.L.
Dunn, William
Dunphy, Richard D.
Edwards, John
English, Thomas
Erickson, John P.
Farley, William
Farrell, Edward
Fassett, John B.
Ferrell, John H.
Fitzpatrick, Thomas
Flood, Thomas
Foy, Charles H.
Franks, William J.

Freeman, Martin
Frisbee, John B.
Gardner, William
Garrison, James R.
Garvin, William
George, Daniel G.
Gile, Frank S.
Graham, Robert
Greene, John
Griffiths, John
Griswold, Luke M.
Haffee, Edmund
Haley, James
Halstead, William
Ham, Mark G.
Hamilton, Hugh
Hamilton, Richard
Hamilton, Thomas W.
Hand, Allexander
Harcourt, Thomas
Harding, Thomas
Harley, Bernard
Harrington, Daniel
Harris, John
Harrison, George H.
Hathaway, Edward W.
Hawkins, Charles
Hayden, Joseph B.
Hayes, John
Hayes, Thomas
Hickman, John
Hinnecan, William
Hollat, George
Horton, James
Horton, Lewis A.
Houghton, Edward J.
Howard, Martin
Howard, Peter
Huskey, Michael
Hyland, John
Irlam, Joseph
Irving, John
Irving, Thomas
Irwin, Nicholas
James, John H.
Jenkins, Thomas
Johnson, Henry
Johnston, William P.
Jones, Andrew
Jones, John
Jones, John E.

Jones, Thomas
Jones, William
Jordan, Robert
Jordan, Thomas
Kane, Thomas
Kendrick, Thomas
Kenna, Barnett
Kenyon, Charles
Kinnaird, Samuel W.
Lafferty, John
Laffey, Bartlett
Lakin, Daniel
Lann, John S.
Lawson, John
Lear, Nicholas
Lee, James H.
Leland, George W.
Leon, Pierre
Lloyd, Benjamin
Lloyd, John W.
Logan, Hugh
Lyons, Thomas
Machon, James
Mack, Alexander
Mack, John
Madden, William
Martin, Edward
Martin, William
Martin, William
McClelland, Matthew
McCormick, Michael
McCullock, Adam
McDonald, John
McFarland, John
McGowan, John
McHugh, Martin
McIntosh, James
McKnight, William
McLeod, James
McWilliams, George W.
Melville, Charles
Mifflin, James
Miller, James
Milliken, Daniel
Mills, Charles
Molloy, Hugh
Montgomery, Robert
Moore, Charles
Moore, Charles
Moore, George
Moore, William

Branch of Service (U.S. Navy)

The Naval bombardment and capture of Forts Walker and Beauregard, South Carolina. Actions, like this one, against Confederate coastal fortifications, resulted in the vast majority of the Medals of Honor awarded by the U.S. Navy during the war (U.S. Army War College).

Morgan, James H.
Morrison, John G.
Morton, Charles W.
Mullen, Patrick
Murphy, Patrick
Naylor, David
Neil, John
Newland, William
Nibbe, John H.
Nichols, William
Noble, Daniel
O'Brien, Oliver
O'Connell, Thomas
O'Donoghue, Timothy
Ortega, John
Parker, William
Parks, George
Pease, Joachim
Peck, Oscar E.
Pelham, William
Perry, Thomas
Peterson, Alfred
Phinney, William
Poole, William B.

Prance, George
Preston, John
Price, Edward
Province, George
Pyne, George
Read, Charles
Read, Charles A.
Read, George E.
Regan Jeremiah
Rice, Charles
Richards, Louis
Ringold, Edward
Roberts, James
Robinson, Alexander
Robinson, Charles
Rountry, John
Rush, John
Sanderson, Aaron
Saunders, James
Savage, Auzella
Schutt, George
Seward, Richard E.
Sharp, Hendrick
Shepard, Louis C.

Sheridan, James
Shutes, Henry
Simkins, Lebbeus
Smith, Charles H.
Smith, Edwin
Smith, James
Smith, John
Smith, John
Smith, Oloff
Smith, Thomas
Smith, Walter B.
Smith, William
Stanley, William A.
Sterling, James E.
Stevens, Daniel D.
Stoddard, James
Stout, Richard
Strahan, Robert
Sullivan, James
Sullivan, John
Sullivan, Timothy
Summers, Robert
Swanson, John
Swatton, Edward

Swearer, Benjamin
Talbott, William
Tallentine, James
Taylor, John
Taylor, Thomas
Taylor, William G.
Thielberg, Henry
Thompson, William
Todd, Samuel
Tripp, Othniel
Truett, Alexander H.
Verney, James W.
Wagg, Maurice
Ward, James

Warren, David
Webster, Henry S.
Weeks, Charles H.
Wells, William
White, Joseph
Whitfield, Daniel
Wilcox, Franklin L.
Wilkes, Henry
Wilkes, Perry
Williams, Anthony
Williams, Augustus
Williams, John
Williams, John
Williams, John

Williams, Peter
Williams, Robert
Williams, William
Willis, Richard
Wood, Robert B.
Woods, Samuel
Woon, John
Woram, Charles B.
Wright, Edward
Wright, William
Young, Edward B.
Young, Horatio N.
Young, William

Names by Regiment and by Naval Ship

Entries on pages 239–253 are ordered alphabetically by state; entries on pages 254–257 are by ship name

Admirals, Generals, Staff
Baird, Absalom
Batchelder, Richard N.
Beaumont, Eugene B.
Beebe, William S.
Benyaurd, William H.
Butterfield, Daniel
Curtis, Newton Martin
Estes, Lewellyn G.
Force, Manning F.
Gillespie, George L.
Gouraud, George E.
Grant, Gabriel
Greene, Oliver D.
Hatch, John P.
Howard, Oliver O.
King, Horatio C.
Lane, Morgan D.
McGonnigle, Andrew J.
McMahon, Martin T.
Porter, Horace
Robinson, John C.
Saxton, Rufus
Sickles, Daniel E.
Smith, Joseph S.
Stahel, Julius
Stanley, David S.
Steele, John W.
Stevens, Hazard
Thompson, J. (James) Harry
Tremain, Henry E.
Von Vegesack, Ernest

Walker, Dr. Mary E.
Webb, Alexander S.
Weir, Henry C.
Wilson, John M.
Woodall, William H.

1st Connecticut Hvy. Art.
Murphy, James T.

2nd Connecticut Hvy. Art.
Briggs, Elijah A.
Gibbs, Wesley
McDonald, George E.

1st Connecticut Cavalry
Lanfare, Aaron S.
Marsh, Charles H.
Neville, Edwin M.
Whitaker, Edward W.

5th Connecticut Infantry
Corliss, George W.

7th Connecticut Infantry
Jackson, Frederick R.

8th Connecticut Infantry
Hickok, Nathan E.

9th Connecticut Infantry
Curtis, John C.

10th Connecticut Infantry
Tucker, Allen

11th Connecticut Infantry
Horne, Samuel B.

14th Connecticut Infantry
Bacon, Elijah W.
Flynn, Christopher
Hincks, William B.

21st Connecticut Infantry
Beckwith, Wallace A.
Buck, F. Clarence
Gray, Robert A.
Hubbell, William S.
Palmer, John G.

25th Connecticut Infantry
Simonds, William Edgar

28th Connecticut Infantry
Fox, Nicholas

1st Delaware Infantry
Mayberry, John B.
McCarren, Bernard
Postles, James Parke
Tanner, Charles B.

3rd Delaware Infantry
Shilling, John

4th Delaware Infantry
Buckingham, David E.
Smith, S. Rodmond

Chicago Merc. Battery, Illinois Light Artillery
Dunne, James
Kloth, Charles H.
Kretsinger, George

McGuire, Patrick
Stephens, William G.
White, Patrick H.

2nd Illinois Lt. Artillery
Churchill, Samuel J.

1st Illinois Cavalry
Palmer, George H.

3rd Illinois Cavalry
Carr, Eugene, A.

8th Illinois Cavalry
Capron, Horace, Jr.

8th Illinois Infantry
Miller, Henry A.
Wheaton, Lloyd

11th Illinois Infantry
Newman, Marcellus J.
Vernay, James D.

13th Illinois Infantry
Josselyn, Simeon T.

20th Illinois Infantry
McDonald, John Wade

21st Illinois Infantry
McKeen, Nineveh S.

23rd Illinois Infantry
Creed, John
Highland, Patrick
McGraw, Thomas

28th Illinois Infantry
Williams, Elwood N.

31st Illinois Infantry
Murphy, Thomas C.

33rd Illinois Infantry
Pike, Edward M.

36th Illinois Infantry
Kelley, Leverett M.

37th Illinois Infantry
Black, John C.
Black, William P.
Blodgett, Welis H.
Payne, Thomas H.L.

39th Illinois Infantry
Allen, Abner P.
Hardenbergh, Henry M.

45th Illinois Infantry
Taylor, Henry H.

52nd Illinois Infantry
Spalding, Edward B.

55th Illinois Infantry
Cox, Robert M.
Fisher, John H.
Haney, Milton L.
Howe, Orion P.
Larrabee, James W.
Lower, Robert A.
Morford, Jerome
Sanford, Jacob
Warden, John

59th Illinois Infantry
Post, Philip Sidney

77th Illinois Infantry
Putnam, Winthrop D.

86th Illinois Infantry
Webber, Alason P.

88th Illinois Infantry
Merrifield, James K.

89th Illinois Infantry
Farquhar, John M.

97th Illinois Infantry
Colby, Carlos W.
Dickie, David
Fraser, William W.
Pentzer, Patrick H.
Vifquain, Victor
Wood, Richard H.

99th Illinois Infantry
Higgins, Thomas J.

104th Illinois Infantry
Gage, Richard J.
Hapeman, Douglas
Holland, Lemuel F.
Houghton, George L.
Marsh, George
Shapland, John
Slagle, Oscar
Smalley, Reuben S.

106th Illinois Infantry
Fox, Henry

113th Illinois Infantry
Burritt, William W.

Darrough, John S.
Gould, Newton T.
Henry, James
Johns, Elisha
Miller, Jacob C.

115th Illinois Infantry
Hymer, Samuel

116th Illinois Infantry
Davis, Martin K.
Geschwind, Nicholas
Johnson, Andrew
Rundle, Charles W.
Schenck, Benjamin W.
Sprague, Benona
Ward, Thomas J.
Widick, Andrew J.

117th Illinois Infantry
Moore, Wilbur F.

119th Illinois Infantry
Cook, John H.
McConnell, Samuel
Rebmann, George F.
Whitmore, John

122nd Illinois Infantry
Callahan, John H.
Stokes, George

127th Illinois Infantry
Bowen, Emmer
Goldsbery, Andrew E.
Hyatt, Theodore
McCornack, Andrew
Murphy, Robinson B.
Toomer, William

147th Illinois Infantry
Powers, Wesley J.

15th Indiana Light Artillery
Fout, Frederick W.

2nd Indiana Cavalry
Ferrier, Daniel T.

3rd Indiana Cavalry
Evans, Coron D.
Holmes, William T.
Jordan, Absalom
Shepard, William

5th Indiana Cavalry
Bruner, Louis J.

Names by Regiment

7th Indiana Infantry
Opel, John N.

8th Indiana Infantry
Hough, Ira

11th Indiana Infantry
Ryan, Peter J.
Seston, Charles H.
Sterling, John T.

15th Indiana Infantry
Banks, George L.
Graham, Thomas N.
Whitehead, John M.

18th Indiana Infantry
Taylor, Richard

19th Indiana Infantry
Buckles, Abram J.

20th Indiana Infantry
Kirk, Jonathan C.
Rood, Oliver P.
Thompson, William P.

27th Indiana Infantry
Box, Thomas J.

30th Indiana Infantry
Lawton, Henry

49th Indiana Infantry
Kendall, William W.

51st Indiana Infantry
Anderson, Marion T.
Russell, Milton

59th Indiana Infantry
Archer, James W.

74th Indiana Infantry
Chamberlain, Orville T.
Kuder, Jeremiah

83rd Indiana Infantry
Armstrong, Clinton L.
Blasdel, Thomas A.
Chisman, William W.
Conaway, John W.
Frantz, Joseph
Helms, David H.
Overturf, Jacob H.
Smalley, Reuben
Steinmetz, William
Stolz, Frank

88th Indiana Infantry
Dougall, Allan H.

100th Indiana Infantry
Brouse, Charles W.
Johnson, Ruel M.

17th Indiana Mounted Infantry
Davis, John
Hudson, Aaron R.

3rd Iowa Cavalry
Birdsall, Horatio L.
Dunlavy, James
Power, Albert
Tibbetts, Andrew W.
Young, Cavalry M.

4th Iowa Cavalry
Bates, Norman F.
Bebb, Edward J.
Cosgriff, Richard H.
Fanning, Nicholas
Hays, John H.
Miller, James P.
Morgan, Richard H.
Swan, Charles A.

5th Iowa Cavalry
Healey, George W.

1st Iowa Infantry
Boquet, Nicholas

2nd Iowa Infantry
Twombly, Voltaire P.

4th Iowa Infantry
Williamson, James A.

7th Iowa Infantry
Smith, Henry I.

8th Iowa Infantry
Bras, Edgar A.

9th Iowa Infantry
Elison, James M.
Herron, Francis J.

11th Iowa Infantry
Herington, Pitt B.
Mayes, William B.

12th Iowa Infantry
Kaltenbach, Luther
Sloan, Andrew J.

21st Iowa Infantry
Hill, James

22nd Iowa Infantry
Godley, Leonidus M.

32nd Iowa Infantry
May, William

4th Kentucky Cavalry
Weston, John F.

1st Kentucky Infantry
Horsfall, William H.

10th Kentucky Infantry
Mattingly, Henry B.

12th Kentucky Infantry
Brown, John Harties
Hughes, Oliver

1st Louisiana Cavalry
Dorley, August
Riley, Thomas

2nd Louisiana Infantry (Colored)
Beaufort, Jean J.

1st Maine Heavy Artillery
Chapman, John

5th Maine Light Artillery
Chase, John F.
Whittier, Edward N.

1st Maine Cavalry
Smith, Charles H.
Thaxter, Sidney W.
Tobie, Edward P.

2nd Maine Cavalry
Spurling, Andrew B.

1st Maine Infantry
Littlefield, George H.
Merril, Augustus

2nd Maine Infantry
Knowles, Abiather J.
Wheeler, Henry W.

3rd Maine Infantry
Haskell, Frank W.

6th Maine Infantry
Clark, Charles A.
Roberts, Otis O.

7th Maine Infantry
Hyde, Thomas W.

9th Maine Infantry
Belcher, Thomas

13th Maine Infantry
Hesseltine, Francis S.

17th Maine Infantry
Haynes, Asbury F.
Mattocks, Charles P.

19th Maine Infantry
Hanscom, Moses C.

20th Maine Infantry
Chamberlain, Joshua L.
Fernald, Albert E.
Morrill, Walter G.
Tozier, Andrew J.

1st Maryland Cavalry
Myers, William H.

1st Maryland Infantry
Cadwallader, Abel G.
Smith, Francis M.
Stewart, Joseph
Taylor, William
Thompson, John

2nd Maryland Infantry
Mathews, William H.

3rd Maryland Infantry
Carter, Joseph F.
McAlwee, Benjamin F.
Plowman, George H.
Schneider, George
Strausbaugh, Bernard A.

4th Maryland Infantry
Tucker, Jacob R.

6th Maryland Infantry
Buffington, John E.

7th Maryland Infantry
Koogle, Jacob
Phelps, Charles E.

2nd Independent Battery, Massachusetts Light Artillery
Marland, William

9th Independent Battery, Massachusetts Light Artillery
Reed, Charles W.

2nd Massachusetts Cavalry
Baybutt, Philip
Crocker, Henry H.

3rd Massachusetts Cavalry
Elliott, Russell C.

4th Massachusetts Cavalry
Downey, William
Duffey, John
Gifford, David L.
Scanlan, Patrick

1st Massachusetts Infantry
Allen, Nathaniel

4th Massachsetts Infantry
Lovering, George M.

5th Massachusetts Infantry
Ellsworth, Thomas F.

6th Massachusetts Infantry
Sweatt, Joseph G.

7th Massachusetts Infantry
Holehouse, James
Luther, James H.
Maxham, Lowell M.

9th Massachusetts Infantry
Tobin, John M.

13th Massachusetts Infantry
Maynard, George H.

18th Massachusetts Infantry
Anderson, Frederick C.

19th Massachusetts Infantry
Adams, John G.B.
De Castro, Joseph H.
Falls, Benjamin F.
Jellison, Benjamin H.
Murphy, Daniel J.
Rice, Edmund
Robinson, John H.

21st Massachusetts Infantry
Plunkett, Thomas

23rd Massachusetts Infantry
Terry, John D.

25th Massachusetts Infantry
Boss, Orlando
Casey, David

29th Massachusetts Infantry
Deane, John M.
Gaylord, Levi B.
Harbourne, John H.
Homan, Conrad
Howe, William H.
Mahoney, Jeremiah
Manning, Joseph S.
Osborne, William H.
Wright, Samuel C.

30th Massachusetts Infantry
Ferris, Eugene W.

32nd Massachusetts Infantry
Gardner, Charles N.

33rd Massachusetts Infantry
Sladen, Joseph A.

34th Massachusetts Infantry
Gardner, Robert J.
Hunter, Charles A.

35th Massachusetts Infantry
Haskell, Marcusw M.
Whitman, Frank M.

37th Massachusetts Infantry
Eddy, Samuel E.

Leonard, Edwin
Taggert, Charles A.
Tracy, Charles H.
Welch, Richard

38th Massachusetts Infantry
Lunt, Alphonso M.

40th Massachusetts Infantry
Cosgrove, Thomas
Deland, Frederick N.
Henry, Guy V.
Lord, William

46th Massachusetts Infantry
Bryant, Andrew S.

49th Massachusetts Infantry
Johns, Henry T.
Strong, James N.
Warren, Francis E.

50th Massachusetts Infantry
Hanna, Marcus A.

54th Massachusetts Infantry (Colored)
Carney, William H.

55th Massachusetts Infantry
Smith, Andrew Jackson

57th Massachusetts Infantry
Karpeles, Leopold
Pinkham, Charles H.

59th Massachusetts Infantry
Chandler, Henry F.

1st Michigan Cavalry
Traynor, Andrew

2nd Michigan Cavalry
Ranney, George E.

3rd Michigan Cavalry
Robinson, James H.

5th Michigan Cavalry
Cole, Gabriel

Fox, Henry M.
Hastings, Smith H.

6th Michigan Cavalry
Crocker, Ulric L.
Custer, Thomas W.
Norton, Elliott M.

7th Michigan Cavalry
Holton, Charles M.

9th Michigan Cavalry
Cristiancy, James I.
Hadley, Cornelius M.
Toban, James W.

1st Michigan Infantry
Willcox, Orlando B.
Withington, William H.

3rd Michigan Infantry
Morse, Benjamin

4th Michigan Infantry
Luce, Moses A.

5th Michigan Infantry
Kemp, Joseph
Menter, John W.
Mundell, Walter L.

6th Michigan Infantry
Hill, Edward

7th Michigan Infantry
Forman, Alexander A.
French, Samuel S.
Shafter, William R.
Smith, Alonzo

11th Michigan Infantry
Whitney, William G.

13th Michigan Infantry
Keen, Joseph S.

14th Michigan Infantry
Clute, George W.
Irwin, Patrick
Plant, Henry E.

15th Michigan Infantry
Sancrainte, Charles F.

16th Michigan Infantry
Sidman, George E.

17th Michigan Infantry
Alber, Frederick

Brandle, Joseph E.
falconer, John A.
Kelley, Andrew J.
McFall, Daniel
Shepard, Irwin
Swift, Frederic W.
Thompson, Charles A.

19th Michigan Infantry
Baldwin, Frank D.

20th Michigan Infantry
Cutcheon, Byron M.
Noll, Conrad

26th Michigan Infantry
Fall, Charles S.
McHale, Alexander U.

27th Michigan Infantry
Dodd, Robert F.

1st Michigan Sharpshooters
De Puy, Charles H.
Haight, Sidney
Thatcher, Charles M.
Young, Benjamin F.

1st Minnesota Infantry
Merritt, John G.
O'Brien, Henry D.
Sherman, Marshall

1st Minnesota Infantry Battalion
Pickle, Alonzo H.

2nd Minnesota Infantry
Burger, Joseph
Cilley, Clinton A.
Clark, William A.
Flannigan, James
Hanna, Milton
Holmes, Lovilo N.
Pay, Byron E.
Reed, Axel H.
Vale, John
Wright, Samuel

3rd Minnesota Infantry
Barrick, Jesse T.

5th Minnesota Infantry
Gere, Thomas P.

1st Missouri Light Artillery
Follett, Joseph L.
Guerin, Fritz W.
Hammel, Henry A.
Pesch, Joseph

3rd Missouri Cavalry
Lucas, George W.

4th Missouri Cavalry
Beiger, Charles
Grebe, M.R. William

12th Missouri Cavalry
Porter, Ambrose

1st Missouri Infantry
Schofield, John M.

3rd Missouri Infantry (Reserve)
Wheery, William M.

6th Missouri Infantry
Flynn, James E.
Frizzell, Henry F.
Hunt, Louis T.
Labill, Joseph S.
Stockman, George H.

8th Missouri Infantry
Ayers, John G.K.
Bickford, Matthew
Cunningham, James S.
Johnston, David
Kirby, Dennis T.
O'Dea, John
Reed, William
Trogden, Howell G.
Wagner, John W.
Wortick, (Wertick) Joseph

11th Missouri Infantry
O'Donnell, Menomen
Parks, James W.
Simmons, William T.
Welch, George W.

24th Missouri Infantry
McCammon, William W.

2nd New Hampshire Infantry
Dillon, Michael A.

6th New Hampshire Infantry
Cohn, Abraham
Hadley, Osgood T.

7th New Hampshire Infantry
Dow, George P.
Little, Henry F.W.
Robie, George F.
Tilton, William

8th New Hampshire Infantry
Nolan, John J.

9th New Hampshire Infantry
Copp, Charles D.
Knight, Charles H.
Simons, Charles J.
Wilcox, William H.
Wilkins, Leander A.

10th New Hampshire Infantry
Brady, James
Coughlin, John

11th New Hampshire Infantry
Barker, Nathaniel C.
Goodall, Francis H.
Rowe, Henry W.

15th New Hampshire Infantry
Tabor, William S.

18th New Hampshire Infantry
Boutwell, John W.
Camp, Carlton N.

1st New Jersey Cavalry
Clancy, James T.
Hooper, William B.
Locke, Lewis
Porter, William
Sagelhurst, John C.
Southard, David
Stewart, George W.
Streile, Christian
Titus, Charles
Tompkins, Aaron B.

Wilson, Charles E.
Wilson, John

1st New Jersey Veteran Battalion
Brant, William

1st New Jersey Infantry
Hopkins, Charles F.

2nd New Jersey Infantry
English, Edmund

4th New Jersey Infantry
Beech, John P.

5th New Jersey Infantry
Sewell, William J.

6th New Jersey Infantry
Conner, Richard

9th New Jersey Infantry
Drake, James M.

11th New Jersey Infantry
Oss, Albert

26th New Jersey Infantry
Cummings, Amos J.

33rd New Jersey Infantry
Magee, William
Toffey, John J.

40th New Jersey Infantry
Fesq, Frank

2nd New York Heavy Artillery
Simmons, John
Davis, Thomas

4th New York Heavy Artillery
Corliss, Stephen P.
Thompson, Allen
Thompson, James

7th New York Heavy Artillery
Begley, Terrence

8th New York Heavy Artillery
Williams, Le Roy

14th New York Heavy Artillery
Hill, James
Houghton, Charles H.

Names by Regiment

15th New York Heavy Artillery
Dickey, William D.
Kauss, August

1st New York Light Artillery
Bronner, August F.
Ginley, Patrick
Smith, David L.

3rd New York Light Artillery
Smith, Wilson

15th New York Light Artillery
Knox, Edward M.

34th New York Battery
Beddows, Richard
Ludwig, Carl
Rossbach, Valentine
Starkins, John H.

1st New York Cavalry
Anderson, Charles W.
Carman, Warren
Morris, William
Norton, John R.
O'Brien, Peter
Pitman, George J.
Savacool, Edwin F.
Thomson, Clifford

2nd New York Cavalry
Benjamin, John F.
Brewer, William J.
Cadwell, Luman L.
Calkin, Ivers S.
Campbell, James A.
Gribben, James H.
Hickey, Dennis W.
Miller, Frank
Payne, Irvin C.

3rd New York Cavalry
Kenyon, John S.

4th New York Cavalry
DeCesnola, Louis P.
Leslie, Frank
Mandy, Harry J.

5th New York Cavalry
Burke, Thomas

Packard, Loron F.
Rhodes, Julius D.
Scofield, David H.
Tribe, John
Walsh, John

6th New York Cavalry
Blunt, John W.
Heermance, William L.
Kelly, Thomas
McEnroe, Patrick H.
Meach, George
Wells, Thomas M.

8th New York Cavalry
Bickford, Henry H.
Compson, Hartwell B.
Goheen, Charles A.
Hart, William E.
Kelly, Daniel
Kuder, Andrew
Madison, James
Miller, John
Niven, Robert
Read, Morton A.
Sova, Joseph E.

9th New York Cavalry
Goodrich, Edwin
Hills, William G.
Lyman, Joel H.
Parks, Henry Jeremiah
Putnam, Edgar P.
Reynolds, George
Rutherford, John T.

10th New York Cavalry
Bringle, Andrew
Carey, James L.
Farnsworth, Herbert E.
Norton, Llewellyn P.
Preston, Noble D.

15th New York Cavalry
Boehm, Peter M.

19th New York Cavalry
Bowen, Chester B.
Lorish, Andrew J.
Winegar, William W.

20th New York Cavalry
Lonsway, Joseph

21st New York Cavalry
Dodds, Edward E.

22nd New York Cavalry
Bruton, Christopher C.
Crowley, Michael
Harvey, Harry
Ladd, George

24th New York Cavalry
Chandler, Stephen E.
Kenyon, Samuel P.
Meyer, Henry C.
Schmal, George W.

1st New York Marine Artillery
Avery, William B.

1st New York Infantry
Levy, Benjamin

2nd New York Infantry (Militia)
Swift, Harlan J.

5th New York Infantry
Webb, James

9th New York Infantry
Langbein, J.C. Julius
Libaire, Adolphe

11th New York Infantry
Brownell, Francis E.

12th New York Infantry
Cross, James E.
Oliver, Paul A.
Rand, Charles F.

13th New York Infantry
Ranney, Myron H.

16th New York Infantry
Allen, James
Gilmore, John C.
Hall, Francis B.
Moffitt, John H.

23rd New York Infantry
Hogarty, William P.

26th New York Infantry
Cleveland, Charles F.
Keene, Joseph
Schubert, Martin

27th New York Infantry
Hall, Henry Seymour

33rd New York Infantry
Carter, John J.
Curran, Richard

37th New York Infantry
Conboy, Martin
Fallon, Thomas T.
O'Beirne, James R.

38th New York Infantry
Murphy, Charles J.

40th New York Infantry
Boody, Robert
Kline, Harry

42nd New York Infantry
Madden, Michael

43rd New York Infantry
Connors, James
Shubert, Frank

45th New York Infantry
Irsch, Francis

47th New York Infantry
Gasson, Richard

48th New York Infantry
Hibson, Joseph C.

49th New York Infantry
McVeane, John P.

51st New York Infantry
Caruana, Orlando E.

52nd New York Infantry
Westerhold, William

55th Ohio Infantry
Stacey, Charles

59th New York Infantry
Embler, Andrew H.
Ludgate, William
Wiley, James

60th New York Infantry
Johnson, Follett

61st New York Infantry
Greig, Theodore W.
Hagerty, Asel
Miles, Nelson A.
Nutting, Lee
Riddell, Rudolph

62nd New York Infantry
Brown, Edward, Jr.
Evans, James R.
Morse, Charles E.

64th New York Infantry
Marsh, Albert

65th New York Infantry
Shaler, Alexander

69th New York Infantry
Donoghue, Timothy
Rafferty, Peter

70th New York Infantry
Coyne, John N.

72nd New York Infantry
Brown, Henri Le Ferve
Haight, John H.
Horan, Thomas
Young, James M.

73rd New York Infantry
Jones, William
Schlachter, Philipp
Wilson, Christopher W.

74th New York Infantry
Brannigan, Felix
Gion, Joseph
Jacobson, Eugene P.
Luty, Gotlieb

79th New York Infantry
Judge, Francis W.

82nd New York Infantry
Carey, Hugh
Cullen, Thomas
Urell, M. Emmet

86th New York Infantry
Newman, William H.

88th New York Infantry
Ford, George W.
Quinlan, James

89th New York Infantry
McKee, George

90th New York Infantry
Wambsgan, Martin

92nd New York Infantry
Shea, Joseph H.

93rd New York Infantry
Robertson Robert S.
Russell, Charles L.

95th New York Infantry
Smith, Richard

96th New York Infantry
Archer, Lester

97th New York Infantry
Burk, Thomas

100th New York Infantry
Kane, John

108th New York Infantry
Raymond, William H.

109th New York Infantry
Catlin, Isaac S.
Tracy, Benjamin F.

111th New York Infantry
Lutes, Franklin W.

112th New York Infantry
Skellie, Ebenezer

115th New York Infantry
Thackrah, Benjamin

116th New York Infantry
Love, George M.

118th New York Infantry
Johndro, Franklin

120th New York Infantry
Plimley, William

121st New York Infantry
Dockum, Warren C.
Gifford, Benjamin
Hawthorne, Harris S.

122nd New York Infantry
Tracy, William G.

123rd New York Infantry
Sartwell, Henry

124th New York Infantry
Bradley, Thomas W.
Freeman, Archibald
Hallock, Nathan M.
Thompkins, George W.
Wisner, Lewis S.

A group of officers from the 61st New York Infantry. Five members of the regiment won the Medal of Honor during the war, including Colonel Nelson Miles, and Lieutenant Theodore Greig. Miles would go on to win his general's stars, and would gain fame as an Indian fighter (U.S. Army War College).

125th New York Infantry
Burk, E. Michael
Clark, Harrison

126th New York Infantry
Brown, Morris, Jr.
Dore, George E.
Wall, Jerry

132nd New York Infantry
Haring, Abram P.

136th New York Infantry
Buckley, Denis

139th New York Infantry
Jamieson, Walter

140th New York Infantry
Shipley, Robert F.

142nd New York Infantry
Anderson, Bruce
Chapin, Alaric B.
Merrill, George
Neahr, Zachariah C.
Walling, William H.

143rd New York Infantry
Collins, Thomas D.

146th New York Infantry
Edwards, David
Grindlay, James G.
Murphy, Thomas J.

147th New York Infantry
Coey, James

148th New York Infantry
Buchanan, George A.
Mangam, Richard C.
Tinkham, Eugene M.
Van Winkle, Edward (Edwin)
Wells, Henry S.

149th New York Infantry
Barnum, Henry A.
Crosier, William H.H.
Goettel, Philip
Kappesser, Peter
Kiggins, John
Potter, Norman F.

152nd New York Infantry
Weeks, John H.

154th New York Infantry
McKay, Charles W.
Welch, Stephen

158th New York Infantry
Grueb, George
Howard, James
Laing, William
Meagher, Thomas
Murphy, Thomas
Schiller, John

164th New York Infantry
Brosnan, John
Doody, Patrick

169th New York Infantry
Freeman, William H.

170th New York Infantry
Murphy, Michael C.

178th New York Infantry
Rockefeller, Charles M.

187th New York Infantry
Orr, Charles A.

1st New York Mounted Infantry
Mills, Frank W.

182nd New York Infantry
Keele, Joseph

185th New York Infantry
Everson, Adelbert

1st Ohio Light Artillery
Dilger, Hubert

11th Ohio Light Artillery
Sears, Cyrus

2nd Ohio Cavalry
Clapp, Albert A.
Gause, Isaac
Hoffman, Henry
Hughey, John
Larimer, Smith
Richardson, William R.

10th Ohio Cavalry
Cockley, David L.

13th Ohio Cavalry
Gwynne, Nathaniel
Peirsol, James K.

1st Ohio Infantry
Porter, John R.

2nd Ohio Infantry
Pittinger, William
Ross, Marion A.
Smith, James (Ovid)
Surles, William H.

4th Ohio Infantry
Holcomb, Daniel I.
Morgan, Lewis

5th Ohio Infantry
Gray, John
Murphy, John P.
Tyrrell, George William

8th Ohio Infantry
Miller, John
Richmond, James
Rounds, Lewis A.

11th Ohio Infantry
Bell, James B.
Green, George
Howard, Hiram R.

12th Ohio Infantry
Inscho, Leonidus H.

15th Ohio Infantry
Brown, Robert B.
Richey, William E.

20th Ohio Infantry
Casey, Henry

21st Ohio Infantry
Bensinger, William
Brown, Wilson W.
Buffum, Robert
Knight, William J.
Mason, Elihu H.
Scott, John M.
Vance, Wilson
Wilson, John A.
Wood, Mark

30th Ohio Infantry
Archinal, William
Brown, Uriah
Campbell, William
Harris, Sampson
Longshore, William H.
McClelland, James M.
McGonagle, Wilson
Pearsall, Platt
Schmauch, Andrew

31st Ohio Infantry
Walker, James C.

33rd Ohio Infantry
Dorsey, Daniel A.
Hawkins, Martin J.
Parrott, Jacob
Reddick, William H.
Robertson, Samuel
Slavens, Samuel
Wollam, John

35th Ohio Infantry
Boynton, Henry V.

37th Ohio Infantry
Frey, Franz
Hanks, Joseph
John, William

Kountz, John S.
Renninger, Louis
Rock, Frederick
Schmidt, William
Schnell, Christian
Torgler, Ernst

41st Ohio Infantry
Garrett, William
Holcomb, Daniel I.

43rd Ohio Infantry
Swayne, Wager

46th Ohio Infantry
Davis, Harry
Sturgeon, James K.

47th Ohio Infantry
Albert, Christian
Ballen, Frederick
Brown, John H.
Davidson, Andrew
De Witt, Richard W.
Guin, Thomas
Hack, John
Hodges, Addison J.
Lewis, Henry
Nash, Henry H.
Peters, Henry C.
Sype, Peter
Ward, William H.

48th Ohio Infantry
Carmin, Isaac H.

52nd Ohio Infantry
Treat, Howell B.

54th Ohio Infantry
Buhrman, Henry G.
Jardine, James
Jones, David
McGinn, Edward
Swegheimer, Jacob
Welsh, Edward

56th Ohio Infantry
Wilhelm, George

57th Ohio Infantry
Ayers, David
Day, David F.
Grimshaw, Samuel

58th Ohio Infantry
Orbansky, David

Names by Regiment

60th Ohio Infantry
Wageman, John H.

63rd Ohio Infantry
Sprague, John W.

66th Ohio Infantry
Cranston, William W.
Heller, Henry
Seaman, Elisha B.
Thompson, Thomas

72nd Ohio Infantry
McCleary, Charles H.

73rd Ohio Infantry
Enderlin, Richard

80th Ohio Infantry
Davis, Freeman

82nd Ohio Infantry
Morey, Delano
Williams, William H.

83rd Ohio Infantry
Stickels, Joseph

91st Ohio Infantry
Cumpston, James M.

95th Ohio Infantry
Colwell, Oliver
Smith, Otis W.

97th Ohio Infantry
Ramsbottom, Alfred

101st Ohio Infantry
Myers, George S.
Yeager, Jacob F.

104th Ohio Infantry
Davis, Joseph
Gaunt, John C.
Greenawalt, Abraham
Hall, Newton H.
Kelley, George V.
Ricksecker, John H.

107th Ohio Infantry
Finkenbiner, Henry S.

110th Ohio Infantry
James Isaac
McMillen, Francis M.

116th Ohio Infantry
Thompson, Freeman C.
Van Matre, Joseph

122nd Ohio Infantry
Loyd, George
Patterson, John T.
Robinson, Elbridge

124th Ohio Infantry
Carr, Franklin

126th Ohio Infantry
Blickensderfer, Milton

133rd Ohio Infantry
Gregg, Joseph O.

Independent Pennsylvania Light Artillery
Carlisle, Casper R.

1st Pennsylvania Cavalry
Davidsizer, John A.
Elliott, Alexander
Higby, Charles
Landis, James P.
Thomas, Hampton S.
Warfel, Henry C.
Young, Andrew J.

3rd Pennsylvania Cavalry
Hunterson, John C.
Miller, William E.

4th Pennsylvania Cavalry
Donaldson, John
Sowers, Michael

5th Pennsylvania Cavalry
McKeever, Michael

6th Pennsylvania Cavalry
Furness, Frank

7th Pennsylvania Cavalry
Davis, Charles C.

8th Pennsylvania Cavalry
Galloway, John
Vanderslice, John M.

11th Pennsylvania Cavalry
Ward, Nelson W.

13th Pennsylvania Cavalry
Caldwell, Daniel
Dougherty, Michael

14th Pennsylvania Cavalry
Kerr, Thomas R.
Schoonmaker, James M.

15th Pennsylvania Cavalry
Anderson, Everett W.
Betts, Charles M.
Bourke, John G.
Palmer, William J.
Taylor, Anthony
Tweedale, John

16th Pennsylvania Cavalry
Rohm, Ferdinand F.
Spillane, Timothy

17th Pennsylvania Cavalry
Bonebrake, Henry G.

22nd Pennsylvania Cavalry
Slusher, Henry C.

2nd Pennsylvania Infantry Reserves
Woodward Evan M.

4th Pennsylvania Infantry Militia
Cooke, Walter H.
Hartranft, John F.

6th Pennsylvania Infantry Reserves
Corson, Stephen P.
Furman, Chester S.
Hart, John W.
Johnson, Wallace W.
Mears, George W.
Roush, Levi J.
Smith, Thaddeus S.

7th Pennsylvania Infantry Reserves
Cart, Jacob

9th Pennsylvania Infantry Reserves
Johnson, Samuel

11th Pennsylvania Infantry
De Lavie, Hiram H.
Howard, Henderson C.
Reed, George W.
Shambaugh, Charles

13th Pennsylvania Infantry Reserves
Lower, Cyrus B.

23rd Pennsylvania Infantry
Fassett, John B.

26th Pennsylvania Infantry
Roosevelt, George W.

28th Pennsylvania Infantry
Orth, Jacob G.

45th Pennsylvania Infantry
Hogan, Franklin
Kinsey, John

48th Pennsylvania Infantry
Blackwood, William R.D.
Monaghan, Patrick
Reid, Robert

50th Pennsylvania Infantry
Brown, Charles
Hill, Henry

54th Pennsylvania Infantry
Evans, Thomas
Mostoller, John W.
Snedden, James

55th Pennsylvania Infantry
Flanagan, Augustin

56th Pennsylvania Infantry
Jennings, James T.

57th Pennsylvania Infantry
Bishop, Francis A.
Brest, Lewis F.

58th Pennsylvania Infantry
Clay, Cecil
Johnson, Joseph E.
McKown, Nathaniel A.

61st Pennsylvania Infantry
Clausen, Charles H.
Fisher, Joseph
Matthews, John C.
Matthews, Milton
Mindil, George W.
Mitchell, Theodore
Orr, Robert L.
Rhodes, Sylvester D.

63rd Pennsylvania Infantry
Kindig, John M.

67th Pennsylvania Infantry
Keough, John

69th Pennsylvania Infantry
McAnally, Charles

71st Pennsylvania Infantry
Clopp, John E.

81st Pennsylvania Infantry
Robinson, Thomas

83rd Pennsylvania Infantry
Grace, Peter
Swap, Jacob E.

85th Pennsylvania Infantry
Leonard, William E.
Morrison, Francis
Shellenberger, John S.

87th Pennsylvania Infantry
Reigle, Daniel P.

88th Pennsylvania Infantry
Clark, James G.
Gilligan, Edward L.
Martin, Sylvester H.
Sands, William

90th Pennsylvania Infantry
Beyer, Hillary
Breyer, Charles
Paul, William
Scheibner, Martin E.
Sellers, Alfred J.
Shiel, John
White, J. Henry

93rd Pennsylvania Infantry
Marquette, Charles

95th Pennsylvania Infantry
Fox, William R.
Galloway, George N.
Wilson, Francis A.

97th Pennsylvania Infantry
Engle, James E.
Lewis, Dewitt Clinton
Pennypacker, Galusha
Wainwright, John
Walton, George W.

98th Pennsylvania Infantry
McAdams, Peter

99th Pennsylvania Infantry
Bonnaffon, Sylvester, Jr.
Fasnacht, Charles H.
Munsell, Harvey M.

100th Pennsylvania Infantry
Chambers, Joseph B.
Oliver, Charles

104th Pennsylvania Infantry
Purcell, Hiram W.

105th Pennsylvania Infantry
Mitchell, Alexander H.

107th Pennsylvania Infantry
Delaney, John C.
Hottenstine, Solomon J.

109th Pennsylvania Infantry
Storey, John H.R.
Veale, Moses

Names by Regiment

114th Pennsylvania Infantry
Collis, Charles H.T.

116th Pennsylvania Infantry
Mulholland, St. Clair A.
Sacriste, Louis J.
Seitzinger, James M.

121st Pennsylvania Infantry
Funk, West

128th Pennsylvania Infantry
Gresser, Ignatz

129th Pennsylvania Infantry
Frick, Jacob G.

134th Pennsylvania Infantry
Quay, Matthew S.

136th Pennsylvania Infantry
Petty, Philip

138th Pennsylvania Infantry
Connell, Trustrim

140th Pennsylvania Infantry
Bingham, Henry H.
Pipes, James
Purman, James J.

141st Pennsylvania Infantry
Bennett, Orren
Rought, Stephen

143rd Pennsylvania Infantry
De Lacey, Patrick
Rutter, James M.

147th Pennsylvania Infantry
Goodman, William E.

148th Pennsylvania Infantry
Ammerman, Robert W.
Brown, Jeremiah Z.

Harris, George W.
Phillips, Josiah

150th Pennsylvania Infantry
Huidekoper, Henry S.
Reinsinger, J. Monroe

155th Pennsylvania Infantry
Pearson, Alfred L.

157th Pennsylvania Infantry
Scott, John Wallace

188th Pennsylvania Infantry
Blucher, Charles
Graul, William
Kramer, Theodore L.

191st Pennsylvania Infantry
Shopp, George J.

205th Pennsylvania Infantry
Lilley, John

207th Pennsylvania Infantry
Ilgenfritz, Charles H.

208th Pennsylvania Infantry
Hoffman, Thomas W.

210th Pennsylvania Infantry
Day, Charles
Raub, Jacob F.

211th Pennsylvania Infantry
Ewing, John C.
Harmon, Amzi D.

1st Pennsylvania Rifles
Thompson James B.

1st Rhode Island Light Artillery
Barber, James A.
Bucklyn, John K.
Childs, Benjamin H.
Corcoran, John

Ennis, Charles D.
Havron, John H.
Lewis, Samuel E.
Molbone, Archibald
Potter, George W.

1st Rhode Island Cavalry
Bliss, George N.

2nd Rhode Island Infantry
Babcock, William J.
Parker, Thomas

4th Rhode Island Infantry
Burbank, James H.
Welsh, James

7th Rhode Island Infantry
Bliss, Zenas R.
Taylor, Joseph

1st Tennessee Cavalry
Collins, Harrison

4th Tennessee Infantry
Lawson, Gaines

2nd United States Artillery
Banjamin, Samuel N.
Immell, Lorenzo D.
Kaiser, John
Kennedy, John
Williston, Edward B.
Woodruff, Carle A.

4th United States Artillery
Cook, John
Fuger, Frederick
King, Rufus, Jr.

5th United States Artillery
Adelbert Ames
Du Pont, Henry A.
McGough, Owen
Uhrl, George

1st United States Cavalry
Harris, Moses
O'Connor, Timothy

2nd United States Cavalry
Hanford, Edward R.
Rodenbough, Theophilus F.

Schmidt, Conrad
Tompkins, Charles H.

4th United States Cavalry
Hedges, Joseph

5th United States Cavalry
Arnold, Abraham K.

6th United States Cavalry
Platt, George C.
Schwenk, Martin

8th United States Cavalry
Seward, Griffin

7th United States Infantry
O'Neill, Stephen

11th United States Infantry
Cutts, James M.
Patterson, John H.
Wood, H. Clay

14th United States Infantry
Cayer, Ovila
Williams, George C.

15th United States Infantry
Carson, William J.

18th United States Infantry
Freeman, Henry B.

19th United States Infantry
Prentice, Joseph R.

4th United States Colored Infantry
Appleton, William H.
Fleetwood, Christian A.
Hilton, Alfred B.
Veal, Charles

5th United States Colored Infantry
Beaty, Powhatan
Bronson, James H.
Holland, Milton M.
Pinn, Robert

6th United States Colored Infantry
Edgerton, Nathan H.

Hawkins, Thomas R.
Kelly, Alexander

30th United States Colored Infantry
Bates, Delavan
Davidson, Andrew

34th United States Colored Infantry
Brush, George W.

36th United States Colored Infantry
Gardiner, James
James, Miles

38th United States Colored Infantry
Barnes, William H.
Harris, James H.
Ratcliff, Edward

39th United States Colored Infantry
Dorsey, Decatur

43rd United States Colored Infantry
Wright, Albert D.

73rd United States Colored Infantry
Merriam, Henry C.
Nichols, Henry C.

102nd United States Colored Infantry
Barrell, Charles L.
Bennett, Orson W.

116th United States Colored Infantry
Evans, Ira H.
Thorn, Walter

2nd United States Infantry
Burke, Daniel W.

10th United States Infantry
Schwan, Theodore

12th United States Infantry
Younker, John L.

13th United States Infantry
Kephart, James

14th United States Infantry
Wright, Robert

16th United States Infantry
Barry Augustus

18th United States Infantry
Phisterer, Frederick

1st United States Sharpshooters
Peck, Cassius
Ripley, William Y.W.
Woodruff, Alonzo

1st United States Veteran Reserve Corps
Wray, William J.

1st Vermont Cavalry
Lyon, Frederick A.
Sweeney, James
Wells, William
Woodbury, Eri D.

1st Vermont Infantry
Dolloff, Charles W.

2nd Vermont Infantry
Clarke, Dayton P.
Harrington, Ephraim, W.
Noyes, William W.
Robbins, Augustus I.
Tracy, Amasa A.

3rd Vermont Infantry
Beatty, Alexander M.
Hawkins, Gardner C.
Johnston, Willie
Pingree, Samuel E.
Scott, Julian A.
Seaver, Thomas O.

4th Vermont Infantry
Coffey, Robert J.
Drury, James
Hooker, George W.
Rich, Carlos H.
Wheeler, Daniel D.

5th Vermont Infantry
Gould, Charles G.
Grant, Lewis A.
Hack, Lester G.
Sargent, Jackson

6th Vermont Infantry
Butterfield, Frank G.
Clark, John W.
Holton, Edward A.
Sperry, William J.

8th Vermont Infantry
Downs, Henry W.
Howard, Squire E.
Ingalls, Lewis J.
Thomas, Stephen

9th Vermont Infantry
Jewett, Erastus W.
Livingston, Josiah O.
Peck, Theodore S.

10th Vermont Infantry
Davis, George E.
Henry, William W.
Scott, Alexander

12th Vermont Infantry
Benedict, George G.

13th Vermont Infantry
Lonergan, John

16th Vermont Infantry
Veazey, Wheelock G.

1st West Virginia Cavalry
Adams, James F.
Anderson, Thomas
Blackmar, Wilmon W.
Boon, Hugh P.
Boury, Richard
Capehart, Charles E.
Capehart, Henry
Cunningham, Francis M.
Houlton, William
Rowland, Archibald H., Jr.
Schorn, Charles
Shanan, Emisire
Shoemaker, Levi
Woods, Daniel A.

2nd West Virginia Cavalry
Kimball, Joseph

McElhinny, Samuel O.
Powell, William H.
Shields, Bernard

3rd West Virginia Cavalry
McWhorter, Walter F.

1st West Virginia Infantry
Burns, James M.

4th West Virginia Infantry
Barringer, William H.
Buckley, John C.
Bumgarner, William
North, Jasper N.
Parsons, Joel
Summers, James C.

11th West Virginia Infantry
Moore, George G.
White, Adam

12th West Virginia Infantry
Apple, Andrew O.
Curtis, Josiah M.
Durham James R.
McCauslin, Joseph
Reeder, Charles A.

14th West Virginia Infantry
Shanes, John

12th Wisconsin Light Artillery
Croft, James E.

3rd Wisconsin Cavalry
Pond, George F.
Pond, James B.

1st Wisconsin Infantry
Durham, John S.
Eckes, John N.

2nd Wisconsin Infantry
Johnson, John

3rd Wisconsin Infantry
Elise, William

6th Wisconsin Infantry
Waller, Francis A.

7th Wisconsin Infantry
Coates, Jefferson
Ellis, Horace
O'Conner, Albert
Sickles, William H.

8th Wisconsin Infantry
Hilliker, Benjamin F.

11th Wisconsin Infantry
Moore, Daniel B.

12th Wisconsin Infantry
Truell, Edwin M

14th Wisconsin Infantry
Murphy, Dennis J.F.

24th Wisconsin Infantry
MacArthur, Arthur, Jr.
Toohey, Thomas

31st Wisconsin Infantry
Anderson, Peter

U.S.S. *Agawam*
Bibber, Charles J.
Conlan, Dennis
Garvin, William
Hawkins, Charles
Hinnecan, William
Montgomery, Robert
Neil, John
Rice, Charles
Roberts, James
Sullivan, James

U.S.S. *Albatross*
Brown, James

U.S.S. *Baron De Kalb*
Cotton, Peter
Leon, Pierre
McDonald, John
Robinson, Charles

U.S.S. *Benton*
Brownell, William P.
Martin, William
Moore, William
Morton, Charles W.
Williams, Robert

U.S.S. *Brooklyn*
Blagheen, William
Brown, John
Brown, William H.

Officers on board the deck of the U.S.S. Agawam. Ten members of the Agawam's crew were awarded the Medal of Honor, primarily for service in the expeditions against Fort Fisher, North Carolina (U.S. Army War College).

Buck, James
Cooper, John
Davis, Samuel W.
Denig, J. Henry
Dennis, Richard
Halstead, William
Hudson, Michael
Irlam, Joseph
Irving, John
Irwin, Nicholas
Kenna, Barnett
Machon, James
Mack, Alexander
Madden, William
Mifflin, James
Nichols, William
Oviatt, Miles M.
Price, Edward
Smith, Willard M.
Sterling, James E.
Todd, Samuel

U.S.S. Calena
Gardner, William
Jordan, Thomas

Kenyon, Charles
Mackie, John F.
Martin, Edward
Young, Edward B.

U.S.S. Canonicus
Stevens, Daniel D.

U.S.S. Carondelet
Arther, Matthew
Dorman, John
Huskey, Michael
Morrison, John G.

U.S.S. Cayuga
Parker, William
Wright, Edward
Young, William

U.S.S. Ceres
Hand, Allexander
Kelley, John

U.S.S. Chickasaw
Jones, Andrew
Seanor, James

U.S.S. Cincinnati
Bois, Frank
Corcoran, Thomas E.
Dow, Henry
Hamilton, Thomas W.
Jenkins, Thomas
McHugh, Martin

U.S.S. Commodore Hull
Colbert, Patrick

U.S.S. Commodore Perry
Breen, John
Lakin, Daniel
Peterson, Alfred
Williams, John

U.S.S. Decotah
Harding, Thomas

U.S.S. Fort Henry
Nugent, Christopher

U.S.S. Fort Hindman
Duncan, James K.L.
Johnston, William P.
Molloy, Hugh

Names by Naval Ship

U.S.S. Galena
Regan, Jeremiah

U.S.S. Hartford
Brown, Wilson
Diggins, Bartholomew
Dunphy, Richard D.
Fitzpatrick, Thomas
Freeman, Martin
Garrison, James R.
Lawson, John
McFarland, John
Melville, Charles
O'Connell, Thomas
Pelham, William
Stanley, William A.

U.S.S. Hendrick Hudson
Mack, John
Schutt, George

U.S.S. Howquah
Connor, William C.
Robinson, Alexander

U.S.S. Hunchback
Barton, Thomas

U.S.S. Isaac Smith
Stout, Richard

U.S.S. John Adams
O'Brien, Oliver

U.S.S. Kearsarge
Aheam, Michael
Bickford, John F.
Bond, William
Haley, James
Ham, Mark G.
Harrison, George H.
Hayes, John
Lee, James H.
Moore, Charles
Pease, Joachim
Perry, Thomas
Poole, William B.
Read, Charles A.
Read, George E.
Saunders, James
Smith, William
Strahan, Robert

U.S.S. Keokuk
Anderson, Robert

U.S.S. Lackawana
Burns John M.
Cassidy, Michael
Chaput, Louis G.
Dougherty, Patrick
Edwards, John
Kinnaird, Samuel W.
McCullock, Adam
Phinney, William
Smith, John
Taylor, George
Ward, James
Whitfield, Daniel

U.S.S. Lehigh
Gile, Frank S.
Irving, Thomas
Leland, George W.
Williams, William
Young, Horatio N.

U.S.S. Louisville
Bradley, Charles
Byrnes, James
Sullivan, Timothy
Talbott, William

U.S.S. Magnolia
Lann, John S.
Pyne, George
Read, Charles
Smith, Thomas

U.S.S. Marblehead
Blake, Robert
Farley, William
Miller, James
Moore, Charles

U.S.S. Marmora
Franks, William J.
Laffey, Bartlett
Stoddard, James

U.S.S. Metacomet
Avery, James
Baker, Charles
Donnelly, John
Harris, John
Johnson, Henry
Murphy, Patrick
Noble, Daniel
Taylor, Thomas

U.S.S. Minnesota
Barter, Gurdon H.
Bass, David L.
Connor, Thomas
Harcourt, Thomas
Mills, Charles
Rannahan, John
Shipman, William
Shivers, John
Thompson, Henry A.
Wilcox, Franklin L.

U.S.S. Mississippi
Brennan, Christopher
Brinn, Andrew
Howard, Peter
Vaughn, Pinkerton R.

U.S.S. Mohican
Thompson, William
Williams, John

U.S.S. Monadnock
Dunn, William

U.S.S. Monitor
Williams, Peter

U.S.S. Montauk
Horton, James
Rountry, John
Weeks, Charles H.

U.S.S. Monticello
Sullivan, John
Warren, David
Wright, William

U.S.S. Mount Washington
Jordan, Robert
Thielberg, Henry
Wood, Robert B.
Woods, Samuel

U.S.S. Neosho
Ditzenback, John
Ferrell, John H.

U.S.S. Nereus
Kane, Thomas

U.S.S. New Ironsides
Barnum, James
Dempster, John
English, Thomas
Haffee, Edmund

Lear, Nicholas
Milliken, Daniel
White, Joseph
Willis, Richard

U.S.S. Oneida
Jones, John E.
Kendrick, Thomas
Naylor, David
Newland, William
Preston, John
Roantree, James S.
Sheridan, James
Woram, Charles B.

U.S.S. Owasco
Farrell, Edward

U.S.S. Pawnee
Swearer, Benjamin
Williams, John

U.S.S. Pensacola
Flood, Thomas
Lyons, Thomas
McLeod, James
Richards, Louis

U.S.S. Peterel
Nibbe, John H.

U.S.S. Picket Boat 1
Denning, Lorenzo
George, Daniel G.
Hamilton, Richard
Harley, Bernard
Houghton, Edward J.
King, Robert H.
Wilkes, Henry

U.S.S. Pinola
Frisbee, John B.

U.S.S. Pittsburgh
Woon, John

U.S.S. Pocahontas
Harrington, Daniel

U.S.S. Pontoosuc
Angling, John
Betham, Asa
Blair, Robert M.
Erickson, John P
McWilliams, George W.
Verney, James W.
Williams, Anthony

U.S.S. Rhode Island
Foy, Charles H.
Griswold, Luke M.
Horton, Lewis A.
Jones, John
Logan, Hugh
Moore, George
Smith Charles H.
Wagg, Maurice

U.S.S. Richmond
Atkinson, Thomas E.
Brazell, John
Brown, Robert
Carr, William
Chandler, James B.
Cripps, Thomas
Cronin, Cornelius
Deakin, Charles
Densmore, William
Doolen, William
Duncan, Adam
Hamilton, Hugh
Hayes, Thomas
Hickman, John
James, John H.
Jones, William
Martin, James
McClelland, Matthew
McIntosh, James
Miller, Andrew
Morgan, James H.
Parks, George
Rush, John
Sharp, Hendrick
Simkins, Lebbeus
Smith, James
Smith, John
Smith, Oloff
Smith, Walter B.
Sprowle, David
Truett, Alexander H.
Vantine, Joseph E.
Wells, William

U.S.S. Santee
Bell, George

U.S.S. Santiago de Cuba
Bazaar, Philip
Griffiths, John

Province, George
Savage, Auzella
Swanson, John
Swatton, Edward
Williams, Augustus

U.S.S. Saratoga
Ortega, John

U.S.S. Sciota
Hathaway, Edward W.

U.S.S. Seneca
Tripp, Othniel

U.S.S. Shokokon
Cliffird, Robert T.

U.S.S. Signal
Asten, Charles
Butts, George
Hyland, John
McCormick, Michael
O'Donoghue, Timothy
Wilkes, Perry

U.S.S. Susquehanna
Webster, Henry S.

U.S.S. Tacony
Brutsche, Henry
Graham, Robert
Howard, Martin
Tallentine, James

U.S.S. Ticonderoga
Bowman Edward R.
Campbell, William
Fry, Isaac N.
Hayden, Joseph B.
Jones, Thomas
Prance, George
Summers, Robert
Taylor, William G.

U.S.S. Valley City
Davis, John

U.S.S. Varuna
Bourne, Thomas
Bradley, Amos
Greene, John
Hollat, George
Martin, William
McGowan, John

McKnight, William
Peck, Oscar E.

U.S.S. *Wabash*
Burton, Albert
Ringold, Edward
Shepard, Louis C.
Tomlin, Andrew J.

U.S.S. *Whitehead*
Smith, Edwin

U.S.S. *Wissahickon*
Shutes, Henry

U.S.S. *Wyalusing*
Baldwin, Charles
Crawford, Alexander
Lafferty, John
Lloyd, Benjamin
Lloyd, John W.

U.S.S. *Wyandank*
Mullen, Patrick
Sanderson, Aaron

Listing by Place of Action

Entries on pages 259–275 are ordered alphabetically by state.

Evergreen, Alabama
Spurling, Andrew B.

Fort Blakely, Alabama
Callahan, John H.
McConnell, Samuel
Merriam, Henry C.
Miller, Henry A.
Moore, Daniel B.
Nichols, Henry C.
Payne, Thomas H.L.
Pentzer, Patrick H.
Rebmann, George F.
Riley, Thomas
Rockefeller, Charles M.
Stickels, Joseph
Vifquain, Victor
Wheaton, Lloyd
Whitmore, John

Mobile Bay, Alabama
Atkinson, Thomas E.
Avery, James
Baker, Charles
Blagheen, William
Bras, Edgar A.
Brazell, John
Brown, John
Brown, Robert
Brown, William H.
Brown, Wilson
Burns, John M.
Carr, William
Cassidy, Michael
Chandler, James B.
Chaput, Louis G.
Cooper, John

Cripps, Thomas
Cronin, Cornelius
Davis, Samuel W.
Deakin, Charles
Denig, J. Henry
Dennis, Richard
Densmore, William
Diggins, Bartholomew
Donnelly, John
Doolen, William
Dougherty, Patrick
Duncan, Adam
Dunphy, Richard D.
Edwards, John
Fitzpatrick, Thomas
Freeman, Martin
Gardner, William
Garrison, James R.
Halstead, William
Hamilton, Hugh
Harris, John
Hayes, Thomas
Hudson, Michael
Irlam, Joseph
Irving, John
Irwin, Nicholas
James, John H.
Johnson, Henry
Jones, Andrew
Jones, John E.
Jones, William
Jordan, Thomas
Kendrick, Thomas
Kenna, Barnett
Kinnaird, Samuel W.
Lawson, John

Logan, Hugh
Machon, James
Mack, Alexander
Madden, William
Martin, Edward S.
Martin, James
McCullock, Adam
McFarland, John
McIntosh, James
Melville, Charles
Mifflin, James
Miller, Andrew
Morgan, James H.
Murphy, Patrick
Naylor, David
Newland, William
Nichols, William
Noble, Daniel
O'Connell, Thomas
Oviatt, Miles M.
Parks, George
Phinney, William
Preston, John
Price, Edward
Roantree, James S.
Seanor, James
Sharp, Hendrick
Sheridan, James
Simkins, Lebbeus
Smith, Charles H.
Smith, James
Smith, John
Smith, John
Smith, Oloff
Smith, Walter B.
Smith, Willard M.

Admiral David Farragut and crew aboard the deck of the U.S.S. Hartford during the battle of Mobile Bay. More than seventy-five Medals of Honor were awarded to participants of the fighting at Mobile Bay (U.S. Army War College).

Sprowle, David
Stanley, William A.
Sterling, James E.
Taylor, George
Taylor, Thomas
Todd, Samuel
Truett, Alexander H.
Ward, James
Wells, William
Whitfield, Daniel
Woram, Charles B.
Young, Edward B.

Mount Pleasant, Alabama
Dorley, August

Red Hill, Alabama
Palmer, William J.

Selma, Alabama
Fanning, Nicholas
Miller, James P.
Swan, Charles A.

Wetumpka, Alabama
Weston, John F.

Chiricahva, Arizona
Seward, Griffin

Arkansas
Elise, William

Arkansas Post, Arkansas
Talbott, William

Benton, Arkansas
Lucas, George W.

Brownsville, Arkansas
Robinson, James H.

Cache River, Arkansas
Pike, Edward M.

Pea Ridge, Arkansas
Black, William P
Carr, Eugene A.
Herron, Francis J.
Power, Albert

Prairie Grove, Arkansas
Black, John C.

Crystal River, Florida
Nugent, Christopher

Fort Gates, Florida
Thackrah, Benjamin

St. Marks, Florida
Lann, John S.
Mack, John
Pyne, George
Read, Charles
Schutt, George
Smith, Thomas

Cherbourg, France
Aheam, Michael
Bickford, John F.
Bond, William
Haley, James
Ham, Mark G.
Harrison, George H.
Hayes, John
Lee, James H.
Moore, Charles
Pease, Joachim
Perry, Thomas
Poole, William B.
Read, Charles A.
Read, George E.

Artist's depiction of the Battle of Atlanta. Eight men won the Medal of Honor in capturing the Gate City of the South, including General Manning Force (Fletcher W. Johnson, Life of William Tecumseh Sherman: Late Retired General, U.S.A., *Edgewood Publishing Company, 1891).*

Saunders, James
Smith, William
Strahan, Robert

Allatoona, Georgia
Croft, James E.

Atlanta, Georgia
Davis, Harry
Force, Manning F.
Grimshaw, Samuel
Haney, Milton L.
Lawton, Henry W.
Murphy, Robinson, B.
Sancrainte, Charles F.
Truell, Edwin M.

Big Shanty, Georgia
Bensinger, William
Brown, Wilson W.
Buffum, Robert

Dorsey, Daniel A.
Hawkins, Martin J.
Knight, William J.
Mason, Elihu H.
Parrott, Jacob
Pittinger, William
Porter, John R.
Reddick, William H.
Robertson, Samuel
Ross, Marion A.
Scott, John M.
Slavens, Samuel
Smith, James (Ovid)
Wilson, John A.
Wollam, John
Wood, Mark

Buzzard's Roost Gap, Georgia
Hymer, Samuel

Treat, Howell B.
Yeager, Jacob F.

Chattahoochie River, Georgia
Keen, Joseph S.

Chickamauga, Georgia
Carson, William J.
Chamberlain, Orville T.
Cilley, Clinton A.
Myers, George S.
Porter, Ambrose
Reed, Axel H.
Richey, William E.
Taylor, Anthony
Whitney, William G.

Columbus, Georgia
Bates, Norman F.
Bebb, Edward J.

Birdsall, Horatio L.
Cosgriff, Richard H.
Hays, John H.
Morgan, Richard H.
Tibbetts, Andrew W.

Culloden, Georgia
Davis, John
Hudson, Aaron R.

Dallas, Georgia
Storey, John H.R.

Decatur, Georgia
Sprague, John W.

Dug Gap, Georgia
McKay, Charles W.
Welch, Stephen

Ezra Chapel, Georgia
Torgler, Ernst

Flint River, Georgia
Estes, Lewellyn G.

Jonesboro, Georgia
Baird, Absalom
Grebe, M.R. William
Irwin, Patrick
Kuder, Jeremiah
Mattingly, Henry B.

Kenesaw Mountain, Georgia
Herington, Pitt B.
Mayes, William B.
Sturgeon, James K.
Webber, Alason P.

New Hope Church, Georgia
Johnson, Follett

Newnan, Georgia
Healey, George W.

Oostanaula, Georgia
Powers, Wesley J.

Peach Tree Creek, Georgia
Baldwin, Frank D.
Buckley, Denis
Crosier, William H.H.
Hapeman, Douglas
Williams, William H.

Resaca, Georgia
Box, Thomas J.
Collins, Thomas D.
Newman, Marcellus J.
Oliver, Paul A.
Ranney, George E.
Sladen, Joseph A.
Tremain, Henry E.
Tyrrell, George William

Ringgold, Georgia
Goettel, Philip

Varnells Station, Georgia
Ferrier, Daniel T.

Waynesboro, Georgia
Cockley, David L.

Baxter Springs, Kansas
Pond, James B.

Drywood, Kansas
Pond, George F.

Osage, Kansas
Dunlavy, James
Young, Cavalry M.

Horseshoe Bend, Kentucky
Cutcheon, Byron M.

Perryville, Kentucky
Durham, John S.
Surles, William H.

Alabama Bayou, Louisiana
Cadwell, Luman L.

Baton Rouge, Louisiana
Curtis, John C.

Bayou Teche, Louisiana
Howard, Squire E.

Boutte Station, Louisiana
Ingalls, Lewis J.

Cane River Crossing, Louisiana
Beebe, William S.

Forts Jackson and St. Philip, Louisiana
Bourne, Thomas
Bradley, Amos

Brennan, Christopher
Buck, James
Farrell, Edward
Flood, Thomas
Frisbee, John B.
Greene, John
Hollat, George
Lyons, Thomas
Martin, William
McGowan, John
McKnight, William
McLeod, James
Parker, William
Peck, Oscar E.
Richards, Louis
Shutes, Henry
Wright, Edward
Young, William

Georgia Landing, Louisiana
Nolan, John J.

Grand Coteau, Louisiana
Marland, William

Harrisonburg, Louisiana
Duncan, James K.L.
Johnston, William P.
Molloy, Hugh

Irish Bend, Louisiana
Simonds, William Edgar

Natchitoches, Louisiana
Elliott, Russell C.

Pleasant Hill, Louisiana
Cook, John H.

Port Hudson, Louisiana
Beaufort, Jean J.
Brinn, Andrew
Deland, Frederick N.
Fox, Nicholas
Hanna, Marcus, A.
Hickman, John
Howard, Peter
Johns, Henry T.
Lovering, George M.
McClelland, Matthew
Rush, John
Strong, James N.
Tabor, William S.

Place of Action

Vantine, Joseph E.
Vaughn, Pinkerton R.
Warren, Francis E.

Red River, Louisiana
Asten, Charles
Brown, James
Butts, George
Hyland, John
McCormick, Michael
O'Donoghue, Timothy
Wilkes, Perry

Ship Island Sound, Louisiana
Seward, Richard E.

Antietam, Maryland
Beyer, Hillary
Carter, John J.
Child, Benjamin H.
Cleveland, Charles F.
Cook, John
Curran, Richard
Greene, Oliver D.
Greig, Theodore W.
Gresser, Ignatz
Haskell, Marcus M.
Hogarty, William P.
Hyde, Thomas W.
Johnson, Samuel
Libaire, Adolphe
Murphy, John P.
Orth, Jacob G.
Paul, William H.
Tanner, Charles B.
Whitman, Frank M.
Wright, Samuel C.

Mason's Island, Maryland
Madden, Michael

Monocacy, Maryland
Davis, George E.
Scott, Alexander

South Mountain, Maryland
Allen, James
Hatch, John P.
Hooker, George W.
Inscho, Leonidus H.

Black River Bridge, Mississippi
Kendall, William W.

Champion Hill, Mississippi
Hill, James
Wilhelm, George

Chickasaw Bayou, Mississippi
Williamson, James A.

Corinth, Mississippi
Archer, James W.
Horsfall, William H.
McCammon, William W.
Murphy, Dennis J.F.
Swayne, Wager

Deer Creek, Mississippi
Huskey, Michael

Eastport, Mississippi
Darrough, John S.

Grand Gulf, Mississippi
Guerin, Fritz W.
Hammel, Henry A.
Pesch, Joseph
Woon, John

Great Gulf Bay, Mississippi
Brownell, William P.

Iuka, Mississippi
Sears, Cyrus

Ivy Farm, Mississippi
Bieger, Charles

Mechanicsburg, Mississippi
Hilliker, Benjamin F.

Tallahatchie River, Mississippi
Porter, Ambrose

Vicksburg, Mississippi
Albert, Christian
Archinal, William
Armstrong, Clinton L.
Ayers, David
Ayers, John G.K.
Ballen, Frederick
Barringer, William H.
Bickford, Matthew
Blasdel, Thomas A.
Bois, Frank
Bowen, Emmer
Brown, John H.
Brown, Uriah
Buckley, John C.
Buhrman, Henry G.
Bumgarner, William
Burritt, William W.
Campbell, William
Carmin, Isaac H.
Casey, Henry
Chisman, William W.
Colby, Carlos W.
Conaway, John W.
Corcoran, Thomas E.
Cox, Robert M.
Cunningham, James S.
Davidson, Andrew
Davis, Martin K.
Day, David F.
De Witt, Richard W.
Dickie, David
Dow, Henry
Dunne, James
Eckes, John N.
Elison, James M.
Fisher, John H.
Flynn, James E.
Frantz, Joseph
Fraser, William W.
Frey, Franz
Frizzell, Henry F.
Geschwind, Nicholas
Godley, Leonidus M.
Goldsbery, Andrew E.
Gould, Newton T.
Guin, Thomas
Hack, John
Hamilton, Thomas W.
Hanks, Joseph
Harris, Sampson
Hathaway, Edward W.
Helms, David H.
Henry, James
Higgins, Thomas J.
Hodges, Addison, J.
Howe, Orion P.
Hunt, Louis T.

Artist's depiction of the Battle of Vicksburg, Mississippi. One hundred twenty-two men won the Medal of Honor during the seige and battles that took place around Vicksburg, including the men who took part in the Forlorn Hope. This is twice the number awarded to participants of the Battle of Gettysburg (U.S. Army War College).

Hyatt, Theodore
Jardine, James
Jenkins, Thomas
John, William
Johns, Elisha
Johnson, Andrew
Johnston, David
Jones, David
Kephart, James
Kirby, Dennis T.
Kloth, Charles H.
Kretsinger, George
Labill, Joseph S.
Larrabee, James W.
Lewis, Henry
Longshore, William H.
Lower, Robert A.
McClelland, James M.
McCornack, Andrew
McGinn, Edward
McGonagle, Wilson
McGuire, Patrick

McHugh, Martin
Miller, Jacob C.
Morford, Jerome
Murphy, Thomas C.
Nash, Henry H.
North, Jasper N.
O'Dea, John
O'Donnell, Menomen
Overturf, Jacob H.
Parsons, Joel
Pearsall, Platt
Peters, Henry C.
Putnam, Winthrop D.
Reed, William
Renninger, Louis
Rock, Frederick
Rundle, Charles W.
Sanford, Jacob
Schenck, Benjamin W.
Schmauch, Andrew
Schnell, Christian
Smalley, Reuben

Sprague, Benona
Steinmetz, William
Stephens, William G.
Stockman, George H.
Stolz, Frank
Summers, James C.
Swegheimer, Jacob
Sype, Peter
Taylor, Henry H.
Toomer, William
Trogden, Howell G.
Vernay, James D.
Wagner, John W.
Ward, Thomas J.
Ward, William H.
Warden, John
White, Joseph
White, Patrick H.
Widick, Andrew J.
Wood, Richard H.
Wortick, (Wertick) Joseph

Place of Action

Yazoo City, Mississippi
Franks, William J.
Laffey, Bartlett
Stoddard, James

Yazoo, River, Mississippi
Cotton, Peter
Leon, Pierre
Martin, William
McDonald, John
Moore, William
Morrison, John G.
Morton, Charles W.
Nibbe, John H.
Robinson, Charles
Williams, Robert

Lexington, Missouri
Palmer George H.

Newtonia, Missouri
Blodgett, Welis H.

Wilson's Creek, Missouri
Boquet, Nicholas
Immel, Lorenzo D.
Schofield, John M
Wherry, William M.
Wood, H. Clay

Brooklyn, New York
Taylor, John

Bachelors Creek, North Carolina
Haring, Abram P.

Beaufort, North Carolina
Harding, Thomas

Bentonville, North Carolina
Anderson, Peter
Clute, George W.
Dougall, Allan H.
Plant, Henry E.

Black River, North Carolina
Smith, Henry I.

Camden, North Carolina
Langbein, J.C. Julius

Cape Hatteras, North Carolina
Griswold, Luke M.
Moore, George
Wagg, Maurice

Elizabeth City, North Carolina
Davis, John

Fort Clark, North Carolina
Swearer, Benjamin

Fort Fisher, North Carolina
Anderson, Bruce
Angling, John
Barnum, James
Barter, Gurdon H.
Bass, David L.
Bazaar, Philip
Betham, Asa
Bibber, Charles J.
Binder, Richard
Blair, Robert M.
Bowman, Edward R.
Burton, Albert
Campbell, William
Chapin, Alaric B.
Conlan, Dennis
Connor, Thomas
Curtis, Newton Martin
Dempster, John
Dunn, William
English, Thomas
Erickson, John P.
Foy, Charles H.
Freeman, William H.
Fry, Isaac N.
Garvin, William
Griffiths, John
Haffee, Edmund
Harcourt, Thomas
Hawkins, Charles
Hayden, Joseph B.
Hinnecan, William
Jones, Thomas
Kane, Thomas
Lear, Nicholas
McWilliams, George W.
Merrill, George

Milliken, Daniel
Mills, Charles
Montgomery, Robert
Neahr, Zachariah C.
Neil, John
Pennypacker, Galusha
Prance, George
Province, George
Rannahan, John
Rice, Charles
Roberts, James
Savage, Auzella
Shepard, Louis C.
Shipman, William
Shivers, John
Stevens, Daniel D.
Summers, Robert
Swanson, John
Swatton, Edward
Taylor, William G.
Thompson, Henry A.
Tomlin, Andrew J.
Tripp, Othniel
Verney, James W.
Wainwright, John
Walling, William H.
Welsh, Edward
Wilcox, Franklin L.
Williams, Anthony
Williams, Augustus
Willis, Richard

Greensboro, North Carolina
Betts, Charles M.

Hamilton, North Carolina
Kelley, John

Nansemond, North Carolina
Thielberg, Henry
Wood, Robert B.

New Bern, North Carolina
Bryant, Andrew S.
Caruana, Orlando E.
Terry, John D.
Thompson, J. (James) Harry

Newport Barracks, North Carolina
Jewett, Erastus W.
Livingston, Josiah O.
Peck, Theodore S.

Plymouth, North Carolina
Brutsche, Henry
Colbert, Patrick
Graham, Robert
Howard, Martin
Tallentine, James

Roanoke River, North Carolina
Baldwin, Charles
Crawfoed, Alexander
Denning, Lorenzo
George, Daniel G
Hamilton, Richard
Hand, Allexander
Harley, Bernard
Houghton, Edward J.
King, Robert H.
Lafferty, John
Lloyd, Benjamin
Lloyd, John W.
Wilkes, Henry

Sandy Cross Roads, North Carolina
Mills, Frank W.

Tranter's Creek, North Carolina
Avery, William B.

Trenton, North Carolina
Kenyon, John S.

Washington, North Carolina
Smith, Wilson

Wilmington, North Carolina
Clifford, Robert T.
Connor, William C.
Robinson, Alexander
Sullivan, John
Warren, David
Wright, William

Fairfield, Pennsylvania
Platt, George C.

Gettysburg, Pennsylvania
Allen, Nathaniel
Bacon, Elijah W.
Benedict, George G.
Brown, Morris, Jr.
Carey, Hugh
Carlisle, Casper R.
Chamberlain, Joshua L.
Clark, Harrison
Clopp, John E.
Coates, Jefferson
De Castro, Joseph H.
Dore, George E.
Enderlin, Richard
Falls, Benjamin F.
Fassett, John B.
Flynn, Christopher
Fuger, Frederick
Furman, Chester S.
Gilligan, Edward L.
Hart, John W.
Hincks, William B.
Horan, Thomas
Huidekoper, Henry S.
Irsch, Francis
Jellison, Benjamin H.
Johnson, Wallace W.
Knox, William J.
Lonergan, John
Mayberry, John B.
McCarren, Bernard
Mears, George W.
Miller, John
Miller, William E.
Munsell, Harvey M.
O'Brien, Henry D.
Pipes, James
Postles, James Parke
Purman, James J.
Raymond, William H.
Reed, Charles W.
Reinsinger, J. Monroe
Rice, Edmund
Richmond, James
Robinson, John H.
Rood, Oliver P.
Roush, Levi J.
Rutter, James M.
Sellers, Alfred J.
Sherman, Marshall
Sickles, Daniel E.
Smith, Thaddeus S.
Stacey, Charles
Sullivan, James
Thompson, James B.
Tozier, Andrew J.
Veazey, Wheelock G.
Wall, Jerry
Waller, Francis A.
Webb, Alexander S.
Wells, William
Wiley, James

Millerstown, Pennsylvania
Schwenk, Martin

Monterey Mountain, Pennsylvania
Capehart, Charles E.

Aiken, South Carolina
Toban, James W.

Ashepoo River, South Carolina
Brush, George W.
Downey, William
Duffey, John
Gifford, David L.
Scanlan, Patrick

Camden, South Carolina
Barrell, Charles L.

Charleston, South Carolina
Anderson, Robert
Gile, Frank S.
Irving, Thomas
Leland, George W.
Williams, William
Young, Horatio N.

Dingles Mill, South Carolina
Finkenbiner, Henry S.

Fort Wagner, South Carolina
Carney, William H.
Hibson, Joseph C.

Hilton Head, South Carolina
Thompson, William
Williams, John

*Confederate assault at Gettysburg. Big Round Top and Little Round Top can be seen in the distance. Sixty-one men won the Medal of Honor for their deeds upon the fields of Gettysburg. Though this is considered to be the greatest single battle of the war, several engagements bested it, in terms of medals awarded (*The History of the Civil War in the United States*).*

Honey Hill, South Carolina
Bennett, Orson W.
Ellsworth, Thomas
Gouraud, George E.
Smith, Andrew Jackson

James Island, South Carolina
Jackson, Frederick R.

John's River, South Carolina
Blake, Robert

Lagareville, South Carolina
Farley, William
Miller, James
Moore, Charles

Pocataligo, South Carolina
Ringold, Edward

Secessionville, South Carolina
Lewis, Dewitt Clinton

Stono River, South Carolina
Stout, Richard

Sullivan's Island, South Carolina
O'Brien, Oliver

Bells Mills, Tennessee
Ditzenback, John
Ferrell, John H.

Brentwood Hills, Tennessee
Holcomb, Daniel I.

Campbell Station, Tennessee
Starkins, John H.

Chattanooga, Tennessee
Barnum, Henry A.
Johnson, Ruel M.
Toffey, John J.

Crosby's Creek, Tennessee
Anderson, Everett W.

Duck River, Tennessee
Barrick, Jesse T.

Elk River, Tennessee
Gage, Richard J.
Holland, Lemuel F.
Houghton, George L.
Marsh, George
Shapland, John
Slagle, Oscar
Smalley, Reuben S.

Fort Donelson, Tennessee
Twombly, Voltaire P.

Fort Henry and Donelson, Tennessee
Arther, Matthew

Franklin, Tennessee
Brown, John Harties
Davis, Joseph
Gaunt, John C.
Greenawalt, Abraham
Hall, Newton H.
Kelley, George V.
Merrifield, James K.
Ramsbottom, Alfred
Ricksecker, John H.
Stanley, David S.
Toohey, Thomas

Harpeth River, Tennessee
Beaumont, Eugene B.
Hedges, Joseph

Jackson, Tennessee
Fox, Henry

Knoxville, Tennessee
Falconer, John A.
Hadley, Cornelius M.
Judge, Francis W.
Kelley, Andrew J.
Mahoney, Jeremiah
Manning, Joseph S.
Shepard, Irwin

Lenoire, Tennessee
Brandle, Joseph E.
Swift, Frederic W.

Lookout Mountain, Tennessee
Kappesser, Peter
Kiggins, John
Potter, Norman

Minville, Tennessee
Lawson, Gaines

Missionary Ridge, Tennessee
Banks, George L.
Bell, James B.
Boynton, Henry V.
Brouse, Charles W.
Brown, Robert B.
Davis, Freeman
Graham, Thomas N.
Green, George
Howard, Hiram R.
Josselyn, Simeon T.
Kelley, Leverett M.
Kountz, John S.
MacArthur, Arthur, Jr.
Schmidt, William
Walker, James C.

Murfreesboro, Tennessee
Magee, William

Nashville, Tennessee
Anderson, Marion T.
Carr, Franklin
Churchill, Samuel J.
Colwell, Oliver
Garrett, William
Gere, Thomas P.
Kaltenbach, Luther
May, William
McCleary, Charles H.
Moore, Wilbur F.
Parks, James W.
Post, Philip Sidney
Simmons, William T.
Sloan, Andrew J.
Smith, Otis W.
Stokes, George
Welch, George W.

Nolensville, Tennessee
Burger, Joseph
Clark, William A.
Flannigan, James
Hanna, Milton
Holmes, Lovilo N.
Pay, Byron E.
Vale, John
Wright, Samuel

Richland Creek, Tennessee
Collins, Harrison

Shelbyville, Tennessee
Davis, Charles C.

Shiloh, Tennessee
McDonald, John Wade
Spalding, Edward B.
Williams, Elwood N.

Spring Hill, Tennessee
Steele, John W.

Stone's River, Tennessee
Bourke, John G.
Farquhar, John M.
Follett, Joseph L.
Freeman, Henry B.
McKeen, Nineveh S.
Phisterer, Frederick
Prentice, Joseph R.
Russell, Milton
Tweedale, John
Whitehead, John M.
Vance, Wilson

Walker's Ford, Tennessee
Bruner, Louis J.

Wauhatchie, Tennessee
Veale, Moses

Galveston, Texas
Bell, George

Matagorda Bay, Texas
Hesseltine, Francis S.

Aldie, Virginia
Di Cesnola, Louis P.

Alexandria, Virginia
Brownell, Francis E.

Alsops Farm, Virginia
Galloway, George N.

Amelia Springs, Virginia
Chandler, Stephen E.
Newman, William H.
Thomas, Hampton S.

Appomattox, Virginia
Anderson, Thomas
Brewer, William J.
Carey, James L.
Donaldson, John
Funk, West
Higby, Charles
Myers, William H.
Read, Morton A.
Schorn, Charles
Shields, Bernard
Sova, Joseph E.
Tobie, Edward P.

Ashby's Gap, Virginia
Dodds, Edward E.

Artist's drawing of the Union attack up Lookout Mountain, at Chattanooga, Tennessee. The capture of Lookout Mountain preceeded the capture of Missionary Ridge, and the breaking of the Confederate seige of the city (The History of the Civil War in the United States).

Back Creek Valley, Virginia
Marsh, Charles H.

Banks Ford, Virginia
Coffey, Robert J.

Bermuda Hundred, Virginia
Drake, James M.
Engle, James E.
Morrison, Francis

Berryville, Virginia
Ferris, Eugene W.
Gause, Isaac

Bethesda Church, Virginia
Gillespie, George L.

Blackburns Ford, Virginia
Cross, James E.
Peck, Cassius
Rand, Charles F.

Blackwater, Virginia
Burbank, James H.

Boydton Plank Road, Virginia
Bonnaffon, Sylvester, Jr.
Embler, Andrew H.

Bristoe Station, Virginia
Corson, Joseph K.
Cullen, Thomas
Hallock, Nathan M.
Hanscom, Moses C.
Urell, M. Emmet

Brooks Ford, Virginia
Clark, Charles A.

Bull Run, Virginia
Conner, Richard
Cooke, Walter H.
Hartranft, John F.
Knowles, Abiather J.
McGough, Owen

Merritt, John G.
Murphy, Charles J.
Ranney, Myron H.
Roosevelt, George W.
Smith, Joseph S.
Webb, James
Wheeler, Henry W.
Willcox, Orlando B.
Withington, William H.

Burnt Ordinary, Virginia
McKeever, Michael

Carrsville, Virginia
Sweatt, Benjamin

Carter's Farm, Virginia
Shanes, John

Catlett Station, Virginia
Batchelder, Richard N.

Cedar Creek, Virginia
Blunt, John W.
Crocker, Henry H.

Crocker, Ulric L.
Du Pont, Henry, A.
Goodrich, Edwin
Henry, William W.
Hough, Ira
Love, George M.
Lyon, Frederick A.
McGonnigle, Andrew J.
Parks, Henry Jeremiah
Reigle, Daniel P.
Scofield, David H.
Sweeney, James
Taylor, Richard
Thomas, Stephen
Tracy, Amasa A.
Walsh, John
Wambsgan, Martin
Wells, Thomas M.

Cedar Mountain, Virginia
Corliss, George W.
Younker, John L.

Cemetery Hill, Virginia
Bates, Delavan

Chamberlains Creek, Virginia
Hooper, William B.
Wilson, John

Chancellorsville, Virginia
Boody, Robert
Bradley, Thomas W.
Brannigan, Felix
Bucklyn, John K.
Chase, John F.
Cranston, William W.
Dilger, Hubert
Gion, Joseph
Goodman, William E.
Heermance, William L.
Heller, Henry
Jacobson, Eugene P.
Luty, Gotlieb
Miles, Nelson A.
Mulholland, St. Clair A.
O'Neill, Stephen
Oss, Albert
Sacriste, Louis J.
Sartwell, Henry
Seaman, Elisha B.
Sewell, William J.

Thompson, Thomas
Thomson, Clifford
Tracy, William G.

Chapel House Farm, Virginia
Wright, Robert

Chapin's Farm, Virginia
Barnes, William H.
Beaty, Powhatan
Belcher, Thomas
Brady, James
Bronson, James H.
Buchanan, George A.
Buck, F. Clarence
Edgerton, Nathan H.
Flanagan, Augustin
Fleetwood, Christian A.
Gardiner, James
Gasson, Richard
Grueb, George
Hawkins, Thomas R.
Hickock, Nathan E.
Hilton, Alfred B.
Holland, Milton M.
James, Miles
Johndro, Franklin
Kelly, Alexander
Kramer, Theodore L.
Laing, William
McKown, Nathaniel A.
Meagher, Thomas
Murphy, Thomas
Pinn, Robert
Ratcliff, Edward
Schiller, John
Shea, Joseph H.
Skellie, Ebenezer
Van Winkle, Edward (Edwin)
Veal, Charles
Wells, Henry S.

Charles City Crossroads, Virginia
Shambough, Charles

Charlottesville, Virginia
Boury, Richard

Chickahominy and Ashland, Virginia
Capron, Horace, Jr.

Cold Harbor, Virginia
Beatty, Alexander M.
Begley, Terrence
Boss, Orlando
Casey, David
Doody, Patrick
Henry, Guy V.
Hill, Edward
Seitzinger, James M.
Tinkham, Eugene M.
Williams, Le Roy

Corbin's Bridge, Virginia
Robertson, Robert S.

Crump's Creek, Virginia
Putnam, Edgar P.

Dabby's Mills, Virginia
Delaney, John C.
Sands, William
Smith, Francis M.

Davenport Bridge, Virginia
Arnold, Abraham K.
Deep Bottom, Virginia
Leonard, William E.

Deep Bottom, Virginia
Hardenbergh, Henry M.
Pickle, Alonzo H.

Deep Run, Virginia
Shellenberger, John S.

Dinwiddie Courthouse, Virginia
Boehm, Peter M.
King, Horatio C.

Drury's Bluff, Virginia
Cosgrove, Thomas
Gray, Robert A.
Kenyon, Charles
Lord, William
Mackie, John F.
Regan, Jeremiah

Dutch Gap Canal, Virginia
Thorn, Walter

Fair Oaks, Virginia
Forman, Alexander A.
French, Samuel S.
Grant, Gabriel

Place of Action

Haskell, Frank W.
Howard, Oliver O.
O'Beirne, James R.
Purcell, Hiram W.
Shafter, William R.

Fairfax, Virginia
Tompkins, Charles H.

Falling Waters, Virginia
Holton, Charles M.

Farmville, Virginia
Galloway, John
Ludgate, William

Fisher's Hill, Virginia
Connors, James
Creed, John
Moore, George G.
Rhodes, Sylvester D.
Whittier, Edward N.

Five Forks, Virginia
Benyaurd, William H.
Blackmar, Wilmon W.
Bonebrake, Henry G.
De Lavie, Hiram H.
Edwards, David
Everson, Adelbert
Fernald, Albert E.
Gardner, Charles N.
Grindlay, James G.
Kauss, August
Koogle, Jacob
Murphy, Thomas J.
Scott, John Wallace
Shipley, Robert F.
Stewart, Joseph
Winegar, William W.

Fort Fisher, Virginia
Littlefield, George H.

Fort Harrison, Virginia
Archer, Lester
Blucher, Charles
Clay, Cecil
Graul, William
Horne, Samuel B.
Hubbell, William S.
Johnson, Joseph E.

Fort Huger, Virginia
Stevens, Hazard

Fort Sedgwick, Virginia
Ilgenfritz, Charles H.

Fort Stedman, Virginia
Carter, Joseph F.
Deane, John M.
Gaylord, Levi B.
Howe, William H.
McDonald, George E.
Pinkham, Charles H.

Franklin, Virginia
Barton, Thomas
Breen, John
Lakin, Daniel
Peterson, Alfred
Smith, Edwin
Williams, John

Fredericksburg, Virginia
Adams, John G.B.
Beckwith, Wallace A.
Bliss, Zenas R.
Brown, Edward, Jr.
Cart, Jacob
Collis, Charles H.T.
Copp, Charles D.
Donoghue, Timothy
Frick, Jacob G.
Goodall, Francis H.
Harrington, Ephraim W.
Holehouse, James
Johnson, John
Keene, Joseph
Luther, James H.
Maxham, Lowell M.
Maynard, George H.
Palmer, John G.
Petty, Philip
Plunkett, Thomas
Quay, Matthew S.
Schubert, Martin
Shaler, Alexander
Shiel, John
Woodward Evan M.

Fredericksburg Heights, Virginia
McVeane, John P.

Front Royal, Virginia
Kelly, Thomas
Leslie, Frank

Mandy, Harry J.
Taylor, William

Gaines Mill, Virginia
Butterfield, Daniel
Hall, Henry Seymour
Hopkins, Charles F.
Moffitt, John H.
Sidman, George E.
Von Vegesack, Ernest
Williams, George C.

Glendale, Virginia
Howard, Henderson C.
Levy, Benjamin

Gravelly Run, Virginia
O'Connor, Albert
Sickles, William H.

Hampton Roads, Virginia
Williams, Peter

Hanover Courthouse, Virginia
Burke, Thomas

Hatcher's Run, Virginia
Cadwallader, Abel G.
Caldwell, Daniel
Coey, James
Day, Charles
Evans, Ira H.
Mangam, Richard C.
Murphy, Daniel J.
Orr, Charles A.
Plimley, William
Raub, Jacob F.
Sagelhusrt, John C.
Smith, Alonzo
Spillane, Timothy
Thaxter, Sidney W.
Thompson, John
Vanderslice, John M.
White, Adam
Woodruff, Alonzo

Haws Shops, Virginia
Christiancy, James I.

Jefferson, Virginia
Dougherty, Michael

Jetersville, Virginia
Lane, Morgan D.

Laurel Hill, Virginia
Luce, Moses A.
Phelps, Charles E.
Robinson, John C.

Lees Mills, Virginia
Holton, Edward A.
Pingree, Samuel E.
Scott, Julian A.

Lewis' Farm, Virginia
Pearson, Alfred L.

Luray, Virginia
Baybutt, Philip

Lynchburg, Virginia
Mostoller, John W.

Malvern Hill, Virginia
Osborne, William H.
Rafferty, Peter
Ripley, William Y.W.
Tobin, John M.
Wilson, John M.

Manassas (First), Virginia
Ames, Adelbert

McDowell, Virginia
Morey, Delano

Mason's Hill, Virginia
Traynor, Andrew

Mathias Point, Virginia
Williams, John

Mine Run, Virginia
Scheibner, Martin E.

Murfrees Station, Virginia
Lonsway, Joseph

Namozine Church, Virginia
Custer, Thomas W.

Nansemond River, Virginia
Jordan, Robert
Woods, Samuel

New Market, Virginia
Burns, James M.

New Market Heights, Virginia
Harris, James H.

Newbys Crossroads, Virginia
Hastings, Smith H.
Woodruff, Carle A.

Nineveh, Virginia
Adams, James F.
Shoemaker, Levi

North Anna River, Virginia
Keele, Joseph
Kirk, Jonathan C.
Murphy, Michael C.

North Fork, Virginia
Hills, William G.

Opequan Creek, Virginia
Lunt, Alphonso M.

Paines Crossroads, Virginia
Davidsizer, John A.
Elliott, Alexander
Landis, James P.
Locke, Lewis
Peirsol, James K.
Schmal, George W.
Stewart, George W.
Streile, Christian
Warfel, Henry C.
Young, Andrew J.

Peeble's Farm, Virginia
Schwan, Theodore

Pegram House, Virginia
Hadley, Osgood T.

Peninsula, Virginia
Hunterson, John C.

Petersburg, Virginia
Allen, Abner P.
Apple, Andrew O.
Appleton, William H.
Babcock, William J.
Barber, James A.
Blackwood, William R.D.
Blickensderfer, Milton
Boutwell, John W.
Brant, William
Briggs, Elijah A.
Brosnan, John
Brown, Jeremiah Z.
Buffington, John E.
Camp, Carlton N.
Catlin, Isaac S.
Chambers, Joseph B.
Chandler, Henry F.
Clark, James G.
Corcoran, John
Curtis, Josiah M.
Davidson, Andrew
De Puy, Charles H.
Dickey, William D.
Dodd, Robert F.
Dolloff, Charles W.
Dorsey, Decatur
Ennis, Charles D.
Ewing, John C.
Fesq, Frank
Fisher, Joseph
Fox, William R.
Gardner, Robert J.
Gibbs, Wesley
Gould, Charles G.
Gwynne, Nathaniel
Hack, Lester G.
Haight, Sidney
Harbourne, John H.
Harmon, Amzi D.
Havron, John H.
Hawkins, Gardner C.
Highland, Patrick
Hill, James
Hoffman, Thomas W.
Hogan, Franklin
Homan, Conrad
Hottenstine, Solomon J.
Houghton, Charles H.
Howard, James
Hunter, Charles A.
James, Isaac
Jamieson, Walter
Kane, John
Knight, Charles H.
Leonard, Edwin
Lewis, Samuel E.
Lilley, John
Loyd, George
Ludwig, Carl
Lutes, Franklin W.
Marquette, Charles
Mathews, William H.

Matthews, John C.
Matthews, Milton
McAlwee, Benjamin
McCauslin, Joseph
McGraw, Thomas
McKee, George
McMillen, Francis M.
Merrill, Augustus
Meyer, Henry C.
Mitchell, Theodore
Molbone, Archibald
Monaghan, Patrick
Murphy, James T.
Oliver, Charles
Orr, Robert L.
Parker, Thomas
Plowman, George H.
Potter, George W.
Reeder, Charles A.
Reid, Robert
Rowe, Henry W.
Sargent, Jackson
Schneider, George
Shubert, Frank
Simons, Charles J.
Sperry, William J.
Strausbaugh, Bernard A.
Swift, Harlan J.
Thatcher, Charles M.
Thompkins, George W.
Thompson, Freeman C.
Tucker, Allen
Tucker, Jacob R.
Van Matre, Joseph
Wageman, John H.
Walton, George W.
Welch, Richard
Welsh, James
Wilkins, Leander A.
Wilson, Francis A.
Wright, Albert D.
Young, Benjamin F.

Piedmont, Virginia
Evans, Thomas
Snedden, James
Stahel, Julius

Port Republic, Virginia
Gray, John

Raccoon Ford, Virginia
Packard, Loron F.

Rappahannock Station, Virginia
Breyer, Charles
Morrill, Walter G.
Roberts, Otis O.
White, J. Henry

Reams Station, Virginia
Ginley, Patrick
Rohm, Ferdinand F.
Whitaker, Edward W.

Richmond, Virginia
Dow, George P.
Gregg, Joseph O.
Kaiser, John
Little, Henry F.W.
Robie, George F.
Tilton, William

Rowanty Creek, Virginia
Buckingham, David E.
Smith, S. Rodmond

Sailors Creek, Virginia
Benjamin John F.
Bennett, Orren
Boon, Hugh P.
Brest, Lewis F.
Bringle, Andrew
Calkin, Ivers S.
Chapman, John
Clapp, Albert A.
Connell, Trustrim
Cunningham, Francis M.
Davis, Thomas
Dockum, Warren C.
Eddy, Samuel E.
Evans, Coron D.
Ford, George W.
Gifford, Banjamin
Gribben, James H.
Hagerty, Asel
Hawthorne, Harris S.
Haynes, Asbury F.
Hoffman, Henry
Holmes, William T.
Houlton, William
Hughey, John
Jordan, Absalom
Kenyon, Samuel P.
Keough, John

Kimball, Joseph
Kline, Harry
Lanfare, Aaron S.
Larimer, Smith
Mattocks, Charles P.
McElhinny, Samuel O.
McWhorter, Walter F.
Menter, John W.
Miller, Frank
Morris, William
Mundell, Walter L.
Neville, Edwin M.
Norton, Elliott M.
Norton, John R.
Norton, Llewellyn P.
Payne, Irvin C.
Pitman, George J.
Porter, William
Richardson, William R.
Riddell, Rudolph
Savacool, Edwin F.
Shanan, Emisire
Shepard, William
Simmons, John
Southard, David
Taggart, Charles A.
Titus, Charles
Tompkins, Aaron B.
Wilson, Charles E.
Woods, Daniel A.

St. Mary's Church, Virginia
Smith, Charles H.
Weir, Henry C.

Salem Heights, Virginia
Butterfield, Frank G.
Cummings, Amos J.
Gilmore, John C.
Grant, Lewis A.
Hall, Francis B.
McAdams, Peter
Wheeler, Daniel D.

Savage Station, Virginia
Quinlan, James

Shenandoah Valley, Virginia
Cumpston, James M.
Hart, William E.

Shepherdstown Ford, Virginia
Burke, Daniel W.

Sinking Creek Valley, Virginia
Powell, William H.

Smithfield, Virginia
Harris, Moses

South Side Railroad, Virginia
Corliss, Stephen P.

Spotsylvania, Virginia
Alber, Frederick
Ammerman, Robert W.
Barker, Nathaniel C.
Beddows, Richard
Beech, John P.
Bishop, Francis A.
Burk, E. Michael
Clarke, Dayton P.
Clausen, Charles H.
Fall, Charles S.
Fasnacht, Charles H.
Freeman, Archibald
Harris, George W.
Jones, William
Kindig, John M.
Kinsey, John
Marsh, Albert
McAnally, Charles
McFall, Daniel
McHale, Alexander U.
Mitchell, Alexander H.
Morgan, Lewis
Morse, Benjamin
Noll, Conrad
Noyes, William W.
Robbins, Augustus I.
Robinson, Thomas
Rossbach, Valentine
Rounds, Lewis A.
Russell, Charles L.
Schlachter, Philipp
Seaver, Thomas O.
Thompson, Charles A.
Tracy, Charles H.
Weeks, John H.
Westerhold, William
Wilcox, William H.

Wilson, Christopher W.
Wisner, Lewis S.

Staunton River Bridge, Virginia
Ward, Nelson W.

Stony Creek Bridge, Virginia
Hickey, Dennis W.

Stony Creek Station, Virginia
Sowers, Michael

Sutherland Station, Virginia
Phillips, Josiah

Swifts Creek, Virginia
Coughlin, John

Thoroughfare Gap, Virginia
Rhodes, Julius D.

Todd's Tavern, Virginia
Nutting, Lee

Trevilian Station, Virginia
Farnsworth, Herbert E.
Furness, Frank
Kennedy, John
Preston, Noble D.
Rodenbough, Theophilus F.
Williston, Edward B.

Vaughn Road, Virginia
Clancy, James T.

Warrenton, Virginia
Clark, John W.

Warwick Courthouse, Virginia
Smith, David L.

Waterloo Bridge, Virginia
Tribe, John

Waynesboro, Virginia
Anderson, Charles W.
Bickford, Henry H.
Bliss, George N.
Bruton, Christopher C.
Carman, Warren
Compson, Hartwell B.

Crowley, Michael
Goheen, Charles A.
Harvey, Harry
Kelly, Daniel
Kuder, Andrew
Ladd, George
Madison, James
Miller, John
Niven, Robert
O'Brien, Peter

Weldon Railroad, Virginia
Anderson, Frederick C.
Brown, Charles
Cayer, Ovila
Drury, James
Ellis, Horace
Hughes, Oliver
Jennings, James T.
Martin, Sylvester H.
Reed, George W.
Shilling, John
Smith, Richard
Taylor, Joseph

White Oak Road, Virginia
Thompson, Allen
Thompson, James

White Oak Swamp, Virginia
Bronner, August F.
King, Rufus, Jr.
McMahon, Martin T.
Uhrl, George

Wilderness, Virginia
Bingham, Henry H.
Brown, Henri Le Ferve
Buckles, Abram J.
Burk, Thomas
Cohn, Abraham
Cutts, James M.
De Lacey, Patrick
English, Edmund
Evans, James R.
Grace, Peter
Hill, Henry
Karpeles, Leopold
Kemp, Joseph
Lower, Cyrus B.
Morse, Charles E.
Opel, John N.

Place of Action

Patterson, John H.
Rich, Carlos H.
Rought, Stephen
Swap, Jacob E.
Thompson, William P.
Tracy, Benjamin F.
Young, James M.

Williamsburg, Virginia
Conboy, Martin
Coyne, John N.
Dillon, Michael A.
Mindil, George W.

Winchester, Virginia
Bowen, Chester B.
Cole, Gabriel
Downs, Henry W.
Durham, James R.
Fox, Henry M.
Lorish, Andrew J.
Lyman, Joel H.
McEnroe, Patrick H.

Meach, George E.
Patterson, John T.
Reynolds, George
Robinson, Elbridge
Ryan, Peter J.
Schmidt, Conrad
Schoonmaker, James M.
Seston, Charles H.
Sterling, John T.

Woodstock, Virginia
Campbell, James A.
Hanford, Edward R.

Yellow Tavern, Virginia
Rutherford, John T.

Fort Stevens, Washington, D.C.
Wray, William J.

Greenbrier River, West Virginia
Capehart, Henry

Harpers Ferry, West Virginia
Fout, Frederick W.
Saxton, Rufus

Moorefield, West Virginia
Kerr, Thomas R.
Slusher, Henry C.

For Actions Over Time
Benjamin Samuel N.
Dorman, John
Fallon, Thomas T.
Haight, John H.
Orbansky, David
Ortega, John
Sullivan, Timothy
Walker, Dr. Mary E.
Woodall, William H.

Listing by Act of Heroism

Advancing the Colors
Adams, John G.B.
Allen, Abner P.
Apple, Andrew O.
Archer, Lester
Babcock, William J.
Banks, George L.
Barker, Nathaniel C.
Belcher, Thomas
Bell, James B.
Blucher, Charles
Brown, Edward, Jr.
Buckles, Abram J.
Cadwallader, Abel G.
Carney, William H.
Clark, Harrison
Cleveland, Charles F.
Copp, Charles D.
Corliss, George W.
Corliss, Stephen P.
Curtis, Josiah M.
Day, Charles
Dorsey, Decatur
Durham, John S.
Edgerton, Nathan H.
Elison, James M.
English, Edmund
Fisher, Joseph
Flanagan, Augustin
Fleetwood, Christian
Freeman, William H.
Frick, Jacob G.
Gasson, Richard

Artist's rendition of the storming of Fort Donelson, Tennessee. Voltaire Twombly received the only Medal of Honor awarded for the fighting that took place there. Twombly served as a corporal in the 2nd Iowa Infantry, and gallantly advanced the colors of the regiment after three color bearers had been shot down (U.S. Army War College).

Gilmore, John C.
Ginley, Patrick
Graham, Thomas N.
Graul, William
Harrington, Ephraim W.
Higgins, Thomas J.
Highland, Patrick
Hilton, Alfred B.
Howard, James
Hunter, Charles A.
Ilgenfritz, Charles H.
Jamieson, Walter
Kane, John
Keene, Joseph
Kirby, Dennis T.
Libaire, Adolphe
Littlefield, George H.
MacArthur, Arthur, Jr.
Marquette, Charles
Matthews, John C.
Maxham, Lowell M.
McCauslin, Joseph
McKee, George
Moffitt, John H.
Morse, Charles E.
Munsell, Harvey M.
Murphy, Dennis J.F.
Nolan, John J.
O'Brien, Henry D.
O'Donnell, Menomen
O'Neill, Stephen
Orr, Robert L.
Parker, Thomas
Paul, William H.
Pearson, Alfred L.
Petty, Philip
Plunkett, Thomas
Sargent, Jackson
Schneider, George
Schubert, Martin
Seitzinger, James M.
Seston, Charles H.
Skellie, Ebenezer
Taylor, Henry H.
Thompson, John
Tracy, Benjamin F.
Tucker, Allen
Twombly, Voltaire P.
Veal, Charles
Wilson, Charles E.

Capturing Artillery

Beaumont, Eugene B.
Bringle, Andrew
Buchanan, George A.
Corcoran, John
Fox, William R.
Gray, John
Healey, Joseph
Lonergan, John
Magee, William
Norton, Llewellyn P.
Peck, Cassius
Reeder, Charles A.
Rhodes, Sylvester D.
Shanes, John
Sperry, William J.
Thomas, Hampton S.
Walker, James C.
Whittier, Edward N.
Wilson, Francis A.

Capturing Enemy Prisoners

Alber, Frederick
Allen, James
Anderson, Everett W.
Baldwin, Frank D.
Barrick, Jesse T.
Betts, Charles M.
Blodgett, Welis H.
Capehart, Charles E.
Carter, Joseph F.
Coffey, Robert J.
Cosgrove, Thomas
Cranston, William W.
Crocker, Henry H.
Curtis, John C.
Dunlavy, James
Elliott, Russell C.
Hart, John W.
Hart, William E.
Hawthorne, Harris S.
Hedges, Joseph
Heller, Henry
Hill, James
Hooker, George W.
Hubbell, William S.
Inscho, Leonidus H.
Irsch, Francis
Irwin, Patrick
Johndro, Franklin

Kelley, Leverett M.
Kirk, Jonathan C.
Knight, Charles H.
Kramer, Theodore L.
Luther, James H.
Lyman, Joel H.
Mathews, William H.
McFall, Daniel
Mears, George W.
Merrill, Augustus
Mills, Frank W.
Morey, Delano
O'Connor, Albert
Palmer, George H.
Parks, Henry Jeremiah
Pentzer, Patrick H.
Plimley, William
Powell, William H.
Putnam, Edgar P.
Richey, William E.
Roush, J. Levy
Rutherford, John T.
Ryan, Peter J.
Seaman, Elisha B.
Sickles, William H.
Simmons, Charles J.
Smith, Richard
Smith, Thaddeus S.
Spurling, Andrew B.
Sterling, John T.
Sturgeon, James K.
Swift, Harlan
Taylor, Joseph
Thackrah, Benjamin
Thompson, Thomas
Wilhelm, George
Wright, William
Young, Cavalry M.

Capturing an Enemy Flag

Adams, James F.
Ammerman, Robert W.
Anderson, Charles W.
Anderson, Frederick C.
Anderson, Thomas
Bacon, Elijah W.
Bates, Norman F.
Baybutt, Philip
Bebb, Edward J.
Begley, Terrence

Act of Heroism 279

A Federal artillery battery in action during the battle of Fredericksburg, Virginia. Forty-three Medals of Honor were presented to men who either captured enemy artillery or saved their own from being taken (U.S. Army War College).

Benjamin, John F.
Bennett, Orren
Birdsall, Horatio L.
Bishop, Francis A.
Blickensderfer, Milton
Bonebrake, Henry G.
Boon, Hugh P.
Boury, Richard
Bowen, Chester B.
Box, Thomas J.
Brady, James
Brant, William
Bras, Edgar A.
Brest, Lewis F.
Brewer, William J.
Briggs, Elijah A.
Brown, Charles
Brown, John Harties
Brown, Morris, Jr.
Brown, Robert B.
Bruton, Christopher C.
Buckley, Denis
Burk, E. Michael
Burke, Thomas
Caldwell, Daniel
Calkin, Ivers S.
Callahan, John H.
Carey, Hugh
Carman, Warren
Cart, Jacob
Chambers, Joseph B.

Chapman, John
Clapp, Albert A.
Clopp, John E.
Clute, George W.
Cole, Gabriel
Collins, Harrison
Collins, Thomas D.
Colwell, Oliver
Compson, Hartwell B.
Connell, Trustrim
Connors, James
Cosgriff, Richard H.
Coyne, John N.
Creed, John
Crocker, Ulric L.
Crowley, Michael
Cullen, Thomas
Cumpston, James M.
Cunningham, Francis M.
Custer, Thomas W.
Davidsizer, John A.
Davis, Harry
Davis, John
Davis, Joseph
Davis, Thomas
De Castro, Joseph H.
De Lacey, Patrick
De Lavie, Hiram H.
Dockum, Warren C.
Dolloff, Charles W.
Donaldson, John

Dorley, August
Edwards, David
Elliott, Alexander
Ellis, Horace
Evans, Coron D.
Evans, Thomas
Everson, Adelbert
Ewing, John C.
Fall, Charles S.
Falls, Benjamin F.
Fanning, Nicholas
Fasnacht, Charles H.
Fernald, Albert E.
Fesq, Frank
Flynn, Christopher
Ford, George W.
Fox, Henry M.
Freeman, Archibald
Funk, West
Gardner, Charles N.
Garrett, William
Gaunt, John C.
Gause, Isaac
Gere, Thomas P.
Gibbs, Wesley
Gifford, Benjamin
Gilligan, Edward L.
Goettel, Philip
Goheen, Charles A.
Green, George
Greenawalt, Abraham

Greig, Theodore W.
Gribben, James H.
Grindlay, James G.
Hack, Lester G.
Hagerty, Asel
Hall, Newton H.
Hanford, Edward R.
Hanscom, Moses C.
Harbourne, John H.
Hardenbergh, Henry M.
Harmon, Amzi D.
Harris, George W.
Harvey, Harry
Haynes, Asbury F.
Hays, John H.
Hickok, Nathan E.
Higby, Charles
Hill, James
Hincks, William B.
Hoffman, Henry
Hogan, Franklin
Holcomb, Daniel I.
Holmes, William T.
Holton, Charles M.
Horan, Thomas
Hottenstine, Solomon J.
Hough, Ira
Houlton, William
Howard, Hiram R.
Hudson, Aaron R.
Hughes, Oliver
Hughey, John
James, Isaac
Jellison, Benjamin H.
Jennings, James T.
Johnson, Samuel
Jones, William
Jordan, Absalom
Josselyn, Simeon T.
Judge, Francis W.
Kaltenbach, Luther
Kappesser, Peter
Kauss, August
Kelley George V.
Kelly, Daniel
Kelly, Thomas
Kemp, Joseph
Kenyon, Samuel P.
Keough, John
Kerr, Thomas R.
Kimball, Joseph

Kindig, John M.
Kline, Harry
Koogle, Jacob
Kuder, Andrew
Kuder, Jeremiah
Ladd, George
Landis, James P.
Lane, Morgan D.
Lanfare, Aaron S.
Larimer, Smith
Leonard, William E.
Leslie, Frank
Lilley, John
Locke, Lewis
Lorish, Andrew J.
Love, George M.
Loyd, George
Lutes, Franklin W.
Lyon, Frederick A.
Mahoney, Jeremiah
Mandy, Harry J.
Mangam, Richard C.
Manning, Joseph S.
Marsh, Albert
Marsh, Charles H.
Matthews, Milton
Mattingly, Henry B.
May, William
Mayberry, John B.
McAnally, Charles
McCarren, Bernard
McCleary, Charles H.
McConnell, Samuel
McDonald, George E.
McElhinny, Samuel O.
McEnroe, Patrick H.
McHale, Alexander U.
McKeen, Nineveh S.
McKown, Nathaniel A.
McMillen, Francis M.
McVeane, John P.
McWhorter, Walter F.
Meach, George E.
Menter, John W.
Merrifield, James K.
Merritt, John G.
Miller, Frank
Miller, Henry A.
Miller, James P.
Miller, John
Miller, John

Mitchell, Alexander H.
Mitchell, Theodore
Moore, George G.
Moore, Wilbur F.
Morgan, Richard H.
Morris, William
Morse, Benjamin
Mundell, Walter L.
Murphy, Daniel J.
Murphy, John P.
Murphy, Thomas
Murphy, Thomas J.
Neville, Edwin M.
Newman, William H.
Niven, Robert
Norton, Elliott, M.
Norton, John R.
O'Brien, Peter
Oliver, Charles
Opel, John N.
Orth, Jacob G.
Parks, James W.
Payne, Irvin C.
Peirsol, James K.
Phillips, Josiah
Pinkham, Charles H.
Pitman, George J.
Potter, Norman F.
Ramsbottom, Alfred
Read, Morton A.
Rebmann, George F.
Reed, George W.
Reid, Robert
Reigle, Daniel P.
Reynolds, George
Richmond, James
Ricksecker, John H.
Riley, Thomas
Roberts, Otis O.
Robinson, John H.
Robinson, Thomas
Rood, Oliver P.
Rought, Stephen
Rounds, Lewis A.
Rowe, Henry W.
Russell, Charles L.
Sancrainte, Charles F.
Sands, William
Savacool, Edwin F.
Schlachter, Philipp
Schmal, George W.

Schorn, Charles
Scofield, David H.
Scott, John Wallace
Shanan, Emisire
Shambough, Charles
Shellenberger, John S.
Shepard, William
Sherman, Marshall
Shields, Bernard
Shilling, John
Shipley, Robert F.
Shoemaker, Levi
Shopp, George J.
Shubert, Frank
Simmons, John
Simmons, William T.
Sloan, Andrew J.
Smith, Alonzo
Smith, Otis W.
Southard, David
Sova, Joseph E.
Stewart, George W.
Stewart, Joseph
Stickels, Joseph
Stokes, George
Streile, Christian
Sweeney, James
Taggart, Charles A.
Taylor, Richard
Thompkins, George W.
Thompson, James B.
Thompson, William P.
Tibbetts, Andrew W.
Tompkins, Aaron B.
Tyrrell, George William
Vifquain, Victor
Wall, Jerry
Waller, Francis A.
Walling, William H.
Warfel, Henry C.
Weeks, John H.
Welch, George W.
Welch, Richard
Wells, Thomas M.
Westerhold, William
White, Adam
Whitmore, John
Wiley, James
Wilson, Christopher W.
Winegar, William W.
Woodall, William H.

Woodbury. Eri D.
Woods, Daniel A.
Woodward, Evan M.
Wright, Albert D.
Young, Andrew J.
Young, Benjamin F.

Capturing an Enemy Vessel

O'Brien, Oliver
Warren, David
Weston, John F.

Carrying Water to Comrades

Hanna, Marcus A.
White, J. Henry

Delivering Messages Under Fire

Gillespie, George L.
Grebe, M.R. William
Hadley, Cornelius M.
Horne, Samuel B.
Howard, Squire E
Keele, Joseph
King, Horatio C.
Murphy, Thomas C.
Phisterer, Frederick
Postles, James Parke
Province, George
Rowland, Archibald H., Jr.
Schwenk, Martin
Shepard, Irwin
Swanson, John
Webb, James
Whitaker, Edward W.
Woram, Charles B.
Younker, John L.

Escaping from the Enemy

Traynor, Andrew

Fighting in the Big Shanty, Georgia, Raid

Bensinger, William
Brown, Wilson W.
Buffum, Robert
Dorsey, Daniel A.

Hawkins, Martin J.
Knight, William J.
Mason, Elihu H.
Parrot, Jacob
Pittinger, William
Porter, John R.
Reddick, William H.
Robertson, Samuel
Ross, Marion A.
Scott, John M.
Slavens, Samuel
Smith, James (Ovid)
Wilson, John A.
Wollam, John
Wood, Mark

Killing a Confederate General

Clancy, James T.
Lucas, George W.

Killing the Murderer of Colonel Ellsworth

Brownell, Francis E.

Pressing an Attack

Anderson, Marion T.
Appleton, William H.
Archer, James W.
Arnold, Abraham K.
Baird, Absalom
Barnum, Henry
Bates, Delavan
Beaty, Powhatan
Beebe, William S.
Benyaurd, William H.
Bingham, Henry H.
Black, John C.
Blackmar, Wilmon W.
Bliss, George N.
Blunt, John W.
Boehm, Peter M.
Bonnaffon, Sylvester, Jr.
Boynton, Henry V.
Bronson, James H.
Brown, Jeremiah Z.
Butterfield, Daniel
Carey, James L.
Carter, John J.
Cayer, Ovila
Chamberlain, Joshua L.

Christiancy, James I.
Cilley, Clinton A.
Clay, Cecil
Cockley, David L.
Coey, James
Collis, Charles H.T.
Conboy, Martin
Cook, John H.
Curtis, Newton Martin
Cutcheon, Byron M.
Davis, Charles C.
Denning, Lorenzo
Di Cesnola, Louis P.
Doody, Patrick
Dougherty, Michael
Drake, James M.
Durham James R.
Embler, Andrew H.
Ennis, Charles D.
Estes, Lewellyn G.
Falconer, John A.
Furman, Chester S.
Gardner, Robert J.
Godley, Leonidas M.
Gould, Charles G.
Grant, Lewis A.
Harris, Moses
Haskell, Frank W.
Hatch, John P.
Henry, Guy V.
Hill, Edward
Holland, Lemuel F.
Holland, Milton M.
Howard, Oliver O.
Hyde, Thomas W.
Johnson, Joseph E.
Johnson, Wallace W.
Kendall, William W.
Kloth, Charles H.
Kretsinger, George
Lawton, Henry W.
Lewis, Samuel E.
Ludgate, William
Marsh, George
Mattocks, Charles P.
McGonnigle, Andrew J.
McGuire, Patrick
McKeever, Michael
Meagher, Thomas
Merriam, Henry C.
Miller, William E.

Mindil, George W.
Molbone, Archibald
Morrill, Walter G.
Mostoller, John W.
Murphy, Robinson B.
Nugent, Christopher
Nutting, Lee
Palmer, William J.
Payne, Thomas H.L.
Pennypacker, Galusha
Phelps, Charles E.
Pingree, Samuel E.
Pinn, Robert
Pond, George F.
Porter, Ambrose
Post, Philip Sidney
Potter, George W.
Preston, Noble D.
Putnam, Winthrop D.
Quinlan, James
Ratcliff, Edward
Ripley, William Y.W.
Robinson, John C.
Russell, Milton
Schofield, John M.
Schoonmaker, James M.
Seaver, Thomas O.
Sellers, Alfred J.
Shaler, Alexander
Stahel, Julius
Stanley, David S.
Stevens, Hazard
Swayne, Wager
Toffey, John J.
Tompkins, Charles H.
Vanderslice, John M.
Van Winkle, Edward
   (Edwin)
Veazey, Wheelock G.
Von Vegesack, Ernest
Webb, Alexander S.
Wells, Henry S.
Wells, William
Wheaton, Lloyd
White, Patrick H.
Willcox, Orlando B.
Williamson, James A.

Procuring Ammunition

Bradley, Thomas W.
Brown, Henri Le Ferve

Chamberlain, Orville T.
Downs, Henry W.
Engle, James E.
Follett, Joseph L.
Furness, Frank
Raymond, William H.
Ringold, Edward
Whitney, William G.
Williams, Elwood N.

Sacrificing One's Safety to Save a Comrade

Anderson, Robert
Avery, James
Baker, Charles
Barton, Thomas
Beatty, Alexander M.
Beyer, Hillary
Bieger, Charles
Blackwood, William R.D.
Boody, Robert
Boss, Orlando
Boutwell, John W.
Breyer, Charles
Brinn, Andrew
Brosnan, John
Brown, Uriah
Brush, George W.
Burk, Thomas
Camp, Carlton N.
Campbell, James A.
Capehart, Henry
Carmin, Isaac H.
Caruana, Orlando E.
Chandler, Stephen E.
Connor, Thomas
Corson, Joseph K.
Curran, Richard
Darrough, John S.
Davis, John
Delaney, John C.
Dodd, Robert F.
Dodds, Edward E.
Donnelly, John
Donoghue, Timothy
Downey, William
Duffey, John
Duncan, James K.L.
Eddy, Samuel E.
Ellsworth, Thomas

Act of Heroism

The Battle of Wilson's Creek. A contemporary artist's depiction of the fighting where Nicholas Bouquet, Lorenzo Immel, John Schofield, William Wherry, and Clay Wood won their Medals of Honor (Orville J. Victor, The History, Civil, Political, and Military of the Southern Rebellion from Its Incipient Stages to Its Close, New York: James D. Torrey, Publishers, 1861).

Enderlin, Richard
Farnsworth, Herbert E.
Ferrier, Daniel T.
Fox, Nicholas
Freeman, Henry B.
Frisbee, John B.
Gifford, David L.
Goodall, Francis H.
Goodrich, Edwin
Grace, Peter
Grant, Gabriel
Gray, Robert A.
Gresser, Ignatz
Grimshaw, Samuel
Griswold, Luke M.
Haight, John H.
Hall, Francis B.
Hallock, Nathan M.
Hanks, Joseph
Harding, Thomas
Harris, John
Haskell, Marcus M.
Herington, Pitt B.
Hills, William G.
Hopkins, Charles F.
Horsfall, William H.
Horton, Lewis A.

Huskey, Michael
Ingalls, Lewis J.
Irving, Thomas
Johnson, Henry
Jones, John
Kenyon, John S.
Kephart, James
Kiggins, John
Knowles, Abiather J.
Langbein, J.C. Julius
Lawson, Gaines
Lewis, Dewitt Clinton
Livingston, Josiah O.
Logan, Hugh
Lord, William
Luce, Moses A.
Madden, Michael
Mayes, William B.
Maynard, George H.
McAdams, Peter
McDonald, John Wade
McKay, Charles W.
Meyer, Henry C.
Mills, Charles
Moore, Daniel B.
Moore, George
Morrison, Francis

Murphy, Charles J.
Newman, Marcellus J.
Nibbe, John H.
Noble, Daniel
Orr, Charles A.
Patterson, John H.
Patterson, John T.
Pickle, Alonzo H.
Pipes, James
Power, Albert
Prentice, Joseph R.
Purman, James J.
Ranney, George E.
Rich, Carlos H.
Robinson, Elbridge
Rohm, Ferdinand F.
Rountry, John
Rutter, James M.
Sagelhurst, John C.
Scanlan, Patrick
Scheibner, Martin E.
Schmidt, Conrad
Schmidt, William
Schwan, Theodore
Scott, Julian A.
Seward, Richard E.
Shea, Joseph H.

Shiel, John
Slusher, Henry C.
Smith, Charles H.
Smith, Francis M.
Storey, John H.R.
Surles, William H.
Sweatt, Joseph G.
Tabor, William S.
Taylor, George
Thorn, Walter
Tinkham, Eugene M.
Toban, James W.
Tomlin, Andrew J.
Torgler, Ernst
Tracy, Amasa A.
Tracy, Charles H.
Treat, Howell B.
Tremain, Henry E.
Vance, Wilson
Wagg, Maurice
Walker, Dr. Mary E.
Walton, George W.
Ward, Nelson W.
Webber, Alason P.
Weeks, Charles H.
Weir, Henry C.
Welch, Stephen
Wheeler, Henry W.
Whitehead, John M.
Whitman, Frank M.
Williams, Le Roy
Withington, William H.
Woodruff, Alonzo
Woods, Samuel
Yeager, Jacob F.
Young, Horatio N.
Young, James M.

Saving Artillery from Capture
Anderson, Peter
Bennett, Orson W.
Boquet, Nicholas
Bucklyn John K.
Carlisle, Casper R.
Chase, John F.
Clausen, Charles H.
Coughlin, John
Cummings, Amos J.
Fassett, John B.
Hastings, Smith H.

Henry, William W.
Knox, Edward M.
Ludwig, Carl
Marland, William
McGough, Owen
Pike, Edward M.
Porter, Horace
Sacriste, Louis J.
Smith, Joseph S.
Smith, Wilson
Starkins, John H.
Uhrl, George
Woodruff, Carle A.

Saving the Command
Batchelder, Richard N.
Catlin, Isaac S.
Clark, Charles A.
Clark, John W.
Clark, William A.
Davidson, Andrew
Dilger, Hubert
Du Pont, Henry A.
Farquhar, John M.
Flannigan, James
Fox, Henry
Galloway, John
Hapeman, Douglas
Haring, Abram P.
Heermance, William L.
Herron, Francis J.
Hyland, John
Hymer, Samuel
Kennedy, John
Mulholland, St. Clair A.
Peck, Theodore S.
Pond, James B.
Porter, William
Robbins, Augustus I.
Rossbach, Valentine
Sprague, John W.
Steele, John W.
Swift, Frederic W.

Saving the Regimental Colors
Allen, Nathaniel
Beddows, Richard
Bickford, Henry H.
Brandle, Joseph E.
Burns, James M.

Carr, Franklin
Casey, David
Conner, Richard
Cox, Robert M.
Crosier, William H.H.
Davis, Freeman
Ditzenback, John
Dore, George E.
Dougall, Allan H.
Drury, James
Evans, James R.
Ferrell, John H.
Goodman, William E.
Hadley, Osgood T.
Hawkins, Thomas R.
Holton, Edward A.
Homan, Conrad
Kinsey, John
Levy, Benjamin
Lunt, Alphonso M.
Madison, James
Monaghan, Patrick
Myers, George S.
Noll, Conrad
Plant, Henry C.
Platt, George C.
Plowman, George H.
Purcell, Hiram W.
Ranney, Myron H.
Roosevelt, George W.
Savage, Auzella
Scott, Alexander
Smith, Andrew Jackson
Strausbaugh, Bernard A.
Tanner, Charles B.
Thompson, Charles A.
Tozier, Andrew J.
Walsh, John
Wambsgan, Martin
Welsh, James
Wilkins, Leander A.

Scouting the Enemy, or Behind Enemy Lines
Brannigan, Felix
Bruner, Louis J.
Dillon, Michael A.
Evans, Ira H.
Finkenbiner, Henry S.
Gion, Joseph

Act of Heroism

Hesseltine, Francis S.
Hibson, Joseph C.
Hunterson, John C.
Jacobson, Eugene P.
Keen, Joseph S.
Luty, Gotlieb
Martin, Sylvester H.
Nichols, Henry C.
Richardson, William R.
Rockefeller, Charles M.
Thompson, Allen
Thompson, James
Thomson, Clifford
Tracy, William G.
Williams, William H.

Serving After Expiration of Enlistment
Cooke, Walter H.
Hartranft, John F.
Quay, Matthew S.
Thaxter, Sidney W.

Showing Gallantry Under Fire
Ahearn, Michael
Albert, Christian
Ames, Adelbert
Anderson, Bruce
Angling, John
Archinal, William
Armstrong, Clinton L.
Arther, Matthew
Asten, Charles
Atkinson, Thomas E.
Avery, William B.
Ayers, David
Ayers, John G.K.
Baldwin, Charles
Ballen, Frederick
Barber, James A.
Barnes, William H.
Barnum, James
Barrell, Charles L.
Barringer, William
Barry, Augustus
Barter, Gurdon, H.
Bass, David L.
Bazaar, Philip
Beaufort, Jean J.

Beckwith, Wallace A.
Beech, John P.
Bell, George
Benedict, George G.
Benjamin, Samuel N.
Betham, Asa
Bibber, Charles J.
Bickford, John F.
Bickford, Matthew
Binder, Richard
Black, William P.
Blagheen, William
Blair, Robert M.
Blake, Robert
Blasdel, Thomas A.
Bliss, Zenas R.
Bois, Frank
Bond, William
Bourke, John G.
Bourne, Thomas
Bowen, Emmer
Bowman, Edward R.
Bradley, Amos
Bradley, Charles
Brazell, John
Breen, John
Brennan, Christopher
Bronner, August F.
Brouse, Charles W.
Brown, James
Brown, John
Brown, John H.
Brown, Robert
Brown, William H.
Brown, Wilson
Brownell, William P.
Brutsche, Henry
Bryant, Andrew S.
Buck, F. Clarence
Buck, James
Buckingham, David E.
Buckley, John C.
Buffington, John E.
Buhrman, Henry G.
Bumgarner, William
Burbank, James H.
Burger, Joseph
Burke, Daniel W.
Burns, John M.
Burritt, William W.
Burton, Albert

Butterfield, Frank G.
Butts, George
Byrnes, James
Cadwell, Luman L.
Campbell, William
Campbell, William
Capron, Horace, Jr.
Carr, Eugene A.
Carr, William M.
Carson, William J.
Casey, Henry
Cassidy, Michael
Chandler, Henry F.
Chandler, James B.
Chapin, Alaric B.
Chaput, Louis G.
Child, Benjamin H.
Chisman, William W.
Churchill, Samuel J.
Clark, James G.
Clarke, Dayton P.
Clifford, Robert T.
Coates, Jefferson
Cohn, Abraham
Colbert, Patrick
Colby, Carlos W.
Conaway, John W.
Conlan, Dennis
Connor, William C.
Cook, John
Cooper, John
Corcoran, Thomas E.
Cotton, Peter
Crawford, Alexander
Cripps, Thomas
Croft James E.
Cronin, Cornelius
Cross, James E.
Cunningham, James S.
Cutts, James M.
Davidson, Andrew
Davis, George E.
Davis, Martin K.
Davis, Samuel W.
Day, David F.
Deakin, Charles
Deane, John M.
Deland, Frederick N.
Dempster, John
Denig, J. Henry
Dennis, Richard

Act of Heroism (Showing Gallantry Under Fire)

Densmore, William
De Puy, Charles H.
De Witt, Richard W.
Dickey, William D.
Dickie, David
Diggins, Bartholomew
Doolen, William
Dorman, John
Dougherty, Patrick
Dow, George P.
Dow, Henry
Duncan, Adam
Dunn, William
Dunne, James
Dunphy, Richard D.
Eckes, John N.
Edwards, John
Elise, William
English, Thomas
Erickson, John P.
Fallon, Thomas T.
Farley, William
Farrell, Edward
Ferris, Eugene W.
Fisher, John H.
Fitzpatrick, Thomas
Flood, Thomas
Flynn, James E.
Force, Manning F.
Forman, Alexander A.
Fout, Frederick W.
Foy, Charles H.
Franks, William J.
Frantz, Joseph
Fraser, William W.
Freeman, Martin
French, Samuel S.
Frey, Franz
Frizzell, Henry
Fry, Isaac N.
Fuger, Frederick
Gage, Richard J.
Galloway, George N.
Gardiner, James
Gardner, William
Garrison, James R.
Garvin, William
Gaylord, Levi B.
George, Daniel G.
Geschwind, Nicholas
Gile, Frank S.

Goldsbery, Andrew E.
Gould, Newton T.
Gouraud, George E.
Graham, Robert
Greene, John
Greene, Oliver D.
Gregg, Joseph O.
Griffiths, John
Grueb, George
Guerin, George
Guin, Thomas
Gwynne, Nathaniel
Hack, John
Haffee, Edmund
Haight, Sidney
Haley, James
Hall, Henry Seymour
Halstead, William
Ham, Mark G.
Hamilton, Hugh
Hamilton, Richard
Hamilton, Thomas W.
Hammel, Henry A.
Hand, Allexander
Haney, Milton L.
Hanna, Milton
Harcourt, Thomas
Harley, Bernard
Harrington, Daniel
Harris, James H.
Harris, Sampson
Harrison, George H.
Hathaway, Edward W.
Havron, John H.
Hawkins, Charles
Hawkins, Gardner C.
Hayden, Joseph B.
Hayes, John
Hayes, Thomas
Helms, David H.
Henry, James
Hickey, Dennis W.
Hickman, John
Hill, Henry
Hilliker, Benjamin F.
Hinnecan, William
Hodges, Addison J.
Hoffman, Thomas W.
Hogarty, William P.
Holehouse, James
Hollat, George

Holmes, Lovilo N.
Hooper, William B.
Horton, James
Houghton, Charles H.
Houghton, Edward J.
Houghton, George L.
Howard, Henderson C.
Howard, Martin
Howard, Peter
Howe, Orion P.
Howe, William H.
Hudson, Michael
Huidekoper, Henry S.
Hunt, Louis T.
Hyatt, Theodore
Immell, Lorenzo D.
Irlam, Jospeh
Irving, John
Irwin, Nicholas
Jackson, Frederick R.
James, John H.
James, Miles
Jardine, James
Jenkins, Thomas
Jewett, Erastus W.
John, William
Johns, Elisha
Johns, Henry T.
Johnson, Andrew
Johnson, Follett
Johnson, John
Johnson, Ruel M.
Johnston, David
Johnston, William P.
Jones, Andrew
Jones, David
Jones, John E.
Jones, Thomas
Jones, William
Jordan, Robert
Jordan, Thomas
Kaiser, John
Kane, Thomas
Karpeles, Leopold
Kelley, Andrew J.
Kelley, John
Kelly, Alexander
Kendrick, Thomas
Kenna, Barnett
Kenyon, Charles
King, Robert H.

Act of Heroism (Showing Gallantry Under Fire)

King, Rufus, Jr.
Kinnaird, Samuel W.
Kountz, John S.
Labill, Joseph S.
Lafferty, John
Laffey, Bartlett
Laing, William
Lakin, Daniel
Lann, John S.
Larrabee, James W.
Lawson, John
Lear, Nicholas
Lee, James H.
Leland, George W.
Leon, Pierre
Leonard, Edwin
Lewis, Henry
Little, Henry F.W.
Lloyd, Benjamin
Lloyd, John W.
Longshore, William H.
Lonsway, Joseph
Lovering, Geoge M.
Lower, Cyrus B.
Lower, Robert A.
Lyons, Thomas
Machon, James
Mack, Alexander
Mack, John
Mackie, John F.
Madden, William
Martin, Edward S.
Martin, James
Martin, William
Martin, William
McCammon, William W.
McClelland, James M.
McClelland, Matthew
McCormick, Michael
McCornack, Andrew
McCullock, Adam
McDonald, John
McFarland, John
McGinn, Edward
McGonagle, Wilson
McGowan, John
McGraw, Thomas
McHugh, Martin
McIntosh, James
McKnight, William
McLeod, James

McMahon, Martin T.
McWilliams, George W.
Melville, Charles
Merrill, George
Mifflin, James
Miles, Nelson A.
Miller, Andrew
Miller, Jacob C.
Miller, James
Milliken, Daniel
Molloy, Hugh
Montgomery, Robert
Moore, Charles
Moore, Charles
Moore, William
Morford, Jerome
Morgan, James
Morrison, John G.
Morton, Charles W.
Mullen, Patrick
Murphy, James T.
Murphy, Michael C.
Murphy, Patrick
Myers, William H.
Nash, Henry H.
Naylor, David
Neahr, Zachariah C.
Neil, John
Newland, William
Nichols, William
North, Jasper N.
Noyes, William W.
O'Beirne, James R.
O'Connell, Thomas
O'Dea, John
O'Donoghue, Timothy
Oliver, Paul A.
Orbansky, David
Ortega, John
Osborne, William H.
Oss, Albert
Overturf, Jacob H.
Oviatt, Miles M.
Packard, Loron F.
Palmer, John G.
Parker, William
Parks, George
Parsons, Joel
Pay, Byron E.
Pearsall, Platt
Pease, Joachim

Peck, Oscar E.
Pelham, William
Perry, Thomas
Pesch, Joseph
Peters, Henry C.
Peterson, Alfred
Phinney, William
Poole, William B.
Powers, Wesley J.
Prance, George
Preston, John
Price, Edward
Pyne, George
Rafferty, Peter
Rand, Charles F.
Rannahan, John
Raub, Jacob F.
Read, Charles
Read, Charles A.
Read, George E.
Reed, Axel H.
Reed, Charles W.
Reed, William
Regan, Jeremiah
Reinsinger, J. Monroe
Renninger, Louis
Rhodes, Julius D.
Rice, Charles
Rice, Edmund
Richards Louis
Roantree, James S.
Roberts, James
Robertson, Robert S.
Robie, George F.
Robinson, Alexander
Robinson, Charles
Robinson, James H.
Rock, Frederick
Rodenbough, Theophilus F.
Rundle, Charles W.
Rush, John
Sanderson, Aaron
Sanford, Jacob
Sartwell, Henry
Saunders, James
Saxton, Rufus
Schenck, Benjamin W.
Schiller, John
Schmauch, Andrew
Schnell, Christian
Schutt, George

Seanor, James
Sears, Cyrus
Seward, Griffin
Sewell, William J.
Shafter, William R.
Shapland, John
Sharp, Hendrick
Shepard, Louis C.
Sheridan, James
Shipman, William
Shivers, John
Shutes, Henry
Sickles, Daniel E.
Sidman, George E.
Simkins, Lebbeus
Simonds, William Edgar
Sladen, Joseph A.
Slagle, Oscar
Smalley, Reuben
Smalley, Reuben S.
Smith, Charles H.
Smith, David L.
Smith, Edwin
Smith, Henry I.
Smith, James
Smith, John
Smith, John
Smith, Oloff
Smith, S. Rodmond
Smith, Thomas
Smith, Walter B.
Smith, Willard M.
Smith, William
Snedden, James
Sowers, Michael
Spalding, Edward B.
Spillane, Timothy
Sprague, Benona
Sprowle, David
Stacey, Charles
Stanley, William A.
Steinmetz, William
Stephens, William G.
Sterling, James E.
Stevens, Daniel D.
Stockman, George H.
Stoddard, James
Stolz, Frank

Stout, Richard
Strahan, Robert
Strong, James N.
Sullivan, John
Sullivan, Timothy
Summers, James C.
Summers, Robert
Swan, Charles A.
Swap, Jacob E.
Swatton, Edward
Swearer, Benjamin
Swegheimer, Jacob
Sype, Peter
Talbott, William
Tallentine, James
Taylor, Anthony
Taylor, Thomas
Taylor, William
Taylor, William G.
Terry, John D.
Thatcher, Charles M.
Thielberg, Henry
Thomas, Stephen
Thompson, Freeman C.
Thompson, Henry A.
Thompson, J. (James) Harry
Thompson, William
Tilton, William
Titus, Charles
Tobie, Edward
Tobin, John M.
Todd, Samuel
Toohey, Thomas
Toomer, William
Tribe, John
Tripp, Othniel
Trogden, Howell G.
Truell, Edwin M.
Truett, Alexander H.
Tucker, Jacob R.
Tweedale, John
Urell, M. Emmet
Vale, John
Van Matre, Joseph
Vantine, Joseph E.
Vaughn, Pinkerton R.
Veale, Moses

Vernay, James D.
Verney, James W.
Wageman, John H.
Wagner, John W.
Wainwright, John
Ward, James
Ward, Thomas J.
Ward, William H.
Warden, John
Warren, Francis E.
Webster, Henry S.
Wells, William
Welsh, Edward
Wheeler, Daniel D.
Wherry, William M.
White, Joseph
Whitfield, Daniel
Widick, Andrew J.
Wilcox, Franklin L.
Wilcox, William H.
Wilkes, Henry
Wilkes, Perry
Williams, Anthony
Williams, Augustus
Williams, George C.
Williams, John
Williams, John
Williams, John
Williams, Peter
Williams, Robert
Williams, William
Willis, Richard
Williston, Edward B.
Wilson, John
Wilson, John M.
Wisner, Lewis S.
Wood, H. Clay
Wood, Richard H.
Wood, Robert B.
Woon, John
Wortick (Wertick), Joseph
Wray, William J.
Wright, Edward
Wright, Robert
Wright, Samuel
Wright, Samuel C.
Young, Edward B.
Young, William

Listing by State or Country of Birth

Alabama
Houghton, Edward J.
Reddick, William H.
Taylor, Richard

Arkansas
Wheeler, henry W.

Austria
Burger, Joseph

Belgium
Oss, Albert
Vifquain, Victor

California
Woods, Samuel

Canada
Asten, Charles
Bois, Frank
Brown, John Harties
Buckley, Dennis
Cayer, Ovila
Chapman, John
Chaput, Louis G.
Coffey, Robert J.
Dodd, Robert F.
Dodds, Edward E.
Fitzpatrick, Thomas
Gilmore, John C.
Hagerty, Asel
Higgins, Thomas J.
Houghton, George L.
McIntosh, James
McMahon, Martin T.
McVeane, John P.
Murphy, James T.
Neil, John
O'Connor, Albert
O'Neill, Stephen
Pelham, William
Pickle, Alonzo H.
Powers, Wesley J.
Rich, Carlos H.
Scott, Alexander
Shivers, John
Young, Benjamin F.

Chile
Bazaar, Philip
Sova, Joseph E.

Connecticut
Babcock, William J.
Bacon, Elijah W.
Beckwith, Wallace A.
Briggs, Elijah A.
Buck, F. Clarence
Burke, Daniel W.
Corliss, George W.
Crocker, Henry H.
Curtis, John C.
Denning, Lorenzo
Ennis, Charles D.
Fox, Nicholas
Gibbs, Wesley
Harding, Thomas
Hickok, Nathan E.
Hooper, William B.
Hubbell, William S.
Jackson, Frederick R.
Jones, John
Lanfare, Aaron S.
Marsh, Charles H.
Neville, Edwin M.
Norton, Elliott M.
Palmer John G.
Peck, Oscar E.
Shaler, Alexander
Swift, Frederic W.
Tinkham, Eugene M.
Tracy, Charles H.
Tucker, Allen
Weeks, John H.
Whitaker, Edward W.

Delaware
Baldwin, Charles
Buckingham, David E.
Du Pont, Henry A.
Hand, Allexander
Mayberry, John P.
Palmer, William J.
Postles, James Parke
Sacriste, Louis J.
Seward, Griffin
Smith, S. Rodmond

Denmark
Irwin, Nicholas
Miller, James
Thompson, John

England
Baybutt, Philip
Beddows, Richard
Beech, John P.
Bell, George
Blagheen, William

289

Bourne, Thomas
Burton, Albert
Cook, John H.
Croft, James E.
Donnelly, John
Dore, George E.
Edwards, David
Elise, William
Erickson, John P.
Garrett, William
Graham, Robert
Green, George
Harbourne, John H.
Harvey, Harry
Hibson, Joseph C.
Hill, James
Holehouse, James
Irlam, Joseph
Irving, Thomas
Jennings, James T.
Judge, Francis W.
Keen, Joseph S.
Keene, Joseph
Kenna, Barnett
Leslie, Frank
Lloyd, Benjamin
Lord, William
Ludgate, William
Machon, James
Madden, William
Mandy, Harry J.
Mathews, William H.
Moore, Charles
Murphy, Charles J.
Parker, Thomas
Plowman, George H.
Powell, William H.
Pyne, George
Roberts, James
Robinson, Alexander
Shapland, John
Shilling, John
Sladen, Joseph A.
Smith, Henry I.
Smith, Thomas
Stacey, Charles
Stokes, George
Sweeney, James
Tallentine, James
Taylor, Joseph
Thompson, Henry A.

Thompson, J. (James) Harry
Vale, John
Wagg, Maurice
Williams, George C.
Willis, Richard
Wilson, John
Wood, Mark
Woon, John
Wright, William

Florida
Post, Philip Sidney

France
Beaufort, Jean J.
Frantz, Joseph
Geschwind, Nicholas
Howard, Peter
Jamieson, Walter
Labill, Joseph S.
Ludwig, Carl
Morse, Charles E.
Prance, George

Georgia
Leland, George W.

Germany
Alber, Frederick
Archinal, William
Ballen, Frederick
Bieger, Charles
Blucher, Charles
Boquet, Nicholas
Bronner, August F.
Dilger, Hubert
Dorley, August
Enderlin, Richard
Fesq, Frank
Fout, Frederick W.
Fox, Henry
Freeman, Martin
Fuger, Frederick
Grebe, M.R. William
Gresser, Ignatz
Grueb, George
Hack, John
Hammel, Henry A.
Hart, John W.
Hoffman, Henry
John, William
Kaiser, John

Kaltenbach, Luther
Kappesser, Peter
Kauss, August
Kline, Harry
Langbein, J.C. Julius
Miller, Andrew
Miller, Henry A.
Miller, John
Miller, John
Mindil, George W.
Nibbe, John H.
Noll, Conrad
Phisterer, Frederick
Rock, Frederick
Rossbach, Valentine
Schiller, John
Schlachter, Philipp
Schmal, George W.
Schmauch, Andrew
Schmidt, Conrad
Schorn, Charles
Schubert, Martin
Schwan, Theodore
Schwenk, Martin
Seitzinger, James M.
Shubert, Frank
Stockman, George H.
Streile, Christian
Swegheimer, Jacob
Thielberg, Henry
Torgler, Ernst
Uhrl, George
Wambsgan, Martin
Wells, William
Younker, John L.

Holland
Burbank, James H.
Mack, Alexander

Hungary
Karpeles, Leopold
Stahel, Julius

Illinois
Allen, Abner P.
Archer, James W.
Bickford, Matthew
Blodgett, Welis H.
Davis, Martin K.
Flynn, James E.
Goldsbery, Andrew E.

State or Country of Birth

Gould, Newton T.
Holmes, William T.
Johnston, William P.
Josselyn, Simeon T.
Kretsinger, George
Lower, Robert A.
Lucas, Geoerge W.
Luce, Moses A.
Marsh, George
McCornack, Andrew
McDonald, John Wade
McKeen, Nineveh S.
Molloy, Hugh
Moore, Wilbur F.
Murphy, Robinson B.
Newman, Marcellus J.
Payne, Thomas H.L.
Pond, George F.
Rebmann, George F.
Sanford, Jacob
Simmons, William T.
Smith, Andrew Jackson
Spalding, Edward B.
Sterling, John T.
Taylor, Henry H.
Vernay, James D.
Warden, John
Whitmore, John
Widick, Andrew J.

India
Simons, Charles J.

Indiana
Anderson, Marion T.
Armstrong, Clinton L.
Banks, George L.
Blasdel, Thomas A.
Box, Thomas J.
Brouse, Charles W.
Bruner, Louis J.
Buckles, Abram J.
Campbell, William
Chamberlain, Orville T.
Chisman, William W.
Conaway, John W.
Dunlavy, James
Evans, Coron D.
Fanning, Nicholas
Ferrier, Daniel T.
Graham, Thomas N.
Hardenbergh, Henry M.

Helms, David H.
Hough, Ira
Hunt, Louis T.
Hymer, Samuel
Johnson, Ruel M.
Kelley, Andrew J.
Kendall, William W.
Mason, Elihu H.
Overturf, Jacob H.
Russell, Milton
Seston, Charles H.
Shepard, William
Stolz, Frank
Tibbetts, Andrew W.
Whitehead, John M.
Wilkes, Perry
Wright, Samuel

Iowa
Bras, Edgar A.
Healey, George W.
Morgan, Richard H.
Twombly, Voltaire P.
Welch, George W.

Ireland
Allen, James
Anderson, Robert
Barry, Augustus
Bass, David L.
Begley, Terrence
Blackwood, William R.D.
Bradley, Charles
Brannigan, Felix
Brennan, Christopher
Brosnan, John
Brown, Edward, Jr.
Burk, E. Michael
Burke, Thomas
Byrnes, James
Campbell, William
Carey, Hugh
Casey, David
Cassidy, Michael
Colbert, Patrick
Collis, Charles H.T.
Connor, Thomas
Connors, James
Cooper, John
Cosgrove, Thomas
Creed, John
Cullen, Thomas

Curran, Richard
Delaney, John C.
Donoghue, Timothy
Doody, Patrick
Doolen, William
Dougherty, Michael
Dougherty, Patrick
Downey, William
Drury, James
Dunphy, Richard D.
English, Edmund
Fallon, Thomas T.
Flood, Thomas
Flynn, Christopher
Ford, George W.
Gardner, William
Gasson, Richard
Ginley, Patrick
Gribben, James H.
Haley, James
Harrington, Daniel
Havron, John H.
Highland, Patrick
Hinnecan, William
Horne, Samuel B.
Howard, Martin
Hudson, Michael
Hyland, John
Irwin, Patrick
Jones, Andrew
Jones, William
Kane, John
Keele, Joseph
Kelley, John
Kelly, Thomas
Kennedy, John
Kcough, John
Kerr, Thomas R.
Laffey, Bartlett
Logan, Hugh
Lonergan, John
Mangam, Richard C.
Martin, Edward S.
Martin, James
Martin, William
McAdams, Peter
McAnally, Charles
McCarren, Bernard
McCormick, Michael
McEnroe, Patrick H.
McGough, Owen

A group of Maine Infantry following the charge against Marye's Heights, in Fredericksburg, Virginia. The bold frontal charges employed in the Napoleonic tactics used by both sides during the Civil War ensured that soldiers would engage in desperate struggles that would create opportunities for individual heroism (U.S. Army War College).

McGowan, John
McGraw, Thomas
McGuire, Patrick
McHale, Alexander U.
McKee, George
McKeever, Michael
Monaghan, Patrick
Montgomery, Robert
Moore, Charles
Morrison, John G.
Morton, Charles W.
Mulholland, St. Clair A.
Murphy, Dennis J.F.
Murphy, John P.
Murphy, Michael C.
Murphy, Patrick
Murphy, Thomas C.
Murphy, Thomas J.
Nolan, John J.
Nugent, Christopher
O'Beirne, James R.

O'Brien, Peter
O'Connell, Thomas
O'Connor, Timothy
O'Dea, John
O'Donnell, Menomen
Platt, George C.
Plunkett, Thomas
Preston, John
Quinlan, James
Rafferty, Peter
Rannahan, John
Reynolds, George
Riley, Thomas
Roantree, James S.
Robinson, John H.
Robinson, Thomas
Ryan, Peter J.
Scanlan, Patrick
Schutt, George
Sewell, William J.
Shields, Bernard

Smith, William
Spillane, Timothy
Stewart, Joseph
Sullivan, Timothy
Tobin, John M.
Toomer, William
Tyrrell, George William
Urell, M. Emmet
Walsh, John
Welch, Richard
Wells, Thomas M.
Welsh, Edward
Welsh, James
White, Patrick H.
Williams, William
Wilson, Christopher W.
Wright, Robert

Italy

Di Cesnola, Louis P.
Hyde, Thomas W.

Kentucky
Black, William P.
Callahan, John H.
Darrough, John S.
Davis, John
Horsfall, William H.
Hudson, Aaron R.
Mattingly, Henry B.
McMillen, Francis M.
Noble, Daniel
Rood, Oliver P.
Steinmetz, William
Weston, John F.
Williamson, James A.

Louisiana
Anderson, Charles W.
Anderson, Everett W.
Leon, Pierre
Williams, John

Maine
Ames, Adelbert
Angling, John
Belcher, Thomas
Bibber, Charles J.
Bickford, John F.
Bliss, Zenas R.
Boody, Robert
Bowman, Edward R.
Chamberlain, Joshua L.
Chase, John F.
Clark, Charles A.
Davis, Samuel
Duncan, Adam
Dunn, William
Estes, Lewellyn G.
Farley, William
Fernald, Albert E.
Frisbee, John B.
Hanna, Marcus A.
Hanscom, Moses C.
Harrington, Ephraim W.
Haskell, Frank W.
Haynes, Asbury F.
Hesseltine, Francis S.
Hincks, William B.
Howard, Oliver O.
Kendrick, Thomas
Knowles, Abiather J.
Littlefield, George H.
Lunt, Alphonso M.

Mack, John
McCullock, Adam
Merriam, Henry C.
Merrill, Augustus
Milliken, Daniel
Morrill, Walter G.
O'Brien, Henry D.
Pike, Edward M.
Poole, William B.
Reed, Axel H.
Richmond, James
Roberts, Otis O.
Savage, Auzella
Seward, Richard E.
Smith, Charles H.
Smith, Charles H.
Smith, Joseph S.
Spurling, Andrew B.
Sterling, James E.
Talbott, William
Taylor, Thomas
Terry, John D.
Thaxter, Sidney W.
Tobie, Edward P.
Tozier, Andrew J.
Tracy, Amasa A.
Tripp, Othniel
Verney, James W.
Whitman, Frank M.
Whittier, Edward N.
Wood, H. Clay
Young, Horatio N.

Malta
Caruana, Orlando E.

Maryland
Barnes, William H.
Brown, William H.
Buck, James
Buffington, John E.
Cadwallader, Abel G.
Capron, Horace, Jr.
Carr, William M.
Carter, Joseph F.
Diggins, Bartholomew
Dorsey, Decatur
Fleetwood, Christian
Harris, James H.
Hayden, Joseph B.
Hilton, Alfred B.
Jones, Thomas

Koogle, Jacob
Lakin, Daniel
Mullen, Patrick
Porter, Ambrose
Ringold, Edward
Schneider, George
Shea, Joseph H.
Shutes, Henry
Smith, Francis M.
Swearer, Benjamin
Truett, Alexander H.
Wagner, John W.

Massachusetts
Adams, John G.B.
Allen, Nathaniel
Anderson, Frederick C.
Atkinson, Thomas E.
Barnum, James
Bond, William
Boss, Orlando
Brady, James
Brown, John H.
Bryant, Andrew S.
Buffum, Robert
Chandler, Henry F.
Chandler, James B.
Davis, George E.
Deane, John M.
De Castro, Joseph H.
Deland, Frederick N.
Dennis, Richard
Dillon, Michael A.
Duffey, John
Ellsworth, Thomas F.
Falls, Benjamin F.
Funk, West
Gardner, Charles N.
Gaylord, Levi B.
Gifford, David L.
Gile, Frank S.
Grace, Peter
Griswold, Luke M.
Harcourt, Thomas
Harrison, George H.
Haskell, Marcus M.
Hathaway, Edward W.
Homan, Conrad
Horton, James
Horton, Lewis A.
Howe, William H.

Hunter, Charles A.
Ingalls, Lewis J.
James, John H.
Jellison, Benjamin H.
Johns, Henry T.
Leonard, Edwin
Lovering, George, M.
Luther, James H.
Lyon, Frederick A.
Lyons, Thomas
MacArthur, Arthur, Jr.
Mahoney, Jeremiah
Manning, Joseph S.
Marland, William
Maxham, Lowell M.
Maynard, George H.
Miles, Nelson A.
Moore, William
Newland, William
O'Brien, Oliver
Osborne, William H.
Parker, William
Pinkham, Charles H.
Putnam, Winthrop D.
Reed, Charles W.
Regan, Jeremiah
Rice, Edmund
Rountry, John
Saunders, James
Saxton, Rufus
Seanor, James
Smith, John
Stanley, William A.
Tabor, William S.
Taggert, Charles A.
Truell, Edwin M.
Warren, Francis E.
Williams, Anthony
Withington, William H.

Michigan
Ayers, John G.K.
Baldwin, Frank D.
Barrell, Charles L.
Bennett, Orson W.
Bickford, Henry H.
Chandler, Stephen E.
Christiancy, James I.
Clute, George W.
Cronin, Cornelius
De Puy, Charles H.

Dunne, James
Falconer, John A.
Fall, Charles S.
Forman, Alexander A.
Haight, Sidney
Hastings, Smith H.
Herington, Pitt B.
Hodges, Addison J.
Lewis, Henry
Mundell, Walter L.
Nash, Henry H.
Peters, Henry C.
Rhodes, Julius D.
Robinson, James H.
Sancrainte, Charles F.
Savacool, Edwin F.
Shafter, William R.
Sype, Peter
Thatcher, Charles M.
Toban, James W.
Ward, William H.
Wheaton, Lloyd
Whitney, William G.
Willcox, Orlando B.
Woodruff, Alonzo

Mississippi
Black, John C.
Brown, Wilson

Missouri
Frizzell, Henry F.
Pentzer, Patrick H.
Wherry, William M.

New Hampshire
Appleton, William H.
Barker, Nathaniel C.
Batchelder, Richard N.
Boutwell, John W.
Camp, Carlton N.
Cilley, Clinton A.
Cohn, Robert J.
Colby, Carlos W.
Copp, Charles D.
Cutcheon, Byron M.
Dow, George P.
Elliott, Russell C.
Evans, Ira H.
Foy, Charles H.
Gage, Richard J.
George, Daniel G.

Goodall, Francis H.
Hadley, Osgood T.
Ham, Mark G.
Harris, Moses
Kimball, Joseph
Knight, Charles H.
Little, Henry F.W.
Melville, Charles
Pingree, Samuel E.
Robie, George F.
Rowe, Henry W.
Sweatt, Joseph G.
Todd, Samuel
Veazey, Wheelock G.
Wilcox, William H.
Wilkins, Leander A.
Woodbury, Eri D.

New Jersey
Brant, William
Carmin, Isaac H.
Davis, John
Drake, James M.
Follett, Joseph L.
Grant, Gabriel
Hopkins, Charles F.
Howard, James
Kane, Thomas
Magee, William
Pitman, George J.
Sheridan, James
Southard, David
Stewart, George W.
Strahan, Robert
Thompson, William
Titus, Charles
Tomlin, Andrew J.
Tompkins, Aaron B.
Traynor, Andrew
Weeks, Charles H.
Whitfield, Daniel
Williams, John
Wood, Richard H.
Young, Edward B.

New York
Anderson, Bruce
Archer, Lester
Barnum, Henry A.
Barter, Gurdon H.
Bates, Delavan
Beebe, William S.

State or Country of Birth

Benjamin, John F.
Benjamin, Samuel N.
Betham, Asa
Birdsall, Horatio L.
Blunt, John W.
Boehm, Peter M.
Bowen, Chester B.
Bowen, Emmer
Box, Thomas J.
Bradley, Amos
Bradley, Thomas W.
Breen, John
Brewer, William J.
Bringle, Andrew
Brown, Henri Le Ferve
Brown, James
Brown, Morris, Jr.
Brownell, Francis E.
Brownell, William P.
Brush, George W.
Bruton, Christopher C.
Buchanan, George A.
Burk, Thomas
Burns, John M.
Burritt, William W.
Butterfield, Daniel
Butts, George
Cadwell, Luman L.
Calkin, Ivers S.
Campbell, James A.
Carey, James L.
Carman, Warren
Carr, Eugene A.
Carter, John J.
Catlin, Isaac S.
Chapin, Alaric B.
Clancy, James T.
Clapp, Albert A.
Clark, Harrison
Clarke, Dayton P.
Cleveland, Charles F.
Coey, James
Cole, Gabriel
Collins, Thomas D.
Compson, Hartwell B.
Conboy, Martin
Conlan, Dennis
Corcoran, Thomas E.
Corliss, Stephen P.
Cosgriff, Richard H.
Cotton, Peter

Coyne, John N.
Crosier, William H.H.
Cross, James E.
Crowley, Michael
Cummings, Amos J.
Curtis, Newton Martin
Densmore, William
Dickey, William D.
Ditzenback, John
Dockum, Warren C.
Dolloff, Charles W.
Durham John S.
Embler, Andrew H.
English, Thomas
Evans, James R.
Everson, Adelbert
Farnsworth, Herbert E.
Farrell, Edward
Flannigan, James
Freeman, Archibald
Freeman, William H.
French, Samuel S.
Gardner, Robert J.
Garrison, James R.
Gere, Thomas P.
Gifford, Benjamin
Goettel, Philip
Goheen, Charles A.
Goodrich, Edwin
Gouraud, George E.
Greene, John
Greene, Oliver D.
Greig, Theodore W.
Grindlay, James G.
Guerin, Fritz W.
Hack, Lester G.
Hadley, Cornelius M.
Haight, John H.
Hall, Francis. B.
Hall, Henry Seymour
Hallock, Nathan M.
Halstead, William
Hamilton, Hugh
Hanford, Edward R.
Hapeman, Douglas
Haring, Abram P.
Harley, Bernard
Hart, William E.
Hatch, John P.
Hawthorne, Harris S.
Heermance, William L.

Hickey, Dennis W.
Hill, Edward
Hill, James
Hills, William G.
Hogarty, William P.
Hollat, George
Holmes, Lovilo N.
Holton, Charles M.
Hooker, George W.
Horan, Thomas
Houghton, Charles H.
Houlton, William
Huskey, Michael
Irsch, Francis
Irving, John
Jacobson, Eugene P.
Johnson, Follett
Johnson, Wallace, W.
Johnston, Willie
Jones, John E.
Jordan, Robert
Kelley, Leverett M.
Kelly, Daniel
Kenyon, Charles
Kenyon, John S.
Kenyon, Samuel P.
Kiggins, John
King, Horatio C.
King, Robert H.
King, Rufus, Jr.
Kinnaird, Samuel W.
Kirby, Dennis T.
Knox, Edward M.
Kuder, Andrew
Ladd, George
Lafferty, John
Laing, William
Lane, Morgan D.
Lann, John S.
Larrabee, James W.
Lee, James H.
Levy, Benjamin
lloyd, John W.
Locke, Lewis
Lonsway, Joseph
Lorish, Andrew J.
Love, George M.
Lutes, Franklin W.
Lyman, Joel H.
Mackie, John F.
Madden, Michael

Madison, James
Marsh, Albert
McClelland, Matthew
McFall, Daniel
McGinn, Edward
McGonnigle, Andrew J.
McKay, Charles W.
McKnight, William
Meach, George E.
Menter, John W.
Merrill, George
Merritt, John G.
Meyer, Henry C.
Miller, Frank
Mills, Charles
Mills, Frank W.
Moffitt, John H.
Morgan, James H.
Morse, Benjamin
Murphy, Thomas
Naylor, David
Neahr, Zachariah C.
Newman, William H.
Nichols, William
Niven, Robert
Norton, John R.
Norton, Llewellyn P.
Nutting, Lee
O'Donoghue, Timothy
Orr, Charles A.
Oviatt, Miles M.
Packard, Loron F.
Palmer, George H.
Parks, George
Parks, Henry Jeremiah
Patterson, John H.
Pay, Byron E.
Pease, Joachim
Perry, Thomas
Phillips, Josiah
Plant, Henry C.
Plimley, William
Pond, James B.
Porter, William
Potter, Norman F.
Price, Edward
Province, George
Putnam, Edgar P.
Rand, Charles F.
Ranney, George E.
Ranney, Myron H.

Raymond, William H.
Read, Charles
Read, Morton A.
Riddell, Rudolph
Robertson, Robert S.
Robinson, John C.
Rockefeller, Charles M.
Rounds, Lewis A.
Russell, Charles L.
Sagelhurst, John C.
Sartwell, Henry
Schofield, John M.
Scofield, David H.
Sears, Cyrus
Shepard, Irwin
Shipley, Robert F.
Shipman, William
Sickles, Daniel E.
Sickles, William H.
Sidman, George E.
Simkins, Lebbeus
Simmons, John
Skellie, Ebenezer
Smalley, Reuben
Smith, Alonzo
Smith, David L.
Smith, Edwin
Smith, James
Smith, John
Smith, Richard
Smith, Walter B.
Smith, Willard M.
Smith, Wilson
Sprague, Benona
Sprague, John W.
Sprowle, David
Starkins, John H.
Stephens, William G.
Stout, Richard
Sullivan, James
Sullivan, John
Swap, Jacob E.
Swatton, Edward
Swift, Harlan J.
Taylor, George
Taylor, John
Thompkins, George W.
Thompson, Allen,
Thompson, James
Thompson, William P.
Toffey, John J.

Toohey, Thomas
Tracy, Benjamin F.
Tracy, William G.
Tremain, Henry E.
Tribe, John
Van Winkle, Edward (Edwin)
Wainwright, John
Walker, Dr. Mary E.
Wall, Jerry
Walling, William H.
Ward, James
Webb, Alexander S.
Webb, James
Webber, Alason P.
Webster, Henry S.
Weir, Henry C.
Welch, Stephen
Wilcox, Franklin L.
Wilkes, Henry
Williams, Le Roy
Williams, Robert
Winegar, William W.
Wisner, Lewis S.
Woodruff, Carle A.
Woram, Charles B.
Wright, Edward
Young, James M.
Young, William

North Carolina
Franks, William J.
Sanderson, Aaron
Stoddard, James
Trogden, Howell G.

Norway
Brown, Robert
Johnson, Henry
Johnson, John
Phinney, William
Williams, Augustus
Williams, Peter

Ohio
Albert, Christian
Ayers, David
Barrick, Jesse T.
Barton, Thomas
Bebb, Edward J.
Bell, James B.
Bensinger, William

State or Country of Birth

Boury, Richard
Boynton, Henry V.
Brandle, Joseph E.
Brown, Robert B.
Brown, Uriah
Brown, Wilson W.
Buhrman, Henry G.
Burns, James M.
Carr, Franklin
Cockley, David L.
Colwell, Oliver
Cook, John
Cox, Robert M.
Cranston, William W.
Crocker, Ulric L.
Cumpston, James M.
Custer, Thomas W.
Davis, Freeman
Davis, Harry
Day, David F.
De Witt, Richard W.
Dorman, John
Elison, James M.
Finkenbiner, Henry S.
Fox, Henry M.
Freeman, Henry B.
Gaunt, John C.
Gause, Isaac
Gregg, Joseph O.
Grimshaw, Samuel
Guin, Thomas
Gwynne, Nathaniel
Hall, Newton H.
Haney, Milton L.
Hanks, Joseph
Hanna, Milton
Harris, Sampson
Hawkins, Thomas R.
Hays, John H.
Hedges, Joseph
Heller, Henry
Henry, James
Holcomb, Daniel I.
Holland, Lemuel F.
Howard, Hiram R.
Howe, Orion P.
Hughey, John
Immell, Lorenzo D.
Inscho, Leonidus H.
James, Isaac
Johns, Elisha

Johnson, Andrew
Jones, David
Jordan, Absalom
Kelley, George V.
Kemp, Joseph
Kirk, Jonathan C.
Knight, William J
Kountz, John S.
Kuder, Jeremiah
Larimer, Smith
Lawton, Henry W.
Longshore, William H.
Loyd, George
Mayes, William B.
McCammon, William W.
McCleary, Charles H.
McClelland, James M.
McConnell, Samuel
McElhinny, Samuel O.
McGonagle, Wilson
McHugh, Martin
Miller, Jacob C.
Miller, James P.
Morey, Delano
Morgan, Lewis
Myers, George S.
Parks, James W.
Parrott, Jacob
Patterson, John T.
Pearsall, Platt
Pinn, Robert
Pittinger, William
Porter, John R.
Power, Albert
Prentice, Joseph R.
Ramsbottom, Alfred
Renninger, Louis
Richardson, William R.
Richey, William E.
Ricksecker, John H.
Robertson, Samuel
Robinson, Elbridge
Ross, Marion A.
Rundle, Charles W.
Schenck, Benjamin W.
Schmidt, William
Scott, John M.
Seaman, Elisha B.
Shepard, Louis C.
Slagle, Oscar
Slavens, Samuel

Smith, Otis W.
Stanley, David S.
Stickels, Joseph
Sturgeon, James K.
Surles, William H.
Swayne, Wager
Thompson, Charles A.
Thompson, Freeman C.
Thompson, Thomas
Treat, Howell B.
Vance, Wilson
Wageman, John H.
Walker, James C.
Waller, Francis A.
Ward, Nelson W.
Wiley, James
Wilhelm, George
Williams, William H.
Wilson, John A.
Wollam, John
Wood, Robert B.
Young, Cavalry M.

Oklahoma
Henry, Guy V.

Pennsylvania
Ammerman, Robert W.
Anderson, Thomas
Apple, Andrew O.
Arnold, Abraham K.
Baird, Absalom
Beaumont, Eugene B.
Bennett, Orren
Benyaurd, William H.
Betts, Charles M.
Beyer, Hillary
Binder, Richard
Bingham, Henry H.
Bishop, Francis A.
Blackmar, Wilmon W.
Blickensderfer, Milton
Bonebrake, Henry G.
Bonnaffon, Sylvester, Jr.
Boon, Hugh P.
Bourke, John G.
Brazell, John
Brest, Lewis F.
Breyer, Charles
Bronson, James H.
Brown, Charles
Brown, Jeremiah Z.

Brutsche, Henry
Caldwell, Daniel
Capehart, Charles E.
Capehart, Henry
Carlisle, Casper R.
Carson, William J.
Cart, Jacob
Casey, Henry
Chambers, Joseph B.
Clark, James G.
Clark, William A.
Clausen, Charles H.
Clay, Cecil
Clifford, Robert T.
Clopp, John E.
Connell, Trustrim
Conner, Richard
Cooke, Walter H.
Corson, Joseph K.
Crawford, Alexander
Cripps, Thomas
Cunningham, Francis, M.
Cunningham, James S.
Davidsizer, John A.
Davis, Charles C.
Day, Charles
Deakin, Charles
De Lacey, Patrick
De Lavie, Hiram H.
Denig, J. Henry
Donaldson, John
Duncan, James K.L.
Edgerton, Nathan H.
Elliott, Alexander
Ellis, Horace
Engle, James E.
Ewing, John C.
Fasnacht, Charles H.
Fassett, John B.
Fisher, John H.
Fisher, Joseph
Flanagan, Augustin
Fox, William R.
Frick, Jacob G.
Fry, Isaac N.
Furman, Chester S.
Furness, Frank
Galloway, George N.
Galloway, John
Gilligan, Edward L.
Gion, Joseph
Goodman, William E.
Graul, William
Gray, Robert A.
Greenawalt, Abraham
Haffee, Edmund
Hamilton, Richard
Harmon, Amzi D.
Harris, George W.
Hartranft, John F.
Hawkins, Martin J.
Hayes, John
Herron, Francis J.
Higby, Charles
Hill, Henry
Hoffman, Thomas W.
Hogan, Franklin
Hottenstine, Solomon J.
Howard, Henderson C.
Huidekoper, Henry S.
Hunterson, John C.
Hyatt, Theodore
Ilgenfritz, Charles H.
Johnson, Joseph E.
Johnson, Samuel
Johnston, David
Jones, William
Kelly, Alexander
Kephart, James
Kindig, John M.
Kinsey, John
Kramer, Theodore L.
Landis, James P.
Lawson, John
Leonard, William E.
Lewis, Dewitt Clinton
Lilley, John
Lower, Cyrus B.
Luty, Gotlieb
Marquette, Charles
Martin, Sylvester H.
Matthews, John C.
Matthews, Milton
May, William
McKown, Nathaniel A.
McWilliams, George W.
Mears, George W.
Merrifield, James K.
Miller, William E.
Mitchell, Alexander H.
Mitchell, Theodore
Moore, George
Morford, Jerome
Morris, William
Morrison, Francis
Mostoller, John W.
Munsell, Harvey M.
Murphy, Daniel J.
Myers, William H.
Oliver, Charles
Orr, Robert L.
Orth, Jacob G.
Paul, William H.
Payne, Irvin C.
Pearson, Alfred L.
Peirsol, James K.
Pennypacker, Galusha
Petty, Philip
Pipes, James
Porter, Horace
Purcell, Hiram W.
Quay, Matthew S.
Raub, Jacob F.
Reed, George W.
Reed, William
Reigle, Daniel P.
Reisinger, H. Monroe
Rhodes, Sylvester D.
Rodenbough, Theophilus F.
Rohm, Ferdinand F.
Roosevelt, George W.
Rought, Stephen
Roush, Levi J.
Rowland, Archibald H., Jr.
Rutter, James M.
Sands, William
Schoonmaker, James M.
Scott, John Wallace
Sellers, Alfred J.
Shellenberger, John S.
Shopp, George J.
Sloan, Andrew J.
Slusher, Henry C.
Smalley, Reuben S.
Smith, Thaddeus S.
Sowers, Michael
Storey, John H.R.
Strausbaugh, Bernard A.
Swan, Charles A.
Tanner, Charles B.
Taylor, Anthony
Taylor, William G.

Thomas, Hampton, S.
Thompson, James B.
Tucker, Jacob R.
Tweedale, John
Vanderslice, John M.
Vantine, Joseph E.
Vaughn, Pinkerton R.
Veale, Moses
Walton, George W.
Warfel, Henry C.
White, J. Henry
Williams, Elwood N.
Williams, John
Wilson, Charles E.
Wilson, Francis A.
Woodward, Evan M.
Wortick, (Wertick) Joseph
Wray, William J.
Wright, Albert D.
Yeager, Jacob F.
Young, Andrew J.

Prussia
Cohn, Abraham
Connor, William C.
Martin, William
Orbansky, David
Pesch, Joseph
Shambough, Charles
Summers, Robert
Westerhold, William

Rhode Island
Avery, William B.
Barber, James A.
Bliss, George N.
Bucklyn, John K.
Child, Benjamin H.
Corcoran, John
Edwards, John
Hayes, Thomas
Lear, Nicholas
Lewis, Samuel E.
McDonald, George E.
Molbone, Archibald
Potter, George W.
Read, George E.
Stevens, Hazard

Russia
Rice, Charles
Scheibner, Martin E.

Scotland
Arther, Matthew
Avery, James
Brinn, Andrew
Brown, John
Davidson, Andrew
Dempster, John
Dickie, David
Dougall, Allan H.
Dow, Henry
Farquhar, John M.
Fraser, William W.
Gray, John
Hamilton, Thomas W.
Harris, John
Hawkins, Charles
Jardine, James
McDonald, John
McLeod, James
Meagher, Thomas
Reid, Robert
Robinson, Charles
Snedden, James
Thackrah, Benjamin
Warren, David

Spain
Ortega, John
Sharp, Hendrick

Sweden
Peterson, Alfred
Read, Charles A.
Smith, Oloff
Swanson, John
Von Vegesack, Ernest

Switzerland
Frey, Franz
White, Adam

Tennessee
Collins, Harrison
Ferrell, John H.
Gillespie, George L.
Hughes, Oliver
Lawson, Gaines
Stevens, Daniel D.

Texas
Holland, Milton M.

Vermont
Bates, Norman F.

Beatty, Alexander M.
Benedict, George G.
Butterfield, Frank G.
Churchill, Samuel J.
Clark, John W.
Coughlin, John
Davidson, Andrew
Downs, Henry W.
Eddy, Samuel E.
Ferris, Eugene W.
Gould, Charles G.
Grant, Lewis A.
Hawkins, Gardner C.
Henry, William W.
Holton, Edward A.
Howard, Squire E.
Jewett, Erastus W.
Johndro, Franklin
Livingston, Josiah O.
Mattocks, Charles P.
Nichols, Henry C.
Noyes, William W.
Peck, Cassius
Peck, Theodore S.
Phelps, Charles E.
Robbins, Augustus I.
Sargent, Jackson
Scott, Julian A.
Seaver, Thomas O.
Sherman, Marshall
Sperry, William J.
Steele, John W.
Thomas, Stephen
Tilton, William
Wells, William
Wheeler, Daniel D.
Williston, Edward B.

Virginia
Adams, James F.
Beaty, Powhatan
Blair, Robert M.
Blake, Robert
Carney, William H.
Dorsey, Daniel A.
Gardiner, James
Garvin, William
Hickman, John
James, Miles
Jordan, Thomas
Mifflin, James

Ratcliff, Edward
Schnell, Christian
Smith, James (Ovid)
Tompkins, Charles H.
Veal, Charles

Wales
Davis, Joseph
Davis, Thomas
Evans, Thomas
Griffiths, John

Washington Territory
Wilson, John M.

Washington, D.C.
Baker, Charles

Cutts, James M.
Force, Manning F.
McAlwee, Benjamin F.
Rush, John
Taylor, William
White, Joseph

West Virginia
Barringer, William H.
Buckley, John C.
Bumgarner, William
Curtis, Josiah M.
Durham, James R.
Eckes, John N.
Godley, Leonidus M.
McCauslin, Joseph

McWhorter, Walter F.
Moore, George G.
Reeder, Charles A.
Shanan, Emisire
Shanes, John
Shoemaker, Levi
Summers, James C.
Van Matre, Joseph
Ward, Thomas J.
Woods, Daniel A.

Wisconsin
Anderson, Peter
Coates, Jefferson
Hilliker, Benjamin F.
Moore, Daniel B.

Listing by Birth Year of Recipient

1804
Shutes, Henry

1808
Buck, James

1809
Baker, Charles
Saunders, James

1811
Sprowle, David

1812
Talbott, William

1814
Freeman, Martin

1815
Sharp, Hendrick
Todd, Samuel

1816
Barnum, James

1817
McDonald, John
Sprague, John W.

1818
Jennings, James T.
Strong, James N.

1819
Davidson, Andrew

English, Thomas
Hyland, John

1820
Ham, Mark G.
Jones, Thomas

1821
Whitfield, Daniel

1822
Eddy, Samuel E.
Frisbee, John B.
Ginley, Patrick
Hatch, John P.
Williams, Anthony

1823
Ferrell, John H.
Murphy, Patrick
Parks, George
Whitehead, John M.
Willcox, Orlando B.
Woon, John

1824
Atkinson, Thomas E.
Force, Manning F.
Haley, James
Johnson, Henry
Phinney, William
Saxton, Rufus

1825
Avery, James

Capehart, Henry
Donoghue, Timothy
Sickles, Daniel E.
Stahel, Julius
Swearer, Benjamin

1826
Benedict, George G.
Brown, James
Brown, John
Dennis, Richard
Jordan, Robert
Lear, Nicholas
Martin, James
May, William
Potter, Norman F.
Smith, Charles H.
Smith, James
Smith, John
Tripp, Othniel
Willis, Richard

1827
Breen, John
Kenna, Barnett
Prance, George
Ringold, Edward
Shaler, Alexander
Smith, Walter B.

1828
Beatty, Alexander M.
Bowman, Edward R.
Buffum, Robert
Chamberlain, Joshua L.

Clark, William A.
Ditzenback, John
Grant, Lewis A.
Melville, Charles
Stanley, David S.
Webber, Alason P.
Williams, John

1829
Brinn, Andrew
Carr, William M.
Crowley, Michael
Howard, Peter
Hymer, Samuel
James, Miles
Larimer, Smith
McGonnigle, Andrew J.
Tracy, Amasa
Williamson, James A.
Wright, Edward

1830
Boury, Richard
Brown, Robert
Carr, Eugene A.
Clark, John W.
Davis, Charles C.
Franks, William J.
Hamilton, Hugh
Hartranft, John F.
Holmes, Lovilo N.
Howard, Oliver O.
Hyatt, Theodore
Knowles, Abiather J.
McCullock, Adam
Murphy, Dennis J.F.
Neahr, Zachariah C.
O'Donnell, Menomen
Shivers, John
Taylor, George
Tracy, Benjamin F.
Walling, William H.
Wilhelm, George
Wilkes, Perry

1831
Barton, Thomas
Boon, Hugh P.
Butterfield, Daniel
Cole, Gabriel
Edwards, John

Hayes, John
Henry, William W.
Jones, William
Lloyd, John W.
Mason, Elihu H.
McClelland, James M.
McGowan, John
Oliver, Paul A.
Robinson, Alexander
Schofield, John M.
Sheridan, James
Shipman, William
Slavens, Samuel
Smith, John
Stanley, William A.
Swift, Frederic W.
Wilcox, Franklin L.
Williams, Peter

1832
Batchelder, Richard N.
Blagheen, William
Brennan, Christopher
Connor, William C.
Cooper, John
Di Cesnola, Louis P.
Gardner, William
Gresser, Ignatz
Haffee, Edmund
Hawthorne, Harris S.
Lorish, Andrew J.
Lovering, George M.
McMillen, Francis M.
Molloy, Hugh
Nichols, Henry C.
Regan, Jeremiah
Ripley, William Y.W.
Robinson, Charles
Ross, Marion A.
Sears, Cyrus
Shapland, John
Shilling, John
Veale, Moses
Walker, Dr. Mary E.
Wells, William
Williams, John
Williams, John A.
Wood, H. Clay

1833
Albert, Christian

Barnum, Henry A.
Birdsall, Horatio
Box, Thomas J.
Capehart, Charles E.
Conboy, Martin
Duncan, Adam
Durham, James R.
Farrell, Edward
Fox, Henry
Greene, Oliver D.
Hamilton, Thomas W.
Harrington, Ephraim W.
Hesseltine, Francis S.
Irwin, Nicholas
McClelland, Matthew
McCormick, Michael
McIntosh, James
Niven, Robert
Phelps, Charles E.
Poole, William B.
Post, Philip Sidney
Quay, Matthew S.
Quinlan, James
Schutt, George
Seanor, James
Seaver, Thomas O.
Smith, Oloff
Stockman, George H.
Sullivan, James
Thielberg, Henry
Treat, Howell B.
Ward, James
White, Patrick H.

1834
Asten, Charles
Belcher, Thomas
Bourne, Thomas
Brown, John Harties
Bucklyn, John K.
Collins, Harrison
De Lacey, Patrick
Densmore, William
Dunn, William
Embler, Andrew H.
Farnsworth, Herbert E.
Hawkins, Charles
Hayden, Joseph B.
Hudson, Michael
Jones, John E.
Lakin, Daniel

Leland, George W.
Logan, Hugh
McAdams, Peter
Kennedy, John
Moore, William
Shopp, George J.
Swayne, Wager
Taylor, Thomas
Thomson, Clifford
Truett, Alexander H.
Vernay, James D.
Verney, James W.

1835
Ames, Adelbert
Arther, Matthew
Bell, James B.
Blickensderfer, Milton
Bliss, Zenas R.
Boynton, Henry V.
Bronner, Augustus F.
Burns, John M.
Catlin, Isaac S.
Chandler, Henry F.
Clifford, Robert T.
Curtis, Newton Martin
Farley, William
Garvin, William
Griffiths, John
Hall, Henry Seymour
Harris, George W.
Hill, Edward
James, John H.
Jones, Andrew
Jones, William
Mitchell, Theodore
Ratcliff, Edward
Richards, Louis
Roantree, James S.
Rush, John
Savacool, Edwin F.
Sewell, William J.
Steele, John W.
Sullivan, Timothy
Toohey, Thomas
Vantine, Joseph E.
Veazey, Wheelock G.
Webb, Alexander S.
Withington, William H.
Woods, Samuel
Wright, William

Young, Edward B.
Young, William

1836
Barker, Nathaniel C.
Boody, Robert M.
Brown, William H.
Cadwell, Lyman L.
Calkin, Ivers S.
Corson, Joseph K.
Cronin, Cornelius
Cutcheon, Byron M.
Dilger, Hubert
Dorsey, Decatur
Guinn, Thomas
Hamilton, Richard
Hand, Allexander
Hedges, Joseph
Ludgate, William
Mack, Alexander
Mackie, John F.
Maynard, George H.
McCammon, William W.
McFall, Daniel
Miller, Andrew
Miller, William E.
Morton, Charles W.
Newman, Marcellus J.
Noll, Conrad
Orr, Robert L.
Palmer, William J.
Perry, Thomas
Rannahan, John
Sellers, Alfred J.
Simkins, Lebbeus
Smith, Joseph S.
Stout, Richard
Swatton, Edward
Warren, David
Wherry, William M.
Wood, Robert B.
Younker, John L.

1837
Arnold, Abraham K.
Ayers, John G.K.
Beaty, Powhattan
Beaumont, Eugene B.
Beyer, Hillary
Bliss, George N.
Bradley, Amos

Brazell, John
Bumgarner, William
Casey, Henry
Cassidy, Michael
Cilley, Clinton A.
Cripps, Thomas
Cunningham, Francis M.
Deakin, Charles
Drake, James M.
Fitzpatrick, Thomas
Frantz, Joseph
Freeman, Henry B.
Frey, Franz
Griswold, Luke M.
Hagerty, Asel
Halstead, William
Harding, Thomas
Heermance, William L.
Herron, Francis J.
Hickman, John
Hubbell, William S.
Ilgenfritz, Charles H.
Jardine, James
Jones, John
Johns, Elisha
King, Horatio C.
Knight, William J.
Lawson, John
Leon, Pierre
Mayes, William B.
McHugh, Martin
Neil, John
Nichols, William
Norton, Llewellyn P.
Porter, Horace
Read, Charles A.
Roberts, James
Sartwell, Henry
Schenck, Benjamin W.
Taylor, Anthony
Thomas, Hampton, S.
Wagg, Maurice
Weeks, Charles H.
Wells, William
Williams, Robert

1838
Alber, Frederick
Archer, Lester
Betham, Asa
Betts, Charles M.

Bibber, Charles J.
Bickford, Henry H.
Blackwood, William R.D.
Bonebrake, Henry G.
Bradley, Charles
Bronson, James
Burbank, James H.
Burger, Joseph
Burton, Albert
Butts, George
Byrnes, James
Campbell, William
Chandler, James B.
Collis, Charles H.T.
Conlan, Dennis
Corcoran, Thomas E.
Curran, Richard
Cutts, James M.
DeWitt, Richard W.
Fernald, Albert E.
Frick, Jacob G.
Goodman, William E.
Grebe, M.R. William
Hadley, Cornelius M.
Hathaway, Edward W.
Holton, Charles M.
Horton, James
Judge, Francis W.
King, Rufus
Kirby, Dennis T.
Lyons, Thomas
McAlwee, Benjamin F.
McKown, Nathaniel A.
McMahon, Martin T.
Milliken, Daniel
Montgomery, Robert
Moore, Daniel B.
Moore, George
Newman, William H.
Pearson, Alfred L.
Peterson, Alfred
Pike, Edward M.
Porter, John R.
Prentice, Joseph R.
Read, George E.
Rodenbough, Theophilus F.
Schnell, Christian
Scott, John Wallace
Seaman, Elisha B.
Smith, Thomas
Smith, William

Sterling, James E.
Stoddard, James
Stokes, George
Summers, James C.
Summers, Robert
Swan, Charles A.
Thompson, John
Titus, Charles
Veal, Charles
Wheaton, Lloyd
Whitman, Frank M.
Woodward, Evan M.

1839

Allen, Abner
Anderson, Everett W.
Anderson, Marion T.
Baldwin, Charles
Banks, George L.
Bates, Norman F.
Bebb, Edward J.
Bell, George
Benjamin, Samuel N.
Bickford, Matthew
Black, John C.
Blodgett, Welis H.
Bond, William
Brandle, Joseph E.
Brouse, Charles W.
Brown, Jeremiah Z.
Brown, Wilson W.
Carey, James L.
Cotton, Peter
Coyne, John N.
Cullen, Thomas
Davis, George E.
Dempster, John
Denig, J. Henry
Donnelly, John
Hapeman, Douglas
Harris, John
Holehouse, James
Horton, Lewis A.
Howard, Henderson C.
Huidekoper, Henry S.
Irving, John
Irwin, Patrick
Jewett, Erastus W.
Kappesser, Peter
Kendall, William W.
Kendrick, Thomas

Lloyd, Benjamin
Lonergan, John
Marland, William
Martin, William
Mifflin, James
Miller, Henry A.
Moore, Charles
Mulholland, St. Clair A.
Mundell, Walter L.
O'Brien, Oliver
Porter, Ambrose
Ranney, George E.
Scott, John M.
Smalley, Reuben
Sullivan, John
Thaxter, Sidney W.
Thompson, Thomas
Vaughn, Pinkerton, R.
Wainwright, John
Woodruff, Alonzo

1840

Allen, Nathaniel
Archinal, William
Avery, William B.
Barry, Augustus
Bates, Delavan
Bensinger, William
Binder, Richard
Bishop, Francis A.
Blunt, John W.
Brownell, Francis E.
Bruton, Christopher C.
Buckingham, David E.
Campbell, William
Capron, Horace, Jr.
Carney, William H.
Carson, William J.
Clarke, Dayton P.
Colbert, Patrick
Compson, Hartwell B.
Copp, Charles D.
Crocker, Henry H.
Cross, James E.
Cunningham, James
Davidson, Andrew
Deane, John M.
Dow, Henry
Dunne, James
Dunphy, Richard D.
Fesq, Frank

Flood, Thomas
Garrison, James R.
Gaylord, Levi B.
George, Daniel G.
Gouraud, George E.
Green, George
Harbourne, John H.
Hayes, Thomas
Herington, Pitt B.
Holland, Lemuel F.
Inscho, Leonidus H.
Irlam, Joseph
Irsch, Francis
Jordan, Thomas
Kenyon, Charles
Lee, James H.
Martin, Edward S.
Mattocks, Charles P.
McFarland, John
McKnight, William
Menter, John W.
Molbone, Archibald
Morgan, James H.
Noble, Daniel
Nugent, Christopher
O'Connor, Timothy
Ortega, John
Payne, Thomas H.L.
Peters, Henry C.
Petty, Philip
Pittinger, William
Postles, James Parke
Price, Edward
Raub, Jacob F.
Read, Charles
Rice, Charles
Rought, Stephen
Rountry, John
Rowe, Henry W.
Sancrainte, Charles F.
Scheibner, Martin E.
Schofield, David H.
Seward, Richard E.
Shoemaker, Levi
Smith, Henry I.
Smith, Willard M.
Spalding, Edward B.
Stevens, Daniel D.
Tallentine, James
Torgler, Ernst
Trogden, Howell G.

Waller, Francis A.
Ward, William H.
White, Joseph
Whitney, William G.
Whittier, Edward N.
Williams, William

1841

Adams, John
Ammerman, Robert
Anderson, Robert
Anderson, Thomas
Ayers, David
Babcock, William J.
Barber, James A.
Barrick, Jesse T.
Barringer, William H.
Beebe, William S.
Bennett, Orson W.
Benyaurd, William H.
Bingham, Henry H.
Bois, Frank
Bras, Edgar A.
Brown, Charles
Brown, Edward, Jr.
Brown, Uriah
Brown, Wilson
Bryant, Andrew S.
Buffington, John C.
Burke, Daniel
Cadwallader, Abel G.
Carmin, Isaac H.
Chamberlain, Orville T.
Chandler, Stephen E.
Clapp, Albert A.
Clark, Charles
Coey, James
Cummings, Amos J.
Davis, Harry
Dickie, David
Doolen, William
English, Edmund
Ferrier, Daniel T.
Ferris, Eugene W.
French, Samuel S.
Graham, Robert
Gregg, Joseph O.
Hack, Lester G.
Haight, John H.
Harcourt, Thomas
Heller, Henry

Hinnecan, William
Hodges, Addison J.
Hughes, Oliver
Huskey, Michael
Jones, David
Kane, Thomas
Kelley, Leverett M.
Laffey, Bartlett
Lawson, Gaines
Madden, Michael
Newland, William
O'Donoghue, Timothy
Oviatt, Miles M.
Palmer, George H.
Preston, John
Pyne, George
Reigle, Danisl P.
Richey, William E.
Rutter, James M.
Schlachter, Philipp
Schwan, Theodore
Smith, Edwin
Sype, Peter
Taylor, William G.
Thompson, Henry A.
Tribe, John
Tweedale, John
Wall, Jerry C.
Walsh, John
Warden, John
Webb, James
Wheeler, Daniel D.
Whitaker, Edward W.
Woodruff, Carle A.
Yeager, Jacob F.

1842

Anderson, Frederick C.
Baldwin, Frank D.
Ballen, Frederick
Barrell, Charles L.
Black, William P.
Boquet, Nicholas
Bowen, Chester B.
Brady, James
Brant, William, Jr.
Brest, Lewis
Brown, Henri Le Fevre
Brown, John H.
Brown, Morris, Jr.
Brush, George W.

Buchanan, George A.
Buckley, John C.
Burk, Thomas
Burke, Thomas
Butterfield, Franklin G.
Caldwell, Daniel
Carter, John J.
Carter, Joseph F.
Casey, David
Clark, Harrison
Clausen, Charles H.
Clay, Cecil
Coffey, Robert J.
Connor, Thomas
Corcoran, John
Corliss, Stephen P.
Crawford, Alexander
Diggins, Bartholomew
Donaldson, John
Fall, Charles S.
Finkenbiner, Henry S.
Furman, Chester S.
Gasson, Richard
Hanna, Marcus A.
Hanna, Milton
Harley, Bernard
Harrison, George H.
Houghton, Charles H.
Irving, Thomas
Johnson, John
Josselyn, Simeon T.
Lafferty, John
Lann, John S.
Lewis, Henry
Little, Henry F.W.
Luce, Moses A.
Madison, James
Martin, William
McHale, Alexander U.
McKeever, Michael
Morrison, John G.
Murphy, Thomas C.
Nash, Henry H.
Nibbe, John H.
O'Connell, Thomas
Peck, Theodore S.
Pickle, Alonzo H.
Platt, George C.
Province, George
Reid, Robert
Rhodes, Sylvester D.

Roberts, Otis O.
Rundle, Charles W.
Sargent, Jackson
Schoonmaker, James M.
Schorn, Charles
Smith, Alonzo
Smith, Francis M.
Stevens, Hazard
Swanson, John
Tanner, Charles B.
Twombly, Voltaire P.
Wheeler, Henry W.
Williams, Augustus

1843

Allen, James
Appleton, William H.
Bass, David L.
Beddows, Richard
Bickford, John F.
Brewer, William J.
Bruner, Louis J.
Buck, Frederick Clarence
Cart, Jacob
Child, Benjamin H.
Chisman, William W.
Coates, Jefferson
Cockley, David L.
Conaway, John W.
Crosier, William H.H.
Davis, Martin K.
Deland, Frederick N.
Denning, Lorenzo
Dorman, John
Durham, John S.
Enderlin, Richard
Ennis, Charles D.
Estes, Llewellyn G.
Fisher, Joseph
Follett, Joseph
Forman, Alexander A.
Goodrich, Edwin
Greig, Theodore W.
Haskell, Frank W.
Hastings, Smith H.
Havron, John H.
Hibson, Joseph C.
Hilliker, Benjamin F.
Horne, Samuel B.
Hough, Ira
Houghton, Edward J.

Howard, Hiram R.
Howard, Martin
Hunter, Charles A.
Johnson, Follett
Johnson, Joseph E.
Keen, Joseph S.
Kelley, George V.
Kenyon, John S.
Kerr, Thomas R.
Kinnaird, Samuel W.
Landis, James P.
Lawton, Henry W.
Lower, Cyrus B.
Lyon, Frederick A.
Mack, John
Madden, William
Mills, Charles
Moffitt, John H.
Monaghan, Patrick
Munsell, Harvey M.
Naylor, David
O'Connor, Albert
Parrott, Jacob
Pinn, Robert
Read, Morton A.
Reeder, Charles A.
Robertson, Samuel
Rohm, Ferdinand F.
Sacriste, Louis J.
Shanan, Emisire
Shepard, Irwin
Shepard, Louis C.
Simmons, William T.
Simons, Charles J.
Smith, Andrew J.
Sweatt, Joseph G.
Swegheimer, Jacob
Swift, Harlan J.
Taggart, Charles A.
Thompson, Charles A.
Walker, James C.

1844

Adams, James
Anderson, Charles
Armstrong, Clinton L.
Baybutt, Philip
Beech, John P.
Bieger, Charles
Bonnaffon, Sylvester, Jr.
Boss, Orlando

The Battle of Perryville. Though the participants who fought there stated this battle was among the most savagely contested of any that took place during the war, only two Medals of Honor were awarded to soldiers who served there: John Durham and William Surles (U.S. Army War College).

A Union assault at the Battle of Antietam. Twenty men won the Medal of Honor for their gallantry at Antietam, a relatively small number considering that this was the bloodiest day of the entire war, and acts of individual courage abounded (The History of the Civil War in the United States).

Bradley, Thomas W.
Breyer, Charles
Brown, Robert B.
Buckley, Dennis
Campbell, James A.
Carr, Franklin
Caruana, Orlando E.
Cosgriff, Richard H.
Curtis, Josiah M.
Day, Charles
Dodd, Robert F.
Dougherty, Michael
Dougherty, Patrick
Evans, Ira H.
Falconer, John A.
Ford, George W.
Fox, Henry M.
Freeman, William
Hays, John H.
Holland, Milton M.
Jackson, Frederick R.
Kemp, Joseph
Kinsey, John
Lloyd, George
Lower, Robert A.
McCornack, Andrew
McWilliams, George W.
Morse, Benjamin
Mullen, Patrick
Murphy, John P.
Nolan, John J.
O'Beirne, James R.
Paul, William H.
Pay, Byron E.
Pennypacker, Galusha
Raymond, William H.
Roosevelt, George W.
Schneider, George
Sowers, Michael
Stolz, Frank
Tabor, William S.
Thatcher, Chrales M.
Toban, James W.

Toffey, John J.
Tomlin, Andrew J.
Wagner, John W.
Whitmore, John
Wright, Albert D.
Young, Benjamin F.

1845
Anderson, Bruce
Apple, Andrew O.
Boehm, Peter H.
Boutwell, John W.
Burns, James M.
Camp, Carlton N.
Chaput, Louis G.
Custer, Thomas W.
Davis, Samuel W.
Dickey, William D.
Dore, George H.
Duncan, James K.L.
Gardner, Charles N.
Gile, Frank S.
Gould, Charles G.
Grace, Peter
Hill, James
Johnson, Samuel
Kelley, Andrew J.
King, Robert H.
Kountz, John S.
Levy, Benjamin
Lucas, George W.
MacArthur, Arthur, Jr.
Manning, Joseph S.
Morrison, Francis
Powers, Wesley J.
Rowland, Archibald H., Jr.
Sidman, George E.
Smith, James (Ovid)
Surles, William H.
Thompson, Freeman C.
Tucker, Jacob R.
Vance, Wilson
Webster, Henry S.

Weeks, John H.
Wilkes, Henry
Williams, LeRoy
Woram, Charles B.
Young, Horatio N.

1846
Bourke, John G.
Bronson, John
Brutsche, Henry
Buckles, Abram J.
Graul, William
Haight, Sidney
Harvey, Harry
Langbein, J.C. Julius
Noyes, William W.
Savage, Auzella
Schmidt, William
Vanderslice, John M.
Wray, William J.

1847
Anderson, Peter
Burk, Michael E.
Collins, Thomas D.
Cook, John
Day, David F.
McKay, Charles
Smith, Thaddeus S.
Thompson, Allen
Woods, Daniel A.

1848
Burger, Joseph
Delaney, John C.
Howe, Orion P.
Machon, James
Parks, Henry Jeremiah
Peck, Oscar E.

1849
Harrington, Daniel

Listing by Year of Issuance

1863
Anderson, Robert
Arther, Matthew
Barton, Thomas
Bell, George
Bensinger, William
Bois, Frank
Bourne, Thomas
Bradley, Amos
Bradley, Charles
Breen, John
Brennan, Christopher
Brinn, Andrew
Brown, Wilson W.
Buck, James
Buffum, Robert
Byrnes, James
Corcoran, Thomas E.
Cotton, Peter
Dorsey, Daniel
Dow, Henry
Farrell, Edward
Flood, Thomas
Frisbee, John B.
Greene, John
Hamilton, Thomas W.
Hand, Allexander
Harrington, Daniel
Hawkins, Martin J.
Hickman, John
Hollat, George
Howard, Peter
Jackson, Frederick R.
Jenkins, Thomas
Johnson, Samuel
Johnston, Willie
Jordan, Robert
Kelley, John

Kenyon, Charles
Knight, William J.
Lakin, Daniel
Leon, Pierre
Mackie, John F.
Martin, William
Martin, William
Mason, Elihu H.
McClelland, Matthew
McDonald, John
McGowan, John
McHugh, Martin
McKnight, William
McLeod, James
Morton, Charles E.
Parker, William
Parrott, Jacob
Peck, Oscar E.
Peterson, Alfred
Pittinger, William
Porter, John R.
Reddick, William H.
Regan, Jeremiah
Richards, Louis
Ringold, Edward
Roberts, Otis O.
Robertson, Samuel
Robinson, Charles
Ross, Marion A.
Rush, John
Smith, Edwin
Sullivan, Timothy
Swearer, Benjamin
Thielberg, Henry
Thompson, William
Vantine, Joseph E.
Vaughn, Pinkerton R.
Williams, John

Williams, John
Williams, John
Williams, Peter
Williams, Robert
Wilson, John A.
Wood, Mark
Wood, Robert B.
Woods, Samuel
Woon, John
Wright, Edward
Young, William

1864
Adams, James F.
Aheam, Michael
Anderson, Frederick C.
Asten, Charles
Atkinson, Thomas E.
Bacon, Elijah W.
Baldwin, Charles
Baybutt, Philip
Begley, Terrence
Bibber, Charles J.
Bickford, John F.
Bishop, Francis A.
Blagheen, William
Blake, Robert
Bond, William
Bowen, Chester B.
Brazell, John
Brown, Charles
Brown, James
Brown, John
Brown, Robert
Brown, William H.
Brown, Wilson
Brownell, William P.
Brutsche, Henry

Picture showing the palisade and several of the traverses of Fort Fisher, North Carolina. Medals of Honor were liberally awarded to both Army and Navy personnel following the capture of this Confederate stronghold. Secretary Welles and Secretary Stanton vied with one another in issuing promotions and medals to the men of their perspective branches. Sixty-seven medals were awarded to soldiers and sailors who took part in the two expeditions, a remarkable number considering the relatively small number of men involved. Note the numerous footsteps in the sand caused by one of the assaulting columns (U.S. Army War College).

Burk, E. Michael
Burns, John M.
Butts, George
Carr, William M.
Cart, Jacob
Cassidy, Michael
Chandler, James B.
Chaput, Louis G.
Clifford, Robert T.
Colbert, Patrick
Cole, Gabriel
Conlan, Dennis
Connor, William C.

Connors, James
Cooper, John
Crawford, Alexander
Creed, John
Cripps, Thomas
Crocker, Ulric L.
Cronin, Cornelius
Cullen, Thomas
Davis, Harry
Davis, John
Davis, Samuel W.
Deakin, Charles
De Castro, Joseph H.

Denig, J. Henry
Denning, Lorenzo
Dennis, Richard
Densmore, William
Doolen, William
Dore, George E.
Dorman, John
Dougherty, Patrick
Drury, James
Duncan, Adam
Duncan, James K.L.
Dunphy, Richard D.
Edwards, John

Ellis, Horace
Evans, Thomas
Falls, Benjamin F.
Farley, William
Fitzpatrick, Thomas
Flynn, Christopher
Fox, Henry M.
Franks, William J.
Freeman, Archibald
Freeman, Martin
Gardner, William
Garrison, James R.
Garvin, William
Gause, Isaac
Gile, Frank S.
George, Daniel G.
Graham, Robert
Gray, John
Haley, James
Halstead, William
Ham, Mark G.
Hamilton, Hugh
Hamilton, Richard
Hanford, Edward R.
Hanscom, Moses C.
Harding, Thomas
Harley, Bernard
Harris, George W.
Harrison, George H.
Hawkins, Charles
Hayes, John
Hayes, Thomas
Hill, James
Hincks, William B.
Hinnecan, William
Hogan, Franklin
Hough, Ira
Houghton, Edward J.
Howard, Martin
Hudson, Michael
Huskey, Michael
Hyland, John
Irlam, Joseph
Irving, John
Irving, Thomas
Irwin, Nicholas
James, John H.
Jellison, Benjamin H.
Jennings, James T.
Johnston, William P.
Jones, Andrew

Jones, John E.
Jones, William
Jones, William
Kelly, Thomas
Kemp, Joseph
Kendrick, Thomas
Kenna, Barnett
Kindig, John M.
King, Robert H.
Kinnaird, Samuel W.
Lafferty, John
Laffey, Bartlett
Lawson, John
Lee, James H.
Leland, George W.
Leslie, Frank
Lloyd, Benjamin
Lloyd, John W.
Lorish, Andrew J.
Lucas, George W.
Lyon, Frederick A.
Machon, James
Mack, Alexander
Madden, William
Mahoney, Jeremiah
Manning, Joseph S.
Martin, Edward S.
Martin, James
Mayberry, John B.
McCarren, Bernard
McCormick, Michael
McCullock, Adam
McEnroe, Patrick H.
McFarland, John
McIntosh, James
Meach, George
Melville, Charles
Mifflin, James
Miller, Andrew
Miller, James
Miller, John
Molloy, Hugh
Monaghan, Patrick
Montgomery, Robert
Moore, Charles
Moore, Charles
Moore, George G.
Moore, William
Morgan, James H.
Morgan, Lewis
Murphy, Daniel J.

Murphy, Patrick
Murphy, Thomas
Naylor, David
Neil, John
Newland, William
Nichols, William
Nugent, Christopher
O'Brien, Oliver
O'Connell, Thomas
O'Donoghue, Timothy
Opel, John N.
Ortega, John
Oviatt, Miles M.
Parks, George
Parks, Henry Jeremiah
Pease, Joachim
Pelham, William
Perry, Thomas
Phinney, William
Plowman, George H.
Poole, William B.
Preston, John
Price, Edward
Read, Charles A.
Read, George E.
Reed, George W.
Reid, Robert
Reigle, Daniel P.
Reynolds, George
Rice, Charles
Richmond, James
Roantree, James S.
Roberts, James
Robinson, Alexander
Robinson, John H.
Robinson, Thomas
Rood, Oliver P.
Rought, Stephen
Rounds, Lewis A.
Rowe, Henry W.
Russell, Charles L.
Schlachter, Philipp
Schofield, David H.
Seanor, James
Seward, Richard E.
Sharp, Hendrick
Sheridan, James
Sherman, Marshall
Shilling, John
Shoemaker, Levi
Simkins, Lebbeus

Smith, Alonzo
Smith, James (Ovid)
Smith, James
Smith, John
Smith, John
Smith, Oloff
Smith, Walter B.
Smith, Willard M.
Smith, William
Sprowle, David
Stanley, William A.
Sterling, James E.
Stoddard, James
Stout, Richard
Strahan, Robert
Strausbaugh, Bernard A.
Sullivan, James
Sullivan, John
Sweeney, James
Tallentine, James
Taylor, George
Taylor, Richard
Thompson, James B.
Thompson, William P.
Todd, Samuel
Truett, Alexander H.
Wagg, Maurice
Wall, Jerry
Waller, Francis A.
Walsh, John
Ward, James
Warren, David
Weeks, John H.
Wells, Thomas M.
Wells, William
Westerhold, William
Wiley, James
Wilkes, Henry
Wilkes, Perry
Wilkins, Leander A.
Wollam, John
Woodbury, Eri D.
Woram, Charles B.
Wright, William
Young, Benjamin F.
Young, Horatio N.

1865
Allen, Abner P.
Ammerman, Robert W.
Anderson, Charles W.

Anderson, Peter
Anderson, Thomas
Angling, John
Apple, Andrew O.
Archer, Lester
Barnes, William H.
Barnum, James
Barter, Gurdon H.
Bass, David L.
Bates, Norman, F.
Bazaar, Philip
Beaty, Powhatan
Bebb, Edward J.
Belcher, Thomas
Benjamin, John F.
Bennett, Orren
Betham, Asa
Bickford, Henry H.
Binder, Richard
Birdsall, Horatio L.
Blair, Robert M.
Blickensderfer, Milton
Blucher, Charles
Bonebrake, Henry G.
Boury, Richard
Bowman, Edward R.
Box, Thomas J.
Brady, James
Brant, William
Bras, Edgar A.
Brest Lewis F.
Brewer, William J.
Briggs, Elijah A.
Bringle, Andrew
Bronson, James H.
Brown, John Harties
Bruton, Christopher C.
Buchanan, George A.
Buck, F. Clarence
Buckley, Denis
Burton, Albert
Caldwell, Daniel
Calkin, Ivers S.
Callahan, John H.
Campbell, William
Capron, Horace, Jr.
Carman, Warren
Carr, Franklin
Chapman, John
Clancy, James T.
Clapp, Albert A.

Clopp, John E.
Cohn, Abraham
Collins, Harrison
Colwell, Oliver
Compson, Hartwell B.
Connell, Trustrim
Connor, Thomas
Cosgriff, Richard H.
Crowley, Michael
Cunningham, Francis M.
Curtis, Josiah M.
Custer, Thomas
Davidsizer, John A.
Davis, John
Davis, Joseph
Davis, Thomas
De Lavie, Hiram H.
Dempster, John
Ditzenback, John
Dockum, Warren C.
Dolloff, Charles W.
Donaldson, John
Dorsey, Decatur
Dunlavy, James
Dunn, William
Edwards, David
Elliott, Alexander
Elise, William
English, Thomas
Erickson, John P.
Evans, Coron D.
Everson, Adelbert
Ewing, John C.
Fanning, Nicholas
Fernald, Albert E.
Ferrell, John H.
Fesq, Frank
Flanagan, Augustin
Fleetwood, Christian
Ford, George W.
Foy, Charles H.
Fry, Isaac N.
Gardiner, James
Gardner, Charles N.
Gardner, Robert J.
Garrett, William
Gasson, Richard
Gaunt, John C.
Gere, Thomas P.
Gibbs, Wesley
Gifford, Benjamin

Goettel, Philip
Goheen, Charles A.
Graul, William
Greenawalt, Abraham
Gribben, James H.
Griffiths, John
Griswold, Luke M.
Grueb, George
Hack, Lester G.
Haffee, Edmund
Hagerty, Asel
Hall, Newton H.
Harcourt, Thomas
Hardenbergh, Henry M.
Harmon, Amzi D.
Harvey, Harry
Hayden, Joseph B.
Haynes, Asbury F.
Hays, John H.
Hickok, Nathan E.
Higby, Charles
Highland, Patrick
Hilton, Alfred B.
Hoffman, Henry
Holcomb, Daniel I.
Holland Milton M.
Holmes, William T.
Hooper, William B.
Horton, James
Horton, Lewis A.
Hottenstine, Solomon J.
Houlton, William
Howard, James
Hudson, Aaron R.
Hughes, Oliver
Hughey, John
Hunter, Charles A.
Jacobson, Eugene P.
James, Isaac
James, Miles
Johndro, Franklin
Jones, John
Jones, Thomas
Jordan, Absalom
Jordan, Thomas
Kaltenbach, Luther
Kane, John
Kappesser, Peter
Kauss, August
Kelley, George V.
Kelly, Alexander

Kelly, Daniel
Kenyon, Samuel P.
Keough, John
Kimball, Joseph
Kline, Harry
Koogle, Jacob
Kramer, Theodore L.
Kuder, Andrew
Kuder, Jeremiah
Laing, William
Landis, James P.
Lanfare, Aaron S.
Lann, John S.
Larimer, Smith
Lear, Nicholas
Leonard, William E.
Levy, Benjamin
Lilley, John
Locke, Lewis
Logan, Hugh
Love, George M.
Lutes, Franklin W.
Mack, John
Madison, James
Mandy, Harry J.
Marquette, Charles
Marsh, Charles H.
Matthews, Milton
Mattingly, Henry B.
May, William
McCauslin, Joseph
McCleary, Charles H.
McConnell, Samuel
McDonald, George E.
McElhinny, Samuel O.
McGraw, Thomas
McKee, George
McKown, Nathaniel A.
McMillen, Francis M.
McWhorter, Walter F.
McWilliams, George W.
Meagher, Thomas
Menter, John W.
Miller, Frank
Miller, Henry A.
Miller, James P.
Miller, John
Milliken, Daniel
Mills, Charles
Mitchell, Theodore
Moore, George

Moore, Wilbur F.
Morgan, Richard H.
Morris, William
Morrison, John G.
Mullen, Patrick
Mundell, Walter L.
Murphy, Thomas J.
Neville, Edwin M.
Newman, William H.
Nibbe, John H.
Niven, Robert
Norton, Elliott M.
Norton, John R.
Norton, Llewellyn P
O'Brien, Peter
O'Connor, Timothy
Oliver, Charles
Parks, James W.
Payne, Irvin C.
Peirsol, James K.
Phillips, Josiah
Pitman, George J.
Porter, William
Potter, Norman F.
Prance, George
Province, George
Pyne, George
Ramsbottom, Alfred
Rannahan, John
Ratcliff, Edward
Read, Charles
Read, Morton A.
Rebmann, George F.
Ricksecker, John H.
Riddell, Rudolph
Riley, Thomas
Robinson, James H.
Rountry, John
Ryan, Peter J.
Sanderson, Aaron
Saunders, James
Savacool, Edwin F.
Savage, Auzella
Schiller, John
Schmal, George W.
Schorn, Charles
Schutt, George
Scott, John Wallace
Scott, Julian A.
Seston, Charles H.
Shanan, Emisire

Shellenberger, John S.
Shepard, Louis C.
Shepard, William
Shields, Bernard
Shipley, Robert, F.
Shipman, William
Shivers, John
Shopp, George J.
Shubert, Frank
Simmons, John
Simmons, William T.
Skellie, Ebenezer
Sloan, Andrew J.
Smith, Andrew Jackson
Smith, Charles H.
Smith, Otis W.
Smith, Richard
Southard, David
Sova, Joseph E.
Sterling, John T.
Stewart, George W.
Stewart, Joseph
Stickels, Joseph
Stokes, George
Streile, Christian
Summers, Robert
Swan, Charles A.
Swanson, John
Swatton, Edward
Taggart, Charles A.
Talbott, William
Taylor, Thomas
Taylor, William G.
Thompkins, George W.
Thompson, Freeman C.
Thompson, Henry A.
Tibbetts, Andrew W.
Titus, Charles
Tomlin, Andrew J.
Tompkins, Aaron B.
Tripp, Othniel
Tucker, Allen
Tyrrell, George William
Van Matre, Joseph
Van Winkle, Edward
  (Edwin)
Veal, Charles
Verney, James W.
Vifquain, Victor
Walker, Dr. Mary E.
Warfel, Henry C.

Webster, Henry S.
Welch, George W.
Welch, Richard
Wells, Henry S.
White, Adam
White, Joseph
Whitmore, John
Wilcox, Franklin L.
Williams, Anthony
Williams, Augustus
Willis, Richard
Wilson, Charles E.
Wilson, John
Winegar, William W.
Woodall, William H.
Woods, Daniel A.
Young, Andrew J.
Young, Cavalry M.
Young, Edward B.

1866
Avery, James
Baker, Charles
Barber, James A.
Brannigan, Felix
Coates, Jefferson
Donnelly, John
Harris, John
Havron, John H.
Lane, Morgan D.
Lewis, Samuel E.
Magee, William
Molbone, Archibald
Munsell, Harvey M.
Murphy, John P.
Noble, Daniel
Plunkett, Thomas
Richardson, William R.
Scott, John M.
Shambough, Charles
Shea, Joseph H.
Shutes, Henry
Taylor, John

1867
Cayer, Ovila
Johnson, Henry
Kane, Thomas
Keele, Joseph
Orth, Jacob G.
Parker, Thomas

Reeder, Charles A.
Terry, John D.
Weeks, Charles H.

1869
Brown, Morris, Jr.
Homan, Conrad
Wright, Robert

1870
Barry, Augustus
Hawkins, Thomas R.
Judge, Francis W.
Karpeles, Leopold
Little, Henry F.W.
McVeane, John P.
Seward, Griffin
Stevens, Daniel D.
Thompson, J. (James)
  Harry
Truell, Edwin M.
Urell, M. Emmet

1871
Chambers, Joseph B.
Myers, William H.
Tucker, Jacob R.

1872
Funk, West
Hart, William E.
Lyons, Thomas

1873
Bryant, Andrew S.
Drake, James M.
Rowand, Archibald H., Jr.

1874
Harris, James H.
Whitman, Frank M.

1876
Luty, Gotlieb

1877
Benjamin, Samuel N.
Brownell, Francis E.

1878
Burke, Thomas

Fasnacht, Charles H.
Kaiser, John

1879
Fox, William R.
Orbansky, David
Pentzer, Patrick H.

1880
Brown, Edward, Jr.
Merritt, John G.
Spillane, Timothy
Wilson, Francis A.

1883
Robie, George F.
Slavens, Samuel

1884
Dow, George P.
Gion, Joseph
Johnston, David
Tilton, William

1885
Littlefield, George H.

1886
Hartranft, John F.
Murphy, James T.
Potter, George W.

1887
Bennett, Orson W.
Bourke, John G.
Cooke, Walter H.
Corcoran, John
Greig, Theodore W.
Lower, Cyrus B.
Rhodes, Julius D.
Roosevelt, George W.
Tweedale, John
Wilhelm, George

1888
Boss, Orlando
Carey, Hugh
Casey, David
Chase, John F.
Coyne, John N.
Haight, John H.

Mangam, Richard C.
Quay, Matthew S.

1889
Barnum, Henry A.
Dillon, Michael A.
Holton, Charles M.
Ludgate, William
Preston, Noble D.
Sacriste, Louis J.
Schwenk, Martin
Tanner, Charles B.

1890
Allen, James
Brown, Robert B.
Caruana, Orlando E.
Cook, John H.
Copp, Charles D.
Durham, James R.
Follett, Joseph L.
Ginley, Patrick
Gould, Charles G.
Haring, Abram P.
Immell, Lorenzo D.
Luther, James H.
MacArthur, Arthur, Jr.
McKeen, Nineveh S.
Mitchell, Alexander H.
Morse, Charles E.
Murphy, Robinson B.
Neahr, Zachariah C.
O'Brien, Henry D.
Powell, William H.
Thackrah, Benjamin
Wainwright, John

1891
Appleton, William H.
Baldwin, Frank D.
Barrell, Charles L.
Bates, Delavan
Butterfield, Frank G.
Carter, Joseph F.
Clark, John W.
Curtis, Newton Martiin
Cutcheon, Byron M.
Cutts, James M.
Diggins, Bartholomew
Elison, James M.
English, Edmund

Fallon, Thomas T.
Grindlay, James G.
Hall, Henry Seymour
Hickey, Dennis W.
Hogarty, William P.
Hooker, George W.
Hyde, Thomas W.
Jewett, Erastus W.
Livingston, Josiah O.
Lovering, George M.
Loyd, George
Matthews, John C.
McMahon, Martin T.
Merrill, Augustus
Moffitt, John H.
Morse, Benjamin
O'Beirne, James R.
O'Neill, Stephen
Peck, Theodore S.
Pennypacker, Galusha
Pingree, Samuel E.
Quinlan, James
Rice, Edmund
Sargent, Jackson
Surles, William H.
Veazey, Wheelock G.
Webb, Alexander S.

1892
Benedict, George G.
Betts, Charles M.
Burke, Daniel W.
Carlisle, Casper R.
Christiancy, James I.
Clark, James G.
Clarke, Dayton P.
Clausen, Charles H.
Clay, Cecil
Coey, James
Coffey, Robert J.
Conboy, Martin
Cox, Robert M.
Cranston, William W.
Crosier, William H.H.
Davidson, Andrew
Davidson, Andrew
Davis, George E.
Ennis, Charles D.
Evans, Ira H.
Force, Manning F.
Frick, Jacob G.

Gilligan, Edward L.
Gilmore, John C.
Green, George
Heller, Henry
Henry, William W.
Holton, Edward A.
Hopkins, Charles F.
Howard, Hiram R.
Irsch, Francis
Johnson, Follett
Keene, Joseph
Kennedy, John
Kiggins, John
Knox, Edward M.
Mathews, William H.
Miles, Nelson A.
Murphy, Dennis J.F.
Noyes, William W.
Oliver, Paul A.
Orr, Robert L.
Oss, Albert
Peck, Cassius
Postles, James Parke
Putnam, Edgar, P.
Robbins, Augustus I.
Rutherford, John T.
Sancrainte, Charles F.
Schofield, John M.
Seaman, Elisha B.
Sears, Cyrus
Seaver, Thomas O.
Sidman, George E.
Smith, Joseph S.
Sperry, William J.
Sweatt, Joseph G.
Thomas, Stephen
Thompson, Thomas
Tracy, Amasa A.
Tremain, Henry E.
Walling, William H.
Wheeler, Daniel D.
Whittier, Edward N.
Williston, Edward B.
Wray, William J.

1893
Anderson, Marion T.
Arnold, Abraham K.
Avery, William B.
Bingham, Henry H.
Black, John C.

Black, William P.
Bonnaffon, Sylvester, Jr.
Boynton, Henry V.
Buckles, Abram J.
Butterfield, Daniel
Carmin, Isaac H.
Chamberlain, Joshua L.
Collis, Charles H.T.
Coughlin, John
Dilger, Hubert
Doody, Patrick
Downs, Henry W.
Embler, Andrew H.
Fisher, John H.
Gouraud, George E.
Grant, Lewis A.
Greene, Oliver D.
Harrington, Ephraim W.
Hatch, John P.
Hawkins, Gardner C.
Henry, Guy V.
Herron, Francis J.
Hill, Edward
Hill, James
Hills, William G.
Howard, Oliver O.
Johns, Henry T.
Johnson, John
Larrabee, James W.
Lawton, Henry W.
Lonergan, John
Lower, Robert A.
Mindil, George W.
Morey, Delano
Morford, Jerome
Murphy, Thomas C.
Nutting, Lee
Petty, Philip
Post, Philip Sidney
Richey, William E.
Ripley, William Y.W.
Rodenbough, Theophilus F.
Sands, William
Sanford, Jacob
Saxton, Rufus
Schubert, Martin
Shaler, Alexander
Stahel, Julius
Stanley, David S.
Strong, James N.
Swayne, Wager

Taylor, Anthony
Taylor, Henry H.
Tomkins, Charles H.
Vanderslice, John M.
Von Vegesack, Ernest
Warden, John
Warren, Francis E.
Wood, H. Clay
Woodruff, Carle A.
Wright, Albert D.
Younker, John L.

1894
Ames, Adelbert
Anderson, Everett W.
Archinal, William
Armstrong, Clinton L.
Ayers, David
Barringer, William H.
Beatty, Alexander M.
Beech, John P.
Bickford, Matthew
Blasdel, Thomas A.
Blodgett, Welis H.
Bowen, Emmer
Brosnan, John
Brown, Uriah
Buckley, John C.
Burhman, Henry G.
Bumgarner, William
Cadwell, Luman L.
Campbell, William
Carr, Eugene A.
Carson, William J.
Chisman, William W.
Conaway, John W.
Cook, John
Cummings, Amos J.
Cunningham, James S.
Davis, Charles C.
Davis, Martin K.
De Lacey, Patrick
Delaney, John C.
De Witt, Richard W.
Donoghue, Timothy
Eckes, John N.
Estes, Lewellyn G.
Fassett, John B.
Fisher, Joseph
Flynn, James E.
Frantz, Joseph

Freeman, Henry B.
Frey, Franz
Frizzell, Henry F.
Geschwind, Nicholas
Goldsbery, Andrew E.
Goodall, Francis H.
Goodman, William E.
Goodrich, Edwin
Gould, Newton T.
Grace, Peter
Grimshaw, Samuel
Guin, Thomas
Gwynne, Nathaniel
Harris, Sampson
Hawthorne, Harris S.
Helms, David H.
Henry, James
Howard, Squire E.
Hubbell, William S.
Hunt, Louis T.
Hyatt, Theodore
Inscho, Leonidus H.
Jardine, James
John, William
Johns, Elisha
Johnson, Andrew
Jones, David
Kendall, William W.
Kerr, Thomas R.
Kirby, Dennis T.
Kirk, Jonathan C.
Knowles, Abiather J.
Labill, Joseph S.
Leonard, Edwin
Longshore, William H.
Lunt, Alphonso M.
Lyman, Joel H.
Martin, Sylvester H.
McClelland, James M.
McGinn, Edward
McGonagle, Wilson
McKay, Charles W.
Merriam, Henry C.
Miller, Jacob C.
Mostroller, John W.
Myers, George S.
O'Dea, John
Overturf, Jacob H.
Packard, Loron F.
Palmer, William J.
Parsons, Joel

Pearsall, Platt
Phisterer, Frederick
Prentice, Joseph R.
Purcell, Hiram W.
Renninger, Louis
Robinson, John C.
Rock, Frederick
Rundle, Charles W.
Schenck, Benjamin W.
Schmauch, Andrew
Schnell, Christian
Sellers, Alfred J.
Smalley, Reuben
Smith, Henry I.
Spalding, Edward B.
Sprague, Benona
Sprague, John W.
Steinmetz, William
Stephens, William G.
Stevens, Hazard
Stockman, George H.
Stolz, Frank
Swegheimer, Jacob
Thomas, Hampton S.
Toomer, William
Torgler, Ernst
Treat, Howell B.
Trogden, Howell G.
Veale, Moses
Wagner, John W.
Ward, Thomas J.
Welch, Stephen
Welsh, Edward
Wheaton, Lloyd
Widick, Andrew J.
Williams, William H.
Woodward, Evan M.
Wortick (Wertick), Joseph

1895
Albert, Christian
Ayers, John G.K.
Babcock, William J.
Batchelder, Richard N.
Buckingham, David E.
Capehart, Henry
Cilley, Clinton A.
Clark, Harrison
Cleveland, Charles F.
Corliss, Stephen P.
Darrough, John S.

Day, David F.
Deane, John M.
Dunne, James
Ellsworth, Thomas
Evans, James R.
Forman, Alexander A.
Fraser, William W.
French, Samuel S.
Galloway, George N.
Gresser, Ignatz
Hanna, Marcus A.
Hesseltine, Francis S.
Hoffman, Thomas W.
Horsfall, William H.
Howe, William H.
Kloth, Charles H.
Kountz, John S.
Langbein, J.C. Julius
Lawson, Gaines
Luce, Moses A.
McCornack, Andrew
McGuire, Patrick
Mulholland, St. Clair A.
Pickle, Alonzo H.
Pinkham Charles H.
Platt, George C.
Powers, Wesley J.
Ranney, Myron H.
Reed, Charles W.
Reed, William
Rich, Carlos H.
Schmidt, William
Shafter, William R.
Sladen, Joseph A.
Smith, Charles H.
Smith, Francis M.
Smith, S. Rodmond
Sturgeon, James K.
Summers, James C.
Thorn, Walter
Tracy, Benjamin F.
Tracy, William G.
Tribe, John
Walker, James C.
Ward, William H.
Wherry, William M.
White, Patrick H.
Whitney, William G.
Willcox, Orlando B.
Williamson, James A.
Wisner, Lewis S.

Withington, William H.
Wood, Richard H.

1896
Adams, John G.B.
Alber, Frederick
Baird, Absalom
Beddows, Richard
Beyer, Hillary
Boody, Robert
Bradley, Thomas W.
Breyer, Charles
Brown, Henri Le Ferve
Brown, Jeremiah Z.
Brown, John H.
Bruner, Louis J.
Burbank, James H.
Burk, Thomas
Burns, James M.
Burritt, William W.
Chamberlain, Orville T.
Clark, Charles A.
Colby, Carlos W.
Collins, Thomas D.
Cosgrove, Thomas
Crocker, Henry H.
Curtis, John C.
Deland, Frederick N.
De Puy, Charles H.
Dickey, William D.
Dickie, David
Dodd, Robert F.
Dodds, Edward E.
Durham, John S.
Elliott, Russell
Engle, James E.
Falconer, John A.
Fout, Frederick W.
Furman, Chester S.
Gaylord, Levi B.
Guerin, Fritz W.
Hadley, Osgood T.
Haight, Sidney
Hammel, Henry A.
Haney, Milton L.
Harris, Moses
Haskell, Marcus M.
Howe, Orion P.
Hymer, Samuel
Irwin, Patrick
Johnson, Ruel M.

Knight, Charles H.
Lewis, Dewitt Clinton
Ludwig, Carl
Maxham, Lowell M.
McCammon, William W.
McFall, Daniel
Merrifield, James K.
Noll, Conrad
North, Jasper N.
Palmer, George H.
Palmer, John G.
Paul, William H.
Pesch, Joseph
Plant, Henry C.
Purman, James J.
Raub, Jacob F.
Raymond, William H.
Rossbach, Valentine
Rutter, James M.
Sartwell, Henry
Scheibner, Martin E.
Schmidt, Conrad
Schneider, George
Sewell, William J.
Shanes, John
Simons, Charles J.
Smith, Wilson
Stacey, Charles
Starkins, John H.
Storey, John H.R.
Tabor, William S.
Thatcher, Charles M.
Thompson, Allen
Thompson, Charles A.
Thompson, James
Thomson, Clifford
Toban, James W.
Tobin, John M.
Wageman, John H.
Wambsgan, Martin
Webber, Alason P.
Wilcox, William H.
Woodruff, Alonzo
Wright, Samuel C.

1897
Archer, James W.
Banks, George L.
Barker, Nathaniel C.
Beaufort, Jean J.
Beckwith, Wallace A.

Beebe, William S.
Benyaurd, William H.
Bieger, Charles
Blackmar, Wilmon W.
Blackwood, William R.D.
Bliss, George N.
Boquet, Nicholas
Brandle, Joseph E.
Brush, George W.
Burger, Joseph
Cadwallader, Abel G.
Campbell, James A.
Carter, John J.
Casey, Henry
Child, Benjamin H.
Churchill, Samuel J.
Clark, William A.
Cockley, David L.
Conner, Richard
Corliss, George W.
Croft, James E.
Day, Charles
Dougall, Allan H.
Dougherty, Michael
Downey, William
Duffey, John
Eddy, Samuel E.
Enderlin, Richard
Ferris, Eugene W.
Flannigan, James
Fuger, Frederick
Gage, Richard J.
Galloway, John
Gifford, David L.
Gillespie, George L.
Godley, Leonidas M.
Graham, Thomas N.
Grant, Gabriel
Gray, Robert A.
Hall, Francis B.
Hallock, Nathan M.
Hanks, Joseph
Hanna, Milton
Harbourne, John H.
Hart, John W.
Hastings, Smith H.
Hibson, Joseph C.
Hill, Henry
Hilliker, Benjamin F.
Holehouse, James
Holland, Lemuel F.

Year of Issuance

Holmes, Lovilo N.
Horne, Samuel B.
Hunterson, John C.
Kenyon, John S.
King, Horatio C.
Kinsey, John
Kretsinger, George
Marland, William
Marsh, George
McAnally, Charles
McGonnigle, Andrew J.
McGough, Owen
McKeever, Michael
Mears, George W.
Miller, William E.
Morrison, Francis
Murphy, Michael C.
Nichols, Henry C.
Nolan, John J.
O'Donnell, Menomen
Patterson, John H.
Pay, Byron E.
Pearson, Alfred L.
Rafferty, Peter
Rand, Charles F.
Rhodes, Sylvester D.
Robertson, Robert S.
Rockefeller, Charles M.
Rohm, Ferdinand F.
Roush, Levi J.
Russell, Milton
Scanlan, Patrick
Scott, Alexander
Shapland, John
Shepard, Irwin
Shiel, John
Sickles, Daniel E.
Slagle, Oscar
Smalley, Reuben S.
Snedden, James
Sowers, Michael
Spurling, Andrew B.
Steele, John W.
Swap, Jacob E.
Swift, Frederic W.
Swift, Harlan J.
Taylor, Joseph
Taylor, William
Thaxter, Sidney W.
Thompson, John
Toffey, John J.

Tracy, Charles H.
Traynor, Andrew
Twombly, Voltaire P.
Vale, John
Vance, Wilson
Ward, Nelson W.
Webb, James
Williams, Elwood
Williams, George C.
Wilson, John M.
Wright, Samuel
Yeager, Jacob F.

1898
Beaumont, Eugene B.
Bliss, Zenas R.
Boehm, Peter M.
Capehart, Charles E.
Chandler, Henry F.
Chandler, Stephen E.
Clute, George W.
Cross, James E.
Curran, Richard
Davis, Freeman
Du Pont, Henry A.
Edgerton, Nathan H.
Farnsworth, Herbert E.
Ferrier, Daniel T.
Finkenbiner, Henry S.
Fox, Nicholas
Hadley, Cornelius M.
Hapeman, Douglas
Haskell, Frank W.
Hedges, Joseph
Heermance, William L.
Higgins, Thomas J.
Horan, Thomas
Houghton, Charles H.
Howard, Henderson C.
Jamieson, Walter
Johnson, Joseph E.
Josselyn, Simeon T.
King, Rufus, Jr.
Libaire, Adolphe
Lord, William
Madden, Michael
Maynard, George H.
McAdams, Peter
McAlwee, Benjamin F.
Mills, Frank W.
Morrill, Walter G.

Murphy, Charles J.
Orr, Charles A.
Osborne, William H.
Payne, Thomas H.L.
Phelps, Charles E.
Pinn, Robert
Pipes, James
Plimley, William
Pond, James B.
Putnam, Winthrop D.
Reed, Axel H.
Robinson, Elbridge
Schwan, Theodore
Slusher, Henry C.
Tinkham, Eugene M.
Tobie, Edward P.
Tozier, Andrew J.
Uhrl, George
Vernay, James D.
Weston, John F.
Wheeler, Henry W.
Whitaker, Edward W.
Whitehead, John M.
Whitfield, Daniel
Williams, Le Roy
Wilson, Christopher W.
Young, James M.

1899
Allen, Nathaniel
Brouse, Charles W.
Bucklyn, John K.
Catlin, Isaac S.
Corson, Joseph K.
Fall, Charles S.
Fox, Henry
Furness, Frank
Grebe, M.R. William
Gregg, Joseph O.
Healey, George W.
Herington, Pitt B.
Ingalls, Lewis J.
Keen, Joseph S.
Kephart, James
Mattocks, Charles P.
Mayes, William B.
Meyer, Henry C.
Newman, Marcellus J.
Patterson, John T.
Pike, Edward M.
Pond, George F.

The sea battle between the C.S.S. Alabama *and the* U.S.S. Kearsarge *that took place off the coast of Cherbourg, France. Seventeen sailors aboard the Kearsarge received the Medal of Honor for their gallantry in this action (U.S. Army War College).*

Power, Albert
Schoonmaker, James M.
Simonds, William Edgar
Weir, Henry C.

1900
Carney, William H.
Houghton, George L.
Johnson, Wallace W.
Kelley, Andrew J.
Kelley, Leverett M.
McDonald, John Wade
McHale, Alexander U.
Moore, Daniel B.
Smith, Thaddeus S.
White, J. Henry

1901
Ranney, George E.

1902
Farquhar, John M.
Porter, Horace
Walton, George W.

1905
Freeman, William H.

Huidekoper, Henry S.
Porter, Ambrose
Welsh, James

1906
Sagelhurst, John C.
Seitzinger, James M.
Smith, David L.

1907
Hack, John
Hodges, Addison J.
Reinsinger, J. Monroe

1908
Ballen, Frederick

1909
Nash, Henry H.

1911
Sype, Peter

1914
Anderson, Bruce
Chapin, Alaric B.
Merrill, George

1917
Barrick, Jesse T.
Lewis, Henry
Peters, Henry C.
Unknown
Bell, James B.
Blunt, John W.
Boutwell, John W.
Bronner, August F.
Buffington, John E.
Camp, Carlton, N.
Carey, James L.
Cumpston, James M.
Di Cesnola, Louis P.
Dorley, August
Hathaway, Edward W.
Ilgenfritz, Charles H.
Lonsway, Joseph
O'Connor, Albert
Sickles, William H.
Toohey, Thomas

Appendices

A: First Six Winners of the Medal of Honor

1st Parrott, Jacob	3rd Buffum, Robert	5th Pittinger, William
2nd Bensinger, William	4th Mason, Elihu H.	6th Reddick, William H.

The locomotive General, *captured by Andrews' Raiders in an effort to destroy railroad track and bridges between Atlanta and Chattanooga. On March 25, 1863, six of the surviving members of Andrews' party became the first to be awarded the Congressional Medal of Honor. They were, in order of award: Jacob Parrott, William Bensinger, Robert Buffum, Elihu Mason, William Pittinger, and William Reddick (U.S. Army War College).*

B: Winners of More Than One Medal of Honor

Cooper, John   Custer, Thomas W.   Mullen, Patrick

C: Posthumously Awarded Medals of Honor

Thirty-two medals were awarded posthumously to Civil War soldiers. The meaning of a "posthumous award" was significantly different for later generations than it was for the Civil War period. It has, over the years, become associated with heroes whose act of bravery, for which the medal was awarded, cost them their lives. In the majority of the Civil War posthumous awards, the individual was killed, or died, following the act that earned them their medal. The following individuals are those who were killed during the execution of the act for which their medal was awarded.

Brown, Morris, Jr.   Logan, Hugh   Smith, Charles H.
Falls, Benjamin F.   McVeane, John P.   Tallentine, James
Gasson, Richard   Savacool, Edwin F.   Wells, Henry S.
Hardenbergh, Henry M.   Seston, Charles H.

D: Civilian Recipients

Walker, Dr. Mary E.   Woodall, William H.

E: Black Soldiers

Barnes, William H.
Beaty, Powhatan
Bronson, James H.
Carney, William H.
Dorsey, Decatur
Fleetwood, Christian A.

Gardiner, James
Harris, James H.
Hawkins, Thomas
Hilton, Alfred B.
Holland, Milton M.
James, Miles

Kelly, Alexander
Pinn, Robert
Ratcliff, Edward
Veal, Charles
Vantine, Joseph E.

Opposite: *Contemporary artist's depiction of the Battle of Chapin's Farm, where United States Colored Troops took a conspicuous role in the Union Victory (Samuel M. Schmucker, The History of the Civil War in the United States, Chicago: Jones Brothers & Co., 1865).*

Index

Adams, James F. 7, 227, 253, 272, 278, 299, 306, 307
Adams, John G.B. 7, 227, 242, 271, 277, 293, 305, 318
U.S.S. *Agawam* 21, 51, 79, 94, 100, 141, 146, 167, 169, 195, 253
Aheam, Michael 7, 235, 255, 260, 285, 309
Aiken, S.C. 203, 266
C.S.S. *Alabama* 7, 22, 26, 88, 92, 95, 122, 142, 156, 160, 165, 175, 184, 190, 194
Alabama Bayou, La. 39, 262
U.S.S. *Albatross* 32, 253
Alber, Frederick 8, 227, 243, 274, 278, 290, 303, 318
C.S.S. *Albermarle* 54, 61, 79, 89, 103, 118, 120, 124, 218
Albert, Christian 8, 227, 248, 263, 285, 296, 302, 317
Aldie, Va. 61, 268
Alexandria, Va. 33, 268
Allatoona, Ga. 55, 261
Allen, Abner P. 8, 227, 240, 272, 277, 290, 304, 312
Allen, James 8, 227, 245, 263, 278, 291, 306, 315
Allen, Nathaniel M. 8, 227, 242, 266, 284, 293, 304, 319
Alsop's Farm, Va. 78, 268
Amelia Courthouse, Va. 40
Amelia Springs, Va. 45, 147, 200, 268
Ames, Adelbert 8, 227, 251, 272, 285, 293, 303, 316
Ammerman, Robert W. 8, 227, 251, 274, 278, 297, 305, 312
Anderson, Bruce 9, 228, 247, 265, 285, 294, 308, 320
Anderson, Charles W. 9, 227, 245, 274, 278, 293, 306, 312
Anderson, Everett, W. 9, 227, 249, 267, 278, 293, 304, 316
Anderson, Frederick C. 9, 227, 242, 274, 278, 293, 305, 309

Anderson, Marion T. 10, 227, 241, 268, 281, 291, 304, 316
Anderson, Peter 10, 227, 253, 265, 284, 300, 308, 312
Anderson, Robert 10, 235, 255, 266, 282, 291, 305, 305
Anderson, Thomas 10, 227, 253, 268, 278, 297, 305, 312
Andrews, James J. 6
Angling, John 10, 235, 256, 265, 285, 293, 312
Antietam, Md. 21, 43, 46, 48, 51, 57, 85, 86, 93, 100, 107, 111, 123, 145, 151, 154, 198, 225, 263
Apple, Andrew O. 11, 227, 253, 272, 277, 297, 308, 312
Appleton, William H. 11, 227, 253, 272, 277, 297, 308, 312
Appomattox Courthouse, Va. 30, 42, 63, 77, 98, 146, 165, 177, 182, 223, 268
Appomattox Station, Va. 10
Archer, James W. 11, 227, 241, 263, 281, 290, 318
Archer, Lester 11, 227, 246, 271, 277, 294, 303, 312
Archinal, William 11, 227, 248, 263, 285, 290, 304, 316
Arkansas Post, Ark. 198, 260
Armstrong, Clinton L. 11, 227, 241, 263, 285, 291, 306, 316
Arnold, Abraham K. 11, 227, 252, 270, 281, 297, 303, 316
Arther, Matthew 11, 235, 254, 268, 285, 299, 303, 309
Ashby's Gap, Va. 63, 268
Ashepoo River, S.C. 34, 65, 66, 80, 175, 266
Ashland, Va. 41
Asten, Charles 12, 235, 256, 263, 285, 289, 302, 309
Atkinson, Thomas E. 12, 235, 256, 259, 285, 293, 301, 309
Atlanta, Ga. 6, 20, 33, 37, 59, 64, 74, 86, 89, 94, 119, 122,

130, 145, 153, 158, 160, 165, 167, 174, 178, 186, 188, 206, 221, 222, 223, 261
Avery, James 12, 235, 255, 259, 282, 299, 301, 314
Avery, William B. 12, 235, 245, 266, 285, 299, 304, 316
Ayers, David 12, 227, 248, 263, 285, 296, 305, 316
Ayers, John G.K. 12, 227, 244, 263, 285, 294, 303, 317

Babcock, William J. 12, 227, 251, 272, 277, 289, 305, 317
Bachelors Creek, N.C. 91, 265
Back Creek Valley, Va. 130, 269
Bacon, Elijah W. 12, 227, 239, 266, 278, 289, 309
Baird, Absalom 12, 227, 239, 262, 281, 297, 318
Baker, Charles 13, 235, 255, 259, 282, 300, 301, 314
Baldwin, Charles 13, 227, 235, 257, 266, 285, 289, 304, 309
Baldwin, Frank D. 13, 243, 262, 278, 294, 305, 315
Ballen, Frederick 13, 227, 248, 263, 285, 290, 305, 320
Banks, George L. 13, 227, 240, 268, 277, 291, 304, 318
Banks Ford, Va. 13, 49, 269
Barber, James A. 13, 227, 251, 272, 285, 299, 305, 314
Barker, Nathaniel C. 14, 227, 244, 272, 277, 294, 303, 318
Barnes, William H. 14, 227, 252, 270, 285, 293, 312, 323
Barnum, Henry A. 14, 227, 267, 281, 294, 302, 315
Barnum, James 15, 235, 255, 265, 285, 293, 301, 312
U.S.S. *Baron De Kalb* 54, 122, 134, 170, 253
Barrell, Charles L. 15, 228, 252, 266, 285, 294, 305, 315

325

Barrick, Jesse T. 15, 228, 243, 267, 278, 296, 305, 320
Barringer, Rufus 223
Barringer, William H. 15, 228, 253, 263, 285, 300, 305, 316
Barry, Augustus 15, 228, 252, 285, 291, 304, 314
Barter, Gurdon H. 15, 235, 255, 265, 285, 294, 312
Barton, Thomas 15, 235, 255, 271, 282, 296, 302, 309
Bass, David L. 15, 235, 255, 265, 285, 291, 306, 312
Batchelder, Richard N. 15, 16, 228, 239, 269, 284, 294, 302, 317
Bates, Delavan 16, 228, 252, 270, 281, 294, 304, 315
Bates, Norman F. 16, 228, 241, 261, 278, 299, 304, 312
Baton Rouge, La. 57, 262
Baxter Springs, Kans. 159, 262
Baybutt, Philip 16, 228, 242, 272, 289, 306, 309
Bayou Teche, La. 105, 262
Bazaar, Philip 16, 235, 256, 265, 285, 289, 312
Beatty, Alexander M. 16, 235, 252, 270, 282, 299, 301, 316
Beaty, Powhatan 16, 228, 252, 270, 281, 299, 303, 312, 323
Beaufort, Jean J. 17, 228, 241, 262, 285, 290, 318
Beaufort, S.C. 91
Beaumont, Eugene B. 17, 228, 239, 268, 278, 297, 303, 319
Bebb, Edward J. 17, 228, 241, 261, 278, 296, 304, 312
Beckwith, Wallace A. 17, 18, 228, 239, 271, 285, 289, 318
Beddows, Richard 18, 235, 245, 274, 284, 289, 306, 318
Beebe, William S. 18, 228, 239, 262, 281, 294, 305, 318
Beech, John P. 18, 228, 244, 274, 285, 289, 306, 316
Begley, Terrance 18, 228, 244, 270, 278, 291, 309
Belcher, Thomas 18, 228, 242, 270, 277, 293, 302, 312
Bell, George 18, 235, 256, 268, 285, 289, 304, 309
Bell, James B. 19, 228, 248, 268, 277, 296, 303, 320
Bells Mills, Tenn. 72, 267
Bells Mills, Va. 62
Benedict, George G. 19, 228, 253, 266, 285, 299, 301, 315
Benjamin, John F. 19, 228, 245, 273, 279, 295, 312
Benjamin, Samuel N. 19, 228, 275, 285, 295, 304, 314

Bennett, Orren 19, 228, 251, 273, 279, 284, 297, 312
Bennett, Orson W. 19, 20, 228, 252, 267, 294, 305, 315
Bensinger, William 20, 228, 248, 261, 281, 296, 304, 309, 320
U.S.S. *Benton* 34, 130, 142, 143, 220, 253
Benton, Ark. 126, 260
Bentonville, N.C. 10, 48, 64, 159, 265
Benyaurd, William H. 20, 228, 239, 271, 281, 297, 305, 318
Bermuda Hundred, Va. 65, 69, 143, 269
Berryville, Va. 73, 79, 269
Betham, Asa 20, 235, 256, 265, 285, 295, 303, 312
Bethesda Church, Va. 80
Betts, Charles M. 21, 228, 249, 265, 278, 297, 303, 315
Beyer, Hillary 21, 228, 250, 263, 282, 297, 303, 318
Bibber, Charles J. 21, 235, 253, 265, 285, 293, 304, 309
Bickford, Henry H. 21, 22, 228, 245, 274, 284, 294, 304, 312
Bickford, John F. 22, 235, 255, 260, 285, 293, 306, 309
Bickford, Matthew 22, 228, 244, 263, 285, 290, 304, 316
Bieger, Charles 22, 228, 244, 263, 282, 290, 306, 318
Big Shanty, Ga. 6, 20, 33, 37, 64, 71, 94, 119, 130, 153, 158, 160, 165, 171, 178, 187, 188, 221, 222, 261
Binder, Richard 22, 235, 265, 285, 297, 304, 312
Bingham, Henry H. 22, 235, 251, 274, 281, 297, 305, 316
Birdsall, Horatio L. 22, 228, 241, 262, 279, 295, 302, 312
Bishop, Francis A. 22, 228, 250, 274, 279, 297, 304, 309
Black, John C. 22, 23, 228, 240, 260, 281, 294, 304, 316
Black, William P. 23, 228, 240, 260, 285, 293, 305, 316
Black River, N.C. 188, 265
Black River Bridge, N.C. 116, 263
Blackburn's Ford, Va. 55, 155, 164, 269
Blackmar, Wilmon W. 23, 228, 253, 271, 281, 297, 318
Blackwater River 29, 125, 188
Blackwater, Va. 37, 269
Blackwood, William R.D. 23, 24, 228, 250, 272, 282, 291, 304, 318

Blagheen, William 24, 235, 253, 259, 285, 289, 302, 309
Blair, Robert M. 24, 228, 256, 265, 285, 299, 312
Blake, Robert 24, 235, 255, 267, 285, 299, 309
Blasdel, Thomas A. 24, 228, 241, 263, 285, 291, 316
Blickensderfer, Milton 24, 228, 249, 272, 279, 297, 303, 312
Bliss, George N. 24, 228, 251, 274, 281, 285, 299, 303, 318
Bliss, Zenas R. 25, 228, 251, 271, 293, 303, 319
Blodgett, Welis H. 25, 228, 240, 265, 278, 290, 304, 316
Blucher, Charles 25, 228, 251, 271, 277, 290, 312
Blunt, John W. 25, 228, 245, 269, 281, 295, 304, 320
Boehm, Peter M. 25, 228, 245, 270, 281, 295, 308, 319
Bois, Frank 25, 235, 254, 263, 285, 289, 305, 309
Bond, William 26, 235, 255, 260, 285, 293, 304, 309
Bonebrake, Henry G. 26, 228, 249, 271, 279, 297, 304, 312
Bonnaffon, Sylvester, Jr. 26, 228, 250, 269, 281, 297, 306, 316
Boody, Robert 26, 228, 246, 270, 282, 293, 303, 318
Boon, Hugh P. 26, 228, 253, 273, 279, 297, 302
Boss, Orlando 26, 228, 242, 270, 282, 293, 306, 315
Bouquet, Nicholas 27, 228, 241, 265, 284, 290, 305, 318
Bourke, John G. 27, 228, 249, 268, 285, 297, 308, 315
Bourne, Thomas 27, 235, 256, 262, 285, 290, 302, 309
Boury, Richard 27, 228, 253, 270, 279, 297, 302, 312
Boutte Station, La. 108, 262
Boutwell, John W. 27, 228, 244, 272, 282, 294, 308, 320
Bowen, Chester B. 28, 228, 245, 275, 279, 295, 305, 309
Bowen, Emmer 28, 228, 240, 263, 285, 295, 316
Bowman, Edward R. 28, 235, 256, 265, 285, 293, 301, 312
Box, Thomas J. 28, 228, 241, 262, 279, 291, 295, 302, 312
Boydton Plank Road, Va. 26, 69, 269
Boynton, Henry V. 28, 228, 248, 268, 281, 297, 303, 316
Bradley, Amos 28, 235, 256, 262, 285, 295, 303, 309

Bradley, Charles 28, 235, 255, 285, 291, 304, 309
Bradley, Thomas W. 28, 29, 228, 246, 270, 282, 295, 308, 318
Brady, James 29, 228, 244, 270, 279, 293, 305, 312
Brandle, Joseph E. 29, 228, 243, 268, 284, 297, 304, 318
Brannigan, Felix 29, 228, 246, 270, 284, 291, 314
Brant, William, Jr. 29, 228, 244, 272, 279, 294, 305, 312
Bras, Edgar A. 29, 228, 241, 259, 279, 291, 305, 312
Braton, Christopher *see* Bruton, Christopher
Brazell, John 29, 235, 256, 259, 285, 297, 303, 309
Breen, John 29, 235, 254, 271, 285, 295, 301, 309
Brennan, Christopher 29, 235, 255, 262, 285, 291, 302, 309
Brentwood Hills, Tenn. 100, 267
Brest, Lewis 30, 228, 250, 273, 279, 297, 305, 312
Brewer, William J. 30, 228, 245, 268, 279, 295, 306, 312
Breyer, Charles 30, 228, 250, 273, 282, 297, 308, 318
Briggs, Elijah A. 30, 228, 239, 272, 279, 289, 312
Bringle, Andrew 30, 228, 245, 273, 278, 295, 312
Brinn, Andrew 30, 235, 255, 262, 282, 299, 302, 309
Bristoe Station, Va. 53, 56, 88, 90, 207, 269
Bronner, August F. 30, 228, 245, 274, 285, 290, 303, 320
Bronson, James H. 31, 228, 252, 270, 281, 297, 304, 312, 323
Brosnan, John 31, 228, 247, 272, 282, 291, 308, 316
U.S.S. *Brooklyn* 24, 32, 33, 35, 52, 59, 61, 88, 106, 108, 116, 128, 138, 147, 152, 162, 190, 193, 203, 253
Brooklyn, N.Y. 199, 265
Brooks Ford, Va. 47, 269
Brouse, Charles W. 31, 228, 241, 268, 285, 291, 304, 319
Brown, Charles 31, 228, 250, 274, 279, 297, 305, 309
Brown, Edward, Jr. 31, 228, 246, 271, 277, 291, 315
Brown, Henri Le Ferve 31, 228, 246, 274, 282, 295, 318
Brown, James 32, 235, 253, 263, 285, 295, 301, 309
Brown, Jeremiah Z. 32, 228, 251, 272, 281, 297, 304, 318

Brown, John 32, 235, 253, 259, 285, 299, 301, 309
Brown, John H. 32, 228, 248, 263, 285, 293, 305, 318
Brown, John Harties 32, 228, 241, 268, 279, 289, 302, 312
Brown, Morris, Jr. 32, 228, 247, 266, 279, 295, 305, 314, 322
Brown, Robert 32, 228, 235, 255, 259, 268, 285, 296, 302, 309
Brown, Robert B. 33, 248, 279, 297, 308, 315
Brown, Uriah 33, 228, 248, 263, 282, 297, 316
Brown, William H. 33, 236, 253, 259, 285, 293, 303, 309
Brown, Wilson 33, 228, 236, 254, 259, 285, 294, 309
Brown, Wilson W. 33, 248, 261, 281, 296, 304, 309
Brownell, Francis E. 33, 228, 245, 268, 281, 295, 304, 314
Brownell, William P. 34, 236, 252, 263, 295, 309
Brownsville, Ark. 170, 260
Bruner, Louis J. 34, 228, 240, 268, 284, 291, 306, 318
Brush, George W. 34, 228, 252, 266, 282, 295, 305, 318
Bruton, Christopher C. 35, 228, 245, 274, 279, 295, 304, 312
Brutsche, Henry 35, 236, 256, 266, 285, 298, 308, 309
Bryant, Andrew S. 35, 228, 243, 265, 285, 293, 305, 314
Buchanan, George A. 35, 228, 247, 270, 278, 295, 306, 312
Buck, Frederick Clarence 35, 228, 239, 270, 285, 289, 306, 312
Buck, James 35, 236, 254, 262, 285, 293, 301, 309
Buckingham, David E. 35–36, 228, 239, 273, 285, 289, 304, 317
Buckles, Abram (Abraham) J. 35–36, 228, 241, 274, 277, 291, 308, 316
Buckley, Dennis 36, 228, 247, 262, 279, 289, 308, 312
Buckley, John C. 36, 228, 253, 263, 285, 300, 306, 316
Bucklyn, John K. 36, 228, 270, 284, 299, 302, 319
Buffington, John E. 36, 228, 242, 272, 285, 293, 305, 320
Buffum, Robert 37, 228, 248, 261, 281, 293, 301, 309, 320
Buhrman, Henry G. 37, 228, 248, 263, 285, 297, 316
Bull Run, Va. 19, 51, 52, 92, 119, 135, 138, 144, 164, 167,

171, 189, 210, 213, 215, 218, 222, 269
Bumgarner, William 37, 228, 253, 263, 285, 300, 303, 316
Burbank, James H. 37, 228, 251, 269, 285, 290, 318
Burger, Joseph 37, 38, 228, 243, 268, 285, 289, 304, 308, 318
Burk, E. Michael 38, 228, 247, 274, 291, 308, 310
Burk, Thomas 38, 228, 246, 274, 282, 295, 306, 318
Burke, Daniel W. 38, 228, 252, 274, 285, 289, 305, 315
Burke, Thomas 38, 228, 245, 271, 279, 291, 306, 314
Burns, James M. 38, 228, 252, 272, 284, 297, 308, 318
Burns, John M. 38, 236, 255, 259, 285, 295, 303, 310
Burnt Ordinary, Va. 136, 269
Burritt, William W. 38, 228, 240, 263, 285, 295, 318
Burton, Albert 39, 236, 257, 265, 285, 290, 304, 312
Butterfield, Daniel 39, 228, 239, 271, 281, 295, 302, 316
Butterfield, Franklin G. 39, 228, 253, 273, 285, 299, 306, 315
Butts, George 39, 236, 256, 263, 285, 295, 304, 310
Buzzard's Roost Gap, Ga. 107, 205, 225, 261
Byrnes, James 39, 236, 255, 291, 304, 309

Cache River, Ark. 157, 260
Cadwallader, Abel G. 39, 228, 242, 271, 277, 293, 305, 318
Cadwell, Luman 39, 228, 245, 262, 285, 295, 303, 316
Caldwell, Daniel 39, 40, 228, 249, 271, 279, 298, 306, 312
U.S.S. *Calena* 79, 113, 116, 128, 130, 225, 254
Calkin, Ivers S. 40, 228, 245, 273, 279, 295, 303, 312
Callahan, John H. 40, 228, 259, 279, 293, 312
Camden, N.C. 121
Camden, S.C. 15, 265, 266
Camp, Carlton N. 40, 228, 244, 272, 282, 294, 308, 320
Campbell, James A. 40, 228, 245, 275, 282, 295, 308, 318
Campbell, William 40, 228, 248, 263, 265, 285, 291, 304, 312
Campbell, William (Ireland) 41, 236, 256, 285, 291, 304, 316
Campbell Station, Tenn. 192, 267

328 Index

Cane River Crossing, La. 18, 262
U.S.S. *Canonicus* 193, 254
Cape Hatteras, N.C. 86, 142, 210, 265
Capehart, Charles 41, 278, 298, 302, 319
Capehart, Henry 41, 228, 253, 266, 275, 282, 298, 301, 317
Capron, Horace, Jr. 41, 228, 240, 270, 285, 293, 304, 312
Carey, Hugh 41, 42, 228, 246, 266, 279, 291, 315
Carey, James L. 42, 228, 245, 268, 281, 295, 304, 320
Carlisle, Casper R. 42, 228, 249, 266, 284, 298, 315
Carman, Warren 42, 228, 245, 274, 279, 295, 312
Carmin, Isaac H. 42, 228, 248, 263, 282, 294, 305, 316
Carney, William H. 42, 228, 243, 266, 277, 299, 304, 320, 323
U.S.S. *Carondelet* 11, 64, 107, 143, 254
Carr, Eugene A. 42, 43, 228, 240, 260, 285, 295, 302, 316
Carr, Franklin 43, 228, 249, 268, 284, 297, 308, 312
Carr, William M. 43, 228, 256, 259, 285, 293, 302, 310
Carrsville, Va. 196, 269
Carse, George B. 26
Carson, William J. 43, 252, 261, 285, 298, 304, 316
Cart, Jacob 43, 228, 249, 271, 279, 298, 306, 310
Carter, Jimmy 211
Carter, John J. 43, 228, 246, 263, 281, 295, 306, 318
Carter, Joseph F. 43, 228, 242, 271, 278, 293, 306, 315
Carter's Farm, Va. 181, 269
Caruana, Orlando E. 43, 228, 246, 265, 282, 293, 308, 315
Casey, David 43, 228, 242, 270, 284, 291, 306, 315
Casey, Henry 44, 228, 248, 263, 285, 298, 303, 318
Cassidy, Michael 44, 236, 255, 259, 285, 291, 303, 310
Catlett's Station, Va. 16, 269
Catlin, Isaac S. 44, 228, 246, 272, 284, 295, 303, 319
Cayer, Ovila 44, 228, 252, 274, 281, 289, 314
U.S.S. *Cayuga* 152, 224, 226, 254
Cedar Creek, Va. 25, 55, 67, 82, 96, 103, 125, 127, 135, 153, 167, 176, 197, 199, 200, 205, 211, 214, 223, 269

Cedar Mountain, Va. 53, 226, 270
Cemetery Hill, Va. 16, 270
U.S.S. *Ceres* 89, 115, 254
Chamberlain, Joshua L. 44, 228, 242, 266, 281, 293, 301, 316
Chamberlain, Orville T. 45, 228, 241, 261, 282, 291, 305, 318
Chamberlains Creek, Va. 102, 221, 270
Chambers, Joseph B. 45, 228, 250, 272, 279, 298, 314
Champion Hill, Miss. 99, 218, 263
Chandler, Henry F. 45, 228, 243, 272, 285, 303, 319
Chandler, James B. 45, 228, 256, 259, 285, 293, 304, 310
Chandler, Stephen E. 45, 228, 245, 268, 282, 294, 305, 319
Chancellorsville, Va. 26, 28, 29, 36, 46, 54, 62, 76, 81, 82, 96, 109, 127, 139, 144, 150, 151, 174, 179, 180, 201, 205, 270
Chapel House Farm, Va. 225, 270
Chapin, Alaric B. 45, 228, 247, 265, 285, 295, 320
Chapin's Farm, Va. 16, 18, 29, 31, 35, 68, 74, 78, 79, 86, 94, 98, 99, 101, 111, 116, 120, 121, 136, 137, 145, 158, 164, 176, 181, 185, 208, 214, 270
Chapman, John 46, 228, 241, 273, 279, 289, 312
Chaput, Louis G. 46, 236, 255, 259, 285, 289, 298, 310
Charles City Crossroads, Va. 181, 270
Charleston, S.C. 10, 80, 108, 122, 220, 226, 266
Charlottesville, Va. 27, 270
Chase, John F. 46, 228, 241, 270, 284, 293, 315
Chattahoochie River, Ga. 115, 261
Chattanooga, Tenn. 6, 15, 20, 33, 37, 64, 94, 111, 119, 130, 153, 158, 160, 165, 178, 187, 188, 204, 210, 221, 222, 223, 267
Cherbourg, France 7, 22, 26, 88, 92, 95, 122, 142, 154, 156, 160, 165, 175, 190, 194, 260
Chicago Mercantile Battery 66, 119, 120, 135, 193, 216, 239
Chickahominy, Va. 41, 270
Chickamauga, Ga. 43, 45, 46, 145, 160, 166, 168, 198, 217, 261
U.S.S. *Chickasaw* 112, 179, 254

Chickasaw Bayou, Miss. 220, 263
Child, Benjamin H. 46, 228, 251, 263, 285, 299, 306, 318
Chiricava, Ariz. 180, 260
Chisman, William W. 46, 228, 241, 263, 291, 306
Christiancy, James I. 46, 228, 243, 271, 282, 294, 315
Churchill, Samuel J. 46, 228, 240, 268, 285, 299, 318
Cilley, Clinton A. 46, 228, 243, 261, 282, 294, 303, 317
U.S.S. *Cincinnati* 25, 53, 65, 110, 135, 254
Clancy, James T. 46, 47, 228, 244, 274, 281, 295, 312
Clapp, Albert A. 47, 229, 248, 273, 279, 295, 305, 312
Clark, Charles A. 47, 229, 241, 269, 284, 293, 305, 318
Clark, Harrison 47, 229, 246, 266, 277, 295, 306, 317
Clark, James G. 47, 229, 250, 272, 285, 298, 315
Clark, John W. 47, 229, 253, 274, 284, 299, 302, 315
Clark, William A. 47, 48, 229, 243, 268, 284, 298, 302, 318
Clarke, Dayton P. 48, 229, 252, 274, 285, 295, 304, 315
Clausen, Charles H. 48, 229, 250, 274, 284, 298, 306, 315
Clay, Cecil 48, 229, 250, 271, 282, 298, 306, 315
Cleveland, Charles F. 48, 229, 245, 263, 277, 295, 317
Clifford, Robert T. 48, 236, 256, 266, 285, 298, 303, 310
Clopp, John E. 48, 229, 250, 266, 279, 298, 312
Clute, George W. 48, 229, 243, 265, 279, 294, 319
Coates, Jefferson 48, 49, 229, 253, 266, 285, 300, 306, 314
Cockley, David L. 49, 229, 248, 262, 282, 297, 306, 318
Coey, James 49, 229, 247, 271, 282, 295, 305, 315
Coffey, Robert J. 49, 229, 252, 269, 278, 289, 306, 315
Cohn, Abraham 49, 50, 229, 244, 274, 285, 294, 299, 312
Colbert, Patrick 50, 236, 254, 266, 285, 291, 304, 310
Colby, Carlos W. 50, 229, 240, 263, 285, 294, 318
Cold Harbor, Va. 16, 18, 26, 43, 63, 96, 98, 179, 203, 220, 270
Cole, Gabriel 50, 229, 243, 275, 279, 295, 302, 310
Collins, Harrison 50, 229, 251, 268, 279, 299, 302, 312

Index

Collins, Thomas D. 50, 229, 247, 262, 279, 299, 302, 312
Collis, Charles H.T. 50, 229, 251, 271, 282, 291, 304, 316
Columbus, Ga. 16, 17, 22, 53, 95, 142, 206, 261
Colwell, Oliver 50, 229, 249, 268, 279, 297, 312
U.S.S. *Commodore Hull* 50, 254
U.S.S. *Commodore Perry* 29, 121, 156, 220, 254
Compson, Hartwell B. 50, 229, 245, 274, 279, 295, 304, 312
Conaway, John W. 50, 229, 241, 263, 285, 291, 306, 316
Conboy, Martin 50, 51, 229, 246, 275, 282, 295, 302, 315
Conlan, Dennis 51, 236, 253, 265, 285, 295, 304, 310
Connell, Trustrim 51, 229, 251, 273, 279, 298, 312
Conner, Richard 51, 229, 244, 269, 284, 298, 318
Connor, Thomas 51, 236, 255, 265, 282, 291, 306, 312
Connor, William C. 51, 236, 266, 285, 299, 310
Connors, James 51, 229, 246, 271, 279, 291, 310
Cook, John 51, 229, 251, 263, 285, 297, 308, 316
Cook, John H. 51, 52, 229, 240, 262, 282, 290, 302, 315
Cooke, Walter H. 53, 229, 249, 269, 285, 298, 315
Cooper, John 52, 236, 254, 259, 285, 291, 210, 322
Copp, Charles D. 52, 229, 244, 271, 277, 294, 304, 315
Corbin's Bridge, Va. 169, 270
Corcoran, John 52, 229, 251, 272, 299, 306, 315
Corcoran, Thomas E. 53, 236, 254, 263, 278, 285, 295, 304, 309
Corinth, Miss. 11, 102, 132, 144, 196, 263
Corliss, George W. 53, 229, 239, 270, 277, 289, 318
Corliss, Stephen P. 53, 229, 244, 274, 277, 289, 318
Corson, Joseph K. 53, 229, 249, 269, 282, 298, 303, 319
Cosgriff, Richard H. 53, 229, 241, 262, 279, 295, 308, 312
Cosgrove, Thomas 53, 54, 229, 243, 270, 278, 291, 318
Cotton, Peter 54, 236, 253, 265, 285, 295, 304, 309
Coughlin, John 54, 229, 244, 274, 284, 299, 316
Cox, Robert M. 54, 229, 240, 263, 284, 297, 315

Coyne, John N. 54, 229, 246, 275, 279, 295, 304, 315
Cranston, William W. 54, 229, 249, 270, 278, 297, 315
Crawford, Alexander 54, 236, 257, 266, 285, 298, 306, 310
Creed, John 54, 229, 240, 271, 279, 291, 310
Cripps, Thomas 55, 236, 256, 259, 285, 298, 303, 310
Crocker, Henry H. 55, 229, 242, 269, 278, 289, 304, 318
Crocker, Ulric L. 55, 229, 243, 270, 279, 297, 310
Croft, James E. 55, 229, 253, 261, 285, 294, 303, 310
Cronin, Cornelius 55, 236, 256, 259, 285, 294, 303, 310
Crosby's Creek, Tenn. 9, 267
Crosier, William H.H. 55, 229, 247, 262, 284, 295, 306, 315
Cross, James E. 55, 56, 229, 245, 269, 285, 295, 304, 319
Crowley, Michael 56, 229, 245, 274, 279, 295, 302, 312
Crump's Creek, Va. 162, 270
Crystal River, Fla. 148, 260
Cullen, Thomas 56, 229, 246, 269, 279, 291, 304, 310
Culloden, Ga. 59, 105, 262
Cumberland River 72
Cummings, Amos J. 56, 229, 244, 272, 284, 295, 305, 316
Cumpston, James M. 56, 229, 249, 273, 279, 297, 320
Cunningham, Francis M. 56, 229, 253, 273, 279, 298, 303, 312
Cunningham, James S. 56, 229, 244, 263, 285, 298, 304, 316
Curran, Richard 56, 57, 229, 246, 263, 282, 291, 304, 319
Curtis, John C. 57, 229, 239, 262, 278, 289, 318
Curtis, Josiah M. 57, 229, 253, 272, 277, 300, 308, 312
Curtis, Newton Martin 57, 229, 239, 265, 282, 295, 303, 315
Custer, Thomas W. 57, 229, 243, 272, 279, 297, 308, 312, 322
Cutcheon, Byron M. 57, 229, 262, 282, 294, 303, 315
Cutts, James M. 57, 58, 229, 252, 274, 285, 300, 304, 315

Dabny's Mills, Va. 60, 174, 188, 270
Dallas, Ga. 194, 262
Darrough, John S. 58, 229, 240, 263, 282, 293, 317
Davenport Bridge, Va. 11, 270

Davidsizer, John A. 58, 229, 249, 272, 279, 298, 312
Davidson, Andrew 58, 229, 252, 263, 285, 299, 301, 315
Davidson, Andrew (Scotland) 58, 248, 272, 284, 299, 304, 315
Davis, Charles C. 58, 229, 249, 268, 282, 298, 302, 316
Davis, Freeman 58, 229, 249, 268, 284, 297, 319
Davis, George E. 58, 59, 229, 253, 263, 285, 293, 304, 315
Davis, Harry 59, 229, 248, 261, 279, 297, 305, 310
Davis, John (Navy) 59, 236, 256, 265, 293, 310
Davis, John 59, 229, 241, 262, 279, 282, 294, 312
Davis, Joseph 59, 229, 249, 268, 279, 300, 312
Davis, Martin K. 59, 229, 240, 263, 285, 290, 306, 316
Davis, Samuel W. 59, 236, 254, 259, 285, 293, 308, 310
Davis, Thomas 59, 229, 244, 273, 279, 300, 312
Day, Charles 59, 229, 251, 263, 271, 277, 298, 308, 318
Day, David F. 59, 229, 248, 285, 297, 308, 317
Deakin, Charles 60, 236, 256, 259, 285, 298, 303, 310
Deane, John M. 60, 229, 242, 271, 285, 293, 304, 317
DeCastro, Joseph H. 60, 229, 242, 266, 279, 293, 300
Decatur, Ga. 191, 262
U.S.S. *Decotah* 91, 254
Deep Bottom, Va. 91, 123, 157, 270
Deep Run, Va. 270
Deer Creek, Miss. 167, 263
DeLacey, Patrick 60, 251, 274, 279, 298, 302, 316
Deland, Frederick N. 60, 243, 262, 285, 293, 306, 318
Delaney, John C. 60, 229, 250, 270, 282, 291, 308, 316
DeLavie, Hiram H. 60, 61, 229, 249, 271, 279, 298, 312
Dempster, John 61, 236, 255, 265, 285, 299, 304, 312
Denig, J. Henry 61, 235, 254, 259, 285, 298, 304, 310
Denning, Lorenzo 61, 236, 256, 266, 282, 289, 306, 310
Dennis, Richard 61, 236, 254, 259, 285, 293, 301, 310
Densmore, William 61, 236, 259, 286, 295, 302, 310
DePuy, Charles H. 61, 229, 243, 272, 286, 294, 318

Devil's Den 92, 190
DeWitt, Richard W. 61, 229, 248, 263, 286, 297, 304, 316
DiCesnola, Louis P. 61, 229, 245, 268, 282, 292, 302, 320
Dickey, William D. 61, 62, 229, 245, 272, 286, 295, 308, 318
Dickie, David 62, 229, 240, 263, 286, 299, 305, 318
Diggins, Bartholomew 62, 236, 255, 259, 286, 293, 306, 315
Dilger, Hubert 62, 229, 248, 270, 284, 290, 303, 316
Dillon, Michael A. 62, 229, 244, 275, 284, 293, 315
Dingles Mill, S.C. 73, 266
Dinwiddie Court House, Va. 25, 118, 270
Ditzenback, John 62, 63, 236, 255, 267, 284, 295, 302, 312
Dockum, Warren C. 63, 229, 246, 273, 279, 295, 312
Dodd, Robert F. 63, 229, 243, 272, 282, 289, 308, 318
Dodds, Edward E. 63, 229, 245, 268, 282, 289, 318
Dolloff, Charles W. 63, 229, 252, 272, 279, 295, 312
Donaldson, John 63, 229, 249, 268, 279, 298, 305, 312
Donnelly, John 63, 236, 255, 259, 282, 290, 304, 314
Donoghue, Timothy 63, 229, 246, 271, 282, 291, 301, 316
Doody, Patrick 63, 229, 247, 270, 282, 291, 316
Doolen, William 63, 64, 236, 256, 259, 286, 291, 305, 310
Dore, George H. 64, 229, 247, 266, 284, 290, 308, 310
Dorley, August 64, 229, 241, 260, 279, 280, 320
Dorman, John 64, 236, 254, 275, 286, 297, 306, 310
Dorsey, Daniel A. 64, 229, 248, 261, 281, 299, 309, 323
Dorsey, Decatur 64, 229, 252, 272, 277, 293, 303, 312
Dougall, Allan H. 64, 229, 241, 265, 284, 299, 318
Dougherty, Michael 64, 65, 229, 249, 271, 282, 291, 308, 318
Dougherty, Patrick 65, 236, 255, 259, 286, 291, 308, 310
Dow, George P. 65, 229, 244, 273, 286, 294, 315
Dow, Henry 65, 236, 254, 263, 286, 299, 304, 309
Downey, William 65, 229, 242, 266, 282, 291, 318
Downs, Henry W. 65, 229, 253, 275, 282, 299, 316

Drake, James M. 65, 229, 244, 269, 282, 294, 303, 314
Drumgould's Bluff, Miss. 143
Drury, James 65, 229, 252, 274, 284, 291, 310
Drury's Bluff, Va. 53, 84, 116, 125, 128, 166, 270
Drywood, Kans. 159, 262
Duck River, Tenn. 15, 267
Duffey, John 66, 229, 242, 266, 282, 294, 318
Dug Gap, Ga. 135, 214, 262
Duncan, Adam 66, 236, 256, 259, 286, 293, 302, 310
Duncan, James K.L. 66, 236, 254, 262, 282, 298, 308, 310
Dunlavy, James 66, 229, 241, 262, 278, 291, 312
Dunn, William 66, 236, 255, 265, 286, 293, 302, 312
Dunne, James 66, 67, 229, 239, 263, 286, 294, 304, 317
Dunphy, Richard D. 67, 236, 255, 259, 286, 291, 304, 310
DuPont, Henry A. 67, 229, 251, 270, 284, 289, 319
Durham, James R. 67, 229, 253, 275, 277, 282, 300, 302, 315
Durham, John S. 67, 229, 253, 262, 295, 306, 318
Dutch Gap Canal, Va. 202, 270

Early, Jubal 35, 50
Eastport, Miss. 58, 263
Eckes, John N. 67, 229, 253, 263, 286, 300, 316
Eddy, Samuel E. 67, 68, 229, 242, 273, 282, 299, 301, 318
Edgerton, Nathan H. 68, 229, 252, 270, 277, 298, 319
Edwards, David 68, 229, 247, 271, 279, 290, 312
Edwards, John 68, 236, 255, 259, 286, 299, 302, 310
18th Alabama Infantry 85, 104
18th Florida Infantry 223
18th Georgia Infantry 55
18th Indiana Infantry 199, 241
18th Massachusetts Infantry 9, 242
18th New Hampshire Infantry 27, 40, 244
18th North Carolina Infantry 73
18th United States Infantry 43, 76, 252
18th Virginia Infantry 40
8th Arkansas Infantry 136
8th Connecticut Infantry 98, 239
8th Florida Infantry 47, 102
8th Illinois Cavalry 41, 240

8th Illinois Infantry 139, 215, 240
8th Indiana Infantry 103, 241
8th Iowa Infantry 29, 241
8th Kentucky Infantry 107
8th Louisiana Infantry 169
8th Mississippi Infantry 129, 224
8th Missouri Infantry 12, 22, 56, 112, 118, 149, 166, 206, 210, 244
8th New Hampshire 147, 244
8th New York Cavalry 21, 50, 81, 92, 116, 120, 128, 140, 147, 165, 191, 245
8th New York Heavy Artillery 220, 244
8th North Carolina Infantry 9
8th Ohio Infantry 139, 168, 172, 248
8th Pennsylvania Cavalry 78, 208, 249
8th South Carolina Infantry 79
8th United States Cavalry 186, 252
8th Vermont Infantry 65, 105, 108, 200, 253
8th Virginia Cavalry 117
8th Wisconsin Infantry 99, 253
80th Ohio Infantry 58, 249
88th Illinois Infantry 138, 240
88th Indiana Infantry 64, 241
88th New York Infantry 75, 163, 246
88th Pennsylvania Infantry 47, 80, 130, 174, 250
85th Pennsylvania Infantry 123, 142, 181, 250
81st Pennsylvania Infantry 170, 250
89th Illinois Infantry 72, 240
89th New York Infantry 136, 246
82nd New York Infantry 41, 56, 207, 246
82nd Ohio Infantry 142, 220, 249
87th Pennsylvania Infantry 167, 250
86th Illinois Infantry 213, 240
86th New York Infantry 213, 240
83rd Indiana Infantry 11, 24, 46, 50, 75, 96, 152, 186, 193, 241
83rd Ohio Infantry 194, 249
83rd Pennsylvania Infantry 39, 82, 196, 250
11th Connecticut Infantry 102, 239
11th Florida Infantry 121
11th Illinois Infantry 146, 209

Index

11th Indiana Infantry 173, 180, 193, 241
11th Iowa Infantry 97, 132, 241
11th Michigan Infantry 217, 243
11th Mississippi Infantry 196
11th Missouri Infantry 150, 152, 184, 214, 244
11th New Hampshire Infantry 14, 82, 172, 244
11th New Jersey Infantry 151, 244
11th New York Infantry 33, 245
11th Ohio Infantry 85, 104, 248
11th Ohio Light Artillery 19, 179, 248
11th Pennsylvania Cavalry 212, 249
11th Pennsylvania Infantry Reserves 60, 104, 166, 181, 249
11th South Carolina Infantry 106
11th United States Infantry 57, 154, 222, 252
11th West Virginia Infantry 142, 216, 253
11th Wisconsin Infantry 142, 253
Elise, William 68, 229, 253, 260, 286, 290, 312
Elison, James M. 68, 69, 229, 241, 263, 277, 297, 315
Elizabeth City, N.C. 59, 265
Elk River, Tenn. 78, 100, 103, 130, 181, 186, 267
Elliott, Alexander 68, 229, 249, 272, 298, 312
Elliott, Russell C. 68, 229, 242, 262, 278, 294, 318
Ellis, Horace 68, 229, 253, 274, 279, 298, 311
Ellsworth, Elmer 34
Ellsworth, Thomas F. 68, 229, 242, 267, 282, 293, 317
Emblen, Andrew H. 69, 229, 246, 269, 282, 295, 302, 316
Enderlin, Richard 69, 229, 249, 266, 283, 290, 306, 318
Engle, James E. 69, 229, 250, 269, 282, 298, 318
English, Edmund 70, 229, 244, 274, 277, 291, 305, 315
English, Thomas 70, 236, 255, 265, 286, 295, 301, 317
Ennis, Charles D. 70, 229, 251, 272, 282, 289, 306, 315
Erickson, John P. 70, 236, 256, 265, 286, 290, 312
Estes, Lewellyn G. 70, 229, 239, 262, 282, 293, 306, 316
Evans, Coron D. 70, 229, 240, 273, 279, 291, 312
Evans, Ira H. 70, 229, 252, 271, 284, 294, 308, 315

Evans, James R. 70, 229, 246, 274, 284, 295, 317
Evans, Thomas 70, 229, 250, 273, 279, 300, 311
Evergreen, Ala. 192, 259
Everson, Adelbert 71, 229, 248, 271, 279, 295, 312
Ewing, Hugh 32
Ewing, John C. 71, 229, 251, 272, 279, 298, 312
Ezra Chapel, Ga. 204, 262

Fair Oaks, Va. 71, 75, 76, 83, 93, 104, 148, 162, 180, 270
Fairfax, Va. 204
Fairfax Station, Va. 16, 271
Fairfield, Pa. 159, 266
Falconer, John A. 71, 229, 243, 268, 282, 294, 308, 318
Fall, Charles S. 71, 229, 243, 274, 279, 294, 306, 317
Falling Waters, Va. 101, 271
Fallon, Thomas T. 71, 229, 246, 275, 286, 291, 315
Falls, Benjamin 71, 229, 242, 266, 279, 293, 311, 322
Fanning, Nicholas 71, 229, 241, 260, 279, 291, 312
Farley, William 71, 236, 255, 267, 286, 293, 303, 311
Farmville, Va. 78
Farnsworth, Herbert E. 71, 229, 245, 274, 283, 295, 302, 319
Farquhar, John M. 72, 229, 240, 268, 284, 299, 320
Farrell, Edward 72, 236, 256, 262, 286, 295, 302, 309
Fasnacht, Charles H. 72, 229, 250, 274, 279, 298, 315
Fassett, John B. 72, 236, 250, 266, 284, 298, 316
Fernald, Albert E. 72, 229, 242, 271, 279, 293, 304, 312
Ferrell, John H. 72, 236, 255, 267, 284, 299, 301, 312
Ferrier, Daniel T. 73, 229, 240, 262, 283, 291, 305, 319
Ferris, Eugene W. 73, 229, 242, 269, 286, 299, 305, 318
Fesq, Frank 73, 229, 244, 272, 279, 290, 304, 312
15th Georgia Infantry 201
15th Indiana Infantry 13, 83, 216, 240
15th Indiana Light Artillery 75, 240
15th Louisiana Infantry 176
15th Michigan Infantry 174, 243
15th New Hampshire Infantry 197, 244
15th New Jersey Infantry 211
15th New York Battery 119, 245

15th New York Cavalry 25, 245
15th New York Heavy Artillery 61, 115, 245
15th New York Light Artillery 119, 245
15th Ohio Infantry 33, 168, 248
15th Pennsylvania Cavalry 9, 21, 27, 152, 198, 206, 249
15th United States Infantry 43, 252
5th Connecticut Infantry 53, 239
5th Illinois Infantry 105
5th Indiana Cavalry 34, 240
5th Iowa Cavalry 95, 241
5th Maine Light Artillery 46, 217, 241
5th Massachusetts Infantry 68, 242
5th Michigan Cavalry 50, 75, 93, 243
5th Michigan Infantry 116, 138, 144, 243
5th Minnesota Infantry 79, 243
5th New Hampshire Infantry 87
5th New Jersey Infantry 180, 244
5th New York Cavalry 38, 152, 167, 176, 206, 211, 245
5th New York Infantry 213, 245
5th Ohio Infantry 84, 145, 207, 248
5th Pennsylvania Cavalry 136, 249
5th Pennsylvania Infantry 92
5th Texas Infantry 174
5th United States Cavalry 11, 252
5th United States Colored Troops 16, 31, 101, 158, 252
5th United States Light Artillery 8, 67, 135, 207, 251
5th Vermont Infantry 82, 83, 87, 174, 253
50th Massachusetts Infantry 89, 243
50th Pennsylvania Infantry 31, 99, 250
50th Virginia Infantry 150
58th Ohio Infantry 150, 248
58th Pennsylvania Infantry 48, 111, 136, 250
55th Illinois Infantry 54, 73, 89, 121, 142, 174, 212, 240
55th Massachusetts Infantry 186, 242
55th North Carolina Infantry 110
55th Ohio Infantry 192, 246
55th Pennsylvania Infantry 73, 250

332 Index

55th Virginia Infantry 101, 202
51st Indiana Infantry 10, 173, 241
51st New York Infantry 43, 246
51st Virginia Infantry 43
54th Massachusetts Colored Infantry 42, 143
54th Ohio Infantry 37, 110, 112, 134, 197, 214, 248
54th Pennsylvania Infantry 70, 143, 190, 250
59th Illinois Infantry 160, 240
59th Indiana Infantry 11, 241
59th Massachusetts Infantry 45, 243
59th New York Infantry 69, 218, 246
52nd Illinois Infantry 191, 240
52nd New York Infantry 215, 246
52nd Ohio Infantry 86, 205, 248
57th Massachusetts Infantry 114, 158, 243
57th North Carolina Infantry 158
57th Ohio Infantry 12, 59, 248
57th Pennsylvania Infantry 22, 30, 250
56th Ohio Infantry 218, 248
56th Pennsylvania Infantry 110, 250
56th Virginia Infantry 221
Finkenbiner, Henry S. 73, 229, 249, 266, 284, 297, 306, 319
1st Connecticut Cavalry 121, 130, 146, 216, 239
1st Connecticut Heavy Artillery 134, 145, 239
1st Delaware Infantry 131, 133, 161, 198, 239
1st Illinois Cavalry 152, 240
1st Iowa Infantry 27, 241
1st Kentucky Infantry 102, 241
1st Louisiana Battery 186
1st Louisiana Cavalry 64, 168, 241
1st Maine Cavalry 146, 242
1st Maine Heavy Artillery 46, 241
1st Maine Infantry 124, 138, 200, 241
1st Maryland Cavalry 146, 242
1st Maryland Infantry 39, 188, 193, 199, 201, 242
1st Massachusetts Infantry 8, 242
1st Michigan Cavalry 205, 243
1st Michigan Infantry 218, 222, 243
1st Michigan Sharpshooters 61, 88, 199, 225, 243

1st Minnesota Infantry 138, 149, 157, 182, 243
1st Minnesota Infantry Battalion 157, 243
1st Missouri Infantry 177, 244
1st Missouri Light Artillery 74, 86, 89, 156, 244
1st New Jersey Cavalry 46, 102, 124, 160, 174, 191, 193, 195, 203, 204, 221, 244
1st New Jersey Infantry 102, 244
1st New Jersey Veteran Battalion 29, 244
1st New York Artillery 30
1st New York Cavalry 9, 42, 143, 148, 149, 158, 175, 202, 245
1st New York Infantry 123, 245
1st New York Light Artillery 81, 87, 245
1st New York Marine Artillery 12, 245
1st New York Mounted Rifles 140, 248
1st Ohio Infantry 160, 248
1st Ohio Light Artillery 62, 248
1st Pennsylvania Cavalry 58, 68, 98, 121, 200, 212, 225, 249
1st Pennsylvania Rifles 201, 251
1st Rhode Island Cavalry 24, 251
1st Rhode Island Light Artillery 14, 36, 46, 52, 70, 94, 123, 140, 161, 251
1st Tennessee Cavalry 50, 251
1st Texas Infantry 165
1st Texas Rangers 112
1st United States Cavalry 92, 149, 251
1st United States Sharpshooters 155, 169, 223, 252
1st United States Veteran Reserve Corps 224, 252
1st Vermont Cavalry 127, 197, 223, 252
1st Vermont Infantry 63, 214, 252
1st Virginia Infantry 45
1st West Virginia Cavalry 7, 10, 23, 26, 27, 41, 56, 103, 172, 177, 180, 183, 223, 253
1st West Virginia Infantry 38, 253
1st Wisconsin Infantry 67, 253
Fisher, John H. 73, 229, 240, 263, 286, 298, 316
Fisher, Joseph 73, 229, 250, 272, 277, 298, 306, 316
Fisher's Hill, Va. 51, 54, 142, 167, 217, 271

Fitzpatrick, Thomas 73, 236, 255, 259, 286, 289, 303, 311
Five Forks, Va. 20, 23, 26, 61, 68, 71, 72, 78, 86, 115, 119, 145, 178, 183, 193, 221
Flanagan, Augustin 73, 74, 229, 250, 270, 277, 298, 312
Flannigan, James 74, 229, 243, 268, 284, 295, 318
Fleetwood, Christian A. 74, 229, 252, 270, 277, 293, 312, 323
Flint River, Ga. 70, 262
Flood, Thomas 74, 236, 256, 262, 286, 291, 305, 309
Flynn, Christopher 74, 235, 239, 244, 266, 279, 291, 311
Flynn, James E. 74, 235, 263, 286, 290, 316
Follett, Joseph 74, 230, 244, 268, 282, 294, 306, 315
Force, Manning F. 74, 230, 239, 261, 286, 300, 301, 315
Ford, George W. 75, 230, 246, 273, 279, 291, 308, 312
Forman, Alexander A. 75, 230, 243, 270, 286, 294, 306, 317
Fort Beauregard, S.C. 201, 219
Fort Blakely, Ala. 40, 133, 138, 139, 142, 147, 154, 156, 165, 168, 170, 194, 209, 215, 217, 259
Fort Clark, N.C. 196, 265
Fort DeRussy, La. 32
Fort Donelson, Tenn. 11, 207, 267, 268
Fort Fisher, N.C. 9, 10, 15, 16, 20, 21, 22, 24, 28, 39, 40, 45, 51, 57, 61, 66, 70, 75, 76, 77, 79, 86, 87, 90, 94, 95, 100, 113, 114, 122, 124, 137, 138, 140, 141, 146, 155, 161, 162, 164, 167, 169, 175, 182, 183, 193, 195, 196, 199, 204, 206, 209, 210, 211, 213, 216, 217, 219, 220, 265
Fort Fisher, Va. 124, 271
Fort Gates, Fla. 199, 260
Fort Gregg, Va. 8, 78, 98, 106, 114, 201, 206
Fort Harrison, Va. 11, 25, 48, 84, 102, 105, 111, 271
Fort Haskell, Va. 60
U.S.S. Fort Henry 148, 254
Fort Henry, Tenn. 11, 268
Fort Hill, Miss. 54
U.S.S. Fort Hindman 66, 112, 141, 254
Fort Huger, Va. 193, 271
Fort Jackson, La. 27, 28, 29, 35, 72, 74, 77, 85, 101, 127, 130, 136, 152, 155, 168, 183, 224, 226, 262

Index

Fort Morgan, Ala. 79, 89, 139, 157, 169, 181, 212, 224
Fort Moultrie, S.C. 149, 220
Fort St. Philip, La. 27, 28, 29, 35, 72, 74, 77, 85, 101, 127, 130, 135, 136, 152, 155, 168, 183, 224, 226, 262
Fort Sanders, Tenn. 71, 113, 129
Fort Sedgwick, Va. 108, 271
Fort Stedman, Va. 43, 60, 79, 105, 134, 158, 271
Fort Stevens, D.C. 224, 275
Fort Wagner, S.C. 42, 98, 104, 266
Fort Walker, S.C. 201, 219
40th Massachusetts Infantry 53, 60, 96, 125, 243
40th New Jersey Infantry 73, 244
40th New York Infantry 26, 119
40th North Carolina Infantry 48
40th Virginia Cavalry 143
48th New York Infantry 98, 246
48th Ohio Infantry 42, 248
48th Pennsylvania Infantry 23, 141, 166, 250
45th Illinois Infantry 198, 240
45th New York Infantry 108, 246
45th Pennsylvania Infantry 100, 118, 250
45th Virginia Infantry 70
41st Alabama Infantry 127, 210
41st Ohio Infantry 79, 100, 248
44th Georgia Infantry 214
44th Mississippi Infantry 114
44th Tennessee Infantry 167
49th Alabama Infantry 200
49th Indiana Infantry 116, 241
49th Massachusetts Infantry 111, 195, 212, 243
49th New York Infantry 137, 246
42nd New York Infantry 128, 246
42nd Virginia Infantry 173
47th New York Infantry 79, 246
47th North Carolina Infantry 144
47th Ohio Infantry 6, 8, 13, 32, 58, 61, 67, 87, 100, 123, 146, 156, 197, 212, 248
47th Virginia Infantry 31
46th Massachusetts Infantry 35, 243
46th North Carolina Infantry 29
46th Ohio Infantry 59, 195, 248
46th Virginia Infantry 77
43rd New York Infantry 51, 183, 246

43rd Ohio Infantry 196, 248
43rd United States Colored Troops 224, 252
14th Connecticut Infantry 12, 74, 99, 239
14th Michigan Infantry 48, 109, 158, 243
14th New York Heavy Artillery 99, 103, 244
14th Pennsylvania Cavalry 117, 177, 249
14th United States Infantry 44, 219, 225, 252
14th Virginia Cavalry 7
14th West Virginia Infantry 181, 253
14th Wisconsin Infantry 145, 253
4th Alabama Infantry 85
4th Delaware Infantry 35, 189, 239
4th Florida Infantry 133
4th Georgia Battery 143
4th Iowa Cavalry 15, 17, 53, 71, 95, 137, 142, 196, 241
4th Iowa Infantry 220, 241
4th Kentucky Cavalry 215, 241
4th Maryland Infantry 206, 242
4th Massachusetts Cavalry 65, 66, 80, 125, 175, 242
4th Massachusetts Infantry 125, 242
4th Michigan Infantry 126, 243
4th Mississippi Infantry 80
4th Missouri Cavalry 22, 84, 244
4th New Jersey Infantry 18, 244
4th New York Cavalry 61, 123, 129, 245
4th New York Heavy Artillery 53, 200, 201, 244
4th Ohio Infantry 142, 248
4th Pennsylvania Cavalry 63, 191, 249
4th Pennsylvania Infantry 52, 249
4th Pennsylvania Militia 92
4th Rhode Island Infantry 27, 214, 251
4th Tennessee Infantry 122, 251
4th United States Artillery 51, 77, 118, 251
4th United States Cavalry 96, 252
4th United States Colored Troops 11, 74, 99, 208, 252
4th Vermont Infantry 49, 65, 102, 168, 215, 252
4th Virginia Cavalry 63
4th West Virginia Infantry 15, 36, 37, 147, 153, 195, 253

Fout, Frederick W. 75, 230, 240, 275, 286, 290, 319
Fox, Henry 75, 230, 284
Fox, Henry M. 75, 230, 240, 243, 268, 275, 279, 290, 297, 302, 308, 311, 319
Fox, Nicholas 75, 230, 239, 283, 289, 319
Fox, William R. 75, 230, 250, 262, 272, 278, 298, 315
Foy, Charles H. 75, 236, 256, 265, 286, 294, 312
Franklin, Tenn. 15, 32, 59, 79, 85, 88, 115, 138, 164, 168, 192, 204, 268
Franklin, Va. 29, 121, 156, 188, 220, 271
Franks, William J. 75, 236, 255, 265, 286, 296, 302, 311
Frantz, Joseph 75, 230, 241, 263, 286, 290, 303, 316
Fraser, William W. 76, 230, 240, 263, 286, 299, 317
Fredericksburg, Va. 7, 17, 25, 31, 43, 50, 52, 63, 76, 82, 91, 111, 115, 127, 131, 132, 152, 156, 159, 163, 177, 181, 182, 224, 271
Fredericksburg Heights, Va. 137, 271
Freeman, Archibald 76, 230, 246, 274, 279, 295, 311
Freeman, Henry B. 76, 230, 252, 268, 283, 297, 303, 317
Freeman, Martin 76, 236, 255, 259, 286, 290, 301, 311
Freeman, William 76, 230, 247, 265, 277, 295, 308, 320
French, Samuel S. 76, 230, 243, 270, 286, 295, 305, 317
Frey, Franz 76, 230, 248, 263, 286, 299, 303, 317
Frick, Jacob G. 76, 230, 251, 271, 277, 298, 304, 315
Frisbee, John B. 77, 236, 256, 262, 283, 293, 301, 309
Frizell, Henry F. 77, 230, 244, 263, 286, 294, 317
Front Royal, Va. 116, 123, 129, 199, 271
Fry, Isaac N. 77, 235, 256, 265, 285, 298, 312
Fuger, Frederick 77, 230, 251, 266, 286, 290, 318
Funk, West 77, 230, 251, 268, 279, 293, 314
Furman, Chester S. 77, 230, 249, 282, 298, 306, 318
Furness, Frank 77, 78, 230, 249, 274, 282, 298, 319

Gage, Richard J. 78, 230, 240, 267, 286, 294, 318

Index

Gaines Mill, Va. 39, 88, 102, 140, 184, 209, 219, 271
U.S.S. *Galena* 166, 255
Galloway, George N. 78, 230, 250, 286, 317
Galloway, John 78, 230, 249, 268, 284, 298, 318
Galveston, Tex. 19, 268
Gardiner (Gardner), James 78, 230, 252, 270, 286, 299, 312, 323
Gardner, Charles N. 78, 230, 271, 279, 293, 308, 312
Gardner, Robert J. 78, 230, 242, 272, 282, 295, 312
Gardner, William 79, 236, 254, 259, 286, 291, 302, 311
Garrett, William 79, 230, 248, 268, 279, 290, 312
Garrison, James R. 79, 236, 255, 259, 286, 295, 305, 311
Garvin, William 79, 236, 253, 265, 286, 299, 303, 311
Gasson, Richard 79, 230, 246, 270, 277, 291, 306, 312, 322
Gaunt, John C. 79, 230, 249, 268, 279, 297, 312
Gause, Isaac 79, 230, 242, 271, 286, 293, 305, 318
Gaylord, Levi B. 79, 230, 242, 271, 286, 293, 305, 318
George, Daniel G. 79, 236, 256, 266, 286, 294, 305, 311
Georgia Landing, La. 147, 262
Gere, Thomas P. 79, 80, 230, 243, 268, 279, 295, 312
Geschwind, Nicholas 80, 230, 240, 263, 286, 290, 317
Gettysburg, Pa. 8, 12, 19, 32, 41, 42, 44, 47, 48, 60, 64, 69, 71, 72, 74, 77, 80, 92, 99, 102, 106, 108, 110, 112, 119, 125, 131, 133, 137, 139, 140, 144, 149, 158, 161, 162, 165, 166, 167, 168, 170, 171, 172, 173, 179, 182, 184, 190, 192, 201, 204, 209, 211, 213, 214, 218, 288
Gibbs, Wesley 80, 230, 239, 272, 279, 289, 312
Gifford, Benjamin 80, 230, 246, 273, 295
Gifford, David L. 80, 230, 242, 266, 279, 283, 293, 312, 318
Gile, Frank S. 80, 236, 255, 266, 285, 293, 308, 311
Gillespie, George L. 80, 230, 239, 269, 281, 299, 318
Gilligan, Edward L. 80, 81, 230, 250, 266, 279, 298, 316
Gilmore, Harry 92
Gilmore, John C. 81, 230, 245, 273, 278, 289, 316

Ginley, Patrick 81, 230, 245, 273, 278, 291, 301, 315
Gion, Joseph 81, 230, 246, 270, 284, 298, 315
Glendale, Va. 104, 123, 271
Godley, Leonidus M. 81, 230, 241, 263, 282, 300, 318
Goettel, Philip 81, 230, 247, 262, 279, 295, 313
Goheen, Charles A. 81, 230, 245, 274, 279, 295, 313
Goldsbery, Andrew E. 81, 230, 240, 263, 286, 290, 317
Goodall, Francis H. 82, 230, 244, 271, 283, 294, 317
Goodman, William E. 82, 230, 251, 270, 284, 298, 298, 304, 317
Goodrich, Edwin 82, 230, 245, 270, 283, 295, 306, 317
Gould, Charles G. 82, 230, 253, 272, 282, 299, 308, 315
Gould, Newton T. 82, 230, 240, 263, 286, 291, 217
Gouraud, George E. 82, 230, 239, 267, 286, 295, 305, 316
Govan, Daniel 109
Grace, Peter 82, 230, 250, 274, 283, 293, 308, 317
Graham, Robert 83, 236, 256, 266, 286, 290, 305, 311
Graham, Thomas N. 83, 230, 240, 268, 278, 291, 318
Grand Coteau, La. 129, 262
Grand Gulf, Miss. 86, 89, 156, 224, 263
Grant, Gabriel 83, 230, 239, 270, 283, 294, 318
Grant, Lewis A. 83, 84, 230, 253, 273, 282, 299, 302, 316
Graul, William 84, 230, 251, 271, 278, 298, 308, 313
Gravelly Run, Va. 149, 184, 271
Gray, John 84, 230, 248, 273, 278, 299, 311
Gray, Robert A. 84, 230, 239, 270, 283, 298, 318
Great Gulf Bay, Mich. 34, 263
Grebe, M.R. William 84, 230, 244, 262, 281, 290, 304, 319
Green, George 85, 230, 248, 268, 279, 290, 305, 316
Greenawalt, Abraham 85, 230, 249, 268, 279, 298, 313
Greenbrier River, W.V. 41, 275
Greene, John 85, 236, 256, 262, 286, 295, 309
Greene, Oliver D. 85, 230, 239, 263, 286, 295, 302, 316
Greensboro, N.C. 21, 265
Gregg, Joseph O. 85, 230, 249, 273, 286, 297, 305, 319

Greig, Theodore W. 85, 230, 246, 263, 280, 295, 306, 315
Gresser, Ignatz 86, 230, 251, 263, 283, 302
Gribben, James H. 86, 230, 273, 280, 291, 313
Griffiths, John 86, 236, 256, 265, 286, 300, 303, 313
Grimshaw, Samuel 86, 230, 248, 261, 283, 297, 317
Grindlay, James G. 86, 230, 247, 271, 280, 295, 315
Griswold, Luke M. 86, 236, 256, 265, 283, 293, 303, 313
Grueb, George 86, 230, 247, 270, 286, 290, 313
Guerin, Fritz W. 86, 87, 230, 244, 263, 286, 295, 318
Guinn, Thomas 87, 230, 248, 263, 286, 297, 303, 317
Gwynne, Nathaniel 87, 230, 248, 272, 286, 297, 317

Hack, John 87, 230, 248, 263, 286, 290, 320
Hack, Lester G. 87, 230, 253, 272, 280, 295, 305, 313
Hadley, Cornelius M. 87, 230, 243, 268, 281, 295, 304, 319
Hadley, Osgood T. 87, 230, 244, 272, 284, 294, 318
Haffee, Edmund 87, 236, 255, 265, 286, 298, 302, 313
Hagerty, Asel 87, 230, 246, 273, 280, 289, 303, 313
Haight, John H. 87, 88, 230, 246, 275, 283, 295, 305, 315
Haight, Sidney 88, 230, 243, 272, 286, 294, 308, 318
Haines Bluff, Miss. 130, 142
Haley, James 88, 236, 255, 260, 286, 291, 301, 311
Hall, Francis B. 88, 230, 245, 273, 283, 295, 318
Hall, Henry Seymour 88, 230, 245, 271, 286, 295, 303, 315
Hall, Newton H. 88, 230, 249, 268, 280, 297, 313
Hallock, Nathan M. 88, 230, 246, 269, 283, 295, 303, 311
Halstead, William 88, 236, 254, 259, 286, 295, 303, 311
Ham, Mark G. 88, 236, 255, 260, 286, 294, 301, 311
Hamilton, Hugh 89, 236, 256, 286, 295, 302, 311
Hamilton, Richard 89, 236, 256, 266, 286, 298, 303, 311
Hamilton, Thomas W. 89, 236, 254, 263, 286, 299, 302, 309
Hamilton, N.C. 115, 265
Hammel, Henry A. 89, 230, 244, 263, 286, 290, 318

Index

Hampton Roads, Va. 220, 271
Hand, Alexander 89, 236, 254, 266, 286, 289, 303, 309
Haney, Milton L. 89, 230, 240, 261, 286, 297, 318
Hanford, Edward R. 89, 230, 251, 275, 280, 295, 311
Hanks, Joseph 89, 230, 248, 263, 283, 297, 318
Hanna, Marcus A. 89, 230, 243, 262, 281, 293, 317
Hanna, Milton 89, 90, 230, 243, 268, 286, 297, 306, 318
Hanover Courthouse, Va. 38, 271
Hanovertown, Va. 173
Hanscom, Moses C. 90, 230, 242, 269, 280, 293, 311
Hapeman, Douglas 90, 230, 240, 262, 284, 295, 304, 319
Harbourne, John H. 90, 230, 242, 272, 280, 290, 305, 318
Harcourt, Thomas 90, 236, 255, 265, 286, 293, 305, 313
Hardenberg, Henry M 91, 230, 240, 270, 280, 291, 313, 322
Harding, Thomas 91, 236, 254, 265, 283, 289, 303, 311
Haring, Abram P. 91, 230, 346, 265, 284, 295, 315
Harley, Bernard 91, 236, 256, 266, 286, 295, 306, 311
Harmon, Amzi D. 91, 230, 251, 272, 280, 298, 313
Harmon, George W. 134
Harpers Ferry, W.V. 75, 175, 275
Harpeth River, Tenn. 17, 96, 268
Harrington, Daniel 91, 236, 256, 286, 291, 308, 309
Harrington, Ephraim W. 91, 230, 252, 271, 277, 293, 302, 316
Harris, George W. 91, 230, 251, 274, 280, 298, 303, 311
Harris, James H. 92, 230, 252, 272, 286, 293, 314, 323
Harris, John 92, 236, 255, 259, 283, 299, 304, 314
Harris, Moses 92, 230, 251, 274, 282, 294, 318
Harris, Sampson 92, 230, 248, 263, 286, 297, 317
Harrison, George H. 92, 236, 255, 260, 286, 293, 306, 311
Harrisonburg, La. 66, 112, 140, 262
Hart, John W. 92, 230, 249, 266, 278, 290, 318
Hart, William E. 92, 230, 245, 273, 278, 295, 314
U.S.S. *Hartford* 33, 62, 67, 73, 76, 79, 122, 134, 137, 149, 155, 192, 255

Hartranft, John F. 92, 230, 248, 269, 285, 298, 302, 315
Harvey, Harry 93, 230, 245, 274, 280, 290, 308, 313
Haskell, Frank W. 93, 230, 241, 271, 282, 293, 306, 319
Haskell, Marcus M. 93, 230, 242, 263, 283, 293, 318
Hastings, Smith H. 93, 230, 243, 272, 284, 294, 306, 318
Hatch, John P. 93, 230, 239, 263, 282, 295, 301, 316
Hatcher's Mill, Va. 39
Hatchers Run, Va. 40, 49, 59, 70, 129, 144, 151, 159, 164, 174, 186, 191, 200, 201, 208, 216, 223, 271
Hathaway, Edward W. 94, 236, 256, 263, 286, 293, 304, 320
Havron, John H. 94, 230, 251, 272, 286, 291, 306, 314
Hawkins, Charles 94, 236, 253, 265, 286, 299, 302, 311
Hawkins, Gardner C. 94, 230, 252, 272, 286, 299, 316
Hawkins, Martin J. 94, 230, 248, 261, 281, 298, 309
Hawkins, Thomas R. 94, 230, 252, 270, 284, 297, 314, 323
Haws Shops, Va. 46, 271
Hawthorne, Harris S. 94, 230, 246, 273, 278, 295, 302, 317
Hayden, Joseph B. 95, 236, 256, 265, 286, 293, 302, 313
Hayes, John 95, 236, 255, 260, 286, 298, 307, 311
Hayes, Thomas 95, 236, 256, 259, 286, 299, 305, 311
Haynes, Asbury F. 95, 230, 242, 273, 280, 293, 313
Hays, John H. 95, 230, 241, 262, 280, 297, 302, 308, 313
Healey, George W. 95, 230, 241, 262, 278, 291, 319
Hedges, Joseph 96, 230, 252, 268, 278, 297, 303, 319
Heermance, William L. 96, 230, 245, 270, 284, 295, 303, 319
Heller, Henry 96, 230, 249, 270, 278, 297, 305, 316
Helms, David H. 96, 230, 241, 263, 286, 291, 317
U.S.S. *Hendrick Hudson* 128, 178, 255
Henry, Guy V. 96, 230, 243, 270, 282, 297, 316
Henry, James 96, 230, 240, 263, 286, 297, 317
Henry, William W. 96, 97, 230, 253, 270, 284, 299, 302, 316
Herington, Pitt B. 97, 230, 241, 262, 283, 294, 305, 319

Herron, Francis J. 97, 230, 241, 260, 284, 298, 303, 316
Hesseltine, Francis S. 97, 98, 230, 242, 268, 285, 293, 302, 317
Hibson, Joseph C. 98, 230, 246, 266, 285, 290, 306, 318
Hickey, Dennis W. 98, 230, 245, 274, 286, 295, 315
Hickman, John 98, 236, 256, 262, 286, 299, 303, 309
Hickok, Nathan E. 98, 230, 239, 270, 280, 289, 313
Higby, Charles 98, 230, 249, 268, 280, 298, 313
Higgins, Thomas J. 98, 230, 240, 263, 278, 289, 319
Highland, Patrick 98, 230, 240, 272, 278, 289, 319
Hill, Edward 98, 230, 243, 270, 282, 295, 303, 316
Hill, Henry 99, 230, 250, 274, 286, 298, 318
Hill, James 99, 230, 241, 263, 272, 278, 280, 295, 311
Hill, James (England) 99, 230, 244, 290, 308, 316
Hilliker, Benjamin F. 99, 230, 253, 263, 286, 300, 306, 318
Hills, William G. 99, 230, 245, 272, 283, 295, 316
Hilton, Alfred B. 99, 230, 252, 270, 278, 293, 313, 323
Hilton Head, S.C. 201, 219, 266
Hincks, William B. 99, 230, 239, 266, 280, 293, 311
Hinnecan, William 100, 236, 253, 265, 286, 291, 305, 311
Hodges, Addison J. 100, 230, 248, 263, 286, 294, 305, 320
Hoffman, Henry 100, 230, 248, 273, 280, 290, 313
Hoffman, Thomas W. 100, 230, 251, 272, 286, 298, 317
Hogan, Franklin 100, 230, 250, 272, 280, 298, 311
Hogarty, William P. 100, 230, 245, 263, 286, 295, 315
Holcomb, Daniel I. 100, 230, 248, 267, 286, 297, 313
Holehouse, James 100, 230, 242, 271, 286, 290, 304, 318
Holland, Lemuel F. 100, 230, 240, 267, 297, 305, 318
Holland, Milton M. 101, 230, 252, 270, 282, 299, 308, 313, 323
Hollat, George 101, 236, 256, 262, 286, 295, 309
Holmes, Lovilo N. 101, 230, 243, 268, 286, 295, 302, 317
Holmes, William T. 101, 230, 240, 273, 280, 291, 313

336   Index

Holton, Charles M. 101, 231, 243, 271, 280, 295, 304, 315
Holton, Edward A. 102, 231, 253, 272, 284, 289, 316
Homan, Conrad 102, 231, 242, 272, 284, 293, 314
Honey Hill, S.C. 19, 68, 82, 186, 267
Hooker, George W. 102, 231, 252, 263, 278, 295, 315
Hooper, William B. 102, 231, 244, 270, 286, 289, 313
Hopkins, Charles F. 102, 231, 244, 271, 283, 294, 316
Horan, Thomas 102, 231, 246, 266, 280, 295, 319
Horne, Samuel B. 102, 231, 239, 271, 281, 291, 306, 319
Horseshoe Bend, Ky. 57, 162
Horsfall, William H. 102, 231, 241, 263, 283, 293, 304, 313
Horton, James 102, 103, 236, 255, 284, 293, 304, 313
Horton, Lewis A. 103, 236, 256, 283, 293, 304, 313
Hottenstine, Soloman J. 103, 231, 250, 272, 280, 298, 313
Hough, Ira 103, 231, 241, 270, 280, 291, 306, 311
Houghton, Charles H. 103, 231, 244, 270, 286, 295, 306, 319
Houghton, Edward J. 103, 236, 256, 266, 286, 289, 306, 311
Houghton, George L. 103, 231, 240, 267, 286, 289, 320
Houlton, William 103, 231, 253, 273, 280, 295, 313
Howard, Henderson C. 104, 231, 249, 271, 286, 298, 304, 319
Howard, Hiram R. 104, 231, 248, 268, 280, 297, 306, 316
Howard, James 104, 231, 247, 272, 278, 294, 313
Howard, Martin 104, 236, 252, 266, 286, 291, 306, 311
Howard, Oliver O. 104, 231, 239, 271, 282, 293, 302, 316
Howard, Peter 104, 236, 255, 262, 286, 290, 302, 309
Howard, Squire E. 105, 231, 253, 262, 281, 299, 317
Howe, Orion P. 105, 231, 240, 263, 286, 297, 308, 318
Howe, William H. 105, 231, 242, 281, 286, 293, 317
U.S.S. *Howquah* 51, 170, 255
Hubbell, William S. 105, 231, 239, 271, 278, 289, 303, 317
Hudson, Aaron R. 105, 106, 231, 241, 262, 280, 293, 313
Hudson, Michael 106, 235, 254, 259, 286, 291, 302, 311

Hughes, Oliver 106, 231, 241, 274, 280, 299, 305, 313
Hughey, John 106, 231, 248, 273, 280, 297, 313
Huidekoper, Henry S. 106, 231, 251, 266, 286, 298, 304, 320
U.S.S. *Hunchback* 15, 255
Hunt, Louis T. 106, 231, 244, 263, 286, 291, 317
Hunter, Charles A. 106, 231, 242, 272, 278, 294, 306, 313
Hunter, David 52
Hunterson, John C. 106, 231, 249, 272, 285, 298, 319
Huskey, Michael 107, 236, 254, 263, 283, 295, 305, 311
Hyatt, Theodore 107, 231, 240, 264, 286, 298, 302, 317
Hyde, Thomas W. 107, 231, 242, 263, 282, 292, 315
Hyland, John 107, 236, 256, 263, 284, 291, 301, 311
Hymer, Samuel 107, 231, 240, 261, 284, 291, 302, 318

Ilgenfritz, Charles H. 107, 108, 231, 251, 271, 278, 298, 303, 320
Immell, Lorenzo D. 108, 231, 251, 265, 286, 297, 315
Independent Pennsylvania Light Artillery 42, 249
Ingalls, Lewis J. 108, 231, 253, 262, 283, 294, 319
Inscho, Leonidus H. 108, 231, 248, 263, 278, 297, 304, 317
Irish Bend, La. 185, 262
Irlam, Joseph 108, 236, 254, 259, 286, 290, 305, 311
Irsch, Francis 108, 231, 246, 266, 278, 295, 305, 316
Irving, John 108, 236, 254, 259, 286, 295, 304, 311
Irving, Thomas 108, 236, 255, 266, 283, 290, 306, 311
Irwin, Nicholas 108, 109, 254, 259, 286, 289, 302, 311
Irwin, Patrick 109, 231, 243, 262, 278, 291, 304, 318
U.S.S. *Isaac Smith* 194, 255
Iuka, Miss. 179, 263
Ivy Farm, Miss. 22, 263

Jackson, Frederick 109, 231, 239, 267, 286, 289, 308, 309
Jackson, Tenn. 75, 268
Jacobson, Eugene P. 109, 231, 246, 270, 285, 295, 313
James, Isaac 109, 231, 249, 272, 280, 297, 313
James, John H. 109, 236, 256, 259, 286, 294, 303, 311

James, Miles 109, 231, 252, 270, 286, 299, 302, 313, 323
James Island, S.C. 109, 267
Jamieson, Walter 109, 110, 231, 246, 272, 278, 290, 39
Jardine, James 110, 231, 248, 264, 286, 299, 303, 317
Jefferson, Va. 64, 271
Jellison, Benjamin H. 110, 231, 242, 266, 280, 294, 311
Jenkins, Thomas 110, 236, 254, 264, 286, 309
Jennings, James T. 110, 231, 250, 274, 280, 290, 304, 311
Jetersville, Va. 121, 271
Jewett, Erastus W. 110, 231, 253, 266, 282, 299, 304, 315
John, William 110, 231, 248, 264, 286, 290, 317
U.S.S. *John Adams* 149, 255
Johndro, Franklin 110, 231, 246, 270, 278, 299, 313
Johns, Elisha 111, 231, 240, 261, 286, 297, 303, 317
Johns, Henry T. 111, 231, 243, 262, 286, 294, 316
John's Island, S.C. 24, 139, 267
Johnson, Andrew 111, 231, 240, 264, 286, 297, 317
Johnson, Follett 111, 231, 246, 262, 286, 295, 306, 316
Johnson, Henry 111, 236, 255, 259, 283, 296, 301, 314
Johnson, John 111, 231, 253, 271, 286, 296, 306, 316
Johnson, Joseph E. 111, 231, 250, 271, 282, 298, 306, 319
Johnson, Ruel M. 111, 231, 241, 267, 286, 291, 318
Johnson, Samuel 111, 112, 231, 249, 263, 280, 298, 308, 309
Johnson, Wallace W. 112, 231, 249, 266, 282, 295, 320
Johnston, David 112, 231, 244, 264, 282, 298, 315
Johnston, William P. 112, 236, 254, 262, 286, 291, 311
Johnston, Willie 112, 231, 252, 295, 309
Jones, Andrew 112, 236, 254, 259, 286, 303, 311
Jones, David 112, 231, 248, 264, 286, 297, 305, 317
Jones, John 112, 236, 256, 283, 289, 303, 313
Jones, John E. 112, 236, 256, 259, 286, 295, 302, 311
Jones, Thomas 113, 236, 256, 265, 286, 293, 301, 313
Jones, William 113, 231, 246, 286, 298, 302, 311
Jones, William (Ireland) 113,

236, 256, 259, 274, 280, 291, 303, 311
Jonesboro, Ga. 12, 84, 109, 120, 131, 262
Jordan, Absalom 113, 231, 240, 273, 280, 297, 313
Jordan, Robert 113, 236, 255, 272, 286, 295, 301, 309
Jordan, Thomas 113, 236, 254, 259, 286, 299, 305, 313
Josselyn, Simeon T. 113, 231, 240, 268, 280, 291, 306, 319
Judge, Francis W. 113, 114, 231, 246, 268, 280, 290, 304, 314

Kaiser, John 114, 231, 251, 273, 286, 290, 315
Kaltenbach, Luther 114, 231, 241, 268, 280, 290, 313
Kane, John 114, 231, 246, 272, 278, 291, 313
Kane, Thomas 114, 236, 255, 265, 286, 294, 305, 314
Kappesser, Peter 114, 231, 247, 268, 280, 290, 304, 313
Karpeles, Leopold 114, 231, 243, 274, 286, 290, 314
Kauss (Kautz), August 115, 231, 243, 274, 286, 290, 314
U.S.S. *Kearsarge* 7, 22, 26, 88, 92, 95, 122, 142, 154, 156, 180, 165, 175, 190, 194, 255
Keele, Joseph 115, 231, 248, 272, 281, 291, 314
Keen, Joseph S. 115, 231, 243, 285, 290, 306, 319
Keene, Joseph 115, 231, 245, 261, 271, 278, 290, 316
Kelley, Andrew J. 116, 231, 243, 268, 286, 291, 308, 320
Kelley, George V. 115, 231, 249, 268, 280, 297, 306, 313
Kelley, John 115, 231, 254, 265, 291, 309
Kelley, Leverett M. 115, 231, 240, 268, 278, 295, 305, 320
Kelly, Alexander 116, 231, 252, 270, 298, 313, 323
Kelly, Daniel 116, 231, 245, 274, 280, 295, 313
Kelly, Thomas 116, 231, 245, 271, 280, 291, 311
Kemp, Joseph 116, 231, 243, 274, 280, 297, 308, 311
Kendall, William W. 116, 231, 241, 263, 282, 291, 304, 317
Kendrick, Thomas 116, 236, 256, 259, 286, 293, 304, 311
Kenna, Barnett 116, 236, 254, 259, 286, 290, 301, 311
Kennedy, John 116, 231, 251, 274, 284, 291, 303, 316

Kennesaw Mountain, Ga. 97, 132, 195, 213, 262
Kenyon, Charles 116, 117, 236, 254, 270, 286, 295, 305, 209
Kenyon, John S. 117, 231, 245, 266, 283, 295, 306, 319
Kenyon, Samuel P. 117, 231, 245, 273, 280, 295, 313
U.S.S. *Keokuk* 10, 255
Keough, John 117, 231, 250, 273, 280, 291, 313
Kephart, James 117, 231, 252, 264, 283, 298, 317
Kerr, Thomas R. 117, 231, 249, 275, 280, 291, 306, 317
Kiggins, John 117, 231, 247, 268, 283, 295, 316
Kimball, Joseph 117, 231, 253, 273, 280, 294, 313
Kindig, John M. 117, 231, 250, 274, 280, 294, 311
King, Horatio C. 118, 231, 239, 270, 281, 295, 303, 319
King, Robert H. 118, 231, 256, 266, 286, 295, 308, 311
King, Rufus, Jr. 118, 231, 251, 274, 287, 295, 304, 319
Kinnaird, Samuel W. 118, 236, 255, 259, 287, 295, 306, 311
Kinsey, John 118, 231, 250, 274, 284, 298, 308, 319
Kirby, Dennis T. 118, 231, 244, 264, 278, 295, 304, 317
Kirk, Jonathan C. 118, 119, 231, 241, 272, 278, 297, 317
Kline, Harry 119, 231, 246, 273, 280, 290, 313
Kloth, Charles H. 119, 231, 239, 264, 282, 317
Knight, Charles H. 119, 231, 244, 272, 278, 294, 318
Knight, William J. 119, 231, 248, 261, 281, 297, 303, 309
Knowles, Abiather J. 119, 231, 241, 269, 283, 293, 302, 317
Knox, Edward M. 119, 231, 245, 266, 284, 295, 316
Knoxville, Tenn. 71, 87, 113, 115, 129, 182, 268
Koogle, Jacob 119, 231, 242, 271, 280, 293, 313
Kountz, John S. 120, 231, 248, 268, 287, 297, 308, 317
Kramer, Theodore L. 120, 231, 251, 270, 278, 298, 313
Kretsinger, George 120, 231, 239, 264, 282, 291, 319
Kuder, Andrew 120, 231, 245, 274, 280, 295, 313
Kuder, Jeremiah 120, 231, 241, 262, 280, 297, 313

Labill, Joseph S. 120, 231, 244, 264, 287, 290, 317
U.S.S. *Lackawana* 38, 44, 46, 64, 68, 118, 134, 157, 188, 198, 211, 216, 255
Ladd, George 120, 231, 245, 274, 280, 295
Lafferty, John 120, 236, 257, 266, 287, 295, 306, 311
Laffey, Bartlett 120, 121, 236, 255, 265, 287, 291, 305, 311
Lagareville, S.C. 71, 139, 142, 267
Laing, William 121, 231, 247, 270, 287, 295, 313
Lakin, Daniel 121, 236, 254, 271, 287, 293, 302, 309
Landis, James P. 121, 231, 249, 272, 280, 298, 306, 313
Lane, Morgan D. 121, 231, 239, 271, 280, 295, 314
Lanfare, Aaron S. 121, 231, 239, 273, 280, 289, 313
Langbein, J.S. Julius 121, 231, 245, 265, 283, 290, 308, 317
Lann, John S. 121, 236, 255, 260, 287, 295, 306, 313
Larimer, Smith 121, 231, 248, 273, 280, 297, 302, 313
Larrabee, James W. 121, 231, 240, 264, 287, 295, 316
Laurel Hill, Va. 156, 170, 272
Lawson, Gaines 122, 231, 251, 268, 283, 299, 305, 317
Lawson, John 122, 236, 255, 259, 287, 298, 303, 311
Lawton, Henry W. 122, 231, 241, 261, 282, 297, 306, 316
Lear, Nicholas 122, 236, 256, 265, 287, 299, 301, 313
Lee, G.W. Custis 94
Lee, James H. 122, 236, 255, 260, 287, 295, 305, 311
Lees Mills, Va. 102, 157, 179, 272
U.S.S. *Lehigh* 80, 108, 122, 220, 226, 255
Leland, George W. 122, 236, 255, 266, 287, 290, 303, 311
Lenoire, Tenn. 29
Lenoire Station, Tenn. 197, 268
Leon, Pierre 122, 123, 236, 253, 265, 287, 293, 303, 309
Leonard, Edwin 123, 231, 243, 272, 287, 294, 317
Leonard, William E. 123, 231, 250, 270, 280, 298, 313
Leslie, Frank 123, 231, 245, 271, 280, 290, 311
Levy, Benjamin 123, 231, 245, 271, 284, 295, 308, 313
Lewis, Dewitt Clinton 123, 231, 250, 267, 283, 298, 318

Lewis, Henry 6, 123, 231, 248, 264, 287, 294, 306, 320
Lewis, Samuel E. 123, 231, 251, 272, 282, 299, 314
Lewis' Farm, Va. 154, 271
Lexington, Mo. 152, 265
Libaire, Adolphe 123, 124, 231, 245, 263, 278, 319
Lilley, John 124, 231, 251, 272, 280, 298, 313
Lincoln, Abraham 4
Little, Henry F.W. 124, 231, 244, 273, 287, 294, 306, 314
Littlefield, George H. 124, 231, 241, 271, 278, 293, 315
Livingston, Josiah O. 124, 231, 253, 266, 283, 299, 315
Lloyd, Benjamin 124, 236, 257, 266, 287, 290, 304, 311
Lloyd, John W. 124, 236, 257, 266, 287, 295, 302, 311
Locke, Lewis 124, 231, 244, 272, 280, 295, 313
Logan, Hugh 124, 125, 236, 256, 259, 283, 291, 303, 313, 322
Lonergan, John 125, 231, 253, 266, 278, 291, 304, 316
Longshore, William H. 125, 231, 248, 264, 287, 297, 317
Lonsway, Joseph 125, 231, 245, 272, 287, 295, 320
Lookout Mountain, Tenn. 114, 117, 161, 268
Lord, William 125, 231, 243, 276, 283, 290, 319
Lorish, Andrew J. 125, 231, 245, 275, 280, 295, 302, 311
U.S.S. *Louisville* 28, 39, 195, 198, 255
Love, George M. 125, 231, 246, 270, 280, 295, 313
Lovering, George M. 125, 231, 262, 287, 294, 302, 315
Lower, Cyrus B. 126, 231, 250, 274, 287, 298, 306, 315
Lower, Robert A. 126, 231, 240, 254, 287, 291, 308, 316
Loyd, George 126, 231, 249, 272, 280, 297, 308, 315
Lucas, George W. 126, 231, 244, 260, 281, 291, 308, 311
Luce, Moses A. 126, 231, 243, 272, 283, 291, 306, 317
Ludgate, William 126, 231, 246, 282, 290, 303, 315
Ludwig, Carl 126, 231, 245, 272, 284, 290, 318
Lunt, Alphonso M. 126, 231, 243, 272, 284, 293, 317
Luray, Va. 16, 272
Lutes, Franklin W. 127, 231, 246, 272, 280, 295, 313

Luther, James H. 127, 231, 242, 271, 278, 294, 315
Luty, Gotlieb 127, 231, 246, 270, 285, 298, 314
Lyman, Joel H. 127, 232, 245, 275, 278, 295, 317
Lynchburg, Va. 143, 272
Lyon, Frederick A. 127, 232, 252, 270, 280, 294, 306, 311
Lyons, Thomas 127, 236, 256, 262, 287, 294, 304, 314

MacArthur, Arthur, Jr. 127, 128, 232, 253, 268, 278, 294, 308, 315
Machon, James 128, 236, 254, 259, 287, 290, 308, 311
Mack, Alexander 128, 236, 254, 259, 287, 290, 303, 311
Mack, John 128, 236, 255, 260, 287, 293, 306, 313
Mackie, John F. 128, 235, 254, 270, 287, 295, 303, 309
Madden, Michael 128, 232, 246, 263, 283, 295, 305, 319
Madden, William 128, 236, 254, 259, 287, 290, 306, 311
Maddox Creek 144
Madison, James 128, 232, 245, 274, 284, 296, 306, 313
Magee, William 128, 129, 232, 244, 268, 278, 294, 314
U.S.S. *Magnolia* 121, 163, 165, 190, 255
Mahoney, Jeremiah 129, 232, 242, 268, 280, 294, 311
Malvern Hill, Va. 151, 163, 169, 203, 221, 272
Manassas, Va. 8, 272
Mandy, Harry J. 129, 232, 245, 271, 280, 290, 313
Mangam, Richard C. 129, 232, 247, 271, 280, 291, 315
Manning, Joseph S. 129, 232, 242, 268, 280, 294, 308, 311
U.S.S. *Marblehead* 71, 139, 141, 255
Marland, William 129, 232, 242, 262, 284, 294, 304, 319
U.S.S. *Marmora* 75, 130, 194, 255
Marquette, Charles 129, 232, 250, 272, 278, 298, 313
Marsh, Albert 129, 232, 246, 274, 280, 296
Marsh, Charles H. 130, 232, 239, 269, 280, 289, 313
Marsh, George 130, 232, 240, 267, 282, 291, 319
Martin, Edward S. 130, 254, 259, 287, 291, 305, 311
Martin, George *see* Schwenk, Martin

Martin, James 130, 235, 256, 259, 287, 301, 311
Martin, Sylvester H. 130, 232, 250, 274, 285, 298, 317
Martin, William 130, 236, 253, 262, 265, 287, 299, 306, 309
Martin, William (Ireland) 130, 236, 256, 287, 291, 304, 309
Marye's Heights, Va. 100, 181
Mason, Elihu H. 130, 232, 248, 261, 281, 291, 302, 209, 321
Mason's Hill, Va. 205, 272
Mason's Island, Md. 128, 263
Matagorda Bay, Tex. 97, 268
Mathews, William H. 131, 232, 242, 272, 278, 290, 316
Mathias Point, Va. 219, 272
Matthews, John C. 131, 232, 250, 273, 278, 298, 315
Matthews, Milton 131, 232, 250, 273, 280, 298, 313
Mattingly, Henry B. 131, 232, 241, 262, 280, 293, 313
Mattocks, Charles P. 131, 232, 242, 273, 282, 291, 299, 305, 319
Maxham, Lowell M. 131, 232, 242, 271, 278, 294, 318
May, William 131, 232, 241, 268, 280, 298, 301, 313
Mayberry, John B. 131, 232, 239, 266, 280, 289, 311
Mayes, William B. 132, 232, 241, 262, 283, 297, 303, 319
Maynard, George H. 132, 232, 242, 271, 283, 294, 303, 319
McAdams, Peter 132, 232, 250, 273, 283, 291, 303, 319
McAlwee, Benjamin F. 132, 232, 242, 273, 300, 304, 319
McAnally, Charles 132, 232, 250, 274, 280, 291, 319
McCammon, William W. 132, 133, 232, 244, 263, 287, 297, 303, 318
McCarren, Bernard 133, 232, 239, 266, 280, 291, 311
McCauslin, Joseph 133, 232, 253, 273, 278, 300, 313
McCleary, Charles H. 133, 232, 249, 268, 280, 297, 313
McClelland, James M. 133, 232, 248, 254, 287, 297, 302, 317
McClelland, Matthew 133, 236, 256, 262, 287, 296, 302, 309
McConnell, Samuel 133, 232, 240, 259, 280, 297, 313
McCormick, Michael 133, 236, 256, 263, 287, 291, 302, 311
McCornack, Andrew 133, 134, 232, 240, 264, 287, 291, 308, 317
McCullock, Adam 134, 236, 255, 259, 287, 293, 302, 311

Index

McDonald, George E. 134, 232, 239, 271, 280, 299, 313
McDonald, John 134, 236, 253, 265, 287, 299, 301, 309
McDonald, John Wade 134, 232, 240, 268, 283, 291, 320
McDowell, Va. 142, 272
McElhinny, Samuel O. 134, 232, 253, 273, 280, 297, 313
McEnroe, Patrick H. 134, 232, 245, 275, 280, 291, 311
McFall, Daniel 134, 232, 243, 274, 278, 296, 303, 318
McFarland, John 134, 236, 255, 259, 287, 305, 311
McGinn, Edward 134, 232, 248, 264, 287, 296, 317
McGonagle, Wilson 134, 135, 232, 248, 264, 287, 297, 317
McGonnigle, Andrew J. 135, 232, 239, 270, 282, 296, 302, 319
McGough, Owen 135, 232, 251, 269, 284, 291, 319
McGowan, John 135, 236, 256, 262, 287, 292, 302, 309
McGraw, Thomas 135, 232, 240, 273, 287, 292, 313
McGuire, Patrick 135, 232, 240, 264, 282, 292, 317
McHale, Alexander U. 135, 232, 243, 274, 280, 292, 306, 320
McHugh, Martin 135, 236, 254, 264, 287, 297, 303, 309
McIntosh, James 135, 236, 256, 259, 287, 289, 302, 311
McKay, Charles W. 135, 232, 247, 262, 283, 296, 308, 317
McKee, George 136, 232, 246, 273, 278, 292, 313
McKeen, Nineveh S. 136, 232, 240, 268, 280, 291, 315
McKeever, Michael 136, 232, 249, 269, 282, 292, 306, 319
McKnight, William 136, 232, 257, 262, 287, 296, 305, 309
McKown, Nathaniel A. 136, 232, 250, 270, 280, 298, 304, 313
McLeod, James 136, 236, 256, 262, 287, 299, 309
McMahon, Martin T. 136, 137, 232, 239, 274, 287, 304, 315
McMillen, Francis M. 137, 232, 249, 273, 280, 293, 302, 313
McVeane, John P. 137, 232, 246, 271, 280, 289, 314, 322
McWhorter, Walter F. 137, 232, 253, 273, 280, 300, 313
McWilliams, George W. 137, 236, 256, 265, 287, 298, 308, 313

Meach, George E. 137, 232, 245, 275, 280, 296, 311
Meade, George G. 216
Meagher, Thomas 137, 232, 247, 270, 282, 299, 313
Mears, George W. 137, 232, 249, 266, 278, 298, 319
Mechanicsburg, Miss. 99, 263
Melville, Charles 137, 236, 255, 259, 287, 294, 302, 311
Menter, John W. 138, 232, 243, 273, 280, 296, 305, 313
Merriam, Henry C. 138, 232, 252, 259, 282, 293, 317
Merrifield, James K. 138, 232, 240, 268, 280, 298, 318
Merrill, Augustus 138, 232, 241, 273, 278, 293, 315
Merrill, George 138, 232, 247, 265, 287, 296, 320
C.S.S. *Merrimack* 220
Merritt, John G. 138, 232, 243, 269, 280, 296, 315
U.S.S. *Metacomet* 12, 13, 63, 92, 111, 145, 147, 199, 255
Meyer, Henry C. 138, 232, 245, 273, 283, 296, 319
Mifflin, James 138, 139, 236, 254, 259, 287, 299, 304, 311
Miles, Nelson A. 139, 232, 246, 270, 287, 294, 316
Miller, Andrew 139, 235, 256, 259, 287, 290, 303, 311
Miller, Frank 139, 232, 245, 273, 280, 296, 313
Miller, Henry 139, 232, 259, 280, 290, 304, 313
Miller, Jacob C. 139, 232, 240, 264, 287, 297, 317
Miller, James 139, 236, 255, 267, 280, 287, 289, 311
Miller, James P. 139, 232, 241, 260, 297, 313
Miller, John 139, 140, 232, 245, 266, 280, 290, 311
Miller, John (Germany) 140, 248, 274, 280, 290, 313
Miller, William E. 140, 232, 249, 266, 282, 298, 303, 319
Millersville, Pa. 178, 266
Milliken, Daniel 140, 236, 256, 265, 287, 293, 304, 313
Mills, Charles 140, 236, 255, 265, 283, 296, 306, 313
Mills, Frank W. 140, 232, 248, 266, 278, 296, 319
Mindil, George W. 140, 232, 250, 275, 282, 290, 316
Mine Run, Va. 175, 272
Minerva 4
U.S.S. *Minnesota* 15, 51, 90, 113, 140, 164, 183, 201, 217, 255
Minville, Tenn. 122, 268

Missionary Ridge, Tenn. 13, 19, 28, 31, 33, 58, 83, 85, 104, 113, 115, 120, 127, 166, 176, 204, 210, 268
U.S.S. *Mississippi* 29, 30, 208, 255
Mitchell, Alexander H. 140, 121, 232, 250, 274, 280, 298, 315
Mitchell, Theodore 141, 232, 250, 273, 280, 298, 303, 313
Mobile, Ala. 29
Mobile Bay, Ala. 12, 13, 24, 29, 32, 33, 28, 43, 44, 45, 46, 52, 55, 59, 60, 61, 62, 63, 64, 66, 67, 68, 73, 76, 79, 88, 89, 92, 95, 106, 108, 109, 111, 112, 113, 116, 118, 124, 128, 130, 134, 135, 137, 138, 139, 142, 145, 146, 147, 149, 152, 153, 155, 157, 162, 169, 179, 181, 182, 184, 187, 188, 189, 190, 191, 192, 193, 198, 199, 203, 206, 211, 214, 216, 224, 225, 259
Moffitt, John H. 141, 232, 245, 271, 278, 296, 306, 315
U.S.S. *Mohican* 201, 219, 255
Molbone, Archibald 141, 232, 251, 273, 282, 299, 305, 314
Molloy, Hugh 141, 236, 254, 262, 287, 291, 302, 311
U.S.S. *Monadnock* 66, 255
Monaghan, Patrick 141, 232, 250, 273, 284, 292, 306, 311
U.S.S. *Monitor* 86, 103, 112, 220, 255
Monocacy, Md. 58, 178, 263
U.S.S. *Montauk* 102, 172, 213, 255
Monterey Mountain, Pa. 41, 266
Montgomery, Robert 141, 236, 253, 265, 287, 292, 304, 311
U.S.S *Monticello* 195, 212, 225, 255
Moore, Charles 142, 236, 255, 260, 267, 287, 290, 311
Moore, Charles (Ireland) 141, 236, 255, 287, 292, 304, 311
Moore, Daniel B. 142, 232, 253, 259, 283, 300, 304, 320
Moore, George 142, 237, 256, 265, 280, 298, 304, 313
Moore, George G. 142, 232, 253, 271, 283, 300, 311
Moore, Wilbur F. 142, 232, 240, 268, 280, 291, 313
Moore, William 142, 237, 253, 265, 287, 294, 303, 311
Moorefield, W.V. 117, 186, 275
Morey, Delano 142, 232, 249, 272, 278, 297, 316

340 Index

Morford, Jerome 142, 232, 240, 264, 287, 298, 316
Morgan, James H. 142, 237, 256, 259, 287, 296, 305, 311
Morgan, Lewis 142, 232, 248, 274, 297, 311
Morgan, Richard H. 142, 232, 241, 262, 280, 291, 313
Morrill, Walter G. 143, 232, 242, 273, 282, 293, 319
Morris, William 143, 232, 245, 273, 280, 298, 313
Morrison, Francis 143, 232, 250, 269, 283, 298, 308, 319
Morrison, John G. 143, 237, 254, 265, 287, 292, 306, 313
Morse, Benjamin 143, 232, 243, 274, 280, 296, 308, 315
Morse, Charles E. 143, 232, 246, 274, 278, 290, 315
Morton, Charles W. 143, 232, 237, 253, 265, 287, 292, 303, 309
Mostroller, John W. 143, 144, 250, 271, 282, 298, 317
Mount Pleasant, Ala. 64, 260
U.S.S. *Mount Washington* 113, 200, 223, 255
Mulholland, St. Clair A. 144, 232, 251, 270, 284, 292, 304, 317
Mullen, Patrick 144, 237, 257, 287, 293, 308, 313, 322
Mundell, Walter L. 144, 232, 243, 273, 280, 294, 304, 313
Munsell, Harvey M. 144, 232, 250, 266, 278, 285, 298, 306, 314
Murfrees Station, Va. 125, 272
Murfreesboro, Tenn. 128, 268
Murphy, Charles J. 144, 232, 246, 269, 283, 290, 319
Murphy, Daniel J. 144, 145, 232, 242, 271, 280, 298, 311
Murphy, Dennis J.F. 145, 232, 253, 263, 278, 292, 302, 316
Murphy, James T. 145, 232, 239, 273, 287, 289, 315
Murphy, John P. 145, 232, 248, 263, 280, 292, 308, 314
Murphy, Michael C. 145, 232, 247, 272, 287, 292, 319
Murphy, Patrick 145, 237, 255, 259, 287, 292, 301, 311
Murphy, Robinson B. 145, 232, 240, 261, 282, 291, 315
Murphy, Thomas 145, 232, 240, 270, 280, 311
Murphy, Thomas C. 145, 232, 247, 264, 281, 292, 296, 306, 316
Murphy, Thomas J. 145, 232, 247, 271, 280, 292, 313

Myers, George S. 145, 232, 249, 261, 284, 297, 317
Myers, William H. 146, 232, 242, 268, 287, 298, 314

U.S.S. *Nahant* 80, 112, 255
Namozine, Va. 57, 272
C.S.S. *Nansemond* 121
Nansemond River, N.C. 113, 200, 223, 265, 272
Nash, Henry H. 146, 232, 248, 264, 287, 294, 306, 320
Nashville, Tenn. 10, 43, 46, 50, 79, 80, 114, 131, 133, 142, 153, 160, 184, 186, 189, 194, 214, 268
Natchitoches, La. 68, 262
Naylor, David 146, 237, 256, 259, 287, 296, 306, 311
Neahr, Zachariah C. 146, 232, 247, 265, 287, 296, 302, 315
Neil, John 146, 237, 253, 265, 287, 289, 303, 311
U.S.S. *Neosho* 62, 72, 255
Neville, Edwin M. 146, 232, 239, 273, 280, 289, 313
New Bern, N.C. 35, 42, 199, 201, 265
New Hope Church, Ga. 111, 262
U.S.S. *New Ironsides* 15, 61, 70, 87, 122, 140, 216, 220, 255
New Market, Va. 38, 272
New Market Heights, Va. 11, 92, 272
Newby's Crossroads, Va. 93, 223, 272
Newland, William 146, 237, 256, 259, 287, 294, 305, 311
Newman, Marcellus J. 146, 232, 240, 262, 283, 291, 303, 319
Newman, William H. 147, 232, 246, 268, 280, 296, 304, 313
Newnan, Ga. 96, 262
Newport Barracks, N.C. 110, 124, 155, 266
Newtonia, Mo. 25, 265
Nibbe, John H. 147, 237, 256, 265, 283, 290, 306, 313
Nichols, Henry C. 147, 232, 252, 259, 285, 299, 302, 319
Nichols, William 147, 237, 254, 259, 287, 296, 303, 311
19th Georgia Infantry 43, 224
19th Indiana Infantry 35, 241
19th Maine Infantry 90, 242
19th Massachusetts Infantry 7, 60, 71, 110, 144, 167, 170, 242
19th Michigan Infantry 13, 243
19th New York Cavalry 28, 125, 221, 245
19th United States Infantry 157, 162, 252

19th Vermont Infantry 96
19th Virginia Infantry 60
90th New York Infantry 211, 246
90th Pennsylvania Infantry 21, 30, 154, 175, 179, 182, 216, 250
98th Pennsylvania Infantry 132, 250
95th New York Infantry 189, 246
95th Ohio Infantry 50, 189, 249
95th Pennsylvania Infantry 75, 78, 221, 250
91st Ohio Infantry 56, 249
99th Illinois Infantry 48, 240
99th Pennsylvania Infantry 26, 72, 144, 250
92nd New York Infantry 181, 246
97th Illinois Infantry 50, 62, 76, 156, 223, 240
97th New York Infantry 38, 246
97th Ohio Infantry 163, 249
97th Pennsylvania Infantry 69, 123, 155, 209, 210, 211, 250
96th New York Infantry 11, 240
93rd New York Infantry 169, 173, 246
93rd Pennsylvania Infantry 129, 250
Nineveh, Va. 7, 183, 272
9th Connecticut Infantry 57, 239
9th Independent Battery, Massachusetts Light Artillery 166, 242
9th Iowa Infantry 68, 97, 241
9th Maine Infantry 18, 242
9th Massachusetts Infantry 203, 242
9th Michigan Cavalry 46, 87, 203, 243
9th Mississippi Infantry 33
9th New Hampshire Infantry 52, 119, 185, 217, 218, 244
9th New Jersey Infantry 65, 244
9th New York Cavalry 82, 99, 127, 153, 162, 167, 173, 245
9th New York Infantry 121, 123, 245
9th Pennsylvania Infantry Reserves 111, 249
9th Vermont Infantry 110, 124, 155, 253
9th Virginia Infantry 19, 28, 72, 183
Niven, Robert 147, 232, 245, 274, 280, 296, 302, 313
Noble, Daniel 147, 237, 255, 259, 283, 293, 305, 314

Index

Nolan, John J. 147, 244, 262, 278, 292, 308, 319
Nolensville, Tenn. 37, 48, 74, 89, 111, 154, 207, 225, 268
Noll, Conrad 147, 232, 274, 284, 290, 303, 318
North, Jasper N. 147, 148, 232, 253, 264, 287, 318
North Anna River, Va. 115, 118, 145, 272
North Fork, Va. 99, 272
Norton, Elliott M. 148, 232, 243, 273, 280, 289, 313
Norton, John R. 148, 232, 245, 273, 280, 296, 313
Norton, Llewellyn P. 148, 232, 245, 273, 278, 296, 303, 313
Noyes, William W. 148, 232, 252, 274, 287, 299, 308, 316
Nugent, Christopher 148, 235, 254, 260, 282, 292, 305, 311
Nutting, Lee 148, 232, 246, 274, 282, 296, 316

O'Beirne, James R. 148, 232, 246, 271, 287, 292, 308, 315
O'Brien, Henry D. 149, 232, 243, 266, 278, 293, 315
O'Brien, Oliver 149, 237, 255, 267, 281, 294, 304, 311
O'Brien, Peter 149, 232, 245, 274, 280, 292, 313
O'Connell, Thomas 149, 237, 255, 259, 287, 292, 306, 311
O'Connor, Albert 149, 232, 253, 271, 278, 289, 306, 320
O'Connor, Timothy 149, 232, 251, 292, 305, 313
O'Dea, John 149, 150, 232, 244, 264, 287, 292, 317
O'Donnell, Menomen 150, 230, 244, 264, 278, 292, 302, 319
O'Donohue, Timothy 150, 237, 256, 263, 287, 296, 305, 311
Oliver, Charles 150, 232, 250, 273, 280, 298, 313
Oliver, Paul A. 150, 232, 245, 262, 287, 302, 316
118th New York Infantry 110, 246
108th New York Infantry 165, 246
188th Pennsylvania Infantry 25, 84, 120, 251
185th New York Infantry 71, 248
182nd New York Infantry 115, 248
187th New York Infantry 151, 248
111th New York Infantry 127, 246
115th Illinois Infantry 107, 240

115th New York Infantry 199, 246
105th New York Infantry 167
105th Pennsylvania Infantry 106, 167, 251
150th Pennsylvania Infantry 106, 167, 251
158th New York Infantry 86, 104, 121, 137, 145, 176, 247
155th Pennsylvania Infantry 154, 251
154th New York Infantry 135, 214, 247
152nd New York Infantry 213, 247
157th Pennsylvania Infantry 178, 251
101st Ohio Infantry 145, 225, 249
140th New York Infantry 183, 247
140th Pennsylvania Infantry 22, 158, 162, 251
148th New York Infantry 35, 129, 203, 208, 214, 247
148th Pennsylvania Infantry 8, 32, 91, 156, 251
141st Pennsylvania Infantry 19, 172, 251
149th New York Infantry 15, 55, 81, 114, 161, 247
142nd New York Infantry 9, 45, 138, 146, 211, 246
147th Illinois Infantry 161, 240
147th New York Infantry 49, 247
147th Pennsylvania Infantry 82, 251
146th New York Infantry 68, 86, 145, 247
143rd New York Infantry 50, 247
143rd Pennsylvania Infantry 60, 173, 251
114th Pennsylvania Infantry 50, 251
104th Illinois Infantry 78, 90, 100, 103, 130, 181, 186, 240
104th Ohio Infantry 59, 79, 85, 88, 115, 168, 249
104th Pennsylvania Infantry 162, 250
119th Illinois Infantry 51, 65, 217, 240
109th New York Infantry 44, 205, 242
109th Pennsylvania Infantry 194, 209, 250
191st Pennsylvania Infantry 183, 251
199th Illinois Infantry 133
102nd United States Colored Troops 15, 19, 252

117th Illinois Infantry 142, 240
107th Ohio Infantry 73, 82, 249
107th Pennsylvania Infantry 60, 103, 250
170th New York Infantry 145, 247
178th New York Infantry 170, 247
116th Illinois Infantry 59, 80, 111, 172, 176, 191, 212, 217, 240
116th New York Infantry 125, 246
116th Ohio Infantry 201, 208, 249
116th Pennsylvania Infantry 144, 173, 179, 251
116th United States Colored Troops 70, 202, 252
106th Illinois Infantry 75, 240
164th New York Infantry 31, 63, 247
169th New York Infantry 76, 247
110th Ohio Infantry 109, 137, 249
113th Illinois Infantry 28, 58, 82, 96, 111, 139, 240
138th Pennsylvania Infantry 51, 251
134th Pennsylvania Infantry 163, 251
139th New York Infantry 109, 247
132nd New York Infantry 91, 247
136th New York Infantry 36, 247
136th Pennsylvania 156, 251
133rd Ohio Infantry 85, 249
112th New York Infantry 185, 246
120th New York Infantry 159, 246
128th Pennsylvania Infantry 86, 251
125th New York Infantry 38, 47, 247
121st New York Infantry 63, 80, 94, 246
121st Pennsylvania Infantry 77, 251
124th New York Infantry 28, 76, 88, 200, 222, 246
124th Ohio Infantry 43, 249
129th Pennsylvania Infantry 76, 251
122nd Illinois Infantry 40, 240
122nd New York Infantry 194, 205, 246
122nd Ohio Infantry 154, 170, 249

127th Illinois Infantry 28, 81, 107, 133, 145, 204
126th New York Infantry 32, 64, 211, 247
126th Ohio Infantry 24, 249
123rd New York Infantry 174, 246
100th Indiana Infantry 31, 241
100th New York Infantry 114, 246
100th Pennsylvania Infantry 45, 111, 150, 250
U.S.S. *Oneida* 112, 116, 146, 162, 169, 182, 224, 256
O'Neill, Stephen 150, 232, 252, 270, 278, 289, 315
Oostanaula, Ga. 161, 262
Opel, John N. 150, 232, 241, 274, 280, 311
Opequan Creek, Va. 126, 272
Orbansky, David 150, 232, 248, 275, 287, 299, 315
Orr, Charles A. 151, 232, 248, 271, 283, 296, 319
Orr, Robert L. 151, 232, 250, 273, 278, 298, 303, 316
Ortega, John 151, 237, 256, 275, 287, 299, 305, 311
Orth, Jacob G. 151, 232, 250, 263, 280, 298, 314
Osage, Kans. 66, 225
Osborne, William H. 151, 232, 242, 272, 287, 294, 319
Oss, Albert 151, 232, 244, 270, 287, 289, 316
Overturf, Jacob H. 152, 232, 241, 264, 287, 291, 217
Oviatt, Miles N. 152, 235, 254, 259, 287, 296, 305, 311
U.S.S. *Owasco* 72, 256

Packard, Loron F. 152, 232, 245, 273, 287, 296, 317
Paine's Crossroads, Va. 58, 68, 121, 124, 155, 176, 193, 195, 212, 225, 272
Palmer, George H. 152, 232, 240, 265, 278, 296, 305, 318
Palmer, John G. 152, 232, 239, 271, 287, 289, 318
Palmer, William J. 152, 232, 249, 260, 282, 289, 303, 317
Parker, Thomas 152, 232, 251, 273, 278, 290, 314
Parker, William 152, 237, 254, 262, 287, 294, 309
Parks, George 153, 237, 256, 259, 287, 296, 301, 311
Parks, Henry Jeremiah 153, 232, 245, 270, 278, 296, 308, 311
Parks, James W. 153, 232, 244, 268, 280, 297, 313
Parrott, Jacob 153, 232, 244, 268, 280, 297, 313
Parry, A.C. 32
Parsons, Joel 153, 232, 253, 264, 287, 317
Patterson, John H. 154, 232, 252, 275, 283, 296, 319
Patterson, John T. 154, 233, 249, 275, 283, 297, 319
Paul, William H. 154, 233, 250, 263, 278, 298, 308, 318
U.S.S. *Pawnee* 196, 219, 256
Pay, Byron E. 154, 233, 243, 268, 287, 296, 308, 319
Payne, Irvin C. 154, 233, 245, 273, 280, 298, 313
Payne Thomas H.L. 154, 233, 240, 259, 282, 291, 305, 319
Pea Ridge, Ark. 23, 42, 97, 161, 260
Peach Tree Creek, Ga. 13, 36, 55, 90, 220, 262
Pearsall, Platt 154, 233, 248, 264, 287, 297, 317
Pearson, Alfred L. 154, 233, 251, 271, 278, 298, 304, 319
Pease, Joachim 154, 155, 237, 255, 260, 287, 296, 311
Peck, Cassius 155, 233, 252, 269, 278, 316
Peck, Oscar E. 155, 237, 257, 262, 287, 289, 308, 309
Peck, Theodore S. 155, 233, 253, 266, 284, 299, 306, 315
Peeble's Farm, Va. 178, 272
Pegram House, Va. 87, 272
Peirsol, James K. 155, 233, 248, 272, 280, 298, 313
Pelham, William 155, 237, 255, 287, 289, 311
Pennypacker, Galusha 155, 156, 233, 250, 265, 282, 298, 308, 315
U.S.S. *Pensacola* 74, 127, 136, 168, 256
Pentzer, Patrick H. 156, 233, 240, 259, 278, 294, 315
Perry, Thomas 156, 237, 255, 260, 287, 296, 303, 311
Perryville, Ky. 67, 196, 262
Pesch, Joseph 156, 233, 244, 263, 287, 299, 318
U.S.S. *Peterel* 147, 256
Peters, Henry C. 6, 156, 233, 248, 264, 287, 294, 305, 320
Petersburg, Va. 11, 12, 14, 23, 24, 27, 29, 30, 31, 32, 36, 40, 44, 45, 47, 50, 52, 27, 58, 61, 63, 64, 70, 71, 73, 75, 78, 80, 82, 87, 88, 90, 91, 94, 98, 99, 100, 102, 103, 106, 109, 114, 119, 123, 124, 127, 129, 131, 132, 133, 135, 136, 137, 138, 140, 141, 145, 150, 151, 152, 159, 161, 166, 172, 174, 176, 183, 185, 191, 194, 197, 199, 200, 201, 206, 208, 209, 211, 214, 218, 221, 222, 224, 225, 272, 273
Peterson, Alfred 156, 237, 254, 271, 287, 299, 304, 309
Petty, Philip 156, 233, 251, 271, 278, 298, 299, 305, 316
Phelps, Charles E. 156, 233, 242, 272, 282, 299, 302, 319
Phillips, Josiah 156, 233, 251, 274, 280, 296, 313
Phinney, William 157, 237, 255, 259, 287, 296, 301, 311
Phisterer, Frederick 157, 233, 252, 268, 281, 290, 317
U.S.S. *Picket Boat* 61, 79, 89, 91, 103, 118, 218, 256
Pickle, Alonzo H 157, 233, 243, 270, 283, 289, 306, 317
Piedmont, Va. 70, 190, 192, 273
Pike, Edward M. 157, 233, 240, 260, 284, 293, 304, 319
Pingree, Samuel E. 157, 158, 233, 252, 272, 282, 294, 315
Pinkham, Charles H. 158, 233, 243, 271, 280, 294, 317
Pinn, Robert 158, 233, 252, 270, 282, 297, 306, 319, 323
U.S.S. *Pinola* 77, 256
Pipes, James 158, 233, 251, 266, 283, 298, 319
Pitman, George J. 158, 233, 245, 273, 280, 294, 319
Pittinger, William 158, 233, 248, 261, 281, 297, 305, 309, 321
U.S.S. *Pittsburgh* 224, 256
Plant, Henry E. 158, 159, 233, 243, 265, 284, 296, 318
Platt, George C. 159, 233, 252, 266, 284, 292, 306, 317
Pleasant Hill, La. 51, 262
Plimley, William 159, 233, 242, 273, 284, 290, 311
Plowman, George H. 159, 233, 242, 273, 284, 290, 311
Plunkett, Thomas 159, 233, 242, 271, 278, 292, 314
Plymouth, N.C. 35, 50, 83, 198, 266
U.S.S. *Pocahontas* 91, 256
Pocataligo, S.C. 168, 267
Pond, George F. 159, 233, 253, 262, 282, 291, 319
Pond, James B. 159, 160, 233, 253, 284, 296, 319
U.S.S. *Pontoosuc* 10, 20, 24, 70, 137, 209, 219, 256
Poole, William B. 160, 237, 255, 260, 287, 293, 302, 311

Index

Port Hudson, La. 17, 30, 60, 75, 89, 98, 104, 111, 133, 173, 195, 197, 208, 212, 262
Port Republic, Va. 84, 273
Porter, Ambrose 160, 233, 244, 261, 263, 293, 304, 320
Porter, Horace 160, 233, 239, 284, 298, 303, 320
Porter, John R. 160, 233, 248, 261, 281, 297, 304, 309
Porter, William 160, 233, 244, 273, 284, 296, 313
Post, Philip Sidney 160, 161, 233, 240, 268, 290, 302, 316
Postles, James Parke 161, 233, 239, 266, 281, 289, 305, 316
Potter, George W. 161, 233, 251, 273, 282, 299, 315
Potter, Norman F. 161, 233, 247, 268, 280, 296, 301, 313
Powell, William H. 161, 233, 253, 274, 278, 290, 315
Power, Albert 161, 233, 241, 260, 283, 297, 320
Powers, Wesley J. 161, 233, 240, 262, 287, 289, 308, 317
Prairie Grove, Ark. 22, 260
Prance, George 161, 162, 237, 256, 265, 287, 290, 301, 313
Prentice, Joseph B. 162, 233, 252, 268, 283, 297, 304, 317
Preston, John 162, 237, 256, 259, 287, 292, 305, 311
Preston, Noble D. 162, 233, 245, 274, 282, 315
Price, Edward 162, 237, 254, 259, 287, 296, 305, 311
Province, George 162, 237, 256, 265, 281, 296, 306, 313
Purcell, Hiram W. 162m 233, 250, 271, 284, 298, 317
Purman, James J. 162, 233, 251, 266, 283, 318
Putnam, Edgar P. 162, 163, 233, 245, 270, 278, 296, 316
Putnam, Winthrop D. 163, 233, 240, 269, 282, 294, 39
Pyne, George 163, 237, 255, 260, 287, 290, 305, 313

Quay, Matthew S. 163, 233, 251, 271, 285, 298, 302, 315
Quinlan, James 163, 233, 246, 273, 282, 292, 302, 315

Raccoon Ford, Va. 152, 273
Rafferty, Peter 163, 233, 246, 272, 287, 292, 319
Ramsbottom, Alfred 163, 164, 233, 249, 268, 280, 297, 313
Rand, Charles F. 164, 233, 245, 269, 287, 296, 319

Rannahan, John 164, 235, 255, 265, 287, 292, 303, 313
Ranney, George E. 164, 233, 243, 283, 296, 304, 320
Ranney, Myron H. 164, 233, 245, 262, 269, 284, 296, 317
Rapppahannock Station, Va. 30, 143, 169, 216, 273
Ratcliff, Edward 164, 233, 252, 270, 282, 300, 303, 313, 323
Raub, Jacob F. 164, 233, 251, 271, 287, 298, 305, 318
Raymond, William H. 165, 233, 246, 266, 282, 296, 308, 318
Read, Charles 165, 237, 255, 260, 287, 296, 305, 313
Read, Charles A. 165, 237, 255, 260, 287, 297, 303, 311
Read, George E. 165, 237, 255, 260, 287, 294, 311
Read, Morton A. 165, 233, 245, 268, 280, 296, 306, 313
Ream's Station, Va. 81, 158, 171, 216, 273
Rebmann, George F. 165, 233, 240, 259, 280, 291, 313
Red Hill, Ala. 152, 260
Red River, La. 12, 32, 39, 107, 133, 150, 218, 263
Reddick, William H. 165, 233, 248, 261, 281, 289, 309, 321
Reed, Axel H. 166, 233, 243, 261, 281, 289, 309, 321
Reed, Charles W. 166, 233, 242, 266, 287, 317
Reed, George W. 166, 233, 249, 274, 280, 294, 298, 311
Reed, William 166, 233, 244, 264, 287, 298, 317
Reeder, Charles A. 166, 233, 253, 273, 278, 300, 306, 314
Regan, Jeremiah 166, 237, 255, 270, 287, 294, 302, 309
Reid, Robert 166, 167, 233, 250, 273, 280, 299, 306, 311
Reigle, Daniel P. 167, 233, 250, 270, 280, 298, 305, 311
Reinsinger, J. Monroe 167, 233, 251, 266, 287, 320
Renninger, Louis 167, 233, 248, 264, 287, 297, 317
Resaca, Ga. 28, 50, 146, 150, 164, 185, 207, 262
Reynolds, George 167, 233, 245, 275, 280, 292, 311
U.S.S. *Rhode Island* 75, 86, 103, 112, 124, 142, 187, 210, 256
Rhodes, Julius D. 167, 233, 245, 274, 287, 294, 315
Rhodes, Sylvester D. 167, 233, 250, 271, 278, 298, 306, 319
Rice, Charles 167, 237, 253, 265, 287, 299, 305, 311

Rice, Edmund 167, 233, 242, 266, 287, 294, 315
Rich, Carlos H. 168, 233, 252, 275, 283, 289, 317
Richards, Louis 168, 237, 256, 262, 287, 303, 304
Richardson, William R. 168, 233, 248, 273, 285, 297, 314
Richey, William E. 168, 233, 248, 261, 278, 297, 305, 316
Richland Creek, Tenn. 50, 268
U.S.S. *Richmond* 12, 29, 32, 43, 45, 55, 60, 63, 66, 89, 95, 98, 109, 113, 130, 133, 135, 139, 142, 153, 173, 181, 184, 188, 190, 191, 206, 208, 214, 255
Richmond, James 168, 233, 248, 266, 280, 293, 311
Richmond, Va. 65, 85, 114, 124, 169, 202, 210, 273
Ricksecker, John H. 168, 233, 249, 268, 280, 297, 313
Riddell, Rudolph 168, 233, 246, 273, 296, 313
Riley, Thomas 168, 233, 241, 259, 280, 292, 313
Ringgold, Ga. 81, 262
Ringold, Edward 168, 237, 257, 267, 282, 293, 301, 309
Ripley, William Y.W. 169, 233, 252, 272, 282, 302, 316
Roanoke River, N.C. 54, 61, 79, 89, 91, 103, 115, 118, 120, 124, 218, 266
Roantree, James 169, 235, 256, 259, 287, 292, 303, 311
Robbins, Augustus I. 169, 233, 252, 274, 284, 299, 316
Roberts, James 169, 237, 253, 265, 287, 290, 303, 311
Roberts, Otis O. 169, 233, 241, 273, 280, 293, 306, 309
Robertson, Robert S. 169, 233, 246, 270, 287, 296, 319
Robertson, Samuel 169, 233, 248, 261, 281, 297, 306, 309
Robie, George F. 169, 170, 233, 244, 273, 287, 294, 315
Robinson, Alexander 170, 237, 255, 266, 287, 290, 302, 311
Robinson, Charles 170, 237, 253, 265, 287, 299, 302, 309
Robinson, Elbridge 170, 233, 249, 275, 283, 297, 319
Robinson, James H. 170, 233, 260, 287, 292, 294, 311, 313
Robinson, John C. 170, 233, 239, 266, 272, 282, 296, 317
Robinson, John H. 170, 233, 242, 280
Robinson, Thomas 170, 233, 250, 274, 280, 292, 311

Rock, Frederick 170, 233, 248, 264, 287, 290, 317
Rockefeller, Charles M. 170, 171, 233, 247, 259, 285, 296, 319
Rodenbough, Theophilus F. 171, 233, 251, 274, 287, 298, 304, 316
Rohm, Ferdinand F. 171, 233, 249, 273, 283, 298, 306, 319
Rood, Oliver P. 171, 233, 241, 266, 280, 293, 311
Roosevelt, George W. 171, 233, 250, 269, 284, 298, 308, 315
Ross, Marion A. 171, 233, 248, 261, 281, 297, 302, 309
Rossbach, Valentine 171, 233, 245, 274, 284, 290, 318
Rought, Stephen 172, 235, 251, 275, 280, 298, 305, 314
Rounds, Lewis A. 172, 233, 248, 274, 280, 296, 311
Rountry, John 172, 237, 255, 283, 294, 305, 313
Roush, J. Levi 172, 233, 249, 266, 278, 298, 319
Rowand, Archibald, Jr. 172, 233, 253, 281, 298, 308, 314
Rowanty Creek, Va. 35, 189, 273
Rowe, Henry W. 172, 233, 244, 273, 280, 294, 305, 311
Rundle, Charles W. 172, 173, 233, 240, 264, 287, 297, 306, 317
Rush, John 173, 237, 256, 262, 287, 300, 303, 309
Russell, Charles L. 173, 233, 246, 274, 280, 296, 311
Russell, Milton 173, 233, 241, 268, 282, 291, 319
Rutherford, John T. 173, 233, 245, 275, 278, 316
Rutter, James M. 173, 233, 251, 266, 283, 298, 305, 318
Ryan, Peter J. 173, 233, 241, 275, 278, 292, 313

Sacriste, Louis J. 173, 174, 233, 251, 270, 284, 289, 306, 315
Sagelhurst, John C. 174, 233, 244, 271, 283, 296, 320
Sailors Creek, Va. 19, 26, 30, 40, 46, 47, 51, 56, 57, 59, 63, 67, 70, 75, 80, 86, 87, 94, 95, 100, 101, 103, 106, 113, 117, 119, 121, 131, 134, 137, 138, 139, 143, 144, 146, 148, 154, 158, 160, 168, 175, 181, 182, 184, 191, 198, 203, 221, 223, 273
St. Marks, Fla. 121, 128, 163, 165, 178, 190, 260
St. Mary's Church, Va. 187, 214, 273
Salem Heights, Va. 39, 56, 81, 83, 132, 215, 273
Sancrainte, Charles F. 174, 233, 243, 261, 280, 294, 305, 316
Sanderson, Aaron 174, 237, 257, 287, 296, 313
Sands, William 174, 233, 250, 270, 280, 298, 316
Sandy Cross Roads, N.C. 140, 266
Sanford, Jacob 174, 233, 246, 264, 287, 291, 316
U.S.S. *Santee* 19, 256
U.S.S. *Santiago de Cuba* 16, 86, 162, 175, 196, 219, 256
Sargent, Jackson 174, 233, 253, 273, 278, 299, 306, 315
Sartwell, Henry 174, 175, 233, 246, 270, 287, 296, 303, 318
Saunders, James 175, 237, 255, 261, 287, 294, 301, 313
Savacool, Edwin F. 175, 233, 245, 273, 280, 294, 303, 313, 322
Savage, Auzella 175, 237, 256, 265, 284, 293, 308, 313
Savage Station, Va. 163, 273
Savannah Guards 63
Saxton, Rufus 175, 233, 239, 275, 287 294, 301, 316
Scanlan, Patrick 175, 233, 242, 266, 283, 292, 319
Scheibner, Martin E. 175, 176, 233, 250, 272, 283, 299, 305, 318
Schenck, Benjamin W. 176, 233, 240, 264, 287, 297, 303, 317
Schiller, John 176, 233, 247, 270, 287, 290, 313
Schlachter, Philipp 176, 233, 246, 274, 280, 290, 305, 311
Schmal, George W. 176, 233, 245, 272, 280, 290, 313
Schmauch, Andrew 176, 233, 248, 264, 287, 290, 317
Schmidt, Conrad 176, 233, 252, 275, 283, 290, 318
Schmidt, William 176, 233, 248, 268, 283, 297, 308, 317
Schneider, George 176, 233, 242, 273, 278, 293, 308, 318
Schnell, Christian 176, 233, 248, 264, 287, 300, 304, 317
Schofield, David H. 176, 245, 270, 281, 296, 305, 311
Schofield, John M. 177, 233, 244, 265, 282, 296, 302, 316
Schoonmaker, James M. 177, 233, 249, 275, 282, 298, 306, 320
Schorn, Charles 177, 233, 253, 268, 281, 290, 306, 313
Schubert, Martin 177, 233, 245, 271, 273, 278, 290, 316
Schutt, George 177, 178, 237, 255, 260, 287, 292, 302, 313
Schwan, Theodore 178, 233, 252, 272, 283, 305, 319
Schwenk, Martin 178, 252, 266, 281, 290, 315
U.S.S. *Sciota* 94, 256
Scott, Alexander 178, 253, 263, 284, 289, 319
Scott, John M. 178, 233, 248, 261, 281, 297, 304, 314
Scott, John Wallace 178, 233, 251, 271, 281, 298, 304, 313
Scott, Julian A. 179, 233, 252, 272, 283, 299, 313
Seaman, Elisha B. 179, 233, 249, 270, 278, 297, 304, 316
Seanor, James 179, 233, 254, 259, 288, 294, 302, 311
Sears, Cyrus 179, 233, 248, 263, 288, 296, 302, 316
Seaver, Thomas O. 179, 233, 252, 274, 282, 299, 302, 316
Secessionville, S.C. 123, 267
2nd Connecticut Heavy Artillery 30, 86, 239
2nd Illinois Light Artillery 46, 240
2nd Independent Battery, Massachusetts Light Artillery 129, 242
2nd Indiana Cavalry 73, 240
2nd Iowa Infantry 207, 241
2nd Louisiana Infantry (Colored) 17, 241
2nd Louisiana Tigers 72
2nd Maine Cavalry 192, 241
2nd Maine Infantry 119, 215, 241
2nd Maryland Infantry 131, 242
2nd Massachusetts Cavalry 16, 55, 242
2nd Michigan Cavalry 164, 243
2nd Minnesota Infantry 37, 46, 48, 74, 89, 101, 154, 166, 207, 225, 243
2nd Mississippi Infantry 211
2nd New Hampshire Infantry 62, 244
2nd New Jersey Infantry 70, 244
2nd New York Cavalry 19, 30, 39, 40, 86, 98, 139, 154, 245
2nd New York Heavy Artillery 59, 184, 244
2nd New York Infantry Militia 197, 245
2nd Ohio Cavalry 47, 79, 100, 106, 121, 168, 248

Index

2nd Ohio Infantry 158, 188, 196, 248
2nd Pennsylvania Infantry Reserves 224, 249
2nd Pennsylvania Provisional Artillery 159, 194
2nd Rhode Island Infantry 12, 152, 251
2nd United States Artillery 19, 114, 116, 220, 223, 251
2nd United States Cavalry 89, 171, 176, 204, 251
2nd United States Infantry 38, 108, 252
2nd Vermont Infantry 48, 91, 148, 169, 205, 252
2nd West Virginia Cavalry 117, 134, 161, 182, 253
2nd Wisconsin Infantry 111, 253
Seitzinger, James M. 179, 233, 251, 270, 278, 290, 320
Sellers, Alfred J. 179, 180, 233, 250, 266, 282, 298, 303, 317
Selma, Ala. 17, 71, 139, 196, 260
U.S.S. *Seneca* 206, 256
Seston, Charles H. 180, 233, 241, 275, 278, 291, 313, 322
17th Indiana Mounted Infantry 59, 105, 241
17th Louisiana Infantry 76
17th Maine Infantry 95, 131, 242
17th Michigan Infantry 8, 29, 71, 115, 134, 181, 197, 200, 243
17th Mississippi Infantry 129
17th Pennsylvania Cavalry 26, 249
17th South Carolina Infantry 131
7th Arkansas Infantry 131
7th Connecticut Infantry 109, 239
7th Indiana Infantry 150, 241
7th Iowa Infantry 188, 241
7th Maine Infantry 107, 242
7th Maryland Infantry 119, 256, 242
7th Massachusetts Infantry 100, 127, 131, 242
7th Michigan Cavalry 101, 243
7th Michigan Infantry 75, 76, 180, 186, 243
7th New Hampshire Infantry 65, 124, 169, 202, 244
7th New York Heavy Artillery 18, 141, 244
7th Pennsylvania Cavalry 58, 249
7th Pennsylvania Reserve Infantry 43, 249

7th Rhode Island Infantry 25, 199, 251
7th South Carolina Infantry 151
7th Tennessee Infantry 131
7th United States Infantry 150, 252
7th Virginia Infantry 42
7th Wisconsin Infantry 48, 68, 148, 184, 253
70th New York Infantry 54, 246
71st Pennsylvania Infantry 48, 250
74th Indiana Infantry 45, 120, 241
74th New York Infantry 29, 81, 109, 127, 246
79th New York Infantry 113, 246
72nd New York Infantry 31, 87, 102, 226, 240
72nd Ohio Infantry 133, 249
77th Illinois Infantry 163, 240
76th Georgia Infantry 181
73rd New York Infantry 113, 176, 221, 246
73rd Ohio Infantry 69, 249
73rd United States Colored Troops 138, 147, 252
Seward, Griffin 180, 252, 260, 288, 289, 314
Seward, Richard E. 180, 233, 237, 263, 283, 293, 305, 311
Sewell, William J. 180, 233, 244, 270, 288, 292, 303, 318
Shafter, William R. 180, 233, 243, 271, 294, 317
Shaler, Alexander 181, 233, 246, 271, 282, 289, 301, 316
Shambaugh, Charles 181, 233, 249, 270, 281, 299, 314
Shanan, Emisire 181, 234, 253, 273, 281, 300, 306, 313
Shanes, John 181, 234, 253, 269, 278, 300, 318
Shapland, John 181, 234, 240, 267, 288, 290, 302, 319
Sharp, Hendrick 181, 237, 256, 259, 288, 299, 310, 311
Shea, Joseph H. 181, 234, 246, 270, 283, 293, 314
Shelbyville, Tenn. 58, 268
Shellenberger, John S. 181, 234, 250, 270, 281, 298, 314
Shenandoah Valley 56, 92, 273
Shepard, Irwin 181, 182, 234, 243, 268, 281, 296, 319
Shepard, Louis C. 182, 237, 257, 265, 288, 297, 306, 314
Shepard, William 182, 234, 240, 273, 281, 291, 314
Shepherdstown Ford, Va. 38, 274

Sheridan, James 182, 237, 256, 259, 288, 294, 302, 311
Sheridan, Philip 135, 223
Sherman, Marshall 182, 234, 243, 266, 281, 299, 311
Shiel, John 182, 234, 250, 271, 284, 319
Shields, Bernard 182, 234, 253, 268, 281, 292, 314
Shilling, John 182, 183, 234, 239, 274, 281, 290, 302, 311
Shiloh, Tenn. 134, 150, 191, 219, 268
Ship Island Sound, La. 180, 263
Shipley, Robert F. 183, 234, 247, 271, 281, 296, 314
Shipman, William 183, 234, 255, 265, 288, 296, 302, 314
Shivers, John 183, 235, 255, 265, 288, 289, 302, 314
Shoemaker, Levi 183, 234, 253, 272, 281, 300, 305, 311
U.S.S. *Shokokon* 48, 256
Shopp, George J. 183, 234, 251, 281, 298, 303, 314
Shubert, Frank 183, 234, 246, 281, 290, 314
Shutes, Henry 183, 184, 237, 257, 262, 288, 293, 301, 314
Sickles, Daniel E. 184, 234, 239, 266, 288, 296, 301, 319
Sickles, William H. 184, 234, 253, 271, 278, 296, 320
Sidman, George E. 184, 234, 243, 271, 288, 296, 308, 316
U.S.S. *Signal* 12, 39, 107, 133, 150, 218, 256
Simkins, Lebbeus 184, 237, 256, 259, 288, 296, 303, 311
Simmons, John 184, 234, 244, 273, 281, 296, 313
Simmons, William T. 184, 185, 234, 244, 268, 281, 291, 306, 314
Simonds, William Edgar 185, 234, 239, 262, 288, 320
Simons, Charles J. 185, 234, 244, 273, 278, 291, 306, 318
Sinking Creek Valley, Va. 161, 274
Sivel, Henry *see* Mathews, William H.
16th Alabama Infantry 168
16th Georgia Infantry 8, 129
16th Michigan Infantry 184, 243
16th Missouri Infantry 68
16th New York Infantry 8, 81, 88, 140, 245
16th North Carolina Infantry 12
16th Pennsylvania Cavalry 171, 191, 249

16th South Carolina Infantry 178
16th United States Infantry 15, 252
16th Vermont Infantry 209, 253
6th Alabama Cavalry 168
6th Arkansas Infantry 131
6th Florida Infantry 189
6th Maine Infantry 47, 169, 241
6th Maryland Infantry 36, 242
6th Massachusetts Infantry 196, 242
6th Michigan Cavalry 55, 243
6th Michigan Infantry 57, 98, 148, 243
6th Missouri Infantry 74, 77, 106, 120, 194, 244
6th New Hampshire Infantry 49, 244
6th New Jersey Infantry 51, 244
6th New York Cavalry 25, 96, 116, 134, 137, 214, 245
6th North Carolina Infantry 117
6th Pennsylvania Cavalry 77, 249
6th Pennsylvania Infantry Reserves 53, 77, 112, 137, 172, 190, 249
6th Tennessee Infantry 137
6th United States Cavalry 159, 178, 252
6th United States Colored Troops 68, 94, 116, 252
6th Vermont Infantry 39, 47, 102, 191, 253
6th Virginia Infantry 100
6th Wisconsin Infantry 211, 253
60th New York Infantry 111, 246
60th Ohio Infantry 209, 249
65th New York Infantry 181, 246
65th Virginia Infantry 113
61st New York Infantry 85, 87, 104, 139, 148, 168, 246
61st Pennsylvania Infantry 48, 73, 131, 140, 141, 151, 167, 250
64th New York Infantry 129, 246
69th New York Infantry 63, 163, 246
69th Pennsylvania Infantry 132, 250
62nd New York Infantry 31, 70, 143, 246
67th Pennsylvania Infantry 117, 250
66th Ohio Infantry 54, 96, 179, 201, 249
63rd Ohio Infantry 191, 249

63rd Pennsylvania Infantry 117, 250
Skellie, Ebenezer 185, 234, 246, 270, 278, 296, 314
Sladen, Joseph A. 185, 234, 242, 262, 288, 290, 317
Slagle, Oscar 186, 234, 240, 267, 288, 297, 319
Slavens, Samuel 186, 234, 248, 261, 281, 297, 302, 315
Sloan, Andrew J. 186, 234, 241, 268, 281, 298, 314
Slusher, Henry C. 186, 234, 249, 275, 284, 298, 319
Smalley, Reuben 186, 234, 241, 264, 288, 296, 317
Smalley, Reuben S. 186, 234, 240, 267, 288, 298, 304, 319
Smith, Alonzo 186, 234, 243, 271, 281, 306, 312
Smith, Andrew Jackson 186, 187, 234, 243, 267, 284, 291, 306, 314
Smith, Charles H. 187, 234, 241, 273, 288, 293, 317
Smith, Charles H. (Navy) 187, 256, 284, 293, 314, 322
Smith, David L. 187, 234, 245, 274, 288, 296, 320
Smith, Edwin 188, 237, 257, 271, 288, 296, 305, 309
Smith, Francis M. 188, 234, 242, 270, 284, 293, 306, 317
Smith, Henry I. 188, 234, 241, 265, 288, 290, 305, 317
Smith, James 188, 234, 256, 259, 281, 296, 301, 312
Smith, James (Ovid) 188, 234, 248, 261, 300, 308, 312
Smith, John 188, 237, 256, 259, 288, 296, 302, 312
Smith, John 188, 189, 255, 259, 288, 294, 301, 312
Smith, Joseph S. 189, 234, 239, 269, 284, 293, 303, 316
Smith, Oloff 189, 237, 256, 259, 288, 299, 302, 312
Smith, Otis W. 189, 234, 249, 268, 281, 297, 314
Smith, Richard 189, 234, 246, 274, 278, 296, 314
Smith, S. Rodmand 189, 234, 239, 273, 288, 289, 317
Smith, Thaddeus S. 190, 234, 249, 266, 278, 298, 308, 320
Smith, Thomas 190, 237, 255, 260, 288, 290, 304
Smith, Walter B. 190, 237, 256, 259, 288, 296, 301
Smith, Willard M. 190, 235, 254, 259, 288, 296, 305, 312
Smith, William 190, 237, 255, 261, 288, 292, 304, 312

Smith, Wilson 190, 234, 245, 266, 284, 296, 318
Smithfield, Va. 92, 274
Snedden, James 190, 234, 250, 273, 288, 299, 319
South Mountain, Md. 8, 93, 102, 108, 263
South Side Railroad, Va. 53, 274
Southard, David 191, 234, 244, 273, 281, 294, 314
Sova, Joseph E. 191, 234, 245, 268, 281, 289, 314
Sowers, Michael 191, 234, 249, 274, 288, 298, 308, 319
Spalding, Edward B. 191, 234, 240, 268, 288, 291, 305, 317
Spanish Fort, Ala. 29
Sperry, William J. 191, 234, 253, 273, 278, 299, 316
Spillane, Timothy 191, 234, 249, 271, 288, 292, 315
Spotsylvania, Va. 8, 9, 14, 18, 19, 22, 38, 48, 58, 71, 72, 91, 113, 117, 118, 129, 132, 134, 135, 140, 142, 147, 148, 169, 170, 171, 172, 173, 176, 179, 201, 213, 215, 217, 221, 222, 274
Sprague, Benona 191, 234, 240, 288, 317
Sprague, John W. 191, 234, 249, 262, 264, 284, 296, 301, 317
Spring Hill, Tenn. 193, 268
Sprowle, David 191, 235, 256, 260, 288, 296, 301, 317
Spurling, Andrew B. 192, 234, 241, 259, 278, 293, 319
Stacey, Charles 192, 234, 246, 266, 288, 290, 318
Stahel, Julius 192, 234, 239, 273, 282, 290, 301, 316
Stanley, David S. 192, 234, 239, 268, 282, 297, 302, 316
Stanley, William A. 192, 237, 255, 260, 288, 294, 302, 312
Stanton, Edwin 46
Starkins, John H. 192, 234, 245, 267, 284, 296, 318
Staunton River Bridge, Va. 212, 274
Steele, John W. 193, 234, 239, 268, 284, 299, 303, 319
Steinmetz, William 193, 234, 241, 264, 288, 293, 317
Stephens, William G. 193, 234, 240, 264, 288, 296, 317
Stephenson, W.C. 170
Sterling, James E. 193, 237, 254, 260, 288, 293, 304, 312
Sterling, John T. 193, 234, 241, 275, 278, 291, 314

Stevens, Daniel D. 193, 237, 254, 265, 288, 299, 305, 314
Stevens, Hazard 193, 234, 239, 271, 282, 299, 306, 317
Stewart, George W. 193, 234, 244, 272, 281, 294, 314
Stewart, Joseph 193, 194, 234, 242, 271, 281, 292, 314
Stickels, Joseph 194, 234, 249, 259, 281, 297, 314
Stockman, George H. 194, 234, 244, 264, 288, 290, 302, 317
Stoddard, James 194, 237, 255, 265, 288, 296, 304, 313
Stokes, George 194, 234, 268, 281, 290, 304, 314
Stolz, Frank 194, 234, 241, 264, 288, 291, 308, 317
Stone's River, Tenn. 27, 72, 74, 76, 136, 157, 162, 173, 206, 207, 216, 268
Stoney Creek Bridge, Va. 98, 274
Stono River, S.C. 71, 194, 267
Stony Creek Station, Va. 191, 274
Storey, John H.R. 194, 234, 250, 262, 284, 298, 318
Stout, Richard 194, 237, 255, 267, 288, 296, 303, 312
Strahan, Robert 194, 237, 255, 251, 288, 294, 312
Strausbaugh, Bernard 194, 234, 242, 273, 284, 298, 312
Streile, Christian 195, 234, 244, 272, 281, 290, 314
Strong, James N. 195, 234, 243, 262, 288, 301, 316
Stuart, J.E.B. 96
Sturgeon, James K. 195, 234, 248, 262, 278, 297
Sullivan, James 195, 237, 253, 266, 296, 302, 312
Sullivan, John 195, 237, 255, 266, 288, 296, 304, 312
Sullivan, Timothy 195, 237, 255, 275, 288, 292, 303, 309
Sullivan's Island, S.C. 149, 267
Summers, James C. 195, 234, 253, 264, 288, 300, 304, 317
Summers, Robert 195, 237, 256, 265, 288, 299, 304, 314
Sumter Flying Artillery 177
Sumter Heavy Artillery 158
Surles, William H. 196, 234, 248, 262, 284, 297, 308, 315
U.S.S. *Susquehanna* 213, 256
Sutherland Station, Va. 156, 274
Swan, Charles A. 196, 234, 241, 260, 288, 298, 304, 314
Swanson, John 196, 237, 256, 265, 281, 299, 306, 314

Swap, Jacob E. 196, 234, 250, 275, 288, 296, 319
Swatton, Edward 196, 238, 256, 265, 288, 296, 303, 314
Swayne, Wager 196, 234, 248, 263, 282, 297, 303, 316
Swearer, Benjamin 196, 238, 256, 265, 288, 293, 301, 309
Sweatt, Joseph G. 196, 197, 234, 242, 269, 284, 294, 306, 316
Sweeney, James 197, 234, 252, 270, 281, 290, 312
Swegheimer, Jacob 197, 234, 248, 264, 288, 290, 306, 317
Swift, Frederic W. 197, 234, 243, 268, 284, 289, 302, 319
Swift, Harlan J. 197, 234, 245, 273, 278, 296, 306, 319
Swift's Creek, Va. 54, 274
Sype, Peter 197, 234, 248, 264, 288, 294, 305, 320
Tabor, William S. 197, 234, 244, 262, 284, 294, 308, 318
U.S.S. *Tacony* 35, 83, 104, 198, 256
Taggart, Charles A. 198, 234, 243, 273, 281, 294, 306, 314
Talbott, William 198, 238, 255, 260, 288, 293, 301, 314
Tallahatchie River, Miss. 150, 263
Tallentine, James 198, 238, 256, 266, 288, 290, 305, 312, 322
Tanner, Charles B. 198, 234, 239, 263, 284, 298, 305, 315
Taylor, Anthony 198, 234, 249, 261, 288, 298, 303, 316
Taylor, George 198, 234, 255, 260, 283, 296, 302, 312
Taylor, Henry H. 198, 234, 240, 264, 278, 291, 316
Taylor, John 199, 238, 265, 196, 314
Taylor, Joseph 199, 234, 251, 274, 278, 290, 319
Taylor, Richard 199, 234, 241, 270, 281, 289, 312
Taylor, Thomas 199, 238, 255, 260, 288, 293, 303, 314
Taylor, William 199, 234, 242, 265, 288, 300, 319
Taylor, William G. 199, 238, 256, 271, 288, 298, 305, 314
U.S.S. *Tecumseh* 92
C.S.S. *Tennessee* 33, 52, 59, 61, 62, 66, 67, 68, 79, 88, 89, 106, 108, 109, 111, 113, 116, 138, 130, 134, 135, 137, 139, 142, 145, 152, 155, 157, 162, 169, 179, 182, 188, 189, 190, 191, 203, 211, 214, 217, 224, 226

10th Connecticut Infantry 206, 239
10th Kentucky Infantry 131, 241
10th New Hampshire Infantry 29, 54, 244
10th New York Cavalry 30, 42, 71, 148, 162, 245
10th Ohio Cavalry 49, 248
10th United States Infantry 178, 252
10th Vermont Infantry 58, 178, 253
Terry, John D. 199, 234, 242, 265, 288, 293, 314
Thackrah, Benjamin 199, 234, 246, 260, 278, 299, 315
Thatcher, Charles M. 199, 234, 243, 273, 288, 294, 308, 318
Thaxter, Sidney W. 200, 234, 241, 271, 285, 293, 304, 317
Thielberg, Henry 200, 238, 255, 265, 288, 290, 302, 309
3rd Delaware Infantry 182, 239
3rd Illinois Cavalry 42, 240
3rd Indiana Cavalry 70, 101, 113, 182, 240
3rd Iowa Cavalry 22, 66, 161, 202, 225, 241
3rd Maine Infantry 93, 241
3rd Maryland Infantry 43, 132, 159, 176, 194, 242
3rd Massachusetts Cavalry 68, 170, 242
3rd Michigan Cavalry 170, 243
3rd Michigan Infantry 143, 243
3rd Minnesota Infantry 15, 243
3rd Missouri Cavalry 126, 244
3rd Missouri Infantry Reserves 215, 244
3rd New York Cavalry 117, 245
3rd New York Light Artillery 190, 245
3rd Pennsylvania Cavalry 106, 140, 249
3rd Vermont Infantry 16, 94, 112, 157, 179, 252
3rd Virginia Infantry 123, 129
3rd West Virginia Cavalry 137, 253
3rd Wisconsin Cavalry 68, 159, 253
13th Alabama Infantry 145, 214
13th Illinois Infantry 113, 240
13th Maine Infantry 97, 242
13th Massachusetts Infantry 132, 242
13th Michigan Infantry 115, 243
13th Mississippi Infantry 79
13th New York Infantry 164, 245
13th North Carolina Infantry 172
13th Ohio Cavalry 87, 155, 248

348 Index

13th Pennsylvania Cavalry 39, 64, 249
13th Pennsylvania Infantry Reserves 126, 250
13th United States Infantry 117, 252
13th Vermont Infantry 125, 253
13th Virginia Infantry 176
30th Indiana Infantry 122, 241
30th Louisiana Infantry 59
30th Massachusetts Infantry 73, 242
30th Ohio Infantry 11, 33, 41, 92, 125, 133, 134, 154, 176, 248
30th United States Colored Infantry 16, 58, 252
38th Alabama Infantry 28
38th Massachusetts Infantry 126, 243
38th New York Infantry 144, 246
38th United States Colored Troops 14, 92, 164, 252
38th Virginia Infantry 106
35th Massachusetts Infantry 93, 217, 242
35th North Carolina Infantry 225
35th Ohio Infantry 28, 248
31st Illinois Infantry 145, 240
31st Mississippi Infantry 36
31st North Carolina Infantry 116
31st Ohio Infantry 210, 248
31st Wisconsin Infantry 10, 253
34th Massachusetts Infantry 78, 106, 242
34th New York Battery 18, 171, 192, 245
34th United States Colored Troops 34, 252
39th Illinois Infantry 8, 91, 240
39th United States Colored Troops 64, 252
32nd Iowa Infantry 131, 241
32nd Massachusetts Infantry 78, 242
32nd Virginia Cavalry Battalion 89
37th Illinois Infantry 22, 23, 25, 154, 240
37th Massachusetts Infantry 67, 123, 198, 205, 214, 242
37th New York Infantry 50, 71, 148, 246
37th Ohio Infantry 76, 89, 110, 120, 167, 170, 176, 204, 248
36th Illinois Infantry 115, 240
36th United States Colored Troops 78, 109, 252
36th Virginia Infantry 134

33rd Illinois Infantry 157, 240
33rd Massachusetts Infantry 185
33rd New Jersey Infantry 128, 203, 244
33rd New York Infantry 43, 56, 246
33rd North Carolina Infantry 40
33rd Ohio Infantry 64, 94, 153, 165, 169, 186, 222, 248
Thomas, Hampton S. 200, 234, 249, 268, 278, 299, 303, 317
Thomas, Stephen 200, 234, 253, 270, 288, 299, 316
Thompkins, George W. 200, 234, 246, 273, 281, 290, 314
Thompson, Allen 200, 234, 244, 274, 285, 296, 308, 318
Thompson, Charles A. 200, 201, 234, 243, 274, 284, 297, 306, 318
Thompson, Freeman C. 201, 234, 249, 273, 288, 297, 308, 314
Thompson, Henry A. 201, 235, 255, 265, 288, 290, 305, 314
Thompson, James 201, 234, 244, 266, 274, 285, 296, 318
Thompson, James B. 201, 234, 251, 281, 299, 312
Thompson, J. (James) Harry 201, 234, 239, 265, 288, 290, 314
Thompson, John 201, 234, 242, 278, 289, 304, 319
Thompson, Thomas 201, 234, 249, 270, 278, 297, 304, 316
Thompson, William 202, 234, 241, 275, 281, 296, 312
Thompson, William P. 202, 234, 241, 275, 281, 296, 312
Thomson, Clifford 202, 234, 245, 270, 285, 303, 318
Thorn, Walter 202, 234, 252, 270, 284, 317
Thoroughfare Gap, Va. 167, 274
Tibbets, Andrew W. 202, 234, 241, 262, 281, 291, 314
U.S.S. *Ticonderoga* 28, 40, 77, 95, 113, 161, 195, 199, 256
Tilton, William 202, 203, 234, 244, 273, 288, 299, 315
Tinkham, Eugene M. 203, 234, 247, 270, 284, 289, 319
Titus, Charles 203, 234, 244, 273, 288, 294, 304, 314
Toban, James W. 203, 234, 243, 284, 294, 308, 318
Tobie, Edward P. 203, 234, 241, 268, 288, 293, 319
Tobin, John M. 203, 234, 242, 266, 272, 288, 292, 318

Todd, Charles H. 8
Todd, Samuel 203, 238, 254, 257, 260, 288, 294, 301, 312
Todds, Tavern, Va. 148, 274
Toffey, John J. 203, 204, 234, 244, 267, 282, 296, 308, 319
Tomlin, Andrew J. 204, 235, 257, 265, 284, 294, 308, 314
Tompkins, Aaron B. 204, 234, 244, 273, 281, 294, 314
Tompkins, Charles H. 204, 234, 252, 271, 282, 300, 316
Toohey, Thomas 204, 234, 253, 268, 288, 296, 303
Toomer, William 204, 234, 240, 264, 288, 292, 317
Torgler, Ernst (Ernert) 204, 234, 248, 252, 284, 290, 305, 317
Townsend, Lt. Col. Edward 4
Tozier, Andrew J. 204, 234, 242, 266, 284, 293, 319
Tracy, Amasa A. 205, 234, 252, 270, 284, 293, 319
Tracy, Benjamin F. 205, 234, 246, 275, 278, 296, 302, 316
Tracy, Charles H. 205, 234, 243, 274, 284, 289, 319
Tracy, William G. 205, 234, 246, 270, 285, 296, 317
Tranter's Creek, N.C. 12, 266
Traynor, Andrew 205, 234, 243, 272, 281, 294, 319
Treat, Howell B. 205, 234, 248, 261, 284, 297, 302, 317
Tremain, Henry E. 206, 234, 239, 262, 284, 296, 316
Trenchard, S.D. 199
Trenton, N.C. 117, 266
Trevilian Station, Va. 71, 18, 116, 162, 171, 274
Tribe, John 206, 234, 245, 274, 288, 296, 305, 317
Tripp, Othniel 206, 238, 256, 265, 288, 293, 301, 311
Trogden, Howell G. 206, 234, 244, 264, 288, 296, 305, 317
Truell, Edwin M. 206, 234, 253, 261, 288, 294, 314
Truett, Alexander H. 206, 238, 256, 260, 288, 293, 303, 312
Tucker, Allen 206, 234, 239, 273, 278, 289, 314
Tucker, Jacob R. 206, 234, 242, 273, 288, 299, 308, 314
Tweedale, John 206, 207, 234, 249, 268, 288, 296, 305, 315
12th Iowa Infantry 114, 186, 241
12th Kentucky Infantry 32, 106, 241
12th Mississippi Cavalry 139
12th Missouri Cavalry 160, 244

Index

12th New York Infantry 55, 150, 164, 245
12th North Carolina Infantry 222
12th Ohio Infantry 108, 248
12th United States Infantry 226
12th Vermont Infantry 19, 253
12th Virginia Infantry 56, 86, 133
12th West Virginia Infantry 11, 57, 67, 166, 253
12th Wisconsin Infantry 206, 253
12th Wisconsin Light Artillery 55, 253
20th Illinois Infantry 134, 240
20th Indiana Infantry 118, 171, 202, 241
20th Maine Infantry 44, 72, 143, 204, 242
20th Michigan Infantry 57, 147, 243
20th New York Cavalry 125, 245
20th Ohio Infantry 44, 248
28th Connecticut Infantry 75, 239
28th Illinois Infantry 219, 240
28th North Carolina Infantry 117
28th Pennsylvania Infantry 151, 250
28th Virginia Infantry 182
25th Connecticut Infantry 185, 239
25th Massachusetts Infantry 26, 43, 242
25th Virginia Infantry Battalion 139
21st Connecticut Infantry 17, 35, 84, 105, 152, 239
21st Illinois Infantry 136, 240
21st Iowa Infantry 99, 241
21st Massachusetts Infantry 159, 218, 242
21st New York Cavalry 63, 245
21st North Carolina 171
21st Ohio Infantry 20, 33, 27, 119, 130, 178, 207, 221, 222, 248
24th Missouri Infantry 132, 244
24th New York Cavalry 45, 117, 138, 176, 245
24th North Carolina Infantry 166
24th Wisconsin Infantry 127, 204, 253
29th Massachusetts Infantry 60, 79, 90, 102, 105, 129, 151, 225, 242
22nd Iowa Infantry 81, 241
22nd New York Cavalry 35, 56, 93, 120, 245

22nd Pennsylvania Cavalry 186, 249
27th Indiana Infantry 28, 241
27th Michigan Infantry 63, 243
27th New York Infantry 88, 245
27th Virginia Infantry 101
26th Michigan Infantry 71, 135
26th New Jersey Infantry 56, 244
26th New York Infantry 48, 115, 177, 245
26th North Carolina Infantry 90
26th Pennsylvania Infantry 171, 250
26th Virginia Infantry 70, 186
23rd Illinois Infantry 54, 98, 135, 240
23rd Massachusetts Infantry 199, 242
23rd New York Infantry 100, 245
23rd Pennsylvania Infantry 72, 250
23rd Tennessee Infantry 87
23rd Virginia Infantry 215
208th Pennsylvania Infantry 100, 251
211th Pennsylvania Infantry 91, 251
205th Pennsylvania Infantry 124, 251
207th Pennsylvania Infantry 108, 251
210th Pennsylvania Infantry 59, 164, 251
Twombly, Voltaire P. 207, 234, 241, 267, 278, 291, 306, 319
Tyrrell, George William 207, 234, 248, 262, 281, 292, 314

Uhrl, George 207, 234, 251, 274, 284, 290, 319
Urell, M. Emmet 207, 234, 246, 267, 288, 292, 314

Vale, John 207, 235, 243, 268, 288, 290, 319
U.S.S. *Valley City* 59, 256
Vance, Robert B. 9
Vance, Wilson 207, 235, 248, 268, 284, 297, 308, 317
Vanderslice, John M. 208, 235, 249, 271, 282, 299, 308, 316
Van Matre, Joseph 208, 235, 249, 273, 288, 300, 314
Vantine, Joseph E. 208, 256, 263, 288, 299, 303, 307, 323
Van Winkle, Edward (Edwin) 208, 235, 247, 270, 282, 296, 314
Varnell's Station, Ga. 73, 262

U.S.S. *Varuna* 27, 28, 85, 101, 130, 135, 155, 256
Vaughn, Pinkerton R. 208, 235, 255, 263, 288, 289, 304
Vaughn Road, Va. 46, 274
Veal, Charles 208, 235, 252, 270, 278, 300, 304, 314, 323
Veale, Moses 208, 209, 235, 250, 268, 288, 299, 302, 317
Veazey, Wheelock G. 209, 235, 253, 266, 282, 294, 303, 315
Vernay, James D. 209, 235, 240, 264, 288, 303, 314, 319
Verney, James W. 209, 238, 256, 265, 288, 293, 303
Vicksburg, Miss. 6, 8, 11, 12, 13, 15, 22, 24, 25, 28, 32, 33, 36, 37, 38, 41, 42, 44, 46, 50, 53, 54, 56, 58, 59, 61, 62, 65, 66, 69, 73, 74, 75, 76, 77, 80, 81, 82, 87, 89, 92, 94, 96, 98, 100, 105, 106, 107, 110, 111, 112, 117, 118, 119, 120, 121, 123, 133, 135, 139, 142, 145, 147, 150, 152, 153, 154, 156, 163, 166, 167, 170, 173, 174, 176, 186, 191, 193, 194, 195, 197, 204, 206, 209, 210, 212, 214, 216, 217, 223, 224, 263
Vifquain, Victor 209, 235, 240, 259, 281, 289, 314
Von Vegesack, Ernest 209, 235, 239, 271, 282, 299, 316

U.S.S. *Wabash* 39, 168, 182, 204, 257
Wageman, John H. 209, 210, 235, 249, 273, 288, 297, 318
Wagg, Maurice 210, 238, 256, 265, 284, 290, 303, 312
Wagner, John W. 210, 235, 244, 264, 288, 293, 308, 317
Wainwright, John 210, 235, 250, 265, 288, 296, 304, 315
Walker, James C. 210, 235, 248, 268, 278, 297, 306, 317
Walker, Dr. Mary E. 210, 235, 239, 275, 284, 296, 302, 314
Walker's Ford, Tenn. 34, 268
Wall, Jerry 211, 235, 247, 266, 281, 296, 305, 312
Waller, Francis A. 211, 235, 253, 266, 281, 297, 305, 312
Walling, William H. 211, 247, 265, 281, 296, 302, 316
Walsh, John 211, 235, 245, 270, 284, 292, 305, 312
Walton, George W. 211, 235, 250, 273, 284, 299, 320
Wambsgan, Martin 211, 235, 246, 270, 284, 290, 318
Ward, James 211, 238, 255, 260, 288, 296, 302, 312

350 Index

Ward, Nelson W. 212, 235, 249, 274, 284, 297, 319
Ward, Thomas J. 212, 235, 240, 264, 288, 300, 317
Ward, William H. 212, 235, 248, 264, 288, 294, 305, 317
Warden, John 212, 235, 240, 264, 288, 291, 305, 316
Warfel, Henry C. 212, 235, 249, 272, 281, 299, 314
Warren, David 212, 238, 255, 266, 281, 299, 303, 312
Warren, Francis E. 212, 213, 235, 243, 263, 288, 294, 316
Warrenton, Va. 47, 274
Warwick Courthouse, Va. 187, 274
Washington, D.C. 6, 224
Washington, N.C. 190, 266
Waterloo Bridge, Va. 206, 274
Wauhatchie, Tenn. 208, 268
Waynesboro, Ga. 49, 262
Waynesboro, Va. 9, 21, 24, 35, 42, 50, 56, 81, 93, 116, 120, 128, 140, 147, 149, 274
Webb, Alexander S. 213, 235, 239, 266, 282, 296, 303, 315
Webb, James 213, 235, 245, 269, 281, 296, 305, 319
Webber, Alason P. 213, 235, 240, 262, 284, 296, 302, 318
Webster, Henry S. 213, 238, 256, 288, 296, 308, 314
Weeks, Charles H. 213, 238, 255, 284, 294, 303, 314
Weeks, John H. 213, 235, 247, 274, 281, 289, 308, 312
Weir, Henry C. 214, 235, 239, 273, 284, 296, 320
Welch, George W. 214, 235, 244, 268, 281, 291, 314
Welch, Richard 214, 235, 243, 273, 314
Welch, Stephen 214, 235, 247, 262, 284, 296, 317
Weldon Railroad, Va. 9, 31, 44, 65, 68, 106, 110, 130, 166, 182, 189, 199, 274
Welles, Gideon 4
Wells, Henry S. 214, 235, 247, 270, 282, 314, 322
Wells, Thomas M. 214, 235, 245, 270, 281, 292, 312
Wells, William 214, 235, 252, 260, 266, 282, 290, 303
Wells, William (Navy) 214, 238, 256, 288, 299, 302, 312
Welsh, Edward 214, 235, 248, 265, 288, 292, 317
Welsh, James 214, 215, 235, 251, 273, 284, 292, 320
Westerhold, William 215, 235, 246, 274, 281, 299, 312
Weston, John 215, 235, 241, 260, 281, 293, 319
Wetumpka, Ala. 215, 260
Wheaton, Lloyd 215, 235, 259, 282, 294, 304, 317
Wheeler, Daniel D. 215, 235, 252, 273, 288, 299, 305
Wheeler, Henry W. 215, 235, 241, 269, 284, 289, 306, 316, 319
Wherry, William M. 215, 235, 244, 265, 288, 294, 303, 317
Whitaker, Edward W. 216, 235, 239, 273, 281, 289, 305, 319
White, Adam 216, 235, 253, 271, 281, 299, 314
White, J. Henry 216, 235, 250, 273, 281, 299, 320
White, Joseph 216, 238, 256, 264, 288, 300, 305, 314
White, Patrick H. 216, 235, 240, 264, 282, 292, 302, 317
White Oak Road, Va. 200, 201, 274
White Oak Swamp, Va. 30, 136, 274
White Oak Swamp Bridge, Va. 118, 207
U.S.S. *Whitehead* 188, 257
Whitehead, John M. 216, 235, 241, 268, 284, 291, 301, 319
Whitfield, Daniel 216, 238, 255, 260, 288, 294, 301, 319
Whitman, Frank M. 217, 235, 242, 263, 284, 293, 304, 314
Whitmore, John 217, 235, 240, 259, 281, 291, 308, 314
Whitney, William G. 217, 235, 243, 261, 282, 294, 305, 317
Whittier, Edward N. 217, 235, 241, 272, 278, 293, 305, 316
Widick, Andrew J. 217, 235, 240, 264, 288, 291, 317
Wilcox, Franklin L. 217, 238, 255, 265, 288, 296, 302, 314
Wilcox, William H. 217, 218, 235, 244, 274, 288, 294, 315
Wilderness, Va. 22, 31, 36, 38, 49, 57, 60, 70, 82, 99, 114, 116, 143, 150, 154, 168, 172, 196, 202, 205, 226, 274
Wiley, James 218, 235, 246, 266, 281, 297, 312
Wilhelm, George 218, 235, 248, 263, 278, 295, 302, 315
Wilkes, Henry 218, 238, 256, 266, 288, 296, 308, 312
Wilkes, Perry 218, 238, 256, 263, 288, 291, 302, 312
Wilkins, Leander A. 218, 235, 244, 273, 284, 294, 312
Willcox, Orlando B. 218, 219, 235, 243, 269, 282, 294, 301, 317
Williams, Anthony 219, 238, 256, 265, 288, 294, 301, 314
Williams, Augustus 219, 238, 256, 265, 288, 296, 306, 314
Williams, Elwood N. 219, 235, 240, 268, 282, 299, 319
Williams, George C. 219, 235, 252, 271, 288, 290, 319
Williams, John A. (LA) 219, 238, 255, 272, 288, 293, 302, 309
Williams, John (NJ) 219, 238, 256, 266, 288, 294, 302, 309
Williams, John (PA) 220, 238, 254, 271, 288, 299, 302, 309
Williams, LeRoy 220, 235, 270, 284, 296, 308, 319
Williams, Peter 220, 235, 255, 271, 288, 296, 302, 309
Williams, Robert 220, 238, 253, 265, 288, 296, 303, 309
Williams, William 220, 238, 255, 266, 288, 292, 305
Williams, William H. 220, 235, 249, 262, 285, 295, 317
Williamsburg, Va. 50, 54, 62, 71, 87, 140, 170, 275
Williamson, James A. 220, 235, 241, 263, 282, 293, 302, 317
Willis, Richard 220, 238, 256, 265, 288, 290, 301, 314
Williston, Edward B. 220, 221, 235, 251, 274, 288, 289, 316
Wilmington, N.C. 48, 51, 170, 195, 212, 225, 266
Wilson, Charles E. 221, 235, 244, 273, 278, 299, 314
Wilson, Christopher W. 221, 235, 246, 274, 281, 292, 319
Wilson, Francis A. 221, 235, 250, 273, 278, 299, 315
Wilson, John 221, 235, 244, 270, 288, 290, 314
Wilson, John A. 221, 235, 248, 261, 281. 297, 309
Wilson, John M. 221, 235, 239, 272, 288, 300, 319
Wilson's Creek, Mo 27, 108, 277, 215, 222, 265
Winchester, Va. 28, 50, 65, 67, 75, 125, 127, 134, 137, 154, 167, 173, 176, 177, 180, 193, 275
Winegar, William W. 221, 235, 245, 271, 281, 296, 314
Wisner, Lewis S. 222, 235, 246, 274, 288, 296, 317
U.S.S. *Wissahickon* 183, 257
Withington, William H. 222, 235, 243, 269, 284, 294, 303, 318

Index

Wollam, John 222, 235, 248, 261, 281, 297, 312
Wood, H. Clay 222, 235, 252, 265, 288, 293, 302, 316
Wood, Mark 222, 235, 248, 261, 281, 290, 308
Wood, Richard H. 223, 235, 240, 264, 288, 294, 318
Wood, Robert B. 223, 238, 255, 265, 288, 297, 309
Woodall, William H. 223, 235, 239, 275, 281, 314
Woodbury, Eri D. 223, 235, 252, 281, 284, 312
Woodruff, Alonzo 223, 235, 252, 271, 284, 294, 304, 318
Woodruff, Carle A. 223, 235, 251, 272, 284, 296, 305, 316
Woods, Daniel A. 223, 235, 253, 273, 281, 300, 308, 314
Woods, Samuel 223, 224, 238, 255, 272, 284, 289, 303, 309
Woodstock, Va. 40, 89, 275
Woodward, Evan M. 224, 235, 249, 271, 281, 299, 304, 317
Woon, John 224, 238, 256, 263, 288, 290, 301, 309
Woram, Charles B. 224, 238, 256, 260, 281, 296, 308, 312
Worrill Grays 59
Wortick (Wertick), Joseph 224, 235, 244, 264, 288, 299, 317
Wray, William J. 224, 235, 252, 275, 288, 299, 308, 316
Wright, Albert D. 224, 235, 252, 273, 281, 299, 308, 316
Wright, Edward 224, 225, 238, 254, 262, 288, 296, 302, 309
Wright, Robert 225, 235, 252, 270, 288, 292, 314
Wright, Samuel 225, 235, 243, 268, 288, 291, 319
Wright, Samuel C. 225, 235, 242, 263, 288, 318
Wright, William 225, 238, 255, 266, 277, 290, 303, 312
U.S.S. *Wyalusing* 13, 54, 120, 124, 257
U.S.S. *Wyandank* 144, 174, 257
Yazoo City, Miss. 75, 120, 194, 265
Yazoo River 54, 122, 130, 134, 142, 143, 147, 170, 220, 265
Yeager, Jacob F. 225, 235, 249, 261, 284, 299, 305, 319
Yellow Tavern, Va. 173, 275
Young, Andrew J. 225, 235, 249, 272, 281, 299, 314
Young, Benjamin F. 225, 235, 243, 273, 281, 289, 308, 312
Young, Cavalry M. 225, 235, 241, 262, 278, 297, 314
Young, Edward B. 225, 226, 238, 254, 260, 288, 294, 303, 314
Young, Horatio N. 226, 238, 255, 266, 284, 293, 308, 312
Young, James M. 226, 235, 246, 275, 284, 296, 319
Young, William 226, 238, 254, 262, 288, 296, 303, 309
Younker, John L. 226, 235, 252, 270, 281, 290, 303, 316

www.ingramcontent.com/pod-product-compliance
Ingram Content Group UK Ltd.
Pitfield, Milton Keynes, MK11 3LW, UK
UKHW041922140426
5217IPUK00014B/269